In the Name of the Gods

The mystery of resonance
and the prehistoric messiah

In the Name of the Gods

The mystery of resonance
and the prehistoric messiah

DAVID ELKINGTON
with
PAUL HOWARD ELLSON

Green Man Press
Sherborne England

Published by Green Man Press 2001

Illustrations by Amanda Patten

The extracts from *Paul, The Mind of the Apostle*
by A. N. Wilson, published by Sinclair - Stevenson,
used by permission of the Random House Group.

A catalogue record for this book
is available from the British Library

ISBN 0 9539930 0 0

Printed in Great Britain by
Creative Print and Design (Ebbw Vale), Wales

Green Man Press
1 The Green
Sherborne
Dorset DT9 3HZ
England

ISIS – a dedication

Within the sheer grasp of beauty
I shivered
as if to meet your smile,
and trembling thoughts
brought to book
the wild audacity of nature.

And then
all the vibrancy of your gift
and this, our world
stirred deep within me
like the last song of the lark
or the blackbird at dawn.

For within my heart
have stirred illusions
as if willing myself
to keep this world at bay,
and ever the tide lapped at my feet.

But solace betook me,
and having broken through,
the wonder of it all
is that all the time
you were there.

For my Mother and Father,
who went through the thick, and the thin.
For Gillian and Bevan for their influence.
For Paul and Fiona for the journey,
and Isabelle for her wonderful gift.
And ultimately for Clare,
for her gift of being there.

Contents

Acknowledgements

I wish to thank those who gave so much of their time and patience; if I have failed to mention anyone it is not intentional and my heartfelt good wishes go with them. My thoughts are also with those in whose absence this book has become complete.

Paul Ellson, for his insight and patience, and, with Fiona, their patience and humour. To Susan Mears and Annie Tatham-Mannall for an excellent production. Clive and Linda Greenslade for their wonderful support. To John Reid for his generosity and honesty. Robin Whitlock for his research skills. Mo and Dave Elkington for reasons that only they will know. Amanda Patton for her excellent illustrations. Joyce Froome for her splendid advice. Lizzie Hutchins for her keen eyes. John Byrnes for his patience. Gillian and Bevan Brooke for their tremendous support. Paul Broadhurst for the genius of his friendship, and Vivienne Shanley for the genius of hers. Mike and Emma Ives for their extraordinary support. Tony Weeks and Sinaan Menheniot Weeks for their perception and shrewdness. Jean Houston, Mike Ibison, Tom Brown, Meg Switzgable, Richard Salmon, Paula Perliss for their time and presence in the USA. To Peter Lacaux and Mai Watts, the best of best friends. Richard Seccombe for the goodness of his spirit (and humour). Isabelle Kingston, Belle and Ed for their advice and their home. Nigel Hill, Dan Hill, Andrea Mitchell and all at Beaver Cabs. Mr Chips, Bella, Bully and Rags for fun in the Underworld. Bryony Glass, Phillip Blair and Jo Blair. Nigel Blair, John Watson and Honor Blair and Nigel Thomas. Kate Fenn. Peter Renton. Violet MacDermot. Sharon Hill. Dr Simon Mottram and Dr Peter Mansfield for altering my life. Ahmed Osman. Tom and Mary Crabtree. The Staff at Thornford Primary School. The Staff at Sherborne Public Library. William and Heather Elmhirst. Ellen Stilwell. Jason Stilwell. Bear. Keith and Araxia Hearne. Pete Lovelock. Shirley Battie. Tony, Amanda, John and Lydia Robinson. Alec and Cathy Simpson. Jerry Bower. Fay Weldon. Sir George Trevelyan. Barry, Deb, Matthew and Emily Slate. Kate and Ian Houston. Geoff and Julia Strong. Tony Barwick. Nicolas Hudson-Cook. Hazel Collett. Henry Bartlett. Chris Turner. Peter Hitchin. Mike and Sylvia Venn. Jon Symes. John and Caitlin Matthews. Joe Hill. Nick Andrew. Anne Barnes. Hamish Miller and Ba Russell. Patricia Law. Chris Herald. Robin and Tricia Heath. David and V. Hemery. Neil and Leslie Beverley and family for their warmth and generosity. Linda Tucker. Gill and Stuart Black. Dawn and Albert Clamp. Suzy Baker and Laurence. Dean Baker. Barbara Clouson. Sacha Damianavsky. Sylvia Francke. Alan Ezen. Paul Ferguson. Adrian and Dee Gilbert. Sue Hill. Lorraine Harris. Eve Nicholl. Jamie Leader and Nicky, Tim and Harriet Leader. Paul Hover. Clare Harvey. Jake King. Bob Rosenthal. Godfrey Rehaag. Melanie Warren. Rhiannon Lloyd. Jose Ferriman. Ken and Angela. Dr Nita Mandell. Dr Bryan Broome. Jude Stammers. Palden Jenkins. Robert Wheeler. The Chairman and Directors of the Green Man Press for their professionalism and wonderfully enlightened approach to publishing.

Author's Note

There is something happening, something deeply profound, and you are a part of it. It is a mystery in every enigmatic sense of the word – one that unites science and spirituality within the context of both history and the human physiology.

Religion is a paradigm, which the modern psychologist is keen to interpret as an inner, archetypal yearning, and to link closely to notions of evolutionary survival. However, this remains a singularly Western view, one which is coming under question in the light of recent researches into the subtler realms of creation and the nature of consciousness itself.

In the Name of the Gods constitutes the results of twenty years of research taking in all of the above and more. I am presenting within this book a chain of proofs, as well as some speculation, in order to demonstrate often surprising connections that, as they build up, supersede mere coincidence. Therefore the reader must forgive me certain liberties. Where I have used an unfamiliar term I have tried to elucidate further on in the text. I make no apologies for my humour and the use of puns: they serve to illustrate the nature of language as it once was: poetic and multi-levelled. I also believe that if one is going to use Occam's razor one should not cut oneself with it; therefore I have given a multitude of sources to back up my argument wherever possible.

Overall, this work has been divided into three parts. Part One deals with the history, Part Two with the science and the connection to us, the human being, whilst Part Three sees us in the land of Egypt, in the realms of the Ancients.

My views of religion and the founding of the Christian religion in particular, are not simplistic and therefore I make no apologies for what might be perceived as a little dryness within the first two or three chapters. All I can say is that perserverance bears great fruit, for once this background – basically the background to Western civilisation – is established, we are free to move forward in breadth and pace.

As a part of laying out my thesis, I am, of necessity, addressing two major reasons why loss of knowledge has occurred. The first is the misrepresentation of history down the ages and the second is the general habit of pigeonholing knowledge into distinctly separate units. Via these practices, ignorance has slipped in through the back door. My aim is to shut that door, tight! However, this is not to arrogantly assume that I have all of the answers, or that all is done and dusted. This is merely the beginning, and in the light of revisions and further volumes, it is going to be quite a journey!

David Elkington, Dorset, January 2001.

Editor's Note

I first became involved with helping to birth this volume in October 1998, using my editing and writing skills and also advising David from my own research into metaphysics, and 'the mindset of the Ancients' etc. Now, in January 2001, I must say that, through the ups and the downs, and the thick and the thin, it has been a great pleasure to work with David and I trust that the reader will find that our cooperation has been worthwhile.

Now, I believe that the prime function of an Editor's Note should be to assure the reader that not every anomaly to be found in the text is an accident. You should know that due to the nature of the work, we have taken one or two unusual steps:

We have taken steps against the overuse of capital letters. This may disappoint those readers who like to see every deity elevated, but there is a fine line between respect for the gods and the gods jealously jostling for supremacy. Too many capitals reduces meaning and we felt that the most important thing to respect was the progenitor of the gods, God. This also helps underline the important point that, in ancient pantheistic systems, the gods were not replacements for the One God, instead they represented God's attributes. Therefore God and prime terms such as Creator have a capital, the prime name of a god or goddess too – but, as for the remainder, we have tried to avoid it.

We have also moved against modern trends and used AD and BC instead of CE and BCE, for reasons that should become obvious. And overall, in order to make the material more accessible, we have portrayed the investigation in more of a linear fashion than occurred, otherwise the weave of the information as it actually did come in would, at times, prove unnecessarily complex.

Finally, I would like to thank my partner and friend, Fiona Everett, for diverse skills, well applied, and also the following for their support and assistance: Geraldine Beare, Bruce Bowden, Peter Brown, Heather Hanson , John and Susan Hindle, Lizzie Hutchins, Liz Hogan, Bev Mills, Garry Oldfield, Nicky Parry, Claire Robinson, Dom Smith and Matt Turner. I would also like to thank all of my teachers including, of course, May Sarah, Becca and Grace.

Paul Howard Ellson

Foreword

by **Jean Houston**

In this astonishing book, the author, David Elkington offers us a life work. With the energy of a true polymath, he weaves together archaeology, mythology, brain research, literature, history, geology, biblical criticism, linguistics, acoustics, physics, metaphysics, and a spate of other disciplines to explore his remarkable thesis: the ways in which the resonance of earth energies informs the names of our gods, sacred space and their functions in our own spiritual progression.

In a foreword one can only give a taste of the feast to follow, but let me here offer some of my own reflections on three of the themes to be found in this work: sacred space, sacred sound, and the passion of Jesus.

It is not uncommon for people who travel to ancient sacred sites to come away with a sense that they have changed, their hearts opened, their spirits rejuvenated, their possibilities extended. How can we explain such miracles, except that the sacred temples – even the Earth beneath one's feet – still reverberate with ancient power, charged by hundreds and even thousands of years of conscious invocation, prayer, incantation, and meditation. It is the author's contention that ancient peoples, especially the Egyptians, were well aware in their construction of temples and pyramids of the nature of sonic frequencies and of geometrical progressions, seeing these as cosmic or sacred powers and employing them as sacred science to effect consciousness. These were people for whom every animal, plant, and stone embodied the divine, a people for whom daily life vibrated spiritual meaning, for whom the mere act of waking from sleep was a resurrection from death, akin to Ra being reborn each morning.

When we view the world as sacred -- when every beast, grain of sand, molecule of air, tree, seed, and river is viewed as being empowered with gods, and we know the name, that is the frequency of these gods, then the world views us as sacred, too and we rise in consciousness accordingly.

For the most part, the temples of Egypt were erected in the centre of the village, with the dwellings of the townspeople built around each temple. Spirit was the keystone of life. The temples were laid down during the dawn of Egyptian history, according to plans designed for them by the mysterious and god-like Companions of Horus. Each new temple was erected on the site of a previous one, with careful observance to all details ranging from architectural structure to astrological significance, from symbolic meaning to functional aspects. Each temple construction began with an invocation to the divine architects of the universe. The invocations called forth the divine powers of universal harmony, mathematics, myth, and symbolism, powers that were then incorporated into the temple design so that the temple on earth would reflect the same design principles used by the divine architects of the universe.

The function of a temple – whether that temple be an actual architectural structure or a group of initiates who form a template, an intellectual structure – is to maintain and perpetuate a vast body of knowledge intact. The establishment and maintenance of any temple requires extraordinary skill by knowledgeable and dedicated individuals who believe that adherence to divine creative principles is the sacred task of all, who view the structure of their temples as well as their daily lives, as artists and craftsmen imitating the creative acts of the divine. They are a fully conscious and deliberate organization who have come together to keep a body of wisdom intact.

In Egypt, it is true that the Colossus of Memnon no longer sings, that the Nile no longer overflows its banks, that the paint is now flaking from the tomb ceilings, that ancient glyphs crumble every day to sand, and that these losses are deeply felt. And still the power thrums beneath the sand and under blue sky, the light of Heaven pierces the hearts of those who come to revere this place. "The gods want you here," a fellahin once told me. "They need someone to speak their names."

In the Name of the Gods, David Elkington does indeed speak their names, and shows how these names the world over are not only similar in pattern but have the same expressive power in form and function.

In this book we have the coming together of world thought, new science, and social artistry is giving us perspectives on what the world and reality may be It presents us with the beginnings of a new natural philosophy. This new philosophy has the potential to evoke and shape our future sciences, arts, economy, politics, technology, psychology and spirituality. It is a view of the world as living within a larger living life – a complex webbing of interdependent relationships – not unlike Indra's net. Within this net, everything is energy, vibration, frequency, resonance. Even the most solid of material objects is ultimately a dance of constantly changing energy patterns. Ultimately it is all rhythm, all music, the world is sound - Nada Brahma - as the classical Sanskrit philosophers put it.

Whereas our eyes can rarely penetrate beyond the three dimensions of space our ears have the capacity for multidimensionality. In Indian music there is the concept of Anahata and ahata, the unplayed and the played note -both are equally important- and the unplayed is often thought to be more important than the played since it provides the foundation for what is actually played. Heraclitus once said that "The hidden harmony is mightier than what is revealed. Not only is the world sound and vibration, but in physical terms there are trillions of possible vibrations. There is a great music master behind it all. Research on harmonics has shown that the cosmos, the universe, and nature have a tendency to select from those innumerable possibilities the few thousand that give rise to proportions of vibration that give us music, architecture, the forms of animal and human bodies, the DNA relationships containing our genetic code, earth magnetism, states of consciousness and access perhaps to higher realities.

The vantage point of this potent book gives us new insight into the Western world's central faith as well. As we move into religious syncretism, many are coming to a new appreciation of the meaning of their Christian roots. As the author shows so brilliantly, Christianity's seminal story, the death and resurrection of Jesus Christ, recapitulates the myth of the dying and rising God venerated in the millennia that preceded his birth, most particularly in Greece and the Ancient Near East. So Isis searches for the scattered parts of her husband, Osiris, binds them together and animates him to produce new life. Demeter calls forth her daughter, Persephone, from her dwelling place in the Kingdom of the Dead. Tammuz, Adonis, Dionysus, all are destroyed, and all are remade. The Christ story is the culminating expression of this cycle, the apotheosis of an ancient pattern celebrated in the ecstatic and highly ritualized piety of the Mystery Religions.

Now, two thousand years later, a new mystery arises and with it a new spiritual myth. The story of Jesus differs from that of the traditional mystery cult figures in that he was a historical person. Because he lived in space and time, Jesus brought the dimension of human experience to the transpersonal and archetypal field of God-Identity. But traditional Christian thought held Jesus to be unique, the only Son of God. The new mythos of or time democratizes divinity. 'That art Thou', as the Hindus put it. Many of us have come to believe that we are all God in hiding, seeded with Christic identity or Buddha Nature, the literal capacity for cosmic consciousness. The single melody under the cacophony of 21st Century spiritual seeking is our collective awakening to the felt and lived awareness that the Divine is not somewhere 'out there' to be supplicated but somehow 'in here' to be discovered.

In Jesus, moreover, as Elkington has shown, two causalities meet: one individual and national, the other collective and universal. On the horizontal level, the Christ story is a Jewish political tragedy. On the vertical, it is a myth that speaks to humankind's yearning for transformation to a higher level of being. Today, all over the world, the same story is being enacted. Our horizontal planet-wide crisis of war and mayhem cries for the vertical solution of universal species transformation. Now the task of transformation does not belong to Christ or Buddha or Quezlcoatl or any of the Saviours alone. We will be equal to the requirements and the responsibilities of the twenty-first century only if we have nurtured the innate seed of our own divinity. The spiritual paradigm has shifted from the One to the many, from the journey that was Christ's Passion, or the passion of the many rising and dying heroes and heroines of myth and legend, to the many existential journeys along the personal and collective mystic path. Like the Passion, this drama of the world's unfolding is a mystery play with several acts. Jesus the Nazarene had his death and resurrection as Christos; our version is the extinction of parts of our limited local self and our resurrection into a unitive reality that is both spiritual consciousness and global spirit, and that is ultimately spiritual resonance, what can be called mysticism or the art of union with Reality.

As you read this book, you enter into a once and future world, and you become the music of the new song...

Introduction

'And he said unto them, "Unto you it is given to know the mystery of the Kingdom of God: but unto them that are without, all these things are done in parables."'

Mark 4:11

SILENCE. Then just one shaft of sunlight and the miracle would be complete. Before me, a pillar of smoke in the dimly lit surroundings of an ancient monument, as I awaited the rising sun with considerable and mounting excitement. Just one sound, a frequency beyond hearing, the gift of God, was what I was searching for. Arrayed behind me a veritable wall of symbology – spirals, zigzags and crosses, all of which, in recent years, had been subjected to a bewildering array of technology and accompanying paraphernalia. It was a cold morning towards the end of December and the air was thick with a freezing mist of the kind that penetrates the deepest layers – and in the deepest sense. I had come here for a confirmation of events that had happened a few months earlier on Egypt's Giza plateau. I was seeking to understand further those events and to put them into a wider perspective. At Giza, wonderful things had happened, but it was here in the gnawing cold of a British winter that I would find the same things, an irony that would not be lost on me. I had left this country some years earlier in pursuit of the seemingly unknowable, only to return, having realised that it was all here – it was only a matter of looking.

At the outset of my adventure I little realised quite what a quest it would be. I did not know where I was going, nor what I was looking for. I had no theories, not even a premise into which I would slot whatever facts came my way. All I had was a suspicion, a dull irritation within my mind, brought about by a sense of enigma, 'wrapped in mystery inside a riddle', but wherever I looked, wherever I witnessed the mystery in an almost infinite series of 'coincidences', the explanations given were at best fanciful, spurious even. And when my deeper enquiries were answered by a universal, nay, catholic, silence, my hackles rose – not so much at the naked silence, but at the fact that the evidence seemed all-pervasive, emerging out of a time when history seemed hardly to have begun. In retrospect, perhaps this was a reason for such ignorance.

My search had been full of rumour. It was a journey across time, across continents and across a wide spectrum of faith. I had seen many strange things.

Along the road I had encountered satanic popes, heretical saints and non-Christian Christians whose faith was stronger than that of the believers. It was remarkable, I thought, that finally a solution to all of these seeming contradictions had been found, one that encompassed them all by the very fact that Christianity was indeed unique – unique to all religions.

Having discovered that the name of Jesus was to be found the world over, and in the context of a prehistoric acoustic phenomenon, was remarkable and unsettling, but I had carried the task through and at last there was light and reality at the end of the tunnel.

The ultimate statement of intent, the secret Holy Name of God – a word uttered from divine 'lips', at the moment of Creation to incredible and powerful effect, the primordial act of awareness, the act that transformed and brought about matter, *ex nihilo* – out of nothing – no-thing – by an effect of consciousness that has forever been reflected in the make up of the universe – the secret of it was writ here, within this chamber and its glory was about to be manifested at sunrise on the winter solstice at a site constructed over 5,000 years ago, as it would be reflected at sites like this elsewhere.

As a schoolboy in Australia I had the opportunity of meeting a native people – the Aborigines – and sampling their culture. I had arrived from England at the grand old age of four and, young though I was, had immediately been impressed by the quiet air of knowing that the Aborigines somehow seem to have. Their beliefs were not a million miles away from the European beliefs that I had left behind, unaffected as yet by them though I was. When I returned to Europe some years later, to all intents and purposes a naturalised Australian, I was surprised at the connections between the two. The most striking was the Aboriginal myth that told of a man who climbed a tree and was killed in it, only to descend from it alive three days later. This strange man was described as a 'son of God', and in other startlingly familiar terms.

Just one shaft of sunlight and the miracle would be complete.

It is now common knowledge that we are made of the stuff of stars. In some vaguely distant past, we too have been shafts of light and something else, something carried within light, something godly and so little understood, yet exquisite beyond knowing. This something, we are told, was the Word upon God's lips, the Word that gave rise to it all, to literally everything, and through all the long ages it has been cherished by man, nurtured by him and to some extent known and described – but not in any language familiar to us.

In fact I had realised from the outset that language, when dealing with the godly, has its limitations. However, these were limits not unknown to ancient man, who crafted language to his needs, so that it became a key to that original, single, unforgettable sound.

Years later, when I was busy working in advertising and the media, I attended the first of many lectures at the Egypt Exploration Society. I began at last to understand, albeit tentatively at first, the mindset of the Ancients and, equally importantly, their mythology. I learned much.

My research continued and I was almost ready to commit it all to paper, but there was something missing, a spark that I just could not find. Until one day it appeared. It is the greatest of secrets.

However, before the secret can be revealed, we have to ask ourselves certain fundamental questions about the way we view the world. For what is a secret worth if it can never be understood? These are questions that I have asked myself time and time again over the years, because, when confronted with the evidence, it was very difficult to accept the notion, not that a man performed miracles, was crucified and rose again from the dead, but that these events took place only 2,000 years ago, in the first century AD – Anno Domini, the year of our Lord.

Years later I have come to accept that a Christlike figure did indeed live in first century Palestine, for the Church that we know today could not possibly exist without that basic fact. The evidence, however, remains at best circumstantial and, as I will reveal, Jesus also lived in Japan, in Britain, in America and in a host of other places, places that are connected to the profoundest sacred technology. In Japan, Britain and America, as well as at innumerable other sites, these monuments take the shape of pyramids. It seems that Jesus lived in some style. Furthermore, he did so many millennia ago. And, if my hunch is correct, by visiting these places in the right state of mind, and by according them the respect that is their due, one may still detect the presence of the greatest of heroes, Jesus himself – a fact that can be attested. (see part two)

This is not fiction. When I finally came to this realisation I was forced to confront the fact that truth is indeed stranger than fiction – and it became ever stranger the more I went on. And so it is with the facts upon which my theories are based.

We now come to another question: if the name of Jesus is to be found the world over, intimately associated with particular sacred sites and temples, what if each sacred site not only shares a correlatory pattern but also served the same scientific purpose? Then our view of history really begins to change.

Therefore, my premise is simple: that all God names are resonances, and that the most significant of those names is the name of Jesus, the name of the healer, the saviour. In this sense, Jesus is a master name, a key to all of the other names of the gods and the heroes that are inevitably associated with them.

Based upon what I had uncovered, I adjusted my view regarding the probability of an historical Christ towards the likelihood that there was an older mythical figure called Jesus, for the Jesus of the gospels seems almost a shadow figure, the man who was not there – like the reflection of someone in a plate-glass window. We, in the modern world, have until recently erred on the side of literal interpretation. There is a tendency to only believe in evidence of a particular 'official' nature, until other evidence is found that simply cannot be ignored – the discovery of the Nag Hammadi and the Dead Sea scrolls are particular cases in point.

It is the winners who write the histories, by putting their own views into the mouths of our ancestors. In this way modern regimes gain their identity and their justification. The Western model bases itself upon ancient Greek, and subsequent Roman, civilisation. The problem with this, as will be discussed further on, is that although the Greeks and Romans themselves looked to Egypt as the prime source of their civilisation, Egypt in the Western consciousness, thousands of years later, has been so far reduced in status as to appear irrelevant, a mere distraction within the historical scheme of things. Therefore, despite the mute testimony of the pyramids, Egypt is dismissed as a barbaric civilisation without knowledge of the fundamentals of Western civilisation: philosophy, mathematics, knowledge of *pi* and of golden proportion and cursive language as written. What would have happened if the Muslims had succeeded in tearing down the pyramids? Would archaeologists have believed quite how massive they truly were? It would be reasonable to suggest that they would not, and who could blame them? However, the pyramids still stand and cannot be ignored – but why do we assume that their builders knew nothing of more import?

Once we see how easily we entered into such a dangerous assumption, we can begin to understand the source of the rise of anti-Semitism in the West and its brutal outcome. 'The gap between a Church-centred religion and a cosmic one is enormous and has had tragic consequences.' These words of Gordon Strachan resonated deep within me from the outset of the last phase of my journey. The winners, in writing history, have inscribed their views indelibly upon the flesh of man's past. However, do the winners of history really succeed with their interpretations?

As I progressed, I came to understand that hidden within the winners' version there are strange anomalies, that slowly begin to rise like bubbles to the surface of a deep and murky pool. A good example is to be found in the writings of Julius Caesar, writings that are generally accepted by historians as having a solid basis in fact. From this launchpad has arisen the Romanocentric view of the founding of civilised Britain. According to this view, Caesar came, saw and conquered in order to show how powerful the Romans really were and having made his point, he withdrew to achieve greater glory on the European mainland and within the Roman Senate.

The emergent truth tells a different story, one that Caesar saw fit to expunge from his dubious text. The Romans came to Britain and in a series of engagements with the British tribes the scorecard read: Romans 0, Britons XI. Caesar's famous utterance, 'Veni, vidi, vici' – 'I came, I saw, I conquered' – was rewritten by satirists in the Roman camp, opposed to Caesar, as, 'I came, I saw, I failed to stay.'[1]

By a strange moral twist that is as organic as it is peculiar, truths seem to emerge in spite of the historical flow. A recent poll by the *Daily Telegraph* newspaper revealed that for as many as 70 per cent of practising Christians the Resurrection was a purely spiritual affair. More pleasing than this was the fact that for many this spiritual aspect had strengthened their faith. Why should I find it 'pleasing'? Because new evidence suggests that the long-neglected spiritual angle is about to come into its own. This angle involves a multiplicity of things scientific, but mainly in the fields of medical science and physics, where the study of energy patterns and their interaction has revealed much that goes against the present established 'mechanical' paradigm. This raises a question: given the style of markings found at so many ancient sacred sites, were ancient peoples to a certain extent aware of these patterns? Is this the reason why they constructed the most impossible monuments at improbable locations – to enhance those sites energetically and, by extension, enhance themselves?

For me, this was the crux of it. I was no longer on a quest for gold and jewels and riches beyond measure – I had grown with the project and my vision now began to see beyond that which is tangible in the sense that it might be material. What I saw was subtle almost beyond knowing and all along I had the feeling that I was not alone in my quest. Often I had that curious 'look over the shoulder' feeling, the sense that someone had been there aeons before and that they were still present. Oddly enough, this presence was more comforting than sinister. A sinister presence would have seemed conspiratorial, but this is the point where we enter a new millennium, not the dark days of the Inquisition. From all the information that I had gathered, there was the uncanny feeling that from the realm of the dead, from history herself, there was a life-force that was sprouting new shoots, revealing that real history never dies, that it is the very structure of society itself, giving us a sense of time and place. However, as physics has revealed, care of Mr Einstein, time is an illusion, and history too is an illusion – but it is one that humanity has shaped very carefully to its complex needs.

Just one shaft of sunlight.

My sense of history, my personal view in the light of religion, philosophy and science, is that we have to acknowledge the illusion, face to face, before we can move on. This is the actual view of many of the religious texts of our world, wherever one might travel. If anything, finally acknowledging the present woeful state of the environment and our misuse of it has actually taught us many necessary things about our relationship with our home planet and quite how much we depend upon it. Man, in seeking to rise above nature, may have fallen below it. We must realise the truth of our role in nature, and the language of this realisation is the language of myth. Understanding myth is a way back to truth.

The language of myth, I believe, gave individuals the ability to attain harmony with themselves and, by extension, beyond themselves. Curiously, it is myth that invariably forms the foundation of much of the world's religious belief. Even more curious is the fact that the term 'religion' carries an undertone of man's Fall and of a long-disappeared Golden Age. The term comes from the Latin *religio*, meaning 'to bind back'. To bind back to what, one might ask? Could it be that the Golden Age of man and the Fall are metaphors for spiritual states of being? The more I sought, the more I realised that this was indeed the case.

In 1983 I had an experience of great profundity, one that I have since recognised as a rare moment when everything changed. This overwhelming feeling of change was accompanied by an acute sense of emotion and of incipient spirituality. I must here emphasise that I am not an emotional person, as an Englishman I am proud of my *sang-froid*.

It was a cold, crisp winter of the sort that brings into focus the glories of the British landscape. Approaching the city of Wells over the flat terrain of the Somerset Levels I was instantly struck by the golden beauty of its cathedral when illuminated by midwinter sunshine. The interior of Wells cathedral is one of the glories of European ecclesiastical architecture and, upon entry, I was much taken with the various elements of it, from the fan vaulting to the stained-glass windows. Walking around the nave it is very easy to miss the door that leads up to the Chapter House. I have to admit that I was in a specific frame of mind as I began to ascend the staircase. 1983 had been a bad year for me, and here, almost at the end of it, I was in a reflective but peaceful mood. It was approximately halfway up the staircase that the music hit me. It was my first conscious experience of resonance and its power to transform. The Wells cathedral choir was rehearsing for a carol concert in the Chapter House and I had just been overwhelmed by the first bars of 'In the Deep Midwinter'. It is difficult for me to describe the experience without appearing to exaggerate, but I am *not* exaggerating. I went weak at the knees and felt myself so uplifted that my very sense of being seemed detached from my body. To say that I was dizzy really is an understatement. I came out of the experience an emotional ruin and yet transformed. It took me years to understand why, but, with your patience, this book will explain.

The key to the whole mystery lies within the landscape. The landscape, mankind's relationship to it and the mystery are one and the same thing. So, too, are landscape and language. And this extends outwards to the cosmos, so that there is an actual link between heaven and earth, that link being ourselves. If you do not believe me, then go to these sacred sites yourself and witness the presence of the hero. He is there, beckoning us on by his example.

Wherever I went, from the pyramids of Giza to the sacred rock of the Aborigines, Uluru, there he was. Myth tells of his arrival in many lands, every inch heroic, arrayed in white, bringing knowledge and peace to a far-flung world and then mysteriously disappearing, promising to return, one day. Very early on I was struck by the similarities of this myth worldwide and by various other aspects too. Only later did it occur to me that this hero might be one and the same person. But others before me have commented upon the universal nature of Jesus' knowledge and words (see for example G. Strachan, *Jesus the Master Builder*, p.189). What was the knowledge that the hero gave to the world?

Perhaps the answer to that really does lie in religion. By the time I had visited a broad swathe of the world's sacred monuments I had come to the conclusion that there was more to religion than met the eye. I had become faintly aware of an underlying spiritual technology, that somehow religion is a lost language of science and that, in another way, science is a rediscovery of religion. Moreover, if this really is true, it begs the question, who or what is the hero – who or what was Jesus?

Just one shaft of sunlight.

Realising that there was a Jesus of history and a separate hidden Jesus of myth had led me up the garden path out of the gate and into an all too real world. I became happy with the distinction between the two Jesuses, because at last the impossibility of much religious belief began to make sense, particularly from the human angle.

My new understanding of Christianity's uniqueness had done away with the need to differentiate between Pagans and Christians. Suddenly the disparate elements took upon themselves a new cohesion, a unity that I discovered was very profound. It was the last thing I had expected to occur. Suddenly, it all made sense: a Name of Power that almost predates history, that occurs in association with particular sacred sites in all of the world's civilisations, all of them linked by a specific set of brain-altering frequencies that give rise to the same beliefs, the same rituals and the same conclusions. Beyond that we breach the official remit of history, going into the realm of the shaman, of the healer and of the scientist, into a fantastic but very real world of practical and spiritual implications. How else can we explain the extraordinary use of stone and sound, as displayed in Egypt, South America and a host of other places? A man transformed does indeed walk with God. The only task left to me now is to explain it. Where to begin?

Just one shaft of starlight and the miracle is complete.

I shall now happily invoke the Muse, knowing that in writing of Christianity as it really is there will be no contradiction.

Prologue

'If the historic Muse hath entrusted me with any secrets, I will by no means be guilty of discovering them till she shall give me leave.'

Henry Fielding, *Tom Jones*, II:6

DEEP in the depths of a British midwinter, when days are short and bleak and nights are a chorus of freezing winds and hard crystalline frosts, we long for Christmas and the lengthening of the days, and we yearn for the optimism that light brings. At that time, psychologically at least, there is the feeling that darkness has been defeated in its eternal battle with light, and that life can be lived to the full as the longer days herald the approach of spring and a renewal.

On a yet deeper level, we are aware that Christmastime is the celebration of the divine child, who brings light and all good things. How poignant that the birth of Jesus, the light-giving Christian hero, coincides with this time when the darkness retreats and the light proves victorious, when nature herself underlines the Christian message. This newborn child will take mankind out of the darkness and will, by example, set us upon the road to salvation, the attainment of heaven. And yet, despite its strong Christian associations, this is a motif familiar to many of the world's religions, one which seems almost omnipresent within the world's mythology – an observation that has not been lost upon generations of scholars.

Among the first to comment in any detail upon the similarities between motif and myth was the great anthropologist Sir James George Frazer. The culmination of his research was the 22-volume *The Golden Bough*, which caused a considerable stir within the circles of high Victorian society. Some even suggested that the death knell for the Church had sounded. However, this observation remained just that, until midway through the twentieth century, when a less strictured, more radical generation, readily influenced by Frazer, came into its own.

This generation of scholars has, with varying degrees of success, been chipping away at the fabric of the Church and its dogma. Even theologians have joined in the sport (Hans Kung and Matthew Fox are among the most prominent), some to the point of heresy, but what may come as a big surprise is that this considerable army of twentieth century scholarship was not the first to arrive in this fruitful territory. The ground had been trodden as long ago as the twelfth, thirteenth and fourteenth centuries, a fact not unknown to the current Church elders, who have a well–documented archive going back to the very period in question.

The archive speaks of heresy, suppression, torture and murder – all of it in the name of Christianity, all of it perpetrated by a Church in crisis. It was during this period that the Church began, effectively, to label itself into a corner. Suppression was rife and amongst those whose beliefs were suppressed, in the early fourteenth century, were the senior hierarchy of the Knights of the Temple of Solomon, the Templars for short. Their crime? The preaching of a broader and deeper Jesus, of an older and greater Christianity. My research told me that as well as having realised the similarities between myth and religion, the Templars were in possession of a more potent, perhaps scientific knowledge, one that they put to profound and practical use. In the chapters that follow, I shall unveil that science – a secret science, one intimately connected with the name of Jesus.

Now, for reasons that will soon become apparent, there is no better way to introduce my investigation into the enigma of Jesus than via tales that seemed to appear in Britain, Ireland and mainland Europe at about the time of the Templar period, the early 1100s. They are folk tales, but ones that many historians believe are based upon actual historical characters.

It may be said, with some confidence, that these tales were given their final shape by the troubadours, and were much approved of by their masters, the Templars. 'Troubadour' was the title given to the wandering minstrels and storytellers who flourished in Western Europe at the time of the Templars.

The medieval period was an age in whch few people ever left their locale to venture outwards into the wider world. Travel was sanctioned by the ruling classes and perhaps the limitations of locality showed themselves to a certain extent within medieval thought, which was perhaps hemmed in by a lack of experience of what the wider world had to offer. This age was a little over 1,000 years after the death of Christ upon the cross and yet, via the troubadour tradition, something older began to stir within the medieval mind, a little something that was stirred by an unerring suspicion – the fact that other men, called 'gods', had long ago been crucified and shared not only the simple fate of Jesus, but also his words, his deeds and, in fact, many aspects of his life. The troubadours were part of an oral tradition, a worldwide tradition that finds its origins in the period that came well before the written word and right up until the twentieth century, with the advent of mass education, television and the microchip, it still had great influence as a tool for enlightening the populace. It is regrettable that, in the present day, many of the tradition's stories are dismissed as old wives' tales.

However, in the Templar period, awkward questions were raised about the nature of these stories and the nature of Christian belief in general. The inevitable occurred – the wrath of the Church was awoken and the era of suppression began its long and bloody reign. The troubadours disappeared from the stage of history, as did many others, long before their time was due, killed in the great upheavals that took place in the aftermath of their doubting – and all because of the rumours of a crucified man and his miracles being well before *his* time, many thousands of years before.

In Gaulish Western Europe he was called Esus and can be seen, in at least one depiction, as a crucified man, nailed to a tree. In Britain, as I will demonstrate, one of his names was Robin Hood. In other myths, he appears mysteriously as 'the Lord', working miracles and wonders that share many uncanny similarities with certain episodes within the Gospels. Furthermore, these characters appear in tandem with specific locations, sites of great sanctity and, as will emerge, great power. Was there, I mused, a connection, one that is intimated in myth? And how recent were these myths that people were so suddenly becoming aware of? As it turned out, they were not that recent at all; they were very ancient indeed.

Looking further abroad, I soon came to realise that these facts and figures were not just restricted to Europe. They seemed to occur everywhere. In Native America, before the arrival of the first Europeans, the hero appears occurs under variations of the name Esa. The same too in Central and South America and other places besides. The range is truly astonishing. Though there are many variants upon a theme, a cursory glance at these legends reveals as many similarities as there are discrepancies when compared to the Gospels. And so it is that the myths do not always come across as obviously as perhaps they should.

It was whilst I was exploring the theme of Robin Hood that I came across a piece of information which surprised me. Apparently the Roman goddess Diana, according to sources contemporary with the Roman period, had a vision of a Virgin and a Holy Child. What is surprising is that there is an exact parallel to this in the Gospels, where St. Anne, mother of the Virgin, has the same vision. Diana and Anna – the same name. In Middle Eastern myth Di-ana is the mother of Mari. On the male side of things there are even more surprises. The Jewish God is called Yahweh and his son Yeshua, or Jesus as he is famously known. Intriguingly, amongst the Native American peoples there are two such characters, called respectively Yawe and Yeshe.

The similarities continue. But more intriguing than all this is the fact that these names were hallowed within certain sacred spaces, and it is this that I have so far omitted, the most beautiful and enduring legacy of the Templar period – the Gothic cathedrals.

These huge houses of worship were erected, on an unprecedented scale, right across western Europe, by vast armies of masons whose training remains largely a mystery – as mysterious as their intent. The care and attention paid to the detail of these extraordinary monuments is, by any standard, remarkable given the time period concerned, and where the money came from goodness knows! But why? Why that design? Why that size? Well, have you heard the acoustics? 'Breathtaking' does not do them justice. These places are monuments to the human voice – to the sheer power of the voice, to be exact. I shall touch upon something of great import.

It struck me that the rituals performed in these places are an expression of the sacred and, ultimately, of the language of the sacred. Words are poetic metaphors and more. They are expressions of the power of sound. The Templars were the 'Poor Knights of the Temple of Solomon', and upon their return to Europe suddenly these temples were everywhere – as if we are being told that somehow the historical Jesus is linked to the resonance of the divine. A resonant Messiah?

I have always noticed how, throughout history, certain syllables have a recurring value and occur on a regular basis, so much so that they seem to make up the foundation of the language of myth. The very names of the gods themselves are composed of such syllables; these same syllables recur throughout ancient language as puns, and in this guise their meanings translate across many contexts, hiding their innate power.

What occurred to me was this: what if the name of God is a sound, a particular frequency, that in the context of religious ritual has the ability to alter brainwave patterns in such a way as to reveal that we do indeed inhabit a conscious universe? What if the real secret of the ancient mysteries was hidden deep inside the divine – in the Name of the Gods?

Part One

The Dying and Rising God

1

The View from Golgotha

'...Commentators refer to Jeshu-ha-Notzri by mention of the wicked Kingdom of Edom, since that was his nation. ... He was hanged on a Passover Eve... He was near to the Kingdom.'

'Balaam the Lame was 33 years old when Pintias the Robber killed him...They say that his mother was descended from princes and rulers, but consorted with carpenters.'

Lexicon Talmudicum, sub 'Abanarbel'
and Talmud Babli Sanhedrin 106b, 43a, 51a[1]

'...it is not easy, to understand the connection between the risen Christ, making his presence felt, and the historical Jesus.'

A. N. Wilson, *Jesus* [2]

In the early years of the first century Anno Domini, in or around the year of Our Lord AD 33, there appeared a 'wanted' poster in the form of a 'hue and cry' notice. It read something like this:

<u>HUE AND CRY NOTICE</u>

WANTED

for sedition against the state

BAALAM THE LAME

also known as

JESUS

'A man of simple appearance, mature age, dark skin, small stature, three cubits high, hunchbacked, with a long face, long nose and meeting eyebrows, so that they who see him might be affrighted. Scanty hair with a parting in the middle of his head, after the manner of the Nazirites, and with an under–developed beard.'[3]

During the latter months of his ministry, Jesus, through his 'wonder-workings' and teachings, had become something of a thorn in the authorities' side. They wanted him out of the way. It is known that 'hue and cry' notices were in regular use at the time and one similar to the above would have been a part of the authorities' offensive against Jesus.

The description given is known to be reasonably accurate, coming from

Josephus Flavius, a Judaeo-Roman historian born around the year AD 37. Josephus is generally regarded as a more trustworthy historical source than the later Christian writers, who were wont to add their own particular slant in the same way that political spin-doctors do today. In comparison with the early Christian sources Josephus had no particular agenda to fulfil.

An official report on Jesus' trial was filed as a part of the *Acta Pilati*, a document which Josephus used as source material. Josephus' description of Jesus remained in circulation for centuries, being commented on, for example, in the eighth century, by the Archbishop of Crete, Andreas Heirosolymitanus, who stated:

> 'But moreover the Jew Josephus in the manner narrates that the Lord was seen having connate eyebrows, goodly eyes, long faced, crooked, well grown.' [4]

Though long since lost, Josephus' description has been reconstructed from many such reputable sources.[5]

The 'wanted' poster, produced from an historical 'identikit', is not given for effect. Instead, I hope that it will help to indicate how our ideas about Jesus have been shaped by numerous influences, many of which have little to do with the facts. The description given is one of Jesus, but it is a far cry from the Western portrayal of him which, all in all, is distinctly Aryan. In contrast to the very human description given by Josephus, Jesus is worshipped and adored as superhuman and, for many, the idea of Jesus being in any way ugly is unacceptable, gross and untenable.[6] Yet the impression of a 'human' Jesus is one attested to by many of the early Church Fathers, a 'human' and distinctly 'ugly' Jesus, 'when in the flesh'.[7] This last comment, also made by the early Fathers, makes an interesting distinction between the earthly Jesus and the heavenly Christ. It is from the idea of the heavenly that we get our ideal image of what God's Son should look like blue-eyed, red-haired, full-lipped, tall, erect; a fine specimen of a 'god made man'. We could hardly expect anything less, but Josephus, so much nearer to the scene and without an axe to grind, tells us otherwise.

It is a strange thing to observe, but the idea of a religion being founded by a mere 'human', and an ugly one at that, is in many ways a turn-off. When I first encountered the description of the actual Jesus, I was a young man, in my early twenties. At the time I was stunned at this description of the person that I had been taught was the Saviour, for my idea of Jesus, before I had encountered Josephus' remarks, was one of Aryan loveliness – a man who was more than half a god. It did not occur to me the least bit that Jesus would have been every inch a man of his time and of his geography – and that both were complicated.

Who Jesus was is the subject of an ongoing historical and theological argument that will, no doubt, continue for quite some considerable time to come. It is a subject upon which many an academic reputation has risen and fallen. Yet, as the arguments rage and the reputation of the Christian Church flinches under the academic and archaeological spotlight, there is a curious reluctance by almost all participants to step back and observe Jesus beyond the context of Christianity, that is, to look into what came *before*.

The Jesus that we perceive, 2,000 years after the events described in the Gospels, is a character that fits numerous identities. There is the Jesus of faith, meek and mild; there is the radical revolutionary, a 'fundamentalist' zealot whose main aim was the stirring of the masses to rise up against the might of Rome; there is Jesus the Jew, to whom the idea of being labelled a 'Son of God' would be blasphemous in the extreme, a character completely innocent of the charge of initiating a new religious belief; Jesus the miracle-worker who raised Lazarus and turned water into wine; and Jesus the Gnostic whose words were wise, profound, simple and deeply personal, a figure who appealed to the sense of individual responsibility in everyone.

These identities are a rich tapestry, interwoven with many coloured, carefully applied strands, but what they actually show us is a reflection of ourselves. These images demonstrate quite clearly the subtle trap of perceiving history through a modern lens where we apply our current experience and values to opinions and judgements, even tales of 2,000 years ago. Naturally, people of every era are prone to do the same.

It was Albert Schweitzer who noted that the 'early lives of Jesus were written by people who looked down the long well of history and saw their own face reflected at the bottom'. He also realised that the world of the New Testament is strange, even alien, to us, because it was dominated by eschatology, namely the belief that creation had come to its climax, that the end of all things was near.[8] This sense of the 'end of times', of impending catastrophe and then, hopefully, a new age, is important in understanding the beliefs and times of ancient Judea, for we can begin to appreciate that the basis of these beliefs was in mythology, including that of the Old Testament; a mythology that certain interested parties in Judea were doing their utmost to fulfil.

Many Messiahs

The word 'Christ' is derived from the Greek *Christos* , meaning 'the anointed one'. This is derived from the Hebrew word for 'anointed', which is *mashiah* in the West spelt 'messiah'. The Jewish concept of messiah is far removed from what has become associated with the Christian idea of a singular Son of God. The messiah was not a singular figure; there could be, and were, messiahs plural. These messiahs were deliverers, they rescued the people from the harsh repressions of foreign invaders and delivered them into a 'land of milk and honey', free of the Pagan influences of self-interested outsiders. These messiahs were, of course, kings, but kings performing God's will.

We should remember that in ancient society, there was no distinction between secular and religious law. The everyday world was seen in a religious context, whereas today, religion is 'something that some people do on Sundays'. The ruler was seen as administering God's laws upon the earth and therefore the rightful king was also of the priestly caste. Of course, there were variable degrees of success in the role. The most successful were called messiahs.

From time immemorial we know that, at least from the Nile to the Ganges and areas to the north, this priest-king rule held true. In practical terms the genealogy of lineage was at work here in that it was believed that a spiritual and organisational caste, a priestly caste, India's Brahmins for example, would pass on its natural tendencies to its descendants. This, in effect, was a managed gene-pool. Special training would build on those genetic tendencies and so the families concerned would be cossetted, for the stresses of living in survival mode, as members of the peasantry, would make successful training very difficult.[9] Hence the royal household had a special advantage and connection regarding the priesthood, and if one of great priestly potential was found amongst the general populace, they would be brought into the system to be trained. Even in times of upheaval, if the throne were seized by the unannointed, the status quo would soon return, either through training of the new lineage or reinstatement of the old.[10]

At the top of the hierarchy were the royal families. Egypt had its Pharoahs, the Hindu messiahs Rama and Krishna were of royal blood and, even to this day, the head of a Bedouin tribe still holds a spiritual title, the Sheikh. All across the Middle East and most likely across the world, the spiritually trained were the élite. They had a certain something that other classes did not. Solomon and David were messiahs, as were the Hasmonean Kings, who delivered the Jewish Kingdom from the grasp of the Seleucid empire, *c*.167 BC. These kings were perceived as being representative of God's power on earth; it is almost as if they were consensus figureheads both of God and God's people, the messiah-king was the point at which God manifested to the people. In this sense they were 'Sons of God'. They were sometimes called 'God incarnate', suggesting that the spirit of God was fully operative inside them from the point of being crowned, so that they were both God and man. In essence, the king represented the spirit of God and all of the attendant gifts associated with such a being, healing included. However, contrary to what was later to become the norm in Christianity, this still did not make the king a divine being, a god in his *own* right. He was, as the Old Testament often relates, very much a human being, even when the man and the myth merged, and the myth went abroad.[11] The most renowned of the Hebrew messiahs was Solomon, a son of David, around whom much myth is wrapped. Famous for his wisdom and for his love affair with the Queen of Sheba, Solomon was also, according to legend, the progenitor of varying foreign types of Judaism. Like his forebears, Solomon was a great 'begatter' of children. The Ethiopian Falasha, who claim direct descent from Solomon and Sheba, are a case in point; as is the claim of a black South African people, the Lemba.[12] The religion of Solomon was widespread and more liberal than the Judaism that holds sway today.[13]

Behind the Christian idea of 'The Messiah', is something which, whilst taking some if its philosophy from ancient Hebrew concepts of God, really stems from other, wider, more archaic traditions, for example, traditions which were carried in the expansion of Hellenism in the late fourth century BC. The impetus behind this expansion of Greek ideas was embodied in a very famous warrior, Alexander the Great.

Alexander, the Macedonian conqueror of the ancient world, achieved his own godlike status as a result of a series of extraordinary campaigns in which he displayed his enormous courage and tactical genius, a genius born not only of blood, but of learning, for in his youth, Alexander's tutor had been the great Aristotle, and Aristotle had been only too keen to inure his fiery pupil with a broad knowledge. Through the interplay of these various factors Alexander came to believe, as did his followers, that he was divine, a living god. This was seemingly borne out by Alexander's deeds.

Alexander claimed descent from Heracles and was deemed to be a child of the father of the gods, Zeus-Ammon. Ammon is the Egyptian equivalent of Zeus (the father of the Greek pantheon), and it was in Egypt, at the remote Siwa oasis, that Alexander's claim was confirmed by the priests of Ammon. Like Jesus, Alexander was 'born of God'. Intriguingly, this term is explained in various of Alexander's biographies as being due to the fact that his mother, Olympias, took part in orgiastic rites wherein she conceived Alexander 'by God, in other words, by a male priest representing the power of the god, possibly a priest related to the Macedonian royal line'.[14] Another shared feature in both stories is the fact that both heroes are said to have died young. Alexander's career is all the more amazing because of its brevity – at 33, the conqueror of the world was dead, as was Jesus, the spiritual conqueror, at around the same age.

The centre of Alexander's empire, in a geographical sense, was the Holy Land and with the irresistible onset of the Hellenistic expansion, Palestine became a veritable melting pot wherein influences of both East and West transmuted and solidified into what were to become Christianity, Rabbinic Judaism and, later, Islam.

It can be understood that some of the ideas familiar to us within Christianity may in fact have stemmed from the great influx of Greek cultural influence beginning from the fourth century BC.

On the whole the Greek influence was given a vote of approval by the more liberal elements of Judaic society, for there was much that appeared familiar to them from earlier times. However, there was also a conservative element to Jewish culture and religion that, as time went on, became ever more rebellious in the face of a perceived cultural invasion. This element centred on Judah and particularly on the capital, Jerusalem. Its leaders began a successful rebellion which culminated in the overthrow of the Seleucid kings (*c.*167 BC). (Seleucus had been one of Alexander's generals and the heir to a large portion of Alexander's vast empire.)

The new Jewish Hasmonean kings, the Maccabeans, firmly instituted a more narrowly prescribed and centralised form of worship, the centre being the Temple at Jerusalem. However, the centrists did not have it all their own way, especially after the overthrow of the Hasmoneans when, under the Romans, the coming of Herod posed a great threat to the religious authorities: the return of earlier beliefs. This is of key importance. However, before looking into Herod and his beliefs, it will be useful to gain an insight into the historical background.

The Early Kingdoms

What I am about to deliberate is at once complex and labyrinthine, so bear with me, particularly as the conclusion is so crucial, so bloody and so human.

From around 2000 BC, when the ancient Hebrews had migrated from Mesepotamia to the region known as Palestine, they had been establishing their ascendency over the indigenous Canaanites. In the region soon to be known as Judea, King David (*c.*1000 BC), united all of the Hebrew tribes into one nation. This union was only to last for one further generation, that of his son Solomon. During this period, we are told that Solomon carried out his father's wish - the building of a great temple, known as Solomon's Temple. After the death of Solomon, the kingdom of Israel was split into two, with Solomon's heir, Rehobcam, becoming king of the southern portion, Judah, and with an old adversary of Solomon's, Jeroboam, becoming the first king of the north kingdom, Israel (*c.* 931 BC)[15] In the meantime, the people of Judah would flourish and, eventually, come to be known as Jews. Unfortunately for the tribes of Israel, things were not so straightforward.

In 722 BC the northern kingdom of Israel fell to the invading army of Assyria and a considerable number of Israelites were deported to other lands.[16] Many of the deportees went to Jerusalem, taking with them their ancient northern traditions.[17] The Assyrians settled others in their stead, often forcibly. Incomers included Greeks and Phoenicians. This land, with its hotchpotch of remnant Israelites and various incomers, became known as Samaria and its inhabitants Samaritans. Samaria has, within its geography, some of the most significant of the biblical monuments and places. Amongst these is Mount Gerizim, which the Samaritans claim is in fact Mount Moriah, *the* place to worship God. The Samaritans accepted the Pentateuch, the five books of Moses, but not the other Hebrew scriptures. Because of these changes, the character of Samaria was perceived to have changed. It was now viewed as a Pagan area by those of the south who, anxious to preserve their culture in such uncertain times, were becoming less tolerant of broader influences.

In later years attempts were made to bring Samaria into the fold of Judah, but all such attempts failed. Tensions between Judah and its northern relation gradually built up as the Samaritans were increasingly looked upon as outsiders. In *c.* 598 BC, the Jerusalem Temple was destroyed by the Babylonians, who also carried off a large part of the population. Many years later, when the exiles, now known as Jews, returned from Babylon (*c.* 539 BC - see chronology), they began a programme of reconstruction, but even at this stage the Samaritans were refused permission to help them. Later still, a failed revolt against Macedonian rule in *c.* 331 BC again resulted in the exile of the local population and the rebuilding of the city under Hellenistic principles.

The Hellenisation of the region was potent and prolonged. Ideas of Greek philosophy and culture presented a huge challenge to the priests of Yahweh, the Jewish God, with the result that certain aspects of Greek thought became embraced within their theology. However, the main thrust of the Hellenizing tradition was brought to a halt in the year 167 BC by one of the defining moments of Jewish history, the Maccabean revolt. In the aftermath of this domestic upheaval, the Temple cult of Jerusalem would reach its zenith and then topple amidst great catastrophe.

Even during this period and beyond, the inhabitants of Judah and of Samaria regarded each other with great unease, for Jews linked Samaritans to the Gentiles and their forms of belief. In the light of Samarian history and tradition, Jesus' parable of the Good Samaritan becomes endowed with new light; for, actually, an older, less constricted belief system was at work in Samaria. Jesus was himself referred to, somewhat contemptuously, as a Samaritan,[18] someone who walked a dangerously fine line between Judaic law and Gentile belief. Of course, in the past, these had been much closer, but the coming of the Maccabean rule would guarantee that they remained divided.

The accession of the Maccabeans would be the signal for an explosive era to begin, wherein the conservative forces of Judaism would rally against the Roman and Hellenistic influences that they held to be detrimental to their homeland. The Hasmoneans, as the Maccabeans should properly be known, hailed from the village of Modein, 23 miles northwest of Jerusalem (1 Macc.2:1). What spurred them on to official legitimacy and the throne were the excesses of the Seleucid rule.

By the time of the Seleucid King Antiochus IV Epiphanes, the region of Palestine was yet again going through a state of great tension. From the death of Alexander until around 200 BC, Palestine had been ruled by the Ptolemies, whereafter it became the realm of the Seleucid kings (these two dynasties were founded by Generals of Alexander; Seleucus and Ptolemy). By about 168 BC there had been a very serious breakdown in relations between the Seleucids and their vassal state of Judah to the effect that Judaism was proscribed. The banning of Mosaic law was the spark that ignited the fuel and under the tutelage of the wily Mattatias, head of the Hasmonean house, the Jews rose up in revolt and overthrew Seleucid rule in Palestine.

The revolt was a final rejection of what had, in effect become, over-Hellenisation. A decree of King Antiochus that sacrifice to the Greek gods be made in every city and every village of Judea was certainly offensive enough, but the final straw came with a Pagan altar being set up on the Temple altar at Jerusalem and the first sacrifice to Zeus being made. The effect of these events crystallised Jewish opinion against the Greek view. To the more conservative forces of Judaism, Hellenism was nothing but a glorified form of nature worship. They saw it as the spiritual continuation of the idolatrous Canaanite religion of Baal, paying little heed to the fact that Judaism too had its idols, for it was the house of David that was most intimately linked to the Canaanite taint. The revolt was triggered when Mattatias killed the first Jew to approach the Pagan altar. Mattatias, already an old man, was soon to pass away, leaving the way clear for the tactical genius of the family, Judas Maccabeus. Judas was elected leader and together the family oversaw the final expulsion of the Seleucids, a victory that was in some part aided by the death of King Antiochus in 164 BC. It is now that we come to a crucial part of this brief history, where some riddles will be set and some answered.

It was Judas who first moved against the southern territory of Idumaea, also known as Edom. These incursions were continued by John Hyrcanus (c.135-104 BC), who eventually forced Edom into the Judean fold, though not until he had asked for help from the Romans to sort out a few matters on the home front. It was an involvement that would eventually prove fatal to the Hasmonean dynasty, for it was with Roman assistance that the most famous Edomite of all ascended the throne: Herod the Great.

It was Herod and his father, Antipater, who engineered the downfall of the Hasmonean dynasty by demonstrating their allegiance to Rome and by ruthlessly crushing dissent at home. Antipater rose from being a courtier in the service of Hyrcanus II to being put in charge of the province of Judea in 48 BC. Five years later he was poisoned and was soon joined by his eldest son, Phasael, also poisoned, leaving Herod alone, a despised Edomite. With further Roman assistance, Herod was able to place himself on the throne as titular King of the Jews, the very title that was placed above Jesus on the cross.

The background details of the story of Herod are, I believe, of fundamental importance to an understanding of the story of the historical Jesus, for there is a puzzle within both stories that links them very explicitly, a puzzle that is generally dismissed because it contains a considerable amount of myth. From early on in my researches I fully realised the need for coming to terms with myth and interpreting properly its hidden messages. I am not talking here of 'gold and treasure' and sensational speculations that can only end up as a handful of dust, I am writing of an often overlooked aspect of myth - the fact that it was quite often used as a code, as a means of concealing information from the prying eyes of any opposition that might happen upon it. I believe that it is in precisely this fashion that the Gospels were originally written, thus by understanding the impetus behind myth, the story of the birth of Christianity begins to fall into place.

Myth Comes to Life

'Not all true things are to be said to all men.' These are the words of one of the Church Fathers, Clement of Alexandria,[19] and he is referring, in a letter, to the secret gospel of Mark, a gospel discovered by the late Professor Morton Smith in a monastery located at Mar Saba, 12 miles southeast of Jerusalem in 1958. As we shall see later on, the very existence of this gospel proves that the accepted Gospels of the canon, those admitted by the Church to be true, are at best inconsistent, at worst riddled with holes.[20]

There are two types of gospel, the official Gospels (hence the traditionally prescribed capital 'G') and those that, for whatever reason, were not accepted by the compilers of the New Testament. All gospels are rather inclined to give a somewhat patchy view of history. Those of the New Testament canon are certainly no exception; if anything, they incline us to a rather vague view of the central character.

Within a very short period of time after the Gospels' completion, certain aspects of Jesus' documented life had become the focus of theological speculation, as the early Church Fathers sought to interpret the sayings and the deeds of Jesus in a form that rapidly metamorphosed into dogma. Further damage was done by the loss of evidence and, quite often, its deliberate destruction . All of this has served to obscure the facts and to heighten the many rumours as to the real nature of Jesus and his deeds. The situation has been well expressed by the pioneering, though harshly critical, scholar, Rudolf Bultmann of the University of Marburg:

> 'I do indeed think that we can now know almost nothing concerning the life and personality of Jesus, since the early Christian sources show no interest in either.'

But I was not to be frustrated, for my own quest was soon to turn into a bigger picture, and, encouraged by insights from myth and philology, I saw that clues remained.

It was the beginning of chapter two of St. Matthew's Gospel, as told in the King James version, that caught my eye. The very first few lines reveal much and I was very surprised at the implications:

> 'Now when Jesus was born in Bethlehem of Judea, in the days of Herod the King, behold there came wise men from the East to Jerusalem
> Saying, "Where is he that is born King of the Jews? For we have seen his star in the East, and are come to worship him."
> And when he had gathered all the chief priests and scribes of the people together, he demanded of them where Christ should be born.'
>
> Matthew 2:1.4

The reference to Christ is interesting, 'Christ' means 'the anointed one', so the second chapter of Matthew's Gospel announces that an 'anointed one' has been born. This birth would be seen as a direct challenge to the throne, a direct challenge to Herod himself, for kings were 'the anointed'. British kings and queens are, to this day, anointed upon coronation.

Having studied a large section of the world's mythology it is very easy to see that the story, as St. Matthew tells it, bears all the hallmarks of other myths. Many of these will be revealed in good time, but there is another very telling factor, from which St. Matthew is a glaring exception: in all of the other myths, whether the Greek story of Perseus, the Akkadian story of Sargon or the Indian story of Krishna, the child whose destiny is foretold is a blood relative of the tyrant who tries to kill him.

The Gospel continues:

'And thou Bethlehem, in the land of Judah, art not the least among
the princes of Judah: for out of thee shall come a Governor, that
shall rule my people Israel.

Then Herod, when he had privily called the wise men, enquired
of them diligently what time the star appeared.

And he sent them to Bethlehem, and said, "Go and search
diligently for the young child and when ye have found him bring
me word again, that I may come and worship him also."

Matthew 2:6 - 8

'And being warned of God in a dream that they should not return
to Herod, they departed into their own country another way.

And when they were departed, behold, the angel of the Lord
appeareth to Joseph in a dream, saying, "Arise, and take the
young child and his mother, and flee into Egypt, and be thou
there until I bring thee word: for Herod will seek the young child
to destroy him."

Matthew 2:12-13

Just as in other mythologies, there is a massacre of the innocents, shortly after
which the old king dies. So, was Jesus a blood relative of Herod? It is only
when we take a close look at Herod's story in detail that the penny finally
begins to drop.

At the opening of this chapter you will have found quotations from the
Babylonian Talmud, a compilation of Jewish writings, some of which go back
as far as the first century AD. These writings include some rather extraordinary
statements made about the figure of Jesus. I repeat some of them here:

'...Commentators refer to Jeshu-ha-Notzri by mention of the
wicked kingdom of Edom, since that was his nation ...He was
near to the Kingdom.'[21] ...His place was near those in power.'[22]

Parts of the Toldoth and a disputed document, the Toldoth Jeshu, date back
to times near contemporary with Jesus. Quite often both have been dismissed
as being either too late or quite simply too exaggerated. However, the late
Hugh Schonfield, in a work of great learning and originality,[23] ,argued that
rather than being a medieval Jewish polemic against Christianity, the Toldoth
was actually based on an early Jewish-Christian gospel. Furthermore,
Schonfield argues that this Jewish counter-gospel was Nazarene in origin (see
chapter eight).[24] What both the Toldoth and the Talmud reveal is the close
connection of Jesus to the House of Herod, for Babli Sanhedrin 43a states that
Jesus was 'near to the Kingdom', in other words he was an heir by blood of

'the wicked Kingdom of Edom', the land from whence Herod came.

What struck me almost instantly was that, in Hebrew, 'Edom' and 'Adam' are the same word, meaning 'red man' or 'man from red earth'. Interestingly, Jesus is often called the second Adam, come to expunge the sins of the first. '...Commentators refer to Jeshu-ha-Notzri by mention of the wicked Kingdom of Edom, since that was his nation'. So, Jesus was of Edom and of Adam.

Myth has an extraordinary habit of being true to the human impulse, to such an extent that actual events can sometimes be played out as if they were myth come to life. From the moment that the Maccabaeans invaded Edom, trouble was in the air. As Edom was assimilated into the realm of Judea, a mythic bargain came into play, for, according to the Edomites themselves and, more importantly, to Hebrew scripture, Edom was the land of the disinherited Esau, the red, hairy man who had his rightful inheritance deceitfully snatched from under his nose by his younger brother, Jacob, in exchange for a bowl of red lentil broth.

It is said that the lineage of Jacob went on to become Israel, whilst the line of Esau went on to become reviled. The myth of Jacob and Esau, as told in Genesis, is one of the classic myths of the fight between rival twins and it was a rivalry reflected in real life, for Edom and Judah were perpetually at each other's throats. Tradition, in the Jewish quarter, places the source of this enmity, in part, on the refusal of the Edomites to allow the Children of Israel to pass over their land after the Exodus from Egypt. Later on, the anger became fiercer still when Edom plundered Judah after the destruction of Jerusalem in 586 BC. Edom features quite prominently in both Old and New Testament prophecy. Isaiah links the messiah explicitly to the land of Edom:

> 'Who is this coming from Edom, from Bozrah, in garments stained with crimson so richly clothed, marching so full of strength?'
>
> Isaiah 63:1[25]

Crimson is the colour of kings and in the ancient world the crimson dye was generally Phoenician in origin. In a recent book, Dr. Nikos Kokkinos, identifies the Edomites very strongly as Hellenised Phoenicians.[26, 27]

Herod was called by some an Ascalonite, his father being Antipater of Ascalon. Ascalon was a Phoenician city and, in fact, the Phoenicians play a significant role at this stage of the investigations. A look at the old religious ways of the region and Herod's ancestral links reveals much.

We have seen how Jewish commentators referred to 'the wicked kingdom of Edom' and yet, in II Samuel 6, Edom is featured very positively in connection with the revered Ark of the Covenant. In line 9 of the Jerusalem version there is the following:

'David went in fear of Yahweh that day. "However can the ark of Yahweh come to me?" he said. So David decided not to take the ark into the citadel of David and took it to the house of Obed-edom of Gath. The ark of Yahweh remained in the house of Obed-edom of Gath for three months, and Yahweh blessed Obed-edom and his whole family.'

These lines reveal much, for although they were compiled much later than King David's reign, they fit with what is known about the historic circumstance of the period. Gath was in the ancient territory of Philistia and Obed-edom would be, to a Philistine, an interesting abode for the seat of God, given that, according to the Jewish scriptures, God would hardly so bless a Philistine!

The Philistines[28] were a part of the confederation known as the 'Sea Peoples' who are known to archaeologists through various inscriptions dating back to the reign of Ramesses III, Pharaoh of Egypt (c.1186–1154 BC). These peoples, it is thought, came from the Aegean basin and were later to ally themselves with the Phoenicians and Canaanites. It is remarkable that the most sacred object of Judaism, the Ark of the Covenant, should have been allowed in the house of Judah's enemy, and entirely with Yahweh's blessing.

What this demonstrates very clearly is the Edomite-Phoenician connection within the old religion of Israel. Contrary to the pious reportage of certain sections of the Old Testament, the House of David was connected very strongly to the worship of the Phoenician gods, and this is where our link becomes significant, for I do not believe that the religious affairs of Israel were as rigorously bound or as adhered to as is made out. However, I do not believe that David and his house were idolaters either. The religion of David's period was broader and less defined by rigid controls and ritual laws, strictures that came to define Judaism. It must be remembered that here, we are looking at the beliefs of the Hebrews – all the tribes, not just the tribe of Judah, who gave their name to Judaism.

The Phoenicians' word for God is 'El' and is a general term for any god.[29] In Hebrew it translates as 'Yah' sometimes 'Ja' The great father god, the highest god in all Phoenicia was called 'El' and he had a son 'Baal', whose name literally means 'The Lord'. This was the religion of David, about which more will be revealed.

When the Ark was placed in the house of Obed-edom it had been brought from Baalim. This and other references confirm the Phoenician connection. 'El' appears in the Old Testament a number of times, for this is the name that is given to God, as in El Shaddai, El Jireh[30] and, most significantly, El Elyon – 'God Most High'. David was a devout worshipper of God in the highest form, of whom, according to recent research, the God of Judah, Yahweh, *was a son*.[31]

The connection of Yahweh's Ark and Yahweh's blessing upon the

Phoenician-Edomite Obed-edom may have provided one small source of justification for Herod claiming the throne of Judah, but there are more, some of which point to the presence of 'God Most High', certainly as Herod would have seen it.

That Israel and its tribes had close Phoenician connections is borne out by some of the names of the people, one of whom appears in the Old Testament Book of Samuel: Ishbaal, whose name means 'man of the Lord'. Earlier, you will have noted a derisory Judaic name for Jesus as 'Baalam the Lame', a follower of the 'lame god' – almost like calling Jesus 'that idolater who won't get very far'. We are told in the Book of Joshua how the Exodus from Egypt resulted in the arrival of the Children of Israel into the Promised Land, called, at the time, Canaan, but there were already Hebrews resident there. They had not been carried into captivity by the Egyptians and had remained in Canaan. It is difficult to know what the real situation was; later texts read like propaganda, condemning the indigenous peoples as 'immoral' and 'idolaters', implying that the invading Israelites despised Canaan and its ways.

The problem with this point of view is that there is no proof of it. Furthermore, such is the association of Israel, in other parts of the scripture, with all things Canaanite, that it is very easy to get the impression that Canaan *was* Israel and that the so-called 'invasion' by Joshua and his hordes was actually a relatively minor affair and to a large extent, the propagandist fantasy of later writers. This is a view that led Professor Keith Whitelam of the University of Stirling, Scotland, to conclude that Palestinian history has effectively been silenced in the search for Ancient Israel as a potent, historical nation:

> 'In contrast to this marginal nature or nonexistence of ancient Palestinian history, we might compare the pursuit of and invention of "ancient Israel". Biblical studies has been dominated from its inception by a concern for the history of ancient Israel as the key to understanding the Hebrew Bible. It has been of fundamental concern for Christian theology since Christianity is conceived of as a religion based upon revelation within history.' [32]

The history is confusing. The 'nation' of Israel was really a name for a loose confederation of tribal or city-states. Regular squabbles and wars within the confederation would bring border changes and these internal enmities made the area susceptible to regular foreign incursion. Furthermore, any documentation of 'who did what to whom' would be subject to the agenda of the scribes; 'spin-doctors' are not a new phenomenon. I believe that any honest historian would admit confusion over Israel, and over distinctions between

Edom, Canaan, Phoenicia and Philistia, as history progressed. More instructive is the knowledge that the Phoenician pantheon, complete with 'dying and rising gods', was common to all except, eventually, Judah, and that Phoenician influence remained strong in the region right up until Christianity prevailed in the fourth century AD.

Judah does seem, by all accounts, to have been very much a separate entity within the loose confederation. I refer to the fact that the Old Testament informs us that before he was King of Israel, David was King of Judah. I was surprised that there was such a difference between the two at that time, for, along with many others, I had been led to believe that the division into two kingdoms only occurred after the close of King Solomon's reign. The difference seems, though, to have been there from the very beginning until David brought about the temporary union. At that time, David, having been acclaimed King of Judah, the southern kingdom, went on to challenge the late King Saul's son, Ishbaal, he of the Canaanite-Phoenician name. David was soon accepted by the northern tribes as King of Israel, and then, in order to help unite his two kingdoms, he created a capital at Jerusalem. Prior to that, David had his capital in Hebron.

Hebron was one of the most important places in the whole of ancient Israel and its strategic importance is demonstrated by its prominence in parts of the Old Testament, where first it is taken by one people, then another, and so forth. In the late second millennium BC, Hebron was captured by the Philistines. Two hundred years further on it was recaptured by the Edomite clan of Caleb, which, at that time, had allied itself to Judah and later, in the era of King Saul, it was captured from the Calebites by the tribe of Benjamin.

Why was Hebron so very important, particularly to the Jews and Edomites? Because it contains the sacred cave of Machpelah, burial ground of the Hebrew Patriarchs. Abraham is buried there, so too Isaac and Jacob. However, it was particularly important to the Edomites because it was the last resting–place of the 'first man', Adam. Now, as I have already noted, 'Adam' and 'Edom' are the same word, meaning 'red'. Thus if this is a factual tradition, Esau, being the eponymous ancestor of the Edomites, might be expected to be associated with the place, too, and indeed there is a reference in the Talmud to Esau's head being buried at Hebron.[33]

When David was made King of Judah, Jerusalem was in Canaanite hands. David's Phoenician ally, King Hiram of Tyre, helped him to take Jerusalem from the Canaanites and David was then named the King of Israel. As we have noted, for the unity of his new kingdom, David removed his capital from Hebron to Jerusalem, with Hiram providing workmen to build David's palace. (Subsequently, under the auspices of King Solomon, the Temple was also built by workmen from Phoenicia.) From this time onwards, David's heirs would be heirs to the entire kingdom, provided they were related to the lineage as it was *after* the conquest, not before. As we shall see, this was to prove a problem for Herod.

Hundreds of strife-torn years passed, during which the kingship of Israel lapsed. Having had the title 'King of the Jews' conferred on him by the Romans, Herod secured the throne by marrying Mariamne, the heiress of the Hasmoneans and one of the last of the line. Much to his chagrin, Herod was not acclaimed King of Judah, for no doubt his claim to this title was stymied by the legally inscrutable high priests who would have been only too keen to point out the fact that there were others with better claims. (It is recorded by Josephus that in order to help his claim, Herod had all the genealogies burned. Even so, he was not acclaimed King of Judah.)

The Outsider

Herod was a driven man. Perhaps he was inspired at an early age. There is a strange tale from Josephus which, true or not, he thought to be remarkable. In the reading of it, we should realise that 2,000 years ago, soothsayers were a part of the social fabric and to be taken seriously. My retelling of the story will also serve to introduce those most enigmatic of people, the Essenes, into the plot:

> 'Now there was one of these Essenes, whose name was Manahem, who had this testimony, that he not only conducted his life after an excellent manner, but had the foreknowledge of future events given him by God also. This man once saw Herod when he was a child and going to school, and saluted him as King of the Jews; but he, thinking that either he did not know him, or that he was in jest, put him in mind that he was but a private man; but Manahem smiled to himself, and clapped him on his backside with his hand, and said, "However that be, thou wilt be king, and wilt begin thy reign happily, for God finds thee worthy of it; and do thou remember the blows that Manahem hath given thee, as being a signal of the change of thy fortune; and truly this will be the best reasoning for thee, that thou love justice (towards men), and piety towards God, and clemency towards thy citizens; yet do I know how thy whole conduct will be, that thou wilt not be such a one, for thou wilt excel all men in happiness, and obtain an everlasting reputation but wilt forget piety and righteousness; and these crimes will not be concealed

from God at the conclusion of thy life, when thou wilt find that
he will be mindful of them, and punish thee for them."[34]

I have given the entire quote because it is extraordinary that a prominent
member of what is thought to be a Jewish sect should acknowledge Herod as
the God-favoured, rightful King of the Jews.

Whether it was the Manahem incident or something else, Herod must have
been impressed by the Essenes for, writing in *The Antiquities of the Jews*, Josephus
comments that Herod tried to enforce amongst certain parties in Judea an
oath of fidelity to himself and his government.[35] However, of all the parties
concerned, the Essenes were excused this oath. Who were the Essenes?
According to the late Robert Graves, they:

> '...appear to have been an offshoot of the Therapeutae, or Healers,
> an ascetic Jewish sect settled by lake Mareotis in Egypt; Pliny
> described them as the strangest religious body in the world.
> Though Jews, and a sort of Pharisees at that, they believed in the
> Western Paradise – these Essene beliefs are given the same
> account by Josephus, Homer, Hesiod and Pindar – and, like the
> later Druids, they believed in the return of the pure souls to the
> Sun, whose rising they invoked every day.'[36]

It is known, mainly from the works of first-century writers, that there were
many facets to the Essenes and their beliefs that, in time, would come to be
recognised as curiously 'Christian'. They practised baptism and the sharing
of communal goods and participated in a ritual meal involving bread and
wine, a meal that was held in honour of the Messiah, when he should come.
Also;

> '..there was a large Oriental element in Essenism, which has not
> been explained. Moffat admits that this cannot be explained
> without going outside Judaism. Epiphanius declares that they
> were Sampaeans, worshippers of Shamash (the Sun-god).[37]

Baptism and a eucharistic meal – this sounds extraordinarily like Christianity.
Equally extraordinary are the words of Epiphanius, Bishop of Salamis (*c*.315 –
403), who in the fourth century wrote:

> 'They who believed in Christ were called Essenes before they
> were called Christians'.

What is of further interest is that the Essenes did not pay homage to the Temple of Jerusalem, instead they bowed their heads at sunrise and sunset in the direction of Egypt, of Heliopolis, home of the oldest of the dying and rising gods.

But we are ahead of ourselves here. What of Herod's reign, did it follow Manahem's prophecy? Although in the early years of his reign Herod did commit some atrocious acts, he was fairly popular because of his huge programme of building projects across the country. Under his watchful eye and cunning genius, Judea once again reached great heights. Herod also demonstrated his shrewd political ability in his dealings with Rome, the ultimate master of Judea. Take, for example, the Roman civil war (31 BC). Herod had first taken the side of Mark Anthony and Cleopatra, the Queen of Egypt, only to switch, in the nick of time, to that of Octavian, the eventual winner. As Emperor, Octavian took upon himself the name of Augustus Caesar and had Herod confirmed in his position as King of the Jews.

Such a state of affairs was outrageous to many inhabitants of Palestine. The idea of being ruled directly by these outsiders, Augustus and Herod, was beyond bearing. To many, these events were a sure sign of God's dissatisfaction with His people, a sign of the coming apocalypse. The Deuteronomic Royal Law had laid down the rule centuries before, a rule that John the Baptist would refer to on occasion:

> 'One from among thy brethren shall thou set over thee; thou mayest not put a foreigner over thee, who is not thy brother.[38]

Herod's position was uncomfortable. For most of his reign he was despised and ridiculed as a foreigner. As noted earlier, he was not a Jew, because all Jews come from either the tribes of Judah or Benjamin. Herod was from neither. He was king by virtue of his links to other Hebrew tribes. Could he then be accepted as a brother? No, not to the many, after all, although Hebrew and royal by blood, his ancestors had fled to Ascalon, Phoenicia, where they had continued to adhere to unacceptable beliefs. But the Romans knew of Herod's lineage and were happy to endorse it. Intriguingly, there is even the possibility that Herod and Caesar were ancestrally related.[39] In his work, Josephus quotes the will of Herod and also the investigations conducted by the Emperor Augustus into Herod's son's claim to the kingship and the counter claims of a Jewish delegation.[40]

What is interesting is that the investigation would have been performed by the Romans with characteristic thoroughness, and the claims of the Jewish delegation have been equally thorough. The relevant section of Josephus is almost a word for word documentation taken directly from Roman records.

The Romans, having proven Herod's claim through Herod's son's claim, would have greeted the Jewish claims with interest and then beaten them at their own game; the law.

It is the genealogy of David that is central to the argument, the line of the House of David. The genealogy of this house was obscured when, after utter defeat at the hands of the Babylonian king, Nebuchadnezzar, in 586 BC, the population of Judah was exported to Babylon in an exile that was to last almost 60 years. As a consequence, upon their release by Cyrus the Great in 539 BC and the return to their Palestinian homeland, it was difficult to tell with any accuracy who really was who.[41]

One people who had, of course, avoided the captivity, were the Edomites. The expedient that they utilised was a simple one. They were a mobile, tent-dwelling people, Bedouin, who easily evaded capture (if and when they were not in alliance with Judah's oppressors). Thus the returning Jewish exiles (the term 'Jew' dates back to Babylonian times and was first used by the Babylonians to describe their captives) found that the Edomite genealogies had remained intact, which is more than can be said for the Jewish line of the House of David. The exile had served to bring Edomite claims a stage nearer power, but, from the time of the return from exile until the period of the Maccabaean ascendancy, there were no kings in either Judah or Israel and when the Maccabees did come to power, they only laid claim to Judah. After the Roman invasion and the fall of the Maccabees, I believe that Herod's overall claim to the kingship of Israel as a whole was stronger than any.

Herod's father, Antipater, was an adopted Idumaean or Edomite, and an enforced Jew – Edom had been forcefully converted to Judaism by the Maccabaean kings some time before – hence the accusations of Herod being a half-Jew.[42] There are various reports of how Herod's father, originally from Ascalon, had become an Edomite. The historian Epiphanius (*c.* 315–403) who was born only a little way from Herod's hometown, tells us:

> '...Herod was the son of Antipater of Ascalon, a hierodoulos[43] of
> the idol of Apollo. This Antipater's father was named Herod,
> and he was the son of Antipas. Antipater was taken prisoner by
> Idumaeans and fathered Herod during his stay in Idumaean.'[44]

The above situation would not be unusual. It was not uncommon for attackers to take the sons of local dignitaries hostage as part of a peace agreement. The point of most interest here is that Herod's father was a hierodule, one of the priestly caste. Earlier we learned that the high priests and royalty were generally of the same blood. Herod's own grandson, Herod Agrippa,[45] was to attest:

'I have kings for my grandfathers, and for my ancestors, the greater part of whom have been called high-priests: looking upon their royal power as inferior to their office as priests, and thinking that the high-priesthood is as much superior to the power of a king as God is superior to man.'[46]

Here is a strong element of Herod's claim; royal blood in priestly service. In Herod's case, his father and those before him served at the temple of Apollo in Ascalon. Apollo was a hero-god, a god of the sun and therefore a dying and rising god.

Although Josephus' presentation of Herod's ancestry has an additional generation, he relates, as do the other sources, that Herod's father, Antipater, attained high rank in governance.[47] It was Antipater who would provide the power base from which Herod acceded to the throne of Judea, for it was he who gave support to the Roman general Pompey, when he invaded Palestine in 63 BC. This alliance was to be exceedingly profitable. Julius Caesar appointed Antipater as Procurator of Judea in 47 BC and conferred Roman citizenship upon him and his family. Herod made his debut in the same year, when he was appointed Governor of Galilee. Six years later he was appointed Tetrarch (a minor king) of Galilee.

When in 40 BC Parthians from the east invaded Palestine and civil war broke out, Herod fled to Rome, whereupon he was subsequently made King of Judea (his father having been poisoned in 43 BC) and given a substantial army with which to make good his claim. He finally became the undisputed ruler when in 37 BC, at the age of 36, he defeated the final pockets of resistance and embarked upon a long and stormy reign.

Before appointing him, the Romans were fully aware of the Herodian claims to the throne, as were certain parties within Jewish high society of the day; quite simply Herod had to have good grounds for being elevated to such a high and very precarious position. On the paternal side of his family, Herod could claim descent from the tribe of Caleb.[48] Caleb was one of the ten champions sent by Joshua to spy out the land of Canaan before its invasion. The Calebites themselves were members of a far larger tribal confederacy called the Kenites, whose ancestor was Cain, the murderer of Abel. The home territory of the Kenites and thus of the Calebites was Edom. At the invasion of Canaan, Hur was one of the Calebite leaders. David, the greatest of all the Israelite kings, also claimed descent from Hur.[49] It is this that links Herod to the House of David, the family of the messiah.[50] This part of Herod's claim would be strongly resisted by the Jewish authorities, for the link went back to the time prior to David's accession as King of all Israel. In these earlier times we know that the religious cultures of all the tribes were similar, but Judah's religious ways had become much narrower as time progressed; nevertheless we know that up until *c.*164 BC, Herod's priestly ancestors were able to continue their ancient ways of worship in Jerusalem.

Herod's Religion

It was to Ascalon that Herod's ancestors fled when their priestly seat at Jerusalem was taken from them by the fundamentalist Maccabaeans. Before this Maccabaean period, *c.*164 BC, Jerusalem still had fairly expansive religious interests, not all of them involving the practice of Mosaic law. Despite the changes in Judah, the religious cultures of the tribes of Israel and their neighbours remained similar (remember that Judah and Israel were not one and the same). The Philistines shared their culture with both the Phoenicians and the Edomites. The Phoenicians and parts of the Philistine culture worshipped a god called 'Hercules-Melkart'. The Herods worshipped this deity in the form of Apollo, second only to Zeus in the Greek pantheon. Hercules-Melkart and Apollo are dying and rising hero-gods, heroes associated with the sun.

The name Melkart translates as 'King of the city'.[51] A famous related hero-god is Melchizedek, meaning 'The King is righteous' or 'The King of righteousness'. Melchizedek was a king of Salem.

Salem or Salma was in ancient times the god of peace and the sacred hill of Jerusalem was sacred to Salma.[52] We have seen how closely Phoenician Tyre and Jerusalem were linked; according to tradition, it was workmen from Tyre who had built Solomon's Temple. Josephus records that the most ancient name of Jerusalem was Solyma; *sol* meaning 'the sun'. Salma was the early Semite god of the dying and rising sun and was Aegean in origin.[53] According to Martin Bernal in his groundbreaking text, *Black Athena*, and to other commentators, the Aegean peoples, whose cultural history included both the Minoan and Mycenean histories, were by origin Canaanite. This, in turn, makes them Phoenician.[54] Melchizedek, who, in the Book of Genesis, is accorded nigh godly status, was also Phoenician. He was a worshipper of El Elyon, God Most High, the God of Abraham. The ancestors of Herod who fled Jerusalem were in all probability priests of either Melkart or of Salma. We must remember here that Herod's father had been a 'hierodoulos', a temple-slave to Apollo, not a slave in the ordinary sense of the word, but a person who, from an early age, belonged to the god, someone whose body and blood was sacrosanct. Why? Because his blood was understood to be *of the god*. It was blood-royal. It may well be that because of his royal blood, Herod's father was kidnapped and taken to Edom.

Herod was a true heir, the right blood was flowing through his veins, but, as we have seen, by his time, just having the royal blood was not enough. Judaic customs had changed too much since the earlier, liberal days. How that had come about in practical terms is of interest.

It would be an understatement to say that Judaism has had more than its fair share of defining moments. There was the Exodus under Moses and then the exile to Babylon and then the Roman oppression followed by the utter disaster of the great revolt and the final diaspora of the Jews, banished from their homeland. These traumas have defined Judaism in an extraordinary way and the religion must be understood in the context of the suffering of this great people. However, the defining moment wherein Judaism became a way of life, central to the people as one whole unit, occurred in the reign of King Josiah (640–609 BC). Under the auspices of the young king and his Regents, a great reform was carried out that not only centralised the religion on the Jerusalem Temple but also banished from it anything regarded as remotely heretical. Even scripture was adjusted to reflect this measure and to this day the authors of these scriptural reforms are called the Deuteronomists. These reforms concerned the Kingdom of Judah only. The separate kingdom to the north, Israel, had been overthrown by the Assyrians in 772–721 BC and a large part of her population exiled. Israel's religion was centred on the presence of the aforementioned God Most High, the progenitor of a pantheon worshipped at sacred sites, groves and stone circles, known as Asherim, dotted all about the countryside. We have already seen that this multifaceted belief system of Israel, accepted by all during the time of Kings David and Solomon was now seen, by Judah, as largely Pagan. This Pagan heritage, though, remained strong in the region. In *The Risen Lord,* Margaret Barker writes:

> 'There were many in first-century Palestine who still retained a world-view derived from the more ancient religion of Israel in which there was a High God and several Sons of God, one of whom was Yahweh, the Holy One of Israel. *Yahweh, the Lord, could be manifested on earth in human form, as an angel or in the Davidic king. It was as a manifestation of Yahweh, the Son of God, that Jesus was acknowledged as Son of God, Messiah and Lord'* .[55] (My italics)

We shall see how this manifestation through the Davidic line interested Herod. But Margaret Barker's research demonstrates another very interesting historical and theological point: that the period of the first Temple, the era of David and of Solomon, was not one of monotheism. Monotheism, the worship of one god, came much later and was introduced under the reforms of the Deuteronomists. As Margaret Barker informs us:

> 'Yahweh, the Lord, had been the second God, the guardian angel and patron deity of Israel, the Son of El Elyon. Once the Deuteronomists had introduced the records of the people of Judah, Yahweh and El Elyon were no longer distinct. The older beliefs, however, did not disappear and the evidence of Philo confirms that this second deity was still known in the period of Christian origins.'[56]

It is in the pattern of these words that we have a major clue as to the real background of the historical Jesus. Margaret Barker illuminates us further about this second deity, Yahweh:

> 'Many of his titles were taken over by the early church to describe Jesus. The earliest Christian beliefs must have been rooted in those of the first temple, and when Jesus was proclaimed as the Lord, the Son of God, the original Palestinian church used imagery derived from the temple cult.[57]

Now I do not want to misrepresent Margaret Barker, so let me state that, in terms of my thesis, this is as far as she goes. For me her ideas are of profound interest and importance, as well as being exceptionally exciting. However, when evidence of a broader nature came to light outside of the field of direct Christian and Old Testament studies, I felt that the only way to explain this evidence was to broaden my own search. In order, though, that the broader picture be understood, we shall continue to look in some detail at certain key elements in the story of Jesus, some of which are deeply intriguing.

The Hidden Conception

In the Gospel of Matthew we are treated to a genealogy called, in the Jerusalem version, 'The ancestry of Jesus'. It is the opening to Matthew's version of events. What is extraordinary about this genealogy is that 40 generations are cited from Abraham through to Joseph, who is then described, in one of the biggest anticlimaxes in religious history, as the husband of Mary. To describe Jesus as the son of Mary, wife of Joseph the Levite, is a very peculiar way of describing Joseph as Jesus' father in a male-dominated scripture, but then, in the next verse (Matt.1: 18:25), we see that Joseph is not the father of Jesus. What I find acutely frustrating about this passage is, if Joseph is not Jesus' father, why go to all the trouble to explain Joseph's lineage?

If we lay aside the theology for a while and concentrate upon the historical Jesus, about whom Matthew purports to write, we find, that the mystery of Jesus' real father is one of history's great enigmas. That the identity of the father should have remained concealed for all this time only serves to heighten the enigma.

That Jesus was born as Son of God is purely theological, it is a matter of faith. The fact, though, that any real trace of a father has been excised from all of the Gospels and from virtually any remaining evidence does, at first hand, seem quite suspicious. The impression that I got from my many readings of this story is that Jesus did indeed have an earthly father and that whoever he was, he was not Jewish, or that, if he was Jewish, he was still an outsider. And yet emphasis is laid upon the fact that Jesus is of high lineage on both sides of his family, including, of course, as St. Matthew's Gospel attests, the line of Joseph *of the House of David*, who Matthew admits, was not Jesus' father! How do we answer this riddle?

It was at this stage that I noticed some of the essential mythic quality to St. Matthew's text, for in choosing the name Joseph, St. Matthew has not made an arbitrary choice; it is a name that I have noticed in other myths of the dying and rising hero-god. There are other myths in other parts of the world, in ages long before St. Matthew's period, in which Joseph appears as a father figure to a holy child.

The oddness of St. Matthew's genealogy is only heightened when one compares it to the ancestry given by St. Luke. In comparing the two, great discrepancies are all too easily found. It was as if the mythic point was being underscored, particularly when St. Luke states:

> 'When he started to teach, Jesus was about thirty years old, being
> the son, *as it was thought*, of Joseph, son of Heli.'
>
> Luke 3:23–24 (My italics)

This is in the Jerusalem version. In the King James the point is emphasised:

> 'And Jesus himself began to be about thirty years of age being (as
> was supposed) the son of Joseph.'

Let us leave the question there for a moment and turn our attention to the idea of the virgin birth.

The term 'virgin' has for the last 2,000 years provoked great dispute. Even the latest breakthroughs in the field of genetics have been used to establish the physical possibilities of whether Isaiah's prophecy could be fulfilled:[58]

> 'Therefore the Lord himself shall give you a sign; behold a virgin shall conceive and bear a son, and shall call his name Immanuel.'[59]

But there were others besides the Judaeo-Christian writers who wrote of the virgin, one being the Roman poet Virgil. Various Christian writers have, down the years, accorded Virgil a unique position among Pagan writers. In his fourth eclogue he writes:

> 'Now the Virgin returns, the reign of Saturn returns, now a new generation descends from heaven on high. Only do thou, pure Lucina, smile on the birth of the child, under whom the iron brood shall first cease, and a golden race spring up throughout the world.'[60]

Virgil is declaring the arrival of a new age, the Age of Pisces, an age heralded by the celestial Virgin. One can see why Virgil, *c.* 70–19 BC, was accorded the status of 'honorary Christian'. The mythic imagery that Virgil uses is not that different to the imagery on display in St. Matthew's Gospel. The signs, both Pagan and Christian, are looking very similar, but Virgil's mention of Saturn tells us that the references are astrological, where the planets and the constellations represent the various interacting forces of life. The virgin here relates to Virgo. To the Ancients, this constellation represented a divine goddess and there are clues as to what her attributes were and how they might be manifest on earth.

The Hebrew word for 'virgin' in the New Testament is *almah* meaning 'a young woman of marriageable age', literally 'girl'. This has been translated in Greek as *parthenos*, meaning 'virgin'. We can see that as the translation has progressed so too has the meaning. The Hebrew does not necessarily mean 'virgin' as we know it. By widening my search and thus my horizons I discovered that the term *almah* was indeed used correctly, but only because it has hidden connotations. In Persian, Al-Mah is the name of the ancient virgin moon-goddess, furthermore in Latin, *almah* means 'living souls of the world' and the syllable *ma*, as in all language, infers 'mother'. Holy Virgins are 'soul-mothers', better known perhaps as *alma-maters*. This is quite different from the modern connotation of 'virgin'.

As we have seen, the Ancients believed that divinity could be incarnate upon the earth. This would be in the form of a messiah-king, not incarnate at the moment of birth but at the moment of coronation, which was an initiation ceremony, an anointing with the power of God. The Jews believed this too and they believed that the line of David hosted these messiah-kings. Now, though, in Herod's reign, their faith was under threat from the old ways. In fact, as we shall see, Herod even fostered his own ideas of messiah-hood. But a greater threat to both was on the horizon: what if another of the royal line had found 'a young woman of marriageable age', a 'soul mother', and what if she were about to bring forth a soul – about to give birth? This is most certainly what was believed by Alexandrian Jews and Christians of the time, a view later suppressed. It was believed that *Jesus was Antipater's son by a secret marriage to Mary*.[61] This Antipater was Herod's eldest son.

All kings within the territory of the Roman Empire had to deposit a copy of their will into the keeping of the Emperor. Herod's will was in the possession of Augustus and, according to Josephus, Augustus decreed that the eldest son of Antipater would inherit the throne. This will was later suppressed and Antipater's children murdered, with the exception of Jesus, whose fate it was to escape.

Knowing Herod

Nowadays, many question the validity of astrology, but to the Ancients it was a revered science. It was almost universally believed that the celestial movements could be interpreted in order to prophecy events on earth. This was part of the 'as above, so below' philosophy. We have seen Virgil's reference, but, of course, the Roman astrologers were not the only experts. Is it any wonder that Herod flew into a rage when the three wise astrologers announced the birth of the new king? The conspiring of princes has never been a rarity and Herod may well have had his suspicions about Antipater. Now he learns that there is to be a 'loose cannon' in the lineage, an unplanned claimant to the throne – with the Magi's blessing!

When the Magi appeared at Herod's court and asked, Where is he that is born King of the Jews? Herod must have given them the oddest look, for he was that king. Why does it seem to have escaped the notice of others that they referred to the child as *the* 'King of the Jews' and not 'King of Judah'? And surely if Jesus was *born* King of the Jews, it means that his own father was not only a king, too, but a dead one, for the child to have inherited his title! Antipater, by the time of the birth of the child, was indeed dead.

When Herod received that visit from the Magi, it could not have come at a worse time. Herod was nearing the end of his life and was in murderous form. The victims were the populous at large and certain members of his own family. His Hasmonean wife, Mariamne, had been killed on his orders, as well as his two sons by her, Alexander and Aristobulos. As regards the populace, a Roman eagle that had been set up in the precincts of the Temple had been cut down by an outraged mob, resulting in the arrest and burning of the majority of them. Of all the people in this story to have smelt a rat, Herod had the nostrils that were the most receptive and the ways that were most bloody. The rat was Antipater and, as we shall see, Herod already had macabre plans for him, but the blood letting would not stop there. We are told that Herod ordered the killing of the innocents, every child in the region under two years old. We have mentioned that this fits in with the ancient mythologies and yet this does not mean that the event never happened. Again, as I remarked earlier, actual events can sometimes be played out as if they were myth come to life. Murder, murder, everywhere: what on earth was Herod up to?

To stamp his beneficent mark upon the world, Herod financed many great public building projects throughout the region, including the rebuilding of Solomon's Temple. Another of his acts, in the run up to his final days, was to sponsor, out of his own pocket, the restoration of the temple of Apollo on the island of Rhodes. Apollo was the senior Son of God of Zeus, the King of the Gods, with whom Ammon of Egypt was equated, as, originally, was Yahweh. Apollo was a sun-god, a dying and rising god. Herod also showed the same generosity to the people of the island of Kos, also devotees of Apollo, as well as various groups of Phoenicians in Tyre, Sidon and Beirut, and other groups of Greek peoples, all of whom worshipped Apollo in one form or another.[62]

Herod was a king on the cusp of a new age. A messiah was expected and the life of the new hero-god would be attached to the mythic as a new version of the old example. This is what any new age is about – a confirmation of the divine order, and the divine potential inside each and every one of us. Herod, particularly with his Phoenician bloodline, knew the old ways well and knew that the time was ripe for renewal. Already he was a king of the line of David and now he saw *himself* as a messiah, a hero-god. He issued coinage with the Greek 'X' imprinted on it – the cross of the saviour. Herod was declaring his intent. Now his motives for rebuilding Solomon's Temple become crystal clear.

In his rebuilding of the Temple, Herod was taking the role of a latter-day David or Solomon. He was imitating the traditional Hebrew messiahs of old, but he was going further. Walking around the temple's huge exterior one can see blocks of stone of huge size, well beyond the skill and affordability of craftsmen in Solomon's time. Herod's building is lavish and it is superlative, a monument to sheer magnificence (see plate). Intriguingly, it is known that the original overall plan of Solomon's Temple owed more to the ancient Egyptians than it did to any indigenous architect. The design was, in all likelihood, based upon the central temple at Amarna in Egypt, built by the heretic Pharaoh Akhenaten.[63] However, following the advice of the prophet Ezekiel, in the era of Zerubabel (*c*. 520 BC) the not inconsiderable Egyptian elements were removed from the old Temple. Significantly, we shall see that a considerable amount of what is known as Jewish ritual has its origins in Egypt.

Herod knew the links between the old Judaism and the dying and rising god and how they had been severed. He knew of the depth and breadth of the David's old religion. After all, Herod's lineage was Phoenician rather than Jewish, and his royal forebears had served the dying and rising god in the temples of Jerusalem before being ejected by his enemies, the Hasmoneans. So, having eliminated the Hasmonean line, even to the extent of his own wife and her children, the ultimate revenge was afoot: Herod's business was to proclaim himself as a messiah. He would be a dying and rising god, a titular Son of the Sun-God, a manifestation of the deity his forbears had worshipped in the temples of Jerusalem. Now, Solomon's Temple was to be returned to its original pantheon, with Herod as divinity incarnate! Knowing Herod's respect for and special treatment of the Egypt-acknowledging Essenes, they may well have been part of the plan.

Indeed, the time seemed ripe for the return of the divine status that the Pharoahs and others had enjoyed. In Rome, Augustus may well have been contemplating the same path, for the Roman Emperors proclaimed their divinity and practised divine rites from the close of his reign onwards. The maniacal inversions of ancient holy lore by the likes of Nero and Caligula were not long to come, but the same dark impulse was already at work in Judea. However, time was short.

Josephus relates how, in the last few years of his life, Herod fell into a 'distemper'. This manifested itself in all sorts of ways – Herod had become prone to great fits of anger, and 'fire glowed in him slowly, which not so much appeared to the touch outwardly, as it augmented his pains inwardly'. The distemper gave Herod a 'considerable appetite, one that could not be satisfied' and, according to Josephus, his 'entrails were exulcerated, and the chief violence of his pain was by his colon; an aqueous and transparent liquor also settled itself about his feet'.[64]

In the closing months of the drama, the murderous king had his son, Antipater, shipped off to Rome. This, of course, would be the period when Mary would gain a ward – one Joseph. Antipater was in Rome to plead for his life on a false charge of plotting to overthrow his father. Once condemned, Herod would be free to do with him as he wished. The view given by Graves and Podro is one that is consistent with the available evidence:

> 'It is clear from the account of his rigged trial that Antipater was innocent of the formal charges brought against him – the Roman Governor of Syria showed his dissatisfaction by leaving the Court before proceedings were over (*Antiquites*, XVII.5.7) – and the reason for Herod's desire to kill his own son was not necessarily that he had committed a crime. It is possible that, suffering from a horrible and incurable complaint, Herod wished to offer Antipater up as a human sacrifice in propitiation to God. Royal

sacrifice of an eldest son in times of crises was a well attested practice.[65] Antipater was Herod's surrogate.[66]

If all of this sounds bizarre and improbable, then there is a copious amount of evidence that such things did indeed go on in Jerusalem. Contemporary sources, though few, give detailed accounts. King Alexander Janneaus, the Hasmonaean (ruled 103–76 BC), defended his throne by challenging all-comers. One year, at the Day of Atonement, he was besieged by palm-branch waving subjects whilst at the high altar. Astonishingly, they demanded his death as a sign of the fertilising of the earth. The king sagely refused the demand, instituting instead a persecution of his own subjects. In another incident, the Hasmonaean Princess Alexandra III married Prince Philippion of nearby Chalcis. Philippion was slain by his own father, the king, who took Alexandra as his wife.[67] Nikos Kokkinos suggests that 'any offspring from this macabre union would be of interest for the last phase of Hasmonaean history and the later acquisition of the area by the Herods'.

These were dark times, life was cheap and those in power used it without restraint. It seems that such deeds, repulsive to us, were part and parcel of the Herodian climb to fame. Around the time that the doomed Antipater returned, Herod ordered the arrest of some 20,000 Jewish notables, mainly priests. It is clear that his rebuilding of Solomon's Temple was not a gift to conservative Judaism, but a platform for theophany with himself as messiah. The priests' removal would erase the basis of opposition. Perhaps they would be slaughtered at the initiation ceremony. It is very possible that Herod planned for Antipater to be the chief sacrificial offering there.

Finally, however, fate took a hand and Herod's attempted theophany would end in disaster. Such was the deterioration of his condition that, unable to bear the pain and on the point of madness, Herod appeared to take his own life. A 'great tumult was made, as if the king were dead'[68] and in the ensuing confusion, Antipater was put to death. Herod temporarily recovered, but his overall design was to fail utterly, for five days later he finally died. The last act in those uncertain times was for Herod's sister, Salome, to release the 20,000 prisoners who were locked in the Hippodrome. Only Herod's death had prevented their massacre. The relatively new religion of Judah had survived the plans of Herod. Soon a very different threat would come: the new Christianity and with it, St. Paul.

Intermezzo

In chapter one we have established that 'things Christian' are not all that they seem and that perhaps we hold certain incorrect assumptions based upon the work of 'spin-doctors' past and present; from the letter of Lentulus to the 'Jesus as Superstar' approach.

Establishing the complete facts after 2,000 years of obfuscation may be impossible, but with a careful, open-minded sift through the available evidence, we have, hopefully, made some headway. Sifting through material both old and new, I have endeavoured to explain the riddle of Joseph, the meaning of the 'virgin birth' and the possible reasons for Herod's vendetta against the newborn child. Much of this is based upon an understanding of the priest-king culture which permeated ancient society and the subsequent gross abuse of near-absolute power.

By understanding the extraordinary events that took place at the Herodian court we can gain an insight into later anomalies in the life of Antipater's son, whom Christianity would have us believe was a mere carpenter. Would a mere carpenter have appeared before Pilate, the Roman Governor-General of Judea? This would be like being caught shoplifting in New York and being taken to see the President of the USA! The answer, of course, lies in the Herodian bloodline: Jesus' game was up, his Herodian origins must have been known, perhaps through the Temple records. The Herod material makes good sense but can never be proven. What it does, however, is emphasise the power of the old lineages and religious beliefs as well as the strength of the 'dying and rising gods' in both religion and mythology. It is indisputable that these hero-gods were already very ancient by the time of Jesus. Furthermore, there is no denying that, in his own way, Jesus himself was a dying and rising god.

You will note that chapter one deals with the time before Jesus and chapter two with the time after. The relevant aspects of events during Jesus' life will be dealt with as the main thesis unfolds in part two of the book. Part one is a preparation and clearly this first chapter raises more questions than it answers, but answers will come. The aim is to build a new understanding, step by step. The crux of this understanding lies not in material facts but in the 'mindset of the Ancients', in as far as we can approach it. Consequently, it will help if the reader develops a little of this mindset and gets into the Ancients' way of thinking, their way of perceiving and knowing. Hopefully, that will come naturally as we progress – and progress we shall, to one Paul. St. Paul, sainted for services rendered in spreading Christianity as no man before or since.

2

One of Us

CHRISTIANITY, as we know it, began with St. Paul. After all, how would the world know Jesus' teachings without a messenger to deliver them? It would be like writing a letter without there being a postman – except that Paul wasn't just the postman, he wrote the letters himself! And which Jesus was Paul writing about, the historical man or the mythic figure – a dying and rising hero-god, a son of El Elyon, God Most High? The enigma is a real one and much is explained by an investigation of it.

Paul first appears within the New Testament in the book The Acts of the Apostles. The authorship of this book is ascribed to Luke, 'the beloved physician' and travel companion of Paul on his final journey to Rome. It is the same Luke who is also recognised as the author of the Gospel of that name. Luke names Paul as Saul, for, in the early years, he had not yet been 'called' and thus, his name was as yet unchanged. Within these pages he shall remain as Saul until that defining moment of the vision on the road to Damascus.

Luke states that Saul was born at Tarsus, the capital of Cilicia in what is modern southwest Turkey. Tarsus was, for its time, truly cosmopolitan. It held a variety of cultures and a wide variety of beliefs, most of them Pagan. It was, though, largely a Greek city, having fallen under the spell of Alexander the Great during the era of the Hellenic expansion. Saul would have been very familiar with the Greek concept of the gods as awesome powers, far beyond the morality of everyday Jewish life. In fact the Greek gods revealed themselves very much as powers of place and of time, but 'time' in the ancient sense – of corruption and regeneration

Saul was born a freeman and a Roman citizen. An educated man of his time, he of course spoke Greek, the *lingua franca* of Rome's Eastern Empire. That Saul/Paul was a sensitive and intelligent man is easy to discern from his letters. His bold mission to the Gentiles demonstrates also that he was cosmopolitan and held a wide view of the world. His knowledge and use of Greek would have been central to this worldview.

> 'Paul thought in Greek. He wrote in Greek. Together with Philo
> of Alexandria, he is the great conduit through which Jewish
> concepts and stories and patterns of thought came to the Gentile
> world. As these ideas came through the channel, they passed
> into a new intellectual world; the attempt to translate Hebrew
> ideas into a Gentile setting, above all a Greek setting... '[2]

This is an important point to remember because it was under the influence of the later Paul that the Gospels themselves would come to be transcribed into Greek, *out of the context of their original setting*. The young Saul, though, did not adhere to the Greek ways and was soon headed for Jerusalem.

> 'I am a Jew, born in Tarsus in Cilicia, but brought up here in
> Jerusalem as a student of Gamaliel ... in the law of our ancestors.'[3]

Born a Jew or not, if Saul really came from Tarsus straight to Jerusalem, he would have been seen as an outsider, a foreigner even, but Roman citizenship would have had its advantages, in getting good employment for example. Roman citizenship meant good connections.

A Family Affair?

There is no explanation given in the Bible as to Saul's Roman citizenship but oddly enough the name Saul seems to have had Herodian connections. Such connections might also explain the power he was able to wield at a comparatively young age in Jerusalem. Family ties are mentioned by Josephus in connection with Herod the Great's brother-in-law, Costobarus.[4] An explanation comes from Nikos Kokkinos, who suggests that Saul's sister provides the Herodian link:

'Although it cannot be proved, it is not impossible that Paul's
sister had been married to a royal courtier or even to a lesser
member of the Herodian family. Such a connection would solve
a number of problems in Paul's life.'[5]

Professor Robert Eisenman raises, as do others, the intriguing opening to
13:1 in the Book of Acts:

'Now there were in the church that was at Antioch certain
prophets and teachers; as Barnabas, and Simean that was called
Niger, and Lucius of Cyrene, and Manaen *which had been brought
up with Herod the Tetrarch, **and** Saul.'*   (My italics)

Herod the Tetrarch was Herod Antipas, a son of Herod the Great and ruler of
Galilee. I agree with Eisenman when he proposes that Saul is this Herod's
foster brother.[6] Incidentally, Herod Antipas was the very ruler to whom Pilate
sent Jesus for questioning before the crucifixion.[7]

Robert Eisenman strengthens the case of Paul's origins by suggesting, in a
genealogy given in *James, the Brother of Jesus* , that Paul is a great grandson of
Antipater, Herod the Great's father. He suggests that the enigmatic Saul of
Acts and of Josephus is a son of Antipater (another scion of the Herodian
family, not Antipater, suspected father of Jesus) and Cypros.[8]

Continuing along the line of further Herodian connections, mention is made
in the Epistle to the Romans of the figure of Herodian and at last we have a
piece of harder evidence, for Paul writes towards the end of his letter to the
Romans:

'Salute Herodian my Kinsman . . .'

'Herodian' may have been a popular name, but in the context of Paul there is
only one natural conclusion: that Herodian was named after the house into
which Saul was born. We should realise that royal families were very large in
those days, kings had many wives and children, so that a significant percentage
of the well-educated administering classes were 'well connected' and loyal.
Herod the Great, in particular, had very many children. It was through his
prolificacy that, in this era, the Herodians were a powerful force who had a
strong presence everywhere in the region.

After all this time, one is not able to prove, indisputably, that Saul was a
Herodian and also a relative of Jesus (see chapter one), but what it does show
is how the system worked and what the roots and deeper affiliations were
likely to be, whether religious or personal.

It is possible that Saul changed his name to create a distance between himself and his roots. As Paul, he seems a little reluctant to disclose them. Saul means 'asked for' and was the name of the first King of Israel, the one who was overcome by David. On the other hand, Paul means 'humble', a fitting name in the light of his conversion.

The most prominent of the gods in Tarsus was Heracles (the Roman Hercules), the great dying and rising hero-god. Tarsus was also a centre for the cult of Mithras, the bull-slayer. The most distinctive aspect of the Mithraic rites was the drinking of the blood of the slain bull, sometimes represented by a symbolic chalice of wine. More dramatic was the blood–bath that followed the slaying of the bull upon a platform, under which initiates stood, bathing themselves in the hot blood, rubbing it into their eyes, ears and nostrils. The *taurobolium* as the Romans called it, like the sacred meals of other cults, symbolised the transfer of life and power.[9] Heracles too was a bull-slayer, for from the blood of the bull flowed life, grain and plenteousness. As A. N. Wilson observes:

> 'The cult owes much to the dying and rising to life again of other Mediterranean vegetation gods - the Syrian Adonis, the Babylonian Thammuz, the Egyptian Osiris.'[10]

At the same time that the Jews were celebrating the Passover, the Tarseans would have been celebrating the rise of life again in the spring, the resurrection of the god, Heracles, the *theoi soteres* of his people, the divine saviour. And so, Saul would have come out of a region steeped in the *taurobolium* and dying and rising gods and entered into the conservatism of the Jerusalem Temple.

The Vision in the Temple

The Jerusalem Temple had been the focal point of worship since the time of Solomon and we have seen that, in those early days, worship was broad in its nature. The evidence is that there was one God who had many progeny, that Yahweh was originally seen as a *son* of God, and that even the hill of Jerusalem had been sacred to Salma, the dying and rising sun god. Now, in Saul's time, the shining white and golden Temple must have been an extraordinary sight. Herod's magnificent restoration was the glory of the Eastern Empire and it was still the focal point for worship but more intensely so, for in the narrower Jewish religion, 'Pagans' were not welcome. They were even persecuted.

It is Saul who in Acts is described as being a member of the Temple police, apparently employed to stamp out all trace of the followers of Jesus and 'the way'. It was within the jurisdiction of the high priest to order the arrest of fomenters of rebellion and disturbers of the peace. Saul carried out these orders.

According to a version of Josephus' works called the *Slavonic Josephus*, there were inscriptions on the temple balustrade. Josephus describes the 'balustrade with pillars on which was given, in three languages, warning of the Law of Holiness whereby no foreigner was permitted to enter the Holy Place, the second enclosure, which was approached by fourteen steps'.[11]

> 'And above these inscriptions a fourth inscription was hung in the same letters saying, "Jesus, a king who did not reign, was crucified by the Jews because he foretold the destruction of the city and the desolation of the Temple.'[12,13]

There is a further clue to the authenticity of Josephus' report. It comes from the writings of Hegesippus, an early Church historian, *c*..AD 108. Hegesippus refers to James, 'brother' of Jesus, spending his days in prayer in the Temple, being disturbed by certain Jews who ask him, Which is the door of Jesus?

It is well known that the Jerusalem Temple remained important to the early Judaeo-Christians and this would help to explain why. Indeed, with Hegesippus' report and the reliability of Josephus, there is little doubt that the name of Jesus was present in the Temple. However, a contemporary carving of the name upon the walls of the sacred Temple seems, given Jewish feelings of the time, to be more than a little dubious, as it would have been a blasphemy. This points to the name already being a sacred one, carved prior to the life of the historical Jesus. It need not necessarily have been greatly sacred to the Jews – after all, the Temple had been restored under the auspices of Herod, whose leanings were not entirely Jewish. In fact, Josephus' reference to a 'balustrade' reveals much. The original Greek, in which Josephus wrote, gives to the word the form *balaustion* – the blossom of the wild pomegranite, sacred to the dying and rising god.

We are now ready to look at what is arguably the most influential event in the history of the Western world: Paul's vision on the road to Damascus. Without it, Christianity's greatest missionary is likely to have continued persecuting Christians rather than embarking on a course of events that would dramatically expand the early Church and eventually bring the Roman Empire into the fold.

Judging from the telling of the experience,[14] Paul must have been in a heightened state of mind. This type of experience is one where the limitations of language make description difficult. However, as we shall see, there were traditional ways around this problem so that more could be gleaned from the words used. Let us look at the core of it, word for word:

'And as he journeyed, he came near Damascus: and suddenly there shined round about him a light from heaven.

And he fell to the earth, and heard a voice saying unto him, "Saul, Saul, why persecutest thou me?" And he said, "Who art thou Lord?" And the Lord said, "I am Jesus whom thou persecutest: it is hard for thee to kick against the pricks."

And he, trembling and astonished, said, "Lord, what wilt thou have me to do?" And the Lord said unto him, "Arise and go into the city and it shall be told thee what thou must do."

Acts 9:3–6

Thereafter Saul is very much the changed man. As Paul, in the Second Epistle to the Corinthians (12:4), he writes of how he had been caught up into paradise and heard things that are not to be told, that no mortal is permitted to repeat. A. N. Wilson observes:

'Journeys from our present earth-bound condition to a different plane of consciousness were possible in the religious tradition of both Jews and Gentiles, and Paul makes clear that their authenticity and reality as spiritual experiences are in no way invalidated by the suggestion that the initiate might not have journeyed to outer space in person in order to reach the 'third heaven.'[15]

And one doesn't have to journey to Damascus either.

Perhaps Saul did journey toward Damascus. Perhaps he was thrown to the ground as the intense light flashed before him, but would Saul really have been given sanction by the Temple authorities to travel to Damascus? It was well beyond their jurisdiction. After years of inquiry into visions and visionaries, I know of no incident like this. All the evidence shows that when the physiology is in a state of demanding activity, such as marching, the senses are not sensitive enough to process information from the non-material realms. The time for visions is when the body is in a restful state, often in a place of comfort, such as the home; in the quietude of the natural environment; or, more usually, in a place of worship.

I admit that, on rare occasions, there are reports of visions seen by groups of people. These visions seem to be from an external source giving a kind of 'all frequencies broadcast', but Saul's vision is a very personal one, where Saul himself is addressed. Then I came upon Paul's own explanation of how such revelations arise:

'For God, who commanded the light to shine out of the darkness,
hath shined in our hearts, to give the light of the knowledge of
the glory of God in the face of Jesus Christ.'

II Corinthians 4:6

He states that revelation is internal, the light shines inside, 'in our hearts', not from the outside. This is when I recognised that 'the road to Damascus' is a metaphor of divine realisation as couched in the terms of the oral tradition. I recognised in the 'Da' and 'ma'[16] a reference to 'Father-Mother', a sure sign of a cipher hidden in the embroidery of the story. I also noted that Saul is temporarily blinded for three days and that he does not eat or drink for three days either. The number three is also equated with deeper meaning in the oral tradition, three being related to the deepest level of manifestation.[17]

I looked more deeply into the name. In the Arabic tongue it is 'Ash Shams' or 'Esh Shems', having the meanings 'the well of the soul' and 'my God is manifest'. Indeed, the holy traditions tell us that, in the well (the depth) of the soul, one's God is manifest.

Before proceeding further on this road to Damascus, now would be a good time to try to understand the 'ancient tradition' and the way that its knowledge was imparted orally. The tradition had been in operation from time immemorial; it had not simply entered Saul's world, it had framed it. The psychology used in the stories of the oral tradition was the prevailing world psychology wherein the highest goal was to bring heaven down to earth through invoking heaven's attributes, represented by the gods. Naturally, being sensitive to the heavenly influences was important in this.

The overriding dictum was 'as above, so below' and the structure of language reflected that. In this way, one level of discourse could be used as a metaphor for another. As an example, we can see this at work in the most ancient language extant, Sanskrit. Here, the word *bhurij* has three levels of meaning – one relates to the body of the universe, one to the body of man and the other to the objective world of man. The link is an association with the concept of 'things which come together', particularly for practical purposes. Therefore, *bhurij* can be translated as 'scissors', 'a carpenter's vice', 'arms' , 'hands' or 'heaven and earth'.[18]

Nowadays it is well accepted that heaven is best described as a state of being, whereas earth is clearly a place. A look at the world's scriptures tells us that the Ancients believed that a better, higher state of being – heaven – could be brought to this place, the earth. They believed that this was (and is), the great long-term goal of mankind. They also believed that, in the meantime, steps should be taken to ensure that everyone entered that state of being after death. This heavenly state was recognised as a state of balance, being 'at one' with all things. The Ancients believed that invocation of the required divine attributes, i.e. particular 'gods', could help to bring the balance required. True balance was seen as a heavenly principle.

In the old languages, the most profound meaning of a word would often describe a state of being, but in order to reflect 'as above, so below' and to remind everyone of the great goal, even localities were named after the heavenly states that they best represented and, as we shall see further on, so were individuals. Geographically speaking, there are a multitude of examples, one being the ancient city of Kasi (now called Varanasi or Benares). Kasi is also a name for the top of the head as well as 'that by which all is illumined'.[19] Illumination is a permanent heightened state, recognised in mystical traditions worldwide.[20] The physical city lies on the river Ganges, and the Ganges itself represents the 'causal waters' of the universe and the Milky Way.[21] In a strikingly similar vein, the ancient Egyptians believed the river Nile represented the Milky Way and that the gods were born from it.[22]

Within the Christian tradition, the principle of Lectio Divina teaches that the literal meaning of the Bible does not reflect its most important purpose. There are deeper levels of meaning inherent, with moral and metaphorical levels leading to unitive experience.[23] The British churchman turned seer the Reverend John Todd Ferrier explains the metaphorical meaning of many of the stories and place names of the Bible in his many works,[24] though not 'the road to Damascus'. However, it is a simple enough cipher to decode.

Saul was a well educated man and, as is evident from his writings, thoughtful, sensitive and a natural contemplative. It is likely that he was already a devout seeker after God in the Jewish mode, using the Jerusalem Temple for prayer and contemplation. This would have been a natural circumstance, for he was employed there as a guard. In that role he became involved in the antagonism between Jews and the followers of Jesus. He was obliged to police the area on behalf of the Jewish authorities. Acts 8:1 is clear about Saul's role in at least one incident, the martyrdom of Stephen: 'And Saul was consenting unto his death.' No doubt Saul was conscientious in his job, desiring to do what he thought was best for his work and his religion, but things went too far and, as attested, his conscience would be pricked.

Within the temple was the aforementioned inscription of Jesus' name at the very gate where most policing would be required. One can imagine Saul standing close to this inscription day after day, very aware of it as he stopped any Christians from going further, noting who they were for possible further action. However, the pricks of conscience would be working away within him, for it was an uncomfortable situation for a man who was conscientious and yet sensitive. Something had to give.

Whilst the Acts of the Apostles portrays an external and materially embroidered view of the conversion, in his letters, Paul himself emphasises the inward character of revelation. It is this, and precisely this, that has so impressed him. Let us now look at the story of his conversion, interpreting it in the light of the oral tradition.

To approach Damascus means to be in a worshipful state, facing, as it were, the Father and Mother ('Da–Ma') of all things. Saul would be doing this in the time-honoured fashion of inner prayer and contemplation. Naturally, given his uncomfortable circumstances, he would contemplate the thought; 'Could this persecution in the name of God be right?' The ancient traditions teach that a prayerful question will be answered, and indeed, an enlightening answer came and Saul was immediately humbled by it. Being thrown to the floor represents a humbling, a move away from arrogant intent.[25]

Saul now becomes Paul, the humbled one, and, surrendering, decides to serve. It is at that stage that he actually enters Da-ma-scus, the state of the Father-Mother. In traditions the world over, humility, surrender and service are prerequisites for entering the deep well of the soul where God is manifest. The story assures us that Paul rests there within the deep fastness of the Holy Trinity, for he is blinded for *three* days. The subsequent healing of his blindness also informs us that he now perceives with different eyes not just this world, but also, at times, other worlds too:

> 'Paul told his followers many things. For example, he boasted that he had been to heaven and seen visions that were incommunicable. He also boasted that he had developed all his ideas about Jesus before he so much as met any of the Galilean dissidents who had known him "in the flesh". Even the idea of the Christian Eucharist, for example, comes not, as modern literalists still claim, from Jesus, but from Paul.'
>
> A. N. Wilson.[26]

The Book of Acts would have us believe that shortly after his 'conversion', Paul went straight to Jerusalem, 'preaching boldly in the name of the Lord'. The main problem with this is that Paul himself firmly denies it! He states quite explicitly that the first thing he did after his vision was to go at once to Arabia, *not* to Jerusalem.

Thinking about this, he would not want to stay in Jerusalem where his relatives and fellow guards would be enquiring after him. The idea was to persecute Christians, not to actually become one! This was a confusing and dangerous situation. Surely Paul would want to know more about the inner revelation, but his old Jewish friends, even in Tarsus, would not be of help – after all, Paul's revelation was about Jesus, the enemy. No, Paul was a changed man and needed time to let things settle and to learn more, but not where he was too well known, that would be foolish in the circumstances. And so Paul avoids the Jerusalem Christians and is clear about what happened next:

> 'I conferred not with flesh and blood.
> Neither went I up to Jerusalem to them which were apostles
> before me; but I went into Arabia and
> returned again unto Damascus.
> Then after three years I went up to Jerusalem...'
>
> Galatians 1:16–18

So here is where Damascus, the actual place, may come into it, for Paul seems to be telling us that on his return from Arabia, he went to Damascus. But is that what he is really saying? Maybe. But that could just be our modern, literal, Western reading. Also, the relative geographical positions, with Arabia to the south, Damascus in the north and Jerusalem between the two, do not make avoidance of Jerusalem, *en route*, a simple issue. Neither does one travel 'up' from Damascus to Jerusalem. These are small points but aid in the idea that something more is meant here. Therefore, it is time to behave like an initiate and to read the piece in the veiled language of the ancient oral tradition. In this reading, Paul is saying that in Arabia, away from the stressful dangers of Jerusalem, he again found the right conditions for inner revelation and entered the deep well of the soul where God is manifest. Notice, once more, the mystic indicator is present, for we are told that he was there for *three* years.

Why Paul chose Arabia and what he found there will be revealed in a later chapter. What is already clear is that when Paul returned and started out on his missionary work, his brand of Christianity spread quickly.

Paul and James

The fundament of the new faith is summarised by the *Encyclopadia Britannica:*

> 'The New Covenant, or Testament, was viewed as the fulfilment
> of the Old Testament promises of salvation that were continued
> for the new Israel, the church, through the Holy Spirit, which
> had come through Christ, upon the whole people of God. Thus
> the Spirit, which in the Old Testament had been viewed as resting
> only on special charismatic figures, in the New Testament became
> "democratized", i.e., was given to the whole people of the New
> Covenant.'[27]

This matches the flavour of Paul's own conversion. His conversion was a very personal occurrence, his testimony was likewise personal, and, even after editorial tampering, it bears the hallmarks of something that mainstream Christianity has sought to expunge – Gnosticism. Gnosticism, a form of individual revelation via means of 'spiritual knowledge', comes from the Greek *Gnosis*, meaning 'knowledge'. It is a heresy and was condemned as such in the years following the great Council of Nicaea (AD 325). It is worth noting that the contents of the New Testament were not settled until this era and, given the negative attitude towards Gnosticism, it is likely that the more Gnostic elements of Paul's theology were removed.[28] But more than this has been hidden; there are references which infer friction between Paul and the Jerusalem Church. Paul was not accepted by the surviving family and followers of Jesus, who were led by James.

> 'And when Saul was come to Jerusalem, he assayed to join himself
> to the disciples: but they were all afraid of him, and believed not
> that he was a disciple.'
>
> Acts 9:26

Acts and Paul's Epistles demonstrate that James was the undisputed head of the Church, but who exactly was he?

James is often referred to as 'the Brother of the Lord' and he may have been a half-brother of Jesus on the maternal side. Perhaps a reference of Josephus to James as 'the brother of Jesus who was called Christ'[29] is evidence of this relationship. However, the proto-evangelium calls St. James both the 'cousin' and the 'brother' of Jesus, clearly using the term 'brother' as one of religious association, and it seems to me that a much more convincing explanation of the epithet 'Brother of the Lord' is that James was a member of the same religious order as Jesus. I believe that this could hold true for others named 'brother' too. This would go some way to explaining why Joseph of Arimathea was cited as the closest blood relative to Jesus and thus able to claim his post-crucifixion remains.[30] The nature of the order and Jesus' membership of it will be addressed as the thesis unfolds.

The fact that Paul's presence in the New Testament is almost overwhelming is testimony to the eventual completeness of the destruction of James' Jerusalem Church. The Christianity of James was doomed and, quite probably, Paul foresaw this; his version of Jesus was not inspired by the Jerusalem Church. Paul was the self-proclaimed 'Apostle to the Gentiles', a market brand that completely horrified both Jews and Judaeo-Christians.

The passion of the Christianity that Paul took abroad was so new, so enticing and so very different from the dryness of its competitor back home. Paul conceived of a world brimfull of his idea of Christ and that world became pregnant with Paul's vision. A major confrontation arose between Paul and James which was brought about by the broader ramifications of Paul's success as a preacher of a universal church – a kind of catholic converter. Paul's Christianity moved power away from Jerusalem but at that time, the Jerusalem Church was the 'Mother Church' and central to it was the Jerusalem Temple. The Acts of the Apostles neither confirms nor denies this, but it is borne out not only by the importance of the Temple inscription regarding Jesus, but also by a statement made by the Christian writer Sulpicius Severus:

> 'Reference had been made to the likelihood that the Christian writer Sulpicius Severus (c. AD 360–430) drew upon the last books of Tacitus. In his *Chronical*, composed in the fifth century, it is recorded that the Romans decided to destroy the Temple at Jerusalem at the end of the siege because it was a source of inspiration both to Judaism and to Christianity. It has been pointed out that Severus would hardly have made such a statement that contradicted Josephus unless he had drawn his information from a source of considerable prestige and authority. The curious fact that the books of Tacitus dealing with the conclusion of the war have disappeared suggests that they may have suffered at Christian hands because they contained just such a passage as Severus records.'[31]

After many travels, Paul returned to Jerusalem and to the Temple where, ironically, he was confronted by a mob and thrown out. As the uproar continued, he was arrested by the Romans and eventually placed on a boat to Rome, there to plead his case. Paul never returned. The field seemed clear for James and his particular version of Christianity. Unfortunately, the Jerusalem Church had a very outstanding Achilles' heel, the fact that its roots were closely entwined around Jerusalem. As Jesus had predicted, Jerusalem would fall, but James would fall first.

Eusebius quotes Hegesippus, the second-century Christian historian, and says that he gave a good account of the end of James. Hegesippus' work now only survives in fragments recorded by other writers, Eusebius amongst them. Hegesippus writes that James was asked in the Temple: "Which is the door of Jesus?" James' response is odd: "That he was the Saviour." Hegesippus continues: "As there were many therefore of the rulers that believed,[32] there arose a tumult among the Jews, Pharisees and scribes, saying that there was a danger that the people would now expect Jesus as the Messiah."[33] James is then compelled to ascend to the roof of the Temple to quieten the gathering mob and he declares, "Which is the door to Jesus that was crucified?" After this, James is hurled down and killed by a fuller's club. James' death was no accident. It was judicial murder carried out as a political act, one that removed a troublemaker who was, rightly or wrongly, seen as acting beyond the law.

James' version of Christianity did not long survive him; within 4 years the Jews rose up in revolt against the might of Rome and the apocalypse, so often predicted, began. Jewish nationalism rose up intermittently over the next 40 years. It made some inroads at first, mostly against the unsuspecting Romans, but ultimately it failed, with Jewish hopes fading away on a tide of blood, most of it perched upon the vengeful swords of merciless Roman soldiery. Finally, one last bout of Latin ruthlessness sent the entire nation – what was left of it – into exile. The Temple was razed and, to the astonishment of the people, God did not intervene. The place groaned and shook, until it all came tumbling down, courtesy not of God but the Romans. At the same time, Judaeo-Christianity was wiped out. Paul's Christianity continued abroad and prospered, but much had already been lost.

Silence Over Sound

A.N. Wilson makes a very shrewd observation of Paul and his version of Christianity, observing that Paul is quite often perceived as one who 'distorted the original message of Christianity'.[34] In fact, there are a number of ancient documents, contemporary to the period of Paul's preaching, which describe him as a 'false prophet'. Amongst them is the *Kerygmara Petrai*, an Ebionite document of the early Judaeo-Christian Church. It dismisses Paul's rank of Apostle and calls him a false prophet who falsified the true teachings of Jesus.

For a few hundred years after the death of Jesus, a remnant of Jewish Messianists known as 'Ebionites' or 'Ebionim' - 'poor men' - survived. They revered Jesus as one of the last of the prophets and within this sect were a select group called the Desposyni, the descendants of Jesus. There is a reference to these descendants by Eusebius[35] in *The History of the Church*.[36] Commenting on the earlier words of Hegesippus, Eusebius writes:

> 'But there still survived of the family of the Lord the grandsons of Jude, his brother after the flesh, as he was called. These they informed against, as being of the family of David; and the evocatus brought them before Domitian Caesar. For he feared the coming of the Christ, as did also Herod. And he asked them if they were of David's line, and they acknowledged it. Then he asked them what possessions they had or what fortune they owned. And they said that between the two of them they had

> only nine thousand denarii, half belonging to each of them . . .
> after this Damition in no way condemned them, but despised
> them as men of no account . . .'[37]

It seems that these people still lived the simple life as advocated by Jesus. But Paul had learned nothing from this line of followers. In Galatians 1:15–17, Paul is adamant: 'I did not go to anyone for advice, nor did I go to Jerusalem'. This is unfortunate because there were things that the Apostles would have learned directly from Jesus that Paul would never know, or at least never understand or tell correctly. These things have been lost to scripture, perhaps because they were only for the ears of the inner circle, but I believe that, now, in the light of emerging science, they are of import. I am thinking particularly of the following report about the work of Jesus, from the *Slavonic Josephus*:

> 'And everything whatsoever he wrought through some invisible
> power, he wrought through some word and a command...Yet he
> himself did nothing shameful or high-handed, but by his word
> he prepared everything ... he accomplished whatsoever he would
> by a magic word...'[38]

I then realised that almost all reference to any such techniques and associated mystical practices must have been expunged from the Bible (an exception would be the use of sound at the Battle of Jericho).

The following, a précis of Acts 19:13–19, from A. N. Wilson, indicates that Jesus' use of words of power must have left a strong impression at the time:

> 'Some wandering exorcists, seven sons of a Jewish high priest
> called Sceva, tried to conduct an exorcism and said over their
> victim, "I adjure you by the Jesus whom Paul proclaims." The
> evil spirit replied, "Jesus I know, and Paul I know, but who are
> you?' The poor lunatic who was possessed of the demon
> overpowered his exorcists and ran through the crowd. Gradually
> it became known that the name of Jesus was the most powerful
> magic of all, and Paul's followers organised a huge public burning
> of magical books.'[39]

These exorcists were clearly not adept in the use of the name of Jesus and, unfortunately, the much needed training was unlikely to be forthcoming: Jesus was gone and the old books were burnt. How ironic that Paul's followers should destroy evidence of practices used by Jesus himself! Paul did not seem to favour or even to know about such things. These practices would be for intimate disciples only; Paul would not have been privy to them.

Unfortunately, we know that things got worse. The failed uprising meant that, along with the Jews, the Judaeo-Christians would be butchered or in flight from the Romans. Any secret knowledge which had been personally handed down by Jesus would be lost or run to ground. The potency of the Christian heritage was therefore greatly lessened.

Obviously, Paul was a potent and inspiring writer and orator who had experienced visions and entered 'the deep well of the soul where God is manifest'. Resting in the deep well of the soul for a time is one thing, but a permanent state of God realisation would be another, and the Bible tells us that only Jesus had that and that the Apostles did not. Paul, in particular, did not even benefit from direct transmission of knowledge from Jesus.

In the wake of his vision Paul's own Gnosticism was there and Paul certainly saw Jesus as a dying and rising god. Even a brief look at his writings shows that Paul was little interested in the mortality of Jesus, for he hardly ever mentions him in an historical context; the power of the risen Christ is the main theme. And where did Paul get the Eucharist from? I would suggest from the rites of the dying and rising gods so prevalent in Tarsus and elsewhere.

In surveying the work of Paul, I had to admit that he had certainly brought his considerable personal knowledge and experience to bear in the rise of the New Covenant. Nevertheless, there was something missing. The stories of Jesus' 'words of power' had served to intrigue me. I had also developed an interest in Gnosticism, that much abused 'heresy' of early Christianity.

Intermezzo

WE have again seen the rising and dying god writ large. We have also seen that the ancient tradition deeply influenced the ways of the various cultures but that Judah resisted this influence and, in doing so, resisted Jesus too.

This past chapter also gave us an opportunity to explore the ways of the oral tradition and to begin to understand how, within a story, many layers of meaning are available, some revelatory. Clearly, Saul had his own revelations and so changed his name to Paul, a humbler title. However, not to enquire of the Jerusalem Apostles, who were the custodians of Jesus' personal knowledge, still seems arrogant in the extreme. Whilst it would be naîve of us to imagine that there was no residue of Saul in Paul, perhaps there was a reason for his attitude. The Jerusalem Apostles had their revelations, though perhaps they were less mystically inclined than Paul, whose vision they rejected. The Apostles were very much followers of the man, not the myth. Perhaps Paul saw his knowledge as something more original than theirs. This we will return to in part two.

Like any accomplished teacher before him, Paul would expect the true seeker to delve into the inner meaning behind his words and we have seen how they could be used as tools to help understand and develop the unitive experience. I gave Paul's famous vision as an example of an internal experience portrayed and usually only understood in an external manner. But, you may ask, internal or external, what difference does it make? I believe that it makes all the difference of the past 2,000 years of Christendom, where, with the power of God portrayed as something largely external rather than internal, potency was taken away from the laity and given to the priests. The Church therefore became potent at the expense of the individual and in doing so prospered materially, becoming, in effect, the world's first and largest ever multinational corporation. Inner revelation and the oral tradition were out; so, too, were other ingredients. Again, I am thinking of the reports of Jesus' use of sound. What was its nature? How could it be used? These questions would eventually help me to fathom the enigma that was Jesus. Meanwhile, I was sure that, as the Church grew into an institution and the non-conformists came under increasing pressure, much was lost. The most prominent of these non-conformists were the various Gnostic sects that arose in the early centuries AD, whose celebration of Jesus Christ was so very different and, to the Church, so very outrageous. Therefore I furthered my research into Gnosticism as well as into the background of the growing Christian Church.

3

A Touch of Heresy

'There is only one religion, though there are a hundred versions of it.'

George Bernard Shaw

.. the essence of true myth is to masquerade behind seemingly objective and everyday details borrowed from known circumstances.

de Santillana and von Dechend[1]

I had now arrived at a point in my journey where things began to get more than a little exciting. Paul's vision had already sparked something off in my own mind, something beyond mere theology and history, something that connected the physical to the spiritual. And then there were Jesus' words of power, the ones that Josephus wrote of. My curiosity was aroused and I began to think that beyond religious mythology there lay a secret language of the psyche, a language of power, a power that spoke in resonant tones, a language that had something to do with names – the name of Jesus and the names of the ancient gods themselves.

My musings took me again to Paul and to his journey to Rome. I wondered particularly about what he had found there, those things that would have been the local influences on the Church of Rome. By the time of Paul there were, of course, many imported religious beliefs already very well established in the city. The orator Cicero (106–43 BC) had praised the Greeks:

'For it appears to me that among the many exceptional and divine things your Athens has produced and contributed to human life, nothing is better than those mysteries. For by means of them we have been transformed from a rough and savage way of life to the state of humanity, and have been civilized. Just as they are called initiations, so in actual fact we have learned from them the fundamentals of life, and have grasped the basis not only for living with joy but also for dying with a better hope.'[2]

We can see that Rome at that time was not averse to external influences. However, the arrival of the first Christian missionaries was neither timely nor welcome, for, in the era after the death of the Emperor Claudius in AD 54 Rome was a very dangerous place, particularly as it was under the aegis of that most notorious of Emperors, Nero.

Throughout the Empire, Roman law had become, to a large extent, the moral law. Even though Rome herself was possibly the most decadent portion of the Empire, she had underpinned all of her provinces with a firm discipline and cultural outlook. If Christianity was to spread then first it had to enter the bloodstream of the Empire, beginning with its heart. After that it was a matter of going to the far-flung corners and asserting the new rules - Christian rules.

The Bones of St. Peter

In the formative years of the Roman Church there were many manifestations of Pagan belief in the city. However, Paganism did not provide the single firm faith or moral guidance that humanity sought in the increasingly uncertain times, whereas Christianity provided one God and a strict morality.

Paul's appearance in Rome would have been decisive in increasing Christian influence, whilst at the same time separating Christianity further from Judaism. A separate priesthood emerged, away from the pattern of the Jewish hereditary Kahens (modern Cohen). However, these new priests were soon to be seen wearing garments and performing rituals patterned upon older Jewish and Pagan models. In effect, Christianity seemed to be making a statement that either it was borrowed, or that in some way it was older.

Pliny the Younger (*c*.AD 61–112) mentions Christianity in his writings, describing the movement as having been founded by 'Christ' and explaining that at that time, the end of the first century, Jesus Christ was already regarded as a god. Jesus was sometimes referred to as Chrestus. According to Suetonius (b.AD 70), Claudius had the Jews expelled from Rome since 'the Jews constantly made disturbances at the instigation of Chrestus.'[3] 'Chrestus' means 'godly man' or 'good man' in the sense of a 'simple man' and may have been a pun used by Suetonius as a satire upon Jesus. However, the good-man, in having been crucified, had become a god-man, a slain messiah. A slain messiah did not fit in well within the context of Jewish messianic nationalism, which looked for a living leader, therefore this crucified god was ultimately a Gentile god and much more marketable in Rome.[4] The fact that the marketing was successful is borne out by the persecutions which were later deemed necessary by Nero.

Significantly, there were Christians in Rome even before Paul had arrived there, although there is no information about the foundation of the churches in Rome or even who the founders might have been. The idea that it was Peter who founded the Church in Rome is based upon a much later tradition, perhaps reflecting the desire of the Roman Church to be associated with Jesus' chosen apostle in a direct way. The link is tenuous to say the least, but there is another association that reveals much and brings us back once again to the pattern of world myth.

Peter was the 'rock' upon which the Church would be built.[5] It comes from the Latin `petra'. Traditionally, Peter's martyrdom involved being crucified upside down during the reign of Nero. Catholic scholars now admit that they have their reservations about the veracity of the myth and even doubt Peter's burial upon the Vatican Hill or at the alternative site in St. John Lateran.[6] Moreover, the slender passage upon which the legend of Peter hangs, in Matthew 16:18–19, is a forgery, inserted into place, quite deliberately, in the third century.[7] Basically it was a ploy to give Rome greater power over its rivals in the East. Rome's St. Peter is, quite possibly, an early example of a Christianised Roman god.

The god of the city of Rome was Pater Liber and here there are links to the Mithraic Pater Patrum, the Father of Fathers, whose name was foreshortened to 'Papa' and eventually 'Pope'. This Peter/Pater was both a rock and a Father God. The Roman god of the underworld – the force within the rock – was called Dis Pater. In Rome he was venerated along with Proserpina, the Roman equivalent of the Greek Persephone. Dis Pater thus corresponds to Greek Hades. The etymology of Hades is interesting, splitting as it does into two syllables, *ha* and *des*. *Ha* is a generic term meaning simply 'lord'. *Des* or *dis* means the 'circle or disc of the underworld'. Julius Caesar reports that the Gaelic Celts claimed descent from Dis. This belief entailed the god being the father of their race by the shedding of his blood. a dying and rising god, symbolised by the setting and rising sun in the form of a cross. This dying and rising divinity I was well used to, but the association with the rock made me think that the reference was about divine forces within the rock. Something deep within told me that this was a kind of key and later I would pursue it.[8]

Rome is said to be named after its founder Romulus, though this is largely disputed. In fact it is more than likely that it was named after its river, the Tiber, which in former days was called the Ruma.[9] Myth also states that Rome was built by pastoralists or shepherds, but this is myth in its purest state; a pastor is, religiously speaking, a shepherd of souls, one who nurtures and guides. According to Professor Mario Attilio Levi, the evidence is that the city was actually built by salt merchants. Levi inclines toward the idea of Rome being named after its river; he states that its former name does not derive from an archaic Etruscan word, *rumon*, but from *stroma*, meaning 'river'. The former was an Etruscan noble name and was favoured by propagandists eager to display Rome's noble origins.[10] What is undisputed is Rome's connection with the hero-gods. The oldest ancient site in Rome is a temple-site dedicated to Hercules. It is not sited on one of Rome's famous hills, but near the ancient river port of Faro Boario.

It is interesting that Rome should have been built by salt merchants. Salt was indispensable for rearing sheep and livestock, as well as preserving meat, and was an essential component in cheese-making. It is very likely that the biggest traders in salt were Phoenician in origin. The Etruscans, one of the great pre-Roman peoples, were closely connected to the Phoenicians, and may themselves have had Phoenician roots. Both were excellent mariners and both traded in the famous murex dye that brought the colour purple to Rome. The Latin for salt is *sal*; in its feminine form we simply add the alphabetic symbol of the crucifix, the sign of the Saviour, the letter 'T'. The hero-saviour comes literally to save, in Latin *salvare*. Bringing 'salvation' reminded me of the Vatican. The verb *vaticinate* means `to foretell by prophetic inspiration'. The singular of this is the Latin *vates*, meaning 'a prophet-poet', and indeed Vatis was the title given to priests of the Vatican Hill in ancient pre-Christian times. The title was Etruscan.

The Etruscan homeland was Etruria, in what is more or less modern-day Tuscany. This was an important area as far back as the eigth and ninth centuries BC, mainly because of its mineral resources. There were three supreme Etruscan deities: Menrva, Tinia and Uni. Of these, Tinia was deemed the most powerful. These three were worshipped as a Trinity in sanctuaries that consisted of three halls. In Roman times these deities are more recognisable as Minerva, Jupiter and Juno.

Minerva was the tutelary goddess of Rome and of wisdom, she was also equated with the Greek goddess Athena. Jupiter was the Roman equivalent of the Greek Zeus and Jupiter's sister/wife was Juno, goddess of marriage and, as Lucina (literally 'light out of darkness'), she is the goddess of birth. Etruscan gods were a meeting-place between Greece and Rome. Etruscan Aplu is Greek Apollo. Nethuns is Roman Neptune, called Poseidon in Greek.

I could not help but notice that some, if not all, of these gods seem to have ancient Egyptian antecedents. Minerva, for example, is very close to the Egyptian Min, the god of fertility who hails from a place called Koptos. Juno or Uno is very like the Egyptian Nu or Nut, wife of Geb, the earth god. Professor Martin Bernal has posited strong linguistic evidence that Neit, another Egyptian goddess, was later translated by ancient Greeks as Athena. Vowels in many ancient languages are indistinct and sometimes disingenuous. In removing them we can see the comparison. Egyptian *HtNt* means 'House of Nut' or Neit. In transcribing this the Greeks added an 'A', hence Ath'n – Athena.[11]

Roman Jupiter, Tinia in Etruscan, becomes, using the same process, *Tn*, which would seem to connect to a particular and precise date in history. Tn in Egypt would be Akhenaten's famous god, the Aten, represented by a disc, symbolising the sun. This would fall within the dates so far given - the Aten was worshipped around 1400 BC, and the Etruscan Tinia appears on the scene some four centuries later.

As we can see, there was a cosmopolitan foundation and feel to Rome, going back to very ancient times. As the nebulous arrangement of clans orbited and hovered about the place soon to be called Rome, their cultures and beliefs altered and adapted as, over time, they collapsed inwards as individual tribes and emerged as a cohesive unit called Romans.

From the very earliest times the Vatican Hill in Rome attracted the faith of believers; no matter what its name, the religious view was much the same. The early god of the Vatican Hill was Attis – a crucified hero–god, who rose on the third day. In a reflection of the Vatican today, the established clans of ancient Rome were called Curiae. It is the Curia who today still attend to the state of faith in Rome.

Faith in another Guise

Before Christianity and right up until the time of Constantine, the main religions of Rome were pantheistic. Pantheism is 'the belief or philosophical theory that God and the universe are identical; the identification of God with the forces of nature and natural substances'.[12] In such religions these forces are recognized as the gods which spring from God.

In the Classical world the deeper levels of religion were known as the Mysteries. The Emperors themselves, most of whom were acclaimed as gods, were initiates of various of the Mysteries. The levels of initiation were related to the levels of self-knowledge, for Pantheism, in holding that divinity is in nature, addresses the idea that divinity is in us, we too being a part of nature

The advent of what was soon to become known as Roman Christianity was to change all that. St. Paul's religion was to motivate the masses, so a sort of buy now, pay later (if at all) contract was preached to the people, who it seems were only too willing to offload all their spiritual angst, some would say responsibilities, on to the suffering figure of Jesus - a new interpretation of the dying and rising hero-god. The existing cults in and around Rome would relate to a dying and rising god and so it is easy to see that what had actually happened was a merging of that which was uniform. The cults came together under the guise of a new religion, Roman Christianity, which was therefore an old belief system in a new guise.

One might say that Christianity had merely swallowed up what its own foundations had given rise to in the deep and ancient past. This also seems to have been the ethic behind the Emperor Constantine's acceptance of the new religion. By all accounts Constantine was an arch-politician and, as one might expect, an unsavoury character. However, as Emperor it was his imperial duty to bring stability to a strife-torn Empire, and he had the genius to see that such stability could be wrought through the offices of religion. Constantine's background is interesting. He was the son of the Emperor, Constantius Chlorus and the revered Christian, St. Helena. The date of his birth is unknown, but is placed somewhere between the years AD 272 and 288.

By this time the Roman Empire had become so massive that its administration had to be split between East and West. From c. AD 286, there was an Empire of the East and an Empire of the West, ruled by two Emperors, both known as Augustus. This practice began under Diocletian and ended with the fall of the Western Empire in AD 476.

In 293 Constantine was sent to the court of Diocletian, the senior Emperor, under whose guidance he learnt the new Byzantine ideas of absolutism. It was whilst Constantine was on a tour of duty in Britain that his father died, and in the same year, 306, he was proclaimed Western Emperor at York, becoming its ruler in 312, after defeating his rival Maxentius at the Battle of the Milvian Bridge. It is interesting that Constantine was proclaimed in Britain, for a popular belief states that both of his parents were British, although this is strongly disputed.[13] It would be later, in AD 324 that Constantine defeated Licinius, the Emperor of the East, to become Sole Emperor.

In the years running up to Constantine's accession there were various incursions into the Empire. From around AD 235 until approximately AD 284 the Goths appeared on the scene, invading large areas, mainly for pillage, not settlement. Through the many Christian captives they took into slavery, the Goths would themselves become converts to Christianity, though their version of it, Arianism, was later declared heretical. Constantine's Christianity was in many ways a compromise, bringing together all of the disparate elements, one of which was Mithraism. Mithraism had been declared the principal religion of the Empire in 274 AD by the Emperor Aurelian and similarities may have played a decisive part in Constantine's decision to promote Christianity as the religion of the Empire.

Perhaps the most outstanding similarity between Mithraism and Christianity is the birthday of Mithras. This day is called `the Birthday of the Invincible Sun' and falls on December the 25th, which was the winter solstice in the Julian calendar. The solstice is the shortest day of the year, after which the sun's sojourn in the day becomes ever longer. This was also a natural date for the celebration of Jesus' birthday and it was finally made official in the middle of the forth century, by which time much of Mithraism had been absorbed into Christianity.

According to later tradition, Constantine had inherited a predisposition toward Christianity from both his parents. Thus it would seem that it was only natural that the new Emperor would embrace it. However, whether he ever did or not is a matter of some debate. The main argument stems from Constantine's now famous vision.

Constantine's vision occurred shortly before the decisive battle with Maxentius at the Milvian Bridge and was reinforced by a prophetic dream of a luminous cross shining brightly in the sky. Across the symbol was inscribed the legend *In Hoc Signo Vinces* – 'By this sign you will conquer.' Ever the practical man, Constantine took note of the dream and had the celestial portent emblazoned upon the shields of his troops. Needless to say, they went out and conquered. The symbol that Constantine saw has been claimed as a Christian symbol, the Chi Rho the first two letters of the name of Christ, as written in Greek. It is pronounced in the same way as the Egyptian city Cairo.

Of course the marketing arm of the Church was quick to capitalise upon the dream, claiming it for its own and celebrating Constantine's victory over Maxentius as the triumph of Christianity over Paganism. According to this interpretation, it was thanks to this divine inspiration that Constantine converted both himself and the Empire to Christianity. This assumption could not be further from the truth. Constantine's vision, if it was Christian, was

The Chi Rho

only so in very much the older sense of the word, in the way with which I was by now becoming familiar, for the then current symbol of Christianity was the fish.

According to a witness in Constantine's army, the vision took place within the precincts of a temple to Apollo, either in the Vosges or near Autun. The vision was very much a 'numinous' experience. According to the witness, the vision was of a sun god, Sol Invictus – the Invincible Sun. The triumphal arch celebrating Constantine's victory was inscribed with the same.

This was fascinating. Like St. Paul's and innumerable others', it was yet another temple-based vision. I was really beginning to think that temple sites themselves had their own input into the visionary experience. Without any hint of irony I thought to myself that God was indeed working in a mysterious way – through particular sites. Constantine was stating that the sun was God, Apollo was a sun god, and so too, it seems, was Jesus.

The Chi Rho is a fascinating symbol. It is also called the Labarum and, as we can see in the illustration, it is a cross surmounted by a 'p'. By the time of Constantine it was already an ancient symbol of the sun god. Labarum means 'the everlasting Father Sun'.[15] Another version of the Labarum is the Christian 'JHS', which is also called the 'Sign of God'. In Greek it spells out the letters iota, eta and sigma – an identification of Bacchus as the sun god. Bacchus is the Roman form of Dionysus. It is believed that the Labarum is a late development of the Egyptian ansate cross, or ankh. I soon came to realise that Bacchus and Dionysus, too, like Jesus, trod the wine press, were crucified and rose from the dead, just like the Egyptian Osiris, whose symbology includes the ankh.

Digging deeper, I discovered that the Chi Rho may have played its part in the earliest Roman times. Romulus, the legendary founder of Rome, was originally spelt Rhomylus. In some versions of his myth he is crucified, thus we have the cross, Chi, and Rho, from his name.[16] Furthermore, the tutor of one of the Greeks' greatest heroes, Achilles, was a centaur by the name of Chiron. So the Chi Rho appears in Greek myth, too, and on the whole appears to be widespread.

Unsurprisingly, the main religion under Constantine was not Christianity but one of sun-worship[17] and Constantine was its chief priest. Sun-worship even featured upon contemporary coinage. The idea that Constantine converted to Christianity is mistaken. He was not even baptised until AD 337 – as he lay on his deathbed. It was under the tutelage of the official cult of Sol Invictus that Christianity grew ever more powerful and absorbant. Mithraism, of which Sol Invictus was a part, contained elements of other religions, those of Baal, Isis, Astarte and so on. The absorbent approach was continued by the Christians and, as Constantine's reign went on, the distinguishing points between these two major beliefs became less and less defined. Both shared

December the 25th as the birthday of its god, both held Sunday as sacred, and so on.

Christianity had its most powerful supporter in the form of Constantine's mother, Helena, and it was perhaps because of her that the religion began to take the shape it did. On a grand tour of the Holy Land, Helena walked in the very footsteps of Jesus, building churches and finding relics, such as the 'True Cross', to bring back to Constantinople, where they were accorded great reverence.

As the various approaches came together under the banner of Christianity, moves were made to enforce uniformity. The motivation for this was political expediency. Ironically, the early Church Father Tertullian (*c.*AD160-*c.*225) had stated only 100 years before the accession of Constantine that:

> 'The world may need its Caesars, but the Emperor can never be
> a Christian, nor a Christian ever be the Emperor.'

In Tertullian's day Christians considered themselves to be like Jesus: humble bringers of peace. Suddenly, and by association with the Battle of the Milvian Bridge, all of that had changed.

The essence of the political was captured and encased at the Council of Nicaea in AD 325. This council was summoned by Constantine to deal mainly with the Arian controversy. Arianism was soon to be labelled a heresy for its belief that Jesus Christ was not fully divine.

The battle between Arianism and Catholicism was a titanic one, for Arianism very nearly became the faith of the Empire. The battle in itself was over the ultimate definition of God. From this point onwards there would be orthodoxy and there would be heresy. Only 60 years before, Christianity had become legalised *en route* to becoming the official state religion; now it was fighting over its identity.

The Trinity had by this time become the official description of God's nature, and an intriguingly Pythagorean one at that. However, by this time it had also become clear that in the various descriptions of God there was a paradox. Christianity still had a strong connection to the Judaic idea that there was only one God and no lesser gods; Christian literature by this time, though, seemed to contradict this by speaking of the Father, Son and Holy Spirit. Thus arose the question; 'How can God be both one and three?'

Various lines of thought, which were soon to be condemned as heresy, came about in order to explain this paradox. Arianism was one of them. Lucian of Antioch (d. AD 312) suggested the idea that the Son was not God but was created by God before the beginning of the world. The Son, who manifested as Christ, was a great supernatural being worthy of worship but was most definitely not the Creator. Arius, after whom Arianism is named, was one of

Lucian's students. Arius started preaching his doctrine at Alexandria, to the great chagrin of the Catholic Church, which believed that describing the Son as something less than God contained problems for Christian doctrine. Only God should be worshipped, not the things he created; worshipping the Son in this way was actually an insult to God and theologically wrong!

Nevertheless, Arius continued to preach his 'offensive' doctrine, and in AD 321 was excommunicated by Bishop Alexander of Alexandria. Arius responded by drumming up the support of the Eastern Bishops of the Empire and Christian communities were soon split into warring factions both theologically and physically. Settlement soon became an urgent priority, particularly as the bemused Emperor was beginning to lose sleep over the issue: 'Give me back my quiet days and carefree nights. Do not let me spend the rest of my days joylessly.'

Going into the conference, Arianism was in a very strong position, but unfortunately for Arius he was outmanoeuvred and the council turned against him. It was decreed that the Father and the Son did have the same divine nature and Jesus was finally voted into the hallowed status of God. It was official. No longer was he a dangerous mortal – but the boundaries between the historic Jesus and his mythical counterpart now became permanently unclear. It was also at Nicaea that the orthodoxies of the Church were confirmed and for the first time the word 'heresy' began an intimate association with the Church. Roman Catholicism 1, Heresy 0. It was a decisive victory. Arius was banished and his followers lost their positions of authority. But it did not go all the Catholics' way. The Arians fought back, appealing to Constantine that it would be less divisive to bring them back. By the time of the Emperor's death in AD 337 no fewer than three bishops had been deposed in favour of Arians.

Over the course of the next 40 years the balance of power tilted this way and that, until by 378 the Empire had been for some time in firm Catholic hands under Gratian. Gratian was succeeded by Theodosius the Great, and although the Arians were still very widespread and powerful, measures were now taken to curb their influence.

In 381 Theodosius hosted a meeting of Church leaders known as the First Council of Constantinople. It was at this meeting that the ultimate triumph of Catholicism over Arianism occurred. The Doctrine of the Trinity – the Deity as one in nature yet three in persons – was proclaimed as the only correct belief concerning God. Arianism went into massive decline. Even the Goths and the Vandals, who had been converted by the Arian missionary Ulfilas, were eventually to convert to orthodoxy. The way in which the Catholic orthodoxy went about this task was inspired – along with the doctrine of the Trinity went hymns and high ritual, elaborate ceremonies and the belief that relics had miraculous powers. Within the sacred site, powerful unified ceremonies took place that had their effect upon those who participated and, importantly for the winning over of the Arians, many aspects of this new heightened sense of ritual came initially from the Arians themselves.

The Defeat of the Past

Our view of early Christianity is derived mainly from the work of Eusebius, an early Church Father and employee of Constantine. Needless to say Eusebius' work appears rather biased towards what had come out of Nicaea as orthodox Christianity. By this time anything that went against such views was condemned. Image, to the new Church, was everything. Eusebius was a godsend to the new Christianity: he lent it a power and authority that it had lacked and very soon it would go on the rampage. It was Eusebius who drew up the Nicene creed, the article of faith that is still used in modern times. Those who objected to it were themselves objected to and ultimately banished. The Christianity of Eusebius decreed what 'Christian' eventually became, it was the new orthodoxy that defined itself by declaring everything else as 'heretical'. And so, under the auspices of Constantine, the united front of Christianity papered over many divisive cracks. Christianity rewrote and even reconstructed its history. When the tomb of Christ at Jerusalem was discovered, a Pagan temple stood upon the site. Special permission was sought from Constantine to demolish it and a new construction was begun. Uniformity was king. Christianity was the new politics.

The political motivations of Constantine and various of his cronies were confirmed to me when I learned that Constantine had rejected the gospel of Thomas on the grounds that it refers to James as the heir of Jesus. Constantine, of course, wanted none of that. His Church was, and had to be, the Roman Church, from the line of Peter.

Strange anomalies began to appear before me like the ghosts of something utterly familiar and yet strange. The poet Virgil (70–19 BC), on the basis of observing a new incoming age, the Age of Pisces, 'a new great order of centuries is now being born', was now accorded the status of a prophet of Christianity. Why? It is obvious from his writings that he was a Pagan. And there was another strange thing too: how was it that Christian churches began to be constructed in the most unlikely of places?

There was a belief that by visiting places associated with Jesus' life and death, pilgrims were put in touch with the Jesus of history. A part of this process was the construction of churches on top of the sites that Jesus had visited. However, I found it necessary to ask myself: did Jesus really visit Mount Pisgah, the scene of Moses' last appearance and the fabled resting-place of the Ark of the Covenant? And why was a church constructed atop the fortress of Masada by Byzantine monks from St. Catherine's monastery on Sinai? Masada had little or nothing to do with Christianity's inception - it is Jewish to the core, the hiding place of rebels after the collapse of the fight against Rome. And what of St. Catherine's itself – is this an attempted confirmation of a direct link between Jesus and Moses upon the common ground of Mount Sinai? It is believed that Jesus went to Sinai, but did he really go this far south? Furthermore, the later Byzantine Emperor Justinian, who was responsible for the construction of a number of these sites, had most of them built upon older, Pagan foundations. Naturally, it would have been expedient to use the old Pagan masonry in the new buildings, but when I heard that St. Sophia, the great cathedral of Byzantium in Constantinople (now Istanbul), included Pagan stones from hundreds of miles distant, I wondered if this was expediency or something more.

Like Rome itself, Constantinople was built upon seven hills, a possible reason why Constantine chose the site. St. Sophia, now known as the Hagia Sophia, is the marvel of the city. Rising like the curvaceous breast of a woman, it presents a remarkable sight. Even more remarkable is its interior – it is like a unity of the world's greatest temples. The rock out of which the cathedral was constructed came from the same quarry that supplied the rest of this great city. The quarry was called 'the quarry of the Mother of God' – Marmara, meaning literally 'Mother Mary'. The sacred columns from the temple of Artemis at Ephesus were rescued from out of its destruction to adorn the interior and red porphyry from the temple of Ra at Heliopolis in Egypt has also been used.

Built in AD 532-7 by the Emperor Justinian, St. Sophia was the central power-point of the Byzantine Empire. It is one of the greatest monuments to Christ and yet it is comprised of components of other, far older temples. Here, there is no gloating sense of Jesus' superiority over other gods, there is no sense of overweening pride that patronises the past, just the mysterious feeling that all of these components in some way reveal the might and the majesty, the ultimate mystery of God. This importation of Pagan masonry was intriguing but no clear answers were yet forthcoming. No explanatory texts emerged. I wondered if they had been destroyed.

Although Constantine may never have personally accepted the Christian faith until he was on his deathbed, he did, however, invest it with great power. It was because of such powers, conferred on the Church first by Constantine, and afterwards by Theodosius (ad 408–450)[18] and Valentinian (AD 425–455), that all manner of records and artefacts were destroyed.

> 'The Codex Justinianus contains the order of these Emperors for
> the burning of the writings composed by Porphyry,[19] in his
> blindness, lest they cause God's anger and scandalise the pious.
> This order renewed the law of Constantine in which the burning
> of the books of the heretic Arius was ordered, and the death
> penalty imposed for the hiding of such books.'[20]

So it is that from this period, other forms of Christianity, other versions of it that might have made reference to older things and alternative avenues of thought, become scarce if not non-existent. The great hegemony of centralised official Christianity had begun; anything else was seen as competition and thus fair game.

Ironically, this course of action was to bring about what Leo X referred to as 'the myth of Christ'. This myth is, to a large extent, the creation of the Church and so different did the myth and the history become, that an historical Jesus really need not have existed. The theology of the Church deals almost exclusively with this myth and has had to fight a rearguard action over the past century and a half against those who refute both the myth and its own subsequent history, a rearguard action that could have been served well by much of the material that has, over the centuries, been lost, destroyed or ignored.

However, my stance, after long years of enquiry, is that the myth of Jesus Christ was not the invention of the Church, it was merely adopted and adapted in a complex weave of truth, ignorance, piety and arrogance. This might go some way toward explaining why there is confusion over whether or not Constantine chose Christianity as his official state religion. It is generally assumed by Christian historians that this was indeed the case, but the jury is still out, for, as I and others have pointed out, the main religion was the cult of the Invincible Sun, Sol Invictus. My position has always been that the early Christian historians were telling the truth, but that the latter view is correct! To clarify, I believe that these early Christian converts saw Sol Invictus as a 'primer' and a more archaic form of their new religion. It is interesting that by this time Christians were known as 'adherents of the message'. What I had begun to realise at this stage was that in a broader context, the 'message' need not be seen as coming from one source in one era; rather, it came from a multiplicity of sources from many eras.

Curia and Curiouser

As Christianity strengthened, the cults diminished, but cults such as those of Artemis at Ephesus and the Eleusinian Mysteries were to continue well into the new era, to the annoyance of the Christians. In the end the situation came to be seen by the Christian hierarchy as intolerable. In AD 396, the temple site of the Eleusinian Mysteries was destroyed by monks, fanatical in their devotion to Christianity. They were probably incensed at the outrageous similarities between their own religion and the Mysteries: the eucharistic rites represented to communicants the flesh and blood of the Divine Child, called Triptolemus, Dionysus or even Iasius, another form of the name Jesus. Like Jesus, this Divine Child, son of Demeter, the earth goddess, entered into the earth and rose again.

In AD 406, on the heels of the Eleusinian débâcle, the temple of Artemis was destroyed after a campaign of spin-doctoring by St. John Chrysostom ('Golden-mouthed John'). The temple was ransacked and was never to rise again.

The means by which the Church's power increased were dubious to say the least. In the year AD 740 a document appeared that seemed to confirm, once and for all, the authority of the Roman Church and, ultimately, its Bishop, the Pope. The document was and is known as the *Donation of Constantine*, and without a doubt it was a forgery, and a crude one at that, though the ruse was not discovered until well after the damage had been done.

According to this document, dated to the time of Constantine's controversial conversion, the Emperor had consigned to the Bishop of Rome his imperial regalia and, more crucially, his symbols and seals. Furthermore, the document declared the Bishop to be the 'Vicar of Christ', equivalent to the status of Emperor. The Church was now positioned at the centre of all ultimate political power, spiritual and secular, though more the latter than the former. The transformation was complete: the Church could now crown kings and depose them, it could choose, stifle, destroy and rewrite regarding matters of doctrine, dogma and belief. Jesus himself had 'wanted no part in the world of power and politics, and preferred to be crucified rather than to impose his views on anyone'.[21] By now, Christianity had lost its innocence; in fact Christianity had itself been lost and replaced by Catholicism.

For obvious reasons, the Church has been condemned and tried by many in the court of revisionism without a second glance at its achievement, but much has been overlooked or misunderstood. I have not the time to go into detail within these pages about the full role of the Church at this time, but it was pivotal in the huge advance of later European history. For, quite simply, the Church was able to take the more positive aspects of European civilisation and, in the aftermath of the collapse of the Roman Empire, to gel them so that they might withstand some of the grosser aspects of approximately 500 years of internecine strife and barbarism. To play down the role of the Church at this period is to fatally undervalue what it did to save the civilisation of the West. This is not to deny that the same institution was guilty of great excess and barbarity itself, but, quite frankly, Christianity is a religion of extremes, bringing out the best and the worst in men.

Many would say, though, that the worst began to predominate. Indeed, as time moved on, the Church conquered not so much in the name of Christ, but in the name of sin. Sin and guilt became the staples of the Dark and Middle Age spiritual diets. Fear of God was a fear of hellfire; to be unshriven, unbaptised or excommunicated was to be damned in the eyes of society and the moral majority. The politics of sin were to reap rich rewards for the Church and this was the era in which the Church began to dismiss anything beyond its immediate sphere of influence as malign or evil.

It was a period of logical inconsistency and ruthless theocratising. In the *Confessions*, St. Augustine relates that he had a mistress 'whom I had chosen for no special reason but that my restless passions had alighted on her'. Once he had converted and become a bishop he had no more time for her, or their son. The Church condemned such things, but it would have been Augustine's mistress who acquired the uncompromising label of evil. Yet all things on earth were created by God, including the lady and her child – how could they come to be regarded by the Church as evil? Such imperfections were to be epitomised by the actions of the Church for well over the next 1,000 years.

Ironically, the early success of Christianity was more or less down to the fact that for the very first time some of the deepest mysteries of man were available to all, through the revelation of Paul's version of Christ. Unfortunately, as the Church became more secular, this became merely a tool for recruitment. The revelation became central to the Church, rather than to man as an individual. However, individual interpretation in the light of personal revelation remained a keynote in the Christianity known as Gnosticism. In Gnosticism the inner experience and the inner tuition (intuition) were nurtured and encouraged under guidance from experienced elders, following the pattern portrayed by Jesus and his intimate disciples. In fact, in the early years of Christianity, either by choice or necessity, personal interpretation was the done thing. Papias, Bishop of Heirapolis *c.* AD 130 , comments on Matthew:

> 'Matthew compiled the oracles in the Hebrew language, but everyone translated them as he was able.'[22]

Regardless of the past, it now became a case of there being one interpretation of the hero myth against another. The Church, through secularism, espoused the outward mysteries of the divine hero, whilst its opponents espoused the very opposite, the inner mysteries. It was the depth of achievement of the latter that lent them such resilience, particularly when it came to facing the oppression of the Roman Church in the form of the stake, the scaffold and the threat of Satan's hordes (see chapter four).

Preaching to the Converted

The above has been a broad overview of the formulation of a faith in which the wholesale destruction of books, records, sites and artefacts played a major role. However, not everything labelled as heresy disappeared forever - and here we begin to get a little more deeply into the realm of Gnosticism. Gnostic texts give all manner of revelations. Much to my amazement I discovered that there is a strong possibility that the Acts of the Apostles is an incomplete book - it is missing a final chapter, number 29. This last chapter was discovered buried deep in the archives of the Greek Orthodox Church in old Constantinople by C. S. Sonnini in the late eighteenth century. Now at this stage it would only be fair to say that this document is not accepted by many authorities; however, its claim to authenticity must be taken seriously. This manuscript leads some to believe that St. Paul survived his sojourn in Rome and went to Britain to preach the Gospel.[23] More importantly, it tells us that the Druids recognised similarities between the Druidic and Christian religions. In verse 13 there occurs the following line:

> 'And it came to pass that certain of the Druids came unto Paul privately, and showed by their rites and ceremonies they were descended from the Jews which escaped from bondage in the Land of Egypt...'[24]

Now I have no intention of going into the possibility of St. Paul in Britain, for it would not have been necessary for Paul to leave Rome in order to commune with Britons; there were Britons in Rome. It is a fact that the first church in Rome was not, as is often assumed, the Vatican, but a British church, founded quite possibly by the first accorded Pope after St. Peter, Linus. This church, 'the Titulas', became known as Palatium Britannicum, today called St. Pudentiana.[25] The Palatium was the residence of the famous King Caractacus (Caradoc) who, after being captured during the British campaign of Claudius, was sent in chains to Rome. There, in front of the Senate, Caractacus delivered an address of studied genius; he was tragic and pathetic by turns, but his standing, his obvious education and his wisdom won him freedom, albeit limited to Rome. The standing of Caractacus' family grew ever higher in Rome, to the point where Claudius adopted Gladys, daughter of the exiled king.[26] The epigrammatist Martial wrote Gladys some of his finest lines of poetry. *Claudia, Rufe, meo nubit Peregrina Pudenti* was written to celebrate her marriage to Rufus Pudens Pudentinus in AD 53. The later name of the church obviously comes from her adopted Claudian name and marriage names. The site of this church is on the Mons Sacer, or Sacred Hill, and it was frequented by Paul and other Apostles.

Paul would have had plenty of time to get to know the expatriate Britons for St. Jerome, amongst others, states that Paul was sent to Rome in the second year of Nero's reign, AD 56. It is likewise thought that Paul died in around AD 62. Six years in Rome gives a man like Paul plenty of scope and not a few opportunities. In fact, Paul mentions Rufus at the end of his letter to the Romans. Rufus Pudens was apparently martyred in AD 86, whilst his wife Claudia (the former Gladys, the Welsh form of the Latin Claudia) died in AD 97. Their daughter Pudentia was martyred in 107.

It seems that the Druids and the Christians had a lot in common, foremost amongst which was a very ancient religion. Tacitus (*Annals* XIV, ch.30) mentions the general massacre of Druids and Christians in which so many suffered martyrdom, thus confirming the presence of both in Rome. This also brings up the point that the Druids may not have been as barbarous as some propagandist Roman authors (Caesar amongst them) and modern historians lead us to believe. Moreover, there is something quite astonishing: in the hope of clinching peace in Britain, the Emperor Claudius proffered the hand of his daughter to King Arviragus the Briton. They were married in Rome in AD 45, but Arviragus was a Christian and what followed was the odd position where a Christian British King was a member of a Pagan family, whose head, the Roman Emperor himself, had sworn to crush both Christianity and Britain.

I suspect that Claudius' oath was a stirring piece of propaganda, mostly for the benefit of the Senate; much like the words of many politicians today – some things just never seem to change. However, what kind of a Christian was Arviragus? There seems to me to be a distinction here between varying Christianities. Arviragus' Christianity would have stemmed from an exceedingly ancient Druidic form of the belief. The Druids worshipped a hero, born of a virgin, who was crucified and rose three days later. That god was called Esus. At this point something else occurred to me - a simple point but an intriguing one. Lucan, the poet and scholar, born in AD 39, lived in the period contemporary with the rise of nascent Christianity. He was fully conversant with all of the political issues of the day and would have been aware of the disturbances caused by 'Chrestus'. Yet Lucan, who in his many writings covers the issues of his day and those before it, makes no mention of Jesus or Christianity. This may not seem so strange, as many contemporary writers and analysts also failed to mention them. What makes Lucan stand out is the fact that in the Pharsalia he makes mention of the Druids and their god Esus. Christianity during Nero's reign must have had a significant presence, or why else should Nero persecute Christians? Why then does Lucan not comment in a comparative fashion between the Druidic and the Christian when the similarity is so striking? Why does he not even mention it? Perhaps at the time they were so close as to be taken as one. It seems that, at least in the case of the Druids, Paul was preaching to the converted.

Further investigation of the British side of things would, in due course, reveal much, for the British Royal Family in Rome must have seen the similarities between the great temples and churches of Rome and their own back home, for they had standing stones like the pierre stones[27] of Rome, and sacred temples too. Later we shall see that the ancient Britons really knew how to use these constructions – that's what much of Druidism was about.

Histories of Mysteries

We have seen that what we might recognise today as Christianity owes more to the influence of the religious Mysteries that permeated Rome than to any original thought and that the idea of a man overcoming death to become a god was common. The reason why Roman critics rounded on Christianity lay in the Christians' belief that a man overcame death and walked again physically and that he was God's only son. To the initiates of the Mysteries this was utter nonsense, immortality was an affair of the soul, not of the physical body, and Gnostic texts, disallowed by the Church, have Jesus himself claiming that there are more Sons of God than he:

> 'The Kingdom of Heaven is within you and whosoever shall know himself shall find it. Strive therefore to know yourselves and ye shall be aware that ye are the sons of the Almighty Father; and ye shall know that ye are in the city of God and that ye are the city'[28]

To the politicians the idea of the physical Resurrection had a dangerous undertone with unsettling implications for the Empire. Jesus was a recent historical figure and his death was by Roman crucifixion; not only that, it was also said that he would return at a time of judgement. Christians were trouble, they 'had an axe to grind', indeed, the sometimes superhuman bravery of persecuted Christians, under the most harrowing of circumstances, only served to underscore the Roman viewpoint. Until the time of Constantine, the persecution button was turned on and off at irregular intervals; ironically to the benefit of Christianity, for in both Roman and Christian eyes a dead Christian was a better Christian. For Christianity, the politics of martyrdom was a breathtaking stroke of genius, one that elaborated on its prime example – the love displayed by a crucified man.

Whilst the Mysteries were certainly not without love, there was an emphasis on wisdom and the greatest minds of the Hellenistic and Roman worlds considered them as the very source of civilisation, of thought and ultimately of science.

> Unlike the traditional rituals of the official state religions, which were designed to aid social cohesion, the Mysteries were an individualistic form of spirituality which offered mystical visions and personal enlightenment. Initiates underwent a secret process of initiation which profoundly transformed their state of consciousness. The poet Pindar reveals that an initiate into the mysteries "knows the end of life and its God-given beginning".[29]

Like most people of their day the Romans believed in a supernatural life force which they called the *numen*. From this we get our modern word 'numinous', meaning 'suffused or pertaining to divinity'. Plato in *Phaedrus* describes how:

> 'We beheld beatific visions and were initiated into the Mystery which may be truly called blessed, celebrated by us in a state of innocence. We beheld calm, happy, simple, eternal visions, resplendent in pure light.'[30]

Numen may emanate from divinities, but it is not them, it is of them. It is also the ineffable spirit of place, the sense that one gets when in a particularly powerful place as at Delos or Delphi. Plutarch (AD 46–120) pointed out that these places, often far from human habitation where undisturbed nature ran wild, were essential to the vitality of the rest of the world.

> 'Numen exudes the atmosphere of "the other world". Ovid, the Roman poet, described an ancient grove of holm-oaks on the Aventine Hill of the Capital, "at sight whereof you might say, 'There is numen here.'"'[31]

The various rituals of the Mysteries paid homage to the Earth Mother and her mystical son. Offerings were made at the correct times of the year so that she would give numen to the fertility of the fields. Oddly enough, when treaties were made with foreign nations, Latin officials were 'first purified and energised by touching the numen-charged soil of the Roman citadel with their heads'.[32]

The numinous was more than a sense, a feeling, it was the all-important ingredient in perceiving a Mystery. Myth and ritual were designed to induce an elevated state of being, a heightened state of consciousness. It was ever so in religion, to such a degree that any serious inquirer cannot overestimate its importance. The earth that featured so considerably in the Mysteries as the Earth Mother symbolised the nurturing womb and compassion; whilst the hero represented conscious breakthrough, an entrance or gateway into the wider cosmos, perhaps even a stargate wherein the soul ascends from within the loving caress of the Great Mother. The stars themselves were gods: the great Father of the Gods was the sky god Zeus-pitar, Father Zeus, Amon, Petra, Pater and so on. It is interesting, further to these symbolic and very physical-spiritual portrayals, that mathematics and music too played their part, possibly the most important part of the whole. Hymns and chants were considered perhaps the most sacred part of any initiation. We know this because in one form or another, despite the officially sanctioned destruction, motifs still survive, as does the knowledge, the gnosis. It is all simply a matter of understanding it. The difference between the necessarily hidden meaning of the Mysteries and that of the new, official revelation of Jesus Christ was one of subtlety as opposed to literalism. The subtlety of the Eleusinian Mysteries, for example, was in their overall approach to the problems of life and the divine potential in life and in death for all. Christianity was centred upon the deeds of God as one man, who literally survived death.

The literalism of Christianity brought about more than its fair share of tragedy and absurdity. The prophet Mani (AD 216–276), founder of dualistic Manichaeism, which rivalled Christianity whilst sharing many similarities (adherents included, before his conversion, St. Augustine of Hippo) and who had been called by a vision to be an 'apostle', was killed, flayed and hacked to bits on the order of the Persian king, Bahram I, so that the idea of bodily resurrection might be disproven.

The origins of the Mystery Schools are not recorded but adherents include famous names:

> 'It is only when we come to the first five or six centuries BC, and
> to the palmy days of Greece and Alexandria, that we obtain a
> definite knowledge of the existence of the Mystery Schools, and
> of some of their more detailed teachings. This period is associated

with such names as Anaxagoras, Pythagoras, Socrates, Plato, Aristotle, and later on, before the dominance of ecclesiastical Christianity had suppressed the Gnosis ... we have such names as Philo Judaeus, Clement of Alexandria, Valentius, Origen, Proclus, Basilides, Iamblichus, and Plotinus, all speaking openly of the existence of the Mysteries and Mystery Schools.'[33]

We only know a certain amount about the Mysteries because, as many Classical authors admit, there was much that they were not permitted to discuss. Some Classical writers, however, give testimony that is contrary to this view. Diodorus Siculus (first century BC) writes:

'They also say that the honours given to the gods and the sacrifices and rites of the mysteries originally came down to other men from Crete, and in making this claim they offer what they believe is an extremely strong argument. The initiation rite that the Athenians celebrate in Eleusis, the most illustrious, one might say, of all rites, and again the Samothracians' rite and the rite begun by Orpheus in Thrace among the Cicones, all these rites are passed on from one initiate to another in secret. But in Cnossos, Crete, it has always been the custom to practise such initiation rites in broad daylight and to let everybody know about them.'

The Eleusinian Mysteries celebrated the advent of the divine child and the word 'Eleusis' was later adopted into the Christian Mysteries. Eleusis was originally a King of Attica and the name was quite probably a title belonging originally to Attis, another crucified god, the equivalent of Adonis, Dionysus, Osiris and Tammuz. Eleusis' mother was Daeira, who was identified with Aphrodite, goddess of love. The Eleusinian Mysteries celebrated the cereal-birth of the corn god, Dionysus, whose celebration took place in late September, the modern Christian Harvest Festival.[34] His father was said to be one Ogyges, King of Grecian Thebes. Ogyges occurs as a name throughout various myths, and means 'giant', but strictly in the sense of 'of the earth'. This fascinated me. Figures such as Ogyges and the Great Mother gave a consistent appearance of divinity related to the earth as well as heaven and, as a result, I became more and more convinced that the heart of the mystery was actually above, below and all around us.

We have seen the relationship of Rome's Pater Liber to rock and the connection to Mithraism. A further study of Mithraism brought more connections. Mithras was a solar hero and according to his legend was born out of a rock. We have here an instance of a motif being united, whereas in

Christianity it becomes separated: Jesus is the hero, whilst Peter is 'the rock', the cornerstone of the Church.

For the Romans, Mithras was a hero in the vein of Hercules, Apollo or Helios. He was the united principle of the sun, and also present in the constellation of Orion. Orion is, to this day, known as 'the hunter'. Mithras was the hunter of one particular animal - the bull. The most popular artistic representation of the god is the depiction of Mithras slaying a bull. This is interesting in many ways. As noted in chapter one, in the ancient Near East the king was often referred to as the bull of his father, as was the hero. The Phoenician-Canaanite hero is called Baal; 'bull' comes from the same root, as does 'bell'. Bells played a significant part in the rituals of the Near East, as they still do today.

Mithras plunges a sword into the very heart of the bull, and from the wound flows a stream of wheat, said to represent the Milky Way. A dog, possibly Canis Major, licks up the blood, whilst standing behind the bull are Gemini, the Twins. The bull, of course, represents Taurus.

In Mithraism, the bull is a wild, fearsome creature eventually slain by Mithras for the good of fertility on earth. The symbolism is obvious and diminishes differences between Mithraism and Christianity, where it is the hero himself who is slain. The bull in Mithraism represents the wild, uncultured self and Mithras the higher ascended soul. Mithras is accompanied by a horned sun and moon. In the legend all living creatures were the progeny of a sacred bull whose sacrificial blood was fructified by the Moon. But what of being born from a rock? Is Mithraism's central mystery the revelation that the life-force of man, the numen, is somehow relevant to both earth and sky?

Jesus shares the same birthday as Mithras - 25th December – and it is intriguing that deep beneath the Vatican to this day there are the remains of a temple to Mithras.

The oracular caves at Cumae, near Naples, Italy, shared the same Mithraic 'earthforce' qualities. The oracle was dedicated to Apollo and was famous for the quality of its pronouncements. The caves themselves have been naturally carved into the side of a mountain, and, as many observers have reported, look very much like the interior chambers of a pyramid. The oracle was one greatly favoured by the Caesars.[35]

We have already considered how Roman Christianity absorbed and extinguished Mithraism and the like. Gnosticism, though, was more honest about its connections, In a Gnostic gospel there occurs the following:

> 'And it came to pass, when the Lord Jesus was born at Bethlehem,
> a city of Judea, in the time of Herod the King; the wise men came
> from the east to Jerusalem; according to the prophecy of
> Zoradascht [Zoroaster], and brought with them offerings: namely
> gold, frankincense, and myrrh, and worshipped him, and offered
> to him their gifts.'[36]

Notice how this passage links the Nativity directly to the founder of another religion, Zoroastrianism. There is a hero in Zoroastrianism, a prophesied liberator named Saoshyans who would destroy the Devil once and for all. Saoshyans is another form of the name Joshua, the Greek version of the Latin Jesus (Hebrew Jeshua).[37] His birthday is the birthday of the Saviour, Saoshyans meaning literally 'the saviour'. No wonder texts such as the above were rejected by the Church Fathers. Gnosticism and Roman Catholicism were diametrically opposite versions of Christianity, with different modes of teaching. Roman Catholicism, after Nicaea, had a position to defend, which was very much a political position. As the official religion of the Empire it now had both the motivation and the ability to fend off other faiths, including Zoroastrianism which, having influenced Christian origins, was, after AD 325, a heresy, particularly as it continued to influence rival Gnosticism.

Hellenism, Heresy and Mania

The word 'gnostic' comes from the Greek gnostikos from where we derive our word 'knowledge'. Gnosticism was actually a fairly wide collection of movements. The Gnostic's common opponent was the Church of Rome, which viewed them as dangerous heretics. This is quite a distinction, for the very word 'heresy' means 'to make a choice', from the Greek hairesis , the act of 'taking a choice'. This implies that being a member of the Roman Church involved being given no choice. To make a choice, one has to know a certain amount, and 'knowing' was something that, in later years, the Roman Church would take bloody steps to repress.

The Church had developed a centralised doctrine, a dogma, that made sure that the sleeper never awoke, that the faithful remained dependent upon the priesthood and the institution behind it, which continued to grow in power. On the other hand, the beauty of the Gnostic way was the lack of a centralised autocracy. There were, of course, types of priest in Gnosticism, but their job was to awaken the soul and to send it on its way. In Gnosticism one was responsible for one's own mistakes and the lessons to be learned. In effect, Gnosticism was an alternative Christianity. Unfortunately, until very recently the greater part of our knowledge of Gnosticism came only from those who opposed it so vehemently.

Among the most vituperative critics was the Bishop of Lyons, Irenaeus (c.AD 130–c.200). Irenaeus utterly condemned Gnosticism. It was he who insisted upon a single, 'Catholic' (meaning universal) Church. It was he who compiled the New Testament canon that is familiar to us today. With Irenaeus, orthodoxy assumed a coherent form.

Gnosticism is less a development of Christianity than the Church is an offshoot of it. It has been criticised for being merely an amalgam of Christianity with Greek philosophy and other miscellaneous theologies, but this is to ignore its background, which features strong Jewish and Egyptian influences.

Simone Weil, who died at the tragically young age of thirty-four, in1943, was a very brilliant philosopher. She was French and Jewish, but was deeply fascinated by all things Catholic. Her work is very valuable in terms of the insights that it offers into Christian origins and thought. In terms of this book, her most important work is *Intimations of Christianity among the Ancient Greeks*, published posthumously in 1951. In it she writes of the philosophy of Pythagoras and its pre-eminence in the Classical world, and points out that this philosophy is, in many ways, the founding mystery of Greek civilisation:

> 'It impregnates almost all the poetry, almost all the philosophy - especially Plato, whom Aristotle regarded as a pure Pythagorean. The music, the architecture, the sculpture, all the sciences of ancient Greece proceeded from it: so did arithmetic, geometry, astronomy, mechanics and biology – that science which is fundamentally the same as ours today. Plato's political thought (in its authentic form, which means as it is formulated in the dialogue *The Statesman*) also derives from the Pythagorean doctrine.'[38]

Furthermore, she observed that it is a philosophy of great antiquity. In *Philebus* Plato accords with this view, writing as he does of a derivation from the Ancients:

> '... the ancients, who were better than we are, and lived nearer the gods, have transmitted this tradition to us. Here it is: that the realities called eternal derive from the one and the many, the determinate and the indeterminate. We should therefore, since this is the eternal order of things, seek to implant a unity in every kind of domain. We shall find it, for it is there.'[39]

Plato and Pythagoras were both held in the very highest esteem in the early Church, whereas Aristotle, the philosopher who eventually was to hold the greater sway, was profoundly distrusted by it as a materialist. Of course, as the Church lapsed further into secularism, Aristotle became ever more popular. It was with St. Thomas Aquinas that the Aristotelean view gained the primacy. Unlike Plato, Aristotle held that the experience of the senses is the only source of knowledge, and thus it is the experience of the individual that gives rise to ideas, which in themselves boil down to a series of causes, which he declared were 'final', 'formal' and 'material'. It is not surprising that Aristotle's view of the physical world should have formed the basis of all subsequent study of the subject: physics. Plato, by contrast, held the notion of forms, which are located beyond the everyday world, forms that are timeless, motionless and absolute. Plato's is a philosophy that rejects scientific rationalism – the establishment of facts through experiment – in favour of dialogue or arguments, because mind, not matter, is fundamental, materialism being an imperfect copy of abstract and eternal ideas. Platonic love seeks to inspire a person's development through their better qualities.

Aristotle remains only a semi-official philosopher in the Catholic Church; the philosophy, because of the influence of Thomas Aquinas, is known as Thomism. It is taken primarily from Aristotle's *Nicomachean Ethics*, a treatise on moral philosophy.

Simone Weil perceived within Pythagoreanism a theology of proportion, and also saw that this theology had significant links with certain sayings of Jesus, particularly within the Gospel of John. These texts, as Gordon Strachan observes, 'all refer to Jesus' sayings about his relationship to God and to his disciples'.[40] For instance, the following from the Gospel of John:

> 'Holy Father, keep through thine own name those whom thou
> hast given me, that they may be one, as we are... That they may
> all be one; as thou, Father, art in me, and I in thee, that they also
> may be one in us.... And the Glory which thou gavest me I have
> given thee; that they may be one, even as we are one: I in them
> and thou in me, that they may be made perfect in one.'
>
> John 17:11,21–33[41]

This intimation of the Trinity, and of proportion, is what lay at the heart of Pythagorean and Platonic thought, and subsequently Christianity too! It is the linking together of the knowledge of all things. By contrast, Aristotle's philosophy, which in places is vehemently opposed to all things Platonic, underlies all the modern-day ethics of empiricism - seeing is believing; if it cannot be experienced it cannot be. This is, admittedly, a simplified view of it, but the overall significant differences between the two became horrifyingly apparent in the years after the Council of Nicaea and will be demonstrated further on when we shall observe the scientific aspect of my hypothesis in part two.

Aristotle's philosophy may be summarised as follows: 'that the purpose of the moral life is to turn "who we are" into "who we ought to be", which provides an objective standard of progress, if not of perfection. The method of progress is by the practice of virtue.'[42] Plato, on the other hand, held that the divine, eternal power of good was already in us, and that if we wanted to improve upon it then we should appeal to the higher qualities within ourselves. Quite plainly, Plato's view is what became known as Gnosticism. It was a Christian philosopher, Justin Martyr, who acknowledged that Plato, whom he labels Pagan, had taught the doctrine that the 'Son of God' was placed 'crosswise in the universe' some centuries prior to Christianity. It is interesting that Justin should entitle that particular chapter 'Plato's Doctrine of the Cross'.[43]

What is also interesting is the use by St. Paul of the Platonic theory of the Logos; Paul's doctrine of the Incarnation is actually Platonic in nature. This is the hidden Paul, the version of Paul that was hidden in the second century by heresiologists keen to substantiate the view of the actual bodily Resurrection, as against the symbolic interpretation of those soon to be deemed 'heretics'.

Sects and Violence

The various sects that may be described as 'Gnostic', and whose members were viewed as heretics by the Catholic Church, viewed Paul as `the Great Apostle'.[44] It is extraordinary to think that Paul, the man so often referred to as a bastion against heresy, should himself turn out to be heretical! If he were quite the scourge of heresy and bastion of orthodox opinion that the Church has made him out to be, then one might have thought that the Gnostics would have had something to say about it. All that they confirm is the mystery of the interpretation of Paul's letters.

The Gnostic Valentinus suggested that Paul 'initiated the chosen few into the deeper mysteries of Christianity which revealed a secret doctrine of God'.[45] The Gnostic view concurs very much with that of Paul in that both seem to be worshippers of a Jesus very much hidden within the Gospels, whose story does not so much contradict the Gospel story, as seems quite separate from it. It is interesting that the letters of Paul and the Gnostic writings fail to mention any of the supposedly historical happenings of Jesus' story: the journey to Bethlehem, the date and place of Jesus' birth, his baptism, the importance of Peter as 'the rock' upon which the Church would be built and so on. Instead, what we encounter is a rather extraordinary, mystical approach to belief. The followers of Marcian (d. AD 160) had a gospel which they claimed had been revealed to, and written by, Paul. Of deep interest to me was a particular scripture called the *Ascent of Paul*, which recalls certain 'ineffable words' which it is not permissable for a man to speak, 'which Paul heard during his famous ascent to the third Heaven, alluded to by the Apostle in his Letter to the Corinthians'. These texts, discovered in 1945-6, at the village of Nag Hamadi in Upper Egypt, got me thinking. Ineffable words and Egypt again. Why?

Gnosticism certainly pre-dated Christianity and essentially, its view is a purely spiritual one, regarding Christ too as pure spirit. The worldview of the Valentinians (followers of Valentinus), *c.* second century) goes like this:

> 'At the beginning there was already an eternity of being, a Pleroma, a Fullness, a Harmony. At the 'centre' was always the Father, perfect and immeasurably profound – a being of whom nothing could be said which would share in the character of the eternity of which he was. Now it is in the nature of the Father to project a series of archetypes. They are Intelligence (Nous), Truth, the Word (Logos), Life, Humanity and Church (an invisible eternal body). These archetypes hold a potential energy and they in turn project a series of archetypes. With each projection the archetype finds itself to be at a 'distance' from the Father – but there is no space and time. All this is happening in a dimension so removed from the one we know that there is no real way of describing it. The whole thing is an intuition – the activity of the nous within the Gnostic's own experience – philosophical poetry. Now it is of the nature of wisdom, when active, to question and strive to understand.
> One of the projections, Sophia (Wisdom), begins to be unbalanced within the Pleroma because 'she' wishes to know the Father – a privilege granted only to Nous, who is closer to the Father... The disturbance within Sophia leads to her conceiving 'substance without form'. It has come from guilty yearning and so is flawed. It is of a lesser substance. The product of her passion is discarded from the Pleroma into the All, a void. The Father sees a necessity to project two more archetypes: Christ and the Holy Spirit, who teach the contents of the Pleroma their true relation to the Father. The Pleroma sings the praises of the Father and the 'Perfect Fruit' of their joy comes into being: the saviour Jesus. All is not well, however. 'Substance without form', exiled from the Pleroma, brings Matter to birth out of her anguish and yearning for Christ as well as a psychic or 'soul' element. 'Christ' has pity for her and descends to put form on her formlessness which in turn brings about *pneuma*: spirit.'[46]

It is out of these elements – soul, matter and spirit – that the world is created. As Tobias Churton comments, 'So solid things owe their source to "broken" ideas.'[47] Sophia forms a 'Demi-urge' – a creator – to make something out of the chaos that has come about. He organises Heaven, earth and the creatures on it.

Overall, it is a profoundly beautiful and somewhat brilliant concept, and even his bitterest opponents acknowledged Valentinus' genius. The teachings of Valentinus are preserved in a Coptic manuscript dating from the mid-second century. In the same collection is the gospel of Thomas, also in Coptic, which purports to be a collection of sayings of the risen Christ, the living Lord, thus giving an overtly spiritual emphasis, as opposed to the materialist outlook of Rome, which insisted on believing in an actual physical Resurrection.

The Gnostic gospel of Philip also denies the Resurrection in a physical sense, stating only that it takes place spiritually – possibly at baptism.

> 'Those who say they will die first and then rise are in error. If they do not first receive the resurrection while they live, when they die they will receive nothing.'[48]

It was in Coptic Alexandria that the importance of Jesus' divine nature was stressed, in the sense that it was an emanation of the Logos, the Word. I was much struck by this, for yet again what seemed to be implied was that Jesus was identified as some kind of resonance. For the Gnostics, Jesus represented some kind of meniscus between the material and the divine. To them the crucifixion was anathema and utterly grotesque. The cross was merely a symbol of matter; if Jesus was killed upon it, it was only materially so. Fundamentally, the Gnostic way was about people as individuals attaining a higher state – about becoming Jesus.

Logia 3 of the gospel of St. Thomas tells us that:

> 'Jesus said, "The Kingdom is in your centre and is about you. When you know yourselves then you will be known and you will be aware that you are the Sons of the Living Father."'[49]

There is some support for this in the New Testament, where, in John 10:33–34, accusing Jews tell Jesus that they are about to stone him because:

> '..thou, being a man, makest thyself God.
> Jesus answered them, "Is it not written in your law, I said, Ye are gods?"'

In the *Pistis Sophia*, a Coptic Gnostic document (fourth–fifth century), Jesus is everywhere pre-eminent. He is here revealed as Saviour and as the first Mystery, who knows all and unveils all. As such he is pre-existent from before the beginning of eternity. This sounds profoundly like present cosmological thinking about the creation of the universe and matter, *ex nihilo*. Intriguingly, there had been a previous civilisation, in the same land, where there was in essence only one mystery, that of the Creation itself, and that, of course, was the civilisation of ancient Egypt. The *Pistis Sophia* was written in Sahidic, a Coptic dialogue of Upper Egypt, and preserves many features of great antiquity. It is as though we are witnessing the transition of ancient Egyptian religion and cosmology into a new, revitalised belief: Christianity.

In the movie *The Matrix* (1999), Laurence Fishburne appears much as a Gnostic priest might perhaps have appeared and tells the character played by Keanu Reeves a few home truths. The Matrix is a world that people inhabit, it is a giant super–computer that gives people the illusion of living in reality. Fishburne, who has managed to escape the clutches of this world, tells Reeves that it is 'the world that has been pulled over your eyes, to blind you from the truth: you are a slave'. This is exceedingly Gnostic.

Gnostics held that the creator of the material world, the Demi-urge, was an evil god, the lowest emanation of God Most High. They even identified this evil creator with the God of the Old Testament.[50] Of course, this is the very thing that most annoyed the Catholic Church.

When I first came across these facts it was more than a little shocking. I've never really been a great attender of church services, but I was still a believer, even if it was really a leftover from my schooldays. My mind had become used to a particular system and now that apparent reality was being peeled back from my eyes. Then I had confirmation directly from the horse's mouth. In 1958, Professor Morton Smith of Columbia University discovered in the monastery library of Mir Saba, in the Judaean desert, a rather compromising document.[51] It is a letter that had been copied on to the back pages of a seventeenth century biography. The letter is from Clement of Alexandria (*c*.AD 150–211), and tells of a secret teaching of Jesus. However, it is not the teaching of Jesus that concerns us, it is Clement's treatment that is revealing. Clement refers to a secret gospel of Mark that was being interpreted by a Gnostic sect, the Carpocratians, according to their own practices. Clement, in writing to a certain Theodore, observes:

'Not all true things are to be said to all men.'[52]

Clement seems to be annoyed to the point of fury, for in his letter he more or less accuses the Carpocratians of huge irresponsibility. However, there is something else that struck me as odd. Clement states that, after St. Peter's martyrdom, Mark went to Alexandria and there left his Gospel to the Church in Alexandria. According to most historians, Peter's death occurred in approximately AD 64, in the reign of Nero, therefore what exactly was this 'Church' in Alexandria? Most historians are doubtful as to whether the Egyptian Church had established itself by then. Clement comments on how Mark compiled two editions, one of which was more 'spiritual' than the other and was for the use of those 'who were being perfected'. What we are talking about here is initiation and, I would suspect, it was initiation into the old, timeless truths.

There are surprises throughout Gnosticism. The Mandaeans of southern Iraq tell how the prophet John was hidden in a mountain by Enoch for 22 years. This suggests that John was anything but a man. They state that after this experience John became a healer and a 'fisher of men'. However, what fascinates me even more about the Mandaeans is that they claim to have existed from a long time before the Baptist. They also insist that they came originally from Egypt. Even their rites and rituals have an ancient Egyptian feel to them, and it is difficult to deny that there is something special about them. They claim to have originated in a mountain region called the Tura d'Madai, a place that has yet to be identified, but there is a clue in the name and in the names of their gods. The Mandaean Demi-urge is called Ptah-il. There is an Egyptian creator god of the same name, and it even made we wonder whether the Tura d'Madai mountains were not mountains but pyramids, for the Egyptian pyramids were mostly cased in white tura limestone.

One of the great heroines of Gnostic tradition is the Greek holy virgin, Kore, whose mother was the earth goddess, Demeter. Kore was a great power within the Coptic religion, and her festival, the Koreian, was celebrated on the same day as the Feast of Epiphany, 6th January. This was the day on which Kore gave birth – virgin birth – to the Aeon. 'Kore' means 'girl', and brings us back to Mary again, for there are huge similarities in what are essentially the same stories, except that the Gnostic version gives a lot more away.

The Kore/Demeter connection takes us back to the rites at Eleusis, where Kore and Demeter were honoured. In these rites Kore is kidnapped by Hades, with Zeus' approval, and as a result Demeter forsakes the gods. She wanders as a beggar-woman looking for her daughter, forsaking also the earth, which dries up and becomes barren. The beggar–woman image is an interesting one, in that it is very reminiscent of the portrayal of Mary Magdalene in both the canonical and non–canonical texts. In some of these Mary wanders, dressed in rags, after the death of Jesus. So the story of Kore is a kind of female parallel to the story of Jesus, except that Kore goes on to give birth to the divine child, the Aeon. In Egypt Kore was equated with Isis, and Isis is stated to have had two sons, Horus and Aeon (sometimes Aion), which sounds remarkably like John. These two closely parallel Jesus in many respects.

However, there is more: Kore's name survives within the word 'corn'. Now it has always struck me that, wherever you go, the hero-gods are associated with cereal crops. This has generally been regarded as being because of the hero's fertile aspect. In the nineteenth century this may have been a satisfactory explanation, but not in the twenty-first. There is something else going on here, something both more explicit and more subtle: we are being told something, of that I am convinced.

A later variation of Kore's name was Ceres – hence 'cereal', 'corn', 'kernel' and possibly 'carnal'– 'Carnal' in the sense of bringing forth into flesh. Kore was a holy virgin who brought forth a son. Ancient cults spoke of an 'ear of corn near a fall of water'. The same symbolism also occurs within Freemasonry, but the chief source was the rites at Eleusis. At Eleusis the divine child was called Iasion, and his flesh was eaten in Eucharistic rites. This was not as horrible as it sounds, for the holy child in this case is the corn.

Copts and Robbers

We have noted the Coptic relationship to Gnosticism. The history of the Coptic Church is interesting. The argument over whether the Copts are linked to the Egyptian town of Koptos, from where the god Min hails (see earlier), is one that has raged for well over a century. Writing in the late 1880s, Edward Lane stated in *The Manners and Customs of the Modern Egyptians*[53] that the Copts had taken their name from the then village, to which many had fled during the Roman persecutions. On the other hand, Baines and Malek are unequivocal over the issue and state quite plainly that the town of Gebtu – in Greek, Koptos – has no connection with the word 'Coptic'.[54]

Eusebius, Constantine's official historian of the Church, states that the Church in Egypt was founded by St. Mark the Evangelist, and thus ranked, from its base at Alexandria, on an equal footing with Antioch and Rome. Because of its suffering under the persecutions of Diocletian, the Coptic Church has ever since reckoned its era from the year AD 248, the year of Diocletian's accession. The most famous export of the Egyptian Church is monasticism - founded in Egypt in the forth century by St. Anthony.

The Egyptian Coptic Church, like the Persian Church, split from Rome after the Council of Chalcedon in AD 451. The schism was caused by an argument over the nature of Jesus: the Persian Church had decided to adopt the view of Nestorius, who in AD 428 was appointed to the powerful position of Patriarch of Constantinople. Once in this post Nestorius nailed his colours to the mast, stating that two persons were incarnate within Jesus, one divine, the other human. This infers that all of humanity is partially divine and that like Jesus we can attain to divinity. For the Roman Church and for the Empire this was too much. Jesus alone was divine, only the Emperor could accede to his spiritual authority (later on it would be the Popes who rose to such spiritual heights) and the rest of us were mere sinners. Three years after his appointment Nestorius was condemned and subsequently excommunicated; the correspondence condemning him labelled him a 'new Jew'. Nestorianism, however, flourished.

Although the Egyptian Coptic Church did not necessarily agree with Nestorius, it could not accept the ruling against him and parted company with Roman orthodoxy. This made it easier for the Copts to preserve their ancient heritage.

It would not be an exaggeration to say that the Coptic Church was the last resting–place of ancient Egyptian tradition, culture and language. It was in the very ancient Coptic/Egyptian language that the last vestiges of the various heretical Gnostic beliefs were preserved. When these documents eventually came to light, modern understanding of Gnosticism was transformed; up until then the only knowledge we had was written by the opposition at the time of the first great schisms and persecutions within the Church.

In a conversation in 1998 with the Egyptian lawyer and writer Ahmed Osman, I discussed the Coptic Church and asked Ahmed for his views and impressions as a native Egyptian. Ahmed is a gentle man, and when he speaks of Egypt and its history, ancient and modern, it is in tones of quiet reverence, tinged with a lawyer's sharp sense of curiosity and investigation. Ahmed has written many books on many aspects of biblical and Egyptian history. I do not always necessarily agree with his views but I respect very much his insight. What he said intrigued me greatly. He said that the Nag Hamadi scrolls are composed mainly in Coptic but that, in essence, they are pre-Christian. Furthermore, they concur with Paul's letters and traces of them are to be found in the earlier Hermetic texts.

Ahmed's view is an important one, although he concludes that the figure of Jesus found in these texts is one and the same as the Biblical figure of Joshua (the Greek form of the Hebrew Jeshua or Yehoshua), Moses' heir and successor. This is a view that I can only half-believe, for by the time I visited Ahmed I had evidence enough to suggest that the answer was older even than Moses. My feelings were a little different, We have all heard the story of how Joshua and his men surrounded Jericho and destroyed its walls with a blast of sound from trumpets; I mentioned it in the previous chapter. Unfortunately, there is no archaeological evidence to back up this wonderful tale, but after my conversation with Ahmed, I began to wonder if the tale was perhaps slightly misconstrued. Is the myth trying to tell us that it is the name of Joshua, so similar to Jesus, that is important? I even wondered whether the trumpet blast could have issued forth a sound related to the name?

Continuing my investigations, I looked into the name 'Copt'. Although I am by no means one hundred per cent certain of this, the Greek word for 'bishop', *episkopos,* may contain an element of Coptic within it – *kopos,* meaning 'watcher' or 'seer', one who knows.

The Copts came to be seen by orthodoxy as Gnostic and thus heretical. The

Gnostics considered the historical story of Jesus as full of encoded mystical teachings and held that these were the real story of Jesus. Gnosticism claimed that it was the authentic Christianity, but it was viewed with more than suspicion by the Roman Church. A concern for the Church was the overtly spiritual vision that the Gnostics had of Jesus, a vision that seemed to betray something very ancient and archaic. It was Ahmed again who set me on the right path by pointing out that St. Paul in his Letter to the Galatians admits that he himself was initiated into the Egyptian Mysteries by the Gnostics at Sinai.

Mystery Schools exist to this day in the Arab world; many of them are Sufi schools. The Sufi traditions are very ancient and include prescribed song and dance. In a Gnostic text (Apocryphal Acts of John, second–third century), Jesus is to be found singing a hymn and dancing to its tune, with the 12 disciples all around him in a circle, all of this hours before he is taken out and crucified.

The dance has all the elements of some kind of initiation: 'Seeing what I do, keep silence about my mysteries.' It is also symbolic of the orbit of the planets around the sun or of sub-atomic particles around a nucleus. It is interesting that this Apocryphal book was used by Manichaean heretics (remember Mani, who was so cruelly killed by the Persian king in order to disprove the reality of the physical resurrection), as a replacement for the Acts of the Apostles. The hymn reads thus:

> 'Glory to thee, O Father.
> (And we, going about Him in a ring, answered Him):
> Amen!
> Glory to thee, Word [the Logos]. Amen!
> Glory to thee, Grace. Amen!
> Glory to thee, Spirit! Glory to thee Holy One! Glory to the Glory!
> Amen!
> We Praise thee, O Father; We give thanks to thee, O Light;
> In whom Darkness dwells not! Amen!
> For what we give thanks to the Word:
> I would be saved and I would save. Amen!
> I would be loosed and I would loose. Amen!
> I would be wounded and I would wound. Amen!
> ...Grace danceth. I would pipe. Dance ye all. Amen!
> I would play a dirge. Lament ye all. Amen!
> The Ogdoad singeth praise with us. Amen!
> The Twelfth number above leadeth the dance. Amen!
> The whole on high hath part in our dancing. Amen!
> Who danceth not, knows not what is being done. Amen!
> I would flee, and I would stay. Amen!

> ...I would be at-oned and I would at-one. Amen!
> I have no dwelling and I have dwellings. Amen!
> I have no place and I have places. Amen!
> I have no temple and I have temples. Amen!
> I am a lamp to thee who beholdest. Amen!
> I am a mirror to thee who understandeth Me. Amen!
> I am a door to thee who knockest at Me. Amen!
> I am a way to thee a wayfarer. Amen!
>
> Now answer unto My dancing! Beholdest thyself in Me who speak; and seeing what I do, keep silence about my mysteries.'[55]

The hymn continues, and ends in this way:

> 'Say thou to me again: Glory to thee, Father, Glory to thee, Word! Glory to thee, Holy Spirit. But as for Me, if thou wouldst know what I was: in a word I am the Word who did dance all things, and was not shamed [or deceived] at all. It was I who leaped. But do thou understand all, and understanding say: Glory to thee, Father! Amen.'[56]

Jesus sings 'I have no place and I have places' and 'I am the word who did dance all things'; this extraordinary work seems to be admitting that the real Jesus is something intangible, something that has no form and yet can give form!

Intermezzo

From Paul's vision and his interpretation of Christianity in chapter two, we have moved into a far broader landscape. Beginning in Rome itself we have seen that, yet again, the cults of the dying and rising god would have been both influential to, and compatible with, the emerging Christianity. Through Gnostic texts we also saw how geographically distant belief systems from Druidism in the west to Zoroastrianism in the east shared much with Christianity.

The later secularisation of the Church and the politics that came into play changed the tenets and policies of the Church for purposes of power and centralisation. We have seen the sidelining of geniuses such as Pythagoras and Plato and the destruction of 'unholy' books, scrolls, artifacts and even buildings. Where are the official explanations of the use of holy words or explanations for the Christian use of masonry sacred to the Pagans? That the Church historian Eusebius was in the pay of that arch-politician, the Emporer Constantine, speaks volumes. Since that time, the fabric of history has long been torn in pursuit of anything other than the truth.

How ironic that heresy should mean 'choice'. From this period onwards, the only Gnostics to be tolerated were those close enough to the Church to be of use or at least not to be too much of a threat. These would be called Christian mystics and an indication of their potency is that most would be either canonised or murdered.

Let us face it, God, the Creative Force - call it what you will - is a mystery, and so Mysticism seems a valid tool with which to investigate that mystery and to gain knowledge of it. Not knowledge merely as intellectual appreciation but knowledge based upon actual experience. This, as we have seen, was the goal of Gnosticism.

Eventually, after rampant editing or outright destruction, only a few Gnostic texts re-emerged to demonstrate an alternative Christianity. And what a different Christianity it was: To me, it seemed that the ways of Gnosticism were the ways of Jesus and later I was to prove it. In the meantime I was to follow the Gnostic trail to its resurgence, of a sorts, in Western Europe in the Medieval Period

In 1095, as the Crusaders set out to take the Holy Land for Christendom, Europe's religious leaders would not have realised the threat that this would pose to the very core of the Roman Catholic Church, for when the cream of Medieval Europe sojourned in the Bible Lands, they discovered that all that they had been taught was not true. Consequently, the Mystery Schools would again make their presence felt, most notably behind the cover of militarism. Prior to this major movement, other esoteric influences had re- emerged, the intriguingly named Alchemy being one of them.

4

The Temple and the Vision

'Set not much faith in this, for it is too young.'

A Templar comment on being shown a crucifix

'The Templars may have been protecting or propagating a banned element in true Catholicism, a something else unknown or forgotten, even in Rome.'

Francis Hitching[1]

The Symbolic Crucible

WHEN I first came across the word .'alchemy', my mind conjured up images of bearded old men, bent double over crucibles containing intriguing mixtures of this mineral and that powder, of steam and strange noises and darkened rooms and parchments adorned with enigmatic symbols. For me, as for many others, alchemy was all about how to transmute base metal into gold. This view is, however, misguided. It is a misconception made on a regular basis by modern writers and journalists, and one used by scientists to illustrate just how foolish medieval man truly was. Alchemy and alchemists make it abundantly clear that the real transmutation, the vital transmutation, is that of man into God.

'There is no God, but God in Man.'

Alchemists were skilled in many things and had a very broad knowledge of many fields. Religion, philosophy, medicine, logic, magic and mathematics were well within this remit. Knowledge was perceived as a unity and the alchemist was both a seeker and applier of it. This suggests gnosis. It is probably this that explains the great misunderstanding that surrounds alchemy. That it was hidden, that its arcane secrets were covered in layers of enigma, riddle and mystery, was because of the sad necessity of having to be secretive due to the attitudes of the Church. One must admit that there were Christian alchemists, too, but they mainly preceded the era of the Inquisition. Gerbert d'Aurillac was one of them.

In AD 999 Gerbert succeeded to the throne of St. Peter as Pope Sylvester II. He was described by contemporary sources as one of the most learned and wittiest men in Europe. Gerbert seems to have obtained just the right qualifications for his career: aside from being sent to study mathematics at Vich in Catalonia, Spain, he was also to find himself studying other subjects at the great Arab universities of Cordoba and Toledo. There are various legends about Gerbert's stay in Moorish Spain. According to one of them – which suits Gerbert's character as a political heavyweight – he seduced the daughter of his alchemist master in order to learn a great secret, the Secret of Secrets, and was expelled from the country. In yet another version of the story he is said to have encountered a very beautiful maiden, whose name was Meridiana, the Lady of the South, who offered him her gold-clothed body, her wealth and her magical wisdom if he would put his faith in her. After agreeing to the bargain Gerbert soon found himself enthroned, first as Archbishop of Reims, then Archbishop of Ravenna and ultimately as Pope.

As Pope he was set upon achieving a greater spiritual purity than the Church had been able to attain for many a year. He condemned the practice of simony – the purchase or sale of spiritual things – and upheld the practice of clerical celibacy, whilst seeking, with the Holy Roman Emperor, Otto III, a greater universality of both Empire and Church. It was Gerbert who introduced Arabic numbers to the West and who invented the clock, the astrolabe and the hydraulic organ.

The story says that Gerbert's trust in the Lady, Meridiana, gave him the gift of genius and a remarkable career. Meridiana would seem to be yet another vision, but this time with an alchemical format. The meridian is the point of a star's highest altitude (as seen from earth). It is also the great circle of the earth or of a celestial sphere. In other words, it is the measure of that sphere. Gerbert was a noted mathematician. What seems to be intimated here is a system of sacred measure especially relating to celestial or planetary measurement. The divine name 'Mary' is present here as 'Meri'. 'Dia' specifically means 'through', 'across' and 'apart'; as a syllable it gives the sense of these things and is often found in English words – 'diameter', 'diapason', 'diadem', etc. However, Diana was also a Roman goddess associated with the moon. Like Mary, she was a queen of heaven, and at Ephesus, in the Christian era, Diana, under her Greek name Artemis, had her temple dedicated to Mary. There is a strong relationship between the two. 'Diana' may also mean 'Goddess Anna', the mythical mother of Mary in the New Testament. The Lady Meridiana seems to be a composite of both. Gerbert was a mathematician, alchemist and Pope. What was his secret – the measurement of the gods?

Much of what was to become European alchemy came directly out of Moorish Spain in the period immediately preceding the Middle Ages as a consequence of the broad areas of study to be found at the great Arab universities of Toledo and Cordoba.[2] Moorish Spain was, by this time, very much separate from the rest of the Islamic world. In AD 750 the Umayyad dynasty had been deposed as supreme rulers of the Middle East by the Abbasid Caliphs. However, all was not lost by the Umayadds. In AD 711 the Umayyads had invaded Spain and when the Eastern dynasty was overthrown it was one of the last their princes who, escaping to Spain, kept the remnant of the dynasty in power for another 300 years. Moorish, alchemy though, had older origins and here we must look again toward Alexandria.

By the time of the irresistible rise of Islam in the AD 600s Alexandria as a seat of learning was at the nadir of a great decline. The famous library, having recovered from damage in a major fire in BC 48, was finally destroyed after the incitement of a mob by the Christian Patriarch in AD 391 Alexandria went into decline as a centre of learning. The new breed of hardline political Christian seeking out heresy and the heretic made Alexandria a very uncomfortable place for many philosophers and teachers. By the end of the fourth century scholars were departing from Alexandria in droves, often as a result of violence. Perhaps the worst example of this violence occurred in AD 415, when a Christian mob, again incited by the Patriarch, Cyril, pursued and captured the most gifted female of her generation, Hypatia. What ensued was to be the defining point in the annihilation of Classical Paganism. Cyril believed that the study of anything other than the Christian teachings was a sinful distraction; Hypatia was his supreme example. She was stripped naked, flayed alive – with oyster shells being used to strip her flesh from her body - dismembered and burned. There were no objections by any Christian leaders to this barbaric act. Cyril and his monks then set out to halt all official investigation of the murder. They succeeded.[3]

Alexandrian knowledge moved on, notably to Edessa, in modern Syria, and then to Harran, in modern-day Turkey. In Harran, an academy was established that lasted until the tenth century. What resurfaced at Harran was an admixture of alchemical symbolism and Hermetism. These subjects very soon began to permeate the whole of what was, by then, the Islamic world, hence Gerbert's knowledge gained from the Moors.

However, for the ultimate answer to the origins of alchemy, we must turn once again to an observation of the word. 'Alchemy' means 'matter of Egypt', and is derived directly from the Arabic '*Al-Khem*', the old Arab name for Egypt. Even the Greeks acknowledged their debt to Egypt by calling the art of transmuting metals into gold '*khemia*'. An ancient name of Egypt was Kemet or Khemet, 'the Black Land.' 'But why,' I thought, 'would the Greeks have given it this name?'

Looking further at the Greek word for metal, μεταλλον, I could see why. In ordinary English it transliterates as '*metallon*'. From it derive many European words for metal. The first syllable, *meta*, is a prefix that denotes 'a nature of a higher order or more fundamental kind'. 'Very alchemical,' I mused. The last syllable, *on*, is sometimes associated with the sun or, at least, is a reference to Heliopolis in Egypt, called in ancient days On or On-Heliopolis. The double 'l' or lambda separating these two syllables has an ancient meaning all of its own. It means, to 'study, learn, teaching, to teach', etc. It could indicate the study of the higher nature of the sun or light itself, or the study of higher nature at On-Heliopolis.

The first great alchemist was said to have been a woman, by the name of Mary the Jewess.[4] Now, alchemical symbolism involves much that is feminine and seems descriptive of the very thing that the Church was busy denying at the time – the female. Mary is said to have discovered the distillation of alcohol in the period of the Islamic Caliphate; it is said that she invented the double-boiler, called the *bain-marie*. But the legend of Mary is obviously much older than Islam, in fact some Christians believed that alchemy was invented by Mary, the mother of God, who in Church dogma becomes transmuted from the flesh into the spirit.

Furthermore, the idea that Mary invented distillation is interesting. Before the ultimate stage of transmutation, the alchemist would have achieved the stage wherein 'red mercury' appears. It is this that completed the transmutation of base metals into gold.[5]

In an old Italian manuscript there is a particularly vivid illustration of two bearded men sucking the breasts of Sapientia, another form of Sophia–Wisdom. This figure was also known as the Siren of the Philosophers, 'born of our deep sea, who pours milk and blood from her paps.'[6] The milk, (the substance that St. Bernard received from the Virgin), is white. Blood, of course, is red. These same colours are to be found in the form of the Flower of the Alchemists, a five-petalled red and white rose, called 'the womb of the *Filium philosophorum*' – the Glorious Child. It is precisely the same rose that symbolised the Blessed Virgin Mary.[7]

Alchemy would therefore seem to be not only heretical, but syncretic, featuring a union of both Christianity and Pagan symbolism. As the mystical forerunner of chemistry, alchemy is trying to tell us that behind religion there lies a science.

Catechism Twenty-Two

Despite Gerbert's Papacy, the overall movement of the Church was toward tighter control. Strict control had proved valuable to European unity during the strife-torn Dark Ages. Now the continent had moved into the medieval period under the calming influence of monasticism and the blanket of security that its influence threw over the entire period. The Church became central to a civilised Europe and, having positioned herself at the heart of Europe, began to further centralise and secularise. Her means of control in the face of new intellectual and cultural fashions, themselves the product of a new, less embattled ethos, can be summed up quite briefly:

> God works in mysterious ways in order to reveal himself to man; but man cannot know him because he works in such mysterious ways!

I shall label this summation as Catechism-22 (with apologies to the late Joseph Heller,)[8] for, according to the Church, because it was such a mystery, only the Vicar of Christ, the Pope, and his appointed clergy were in any way fit to lead the way. Others, though, thought differently and they were therefore labelled heretics and became endangered. The Albigensians or Cathars, Western Europe's last remaining Gnostic peoples, were soon to pay for their heresy with their very lives – which they gladly parted with, seeing life as a burden created by a false god. The Roman Church, for its part, would happily play the role of Grand Inquisitor, performing its task with amazing zeal and not a little relish.

There was, however, a less callous influence at work within the Church, an influence that, until recently, has barely raised any questions, and yet it was so striking in its originality and breadth of vision that one must wonder if it encompassed a vision wider than that of the Church, Catholic though it was.

The influence was derived in part, both directly and indirectly, from Islam and other beliefs outside the Christian remit. This influence is personified in one of the giants of the era, a leviathan in his time, a man whose picture of Catholic reality was inspired not only by a breadth of vision but by a vision in itself. That man was St. Bernard of Clairvaux.

St. Bernard's Visionary Purpose

St. Bernard of Clairvaux (c. AD 1090–1153) is one of the most extraordinary figures of the medieval period. Even before he was born he was singled out for particular attention, his parents having been told by an oracle that his destiny would be great. The third of seven children, he had particular care paid to his education, at which he excelled. At the age of nine he was sent to the renowned school at Châtillon-sur-Seine, where Bernard's taste for literature expanded along with an extraordinary devotion to the Blessed Virgin. He became known as a young man of great charm and wit, whose learning seemed almost unbounded. And yet Bernard could be abusive and manipulative when he wanted to be. He became, in the eyes of his contemporaries, a man of great gifts, but also someone who could be devious and unscrupulous in the face of opposition. Indeed, Bernard, in the true vein of the knightly family that he came from, was a man of extraordinary energy who seemed to thrive on conflict. Renowned for his wisdom, he was called 'Mellifluous Doctor', meaning that he was honey–tongued and one of his chosen motifs was the bee. The other motif was the dragon, a motif associated with the suppression of heresy. What I wondered about here was the nature of that suppression, for it seems, in the light of Bernard's activities, that all that was suppressed was suppression itself!

Having viewed the Albigensian heresy at close quarters, St. Bernard was honest enough to admit that it was morally unimpugnable and refreshingly free of the corruption rife within the Roman Church. This does not necessarily mean that St. Bernard was a sympathiser of the Cathar heresy, as some make out: he was giving an honest assessment of all that was wrong with Rome.

I am not linking St. Bernard to any heresy, nor am I suggesting that he had a secret political agenda, for through and through Bernard was a man of the Church, as Catholic as can be, but it seems that at an early age he experienced something that set him upon a path that was to stretch the boundaries of Catholicism.

The key lay in an incident that took place when he was a boy. In the school at Châtillon-sur-Seine there was a statue of the Holy Virgin, and it was black. As Bernard looked upon this Black Madonna, from her breast came the miracle that would transform his life: three drops of milk.

Now the medieval period is often dismissed as an age of superstition. In many ways this may be true, but if we can, even momentarily, put ourselves in the mind of medieval man, we will see more than mere superstition, we will see an age of faith exemplified in monasticism. The strength of the monastic movement was driven by practicality. Many young men of aristocratic lineage of the period became monks. The foremost reason was the simple fact that the young man himself may have been only a second or third son of his family and his chances of inheritance were thus slim. The alternatives were war or ministry, a life in the saddle or a life in the cloth. Choosing the latter entailed all manner of disciplines, from the rigours of ritual to the night-long vigils of prayer. The fundamental rules of monasticism were those of chastity, poverty and obedience.

Evelyn Underhill, in her classic work *Mysticism*, succinctly explains the motive behind the rules:

> 'It is not love but lust – the possessive case, the very food of selfhood – which poisons the relation between the self and the external world and immediately "fatigues the soul".'[9]

To help explain this further, Underhill quotes the Muslim theologian and mystic Al Ghazahli (1058–1111) on the Sufis:

> 'Their science has for its object the uprooting from the soul of all passions, the extirpation from it of vicious desires and evil qualities; so that the heart may be detached from all that is not God, and give itself for its only occupation, meditation on the Divine Being.'[10]

In short, rules were there to foster a strength of spirit and to open oneself to the divine influence. The devout Christian monk could expect divine assurance and guidance in many forms; often intuitive, sometimes visionary. Bernard's experience though, smacked of the archaic, the Black Madonna. His entire life was afterwards devoted to the Virgin, the Black Virgin at that. Although, as a man of the cloth, he had to be seen to be working within the dictates of Rome, the influence comes through in his writings (his famous treatise on the Song of Songs is still renowned throughout the Church) and most potently in the great works that he initiated and supported. Bernard was a man of great vision and energy – his reforming zeal completely transformed the Cistercian movement from a dwindling backwater into the largest monastic movement in Europe. However, it was his involvement with the Order of the Temple of Solomon – the Knights Templar – which most displayed the nature of his ambitions, for with his support, Bernard's friends within the Order changed the course of history, by transforming both the architectural and intellectual landscape of Western Europe through the creation of the great cathedrals and their schools.

Templar Travails

The era of St. Bernard saw a spectacular growth in cathedrals and cathedral schools. The inspiration behind these schools derived directly from two areas, the foremost being the first of the Crusades, which from 1095 had opened Europe up to influence from the East, and the second being the influence that came out of Moorish Spain. Bernard himself had regular contact with a Jewish settlement as far south as Cordoba in Moorish Spain. The settlement had been founded in pre-Solomonic times and therefore would have followed the traditions of the ancient Israelites. In this connection, Bernard would also have experienced Moorish influence. To this day the Moorish architecture of Cordoba is marvellously inspirational. Who knows to what depths these things influenced Bernard? Certainly something radical was directing his ambitions. In the introduction to the Rule of the Templars, which Bernard was asked to compose at the inception of the Order of the Temple of Solomon, Bernard writes of the figure of 'Damedieu'. This word would appear to be the medieval French word for the Mother of God, or Goddess. In fact the entire passage is at odds with what St. Bernard goes on to write within the Rule Addressing the first Templar Grand Master, Hugues de Payens, Bernard writes:

> 'Well has Damedieu wrought with us and our Saviour Jesus Christ; who has set his friends of the Holy City of Jerusalem on march through France and Burgundy... The work has been accomplished with our help. And the knights have been sent on the journey through France and Burgundy, that is to say Champagne, under the protection, as we shall see, of the Count of Champagne, *where all precautions can be taken against all interference by public or ecclesiastical authority*; where at this time one can best make sure of a secret, a watch, a hiding place.'[11]
>
> (My italics.)

What was the secret spoken of in this text? And what exactly was the 'work' that had been accomplished? The air of intrigue and suspicion is only heightened by perhaps the most tantalising part of the statement, the section that speaks of ecclesiastical interference. At the time of writing, Bernard of Clairvaux was only around 30 years of age, and yet, for all his youth, he was a man of quite considerable influence. What is obvious from the passage, and what fits all of the available evidence about this remarkable man, is that St. Bernard was a man very much on a mission.[2]

Why was such an organisation encouraged by the Church? A part of the answer lies in the attempt by the Church, at the close of the Dark Ages, to direct the testosterone-driven lust for blood into something for the common good. The bloodshed, mainly within the aristocracy, seemed unending and unnecessary; whilst peasants were forced into common labour, the aristocratic landowners squabbled over ownership in the bloodiest way possible. So desperate was the Church that it even attempted to call a 'Truce of God', which specified days on which noblemen were not to fight. The overall policy of the Church was to create a sort of code, one that was eventually to be called 'chivalry'. However, along with chivalry came courtesy and courtliness, the adoration of the Lady, a moral code that appeared at roughly the same time as St. Bernard was also extolling the Lady's virtues. The Church would later become unhappy with this state of affairs, as gradually elements of perceived heresy crept into such adoration, elements of an older system of belief, though one not too far removed from Christianity.

The knights of the First Crusade won Jerusalem for the West in the summer of 1099, but in doing so they demonstrated huge ferocity and barbarity, slaughtering the entire population of 70,000 in three days. The Templars, founded in 1118, after the First Crusade, had a different behavioural code. Arrogant they could be, but the Order was mightily ascetic – a knight was expected to pray several times a day and was not allowed to marry. They had to sleep in lit rooms, not in darkness, in order to discourage sexual misbehaviour. They slept with their boots on in case they were roused to fight, and their discipline and fighting prowess were renowned.

An indication of quite how different they were may be found in the Templar motto, dating to their founding in 1118. It reads:

'Not unto us, O Lord, not unto us, but to thy name glory.'

This was taken from Psalm 113 and reflects a less arrogant mentality than that of the average crusader.

The Templar way of life was attractive to the aristocratic male. Formerly, many had to choose between the saddle or the cloth, the Knights Templar offered both in one. The discipline of the Templars and their service in the name of God made them the perfect vehicle for St. Bernard's cause: the creation of a broader, more Christian Europe, one based upon a mystical, enquiring view of God. As warrior monks, they represented what might be termed 'a mystical army of God'. Their cause was St. Bernard's cause; his insight was their insight.

The first of the Templar Grand Masters, Hugues de Payens (1070-1131), was also known as Hugo de Pagano – Hugh of the Pagans. The reason for this name could simply be the fact that Hugues' grandfather was Moorish. This in itself is interesting for it would have given Hugues an in–depth knowledge of the Islamic mind and the workings of Islamic culture - ideal for those who were about to search the Holy Land for secrets, for this was the Templar brief. Furthermore, it seems that they were given instructions to look for something beneath Jerusalem. What that something was has been much speculated upon. Ideas range from the Holy Grail to the Ark of the Covenant.

It was important from my perspective to seize upon any hard evidence that I could and to remain as distant from wild speculation as possible. So from this perspective I decided that the best course of action was to take a look at what Jerusalem is most associated with – the Rock of Sion.

Certainly, Solomon's Temple would have been a focus of investigation for the Order. Although no sign of this Temple has ever been unearthed archaeologically, the Templars believed that when they first began to reside in the Holy City it was within the environs of the original Temple. Actually, the ruins that they settled into are likely to have been those of Herod's great edifice, a massive site thought to more than encompass the original Temple.

The original Temple stood upon a rock. This rock was situated, according to the old Hebrew traditions, at the centre of the world, and it contained God's Covenant. This was the very same rock upon which Abraham is said to have attempted to sacrifice his son Isaac.

In his telling of the Grail myth Wolfram von Eschenbach goes into some detail about and what the Grail is. Primarily, it is a stone, he tells us, a stone fallen from Heaven, *Lapis Exilis* (according to the alchemist Arnold of Villanova). What Wolfram writes about the stone's powers, turned out to be quite significant for me. He tells of its effect upon the Knights of the Grail:

> 'By a stone they live,
> And that stone is both pure and precious
> – Its name you have never heard?
> Men call it Lapis Exilis –
>
> If you daily look at that stone
> (If a man you are, or a maiden) for a hundred years,
> If you look on its power, your hair will not grow grey, your face appears
> The same as when you first saw it, your flesh and your bone will not fail
> But young you will live for ever
> – this stone all men call the Grail.'[13]

Wolfram goes on to describe how on Good Friday a dove flew down with the Host and laid it upon the stone. And so upon the same stone that Abraham attempted to shed the blood of his son Isaac, we have the Blood and Body of Christ.

'The stone from the Host receives all good that on earth may be.
Of food or drink, which the earth bears as the bounty of Paradise.
All things in wood or water and all that fly beneath the skies.'[14]

Quite clearly, these words are not all meant to be taken literally. The sense that I got from this was that the Temple on its central rock was the special dwelling-place of God. Thus there is an overwhelming sense of immanence, of the numinous, that God somehow is in the rock.

Jerusalem was described by Pope Urban II, in his call for the First Crusade in 1095, as 'the navel of the world, a land which ... the Redeemer of mankind illuminated by his coming'. The original Latin described it as *umbilicus terrae*. I wondered about that; an umbilicus could be 'from' or 'to' something. Recalling that the early name for Jerusalem was Solyma and related to the sun (see chapter one), the umbilicus could be from the sun with the earth seen as the child. Alternatively, the meaning could be regarding an umbilicus from the earth to humanity, or both.[15]

City Knights

The Templars guarded the pilgrim routes to and from the Holy Land; the information that I had so far accrued demonstrated that there was at least the possibility that what they were protecting was actually the sacred sites.

I decided to look just a little further to see if I could uncover anything more specific. The word 'Jerusalem' seemed a good place to start. Jerusalem is the 'city of peace', the Holy City or City of David.

Today, in certain European countries, it is spelt as Gerusalem and in older manuscripts it is sometimes found as 'Garisalem' or Garesalem. However, a still older form of the name is Uru-shalim, from the Amarna letters of Akhenaten (c.1400 BC). This raised some interesting points. The added letter 'J' or 'G' is indicative of the ancient spelling of God – Yah or Jah. Both 'J' and 'G' are cognate (see chapter eight). *Gar*, which is the first syllable of the name, means 'stone' in Greek. The last syllable may perhaps have formed the basis of the Greek verb *lemma*, from *lambanein*, meaning 'to take'. This leaves us with the middle syllable, *esa* (*esa or usa*). The whole would give the meaning 'Esa's' stone takes' or 'Esa's stone is taken'. Now, I hasten to add that this was all speculation, but a possibility nevertheless.

I looked again. The word 'peace' in the Hebrew is *'shalom'*. Within the name of the city we find 'salem'. Hebrew and Greek share very many similarities, particularly the language within the Bible, which Professor Joseph Yahuda states is 'camouflaged Greek'.[16] the only difference between them being a matter of pronunciation. So 'salem' means not only 'peace' but in Greek 'take blood' or 'blood taken', which seems to describe the precise purpose of the rock within the Bible texts. However, I did not want to take this literally - I knew too much about the ancient oral tradition to do so – but, as yet, I did not know the meaning. Finally, I considered Jerusalem's earlier name of Solyma and its relation to the sun. Did this somehow relate to a sun-like energy thought to be in the rock? No solid answers came, so I investigated from a slightly different angle.

That the Temple Mount is a very holy place cannot be doubted. However, I was being drawn to speculate on the actual nature of such holiness – the fact that such places are holy simply could not be taken for granted. After the rise of Islam in the late 600s, Jerusalem became the third holiest site to Muslims after Mecca and Medina. It is said that the Prophet ascended to heaven atop Mount Moriah and that this is the reason why the Dome of the Rock was built there. It is a curious fact that on the Temple site, built by Solomon son of David, the Dome too is said to have been constructed by Suleiman ben Daud, that is to say, Solomon son of David.

If the Templars were there looking for something, was it treasure? No great Templar treasure in the standard form of gems or gold etc. has ever been found in relation to their activities in the Holy Land. Rumours abound for a variety of reasons and much has been written that remains firmly within the boundaries of speculation, and sometimes total fantasy. However, the rumours are difficult to dismiss. We have already viewed the comments of St. Bernard about precautions against interference by public or ecclesiastical authority. Many have stated, with varying degrees of evidence, that that secrecy was required because the Templars were heretics, Cathar sympathisers, secret idolators or worshippers of St. John. Others, using the claims of Freemasonry, have suggested that underneath the Temple Mount secret archives were unearthed that gave the Templars great knowledge which they put to extremely good use. How much of this is true is highly questionable. One thing that cannot be denied is the rapid growth of the Order within the first two decades of its inception. Whatever it was that they discovered it was almost certainly the key to greater knowledge and, ultimately, great power.

I decided to approach the question of treasure from another angle. In the days of Solomon, the priests of the inner temple, the Holy of Holies, were called *nabi*, meaning 'prophet'. They were oracles of God. It was the job of the nabi to tune in to the divine voice and interpret what it said through a careful and considered use of language. So, taking a lead from this, I once more delved into a careful and considered interpretation of the words at hand.

Freemasons have said that the Templars found secret archives. The word 'archive' is interesting. Etymologically, it derives from the Greek *arkheia*, meaning 'magisterial residence'. There is no better way of describing the abode of God. It is formed upon the root *arkhe*, which is very reminiscent of the word 'ark'. The Ark of the Covenant, which resided in the Holy of Holies, was said to have been secreted beneath the Temple Mount shortly before the destruction of Jerusalem in AD 71. It is this that some claim was found by the Templars. Again, I have to say that the Templars have never been identified with a physical treasure. The word 'treasure' is derived from the French *trésor*. In Old Spanish and Old Italian it is *tresoro*, though in Catalan it is also *tresor*. In Provencal it is spelt *tezaur*. This demonstrates the wide distribution of the word throughout Europe. The root is Latin, *thesaurus'*, which in Portugese is translated as *thesauro*. Of course, a thesaurus is something that every writer is familiar with – it is 'a storehouse of knowledge', especially 'of words'.

This for me was remarkable; we began with a search for treasure only to end up with a veritable thesaurus! It seemed to me that the fact that ancient words which today relate to physical things originally related to more subtle things inferred that the treasured things of the Ancients were subtle and that the subtle realms were where one should be looking for those secrets.

A further look at words brought more intrigue: Jerusalem was called Sarras by the Grail romancers and indeed, until the close of the First Crusade it was inhabited by Saracens. A fraternity of the Saracens upon which the Templars based certain elements of their organisation were the Assassins, who later on became better known as the Ishmaeli Muslims.[17]

The Assassins are known to have made alliances with both the crusading Franks and the Templars against their mutual enemies, the Sunni Muslims. It is to be expected that where the Templars were involved they made more than simple alliances with these highly cultured and highly educated people. Through these cross-cultural opportunities I was convinced that in Islam, and perhaps in other Eastern beliefs, the Order discovered much that could be reconciled within a broader vision of Christianity.

With the word 'Saracen' we now come to another aspect that was to literally crop up with increasing regularity – the appearance of some kind of cereal associated with the hero.

The name Saracen appears in many guises. In Europe it came to mean 'Pagan' or 'Infidel', and was cognate with the Arabian peoples who had the mastery of Jerusalem.[18] 'Saracen' probably derives from the Arabian *sharqi* meaning 'easterner', the root of this is *sharq* , 'sunrise'. Sunrise, you will recall, is symbolic of the hero, the dying and rising god. The Templars celebrated their rituals at sunrise, which, in keeping with the tradition of dying and rising gods, is symbolic of the resurrection of Christ. Sunrise is also symbolic of fertility, especially of the crops. Imagine my surprise when I learnt that in French *sarrazin* is buckwheat. 'Saracen corn' and 'Sarrasin wheat' are terms common in both English and French. Another derivative that I found equally astonishing is 'sarsen', as in boulder or huge chunk of granite - it too is a variation upon the theme of Saracen.

I was fascinated by all of these connections. Indeed, the anomalies connected with the Templars had raised many questions to which I, as yet, had no answers. By now, though, I was convinced that they had made a great discovery in the East, something worth more than a clutch of king's ransoms, for, quite quickly, the Order had become very wealthy, mainly from donations of land and their establishment of the first successful credit system. It has been calculated that the worth of the Order at their fall on 13th October 1307 was a staggering £692 billion, roughly a thousand billion dollars.[19]

The Templars had scoured Jerusalem and, having done this, they travelled as far afield as Egypt and Ethiopia and yet, I repeat, there is no record of any great treasures having been brought back, nothing that would accord with this reputation of material wealth. What did they have that princes and kings should heap wealth upon them? In all likelihood, that 'something' was knowledge, and it would have to be a great knowledge, sought after by all. Perhaps, I mused, the Templars discovered something which could bring people closer to God or even give them some direct experience of the divine.

Here we must recognise the immense influence that religion had over life in those times. Not only was it necessary for the ruling classes to be associated with the Church in order to maintain their positions of power, but it must be understood that virtually every citizen sincerely looked to the divine for redemption from all earthly woes. To be closely associated with the most holy not only held a promise of blessedness in the hereafter, but was also a most practical move for those who wished to maintain their status and control.

Of course, the Templars became overweening, overbearing and arrogant: pride led to a fall. So worried was the Church that in 1274, at the Council of Lyons, Pope Gregory X proposed a merger between the Templars and the Roman Church. Not surprisingly, it was rejected. Instead, the Order had to be erased, but this did not happen immediately. They eventually fell from grace in 1307, at the instigation of the King of France. The fall was entire and much that emerged in the process was intriguing. Many of the knights were put to the Inquisition and what was revealed under torture would no doubt have shocked medieval society. 'You believe wrongly because [Christ] is indeed a false prophet' was a Templar admission under torture. And it was revealed that at his induction into the Order, one Fulk of Troyes was told of a crucifix: 'Set not much faith in this, for it is too young.'

The Templars apparently repudiated the crucifixion, though in what sense is not known. Did they repudiate Christ or simply the mode of his death? The Templar trials opened up a broader field. As Paul Broadhurst and Hamish Miller make clear in their book *Dance of the Dragon*:

'One of the charges levelled at the Templars during their persecution was that they were involved in unusual sexual rites that were overtly Pagan in character, and that, because of their contact with Eastern mystical sects, they practised Tantrism.'[20]

'In the Eastern world there has always been a strong current of mystical sex, and the Tantric tradition is well documented, with its temples famous for the explicit and orgiastic nature of its artistry. It is quite wrong to dismiss such examples of erotic art as pornography, for these temples, as with many such places in the ancient world, were the focus for mystical initiation through the control and use of the sexual energies. The prime purpose was to unleash the mystical fire-serpent of the Kundalini, the divine energy symbolized as a snake, which lies coiled at the base of the spine of every human being. As this Kundalini/sexual energy is slowly awakened, so it rises up through the chakras, the whirling energy centres of the body, bringing with it enhanced spritual perceptions. When it reaches the crown of the head, true union with the divine is said to take place. This is the meaning behind the crown of kings and queens, who represented the divine on Earth, with the crown signifying spiritual vision, symbolized in Ancient Egypt by the uraeus serpent positioned over the pharaoh's third eye.'[21]

One day, I received a call from a close friend, the writer and researcher Robin Whitlock. He was in an excited frame of mind. Robin had found the following words of St. Bernard of Clairvaux:

'*Vicarius Christi Christus Domine deus Pharaonis.*'

This translates as:

'[St Bernard exalted the Pope as] the representative of Christ, the Lord's anointed, the God of Pharaoh.'

When the Order of the Temple was blown wide open by the Church and State, many questioned the Templars' faith and activities and condemned them, without acknowledging how much the Order had contributed to the change in Europe's fortunes. The floodwaters from the East were dammed and, over the next 200 years, Europe would begin to transmute all that it had absorbed from Islam into a European identity.

Any remaining Templar groups disbanded or at least changed their name and maintained a somewhat reduced presence. France, which pursued a policy of active persecution, was to be avoided. In Spain a new Order was created, primarily as a refuge for ex-Templars; it was called Montesa. Even in their demise they left me clues to follow, for Montesa is simply Mount Esa – perhaps related to the 'Usa's stone' of my earlier musings.

Templars in the Telling

We have seen that running beneath the seemingly strictly controlled culture and religion of the medieval period there was a thick vein of heresy that ran counter to the belief of Rome. However, as the era drew to a close, a savage backlash came into force. Heresy was widened to include anything un-Catholic: witchcraft, herblore, folklore and even myth. St. Bernard's common touch was lost; the dream of a broad, Catholic Church, universal in its truest sense, began rapidly to diminish.

> 'Under the influence of the academics, discourse about God very soon tended to become unintelligible to non-specialists. St. Bernard's exclamation that "people discuss the Holy Trinity at every crossroads and the simple claim to have access to the most secret mysteries of the faith" was no longer valid.' [22]

There was to be no conjecture for the public at large, their faith was prescribed and anyone out of line could expect the Inquisition. The outlook of Bernard's era went underground.

> '..I can verify that these are tenets of a heresy widely believed in the Middle Ages; that the fossils of the heresy can be found in numerous works of art and literature; that it was vehemently attacked by the hierarchy of the established Church of Rome; and that it survived in spite of relentless persecution.' [23]

Much of it survived under cover of the oral tradition where the initiate must 'read between the lines'. There is no better way to introduce this idea than via a tale which the Templars brought back with them from the Holy Land in the twelfth century. It may be said, and with some confidence, that this tale was given its final shape by troubadours, wandering minstrels and storytellers who flourished in western Europe at the time of the Templars, and was much approved of by their masters, the Templars. Unfortunately, with the fall of the

Order, the story's true message was lost.

In an age when most commoners never left their locale and travel was sanctioned by the ruling classes, those who travelled generally had something of value to travel for. A troubadour offered far more than entertainment and local gossip. These travellers had originated in Provencal France, an area intimately associated with heresy and papal suspicions. The name troubadour comes from the French verb *Trouver*, to find. This is an interesting indicator. The intimation here is that something has indeed been found and, given the troubadours' Templar connections, it is a thing of great import.

Troubadours were a part of the oral tradition. As we have seen, this worldwide tradition has its origins in a period well before the written word and, up until the twentieth century, with the advent of mass education, television and the microchip, it still had great influence as a tool for enlightening the populace. It is regrettable that, in the present day, its stories are dismissed as 'old wives' tales'. But what would be the crowning value of that tradition, the value which sustained it for so long? It would be the same as in any situation where a listener may ask: 'What does that mean to me? How does that help me in my life?' For we all want wisdom, fulfilment and happiness. As a tradition that was sustained for thousands of years, the oral tradition must have delivered stories that, as well as being entertaining, satisfied those high demands. Not least amongst the stories would be those which answered those most natural of questions: where do we come from and where are we going to?

It can be understood that tales of mankind's origins and history might keep their settings over aeons, whereas those explaining human conditions and directions for advancement may be dressed in the clothes of the day. In this way the storyteller could offer tales of enlightenment using symbols both old and new. These tales may be taken by the listener simply as entertainment but, hidden within, the more discerning seeker would find direction for life. Here we have another reference to *trouver*, 'to find'. A function of the oral tradition has always been to find 'seekers after truth', those who will respond to the deeper message; and so it was with the troubadours and their work.

Puns and punning are the best way of concealing secrets deep within words and within myth, and this is where the fun begins. The following pun is a simple one and may offer us, via its ambiguous meaning, the origins of the term 'hoodlum', for it is to be found within the story of that most English of heroes, Robin Hood. Robin was in every sense a 'Robbing Hood' – he robbed from the rich and gave to the poor. Now the *Oxford Dictionary of Etymology* suggests that the term 'hoodlum' is of unknown origin. I would like to suggest that Robin Hood was a name that crossed Europe with Templars and troubadors in tales that the secret Gnostic-leaning societies of southern Italy understood only too well. These same societies were later to gain notoriety as the Mafia. This is not the first time that the fallen Templars have been accused of resorting to crime. It has been suggested that Templars on the run turned to piracy in order to survive and that the sign of the 'skull and crossbones' is a Templar legacy.[24]

The legend of Robin Hood is only second in importance to that of King Arthur and the Knights of the Round Table in the popular British mythology. The stories of an outlaw of aristocratic origin robbing the rich and giving to the poor have a mass appeal that goes to the heart of every Englishman. Beyond this there is the nostalgic idea of 'Merrie England' with her deep swathes of greenwood, her shires and her traditions of kingship, nobility, romance and revelry. Given his noble standing, his exquisite good manners and his ability to fight for the 'common man', it may be said without exaggeration that Robin is a sort of 'greenwood messiah'.

A cursory glance at the legend reveals as many similarities as there are discrepancies when compared to the Gospels of Matthew, Mark, Luke and John. What emerges is the similarity of the character of Robin to Jesus himself. We have a vague mention of Robin's real father, as vague as the mention of Jesus' father in the Bible. Both Jesus and Robin have a precursor in the form of a 'wild' man called John and both are baptised by John. In the Robin Hood myth this occurs when Robin is 'ducked' by John during a rather amiable but nonetheless competitive fight. Jesus is associated with the Virgin Mary, Mary Magdalene and Mary, sister of Martha. Mention is also made of Jesus' grandmother being a woman called Anna. Robin's story captures these associations within one name, that of the maid, Marian (also note the similarity with Gerbert's Meridiana). Both men have followers, Jesus, the Apostles; Robin, his Merrie Men. Furthermore, both Robin and Jesus speak in favour of the poor and the disinherited and, where Robin operates outside the law, Jesus operates beyond it. Both are condemned.

In this scheme of things Prince John plays the Devil himself, for the Devil is often portrayed as a usurper in biblical texts and he is also portrayed as red, as is Prince John. Furthermore, the Devil tempts Jesus in the wilderness whilst Prince John tempts Robin in the greenwood. On the other hand, King Richard[25] the Lionheart's symbol is a cross, the famous red cross of the Templar order. He represents God, the most high, omnipotent and invisible. He bears ultimate jurisdiction over the land and its people and appears only at the close of the tale, to reward Robin for his heroism and fidelity.

There are additional aspects to the story of Robin that would appear to further encourage the comparison with Jesus. Both are 'hooded' men, for, after his disappearance from the tomb, Jesus reveals himself to his disciples at the supper of Emmaus by removing his hood. As a further hint, in some versions of the legend, the name of Robin's father is given as Adam.[26] Are we being told something here via the mythic language? Was Robin by virtue of his father's name the second Adam, as was Jesus, who had come to expunge the sins of the first Adam? Note that Robin's Saxon name was Rof Breoht Woden – 'Bright Strength of Woden'. Woden was the most senior of the Aesir, the Norse gods. He crucified himself in order to save his people and to renew himself; thus it is that this Robin is a son of God. A further clue lies in his other name; Robin Goodfellow or Godfellow.

If this comparison was encouraged by those behind the myth of Robin, the intimation might be that there is much to be revealed – and indeed there is, for it is at this point that one very important difference arises between the two myths. In some tellings of the legend, Robin's father, the rightful Earl of Huntingdon, is unjustly killed by the soldiers of King John. If this is a covert statement about the Gospel figure of Jesus, then what we are being told is that Jesus' earthly father was a man of some considerable standing, a man who was killed in order to preclude him from what was rightfully his (see chapter one), for in the legend of Robin Hood, the wicked Sheriff appropriates Huntingdon's lands for himself. What, you might ask, is going on? Strangely, in the English language the term 'Sheriff' means 'representative of the royal authority in a shire or county'. This is close to the meaning of its Arabian counterpart, *Sharif* meaning 'noble, high born' or 'ruler'. Suddenly, we have a direct connection between Britain and the Holy Land.[27]

A significant clue to the unravelling of this mystery came in the form of an article in *The Sunday Times* in December 1997.[28] In it the scholar Professor Stephen Knight propounded the theory that the myth of Robin Hood was Scottish in origin and that the original name of Robin Hood was in fact 'Rabbie Hood'. Now I do not believe this to be at all the case,[29] especially as since that time Professor Knight has goe on record as saying that Robin and his Merrie Men were a band of homosexuals. Needless to say, his idea gained good press coverage. However, although there may well have been some gay outlaws, the emphasis of Professor Knight's interpretation does not reflect the nuances of the oral tradition. Merrie Men, for example, seems to imply a meaning well outside modern impositions upon the past. Quite simply it means 'Mary's Men'. We are now deep within the realm of ancient myth, as I'm sure the Templars well knew!

What really sparked my interest was the name Rabbie. For 'Rabbie' read 'Rabbi', for 'Hood', read 'Yahud' – Rabbi Yahud. Much to my astonishment, such a character did exist a few thousand years ago in a region today known as Yemen. Although the details are sketchy, there are distinct Essene connections.[30] Other than that, Rabbi Yahud seems to be as much a figure of legend as his British counterpart.[31] In fact, the name may refer to a whole tribe of Jews in Yemen, as the recent work of Dr. Tudor Parfitt has shown.[32] To scrutinise the name more closely reveals much: it translates as 'The Master' or 'Our Master the Jew'. As we know, Jesus was a Jew and was addressed by his disciples as 'Master'. Significantly, in early English, the word 'Hood' is a title of the Welsh hero, Hu. It means 'The Lord', being a variant upon Hu's name. I was intrigued that Jesus' name in Hebrew and Aramaic is Yeshua or Jeshua!

I was aware that this sound 'hu', as in 'Hood',[33] is still in use as a specified sound today, both in Hindu 'Kriya Yoga' and the Sufi 'Zhikr', as part of the initiates' purification technique.[34] Here then, was another connection with the Middle East and it seemed to me that during the occupation of Jerusalem, the Templars may well have come under Sufi influence, gaining knowledge which stretched back beyond the Islamic and Christian eras to the Essenes and, maybe, further.

I wondered about our cry of joy, 'Yahoo!' (a Middle Eastern word meaning 'God'), and our tradition of blessing after a sneeze: 'Atchoo!' It seems that these knights of old had a merry sense of humour! Indeed, it is no exaggeration to say that such puns offer us great insight. Puns are an essential form of 'humour', a word that breaks up into two syllables, *hu* and *mour*, as in *amour*. Quite literally, 'humour' is 'the love of the Lord' – *Hu* meaning 'Lord and *amour* meaning 'love'. Love and laughter figure prominently in the world's mythology, particularly in the Middle East.

Then I learned something of deeper interest: of all sounds, 'hood' lies absolutely central to the male voice range.[35] We are told that the baffling complexities of the human voice were first explained by Lord Rayleigh only a century ago. Was this earlier emphasis on 'hu' and 'hood' incidental, or was there real knowledge in practice here?

Robin's name in Old English, the language present at the time of the Norman Conquest,[36] is Hreodbeorht. The final syllable of the name, *beorht*, means, 'bright',[37] coming from the Saxon *berhta*. The first syllable officially derives from Saxon *broth*, meaning simply 'fame'. These derivations stem from the language called Old German. However, what is of interest in the light of Robin Hood's closeness in comparison to the figure of Jesus is that at some stage in its linguistic development, the name seems to have been purposefully tampered with. The syllable would have been spelt not as Hrod or Hreod, but as Herod.

The name Robin may therefore mean 'Herod's brightness' – perhaps a reference to a little child, one of Herod's offspring. In the light of the legend of Robin Hood and its similarity to the four Gospel texts, we know exactly who that little child is – it is an intriguing inference of Jesus' lineage. The Templars and troubadours may be long gone, but in the story of Robin Hood they are still whispering their secrets.[38]

Afflicting the Converted

One of the things that had most intrigued me from the Robin Hood material was the fact that the purification sound 'hu' was to be found as central in the male voice range. Here, as in Jesus' words of power, was another secret connected with sound. I was very interested therefore, to learn that in the twelfth century the Roman Catholic Church took it upon itself to ban a particular musical note. The augmented fourth interval (F natural and the B natural above it, sounded at the same time) was so hated by the Church that it was given the label the 'Devil's Chord'.

This chord is the particular speciality of the brass section of the orchestra, trumpets and the like.[39] This is interesting because much iconography from before the 1100s portrays angels, seraphim and cherubim playing trumpets – but trumpets and other brass instruments were now banned by the medieval bishops because of their 'Satanic' music.

The prohibition against the Devil's Chord was just the beginning of yet another dark period of European history. This was an era in which hysteria about 'Devil' worship came to a height. Europe had been conquered, both culturally and psychically, by the Church which had gained the monopoly on religious belief in Europe. Any injuries that it might sustain would now come from within until it splintered irreparably. Devil worship would then be used as a weapon by the emerging Protestant Church in its anti-Catholic polemics, leading ever onwards to greater exaggerations and conspiratorial claims and counter-claims until the Churches settled down into the forms that are recognisable to us today.

As for me, my researches into early Christianity seemed exhausted and I still had far more questions than answers. Little did I know that Science beckoned.

I was mulling over the banning of the Devil's Chord. At first I was surprised - on the one hand we had the expansion of cathedral building throughout the length and breadth of Europe, and on the other we suddenly had a suppression of musical sound. Surely, I thought, the new cathedrals of the time would have been marvellous places to bring out the power of such music.

There is a well-known phrase often used when one is asked to remember something: Does that ring a bell? Many clues had been given to me: gods of the earth and of the sun, hero-gods, sunrise and sunset, power in the stones, temples, visions, secret words and Jesus as 'the Word who did dance all things'. Now here I was musing upon cathedral acoustics when suddenly a deep, clear, resonant bell rang within. Soon bells were ringing everywhere for me, especially a sonorous one below. I was on a new phase of the research.

Part Two

In Search of a Sacred Technology

5

Secrets of Life

'I sing the body electric.'

Walt Whitman[1]

'The singing of words reveals their true meaning directly to the soul through bodily vibration.'

Hildegard of Bingen

HURTLING through the cosmos at great speed is a crystalline living rock, in orbit about the sun. Since the formation of the solar system approximately 4,600 million years ago, our home, the earth, has developed in a profoundly different way from all of the other planets in our solar system. By virtue of being the third planet from the sun, with a unique axial tilt and a 24–hour spin, earth is subject to precisely the right conditions for carbon-based life forms, life as we know it, to thrive, away from the dangers that lurk in space. By a curious twist of fate, the planet is shielded from a majority of incoming meteors and other potential hazards by the gravitational pull of the great planet Jupiter.

However, we have created hazards of our own. For years, the indigenous peoples of the world, from the Kogi of Colombia to the Aborigines of Australia, have warned the Western peoples about their ignorant, wanton ways, justifying their comments with the threat that the Earth Mother won't like it, that she will fight back. They seem to mean this literally. Can they possibly be correct? Is she really a 'being' in her own right?

At the 1995 Rio Summit, the world's industrial nations agreed that they were going to have to clean up their act. Agenda 21, as it was called, was the long-awaited document that would set the environmental themes for the twenty–first century, with all countries agreeing to cut their industrial emissions by at least a third within a decade. The warnings were at last being heeded. The conference, though not achieving much in substance, had broken new ground in admitting the folly of our ways. The world's indigenous peoples were, however, not only correct in their observations about worldwide pollution, conclusions now supported by science, but they are also gaining support for a deeper, more profound observation - that the Earth lives and that we live within her care.

Good Vibrations

As we begin this new millennium, man's age-old need to find a reason for his existence is pulling the realms of science and religion closer together. The question of 'What is God?' has, in the past 60 years, been largely replaced by 'What is consciousness?' The views of the great Jesuit scientist Teilhard de Chardin now seem commonplace. Teilhard, whilst sojourning in England in the early 1900s, had a mystical experience in which he became aware of the universe no longer as an abstract notion or a machine, but as energy transformed into a presence, of which he was a crucial part.[2] Ideas such as this, once considered to be foolish, now seem to have the support of scientific data. Laboratories are now abuzz with speculations about the nature of consciousness and many organisations are dedicated to learning more about what is, in effect, super-nature.[3]

Beyond the laboratory, James Lovelock's Gaia hypothesis, that the earth is a single, self-regulating organism, has caught the popular imagination and this feeling has been carried forward to maintain that planet earth is sentient. Many are becoming more and more convinced that we inhabit a living, breathing world and that, rather than being a dead piece of rock floating through space, our planet may well be a being in itself. Though this is not yet scientifically proven, there is no doubt that we live in earth's embrace, her atmosphere, her vibration. The term 'vibration' is a truism in every sense of the word, hence its popularity with new agers and the hippies before them, moreover it is a remarkably astute way in which to describe the state of matter within the entire universe.

Matter, in order to exist, must vibrate, and anything that vibrates has a frequency of vibration. When a string is plucked, its rate of vibration is measured and if it should happen to vibrate ten times a second, then it may be said to have a frequency of ten cycles per second or 10 Hertz (Hz), after Heinrich Hertz (1857-94). More familiar to radio users and astronomers are the terms Kilo-Hertz (kHz) and Mega–Hertz (MHz). These are thousands and millions of Hertz. We can see therefore that the wavelength of one Hertz must be very long (the higher or faster the frequency, the shorter the wavelength).

Within the known universe there are literally billions of frequencies, as matter vibrates not only from within but also by being struck from without. The earth resonates, or vibrates, at an extremely low frequency, or ELF for short. This resonance is produced from a variety of sources, but the most influential are from space: electromagnetic radiation from the sun and cosmic rays, which are actually high energy particles coming in from all over the cosmos. The origins of these particles are many and varied, from the result of a supernova to something much more violent – gamma ray bursts, possibly the most explosive events in the universe. Another source could be the background radiation of the 'Big Bang' itself, resonating from one end of the universe to the other, like the ripples in a pond.

The best way to describe earth resonance is to picture the planet as a gigantic bell. We know that the earth is not actually hollow but it is much less solid – fluid, even – beneath the crust. Indeed, Mother Earth was described by the ancients as an orb, meaning literally 'hollow sphere', not unlike a bell. When a church bell is struck by a hammer, it vibrates, and no matter how loud it might seem, the frequency of vibration always remains the same. There may however, be overtones, or undertones, which are variations on the resonant frequency. These are dependent upon the shape of the bell, the material, and any cracks or other anomalies. Similarly, our earth is struck by the incoming energies and therefore vibrates at a particular frequency along with its overtones. Thus it is that everything resonates, beats to its own rhythm and in the process gives off energy that remained until fairly recently imperceptible. Now there are ways of measuring it, even at incredibly low frequencies.

Whilst the seismic (underground) vibration of the earth is 32Hz, the primary, above ground vibration of our planet resonates at ELFs of between 7 and 10Hz. These frequencies are measured as fluctuations in the planet's magnetic field. ELF wavelengths are extremely long; in earth resonance they approximate the circumference of the planet. This is known as the Schumann resonance, after W. O. Schumann, who first demonstrated in 1952 that the atmospheric cavity, known as the ionosphere, was in fact a gigantic electrodynamic resonator. It is this region which, in resonating at around 8Hz, dominates all the above ground frequencies.

Ions are atoms that by virtue of gaining or losing an electron have become negatively or positively electrically charged. As the name 'ionosphere' implies, it is a highly electrically charged area of the atmosphere, caused mainly by the incoming ultraviolet radiation from the sun. Incidently, the layers within the ionosphere, the magnetosphere and the troposphere, are also responsible for the reflection of radiowaves and are thus very important to long-distance communication.

By a curious turn of nature, certain frequencies emitted by the brain fall within the band of earth resonance. The brain has varying bands of frequency, reflecting different activities at different times of the day. The lowest of these bands is the Delta rhythm: 0.5–4Hz. The association here is with deep sleep and there is also a link to the onset of paranormal experiences. Theta waves occur between 4–7Hz, when we are only half-awake, dreaming or musing meditatively. Alpha rhythms, at 7–13Hz, are states of passive alertness, wherein the mind is relaxed to the point of emptiness. Intriguingly, Alpha is the wavelength associated with altered states of consciousness, the frequency of expanded awareness. The fourth level of brainwave activity is Beta at 13–30Hz. This is the frequency of normal everyday wakefulness, of active thinking and interaction with the physical world.[4]

So, the brain contains electrical frequencies that occur naturally in the energy fields of the planet itself. This state of affairs may have been the natural result of life evolving to respond rhythmically to the pulses of Mother Earth. The fact that certain frequencies coincide with earth resonance means that, in effect, the Ancients were correct in calling this planet the Earth Mother. Indeed, this connection between earth frequencies and our own Alpha brainwave frequencies is like an unseen umbilicus. Coincidentally, to a degree, all animal life seems to share Alpha frequencies of around 10Hz, significant evidence that:

> ...every creature is hooked up to the earth electromagnetically through its D.C. system.[5]

Much of what is talked of as animal intuition or instinct is in fact an acute sensitivity to electromagnetic fields both within the body and without. It is well known that whales and dolphins navigate the world's oceans by detecting magnetic stripes on the sea floor. What is less known is the acute sensitivity of land animals to changes in the pulse of the earth. Days before an earthquake is due to hit a locality, animals will be seen vacating it, slight variations in frequency having warned them of impending danger. The signature of an oncoming earth tremor or quake falls within the ELF range of 1.6 to 3.2Hz, very long wavelengths indeed,[6] Animal senses must be very highly evolved in order to be able to detect them.

Experimentation has shown that humans, too, are sensitive. Researchers have found that a 10Hz band can restore normal metabolic rhythms in people denied access to the natural fields of earth, sun and moon, and that electrical stimulation of the region of the brain known as the hippocampus, again to around 10Hz, can lead to alterations in the perception of time and space, leading also to 'apparitions'. Alpha states can be induced in all sorts of ways; the very act of staring into space, of observing nature and natural sounds can lead the brain into the Alpha/Theta frequency range. Measuring brainwave patterns via electroencephalograms, researchers have discovered that simple meditative states coincide with earth resonance, particularly the Alpha frequencies. In fact there are frequencies to be found at points all over the brain that relate to those that occur naturally within the energy fields of the wider planet. In short, the 0.4–30Hz waveband, particularly the Alpha waveband within it (8–13Hz) remains supremely important for all earth-based lifeforms.

A Crystal Called Home

The earth is essentially crystalline in nature and, in response to incoming electromagnetic waves, namely the various spectra of light, it exudes a natural radiation. There is also evidence to suggest that this incoming energy interacts with the earth's own energy fields, leading to heightened sensitivities at locations wherein the interaction of the two forms of energy is particularly lively. But not only is the earth crystalline in nature, it also seems that her offspring are. Within the cells of living organisms a certain amount of self-luminosity has been located and this offers a clear indication of the crystalline make-up of organic structures.[7]

Crystals have the ability to convert certain frequencies of light and sound – vibrational energy – into electromagnetic and electric energy. They have the ability to absorb, transduce, amplify and transmit these energies. The primary component of the earth's crystalline make–up is silicon dioxide (SiO^2), better known to us as quartz. In the world of microchip technology it is the wonderful ability of quartz crystals to store energy that is used to great effect. Quartz is electrostatic – rub two pieces together in a darkened room and you will soon see a warm glow. The same effect comes from rubbing amber, or even ebony, with fur or some other material. Significantly, the Greeks called amber *elektron*. This electric charge can be transmitted through the human body, water or even certain metals, a property that makes them natural conductors. Silicon is a natural semiconductor; electricity flows through it with moderate resistance.

As sand, silicon or quartz is found in nearly all stones, but it is for a specific quality that quartz is put to good use in the world's kitchens: the spark that comes from pressure exerted upon a tiny crystal is used to ignite gas. The effect of vibration upon a crystal is one that alternately compresses and decompresses it as the waveform strikes the crystalline surface in a series of rhythmic pulses. The result of this energy transference process is electrical output: 'piezoelectricity'. The spark that arises in the world's kitchens is due to the 'piezoelectric' effect.

On a much larger scale, the tectonic level, where huge continental landmasses rub together, friction is produced in the form of earthquakes and every so often strange phenomena called 'earthlights' are witnessed. These earthlights have recently become the subject of much research and have even been captured on film.[8] It has been suggested, and with good cause, that these strange lights are in fact balls of plasma or superhot gas, sometimes familiar to us as ball lightning. They are, in effect, gas ionised by electricity coming from quartz-bearing rock, mainly granite. These extraordinary effects would therefore show that quartz is also a transducer, the property of transferring one form of energy, electromagnetism, into another, plasma in this case, with spectacular results.

The human body is itself largely crystalline in its structure and organic make up. The blood flowing through our veins is in reality liquid crystal. This is easily demonstrated when the skin is broken. Blood seeps out of the wound and separates into blood-plasma which forms a lattice, interlinking all areas of the wound and sealing off any outward flow. In response to outside exposure to the air, iron crystals, which colour the blood blue inside the body, oxidise and turn red, in the process crystallising and forming a hard shell over the wound. Another example of the crystallisation of certain body parts occurs around puberty when the pineal gland, located near the forehead, begins a process of calcification. The reason for this remains unknown, but it is as if softer parts of the body tissue suddenly turn to bone. Bone is primarily calcium, as can be seen by looking at the teeth, the only bones directly accessible to the outside world.

The bone structure of the body has long been recognised as crystalline in nature; it is a solid crystal structure complete with piezoelectric energy transference properties. Recent research has shown that energy transference in crystals is to a large extent ruled by the geometric structure of the individual crystal. Indeed, crystals are organised structures which, when not in a liquid state, may take one of seven different shapes, according to the atomic make up of the crystalline substance. Whether cubic, tetragonal, orthorhombic, triclinic, monoclinic, hexagonal or trigonal, crystals seem to arise spontaneously, always in the same pattern. Furthermore, when a piezoelectric crystal such as quartz is exposed to an electromagnetic field (EMF), the crystal will change shape and generate an EMF of its own.

Other crystals with this property of piezoelectricity and shape-shifting are tourmaline and bone. The teeth and cartilage around bone and muscle have these properties too. The forces that produce the piezoelectricity in these areas are particular forms of muscle movement and the rhythmic beat of the cardiovascular system; the environment, too, plays its part. EMFs promote crystal growth and tighter bonds between crystals, and therefore have the ability to effect a greater rate of growth in bone structure. Crystals, like very finely tuned violins, are constantly murmuring to themselves, an environmental response and one easily detected. It is this very murmuring that heightens the magnetic forces of attraction, thus aiding the healing process by mending bone fractures through growth. When subjected to a greater intensity of magnetism, bone fractures mend at a quicker rate.[9]

A liquid crystal may be defined as having form, but in the shape of stored information; in fact, it may act simultaneously as a liquid or as a crystal. Fatty tissues, nerve tissues and muscle, the lymphatic system, white blood cells and pleural linings are all liquid crystal systems, all held in place by an overall solid crystal structure – the skeleton. All of this is then held in shape by the skin, which itself exudes, on occasions, copious amounts of liquid crystal through the pores – perspiration.

Further to this, all of the bodily cell structures are considered as being liquid crystal in form. Cellular membranes operate as typical liquid crystals, as do plasma membranes, mitochondrial membranes and the nuclear membranes. As Gabriel Cousens, MD points out:

> Bodily fluids also have crystal qualities. The water molecule contains in itself the potential forms of all crystals in its primary form of a tetrahedron. Water can bring all different forms of ions into a crystalline state and hold them in solution. In addition, the more structured the water is, the higher concentration of ions it can hold. One of the most important of these ion solutions is the dissolved cell salts.[10]

In terms of the pattern of life, water has its own structure and, as has recently been discovered and acknowledged, is able to store data.[11] This data is then organised around particular ions and once it is located within particular cells is able to attract other ions or even cell salts into the same cell.

It is held that life adapts to physical circumstance via a process known as natural selection. Over the course of millions of years, environmental changes have produced variations within life as its forms have adapted, allowing the profusion of different life forms scattered across the entire surface of the planet. However, in the beginning, the very device of adaptation, DNA, if it existed at all, was far too fragile to have been solely, if at all, responsible for the adaptations. Ultraviolet radiation was very profuse upon early earth and DNA is all too easily damaged by it. The earth's protective ozone filter had yet to become formed. Something else must have existed in its stead, something that was adaptable, something that would not simply wear away but would replicate with almost precise accuracy and yet contain the capacity to evolve.

Only one state of matter in the early world contained all of the necessary ingredients – the matter of the earth itself, its very substance – dust, otherwise described as sand, silicon or crystal. Crystals are self-organising lumps of matter. They are regular geometric forms and are able to replicate themselves in a fairly stable manner. Nevertheless, it is *what* they contain that provides deeper answers to the question of life.

The Life Force

As we have observed, crystals are continuously murmuring; that is, they are resonating in response to incoming frequency pulses of electromagnetic radiation. The fact that they respond by giving off their own magnetic energy tells us that they are also surrounded by an electromagnetic field.

Einstein was at particular pains to point out (as in his Unified Field Theory), that it is precisely this kind of energy field that creates the form. In other words as matter is created out of nothing, a zero-point, it becomes defined within the limits of space and time. Space-time gives what was non-linear a set of coordinates: direction, mass, breadth and velocity. No-thing becomes a thing. The Russian scientist and pioneer in the study of organisms and geomagnetism, A. P. Dubrov, underlined Einstein's observation when he wrote … life became into being and has evolved in the presence of the geomagnetic field.[12] Only recently have we been able to measure the extraordinary subtlety of this EMF.

Regarding organisms, it was the pioneering work of Harold Saxton Burr in the 1930s and 40s that first brought to the attention of the world the concept, and the initial evidence, for what he called 'L-fields'. Burr found that where there is life there is a field. He found fields on a wide range of organisms and made meticulous observations of them for a period of over twenty years. As Professor of Anatomy at Yale University, he mounted an extensive campaign of research to investigate this phenomenon. Using extremely sensitive equipment he located minute EMFs on every living thing that came his way, whether it was newt eggs, leaves or human beings.

It was not until the 1960s and 70s that two Russian scientists, Semyon and Valentina Kirlian, developed the means to take actual photographs of these fields. Kirlian photography is dramatic in its support of Saxton Burr's work. It even goes so far as to suggest that if tissue is removed from a living organism, its field persists for quite a time after removal.

Saxton Burr saw these EMFs as organising fields that were just as valuable a part of the living make-up as the genetic code within it; and it is here that I wish to make a rather obvious point: we can see that living things are, to a significant degree, crystalline in nature. In response to incoming electromagnetism, crystals give off their own fields; *en masse*, crystals produce an EMF; Saxton Burr's L-field. However, Mother Earth too is crystalline and so it follows that she too has a field – the geomagnetic field. A huge EMF, this field is just as 'organising' as Saxton Burr's original L–field, thus giving rise to life on earth. Unfortunately, western science has been slow, at times reluctant, to imbibe the extraordinary implications of this research whereas, by contrast, a lot of work has been done from within the old Soviet bloc and the new Russian state. Now, however, in the West, the work of a number of researchers is bearing fruit.

The new work, performed by such pioneers as Rupert Sheldrake, Cyril Smith and A. J. Scott-Morley, has shown that all organisms are surrounded by electrical fields which guide the direction of shape and form of growth. Furthermore, such work has promoted a greater awareness that electrical fields in the environment have an effect upon growth, health and vitality. Distortions within these fields, leading to a breakdown of order within them, may arise from time to time. Modern technology uses overwhelming doses of electrical power that may create such distortions. This in turn might lead to over-strong fields whose influence upon life and subtle organising fields is massively out of balance, leading to biological damage on a cellular level, wherein tissue grows out of control and beyond the control of other factors. It is an uncomfortable fact that cancer is endemic within the Western industrial world whereas in non-industrialised areas, beyond the reach of pollution and technology, it is much less in evidence. Furthermore, it has been shown that exposure to strong energy fields, for instance powerlines, can produce a wide range of unpleasant effects, from headaches and nausea to blackouts, genetic damage, epilepsy and leukaemia.

Exposure to the lower energy fields for long periods at a time, such as watching television or working on a computer, can reduce blood sugar levels and lead to nervous disorders – Chronic Fatigue Syndrome, ME and also epilepsy. Such fields reach well beyond the appliance. In 1987 a major report revealed that computer systems create a field that extends even through and beyond the walls of the building in which they are housed.

In 1996 a report published by the University of Bristol, England, caused widespread consternation amongst politicians and scientists when it was suggested that large concentrations of radon gas, having seeped from the ground, were to be found in close proximity to electricity pylons, with detrimental effects upon human health. Two influential fields were coming together and bringing imbalance.

Radon gas is a natural form of radiation. It is one of the noble gases (gases that rarely react with other elements) and is found in quantity at the earth's fault lines. Other places of seepage are water wells and underground streams. Moreover, wherever there is radon, there is quartz. Natural radiation is a fundamental force of the universe, radiation being, in one sense, a type of resonance on the ultrascale (higher scale) of frequency. In addition to these radiations, we must also remember that the earth is similar to a giant bar magnet and that together, electricity and magnetism permeate all matter and thus all life on earth has an electromagnetic field.

Having drawn attention to the dangers of field imbalance, I should reiterate that electromagnetism is, on the whole, natural, balanced and life supportive. Electromagnetism has the ability to heal. We have already seen how it can promote growth of bone in cases of fracture or breakage. Magnetic fields can also help to treat various forms of cancer and, indeed, rhythmic pulses of electromagnetism have been shown to generally encourage the body's own defences to heal and grow stronger.

Our scientific age, with its increasingly sensitive technology, has led us to these subtle realms of vibrating energies. One might think that with our rising knowledge of the earth's fields and frequencies, our own fields and brainwave frequencies, and investigations into heightened sensitivity, mankind stands of the edge of a breakthrough in the study of earth science and perhaps an understanding of consciousness itself. However, recent experiments at sacred sites tell us that this knowledge is not being discovered for the first time.

Revelation at Newgrange

In 1994, in association with British–based researcher Paul Devereux, Professor Robert Jahn and Dr. Michael Ibison of the Engineering Anomalies Research Department of Princeton University, USA, carried out a series of experiments at selected ancient sacred sites in Britain and Ireland. Bob Jahn had been to Ireland the year before and whilst on a visit to the famous Neolithic cairn at Newgrange had come across a much noticed but little investigated effect. There, in tandem with a still and heavy atmosphere, weird and wonderful things happen when you light up a cigarette. The smoke seems to respond in a resonant fashion. Acting on a hunch, Jahn returned a year later, this time with a large array of equipment in tow .[13]

Newgrange dates to around 3500 BC and, as a cairn, is much like an underground church. The interior is cruciform – indeed, Newgrange is the largest structure of its sort in Europe, a Neolithic cathedral. Carved into both the interior and exterior of the monument - famously in front of the entrance to the passage grave - are a series of concentric spirals

Spiral-etched stone from Newgrange entrance.

Many theories have been put forward in order to explain these vivid but enigmatic symbols. Some researchers believe that they are astronomical markers with perhaps an agricultural purpose in mind, others pass them off as mere ornamentation. Such theories are in many cases accommodating but nonetheless inadequate.

The structure is orientated so that at dawn on the midwinter solstice, the rising sun shines beyond the doors and into an aperture, small in size but covered in spiral motifs; the result is that a shaft of sunlight penetrates deep into the passage, to the very heart of the chamber.

Inside Newgrange there are large water basins, rather like the baptismal fonts inside churches. In the days when Newgrange was in full use, these would have been filled with water to induce the still and heavy atmosphere mentioned earlier. This is a very damp setting in which water vapour plays a key role. As I have said, smoke, in this circumstance, does some very strange things and it has been noted that deep inside the cairn, it can take on a spiral form, seeming to 'respond' to the frequency of sound.

Jahn, Ibison and Devereux found that the resonant frequencies at Newgrange were well defined, the chamber behaving like an acoustically designed building. When they compared their newly gained data with the chamber's carved decorations, they were intrigued. Such is the accuracy of these carvings regarding the chamber's acoustic value that they even reflect such acoustical niceties as nodes and antinodes – the actual construction of a standing waveform or wave pattern (see illustration below).

One can see the way that a waveform works by using a piece of string. If the string is attached to two fixed ends and plucked, waves are sent along it in both directions. They are reflected at both ends and, as they return along the string, they pass through each other and combine, producing a standing wave.

Example of a standing wave pattern between two walls.

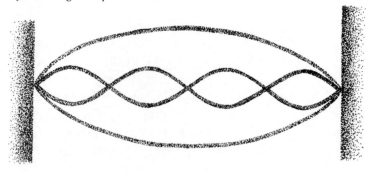

Acoustically speaking, a standing waveform is a wave that is in harmony with the interior, rather like bubbles of vibration within a fixed space. Once a pattern is established, sound reverberates from wall to wall, and as it does so its frequency diminishes by a harmonic with each reverberation. Normally, due to poor acoustic design and an inappropriate volume, sound will dissipate in a building, or the attempt to achieve a standing wave will result in a cacophony of noise. However, in the right conditions, one can easily be formed.

Besides Newgrange, tests were made at Loughcrew, also in Ireland, and at Carn Euny in Cornwall, as well as Chün Quoit (Cornwall) and Wayland's Smithy (Berkshire). The Princeton team's conclusions were dramatic and certain features were clearly established:

1. Despite the substantial small-and large-scale irregularities in the boundary walls of these structures, their resonant frequencies were well defined. After very little practice, the experiments could 'blind-tune' the source frequency to a clearly audible resonance with a reproducibility of +/–1 or 2Hz with little ambiguity.

2. Although many shapes and sizes of cavity were presented, the resonant frequencies of *all* of them lay in the range between 95 and 120Hz (my italics).

3. In all cases, principle antinodes of resonant standing-wave patterns were established at the outer walls, as would be expected theoretically. The number, configuration and relative magnitudes of the other antinodes and nodes leaning back to the source depended on the particular chamber configuration.

4. In some cases, rock art on the chamber walls bore some similarity to the observed standing-wave patterns.[14]

Given that Newgrange, Loughcrew and the other monuments were constructed 5,500 years ago, this is extraordinary stuff, especially the latter point. But the Princeton report goes further:

The Newgrange and Loughcrew sites present extraordinary and well-known examples of diagrammatic rock etchings conventionally regarded as astronomical, seasonal or environmental representations. In several cases, however, the experimenters were also struck by the similarities of certain sketches with the resonant sound patterns characterising these chambers. For example, a number of these sketches feature concentric circles, ellipses or spirals that are not unlike the plan views of the acoustical mappings. In other sketches, sinusoidal or zigzag patterns resemble the alternative nodes and antinodes... Note especially that the two zigzag trains etched on the corbel at the left side of the west subchamber of Newgrange have precisely the same number of 'nodes' and 'antinodes' as the resonant standing-wave pattern we mapped from the chamber centre along the passage... Conceivably, the triple spiral configurations sketched on the magnificent entrance stone and elsewhere could be somewhat more metaphysical representations of the interactive resonances of the three subchambers.[15]

I wondered, how could the Ancients have known about such properties of acoustics and architecture? And why was it important to them to create such places and to mark out acoustic qualities as if to define a building's attributes? These questions sprang to mind as I heard of the Newgrange experiment first hand from Dr Ibison.

I had just finished a public lecture where I had suggested that the various sacred names of the heroes in myth were linked by a common thread and that these names were somehow names of great potency, uttered to powerful intent. Mike Ibison introduced himself and said he felt there was some link between the theme of my lecture and his work.

Although located at Princeton, Mike, as an Englishman, still had a firm foothold in Britain. He was about to immerse himself in the data from the series of experiments described above, in an attempt to make sense of it all. It was a moment of pure synchronicity that he should find himself at my lecture: Since the late 1970s I have been researching the subject of the hero in myth and in the world's oral traditions. What particularly intrigued me were the actual names of the hero and the god he was associated with. In many of the world's great mythic and religious traditions, God has a secret holy name, a name that is ineffable, that is to say it was unspeakable except upon specific days or festivals, and even then it was limited to the high priest, who would utter it under his breath. According to these traditions the name was a name of power, a dangerous thing. I had often wondered if there was more to this than met the eye and from the time of my meeting with Mike Ibison, the acoustic link led me further along the path of enquiry. I proceeded to look at the names, languages and places involved. Were they in some way connected and could it be that the vital clue for which I had been searching was resonance? The time had come for a closer look.

Resonance

One of the most interesting observations made by the team from Princeton was the comparison of Newgrange to some gigantic musical wind instrument.[16] The most significant factor of all of the sites described was that they were constructed with a view to human interaction with the numinous. Newgrange, in acting like a giant flute, was aiding this process, the 62 foot long entrance passage accentuating any sound that entered. In fact, the whole edifice was constructed to a pattern, with everything from the giant stones to the huge water basins placed with a particular purpose in mind.[17] The builders were very careful to maintain a strict acoustical balance, as revealed by the experimental results, and as the interior was constructed with a view to acoustic interactions, it is significant that the whole was built to within the human male voice range, to within 95–110Hz.

It is now necessary to understand more deeply, the concept of resonance and how we as humans interact with it.

All things in the known universe have their resonant frequencies; a resonant frequency is a frequency of vibration that interacts with other frequencies of vibration. If we pluck a guitar string it will be seen to vibrate up and down; one complete cycle, from up to down and up again, gives us a wavelength. Should the guitar string move up and down ten times a second its cycle is described as 10Hz, if 100 times a second then 100Hz, and so on. There are billions of different wavelengths in the known universe, from billions or even trillions of cycles a second down to sub-Hertzian wavelengths. Thus it is that every chemical element, every crystal and every living thing has a signatory vibration, its individual wavelength.

On a quantum level, the structure of a wave pattern is seen not as a movement by an actual physical wave, like the rushing sea for instance, but as the passage of energy through a series of individual oscillating (vibrating) particles, moving at a fixed point. What is being described is called 'kinetic energy' (from the Greek *kineein*, 'to move'). The same effect is better demonstrated using a line, of pool or snooker balls. When the cue-ball hits one end, its *energy is transferred* down the line with the result that it is the last ball, at the other end of the line, that is ejected (hopefully into the pocket!)

Sinusoidal waves (all of the acoustic waves, propogated and studied during the Princeton University survey at Newgrange were of sinusoidal form) are waves that oscillate regularly at a fixed frequency. It is in this way that radio waves are transferred via radio antenna in a form known as longitudinal waves.

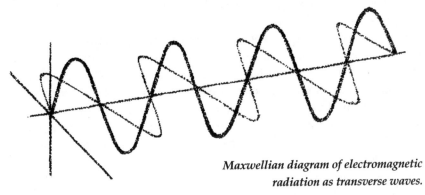

Maxwellian diagram of electromagnetic radiation as transverse waves.

These are waves that we as humans sense as sound. Sound waves occur within a limited frequency band – fixed, of course, by the human inability to hear above or below a certain measure. Transverse waves are of the sort found in water. They are transverse because individual particles move perpendicular to the direction of travel, in other words left and right, whilst the direction is ahead. All electromagnetic energy travels in this way (see illustration) and it is in this form that they can be seen to give off fields that are themselves resonant as well as being the result of other resonating waves, a sort of harmony meets harmony to create yet more harmony. Waves can be reflected when they meet an obstacle, such as a wall; upon reflection they will follow the original path they came in from, thus incoming waves will meet outgoing waves creating a standing-wave pattern, hence the illusion of one's voice being 'thrown' (echoing), in certain types of landscape.

> Resonating frequencies are primary physical bonds in nature.
> For every frequency or frequency bond, there exists natural or
> created resonators. In other words, a field's frequency pattern at
> a given time is a resonating structure that determines the energy
> it will absorb or by which it will be affected[18]

Basically, it can be seen that resonance is implicit in the nature of matter. Indeed, recent research and experimental data have shown that all matter may be nothing other than an interlocking pattern of standing waveforms[19]

Described in the *Oxford English Dictionary* as 'sympathetic vibration', resonance may be seen as the reinforcement or prolongation of sound by reflection, 'as from the walls of a hollow space'. An example of sympathetic vibration can be seen in the phenomenon of tuning forks singing to each other – if one tuning fork calibrated to 440 cycles a second is sounded anywhere near another fork with the same frequency, the second will begin to vibrate in sympathy with the first; without touching, energy has been transferred from one to the other.

In precisely the same way, a cosmic event, for example a supernova (the explosion of a giant star), sets off a string of vibrations, electromagnetic waves, that travel across space and upon striking the earth set up a sympathetic vibration within her that of her natural frequency. This frequency will be a harmonic of the original incoming frequency. In music these harmonics are often called 'undertones' or 'overtones' and they are in proportion to the original incoming frequency of vibration. These harmonics may be multiples of the basic frequency or divisions, for instance a frequency of 32Hz will respond to an incoming frequency of 16Hz, and so on. In this sense harmonics can be seen as colours on a paint chart – there is the primary colour and, surrounding it, the various tones, lighter and darker, of the basic colour scheme.

Perhaps the best demonstration of the sheer power of low-frequency resonance comes from an experiment performed by Professor Gavraud, an engineer from Marseilles, France. Fascinated by the phenomenon of low-frequency vibration, Gavraud set out to construct a machine that could produce infrasound. Infrasound is sound that occurs below the normal limits of human hearing. Gavraud took as his model the pea-whistle used by all French policemen of the time. He found that the pea in the whistle helped to produce a wide range of low-frequency sounds, infrasounds; it was all a matter of building a larger whistle, one exactly six feet in length and powered by compressed air. What happened next is the stuff of modern horror movies: a technician was instructed to give the whistle its first trial blast and upon doing so he collapsed dead on the spot. A post-mortem examinationfollowed and revealed that the cause of the unfortunate man's death was resonance; it had very effectively turned all of his internal organs into jelly. Death was instantaneous. Undeterred, Gavraud has since developed machines that can aim low-frequency sound waves sufficient to demolish entire buildings.

As we have noted, everything in the universe resonates; for every frequency of vibration there is something that vibrates in sympathy with it. So, to call something specific 'a resonator' is perhaps misleading, however, some things connect to our frequency ranges more than others, and so, literally, to us they are more resonant. This sympathetic connection can bring attention to very subtle phenomena. We sometimes call this 'the supernatural'.

'Life may respond to these stimuli directly, but more often it reacts by resonating in sympathy with part of its immediate environment… A very weak electrical or magnetic field becomes noticeable because it resonates on the same frequency as the life field of the organism reacting to it… The supernatural becomes part of natural history.'[20]

Organisms, then, can become aware of very subtle fields through a process of sympathetic resonance. We humans are used to sensing life's rhythmic vibrations through smell, taste, touch, sight and sound. However, not only do each of these senses pick up wide bands of vibrations, but they can also interact across their distinctive boundaries. Certain sensitives, often indigenous peoples, particularly Australian Aborigines, have the ability to 'smell' colour, 'see' sound and 'hear' sight. This indicates that the human body is a good versatile resonator with excellent potential for sensory refinement and adaptation.

The Soviet Academy of Sciences has researched these realms of subtlety. Dermochromatics is a prime example – the ability to feel the different vibrations of light known to us as colour. Colours absorb and refract different levels of electromagnetic energy; the sensation of colour is the different oscillatory reactions of matter (atoms) to incoming frequencies of energy. The more sympathetic the frequency, the more sympathetic the reaction. Different colours have different levels of energy refraction; for example, black totally absorbs and white reflects. Dermochromatics is the sensory ability to observe the energy refraction of different colours by touch, thus realising what those colours are. Thus red burns, yellow is warm, blue is cold and so on (exactly the way an artist uses the palette). Sensing colour in this way is achieved by the use of the fingertips. In a further, striking example of sensorial refinement, certain students, completely blind, could read newspapers and books in prodigious feats of eyeless vision![21]

Earlier, I mentioned that some sensitives have the ability to 'see' sound. Now, in the West, recent research has shown that young children also have the ability to see sound as colour and visa versa.[22] According to the *Oxford Companion to Music*, sound is not a 'thing', it is a sensation that occurs as a series of vibrations that cause a tingling of the ear. Sound is created in the brain as a result of the movement of air pressure as it enters the ear. We are then able to attune ourselves to various rhythms within sound. These rhythms act upon the brain as stimuli, causing it to adjust frequency, just as a radio might be attuned to specific wavebands. Along the same lines certain 'complementary' healthcare systems encourage patients with heart defects to stroke cats. The idea is that the cat's purr has the ability to induce Alpha states in the brain, thus relaxing the patient. A further example is the ability of some musical works to pacify overactive states of mind. In an effort to calm a class of unruly children in 1998, a schoolteacher in Wales[23] introduced them to tape-recorded music of Mozart. The effect was, in her own words, 'awesome'. Not only did the music calm their minds, it improved their learning ability. Physiologically, music has the property of working on the brain's limbic system, thus soothing endorphins are released into the blood. Music triggers memories, all sorts of them, and this also helps to release endorphins. Literally, in response to rhythmic vibration, the brain changes its frequency.

Anecdotal evidence of altered states whilst making or listening to music is rife. Many elements may come into play in creating these experiences, but my own enquiries indicate that certain types of music in certain types of building produce more consistent results than others, the effects upon choir members singing Plainsong chant in Gothic cathedrals being particularly notable. And then there is the accompanying aspect of good health, highlighted in the interesting case of the monks of a Benedictine monastery in France who had abandoned chant altogether. Soon the monks could not operate on their customary three to four hours sleep per night. Now, however long they slept, they remained tired. Meat was introduced to their meals in case the vegetarian diet was at fault (after a tradition of 700 years, this was unlikely). Eventually, Dr. Alfred Tomatis was called in to help solve the problem. Upon examination, he found that many monks were not only tired but their hearing had also suffered. Taking steps to improve their hearing, he also suggested that chant be reinstated at the monastery. This was done, and within a few months the majority of monks were healthy again on the short sleep, frugal diet and hard physical work routine. Dr. Tomatis believes that, through the ear, sound can stimulate brain activity through charging the cerebral cortex with electrical potential.[24,25]

It seemed to me that if the quality of the sound was important, then the acoustics of the space the sound was made in would also be very important. This would make a great deal of sense regarding theNewgrange research; in the world of music, acoustics are all too important to leave out of the equation. This realisation helped me to understand just what the ancient worshippers were up to in their sacred buildings: transformation! I became convinced that they used specifically chosen sounds – words of power, at specifically sited and designed locations - places of power, to attain at-one-ment – states of power! My work was evolving. I was now researching an ancient, sacred technology.

Coils and Transformers

The human organism resonates and in doing so it interacts subtly with the phenomenal world about it. Within that same human organism the many parts which make up the whole are also resonating, with the result that together they can form a harmonious whole. A radio, in order to receive a signal, contains a tuned coil that resonates to the various signals that come through it. These vibrations are then processed by other electronic components, resulting in sound being transmitted from the speaker. In their 1990 book *Science of the Gods*, David Ash and Peter Hewitt make the important analogy of the DNA coil to the coil in a radio.[26] Since the discovery of its double helical form by Crick and Watson, not much attention has been paid to its actual shape, only to its component parts. As Ash and Hewitt point out, the DNA molecule, 'acting as a resonant coil, could receive vibrations from a field of super energy, in this way DNA could bridge the gap between the super-physical world and our own'.[27]

Within our own finely-tuned bodies the fact that DNA might act as a resonator makes sense in that, in line with the rest of the body, DNA is largely crystalline in nature and is to be found everywhere in the make up of our life, whether in the blood, hair or individual skin cells. As a resonator, it would also be responding to other vibrant influences within the body:

> Each organ system or subsystem gives off a specific measurable electromagnetic field. The E.M.Fs are measurable, subtle, vibratory fields that can have a great effect upon the behaviour of an organism.[28]

It is electromagnetism that stimulates the very process of life in all its various forms. The work of Dr. Michael Shallis has shown how sensitive the human being really is to the surrounding fields. Shallis' work has shown that we are naturally inclined to orient ourselves along the north-south axis in line with the earth's magnetic field. It has even been suggested that by orienting ourselves conversely to the Earth's field, we might compromise the information system and circuitry that is the human body.[29] Much of this circuitry is of course in the brain. Brain cells too, act like the coils in radios and in response to a small incoming magnetic field produce small amounts of electricity. Of additional interest is their own source of magnetism: brain cells contain microscopic particles of magnetite (naturally occurring magnetic iron oxide). In 1983 Dr. Robin Baker, a reader in zoology at Manchester University, located another human magnetic source within the ethmoid bone, which is located close to the pituitary and pineal glands in the brain. Although modern science is not certain of their role in the functioning of the body, these glands are traditionally associated with psychic activity and transcendental experience.

The Vibrating Brain

Clearly, resonance plays a hugely significant part in the everyday process of life and what we perceive as material reality. As incoming waves of electromagnetism encounter our planet, a sympathetic vibration is set up – earth resonance, to which life on earth also resonates. This 'life-resonance' is an effect of vibrational pressure upon the crystalline make up of life and of matter in general. As it resonates, this energy radiates outwards, causing living things to have subtle interaction with other living things and with the environment at large.[30] It is significant that the human head, our communication centre, is surrounded by a measurable electromagnetic field – one much stronger than the field around the rest of the body. It is here that the subject of humans and lifeforms in general having auras comes into its own and I find it intriguing that, just as a computer's memory is stored in the electrical field of its crystal-based technology, to be read on command, so psychics say that they can read 'memories', records of interactions, from the aura surrounding an individual's crystal-based body. To do this, the psychic must be in a relaxed but alert state, a state that science associates with Alpha rhythms, brainwave activity at 7 to 13Hz.

We have already seen that there is a relationship between earth resonance and Alpha rhythms of the brain. This relationship can be tested by denying an individual the requisite rhythm. ELF waves directly connect man to earth and to his environment, and once he is removed from that environment he is being excluded from the embrace of the earth's electromagnetic fields. Within man it is the temporal lobe section of the brain that is acutely sensitive to these fields. Deep inside the temporal lobe is the hippocampus, which is associated with memory and dreaming. Stimulation of the same, via tiny currents of electricity, can induce various altered perceptions including distortion of time and space, the appearance of apparitions and various effects upon the ability of hearing. The key frequencies of Schumann Resonance are altered. ELFs are thus intimately associated with key areas of the brain. As mentioned earlier, neural stimulation within the hippocampus connects to Earth frequencies at around 10Hz.[31] Furthermore, as Michael Persinger suggests, the amygdala, which is allied to the hippocampus (in that it is associated with emotional experiences), may use the earth's ELF channel and interact via the temporal lobe area of the brain. It is here that we enter into a broad range of paranormal experiences and out-of-body sensations, such phenomena lead some to believe that our physical bodies may be used as channels for ever higher degrees of conscious experience.[32]

Though often derided, this view is borne out by a recent discovery by geneticists called the 'God spot'. What is being suggested by scientists at the University of California in San Diego is that a particular region of the brain is associated with religious and mystical experiences. Crucially, this region is:

> ...particularly active in people who suffer from Temporal Lobe epilepsy, sufferers of which are often deeply religious and subject to transcendental experiences. The theory is that epileptic seizures strengthen the formation of neural connections between the region known as the Inferior Temporal Cortex and the region devoted to emotion – the Amygdala.[33]

However, in contrast to epilepsy, there is plenty of evidence that religious belief is linked with improved health, happiness and a longer life.[34] Certainly, religious or not, within many there is a passionate yearning to experience the unknown and to be more aware of the subtle, ongoing, everyday experiences that most of us, quite simply, have neither the time nor the sensitivity to notice. Often, when wishing to experience more sensitivity, to be inspired, or to enhance or change atmospheres, we humans take recourse to music.

Music is not an irregular mass of different wavelengths, it is a collection of tones with measured intervals between them, for sound, when mathematically proportionate, is harmonious. This is pleasing to the ear, it appeals to our innate sense of rhythm, it is interactive, and thus it inspires; the muse is upon us. We know how music can change our mood and uplift us, and that harmonious sounds have been used for spiritual purposes from time immemorial. The Newgrange experiments had shown me that to the Ancients, these things went beyond mere harmonious sound and into a practical knowledge of acoustics, architecture and EMFs.

Components of an Ancient Technology

According to mythology, various religious teachings and the evidence of archaeology, the temple is the meeting-place of the human and the heavenly. The temple is a place wherein the devotee may encounter their god or goddess. But, in order to interact, to commune, one's mind must open up beyond the daily material environment to the wider influences of the cosmos. Sacred structures were built with this very purpose in mind. We have already seen how the atmospheric and acoustic pattern of the interior of Newgrange reflects, with uncanny accuracy, the spiral representations carved into the walls inside and outside the cairn. These Neolithic artists seem to be saying, 'We were here, and to great purpose.'

The Ancients, by a process of ritual chant attuned to the resonant frequency of the interior chamber, plugged their brains into a sort of 'harmonic overdrive'. This produced an altered state, wherein awareness and, consequently, psychic activity were greatly enhanced. Following on from my musings upon acoustics and a possible spiritual technology, I now began to realise a deeper relationship between the brain's mind-expanding Alpha rhythms at 7 to 13Hz and the complementary ionosphere-centred earth resonance of 7 to 10Hz. The physical position of the ionosphere is in itself the natural link between the cosmos and the earth. Here, in this spacious and refined realm, the gifts of the heavens, those 'messengers of the gods', the cosmic and, particularly, the dominant solar rays pour in to feed our world with power and light. I contend that, by virtue of this sympathetic resonance, literally, through frequency, associated with the sky and the incoming rays, the practitioner of rites was brought to the gates of heaven.

Further evidence came to me regarding sacred sites and psychic activity. At the height of the Cold War, scientists on both sides of the Iron Curtain were involved in a programme of experimentation today called 'remote viewing'. Although it is now well known that the CIA was involved in its own series of investigations, the Russians have been a lot more forthcoming with information. Towards the end of the 1980s a Soviet scientist performed a multitude of experiments at various Neolithic sites throughout Europe. Much to his astonishment, he came to realise that telepathy can be enhanced many thousands of times at these sites.[35] The choosing of the sites and the design and the building of those ancient structures must have been based upon a profound knowledge and diverse traditional lore tells us that, worldwide, this knowledge was indeed resonance-based.

> In both Mexico and Peru there is a legend which tells that the ancient peoples were scientists of "sound", with which skill they had no need of technological impedimenta. They could split massive stone slabs along precise harmonic lines with sound alone, and then "resonate" them into position. Thus the vast and precisely laid temples of Uxmal and Machu Picchu were raised and patterned – according to this legend - in symphonies of sound. Their religion recognised each individual as having a particular note and pitch. With the "sound knowledge" a man could be "purified" and raised by vibrationary mantras or

conversely, slain by a single note. An echo of this is found in the "kiai" of the samurai warriors in mediaeval Japan. The biologist Dr Lyall Watson suggests that when uttered at the correct pitch the "kiai ... produces partial paralysis by a reaction that suddenly lowers the arterial blood pressure".[36]

In northern India, Thailand and Tibet there is a tradition, just as insistent as in South America, wherein it is said that the largest of the monuments were raised by means of sound. Unfortunately, myth, no matter how stubborn, remains unsubstantiated. However, investigation of its constituent parts does reveal that 'sound technology' is a distinct possibility.

Certain shapes and forms have the ability to reflect and radiate energy in different ways, for example, crystal structure varies, as does crystalline resonance. Some crystal forms radiate electromagnetic energy at different levels from others. A prism, for example, has the property of splitting light into its separate wavelengths of colour – the spectrum. Other crystals can focus light, some being more effective than others; the lens is a good example. On a microcosmic scale, different elements exude different properties by virtue of their atomic make up. Water doesn't become water until its molecular structure is correct. If it has only five molecules or fewer it acts as a film rather than a liquid. With six molecules it suddenly acts in three dimensions instead of two. Also, many radioactive elements such as chromium have isotopes with variations in the number of neutrons. I pondered upon these building blocks of nature, upon how certain numbers and configurations create particular effects. I wondered why not certain numbers and configurations of objects, buildings or blocks, as at Stonehenge and Avebury, for example?

What would be at work is a concept first raised by Herbert Weaver in *Divining the Primary Sense* [37] and since expanded upon by others.[38] He suggests that by virtue of their form and location, all buildings, sacred or otherwise, give out a specific type of energy. Weaver categorises this energy into three different types: Signalling (radiating energy), Suppressing (non-radiating) and Suppressing Locally (within observable boundaries). Indeed, if sacred sites such as temples and cathedrals can resonate internally, then this does not preclude the idea that they resonate externally. This is the basic philosophy behind the Chinese practice of Feng Shui – the balancing of two opposing forms or principles of energy radiation, Feng Shui meaning literally 'wind and water', and the tenet being to bring about harmony between opposites. Rectangles and squares were seen as radiating energy and therefore as bright signals, whereas six-pointed stars, pentagrams and cruciforms were seen as widely suppressing energy. Weaver found that configurations of monuments and sacred sites had specific effects too. In an observation that lends credence to the idea of ley lines, Weaver noted that when configurations of sites were joined by a straight line, energy radiation was confined to *within* those sites. Perhaps the most startling confirmation of this observation comes from such sites as the Castlerigg stone circle in Cumbria, and the Rollright Stones in Oxfordshire, both of which are on straight line configurations and which have remarkably different energy levels inside and outside the circles. Readings of electromagnetic energy suddenly go off the scale when the circles are entered.[39]

Purposeful Power

At the outset there is one thing that distinguishes the sacred site from any other site: sheer power. These sites are made distinct by the presence of ELFs and electromagnetic fields. Significantly, the presence of specific types of architecture at these sites suggests an awareness of these forces and of their manipulation. Pyramidal structures and domed structures, such as those at Newgrange and a host of other locations, hermetically seal off a space, not just aurally and visually, but also electromagnetically[40] – the power of place was confined to within strict boundaries. Furthermore, a majority of sites have focal points. In the majority of religious beliefs, focus is stressed, both physical and spiritual. The physical point of focus is usually the altar on which the sacrament is given. It is a point of concentration at which prayers are offered. In the same ways that energies are focused, concentration of mind is too.

As highlighted by Russian research, absence of interference at sacred places makes the process of thought transference many times more efficient. There, results can be quite dramatic; with the 'airwaves' unsullied, man's link to the gods is more direct. The wearing of special costumes and decoration by indigenous peoples can also be understood in this context. Bone, feathers, horn and hair can produce their own electrical fields, thus Indian headdresses really did have a technological purpose:

> The structure of tents, wigwams and hogans provided the American Indians with protection and suppression when needed. The horns and antlers worn by the warriors also provided protective force fields which prevented chemical emissions from attracting distant foes. Not only were animals and enemies blocked but it was possible to protect individuals from the influence of the gods.[41]

The stronger energies, though, electromagnetism in particular, stem from the actual site. Measurements of radon gas emissions have a tendency to be greatly increased at these locations. This is primarily because of a geological condition known as 'faulting'. Fault lines are fractures deep within the earth's crust and are areas of tectonic or seismic activity. At such places there is a greater amount of mineral encrustation than normal. Minerals, of course, have varying magnetic and electrical properties and, as Paul Devereux points out, 'different minerals have different densities, so the value of gravity can change at such places'.[42] The electrical properties of areas also attract electric currents such as lightning. In simple geological terms these are very special places. Creatures have the ability to recognise these powerful places – animals are acutely sensitive to fluctuations in electromagnetic fields – and, living more 'at one' with nature, ancient man was too. Having recognised the spots, it was all a matter of enhancing the effect.

Besides being located near to geological faulting, the sacredness of a place was marked out by other factors. Some gods were even believed to inhabit individual stones. These stones were often labelled 'omphalos' stones (meaning 'navel' stones). They demarcated a certain area as the 'world centres' – to the Ancients, a god-meets-man interaction point. Although not a specific requirement, these places are almost always linked to sources of water, sacred springs and wells. It was at such places that oracular priests and priestesses communed with the resident deity. Interestingly, stones can 'speak' – they can give off varying signals. A curious confirmation of this is, again, a particular stone within the Rollright Circle in Oxfordshire. This stone was found to emit a signal of 37Hz - but only at a certain time of the year.[43] Signals from stones elsewhere have also been picked up on sensitive equipment. These signals can measure a few feet across and be a few feet above ground level. Beyond this, some stones have even been found to exude strange haloes, affecting photographs that have been taken of them. Certainly, these are fascinating phenomena, giving some credence to traditional lore that the monuments concerned were entrances to the mythic realms, the domain of the gods and their powers.

Quite who these gods were is to be discussed later, however, what is important to realise is that their sacred status drew upon more than just earth energies. Astronomers have discovered that many megalithic burial mounds and stone circles are either astronomically aligned or have astronomical significance. Aside from being aligned north–south and east–west, Newgrange, Stonehenge, Knowth and other monuments built around 3500 BC are very accurate measures of solar and lunar movements. As we have seen at the winter solstice (21st December), a beam of sunlight penetrates the inner sanctum of Newgrange, illuminating it to wonderful effect. The combination of all of these details reveals to us a unique sense of cosmology, a cosmology that was geared ultimately to mind-state enhancement. By tapping into an array of specific energies that were made all the more numinous by the quality of the site, the style of building and the time of year, devotees resonated and attuned their consciousness to what they considered the divine.

Divinity was believed to reside in these places, but were the energies we have described, the local electromagnetic fields and radon emissions, the actual gods concerned, or does the answer lie deeper than that? I have expressed my realisation that earth resonance could be used as a 'gate' to the heavens, but I was left to wonder why 'the gods'? Surely, a frequency is a frequency, the ionosphere is the ionosphere. Why did the Ancients make everything so personal? It was around this time that I found myself again at Newgrange.

There is something powerful about Newgrange, something that draws you in. I have been there many times during the course of this research. On this visit, as usual, I found myself walking the site and musing upon the mystery of the place when I was stopped in my tracks by a rapid sequence of thoughts – thoughts that excited me. If the earth was seen as a living, breathing, sentient being, why not the rest of the cosmos? After all, mythology never suggests that Mother Earth is alone in the cosmos. Therefore, could it be that we inhabit a conscious universe? Full of *conscious* frequencies? That this was the tenet of ancient man's thinking, I was certain: consciousness fills all of space!

Superscience, Suprasense

As well as gateways to the heavens, in the world's mythologies sacred sites are often said to be gateways into the underworld. The underworld means the substratum, the subtle realm which pervades all and, in doing so, links the heavenly and earthly worlds. One well-known journey to the underworld is that of Hercules. who goes there in order to capture and bring to earth Cerberus, the Hound of Hell. Hercules enters into the underworld via an oracular cave, an abode guarded by various forbidding priestesses. Mythology gives countless examples of the same kind of journey, but all of them are linked by the location of the gateway. Be it a temple, cairn, cave or grotto, it is always a location chosen for its sacred properties.

A key to this gateway is hidden within language itself. The word 'entrance' is also 'en-trance'. It comes from the Latin *transire* meaning 'to pass over'. The entry into this trance was, in all likelihood, induced by ritual chanting, as in 'en-chant-ment', meditation or the controlled use of drugs. In many regions of the world these factors still play a vital part in religious tradition and belief; they are associated with altered states, usually induced at sacred sites.

> The temple might be held to have a relationship with the powers
> of the underworld. Libations were poured to them, possibly
> down actual drainpipes. Hence, the temple was the binding post
> of the underworld. The numen (presiding deity) extended into
> the depths like an unseen pillar. It was a vertical bond.[44]

The siting, the shape and the materials used in the creation of holy buildings were a key part of the technology of the sacred. Temples were purposefully built to enhance the state of mind by carefully nurturing its sensitivity to the resonant electromagnetic universe.

As we know, everything in the universe is resonant, for the universe is made up of frequencies of rhythmic vibration; all things both radiate and absorb, transmit and receive energy in this fashion, and it is recognised that energy and information are one and the same. Thus it is conceivable that, with the correct knowledge, anything and everything can be consciously 'tuned into'. I have suggested that by linking with the earth's resonance, mankind was tapping into a wider universal resonance after all, earth's own resonant rhythmic vibrations are largely a response to incoming waves of cosmic energy. Rhythmic vibration, as any radio or software specialist will admit, is the most efficient way to transfer information. As the universe is made up almost entirely of various frequencies of rhythmic vibration, i.e. information transfer systems, the prospect is raised that we may be inhabiting what theorists call a 'mind-state universe', for what is information without mind? A mind-state universe makes the mind far more than just an offshoot of the brain. In *The Doors of Perception*, Aldous Huxley quotes the philosopher C. D. Broad:

> Each person is at each moment capable of remembering all that
> has ever happened to him and of perceiving everything that is
> happening everywhere in the universe.

In the view of Huxley, consciousness extends beyond human boundaries to the universe at large. 'The brain', in his words, 'does not produce mind, it reduces it' and into manageable portions. Dr. Keith Hearne has made the significant point that:

> There is no doubt that a mind-state universe is capable of
> accepting all the peculiar phenomena studied by
> parapsychologists, not to mention all the inexplicable phenomena
> and beliefs of the various religions. We should start to theorise
> more along the line that we share an existence in a mind universe.
> It need not be an unprovable assertion...[45]

If the mind-state universe could be proved, attitudes would change and the ideas of religion could gain renewed currency, underpinned by the knowledge that there is consciousness beyond death, even beyond all things. Research has led Antonio Damasio of the University of Iowa to break the human self into three elements; the 'proto self', 'core self' and 'autobiographical self'.[46] His description of the 'core self' or 'core consciousness' as a sort of pure awareness, uncomplicated by any autobiographical knowledge interests me, for such a description fits well with the Buddhist's Nirvana, the Hindu's Silent Brahman, the Chinese Tao and the Impersonal Transcendent of the Western mystics.

Despite recent researches and scriptural reference to an all-permeating transcendental consciousness, we are still held in the overriding scientific paradigm that there is little connection between separate phenomena. I am, of course, generalising, but the 'separate' view of science in the observation of 'life, the universe and everything' presents very much an 'it' and 'us' situation. By contrast, we know from studies of archaeology and the evidence of history that ancient man believed in a 'connected' universe wherein 'separateness' only went as far as identity. Indeed, we perceive solid objects as separate items. In this way, all things are unique, everything has its individual identity. But ultimately, on a quantum level, it is all frequency, with the frequencies giving rise to the difference. In 'reality', we perceive that difference, but in this act we have our own involvement. It is an interactive moment, we relate on a subjective, personal level, we are in the process of inviting, receiving, filtering and interpreting information. The study of language confirms that earlier civilisations recognised this. The words 'objective' and 'subjective' describe the sense in which we see things. Both are derived from the Latin, *jacere*, 'to throw'; we are throwing out a line in the hope of retrieving something. To make sense of the world we throw out signals and gather them in again and again.

This gathering in means that we put our preprogrammed self into the equation, not least of which is the way in which our sensory equipment tends to work. Matter, according to physical law, is illusory; it is over 99.9 per cent space where millions of atoms race around each other at phenomenal speeds to give the appearance of a solid. This limited appearance is what is registered by the eye, which itself makes many thousands of muscular movements per second in order to record the illusion. It is possible then, in keeping with the ancient tenets, that consciousness may not only fill the space within all things but also the space between all things, as a field of potential from which the illusion arises. Paul Devereux's personal viewpoint is one that I share:

> ...consciousness itself does not have a skull-centred source. It is
> processed rather than produced by the brain, and it is that

processing which gives us our unique human dimension of consciousness. Consciousness could be a potential field, non-physical in itself, that manifests at different levels...In such a view, consciousness is not restricted to the human brain, but can occur in all matter. It may seem bizarre to think of a rock as possessing consciousness, but even a rock is not solid or inert. All matter dissolves into energy fields, which dissolve into the more fundamental and mysterious quantum fields.[47]

Here, consciousness is non-physical in itself, manifesting at different levels, that is, at different frequencies of vibration or resonances. In other words, one shared consciousness is given apparent individuality through a hierarchy of frequencies. could this be the reason why man, apparently individual and of solid body, shares the same resonance as the earth? Teilhard de Chardin thought so. He believed that as the planet evolved and bore life, it passed on a little of its consciousness into its biosphere. He was of the opinion that the whole universe vibrated, even though 'things' retained definition. Teilhard came to believe that the earth was imbued with, and surrounded by, an evolving terrestrial field of consciousness, and that consciousness was a vital component in the phenomenon of nature and of the universe, that probably the universe was conscious, but also that it was living. In this light, consciousness is an act of the ultimate creative imagination, the mind of God, God being the origin and sum total of consciousness. Is the universe a consciousness, made manifest by an enigmatic, vibrating thing that we call energy?

Stardust Memories

Whilst the purpose of this chapter is to move my findings forward rather than be a compendium of theory, it might serve some purpose here to illustrate how science's latest understandings of the nature of the universe give us clues as to how 'perceiving everything that is happening everywhere in the universe' – to reiterate Huxley - might be facilitated.

Because this universal consciousness would not be an object, it is unlikely that modern science could prove its existence by objective criteria. The current impression given to us by science is that the universe was created in chaos and that ever since, it has, by the process of physical law, been sorting itself out. However, as the physicist David Bohm pointed out in 1980 in *Wholeness and the Implicate Order*, space, rather than being chaotic, does have an underlying order, an order that has, from the very outset of creation, guided physical law. Space, according to Bohm, is not a vacuum, but its very opposite, a plenum, and it is full of something called 'zero-point energy', energy that exists in space even at temperatures of absolute zero (-373 C). Zero–point energy will be discussed much later, but its most familiar description to the layman is *ex-nihilo* – something out of nothing. This is also a fair description of consciousness and the finest levels of creation – something that, however inexplicable, seems to come from nowhere.

Bohm made further postulations. Until fairly recently, the swiftest movement was thought to be the speed of light. However, there is a phenomenon that does suggest that somehow light's great speed can be exceeded. The example is very simple: two photons flying apart at the speed of light will each make exactly the same movement or change in direction if one or the other is shifted. This orderly information transfer is instantaneous, even should the two particles be many hundreds of billions of miles apart! I have heard that Einstein called this spooky action at a distance! Its discovery led Bohm to the idea that we just might inhabit a holographic universe, a hologram that arises from out of an underlying and ordered reality. From out of this underlying order may come all of the information, all of the manifestations that are known to our consciousness. Furthermore, the holographic model gives us an example as to how, as Huxley and Broad suggested, all of the information in the universe may be available to us – if we can only tune in to it!

In this light, I would suggest that our normal mode of consciousness is like a partial hologram, one that can only view certain frequencies unless an effort is made to perceive more. We seem to be like television sets, perpetually tuned into one mundane programme, whilst an infinite number of other interesting transmissions are available, but not yet tuned in to. These latter suggestions, which may help to explain the mystery behind the spiritual technology which I shall continue to unveil in these pages, are based upon theoretical sides of science. However, there is a more tangible and easily understood energy that links us to all of life.

Whilst engaged upon research for the present work, I recalled a well-known but nonetheless astonishing fact – that we are made of stardust. The likely process can be briefly summed up as follows. Billions of years ago a massive star exploded in an event called a supernova, sending shock waves and stellar matter out over a wide expanse of space. Eventually, some of this matter was reconstituted in a vast cloud of dust that became the primordial solar system. Shock waves from other novae ignited the core of this dust cloud, giving rise to a star, our sun, whilst other clumps of dust and matter accreted to become the planets and, upon the earth, life itself. Everything in the universe is recycled, and man, in this context, is recycled stellar matter. Every particle that constitutes our physical selves was once fuel that could be found deep in the heart of a star. Man is laden with stardust memories, he is made of the stuff of the very gods themselves and perhaps we still share a little of their resonance.

The Measure of Communion

That man has, in the past, used the sacred site as a place of communion with God or the gods is now beyond doubt. Mythology and archaeological evidence tell us so. Furthermore, the evidence points to the act of communion as being related to an altered state of mind. I find it interesting that the ancient 'altar' was sited on what we now find to be the spot whose radiations were most likely to 'alter' our brainwave patterns; did this word association begin as a subtle pun long ago?

I have always felt drawn to sacred sites and like a majority of others whom I have spoken to, I feel that the best time to visit any of these places is at sunrise or sunset. There is something contemplative about watching the sun, in the last act of the day, setting over the quiet enigma of a holy place. For me, it is a time of reverence, but beyond that, it is almost as if, somehow, fearful of darkness, I wish to soak up the last of the sun's enriching light. Sunsets are very particular, very special times of the day, as is the dawn, though I have to admit that, regretfully, I am hardly ever around to see it.

There is a physical phenomenon that goes some way to explaining my sunset state of mind. In 1938 the Japanese physician Maki Takata developed a test known as the 'Takaton reaction'. It was a test for albumin (the coagulating part of blood) in blood serum. Albumin has a propensity to curdle into small lumps, This process is known as flocculation. In men it is consistent but not in women. However, in January 1938, researchers began to notice that the flocculation indices of both men and women were rising. Detailed analysis showed that the primary agent of influence was the sun. Whilst being very low at night, the index showed a sudden rise at dawn and, what is more, the changing index for both women and men precisely coincided with the appearance of sunspots; 1937 had been a vintage year for sunspots. Clearly, such solar activity has a hidden and yet significant effect on the physiology.

Some scriptures indicate that the Ancients saw a relationship between the sun and consciousness. Vedic texts tell us that the conscious, all-pervasive, reality known as Perusha, '...identified with the Sun, is the Self of all beings, mobile and immobile'.[48] Significantly, a majority of ancient sacred buildings are geared towards specific sun-related times of the year – the solstices and the equinoxes. The solstices mark out the longest day in summer (21st June) and the longest night in winter (21st December), whereas the equinoxes are the only days of the year when daylight is of equal length to darkness. Many sites, Stonehenge for example, have a particular stone that marks out the rising sun of a solstice. Such a stone casts a long shadow, often deep into the interior of the monument. Stonehenge is, of course, both a solar and a lunar calendar of considerable accuracy.[49] Another example is the temple of Luxor in Egypt, where the central axis of the monument is oriented to the midsummer sun. However, on a daily level, it was the rising and setting sun that was of equal, if not more, importance at the same site.[50] The specifics of these sites are telling us one thing: that to ancient man, geometry was all-encompassing, all-important; that it linked heaven and Earth, but that the ultimate link was man himself in his use of these places, places wherein he applied a deep and resonant spiritual technology in order to unlock his stardust memories.

It is interesting that when the sun rises and sets there is much less incoming ionic radiation and earth resonance stabilises at 8Hz. Perhaps the Ancients knew this and felt that this period of equilibrium was advantageous. Since the earliest of times, sunrise and sunset have been particularly designated for prayer, chant and meditation. With hardly an exception to be found worldwide in any era, the most sacred rituals of the day have always been celebrated at these times. These rituals are to be found in the vast corpus of the world's mythology and the great body of sacred literature scattered about the world's religions. We know that the word 'religion' is derived from the Latin *religio* meaning 'to bind back'. If we are 'binding back' every time we sing a hymn or give praise to the Lord, are we, in reality, seeking to resonate with creation, perhaps linking with the universal hologram or communing with the stardust of which we are made?

As previously noted, in Newgrange's interior, smoke, when influenced by a sound frequency appropriate to the building, takes particular shapes and forms (see illustration). This is an ample demonstration that form is a function of frequency, of rhythmic vibration, and the fact that these forms can be seen carved into the interior and exterior of the monument shows that the Neolithic builders were well aware of this. Further demonstrations of the relationship between sound and form have been undertaken in laboratory conditions with sound equipment and smoke chambers. These are revealing. As a simple example, when the sound for the letter 'o' is spoken into the microphone, it is precisely an 'o' that is formed within the smoke!.[51] As the Neolithic researchers sat in their 'smoke chambers' and used their sound equipment (the voice), it is unlikely that such examples would pass them by.

This brings us to language. Indeed, the most common and important use of vibration for mankind is as the sounds and rhythms which make up formal language. Language, even modern language, comes from most ancient roots. Mundane as daily language seems, it is from this point that we embark upon an adventure into a different world, one of profundity, a world wherein language becomes the key to unlock the door of ancient man's mind.

Some commentators upon Sanskrit, the world's most influential and intact ancient language, speak of its origins being rooted in a science of name and form. In keeping with them, I believe that language did not emerge haphazardly from bestial grunts, but that its syllables and words were chosen fittingly and wisely. We utter sounds as resonances that emanate from the region of the throat, mouth and the nasal passages. These resonances are then modified by bringing pressure to bear on them from the palate, the tongue, the teeth and the lips. Human sounds come in two distinct forms: vowels and consonants. Vowels are sounds that have no stricture, in other words they are not strangled into shape by tongue, palate or lips. Air merely escapes in a relatively unimpeded way. By contrast, consonants can easily be 'felt' by the way in which they have been shaped by the mouth before utterance. Consonants are squeezed and distorted into particular patterns. Vowels, being open and sustained, range in power from 9 to 47 microwatts, whilst consonants are restricted to a limit of 2 microwatts, seldom reaching above that threshold.[52] Intriguingly, the various god names held in such awe and esteem by the Ancients had very few consonants. The power of vowels is easily demonstrated by their use in music, where a good soprano can easily shatter glass or rattle a chandelier. This is an extreme example, but it does demonstrate why we should not undervalue the use of sound in ritual.

Back at Newgrange, walking in the mists of an Irish early morning, I could not stop myself thinking of the purpose of the place, and of the gods and heroes associated with it. Having discovered that these profoundly complex sites were the emanation of profoundly wise minds, I realised with some amusement that our pervading view of the ancient ancestors, as it was taught to me at school, was nothing other than a view of ourselves; these sites are now a mirror held in the face of our civilisation by an ancient peoples about whom we know so little because we know so little about ourselves, our full potential. As I walked around the perimeter of the site, I realised, with mounting excitement, that the most revealing clue lay within its measure. Language holds so much. Language itself is based upon measure, upon frequency of rhythm and sound. Ancient chants were all, like poetry, chanted in meters, rhythmical patterns. It is said that the meters were designed to change atmospheres and it is significant that meteorology is the science of the atmosphere. However, the important word here is 'geometry'.

Geometry is two words, 'geo' meaning 'earth' and 'metry' meaning 'measure'. It cannot be a coincidence that the syllable ge makes up the word for 'earth' in not a few languages. *Geo* and *Ge* are Greek words meaning 'earth', and again in Greek we have the famous *Gaia* , meaning literally 'Divine Earth' or 'Earth Goddess'. This linguistic connection, I believe, comes directly from

Geb, the name of the ancient Egypt god who represented the earth. Together these roots give us words such as 'genesis', 'generate', 'gene', 'geology', 'genus' and 'general'. The Latin word *Genus* is from the Greek and means 'of the earth'.

As far away as Papua New Guinea, the creator god is called Geb. In Scottish-Irish Gaelic *Gael* is 'love' and so on (see Glossary and the Anatomy of the Hero). Until recently, linguists believed these roots to be unconnected, a belief that is being revised radically. In Gaelic *Gu* means 'go, to' in the sense of return, thus implying that man comes from the earth and returns to the earth.

As demonstrated by solar and lunar alignments, the sacred measure encapsulated within ancient monuments displays a deep and profound knowledge of geometry; however, such geometry is to a large degree beyond the remit of the present work. In a purer sense, what I was interested in, beyond measure, as it were, was its expression. As we have just seen, language *is* its expression; geo*metry* suddenly becomes an organic principle where meter, rhythm, measure, connect the sun to the site and the sacred atmosphere of the site to language itself. We are beginning to understand that words can have an actual power, a power that contains the creative principle and can describe it so wonderfully well. Who would have thought that not only does the word 'geometry' mean 'measure of the earth' but that this measure, as the design and purpose of the monuments tell us, was quite specific on a vibratory level. Suddenly, just as the rising sun dispersed the mists of the morning, the vibrating, resonating gods were becoming clear and enlivened within my mind's eye!

Tradition tells us that the god who inhabited Newgrange was known as the Dagda. He was called 'The Good God' and he was involved with the use of sound, for he played upon a living harp and as he played upon it the seasons came and went in due order. His wife was Boann and his son was Angus, god of love, very probably a dying and rising god, that is, of the sunrise and sunset. The linguistic root of the Dagda's name is shared with the Greek and it is from the Greek tongue that we come across an interesting clue. *Da* in Greek means literally, 'O earth' and was used for ritual purposes. It is an invocation. The central portion of the name also means 'earth' and, if my assumption is correct, the Dagda's name invokes Mother Earth thrice: 'Da-g(a)-da', O Earth, Earth, O Earth. As if in confirmation, in the ancient myth of this site, she was known as the triple goddess.

The Dagda's name was a powerful one. In the context of being uttered deep inside the Newgrange cairn its effect, as a continuous chant or invocation, must have been profound indeed. At sunrise and sunset, when the landscape mists arose, the effect would be intensified. Imagine then, the further potency, at the winter solstice, when the air was crisp and the atmospheric moisture had penetrated deep inside to the hidden chambers. There would be gathered together devotees of the Dagda. Through concordant ritual of rhythmic chant, the atmosphere would be potentised with the name of the god, when lo! A penetrating, clear shaft of sunlight would break through the mists and into the dim interior, highlighting carved motifs upon the rock and within the air itself, those swirling mists now not only resonating to rhythmic chant, but also to midwinter sun. The elation felt by the congregation, as their brainwaves tumbled into the lower frequencies and their awareness was opened up, merging, at one with the subtler, greater environment, must have been ecstatic. Through the portals of consciousness, by way of the Dagda, they and the Great Mother would be one.

Intermezzo

Stars, planets, human beings and everything else, indeed, everything that exists does so because of vibration. Matter comes into being because energy vibrates and to the benefit of us all, science unlocked many secrets of this energy during the twentieth century. Material progress took a great leap forward as energy was harnessed in the form of electricity and we also began to understand the electrical fields of the solar system, the earth and our own bodies.

We opened chapter five with a catalogue of those discoveries, focusing especially upon the crystalline nature of life, and also suggested that, like us, our planet may be a sentient being. Having established the paramount importance of vibration to life, it was shown that our own Alpha brainwave frequency, the frequency which is associated with altered states of consciousness, coincides with earth resonance.

Having thus created a backdrop, the extraordinary conclusions gained from the Princeton University research at Newgrange and other sites were introduced. These revelations lay bare many misconceptions about our anscestors. The reader should be in no doubt that the Ancients knew a thing or two about acoustics and that many sacred sites were purpose-built acoustic chambers. But why?

Our search for an answer focused on the relationship between the buildings and the builders, set within the all-encompassing planetary atmosphere. The science of acoustics is based upon vibration and the link between brainwaves and the greater environment – at-one-ment – is due to sympathetic or synchronous vibration: resonance. The crystalline nature of life was shown to be a major factor in information exchange and evolutionary growth and we found that the role of resonance was important in this, as well as being a key to understanding the 'supernatural', for amazing changes can occur in response to particular frequencies. Pioneering research was cited, including theories and work featuring some of our own bodily apparatus which may help us to 'tune in'. Empirical evidence was also cited, a notable incident being the monks who found that they needed to chant in order to stay healthy. Subsequently, we looked at the relationship between various practices and beliefs within religion and various elements within science, including the phenomena of radiation, electromagnetism and, of course, resonance. Introducing a strand of etymological enquiry, we began to exchange scientific terminology for the ancient terminology as a sacred science based upon the human voice and acoustic chambers began to reveal itself.

We are now ready to explain much in the way of 'supernatural' phenomena and also to begin to link up with material featured in part one.

6

The Branches of a Tree
Long Forgotten

'Religion is the frozen thought of men out of which they build temples.'

Krishnamurti

'If religion is only a garment of Christianity – and even this garment has looked very different at different times – then what is religionless Christianity?'

Dietrich Bonhoeffer

A Haunting Melody

In the context of religious history and phenomena, the term 'ecstasy' has been given supernatural status, supernatural in the sense of being, so far, inexplicable by any known scientific hypothesis. In seeking to explain the inner workings of nature mankind has, to all intents and purposes, demystified it and some, would argue, despiritualised it. We are no longer comfortable with the unknown, thus when we are faced with 'super-nature' our first reactions may be alarm and fear. Fortunately, following on the heels of these two interlopers comes curiosity. Sad to say, many of us never get as far as this third impulse, preferring to ignore the mystery or explain it away by being 'logical'. Logic, of course, has its limits when we starve it of fresh information. We can keep our equilibrium by using the same old arguments and ignoring, or even ridiculing, the new knowledge. There we remain, behind our barricades, and our world does not really move forward. It is blocked. I feel fortunate that I made it to the third impulse – curiosity – and applied it through one of my favourite disciplines, etymology, the study of the origin and history of words.

Alarm and fear – in the light of these typically human responses, language becomes ever more revealing, displaying to a great degree the balanced way in which our forebears thought about exactly the same phenomena that today we label as the supernatural – paranormal, occult and so on, the very labels and phenomena that today trigger alarm and fear.

Ecstasy is from the Greek, *ekstasis*. The older form of the word is *exstasie* and reveals much. *Ex* is literally 'out of', in this case, 'out of stasis'. 'Stasis' is a commonly used word meaning 'cessation, stoppage, stationariness'. Thus ecstasy infers an 'un-stoppage', an unblocking. Down come the barricades and then comes change, the movement into a peak experience. This movement 'out of' may not always be comfortable – after all, we are leaving our comfort zones – but the result is a joyous or blissful affair; burdens are, at least temporarily, shed. Certainly one is taken out of normal everyday perceptions and, perhaps briefly, made aware beyond one's normal capacity. But it is clear that because of this shift, permanent changes can occur, perhaps a permanent expanded awareness.

Why is this important? Because it appears on a regular basis within religious circles and, beyond that, in an everyday context. When your team wins the competition or when an ordinary, everyday Joe wins the lottery, feelings can be ecstatic; this is a state out of the ordinary, wherein awareness is heightened, awareness of the internal, such as emotions and physical sensations, and awareness of the external – sometimes one's surroundings appear clearer, colours more intense. Ecstasy is often associated with music, with anthem and hymnal, but more than this, the state of ecstasy is associated with the hero of world mythology,[1] the hero who performs superhuman and supernatural deeds. Perhaps by achieving a state of ecstasy, we are communing with the heroic and the heroic state of mind. Certainly when in an ecstatic state, an illusory feeling of invincibility is common. In such moments, dangerous things are often done without a hint of nervousness.

In ages past and in times of crisis, it was customary for civic leaders, kings and potentates to consult the shades of the dead. More often than not these shades were the souls of heroes. In Greek and Egyptian mythology there are detailed descriptions about these encounters; the meeting of Orpheus and Eurydice is amongst the most famous. In Hebrew myth, King Saul consults the shade of the prophet Samuel, aided and abetted by the Witch of Endor.

These stories tell us that spirits, ghosts and apparitions were a common feature in ages past; more so than today, where adherence to dogma, be it scientific or religious, has replaced acceptance that there is something further, something 'hidden'. The problem is that the hidden, or 'occult',[2] is influential. It occurs regularly in everyday life, almost in spite of the presence of the scientist. Science, however, is at last beginning to come to terms with the idea that there may be more to such phenomena than meets the eye.

On 23rd December 1998 at Belgrave Hall in Leicestershire, England, two spectres decided to go for a stroll in the grounds, perhaps little realising that as they were doing so, they were being observed. In an episode not too far removed from Oscar Wilde's *The Canterville Ghost*, it was the ghosts that were being haunted, by security surveillance cameras. One of the figures captured on camera was apparently a woman in a Victorian dress with a bustle. She was identified as Charlotte Ellis, who, in her lifetime, had a deep and abiding love of the place. According to Stuart Warburton, the Hall's managing curator, the images appeared from nowhere. They make no entrance or exit but just appear and disappear. The video equipment was duly inspected and found to have no fault. Belgrave Hall already had a firm reputation for being haunted, but the appearance of the ghosts was the cherry on the cake. The film remains fascinating and unique; hauntings are only just beginning to be understood.[3]

Scientists are discovering that ghostly apparitions most probably have a logical explanation and are not, as has been too often suggested, the result of an overactive imagination.

In February 1998 Vic Tandy and Dr. Tony Lawrence of Coventry University decided to look into the case of a haunting at a local business premises, a medical manufacturing company based in the English Midlands. Tandy, an expert in computer-assisted learning at Coventry University, had been told that the building was haunted. His initial response was to dismiss it as a joke, that is, until he himself became a witness:

> 'As I sat a the same desk writing, I began to feel increasingly uncomfortable. I was sweating, but cold, and the feeling of depression was noticeable – but there was also something else. It was as though something was in the room with me.
> Then I became aware that I was being watched and a figure slowly emerged to my left. It was indistinct and on the periphery of my vision, but it moved just as I would expect a person to. It was grey and made no sound. The hair was standing up on the back of my neck – I was terrified.'

Caught between the compelling nature of the apparition and sheer terror, Vic summoned the courage to look at the spectre face on, only to see it fade and vanish.

> 'I decided I must be cracking up and went home.'

Returning the morning after, he soon had an answer for the events of the night before. As a fencing enthusiast, Vic decided to make use of a vice that was set up in the room. He was adjusting one of his foils and had left the blade clamped in the vice whilst he went on a search for some oil. Upon his return he noticed that the free end of the blade was vibrating up and down in somewhat frantic fashion. It was possible, thought Tandy, that the blade was responding to very low frequency sound waves filling the laboratory, sound waves so low that they could not be heard.

It was discovered that 'trapped' within the laboratory was a standing-wave pattern, a pattern that just happened to reach a peak of intensity near the desk where Vic had been sitting on that hair-raising night. A standing-wave pattern, in this case an extremely low frequency sound (ELF), caused by a oscillations between a newly installed extraction fan and its mounting, was making air vibrate at19 cycles per second, or 19Hz. When the fan's mounting was altered, the standing wave stopped and so did the hauntings.[4]

Working in tandem with Dr Tony Lawrence of the University's School of Health, Vic found that this rate of vibration, called 'infra-sound', plays host to a whole range of physiological effects, including breathlessness, shivering and levels of fear. More significant research by NASA, the American space agency, had already established that if the human eyeball is led to vibrate in sympathy with infrasound at a resonance of around 17–19Hz, smearing of vision would result. When man's 19Hz meets the world's 19Hz it vibrates in sympathy, rather like the effect of a vibrating tuning fork upon other tuning forks. Thus it is that man vibrates in sympathy with his environment and otherworldly effects begin.

Lawrence and Tandy have since come across at least two other 'hauntings' wherein ELFs can be blamed. However, certain fundamental questions must be raised at this point, for we have the *vehicle* of the apparition, but not its provenance, or its origin. Is what we are looking at rather like a pre-recorded message, one that in the right conditions, or frequencies, can be played back? Regarding these conditions, and given what we have already discussed in the context of Newgrange and the extraordinary findings made there, what, we might ask, are the ramifications for architecture in general and our ideas of the cosmos at large?

Lawrence and Tandy pointed out that, if a building acted like a wind instrument, creating standing waves (rather like blowing over the neck of an empty bottle), apparitions could quite possibly occur and in certain conditions, perhaps the long corridor of a tall, dark nineteenth-century house, they were probable. We must think here of Newgrange and the host of other sites. Tandy's and Lawrence's work casts new light on 'otherworldly' experience, but a very important factor is left unaddressed. As Professor David Fontana, former Chairman of the Society for Psychic Research, pointed out:

'It cannot explain those cases where there is some interaction between the person and the apparition – as there is with poltergeists for example. The problem is that whenever you get a potential explanation like this, you find that there is a whole lot of things it cannot account for.'[5]

Visions of the Queen of Heaven

During times of crisis and transition, either individual or national, we are often compelled to look beyond everyday experience and are given to reflect inwardly upon our disquieted feelings. It is almost as if the outer tumultuous events of life are forcing us to look internally. This inward-looking contemplation often brings about yearnings for 'something other', and in its deeper manifestations, a momentary sense of 'oneness', an all too brief, innocent sense of peace. Under such conditions, visions can appear. Remarkably, a vast majority of these visions take on a feminine hue and appear in all manner of guises and across a broad spectrum of cultural beliefs. Of late, these visions of transcendence have occurred with regularity. One simple observation to be made is that visions appear to be tailor-made to the culture or belief in which they are set. Increasingly often, individuals of varying faiths are experiencing the presence of the divine feminine. To many in the West she is the Blessed Virgin Mary, the Mother of God, further east, she is Fatima, daughter of Mohammed.[6]

To the Roman Lucius Apuleius, author of *The Golden Ass*, she was Isis, whereas the Greeks adored her in their many visions of Artemis. Wherever she is and whatever she is called, she is always the Queen of Heaven. Although often described as a 'White Lady', she sometimes appears as the 'Black Madonna'. To some, she is seen to shed blood-red tears amidst her heavenly white garb, whilst to others she sheds ordinary tears down her dark robes; this Black Madonna is often taken for being the Magdalene, the whore who regained her purity through Christ. Thus, by their cultural nature, visions are linked to history; often they were associated with a sense of warning and, aside from feelings of awe and wonder, a deep sense of foreboding. The impression is given that something profound is being said, something from the depths of our archaic past.[7]

Such experiences are often deeply powerful, even completely overwhelming. Others often dismiss them as mere hysteria, though in the context of the visionary phenomenon, hysteria has a tendency to become a mass phenomenon that occurs only after the initial 'real' event. Whatever others may say, to the recipient, the experience remains deeply. It is this sense of the individuality of the experience that is most likely the key to understanding the phenomenon as a whole, hence the fact that they seem tailor-made to the respective cultures concerned.

Sri Aurobindo, an Indian sage who was well used to such phenomena, comments upon the mechanics involved:

> 'The wall between consciousness and force, impersonality and personality, becomes much thinner when one goes beyond the veil of matter. If one looks at a working from the side of impersonal force one sees a force or energy at work acting for a purpose or with a result, if one looks from the side of being one sees a being possessing, guiding and using or else representative of and used by a conscious force as its instrument of specialised action and expression... In modern science it has been found that if you look at the movement of energy, it appears on one side to be a wave and act as a wave, on the other as a mass of particles and to act as a mass of particles each acting in its own way. It is somewhat the same principle here.'[8]

Aurobindo's biographer, Satprem, elucidates further:

> 'A Christian saint who has the vision of the Virgin, say, and an Indian who has the vision of Durga may be seeing the same thing, they may have contacted the same plane of consciousness and the same forces; but quite obviously Durga would mean nothing to the Christian, and moreover, were this force to manifest in its pure state, that is, as a luminous impersonal vibration, it would not be accessible to the consciousness of either the worshipper of the Virgin or the devotee of Durga, or at any rate would not speak to their hearts.'[9]

Although the apparition is usually given whatever name or form accords to the religious belief of the observer, on the wider levels of gender, purpose and demeanour, she remains remarkably uniform in her appearances worldwide, a fact that points to a common origin. This is reflected in the history of belief. Folk religions have, through the ages, calcified as history marches on. Where a new belief has not been brutally imposed, it has changed its shape to suit the cultural ethos in which it is set. Even so, the imposition of a rigid faith has done little to curb the re-emergence of the older ways in one way or another, revealing the roots of the folk tradition. This was a point recognised by C. G. Jung, who wrote of it at some length. His term for it was 'the collective unconscious'. For him, the process of metamorphosis was alchemical and the visions came to be known as 'archetypes', as primal manifestations of the collective unconscious. Jung was no fool and saw the manifestation of phenomena – visions, UFOs and the like – as a continuation of a very old theme.

One of the fundaments of the past is that ancient man saw the earth as feminine and very much alive. This is a view that in the late twentieth century has been given newfound credence by a broad diversity of writers, Teilhard de Chardin, Carl Jung, James Lovelock and Rupert Sheldrake amongst them.

In June 1981, in the Balkan territory of Bosnia-Herzegovina, the Virgin Mary began appearing to six young Croatians, the first of whom was Ivanka Ivankovic,15 years old at the time. As at other times and in other places, the Blessed Virgin appeared as a young woman hovering above the ground and she appeared to beckon Ivanka to her. Ivanka was unafraid, although days later another of the group was physically thrown into a thorn bush by an unseen force when he either refused, or forgot, to kneel. The description of the Virgin, as given by the young people, is particularly interesting. She was a young woman of 19 to 20 years, extraordinarily beautiful and wearing a crown of stars, a long silver dress and a white veil. This is a picture spoken of many years before by Dante Gabriel Rossetti in a poem entitled 'The Blessed Damosel':

> 'The blessed damosel leaned out
> From the gold bar of Heaven;
> Her eyes were deeper than the depth
> Of waters stilled at even;
> She had three lilies in her hand,
> And the stars in her hair were seven.'[10]

A team led by Professor Henri Joyeux of Montpellier University, France, undertook scientific and medical studies on the children. They found that whilst there were no clinical signs of hallucination, hysteria, neuroses or psychosis, EEG recordings clearly indicated the prescence of Alpha rhythms during the visions.[11]

The visions would last from 10 and 20 minutes after which the children would be blessed with the words: 'Go in peace with God.' From here on, as with instances at Fatima, Portugal, in 1917, at Lourdes, France, in 1858, and at Zeitoun, Egypt, from 1968 to 1971, the visions took on a whole new aspect, seeming to cause considerable environmental change. For example, the sun began to dance and spin, and the word *Mir*, meaning 'peace' in Croatian, appeared in the sky above a large cross, which was situated on a nearby mountain.

Quite often the visions come with grave warnings. At Fatima, three momentous secrets were imparted to three young children. At Akita, Japan, in 1973, a nun was warned of the terrible punishment that awaits humanity, a punishment more terrible than the flood. Only believers would be spared. Incidentally, this became one of the few modern apparitions approved by the Roman Catholic Church.

Even to a non-believer, the words of Conchita Gonzalez from a vision of Mary at Garabandal, Spain, 1961–5, are very forbidding; they speak of dreadful catastrophe. The third secret of Fatima has recently been revealed as a prophecy of doom, if we do not mend our ways.

Others of a more agnostic mien have shared much the same experience, if only a little less dramatic. White ladies, and there are several, have appeared to various people down the ages. To Keats she was manifest as 'La Belle Dame sans Merci', to Robert Graves she was the utterly ruthless White Goddess, whilst to Lucius Apuleius of second-century Rome she was none other than the great Egyptian goddess, Isis. All of this is made more intriguing when one considers that the Femina Alba, the White Lady, is actually the goddess of love. In this, the message of dire warning is a paradox that can easily be explained. The only other juncture in nature where love speaks harshly to the loved one is the parent–child relationship, more specifically that of mother and child – the most important, most natural and sacred relationship in physical life. And so we see that these visions share much in common. One wonders, do the sites share commonality?

In this light, it is interesting that the specific locations of these visions should be at places of particular numinosity – temples, churches and sacred sites in general. As we shall investigate, temples, churches and the like, by virtue of being constructed in certain ways upon particular places, capture the subtle vibrating fields of the Earth and enhance them. These buildings are resonant places where acoustic patterns, including standing waves, can be set up. We know that standing waves of around 19Hz resonate with the human eye and I believe that, under those conditions, if there is a subtle form present, it may be seen. To clarify: this type of experience is not 'all in the mind', there is a presence which interacts with the mind, often being 'culturally clothed' by it. Come the vision, cometh the church, but we should note that where there are churches there is always water.

There are many myths, stories and actual experiences that relate to the power of water at sacred sites. Sacred waters are traditionally symbolic of the great Earth Mother, of her fertility, of the womb and of life itself. A great majority of Marian visions have taken place at locations associated with water; pilgrims still travel en masse to Lourdes to partake of its healing waters. The same is true of Knock in Ireland. There are many holy wells in Devon, Cornwall and other British counties.[7] I have personal experience of the languidness of the sacred wells scattered over Dartmoor. Holy wells are known for inducing sleepy states, a change of brain pattern. These waters are relatively high in natural radiation, as they seep forth from granite.

Holy waters have been shown to be different from ordinary water, tap water for example, by the fact that they have different frequencies involved in their make up. Using a technique called infrared spectroscopy, a beam of infrared light is shone through the water. In absorbing some of this light, the water can then be measured via its spectrum. Holy water absorbs light at different frequencies from ordinary water and its properties were quite obviously known by the Ancients.

In early 1999 experts from Anglian Water were called to the site of St Withburga's well at East Dereham, Norfolk. The well is known over a wide area for its healing powers, notable in the treatment of skin ailments. The experts tested six litres of the water and in their report they confirm that 'the water contains naturally occurring minerals, such as potassium and calcium, which are known to be beneficial to health. The water is free of bacteria.'[12] The presence of these minerals and the lack of foreign bodies is a testament to the extraordinary purity of sacred well water. Water from such sites has greater properties of spin than is usual. It is literally composed of tiny vortices that in the process of spinning give off an electric charge and hence an electromagnetic field, minute, but enough to transform it into something very different from ordinary water.[13] Incidentally, quite often, and usually for the use of kings and queens only, rock crystal bowls and chalices were carved in order to help maintain the purity of the well water.

The Ancients are also known to have deliberately increased the potency of water by the use of crystals. In 1974 Dr Patrick Flanagan, an expert on the structure and properties of crystals, undertook research and found that 'crystals of all kinds, such as quartz and precious gemstones, have a marked effect on water surface tension, a characteristic known to ancient Tibetan physicians who applied it to make crystal-affected water potions for their patients.'[14] The water, when poured on food crops such as wheat, alfalfa and mung beans, produced more vigorous growth and a substantial difference in taste. Dr Flanagan believes that crystals are resonators of cosmic energy impulses[15] and that the origins of these incoming energy fluctuations are supernovae and quasar activity. Indeed, it is known that the rate of chemical reactions in water can be affected by sunspot activity (as discovered by G. Piccardi in the 1930s), solar eruptions and incoming showers of cosmic rays. Water is incredibly sensitive to environmental stimuli and, in making up 80 per cent of the human body, must therefore help make us sensitive too.

Water also retains electromagnetic information and by the very act of drinking from a sacred spring, one is literally drinking in the information contained in it.[16] In 1988, Jacques Benveniste and his colleagues put themselves firmly in a position of heresy, for it was with some reservations that the science journal, *Nature*, published the results of a remarkable experiment. Benveniste found that:

> 'They could affect white cells in the blood with antibody solutions so diluted that not a single molecule of antibody could possibly be present in the water. They suggested that possibly water could act as a "template" for the basic molecule of the antibody, and were convinced that "transmission of the information depended on vigorous agitation, possibly inducing a sub-molecular organisation of water".'[17]

In effect, homoeopathy. Homoeopathy uses incredibly diluted solutions of various substances which are used to combat the presence of far larger amounts of the *same* solution in the body – fire to fight fire, in this case a match against an inferno. For various reasons, these principles are much derided by mainstream science, even though there is plenty of evidence to support them.[18]

> 'The editorial of that issue of *Nature* made it clear why the results reached by Benveniste *et al* were unlikely to be accepted; they were "startling not merely because they point to a novel phenomenon, but because they strike at the roots of two centuries of observation and rationalisation of physical phenomena".'[19]

Many others have since arrived at the same conclusions as Benveniste and his team, by the same process of adding a dilution and then halving and adding water, a process repeated, in some cases, countless hundreds of times but with the same effect – the chemical message remaining in the water. Eleven years later, Benveniste's results have been admitted and acclaimed in a new series of experiments announced in the national press.[20]

Further to these revelations, current investigations are revealing that the energy field of water may, in some way, respond to thought. This is not as strange as it might seem. In our own physiology, water appears as a response to thoughts and feelings – in times of sadness or joy it flows from the eyes. What of other subtle interactions? Can weather patterns, for instance, respond to thought? Any time-served shaman would say, yes, most certainly. In fact, on 28th November 1999, in order to help end a drought, a group of Rabbis boarded a plane and circled Israel, spiralling around it seven times whilst praying for rain. It rained!

Nowadays we recognise that this earth is one organic whole. As it becomes apparent that we can interact with its component parts on the level of thought, we should seriously consider the possibility that the earth is a conscious being.

The ancient traditions insist that the earth and indeed the heavens will respond to prayer and affirmation. We must realise that these old sacred monuments were places designed and built specifically for this type of activity; interaction with the conscious being called earth, and beyond that - not necessarily in distance, but in vibration – with the subtler universal consciousness.

The heavens descending in response might go towards explaining the mysterious thunderclap that was heard before the extraordinary vision of the Blessed Virgin at the Coptic church of Zeitoun in 1968, as well as thunderclaps heard elsewhere. Gathered around the dome of the church was a strange mist of the sort that often seems to accumulate at sites of this nature. It is as if here we have an example of the descent of the higher – the godly – spiralling down into the frequencies of the lower, by somehow utilising the site itself.

We are all aware, to some extent, that the dominating movement in the universe is spiral. From galaxies to atmospheric conditions, where satellite photographs now show us spiral cloud formations in all their glory, the spiral is the natural way. In archaic myth, the divine feminine, the goddess, is often represented as a spiral and this is a symbol to be found at a plethora of ancient sites, Newgrange, for instance. At particular sacred sites, it has been shown that:

> '...the vectors of electromagnetic force would have favoured spiral shapes twisting in one direction or the other...'[21]

The spiral may also be seen in water as vortices spinning in clockwise or anticlockwise directions – yet again we have the property of spin, which gives off a magnetic field, adjusting to varying degrees the electromagnetic information retained within. Water is a component of blood; blood spins, and by consuming water from a pure source, we can adjust the varying frequencies and spin ratios of the blood, thus altering the information it contains,[22] a property announced by the medical world in 1998,[23] It would seem therefore that the advanced chemical technology that is our body does, to a certain degree, create the proper circumstances of visions. Therefore, in tandem with the earth and her electromagnetism, our bodies, particularly our brains and sensory faculties, have to be in a certain condition in order to receive information.[24]

Water, in having a memory, is collecting and storing data wherever it is present upon the earth, and when its frequency patterns meet other traces of water, in the human body for example, under particular circumstances, sympathetic vibration can take place. We have seen how the builders of Newgrange seemed to encourage a damp atmosphere. They had a head start; the British Isles are world renowned for their damp climate, in fact, many seers and clairvoyants have said that these islands have so many visions and visionaries because of this.

As already mentioned, spirals and vortices were also associated with water, which in every single ancient belief, without exception, was referred to as female. In Hebrew, the sea is female, in European languages it is female; in French it is *la mer* , for example. Ships that float upon it are 'she' and so on. Water is also associated in myth with space, being referred to as 'the primordial waters'. This may be a metaphor perhaps relating the amniotic fluids of the womb to space as the womb of life;[25] but actually, water and the essential ingredients in its make up are found in space. What I am indicating here is that we have all of this data stored in the feminine waters, molecule by molecule, and yet beyond mere data we have the haunting but interactive presence of the Virgin. The Virgin, though, is not the only interactive vision.

The Abducting Angels

All of humanity is interconnected by virtue of the common habitation of a single planet, earth, but in evolving within her embrace we are even more connected than might seem to be the case. We are by nature, mental, emotional and physical bundles of water and carbon, vivified by healthy doses of magnetism and electricity, which are themselves forms of rhythmic vibration. We are like tuning forks which react to incoming vibrations; the music of the universe. At the same time we are trying to make sense of it all – and, by enquiry, we are aspiring. That which a*spires* is *spi*ritual, it is of the spirit.

A series of experiments in the 1970s demonstrated subtle levels of connectivity in a surprising way. Russell Targ and Harold Puthoff of the Stanford Research Institute took pairs of people who were already fairly familiar with each other's habits and character traits – they knew each other well and they had an emotional affinity. They were separated and put in rooms at opposite ends of the building, thus ensuring complete isolation from one another.

At randomly selected intervals a rapidly flashing light was shone into the eyes of one of the pair. The effect was to reduce Alpha activity, the brainwave pattern associated with relaxation. Meanwhile, the partner was supposed to say when the other was experiencing the flashing sensation. In the event, the responses failed to pinpoint when the effect was taking place, at higher levels than would normally be expected. This might confirm the general opinion that a relaxed condition is required for heightened ESP. However, although one was not able to 'say' when the other was experiencing the flashing, both brains showed a reduced level of activity at precisely the same time. This, remember, was when only one was physically subject to the flashing. A subtle link, not predicted, was showing itself. Could it be that we are linked to each other on many levels? If this is so, surely it is likely to be via the earth and her subtle atmospheres. When it comes to weird phenomena, to coincidences, hauntings and interactive visions, is it not the biosphere that we call earth that is key?

Research indicates that when the body's essential biorhythms are at a maximum, so is psychic activity. On a natural basis this peaking occurs at all three levels – physical, emotional and intellectual – roughly every 45 to 46 years, but perhaps, this state could be induced, let us say, almost religiously.[26]

Religion as we have come to know it has been in decline in the West for years, with the telltale signs of a hardening of belief at the outer extremes - gross materialism and 'new age' fantasy. Meanwhile, faith has to a large extent been replaced with technology. Science would seem to have won the day – or has it? We have already seen how an apparition will 'fit' the society in which it is set, and, with the decline of faith over the years, the ability to see angels has been replaced by the ability to see aliens. What is of great importance is that, if angels and the supposed aliens are the same, there appears to be little difference between the two – except that, in the newer guise of aliens, angels have become a lot more interactive, by some accounts even abductively so.

It is important to admit that the human mind is more incredible than we seem to realise; the UFO/visionary phenomenon has had an impact on regions of the brain about which we know so little. The fact that the form of visions seems to be dictated by one's own personal beliefs and cultural identity has great implications, and it is a shock to realise that what we perceive as being 'out there' may in fact be 'in here'. Jung had the notion that UFOs could be 'projections' of the unconscious mind. This is not to reduce their importance as a phenomenon for, if life does exist elsewhere, our way of communicating with it will only come from a greater understanding of what is going on here, within ourselves and within our own planetary atmosphere.

The Cold War, at its height, induced a state of paranoia the world over. But of all the startling imagery of monolithic government, the black and white imagery of various military struggles, of good against evil, it is the science fiction movies that had the greatest effect, an effect that remains ingrained in our consciousness. We are still wary of the 'stranger from outside', the alien from the great unknown. Early science fiction films include *Red Planet Mars, Invasion of the Body Snatchers* and *The Day the Earth Stood Still*. By today's high technological standards they seem primitive, if not a little crude. But they worked.

Of course, the gist of it in the 1950s was that 'they' were really the communists. Many films from that era still have a McCarthy witch-hunt feel about them, the US military were the 'good guys', the Soviets were the 'bad guys' and, actually at that time, a lot of the UFO phenomenon was thought to emanate from behind the Iron Curtain. Many years later, when the Cold War had been consigned to history, the writer John le Carre asked the Russians about their role in the paranoiac 50s and 60s. They too, had been convinced that they were the good guys. Furthermore, they were just as intrigued by the flying saucer phenomenon as the Americans.

UFOs quite often appear as lights in the sky and as silvery metallic objects. Generally dismissed as satellites in orbit about the earth or as tricks of the light, these objects have been seen by too many people, and too often, to be dismissed out of hand. There always remains a significant percentage that cannot be explained away. In fact a national poll taken in 1998 by *Time* magazine suggested that 22 per cent of the American people believe in 'visitors from another planet'. This same group shared the belief that other planets have been in contact with humans. 17 per cent said that intelligent life had abducted humans in order to experiment on them.

Since the 1970s there has been a huge wave of reported cases of alien abduction, literally hundreds of thousands of them. In the classic abduction case, the victim remembers seeing strange lights and that's about it, but then the nightmares begin and therapy is required. Often, in an attempt to solve the problem, the patient is hypnotised and, during what is usually revealed to be a traumatic episode, can at last unlock a sealed compartment of the memory. However, for all its beneficial uses, hypnosis can only reveal what the subject *believes* might have happened.

Another aspect of abduction cases involves the implantation and later removal of foetuses for alien use, the bereft and confused victim being informed that they are helping to create a kind of racial improvement, a genetic modification upon the old model. Understandably, victims are generally left with painful emotions after these experiences, but also with a higher psychic sense and a greater sense of awareness. These apparitions or encounters are of an extreme psychological complexity, and all may not be as it seems.

The actual experience, as described by the many people who have had them, most certainly involves a change in awareness, where the individual is knocked out of this reality and into something that under normal circumstances would take considerable adjustment. Equally strange is the 'healing' consequence of the abduction experience. Complaints that have been there for years simply vanish: arthritis, rheumatic disorders, even cancer can just disappear when the 'little bug-eyed monster' comes to play. But are abductees 'victims' or do such uncomfortable experiences have more to do with confused belief systems, uncomfortable readjustments of our internal programming, than an episode of interstellar intervention?

At the Fatima vision of the Blessed Virgin in 1917, there were many instances of UFO sightings, all of which were attributed to the divine.[27] Eighty or so years later, is it any different? The only thing that has changed is the nature of belief. At the third sighting at Fatima, thousands of people heard a buzzing noise and heard an explosion, a sonic boom. By the time that I had reached this stage of my research, I could not help wondering whether all of the divine visions and all of these UFOs are part of one and the same thing and related to earth resonances.

Through these pages, it will become clear that we can consciously interact with electromagnetic frequencies or energies with a view to transforming our awareness. But might these frequencies also be interacting with our subconscious, and if so, how would these interactions manifest themselves to our conscious state? Furthermore, are these energies really separate from us? Perhaps by looking into space we are leading ourselves 'up the garden path'. Surely the answer is much closer to home. If so, one would expect that religion and myth should have some, if not all, of the answers.

In February 1997 at a meeting of the American Association, a Vatican astronomer, Dr Christopher Corbally, conceded that the discovery of alien life would necessitate a wider concept of God: 'We need a proper sense of God, one derived in the dialogue between religion and science.' This is stirring stuff, but raises a point of contradiction: given that the word 'catholic' means 'universal', what can possibly be meant by 'a wider concept of God'? It seems to me, that in the light of recent scientific discoveries regarding the powers of the mind, the revelations of quantum physics and so on, we should be looking for depth rather than width, and experience rather than concepts. As mystics and saints have testified throughout the ages, depth of experience is gained by consciously looking within. Yet these words from the scientific arm of the Roman Catholic Church demonstrate that the Church itself is looking anywhere else but there. Mainstream religious thought has for some time been given over to ideas of a God separate and 'out there'. It seems that, officially, a change is not on the agenda. However, the Anglican Bishop of Oxford, the Right Reverend Richard Harries, does seem to have brought some depth to the debate, by describing aliens as angels. He could be uncannily close to the point.[28] During the Middle Ages, in a society that was deeply religious, any vision was willingly interpreted in a biblical light. You already know my thoughts – it is quite possible that what to us are aliens were angels to medieval man.

Science and Western Christianity meet on two points: one, both are doctrinal, sometimes to the point of exclusion, and two, both seem to view the universe and creation in general as separate from human experience. If human experience is informed by current scientific and religious dogma, then this more than implies a loss of contact, not only with ourselves but with the planet and the greater reality.

We will certainly have to look more deeply to find our truths. But there is always help at hand. The great dictionaries have often offered me insights and prompted much deep contemplation. Here is an interesting fact that may yet reveal much: The word 'alien' breaks up into two very interesting and very ancient words: *El Ayin*. *Ayin* is the sixteenth letter of both the Hebrew and Greek alphabets. It has the value of 'o', which stems from the ancient Egyptian hieroglyph for the third eye. The letter *Ayin* or 'o' represents and means 'eye'. *El Ayin* means 'The eye of God'[29] and refers to the third eye or pineal gland. The third eye in ancient Egypt was the eye of Horus, the ultimate source of light or enlightenment. The symbol of the cobra or uraeus upon Pharaoh's brow is also representative of the third eye. As we shall see later, to the Egyptians, angels and gods performed divine acts of healing, miracles were seen as being resonant with godly things, and the gods themselves were seen as resonances. Aliens, though, are not the only contemporary mystery manifestations.

Cereal Graphics

From ancient times, through myth, folk tales and other media, mankind has left us plenty of evidence of the appearance of paranormal happenings, often in association with sacred sites such as ancient tumuli, long barrows and cairns. It is also obvious that in the past, humanity was more than aware of these, by our standards, peculiar events. There was a language for it. In fact, markings at ancient sites, and the designs to be found in churches and cathedrals are prt of that language – the language of pictograms. A language of shape, a mathematical language. This language is now returning to us every summer, bringing with it strange lights over the landscape and annoyance to farmers. It comes in the form of crop circles.

It has been maintained in the popular press that crop circles are the result of hoaxers working late at night. The evidence for this is largely contrary; it is quite impossible to reproduce the creations within the time-frame generally agreed, and those circles that are known to be of human provenance are quite different and of a far lower standard than those that appear quickly and mysteriously.

The modern crop circle phenomenon began to come to prominence in the 1980s, generally in southern Britain near the prehistoric monuments of Stonehenge, Avebury and Silbury. The first circles were rudimentary whorls of impressed cereal. By 1997, the complexity of the imprints had excelled all expectations of what was by now a commonly awaited phenomenon. The culmination came in 1991 with a superb Mandelbrot Set in a wheat field at Ickelton, near Cambridge, England. The sheer complexity of this design ruled out any physical human origin, but what really stood out was the fact that a Mandelbrot Set,[30] a complex element of chaos theory discovered by Beniot Mandelbrot (who taught for a number of years at the nearby University of Cambridge) cannot be drawn freehand. It has to be built up, point by careful point, a process that, even when using a computer, can take days if not weeks.

The phenomenon and its following have grown, and aliens are the favoured explanation, that somehow an extraterrestrial intelligence is manipulating the earth's energies. Strange balls of light have been seen in conjunction with crop circle formation, and some have even been captured on film; spritelike, mercurial and mischievous.

The circles themselves have the appearance of being gigantic hieroglyphs, and in this sense perhaps they are a reference to something deeply unconscious. The twentieth century surrealist painter Rene Magritte used various heiroglyphs in his works to illustrate the dream language of the unconscious mind, a language much commented on by Freud and Jung in their work on psychoanalysis. The hieroglyphic language, I believe, springs from the unconscious and we have already seen the origins of the word 'Alien' in the hieroglyphic letter, *El Ayin*. If *El Ayin* is the 'third eye' or inner visionary centre through which, it is said, we can look into other worlds, what really are these things that the 'see-ers' look upon and on occasion, interact with? They must be subtle energies, likely to be connected with electric and magnetic fields which penetrate and encompass physical life. Do you recall the traditional fairy tales of old? We have seen that there is more to many old tales than meets the eye – but perhaps they meet the third eye? Now, in the light of science, let us take these tales seriously for a moment. Perhaps there is a hierarchy of these energies, which follow the traditional family names, dwarfs and gnomes being the energies inside or nearest the earth, elves, pixies and fairies being more airborne, and angels, as messengers from beyond, more associated with the forces of the sun as they enrich the earth's atmosphere, all of them electromagnetic and all from an alien world, that is, one seen by the *El Ayin*, the third eye, the perceiver of the subtle, quantum realms. And as these visions move into our consciousness, we clothe them with our preconceptions, as we have seen with the visions of the Queen of Heaven. In this way, one may see an angel where another sees ET or the Devil! (Intriguingly, a 1678 woodcut shows a 'mowing devil' in the midst of what

looks like a crop circle.) The way we chose to percieve these energies may be
due to a process operating at a very deep level.

> ' ..at the finest level of description of the mind, the swift
> construction, manipulation and superposition of many images,
> might require explanation at the quantum level.'[31]

But what of the circles themselves? The more serious researchers are
convinced that they are created by powerful electrical forces. Massachusetts
biologist Dr William Levengood has found that both the plants and the soil
within crop circles exhibit very strange structural changes, as if they have
been hit by a massive but intense burst of energy. There are chemical changes
and bizarre anomalies at a molecular level: the nodes of the plants are swollen
to the point where, quite often, they burst or split. They bend at 90° angles
and seedlings are stunted. The effects of human hoaxers are quite contrary –
smashed stalks, broken off at many heights and many angles, and all too
obvious effects of destruction.

In shape, we shall soon see that these crop-glyphs are mathematical, but it
has also been pointed out by various researchers that some appear to spell
out the names of Sumerian and Egyptian deities. This could be a sign that the
Ancients, being more sensitive, could see these energies as a matter of course
and even understand their functions – for ancient gods and goddesses
invariably were functional, representing attributes of what might be called
the Ultimate Creative Force. It is worth mentioning that, in the older religions,
the Vedic for example, force is equated with the Divine Mother.

Now it is easier to see the connections between the circles and ideas that
Mother Earth is somehow communicating with us, and not just through crop
circles. In arctic Canada, ice circles have begun to make their appearance in
the midst of thin coats of lake ice. No hoaxers here – the surrounding ice is a
clear unbroken sheet with not a footprint in sight. Latterly, circles have also
become an 'underground' phenomenon, for dust circles of varying complexity
have been discovered by commuters on the world's underground systems.

Cereal Sound

There is something else which is strongly associated with these phenomena.
In the middle of summer in 1997, as twilight began to fall, Jack Spooncer was
driving home to his farmhouse deep in the heart of west Dorset. The light
was fading fast and Jack flicked on his headlights. Turning a corner he came

upon an extraordinary sight: there in the corner of one of his fields, amidst the crops, was a dome-shaped object that quite took his breath away. His description is intriguing:

'It was like a million icy droplets, glistening, like a hologram, shimmering.'[32]

Jack also noticed a high–pitched sound. He hurried home to fetch his wife, but upon their return there was no sign of the strange dome-shaped object. However, there was something of a signature: half a crop circle, incomplete but a circle all the same.

In another of the many incidents where sound has been reported, one night in 1990, a small group of people, George Wingfield, John Haddington and Michael Cox, gathered together at a location near Silbury Hill, Wiltshire. On consecutive evenings they witnessed lights and heard a strange 'trilling' noise:

'To the human ear this most musical sound has the most beautiful bell-like quality, really indescribable as it is so high-pitched.'[33]

Indeed, the sound was so high pitched that all of them were overtaken by a strange sensation, in one case a feeling of nausea and vomiting, quickly followed by a weakness in the knees.

Strange lights and otherworldly music are a common link between crop circle discoveries and UFO sightings. These sights and sounds also link to visions where the viewer sees, not so much a form, but a 'large globe of golden light', as at Knock, Ireland, in 1879, which appeared to the accompaniment of what was described as 'a heavenly choir'. Significantly, in mythic and other traditions, the otherworldly is associated with music. Pan played his pipes; Orpheus, the harp; there were the sirens of Greek myth; faeries who used music as a means to charm; and the Pied Piper who used his musical magic to lead children into a new world within the rock. There are so many tales bearing the hallmark of music, the gift of the muse.

Music is frequency in harmonic form. The eight notes of our musical scale are familiar to all. Each sound is different because of pitch, the number of vibrations per second, and these in turn are related to each other via a series of fractions or intervals. One might think that the interval between notes is spaced perfectly, but it isn't. The fractions are one and an eighth, one and two eighths, and so on. It is these fractions that are important, in that the 'music' that Jack Spooncer and others have heard at crop circles and during UFO sightings, etc., seems to be expressions of these fractions.

Regarding crop circles, it might be said that it is the music that is laying them down. *Crop circles are harmonic patterns.* This discovery was made by

Gerald Hawkins, author of *Stonehenge Decoded* and a number of other groundbreaking works. He is a respected astronomer and understands the importance of Euclidean geometry, both in terms of astronomy and latterly, corn circles. In realising that fractions of the musical diatonic scale were appearing in the make up of corn circles, Hawkins also realised that we are dealing with something intelligent. Furthermore, new evidence has come to light that in crop circle formations, we are dealing with a phenomenon of infinite harmonics, of vibrations within vibrations, of frequencies within frequencies.[34]

The 'noise' found at these sites is, in fact, rhythmic vibration, which, to all intents and purposes, is birdsong speeded up. What is extraordinary is that birdsong is symphonic. The work of David Hindley, a Cambridge musician, has shown that the songs of birds relate precisely to the rules and principles of human musical composition. Birdsong is a highly compressed sequence of notes. A 48-second song of a skylark ran to nearly 13 minutes when transcribed to human speed by Hindley. Also, it became apparent that the composing skills of Mozart and Beethoven had found a sparring partner![35]

Following on from the earlier revelations of an ancient acoustic science in chapter five, this brief journey into the strange world of crop circles should help us to understand that sound, electrical and magnetic forces can be applied together with intelligence to give rise to form – not only in the mind, where the tendency is to mentally clothe the subtle images, but also physically. Here we approach the ancient dictum that, in truth, name (sound) and form are one. In the ancient traditions, this science of name and form is the realm of the shaman.

The One Who Names

Various theories have been put forward regarding the origins of shamanism. Some authorities believe that the first shamans came from the Altai Mountains in Siberia, others that they emanate from Tibet or other remote areas. However, it is now generally accepted that shamanism is a worldwide phenomenon whose beginnings are hidden in the impenetrable mists of deep antiquity.

Enuma Elish-la nabu shamanu begins the great Mesopotamian story of creation,[36] and in it there is a key word, *Shamanu*. The whole line read:

'When, on high, the heavens were not yet named...'

The shaman is 'the one who names' and this corresponds to native traditions worldwide, particularly those with a tradition that refers to the 'first time', otherwise called the 'dreamtime'. This is an appropriate way to describe the 'other' world, for here, at the finer levels of creation, where electromagnetic fields constantly interact, there is a blurring of identities. In this realm, the journeyman must keep a clear and focused mind, and, like the hero, harrow 'hell' to enter the underworld, the region that underpins physical life, the region where spirits may be consulted. But if the shaman is the traveller to other realms, then the sacred site is the gateway. In the previous chapter, we gained an insight into how sacred atmospheres can elevate sensitivities. They are a means of entrance to the nether realms.

In modern parlance, the shaman can be seen as a frequency modulator, tuning in to the waveband and travelling in consciousness, going where he chooses, even up into the sky. Shamans claim that they can do this. Perhaps consciousness, when unfettered by the body, can go where it wills. Certainly, many people have out of the body experiences. I myself have had a profound near-death experience where 'I', my consciousness, left my body and yet I retained my identity. The realm of consciousness, though, is highly subjective and proving such experiences, in current scientific terms, is virtually impossible. Mainstream science will have to jettison much of its 'objective' dogma before serious study of the nature of consciousness can be undertaken. In the meantime, it is fortunate that a number of sacred sites support the claims of the shaman.

The most famous of these sites is the Nazca lines in South America. These vast geoglyphs were most certainly designed to be seen from the air, from the shamanic mind's eye. Unintelligible at ground level, except as a series of dusty pilgrim processional routes, these spectacular lines, from an aerial viewpoint, form spirals, vast animals, birds and most famously, a spider. They have been subjected to many a hypothesis, even forming the central theme of a book by von Daniken, arguing that they are alien landing sites. Contrary to von Daniken's view, is the evidence on the ground.

Nazca is situated high up in a desert region in southwest Peru. It is an arid region with traces of ancient irrigation and thus early civilisation. The markings, covering a vast expanse, lie on reasonably flat land that is perfect for sightseeing from above – aerial photography has long revealed the wonderful glyphs for what they are. The Nazca culture created the markings over a period of roughly 1,000 years from 400 BC until drought and the subsequent collapse of the culture brought all activity to a close, *c.* AD 600.

The Nazcans themselves lived not far away, on lower ground, closer to the sea. These locations were, and still are, water catchment areas, in complete contrast to the arid plateau some miles away. The water catchment areas have been called 'irrigation channels', which they undoubtedly are, but upon closer inspection they may also have served another purpose. By the indigenous peoples they are still called *Pukas*, a word that is extremely similar to the Gaelic, *puca* (English 'Puck'), meaning 'mischievous sprite', and many of them are fashioned as spiral walkways that descend gradually to the height of a well from wherein holy water was drawn. In these pages, you will notice recurring instances of water, spirals and folklore.

The local pots and shards that have been excavated picture some animals that are not local to the area: monkeys, killer whales and certain species of bird. These animals are also depicted high up on the arid plain. Perhaps these distant species were first seen through shamanic flights.The most compelling piece of evidence, however, is the depiction, upon pottery, of a flying green man, spewing vomit and mucus from mouth and nostrils.

Sacred site and holy water alone did not induce the shaman to fly, for in order to travel to the gods, he imbibed the local narcotic: the juice and flesh of the San Pedro cactus (named after St. Peter – in his role of Guardian of the Heaven's Gates perhaps?) In flying to the realm of the gods, the shaman would negotiate various obstacles by taking the shape and aspect of many and various animals (very reminiscent of Mowgli in Kipling's *Jungle Book*). In this guise he would use their various properties to fight demons and negotiate with the gods for various cures, for rainfall and even a good harvest.

Broadcast in 1998, a television programme, *Flightpaths to the Gods*, presented by Dr Anthony Spawforth, featured a prominent shaman and healer brought up within the Nazca locale, who stated, very significantly:

> '..We need the vibration of the humming bird to help us to tune into the universe, to give us a better understanding of illness and the evil spirits that lay behind it. We need its beak to tap into the wisdom of the sun-god.'

The humming bird forms one of the largest of the Nazca geoglyphs. The same shaman also told how they admired the condor because it spirals up into the sky; shamans say that they 'themselves take off' in spiral fashion. The geoglyphs were processed or walked by the ordinary populace at large, music was played whilst walking the lines and decorated pots would be smashed as if in sacrifice to the gods. This latter ritual also took place on a grand scale in dynastic and predynastic Egypt. The aim of these rituals was literally to massage the earth, to placate her into providing water. These lines were the 'soul paths' of the shaman and lines like them are to be found the world over. A lot of them are pilgrim routes. But whilst the pilgrims walked the lines, the shamans saw them from above. It seems that shamans have ways of gaining knowledge that we are not fully aware of, invisible ways, sensitive ways.

And so it is that man *is* sensitive, and I would venture that this sensitivity was not necessarily drug dependent from the outset. Sophisticated ritual techniques and controlled dietary regimes seem to have been the favoured techniques within ancient societies. Archaeological evidence and analysis of site and of individuals[37] have proven that fasting and dietary techniques were a hallowed part of ritual and of living.[38] Within this sphere, the spiritual 'technology' appears to have been highly developed from the outset of civilisation. If there is evidence of drug usage, it has a tendency to be late on the scene and reflects the general decline that befalls every civilisation. As this happens, clarity is lost and so is depth of knowledge. With this loss comes a facile interpretation of events and even language takes on a new meaning. For example, the idea of the shaman and the hero harrowing hell can tell us a lot about this change of interpretation.

Earlier I referred to the underworld as the subtle substratum which underpins physical life. In ancient Greece, the underworld was called 'Hel' or 'Helle', and here we see the multiple associated meanings which frequently appear in ancient languages, for these words also mean both 'womb' and 'sun', in that womb and sun both underpin, or come before physical life. A further extension of the word *hel*, or *helle* means equally simply but profoundly, 'change'. Thus it is when you are going through hell, you are in fact changing. In its religious context, this is change associated with the element fire – 'a baptism of fire' as one might say. To the Ancients, the sun not only upheld life, it was also the great purifier, and to pass through hell was to pass through the fires of purification. Having been purged, their senses and systems purified, the 'Pure Ones' were then able to commune with the gods, for they could now operate on a more refined level.

Goddess and Son

As we have already seen, the Greek name *Ge* or *Gaia* meaning 'earth', was derived from the Egyptian, 'Geb'. It is echoed to this day in many familiar words – 'geometry', 'geology', 'geomancy', 'geophysics', all earth-based subjects. Again, it is geometry that reveals the most about the earth and her true relationship with the sacred site. As revealed by Alexander Thom, the sacred site is not a haphazard siting upon an earth fault or spring, it is a precisely measured phenomenon that adheres very closely to what Thom discovered to be a precise measure, the megalithic yard.[39] We shall not delve too closely into measure – at this point it is enough to realise that geometry goes beyond measure. It is the language of circles, spirals and ellipses, and therefore a language of movement, especially of heavenly bodies, a language that speaks cryptically of the true nature of the divine, particularly of the divine here on earth. It speaks of the real and ancient history now expressed within the world's religions and mythologies, a language of pattern, rhythm and number, obscured and unjustifiably dismissed.

See now how the mind can work through language. We have noted that the sixteenth letter of the Hebrew and Greek alphabets ,'o', represents the third eye.[40] The Greek prefix *Geo* thus reveals a hidden meaning: that as far as the Greeks were concerned, the Earth, *Ge* is only really perceived or measured via the gateway of the third eye – the letter 'o', which is a perceptual gateway between earth and the way in which we 'have the measure' of it – ge-o-metry. The earth goddess is in this way the subject of contemplation, and that brings her measure to us, the measure of rhythms, vibration and metre. To the human mind, such understandings were a guiding light in the darkness.

Further to Gaia, the Greeks had another name for Mother Earth, one that was older, one that linked her directly to heaven and the cosmos; the name is Maia, or Mara. However the name is spelt, this particular aspect of the goddess is the one that reveals her as the mother of the redeemer, the one who will come, the hero. She is the 'Queen of Heaven' and, as noted previously, she has been witnessed in a vast profusion of visions.

Mary as the mother of the hero is famous and esteemed in the Roman Catholic Church as the 'Mother of God'. Indeed, she was proclaimed as Theotokus, 'God-bearer', at Ephesus in AD 413 by the newly powerful Church. A significant point must be that Ephesus, where the Holy Virgin was assumed body and soul into heaven, was also the cult centre of the goddess Artemis, another divinity often seen in visions. Given the way in which early Christianity absorbed and mimicked local Pagan beliefs, the evidence would suggest that Mary was also an Earth goddess, as was Artemis.

To go even further, the Vatican Office of the Virgin has described her as the primordial being, 'created from the beginning and before the centuries'. In the *Speculum beatae Mariae*, attributed to the thirteenth–century saint, Bonaventura, Mary is said to be:

> '...queen of heaven where she is enthroned in the midst of the
> angels, queen of earth where she constantly manifests her power,
> and queen of hell where she has authority over the demons.'

In effect, the goddess is seen as a creatrix, a force, one of the two prime interacting aspects (male and female) of the Absolute. In native myths of the dreamtime, all life, all humanity, inhabited the womb of the goddess in an ever-present state of wonder and totality. The goddess was what science would call 'causality'; from her came everything. Quite often within myths the goddess is seen as a huntress, armed with a bow and arrows. In this guise she was called Artemis by the Greeks and Diana by the Romans. An essential aspect of the myth of the goddess was that each year she would give birth to a son, whose destiny it was to be cut down in his prime and, having harrowed Hell, be reborn as the goddess's lover. She was the giver and the taker of life, and by the same token she could bestow immortality. Thus in ancient societies, embedded deep within their mythos is the identity of the goddess as creatrix of all.

The Great Goddess has many names and forms, stretching far back into antiquity. As Cybele she makes frequent appearances in Greek mythology and is known to have been the great mother goddess of the Mediterranean. Her name is Anatolian[41] and is to be traced back as far as Catal Huyuk in Anatolia (now in southern Turkey), where a shrine dating to *c*.6,500 BC shows her giving birth to a bull's head with horns, the bull being symbolic of her son, the hero.

Cybele's name has a variety of meanings, each of which is valid, particularly as each goddess had a multitude of functions. One of her names is 'She of the hair'. This is a specific reference to her portrayal as, literally, hairy – just as the Magdalene and others are represented covered head to foot with hair. She (and probably a host of other goddesses) was the protectress of the chasms and clefts of Gaia; it can be said that both she and Gaia are one with Mother Earth.[42] Within this remit she was also the guardian of the bears that hibernated in her caves during the long winter months – they, too, are hairy. Cybele had oracles at various sacred sites, the most famous of which was the Sibyl at Delphi. Sibyl is another spelling of Cybele. Oracles were famous prophetesses, the Gypsy palm-readers of their day.

Literally, Cybele splits into two syllables, *Cy* and *bele*. *Bele* means the same as its male counterpart *Baal* meaning 'lord', but emphasises beauty, the feminine aspect.[43] It is the first syllable that is of prime interest. One translation is 'desert' or 'barren place'. I was surprised to learn, whilst reading one day through a book on the myths and legend of early Christianity, that at least two Marys were associated with arid places: St. Mary of Egypt and St. Mary Magdalene, whose apparent desert experience was in the wilderness of southern Provence in the years after the crucifixion.[44] Intriguingly, the festival of Cybele always fell on 4th April and was called the Megalensia. Given the similarities to the Magdalene, this seems to be a related name. It could be that someone, a Christian copyist perhaps, had sought to limit the similarities between Cybele's festival and the Magdalene by the simple but effective removal of the letter 'd'. More intriguing is the fact that *Cy* also means, in Greek, 'waves', hence cymatics, the study of waveforms. Cybele, in being the goddess, 'lady or beauty of the waves', seems to be making a direct reference to sound, a point borne out by the name of her son, who seems to have inherited something of her music. The son was called various names – Attis, Adonis, Anchises. In his original archaic Syrian homeland he was Dumuzi, known to us as Tammuz.

Tammuz is a shepherd-god, one whose influence on later Christian literature has been noted by scholars. Called an early 'prototype' of Jesus by Christian apologists, Tammuz is most frequently known as the 'dying and rising god'.[45] Shared similarities with Jesus include the fact that he was known as 'the only begotten son', 'the saviour', 'the healer' and 'the Heavenly Shepherd'. A month of the Jewish calendar is still named after Tammuz.

'Tammuz', when divided into its component parts reveals much: *Ta* and *muz*. The second syllable is more familiar to us as 'Moses', meaning literally 'child of'. Thus we have 'child of Ta'. 'Ta' or 'Te' is the seventh note of the musical scale. So too is 'Si', the little known and infrequently used equivalent of 'Te'.[46] Tammuz and his mother, the Sibyl or Cybele, share the same musical note: Tammuz is the child of the seventh, and Cybele is the lady of the seventh. The number seven occurs countless times in religious literature. It was Jesus who, in one of the most famous episodes of his short life, cast out of Mary Magdalene seven devils. Are these seven related to musical notes?

On the occasion of Tammuz' death, the Babylonians would ring out great 'ululations' of despair, a tradition still held in Bedouin custom (under a different, Islamic, guise). The cry of the people, as described by Babylonian chroniclers, was 'alalu', in other words 'halleluiah'; Tammuz had gone to intercede on their behalf. Was it not the 'alalu' of the Babylonians that went on to become the *Te Deum*, the supreme expression of rejoicing in the Roman Catholic and other Churches?

Te Deum Laudamus, 'We praise thee O God, halleluiah' – is the true age of Christianity being revealed here?

Not surprisingly, there were many variations upon the theme of Christianity, some of which came to be seen as heretical. In the second–century AD, a new heresy arose, Montanism. Its founder, Montanus, was a Phrygian of Anatolia, homeland of Cybele. Through Montanus, the Holy Spirit is said to have stated:

'Behold, man is like a lyre, and I fly over it like a plectrum.'[47]

By extension, it seems to me that the Holy Spirit is imparting an exceedingly precious morsel of knowledge: understand waveforms, frequencies, sound – the stuff of music – and not only do you have an understanding of the Divine and its relationship to humanity, but also a key to opening up that relationship! It seems that the Ancients used this knowledge and now so do the crop circle makers. Both, though, are beyond our reach. Fortunately, there is another clear demonstration of this wisdom, one that we can encounter now, ourselves.

The Rise of the Godly

In the years preceding the First Crusade of AD 1095, elements of a new and vital energy began to creep across the threshold of the newly emergent Europe. In the wake of the Dark Age terrors, when the power of Rome had become transformed into a nascent European cultural identity, the heaviness that was the Romanesque design of sacred buildings was about to be replaced by an abundance of lightness and measure.

The Romanesque seems to epitomise the darker age that preceded the medieval period. Light seems constrained within its walls, whose apertures barely deserve the description of windows. Within the Romanesque there is a limited sense of the soul and perhaps of the soul's purpose. There is a strange leaden feeling, a heaviness. Psychologically, and in the context of the period in which they were constructed, this is all too revealing. They are hallowed temples and deserve much good comment, but are outdone by the Gothic – a framework within which light and sound do very profound things.

The Dark Ages had wrought much havoc upon the European landscape, but in their wake there arose much to wonder at. Whilst the feudal system had become firmly established, transforming both culture and landscape into an organised and efficient system of management, the Church itself, having undergone centuries of upheaval, was now subject to a more subtle revolution. This was the era of the great Catholic hegemony, to whom even kings were answerable upon fear of excommunication and consequent removal. During this period (AD 900–1500) the Dark Ages were at last banished as a distant memory as individual nation states arose from the debris, guided by the principle of Christian law.

Scholars often speak of the 'death of the gods' amidst the decline of the ancient world and of their subsequent resurrection during the early to middle years of the Renaissance. But surely this is an irony? If the Pagan gods had died out, so too would the very ideas that they represented. The Greeks had made the concept of deity 'human', that is to say, they had gods with foibles and faults, they were fallible. According to this model, the concept of the gods and the language of myth is the history of life itself, it is the history of human impulse and the discovery of self and identity. Consequently, when the idea of 'one god' came along to replace the idea of 'many gods', the many gods were easy to dismiss as mere aspects of human fallibility. But is divinity something that is purely superhuman? According to many religious ideas, there is a part of God in each and every one of us – we are linked to the cosmos by God who created it. God is in everything, therefore everything is related; everything is relative. Myth, with its many gods, is about relationship and is there to be used as a tool. It is about man reaching out and exceeding his state of humanity, to realise his oneness with God. To clarify: the gods were more than a simple idea, a fad whose time ran out as quickly as Christianity came into fashion, and in point of fact, any idea of *Götterdämmerung* (the death of the gods) must surely imply the demise of humanity also. Fortunately, although we may have slipped, we have certainly not perished.

Humanity is still here, relationship is still here and so are the gods, but their language has changed with the course of history, ebbing and flowing in response to humanity's need. How else can we explain the predominance of 'Pagan' imagery to be found within Christian sanctuaries?

> 'How extraordinary were the adventures in space and time of these gods of the Middle Ages – these hybrid and phantom gods – and how much may be learned of the history of civilisation from a study of their metamorphoses and reincarnations.'[48]

By the same token, what is immediately apparent from a study of the history of the period is that a quite tangible change occurred: in cultural, intellectual and spiritual terms, Europe at last achieved self-identity. The rise of the Gothic is a starting-point, for, from its inception in the 1100s, it marked a transformation of conscious intent, the beginnings of a change in consciousness itself, in a way that is unparalleled in European history.

It was a full two decades before the First Crusade that elements of the Gothic arrived in Europe, at the Benedictine monastery of Monte Cassino, Italy, from 1066–1071. During this time Europe was still throwing off the physical presence of Islam whilst adapting and absorbing into its own culture all that it had learned from the invaders. At its centre in the Middle East, the Islamic culture was still far ahead, in science, philosophy, law, the arts and a host of civiliing disciplines. Exposure to this rich culture during the first of the crusades was to create an unprecedented explosion of creative thought and activity in Europe at the outset of the twelfth century. The Gothic cathedral was the foremost expression of this activity and enthusiasm for the style was boundless. In France alone, between 1170 and 1270, as well as around 500 Gothic-style churches, an astonishing 80 cathedrals were constructed. From the east to the west, medieval Europe was festooned in an abundance of gigantic palaces of light. These great towering masterpieces still display a richness unsurpassed and, as we shall see, embody profound ideas which serve to illumine the mystery of life.

Much that had been lost in the Dark Ages was being rediscovered, if not wholly re-invented, for a terrible price had been paid in knowledge lost during that time. In the words of the late William Anderson, the appearance of the Romanesque alone was an act that was nothing short of heroic, therefore the rampant march of the Gothic was, by the same standards, miraculous.

Contrary to much scholarly opinion, a view is arising, with evidence to support it, that the Romanesque appeared upon the stage only shortly before the Gothic.[49] William Anderson, whose work *The Rise of the Gothic* is a landmark, sees both styles born of:

> 'the explosion of new thoughts and new feelings that erupted in the twelfth century, with the birth of scholastic philosophy and the rediscovery of the eternal feminine that was manifested in various forms such as Mariolatry and the lyrics of the Troubadours. The sculptors of the Romanesque had also released the latent archetypal powers of the ancient gods and a new indigenous style was necessary to contain and reconcile these powers...'[50]

Once the Romanesque style had released these powers its job was effectively done and the stage was set for the total domination of a style devoted to letting in the light, for not only is the Gothic a considerable intellectual and aesthetic achievement, but greater than these is its sense of the spiritual. The observation that the Gothic was concurrent with the Romanesque leans toward the view that the latter arose out of historical consequence whilst the former arose out of a school of learning where many strands of older beliefs and traditions were being drawn together into a unified whole. The sense that I got, particularly from that greatest of Gothic cathedrals, Chartres, with its plethora of unlikely imagery, was that fundamentally, this combined ancient knowledge was Pagan and from out of that, Christianity had arisen. Quite possibly this is how it was meant to be read by the lowly peasantry of the day – that Christianity is the culmination of all that has gone before – but, as we have noted, initiating this activity was the influence of Islam.

In 1064, many thousands of prisoners were taken at the siege of Barbastro, a village in Aragon, Spain. Amongst these prisoners were many Moslem craftsmen. The Moorish-Islamic style of architecture of the preceding centuries was very distinctive and made use of many features, foremost of which is the famous pointed arch. It was the sudden influx of these Moslem prisoners that set the scene for the transformation of European architecture. Over the next 70 years, their ideas would enfranchise and permeate the Guild of Masons. Again, in the words of William Anderson:

> 'The architects who created the Gothic style were men of exceptional boldness and originality and they achieved something extraordinary. They were to form an international organisation that for four hundred years, from about 1140 to 1540, trained through succeeding generations artists of genius who

could maintain the standards of their art and at the same time develop it...'⁵¹

The continuity of Moslem tradition, allied to the new and exciting spiritual revolution of Christian Europe, began to yield swift results. A new style emerged, already with a surprising wholeness. At Monte Cassino, the Moorish tradition of Spain was linked harmoniously with the new knowledge then coming from the Holy Land. However, it was at the rebuilding of the cathedral of St. Denis, north of Paris, that the Gothic really began to emerge, and in truly remarkable fashion. The rebuilding of St. Denis was undertaken by the Abbot, Suger.

Born of a peasant family in 1081, Suger was a modest man who had become the confidant of kings. During the year 1147 he was even Regent of France, whilst its king, Louis VII, was on crusade. By all accounts a good conversationalist and very good company, Suger withdrew from the royal court in order to concentrate upon the rebuilding of his beloved St. Denis. Intriguingly, his first action in undertaking such an immense task was to employ a group of monks to research into the early Christian writings. He specifically enjoined them to look out for anything that commented or revealed any insight into the use of light, and into its magical and transcendent qualities. Abbot Suger adopted the motto, *Ars sina scienta nihil est* – 'Art without knowledge is nothing'. But the Abbot's passion stretched beyond knowledge and art for their own sake. He was reaching for something higher still. He was to write:

> 'When out of my delight in the beauty of the House of God – the loveliness of the many-coloured gems has called me away from external cares, and worthy mediation has induced me to reflect, transferring that which is material to that which is immaterial, on the diversity of the sacred virtues: then it seems to me that I see myself dwelling, as it were in some strange region of the universe which neither exists entirely in the slime of the Earth nor entirely in the purity of Heaven; and that by the grace of God, I can be transported from this inferior to that higher world in an anagogical [mystical] manner.'⁵²

Such intensity bore fruit at St. Denis.

The new west front, begun in 1137, includes the first rose window. The west front itself, the northex, the choir and the crypt are the only surviving elements of Suger's innovations, but these are enough to tell us that the Gothic had at last emerged. Here, instead of the old feeling of monumental architecture coupled with constraint and foreboding, we have a new climate, one of reconciliation and of consolation. Thus the entrant into such an atmosphere feels reassured and at ease. The interior is unburdened by darkness, the columns in the choir are slim, the arches are high and the space between them is broad. Furthermore, here is another element that is central to all Gothic architecture: the 'axes' are aligned to the centre of the choir so that coloured light from the surrounding stained glass is able to penetrate, unhindered, into the deeper recesses. The simplicity of design is startling, its approach quite breathtaking. At St. Denis the new style is emergent, however it is at the cathedral of Sens that is it born.

In 1128 the old cathedral of Sens was destroyed by fire and its Archbishop, Henri le Sanglier, was confronted with a greater task than his compatriot, Abbot Suger at St. Denis. At Sens, a phoenix arose from the ashes. Significantly, the new design incorporates the skeleton as a major element. This is expressed through the use of ribs, arches and piers (see illustration). Here we see, for the first time, the interplay of forces that are in direct opposition to each other, to give a lightness of touch and of style. It is at Sens that we have the opportunity to appreciate its simple musical proportion. Its unity is expressed in the octave 1:2, an example being that the aisles are half the width of the nave. The structure

The Gothic structure

rises upwards in three stages, rather than the four of the Romanesque, and wherever one looks there is rhythm – vertically and horizontally. Also there is a deliberate play on numbers. For example, with the three upward stages we have the Trinity and, with the use of the 1:2 ratio, duality. These buildings were becoming homes of true metaphysical thought.

Within a short time, the new style developed and reached its apogee in one of the greatest masterpieces of historical architecture, Chartres.

Frozen Music

It is a little known fact that when Chartres cathedral came to be built, monarchs from all over Europe gave financial support and manpower for its construction. Built over a period of 26 years, it is a visually stunning work of art and yet, on approach, the first thing that assails the senses is something non-visual. It is a great sense of the 'power of place'. So striking is this sense that, allied to the visual richness, one is considerably aware of a deep feeling of antiquity, an ancient sense of belief and of spirituality. There is a sense of 'something other', something far greater than that which is on display. The oldest and greatest of divinities is implicit in everything at Chartres. It is invisible, but I shall try to reveal it to you.

At Chartres, as at Reims and Amiens and a host of other European sites, the place is dripping with statues. No mass production here, no use of moulds, no uniformity, just thousands of individually carved faces, human, animal and vegetable, figures real and mythical, with flora and fauna equally symbolic. Here, everything is crucial, everything has its role. There is a sense that all is vital and there to be read. But, stand back, until all that has struck the eye as individual has merged into an overview, and then, only then, does one gain a purer insight into the broad magnificence that is the Gothic. For rising out of the ground is the sense of something organic, something that has grown to towering proportions and yearns to grow further still. We are already aware of granite's crystalline properties and we will look more deeply into these later. Parts of Chartres' interior are made of granite, particularly in the altar area. The exterior is limestone. The entire building is like a huge crystal, created to resonate to the sound of praise; praise to the Eternal, to Jesus and to Mary, Mother of God. True sacred sites are designed to be alchemical transmutation points of the soul. They are interactive, Chartres particularly so. Simply walking through the building can be an emotional experience. Gothic cathedrals have been called 'books in stone'. Chartres is more like a huge interactive library!

Here, as at Neolithic sites, sound is the interactive element, and the sciences of acoustics and geometry come together through the architecture to create what John D Barrow sums up as 'the unreproducable acoustic qualities of the Gothic'.[53] Ancient Newgrange gives its acoustic clues in simple carvings; Chartres' carvings are more sophisticated. Above the main door of Chartres,

*Christ enthroned upon
the Tympanum at Chartres*

as well as a host of other cathedrals, can be found the Tympanum. This takes its name from the Greek *Tympanon* , meaning 'kettle-drum', and is derived from the verb *typtein*, 'to strike'. The Tympanum displays Jesus in all his glory, for there, in its midst, is Christ enthroned. Upon further reflection this design looks to all intents and purposes like a standing-wave pattern, with associated nodes and antinodes. There are yet more clues: gargoyles stare down, mouths open as if spewing forth sound. Above the central door of the royal portal is a musician-king who conceals under his robes a matrass – a long-necked chemical flask, symbolic of the alchemist. Also in the royal portal, Pythagoras can be seen in a pose of utter concentration, playing a tintinnabulum – a high-pitched bell. Thereupon follow more learned 'pre-Christian' figures striking the appropriate themes: Euclid, Cicero, Aristotle, Ptolemy, Boethius and Priscian. Interspersed around them are various Biblical prophets: Jeremiah, Moses, Isaiah, Elijah and others.

Looking upwards and away from the royal portal we see the magnificence of Chartres' flying buttresses, which serve to add to the impression of the whole as a heavenly crystal. The buttresses draw the eye further up, until at the pinnacle of the towers we see the full glory of the pointed arch (see illustration). Within these pointed arches, illuminating the entire space of the interior, are an astonishing range of stained-glass windows. Gothic stained–glass is very special and has peculiar properties. The secrets of its manufacture have since been lost to the world. Once I became aware of its properties, my estimation of the humble medieval craftsman soared to new heights. Was he aware of the fact that the stained-glass windows of Gothic cathedrals filter out the harmful ultraviolet of the sun's rays?

Glass is an insulator, a supercooled liquid that has turned solid upon cooling, without crystallisation taking place. It is not a true solid, which is why it is often referred to as 'amorphous'. The amazing qualities of Gothic stained glass are due to the fact that these windows are, literally, sandwiches of super-ground crystalline contents, though where this knowledge came from is an abiding mystery. The effect of this is vital upon the final quality of refraction; Gothic stained glass has a high refractive index. This gives the glass its exquisite jewel-like quality. It is widely believed that this is a purposefully created effect, one that serves to aid the state of mind by the application of only specific types of light, most of it coloured. The work of Blanche Mertz has shown that there is 'neutralisation in that zone which is directly related to the filtering effects of the stained glass windows, creating a wavelength of light that can harmonise with the natural vibrations of human cellular tissue...'[54]

Glass-making of this calibre was a heavily-guarded secret during the Middle Ages. It was the realm of the alchemist and of the secret arts. The results are strikingly impressive – this technology of coloured glass sends the achievement of the Gothic up into rapturous heights. The rose windows, north, south and west, are the glory of Chartres, each one a geometric masterpiece.

Chartres is a temple fine-tuned to an exceptional degree and I use the word 'temple' purposefully. As at Sens, the choir of Chartres cathedral is a double square, 'the ratio of 2 to 1 is exactly that of the Egyptian and Greek Temples ... likewise of Solomon's Temple as far as the Holy of Holies'.[55] This fine-tuning is also demonstrated in a phenomenon again reminiscent of Newgrange and other sites. Every year on 21st June – the summer solstice, the day when the sun reaches its highest point in the sky – a ray of light shines through a spot in the stained-glass window dedicated to St. Apollinaire. The beam descends to a specific place, a flagstone on the western side of the south transept. The stone, larger than those around it, has set within it a small metal tenon; it is this that is illuminated precisely at 12.45 p.m. local time. Because the height of the sun is now at its peak, this can only happen once a year on this solstice day. Note that Apollinaire is another version of Apollo, the Greek sun god.

Nothing was completed at Chartres without precise purpose and planning. So, too, the labyrinth. The labyrinth, as a symbol, is a curious phenomenon. It has its origins way back in the depths of prehistory. By the time its symbolic purpose was revived in the Middle Ages, its Pagan roots had melted into the shadows. Of all the labyrinths at cathedral sites, the one at Chartres is the most famous and it will be discussed further in the following chapter. In the meantime, know that it was constructed as an object of mysterious ritual, said to be a penance path used by devotees as a substitute for an actual pilgrimage to Jerusalem. Upon first seeing it I thought of both Newgrange and Nazca. At Newgrange, these enigmatic shapes are to be found everywhere, whilst at the site of the famous Nazca markings evidence has come to light that they, like the labyrinth of Chartres, were used for processional purposes. Indeed, the labyrinth at Chartres does have a ritual 'feel' to it. To me, it is as if it were the path of a ritual dancer.

There was a similar labyrinth at Auxerre cathedral and a well-authenticated story tells us of a ritual associated with it. On the afternoon of Easter Sunday, the Dean and his chapter were to be found standing upon the Auxerre labyrinth, singing the hymn *Victimae Paschali laudes* , whilst the Dean himself threw a golden ball to each member of the chapter as they danced the labyrinth. They danced in a triple rhythm to the hymn.[56] What I found of great interest was the probability that this ceremony dated back at least to the early Bronze

Age. The maze was an emblem of this age, although its origins may go back farther still. In fact, there may be a link here to what is reputed to be the oldest hymn in the world, the Vedic Gayatri, known as the 'triple song' or 'solar hymn', for here the golden ball of the sun is praised in a triple rhythm.[57]

High above the labyrinth at Chartres, pillars rise up into the ceiling of nave, choir and chapel, spreading outwards like the branches of a grand and great oak. Looking up at Chartres' vaulting I recalled that at Dodona, the oldest of the Greek oracle sanctuaries, the father god, Zeus, was worshipped as being immanent within the Sacred Oak; the rustling of its leaves in the wind was said to be his voice. Similarly, to me, the great cathedrals are rather like petrified forests echoing with the divine sound. Perhaps Goethe, the eighteenth–century philosopher, had this in mind when he likened architecture to frozen music. Maybe he knew that during the course of construction, masons would quite often tap a pillar in order to hear its tone.[58] (I have done the same to Hatshepsut's fallen obelisk which lies in the temple grounds at Karnak, Luxor, Egypt. Its tone is a low but very resonant hum). That day at Chartres, I developed a neckache from constantly gazing upwards. I'm sure that the pain distracted me from seeing the obvious (well, that's my excuse anyway!), as it was only later, when looking at photographs, that I realised that the vaulting, when seen as a whole, from end to end, seems to describe an acoustic wave pattern! (See chapter five.)

Spirit-Breath-Wind

If you think that all of these acoustic connections are simply the result of my own imaginings, there are more, including, evidence from experiments clearly linking church and cathedral ornamentation to the science of sound. The experiments also answered a question I had often raised about some of the curious forms to be found carved into many an ecclesiastical interior. Generally, these forms are organic, plant-like, in fact they bear a reasonable resemblance to ferns found in the forest. My question was: 'What do they really represent?' As we have seen, everything in a Gothic cathedral has its deeper purpose.

The original experiment was performed by Father Andrew Glazewski, a Polish physicist based in Britain. Father Glazewski was also a Jesuit priest, whose main interest was crystallography and plant growth and their relationships to sound. All organic matter is made up of crystals and compounds; what Glazewski set out to demonstrate was that plants composed of specific crystals followed the same harmonics as the crystals themselves, extending offshoots from their stems proportionate to the same musical phases and tonalities.[59] His experiments showed that the flutings on the columns of Gothic cathedrals also follow the harmonics. He demonstrated this by use of a smoke-filled chamber placed near to a music speaker. The frequencies emitted from the speaker passed through the thin transparent walls of the chamber and affected the smoke. Various photographs (see plate) show the response to a well-bowed violin, a badly bowed violin, a flute, and so on. When the harmonic is played, the smoke looks just like our fern.

> 'There is strong evidence that they reflect the same ratios in the swelling and narrowing of growing plant stems, as well as the flutings on the columns of Gothic cathedrals such as Chartres.'[60]

This experiment reflects those undertaken by the Princeton team at Newgrange and other Neolithic sites (see chapter five). The conclusion is the same: the builders had an in-depth knowledge of the science of acoustics and they left their clues in the ornamentation.

Sacred buildings are created to bring the faithful closer to God. Souls enter to be unburdened and uplifted by refined atmospheres. It is very clear that these beautiful Gothic cathedrals were dedicated to creating such atmospheres and that to do this, the buildings were specifically designed with frequencies in mind, frequencies of light and sound. sound was the interactive level, There is no shortage of evidence that sound was the interactive level.

One summer, whilst visiting Corpus Christi College, Cambridge, I was given further evidence. In the library there is a text written in 1230, with information dating back to 1140, the era when cathedral building was at its height. In *De Organis,* Wulfstan of Winchester exudes praise at the building of a powerful organ. He goes on:

> 'You have built here such an organ as is nowhere else seen, built with a double foundation. Twelve bellows are combined above in order, and below lie fourteen. With alternative blasts they *produce the greatest of resonances.*
> 'Seventy strong men operate them, pulling their arms and being drenched with much sweat; eagerly they each exhort their companions so that with all their strength they may drive the blast upwards so that the blast bag may roar with full throat.'[61]
>
> (My italics)

An organ of such giant proportions is fit only for a cathedral, what is more, it would be capable of very low frequencies, which would create powerful resonances within the building.

'...and the seven distinctions of sound strike up the "jubilus" with the chant of the lyric semitone mixed in. And in the manner of thunder an iron voice struck the ear, so that besides this the ears take in no sound. The sound roared to such an extent, reverberating here and there, that everyone would close his ears with his hands, in this way being able to tolerate the roar when drawing near which the various sounds produce in their noise.'[62]

One expects that the power of such a resonance would have been stronger than the deep Hindu and Buddhist 'Aum' which, when practised correctly, produces refined atmospheres and clarity of mind. Wulfstan goes on to intimate that the organ did indeed have a cathedral purpose. The original document was composed in Latin and the Latin word for 'resonance' is a very descriptive one, *spiracula*, which, of course, is related to the word 'spirit'. We have looked at 'spirit' before and we shall look again; at this juncture, however, it is instructive to investigate early understandings of the word. Much of what has come down to us from the archaic past suggests that for 'spirit' we should perhaps read 'breath', as in 'holy breath', and 'movement', as in 'vibrations'. The lack of a clearly defined distinction was ably summed up by the late Owen Barfield:

'When we translate Latin "spiritus" we have to render it either as "spirit" or as "breath of" as "wind"... But early users of language would not have made any such distinction between these meanings. To them a word like "spiritus" meant something like "spirit-breath-wind". When the wind blew it was not merely like someone breathing: it was the breath of a god. And when an early speaker talked about his soul as "spiritus" he did not merely mean that it was "like a breath": it was to him just that, the breath of life.'[63]

To extrapolate: spirit is the breath of life, it moves, and, as the breath of life, it is within the individual. This sounds like the qualities of frequency or vibration to me, for we know that without this movement, there is nothing; where there is no vibration, there is no life. This vibratory movement of life is present on all levels, from the orbit of an electron around a nucleus to the movement of great fields of energy radiating out from a sun or the earth, or even out from the beginnings of time and space. It is also the movement of localised yet potent fields, for instance, emanating from a type of stone or the human voice. Everywhere this energy is moving, everywhere it manifests differently, but its attributes, so ably described by those early scientists as 'spirit-breath-wind', are always the same: life giving, life sustaining and life transforming.

Now, as then, the wise give praise at the wonder of life and thanks for the mercy of sustenance, but they also hope and pray for the joy of transformation. The aspirations across the ages are the same; the difference is, the masons and their ancient predecessors knew what they were doing, whereas we are only just beginning to discover their secrets. One of the most important things that we now know in this regard is the fact that our own Alpha states can bring us into alignment with Mother Earth's own resonant atmosphere. Such is the effect that, as far as frequency is concerned, man and his environment can become effectively one and the same thing. Pressures and stresses fall away and the mind enters a state of transcendent calm, whilst at the same time remaining alert. Traditionally, this is the condition wherein the third eye, *el Ayin*, begins to open up and with dedicated practice, the subtle realms can be entered.

> '....the brain and mind are not a monolith: they have multiple structural levels, and the highest of those levels creates instruments that permit the observation of the other levels'[64]

When we look upon the carved spirals of Newgrange and the fernlike designs from the Gothic, we need no longer ask: 'How did these people know what to carve?' They would have no need for the assistance of smoke chambers and the like, for mystics and clairvoyants throughout the ages have told us that when the subtle realms are entered, the finer energies can be seen. By extension, one who had developed such a gift could witness the relationship between sun rays, earth energies, and specific local emanations. By introducing mankind's own interactive tool, the human voice, best vicinity, best design and best practice for further transformation could be ascertained. I believe that a few individuals may well have attained this level of knowledge in the past. They would know beyond a doubt that form is a function of frequency. But as initiates, secrecy would be sworn and this powerful knowledge remained hidden.

This ancient, sometime 'Pagan', sometime Christian, knowledge was not 'devil worship', it was a divine science. The people of 'spirit-breath-wind' knew the power of the Word, for their terms also describe the movement of great fields of energy radiating out from the beginnings of time and space, as in:

> 'In the beginning was the Word, and the Word was with God.'[65]

The Word of God

As a philologist, specialising in etymology, who has, at one lecture, been introduced as an entomologist (an insect specialist!), I know the importance of language and its correct interpretation. Knowledge of the origins and meanings of words is fundamental to a quest of this nature. Unfortunately, we are all so close to language that we take meanings for granted, therefore, without constant enquiry and a shift in mindset, the obvious passes us by unrecognised. I had never set out to discover these things that I now lay before you, my goal was never to fathom the meaning of life. In fact I didn't have a goal, but curiosity just took me from one step to another and then one day I realised where I was. All of this evidence of Christian acoustic motive had really set me pondering. Where was a science of sound referred to in the Bible? The walls of Jericho, yes, but this masonic obsession with resonance seemed fundamental - it was back to basics, back to the beginning, and 'in the beginning was the Word'. And so it was that as I contemplated the above quotation from St. John, the obvious appeared. Some key words hide the truth so simply: the word 'universe' means literally 'one word'. 'OK', I thought, so the Word is the universe. Then who, or what, is God? And by the same token who was/is God's son?

Here at last was the reason, the very motive of my quest. Here, to me, were the two most fundamentally important questions, questions that at first I had never even dreamed of asking, let alone coming anywhere near to answering.

These are daunting questions and I make no claims to know all the answers. All I have really studied, throughout these years, is their language – but each time I have taken a step further. I can remember being told years ago that the answers are out there, somewhere, and in the most obvious places. So I set to work.

The word 'God' has an interesting past (see Glossary). Its etymology reveals an extraordinary origin. The letter 'd' in many old languages of Middle Eastern or Indo European origin is interchangeable with a 't', hence English God becoming German *Gott*. This derives from the Old Norse *Goth* 'and this in turn gives us the familiar term *Gothic*. However, there is a much more intriguing and ancient origin to this word. I traced it back to the much older Old High Norse, *Guth*, ...and *Guth* literally means *'voice'*. This is saying that the Gothic is the godly – it is 'vocal', it is the word of God. Thinking back to Goethe's quote about architecture being frozen music, where then is the *un*frozen music? For years I had heard the terms 'the music of the spheres' and 'the music of the universe'. I had always taken these sayings for granted or even dismissed them, whereas in fact, music is all around us, everything vibrates to its own frequency and resonates with all . The universe *is* this music, and the Ancients were saying it is God's sound, from God's voice. They were saying, *are* saying, that God is voice.

Have we now revealed that the true meaning of the word 'God' is 'voice'? If so, Jesus, it would seem, is the son of The Voice. Could that be sound itself? We know that 'son' is the feminine of 'sound' in French, and that 'sound' in Scandinavia is *sund*. These are quick thoughts, but they bring to mind the hero's link to the sun and reaffirm the connection to the goddess and to sound. However, one must be more circumspect. 'Voice' in itself might mean 'sound', then the son of sound might be a particular frequency or effect, or something more abstract. Certainly, there is more to be unravelled here!

Intermezzo

As chapter six opened, the original meaning of words framed deep in the past again provided fascinating clues for the quest. From thence, we entered the unseen subtle realms of ghosts and visions, particularly Marian visions and we saw the role that sympathetic vibration and Alpha states play in these experiences. That the laws of quantum electrodynamics, where energy may appear as either a particle or a waveform, may figure in the visionary experience, perhaps giving aid to the subjective nature of the vision, is significant.

This offers the beginnings of a scientific explanation, which may allow for a personal interpretation of something very subtle and yet very real. A look at UFOs in that context showed that they may well be variations on the divine theme, with resonace playing its role. The associated and more physically manifest anomaly of crop circles was also linked to sound.

We began to unravel the secrets of sacred sites in terms of their mythology, positioning and physical make-up. The power of place, particularly in relation to water courses and the hidden attributes of water were highlighted.

If sound is so important, then names must be important too. Through the Shaman, 'the one who names', we were brought again to the ancient times and through the myths and names began to be linked back more clearly to the Christian material in part one. We were quickly brought through the Christian period to return to the age of the Templars, but this time, in the wake of Newgrange's acoustic revelations, our focus was on the great buildings of the period, the Gothic cathedrals. Now, in the light of the ancient sacred technology, the buildings speak volumes within their architectural design, construction and decorative art. Furthermore, that old genius Pythagoras has returned.

We should remember that sound and light are different levels of the same phenomenon: frequency of vibration.This was the secret of the Templars, the secret of sound, vibration – voices in the cathedral chanting in the name of God. How perfect, that at its Gothic root, 'God' should mean 'voice'.

7

The Power and the Place

*'The nature of God is a circle of which the centre is everywhere
and the circumference is nowhere.'*

Attributed to Empedocles, 493-433 BC

'It has served us well, this myth of Christ.'

Pope Leo X, 1475-1521

The Sanctity of Place

IN April 1980 the Vatican, perhaps in recognition of the rise of the new
environmental awareness in the West, adopted St. Francis of Assisi as the
patron saint of ecology. The significance of this gesture is considerable and it
is reasonable to suggest that in choosing St. Francis, the Vatican was tacitly
giving its sign of approval to the idea of the earth as a living organism; after
all, St. Francis is renowned for his canticle of 'Brother Sun, Sister Moon' wherein
these heavenly bodies are addressed as beings. This is not only supportive of
Sir James Lovelock's 'Gaia' hypothesis, which postulates that the earth is a
single organism, but also introduces the idea of divinity into our relationship
with the planet. We know that the word Gaia, of course, is the Greek name for
the goddess of the earth.

Of all the saints in Christendom, it is generally agreed that Francis, the
merchant's son from Assisi, was the nearest, both in spirit and personality, to
Jesus. Francis renounced earthly wealth but, to the rich in spirit, material
poverty is no great hardship, and it can open the eyes to what is real and
essential, the greatest treasures of Mother Nature herself. In the medieval
period it was St. Francis who most successfully espoused the sheer beauty of

the planet. 'Brother Sun, Sister Moon' speaks of the planet, the cosmos and life in general as a miracle beyond knowing, and in a biographical way we get a great sense of Francis's awe at the wonder of creation.

'Oh, Most High, Almighty, Good Lord God,
to Thee belong praise,
glory, honour and all blessing.

Praised be my Lord God, with all His creatures
and especially our brother the Sun,
who brings us the day
and who brings us the light: fair is he,
and he shines with a very great splendour.
O Lord, he signifies us to Thee!

Praised be my Lord for our Sister the Moon,
and for the stars,
which he has set clearly and lovely
in the Heaven...'

The medieval period had opened up as one of foreboding for the inhabitants of Europe. There had been a sense of doom in the air, a pre-millennial fear that at any moment the four horsemen of the Apocalypse would spring forth from the gates of Hell, bringing with them the last judgement of God. The air was abuzz with rumour, and the freedoms that had emerged from the ruins of the old Roman Empire were threatened by dark clouds of doom. Not only were the Moslem hordes knocking at the door of the Christian West, so too, it seemed, was the Antichrist. This sense of despair and the occasional accompanying outbreak of hysteria can quite firmly be put down to the medieval sense of millennium, the feeling that a time of tribulation was near.

In retrospect it can be seen that millennial tensions only served to focus the mind upon the intangible, for if doom was in the air, it was in competition with a spate of miracles. The blood of long-dead saints miraculously turned to liquid upon their feast days: the ampoule of blood belonging to St. Januarius, patron saint of Naples, still does this every year on 19th September. Visions of the Holy Virgin occurred and some even claimed to have seen whole armies of angels, led by none other than St. Michael himself.

Standing back to admire the grand view of these disturbed times, we may see a mass of superstition, rumour and belief giving rise to illusion, but we also see the numinousness of the period and how the ultimate mystery of the Christian revelation had, in the majority, evoked a sympathy of the soul to ritual that, quite simply, is unintelligible to us today.

The year One Thousand came and went, and gradually, very gradually, the millennial tensions ebbed away. Indeed, the lifetime of St. Francis (1181-1226) can be taken as a marker for the emergence of a new era, one where ritual was given accentuated potency through power of place. As we have seen, this was the great era of cathedral building, the rise of the Gothic, those awe-inspiring buildings that so magnificently encapsulated the sacred within the site and passed it on for the benefit of man.

Now, gloom had given way to divine possibilities, to the transcendent experience of becoming at one with the sense of God. In this way, identity could almost be left behind as a result of divine possession. Even today, one can sense this when visiting one of the great cathedrals or listening to inspired music of the period. It was possibly within this context that, towards the end of the short life of St. Francis, there began to be manifested upon him one of the more inexplicable of the great miracles, the stigmata.

Stigmata are marks that appear upon the body and they resemble the wounds that Christ suffered at the crucifixion. However, this enigma is not restricted to the pious; the marks have also appeared upon the bodies of those whom we might call 'less than holy'. Could these extraordinary manifestations be caused not so much by faith as by place? *The Oxford Dictionary of the Christian Church* describes how the phenomenon is often accompanied by other, seemingly paranormal, events, such as levitation, bilocation (the ability to be in two places simultaneously), and telepathic faculties. Furthermore, stigmata disappear as quickly as they appear, without leaving the slightest sign of their presence. Neither do the wounds become septic, and when treated, they do not respond.

The fact that the great majority of these phenomena actually occur inside churches, cathedrals and temples has, to a large extent, been taken for granted. Whilst I agree that all of these symptoms bear the hallmarks of the numinous and a sense of the divine, I would suggest an emphasis on the divine *in situ*. I have myself seen what was to all intents and purposes blood seeping forth from wood within a particularly powerful church site. I am convinced that the key to the phenomenon lies within altered states of consciousness brought about by exposure to these sites.

We have already seen how the divine is intimately linked with the sacred site; in human terms such intimacy is an acutely powerful thing, indeed, so powerful that the human electromagnetic field changes dramatically in its presence. In fact, changes in field structure occur *before* any change in brainwave frequency.[1] The implication is that it is the field that gives the body's primary response to any outside interaction. Interestingly, the measurement of this field by telemetry also reveals a person's response to his or her environment. When near the mountains or by the sea this field has a tendency to expand, whereas by contrast, a person's individual response to rushing winds makes the energy field contract.

The difference between these conditions can be attributed to positive and negative ions. In a field of negative ions the body thrives. It is for this reason that 'ionisers' have been recommended for use in certain environments, as a means of recharging the air with negative ions. Furthermore, research and experimentation performed over the last ten years have shown that the human electrical field is, in certain situations, more than capable of responding to the wider atmospheric field, that is, with the earth itself. In induced circumstances of electromagnetic deprivation, the body's response was dramatic – interaction and thinking were at best confused. However, when normal electromagnetic levels were restored, the body responded positively, thinking became lucid. Going further, when electromagnetic levels were increased beyond normality, subjects reported an increased awareness and heightened consciousness. This demonstrates that, amazingly, the whole process of bodily movement and coordination is closely linked to the interaction with the electromagnetic pulse of the environment.

It has been tacitly accepted by a group of scientists in Britain and America[2] that the earth and the human body have meridian points which external electromagnetic energy penetrates in order to flow throughout the entirety of both. In the human body, such energy penetrates at the acupuncture points and flows through the connective tissues. Connective tissue is to be found in the body most notably in the form of tendons and cartilage as well as in the non-muscular structures of arteries and veins and bone.

> 'We concluded that the electromagnetic environment is a milieu in which life and physiological happenings occur. Apparently, for all systems to be "go", a rich electromagnetic field must be present.
>
> 'If further studies verify these findings, the implications are staggering.'[3]

Acupuncture uses a knowledge of electromagnetic fields, the origins of which are lost in the deeper recesses of history. Perhaps the knowledge goes back as far as megalithic and Neolithic times. At any rate, it can now be shown that the importance of the electromagnetic environment was not lost upon the sacred site builders of the past. We shall see that they were aware of the power of radiation and sought to use it to advantage.

To recap: everything in the universe resonates in some form and fashion, resonance can quite simply be described as the radiation and absorption of energy by vibration. Our planet sings to the rhythm of the cosmos by being struck (or, some would say, played) by cosmic waves, much like a bell being struck by a hammer. In this way the earth gives off her own vibratory rhythm, a rhythm to which, as testified by the brain's Alpha waves, we may become attuned. The prescribed place of attunement for the Ancients was the sacred site.

It seems to me that when visiting such sites, the potent atmosphere communicates with us. We are being told; 'You are here' and 'This place is particular, something can happen here' – in other words, these are places of power. The sites are, in a way, speaking to us and so are the builders. This has enormous implications. The builders are saying, and forcefully, 'We know what we are doing.'

The Builder's Choice

Sacred sites are effectively meeting-places of time, space and experience. They are totally oriented to the pragmatic and it is with this in mind that we must regard not only the site but also the mythos associated with it (this we will do later). Not only are thousands of these sites dotted across the landscape of Britain and Europe, they are to be found across the entire face of the planet. Almost all of them are affected by high levels of natural radiation arising from the decay of uranium both in the ground and in the rocks used to build the monuments.[4]

Significantly, on the site of the world's greatest megalithic complex, at Carnac in Brittany, France, there is a high level of granite, so too uranium. Granite is a radioactive rock - it has a higher than normal radiation emission. It is to be found at a high proportion of sacred sites across the world from Stonehenge to the pyramids of Egypt. Granite's use by the Ancients is a testament to its properties and to their sensitivity and innovation. How interesting that so many sacred buildings should be constructed of granite and should also be located in close proximity to uranium deposits. Atmospheric tests inside these monuments register radon levels that are often two to three times higher than normal and in some cases, as with the Sekhemkhet pyramid, Saqqara, Egypt, over 30 times higher![5]

These constructions manipulate the electromagnetism of their environment in a very subtle and beneficial way. But the effects sometimes give results which are confusing to the uninitiated; for those who are stressed, heightened states of awareness can quickly give way to symptoms of fatigue. Basically, when individuals attain a high level of attunement with the sacred environment, the body becomes subject to forces that have, until recently, been little understood by science. Given their effects, it is hardly surprising that these places should be associated with spirits and divine presences. Even today, the enhanced state of environmental energies, perhaps aided and abetted by ritual, can create the perfect example of the sanctity of place, and demonstrate the ability of certain locations to change our perceptions. One need not be mystically inclined to bear witness to this power, in fact it is most often the no-nonsense, non-mystically oriented who are most vociferous in their praise of these sites.

Granite itself gives clues to its powers in a very down to earth, visual way. The rock, because of its radioactivity, produces fertile, higher than average growth in plants. Bulbs, by being planted near granite, can be induced to flower early.[6] Is it not likely that rapid growth in the vicinity of granite had been noted by early civilisations? Surely, then, the effect would be associated with divine beneficence and its potential further explored.

Evidence of the use of natural radiation in the sacred landscape is not confined to Britain and Europe, it is to be found at sites throughout the Americas, Australia, Africa and Asia, where, for example, some of the greatest of the Tibetan monasteries are located in places of higher than usual radioactivity. That being the case, perhaps it is not surprising that certain mountains held in great esteem by Buddhists and Hindus have been found to be rich in uranium deposits.

A mysterious and seeming deliberate use of granite's properties of radiation was related to me in a remarkable story that, coming from any other man I would surely have dismissed. My friend, Dr. Tony Scott-Morley told me of a phenomenon to be found at the Temple of Karnak in Egypt. The story reminded me of the fabulous monolith in Arthur C. Clark's *2001: A Space Odyssey*. Tony was invited to go to Egypt by a group of friends who were investigating various scientific aspects of the Karnak temple. On the last day of his visit, he was asked to take some magnetic readings of one of the altar stones. To his immense surprise, when it came to applying the magnetometer to the stone, Tony could only get a reading off one side. When he related the story to me, he was at great pains to point out that he had checked and rechecked his equipment and that, yes, it was in full working order; however, the stone would still only give one reading! In Clark's novel, and to great effect in Kubrik and Clark's film, the enigmatic monolith does precisely the same thing. Prescience? Or has Clark been to Karnak? I have yet to find out.[7]

If the Ancients were clever enough to make a stone behave in that way or sensitive enough to find one that did this naturally, then they knew a thing or two that we don't. Certainly their ingenuity is underlined by the incredible lengths taken to get materials of exactly the right resonance and also by the construction techniques used in order to optimise the atmosphere at sites. Materials used in the construction of a majority of these sites came from far and wide. The example of Stonehenge is amongst the most famous, with blue

Presceli sarsen stones being hauled from the extreme end of southwest Wales across the Severn estuary and overland to Salisbury Plain. Even much of the stone used to build the Giza pyramids is not indigenous to the Giza Plateau; it was hauled hundreds of miles up the Nile.

As we have seen, the materials were silicon-quartz rocks, and granite was especially prized. Silicon is a semiconductor and electrical circuits can be created within the material itself, thus they are sensitive to electromagnetic fields; also they resonate with the earth. The distances travelled show how important it was to get the right stone. But having the right materials is only part of the story. What is done with them in terms of construction is also important. For instance, prehistoric burial chambers, usually sited at power spots, are constructed of layers of organic and inorganic matter. It is believed that these 'clays, built sandwiched between an inner stone layer and the outer grass covering, act to shield the inside of the chamber from geo-magnetic fields'. Serena Roney-Dougal gained this insight from her days at university, where she did research inside a Faraday chamber. Faraday chambers, in being made of a fine copper mesh, screen out unwanted electromagnetic waves such as those from radio or television.[8] An atmosphere 'cleaned' of all interference would be all the better for the performance of sympathetic resonance – acoustic and ritual chants. The cleaner the atmosphere, the greater the change of state, the more ecstatic the feeling of 'oneness' or attunement with the earth.

The mound at Knowth, Ireland, and the covered pyramid at Silbury Hill in Wiltshire in England are classic examples of this layering technique. Perhaps the greatest example of all is the Great Pyramid of Giza, Egypt. It too has layers, the inner layer being granite and the outer limestone, which is the main material used in construction. It would be good, at this stage, to present a conflicting, more simplistic, view, one that to my mind reduces the achievement of the Ancients down to a matter of aesthetics:

> '...the mound at Knowth was decorated not only with quartz and granodiorite but also with blue and white striped siltstone cobbles. These colourful cobbles were collected from near Dundalk and were found near the entrance to the Eastern and Western tombs. It is not clear exactly how they were used but evidently they were chosen for their attractive colour.'[9]

The problem with such a comment is that this is about as far as it goes. Did megalithic man really go shopping for attractive colours? Or is there more to it?

Wilhelm Reich, who earned notoriety in America for his unfashionable and 'unscientific' ideas, died in a US penitentiary because of a little thing called

'Orgone energy'. Reich maintained that the Orgone was the life force and he constructed Orgone accumulators to prove it. Interestingly, these featured layering similar to that found in mounds and pyramids. Whether Reich truly was mad or not is a matter of conjecture, what cannot be doubted is the strange properties of his little box. When looking into an Orgone accumulator, what can quite clearly be seen is a strange spiral of greenish light. Such a light has never been adequately explained.[10]

Just like Reich's box, pyramids, mounds, cathedrals, churches and long barrows all have their hidden dark-as-night chambers and very often witnesses speak of a greenish light. This includes reports from the Great Pyramid, from the interior of which, the French Emperor, Napoleon Bonaparte, is known to have emerged from the interior, visibly shaken. He had expressly commanded that he be left alone there for some time, in imitation of another conqueror, Alexander the Great. Perhaps an eerie green light would not be enough to spook the wilful Emperor and quite what Napoleon saw was never recorded, but the story adds further mystique to the building's considerable reputation. Reich's work has not been taken up by mainstream science, but another aspect of ancient knowledge is at the leading edge of scientific application, that of quartz and silicon technology.

At a number of sites, quartz itself is used alongside granite. At Newgrange the easterly walls are entirely faced in white quartz. Archaeological evidence suggests that in its heyday it may have been covered everywhere with this material. To various of the world's indigenous peoples, for example, the Australian Aborigines, quartz was actually 'solidified light', whilst to some Native North Americans it was—'holy ice'. Quartz was held to induce or enhance states of consciousness. Rock crystal was particularly useful for this purpose. It was believed that spiritual and emotional forces could, by the use of rock crystal, be transformed. In recalling that when a charge passes through quartz, pressures arise and it begins to vibrate at higher frequencies,[11] one wonders, did ancient traditions have knowledge that we are only beginning to recover?

Within world technologies there is a rapidly growing awareness of the use of crystals to transmute and transform electromagnetic energy. It is estimated that the silicon-based technologies of computer systems will be replaced by the use of a new species of laboratory-produced diamond of great purity (they have no faults) which can easily outdo silicon.[12] If, as the works of the Ancients seem to be telling us, there is a connection between natural forms of radiation, consciousness and the structure of buildings, the effects of incredible breakthroughs in technology may also serve to transform our ideas of consciousness and, by extension, our understanding of sacred sites and the technology of the spirit. For example; it was a ruby crystal that was fundamental in the breakthrough of the first laser technology. This led to the production of the first holograms, which are essentially energy interference patterns, and holograms have now been adopted by scientists in developing and explaining such theories as memory storage in the brain and holographic models of the universe.

Looking at the evolution of a scientific development given above, one can imagine a scenario for the early development of sacred sites and ritual. The evidence tells us that our ancestors were aware of these sites and, with the limited building technology of the time, they did their very best to enhance them. This awareness may have initially been derived by a particularly sensitive woman or man, standing at one of these sites and imbibing the heightened atmosphere, which then led to construction programmes aimed at 'capturing' this feeling. As the Ancients became more adept at building, they would be able to enhance the feeling with precision, using, for example, the power of quartz-bearing rock. A continuing quest for finer attunement to Mother Earth and the cosmos would in turn lead to acoustic-based practices that would 'bind back' *(religio)* the soul to its source.

If this seems improbable, we have only to look at the resonances involved at these sites to see that they are very specific indeed (see chapter five). Newgrange is not the only example of purposely attuned resonance. Incredibly, no matter where in the world we go, sites fall within bands of earth resonance (see the Anatomy of the Hero). From Newgrange Knowth, and Dowth in Ireland to Stonehenge, West Kennett Long Barrow and Chun Quoit in England and the pyramids of Egypt and Mexico the relevent frequencies are found.[13] Also, worldwide, there is an underlying mutuality of form; where structures are not circular, they are cruciform and, very often, pyramidic in some way and, as stated earlier, many of these buildings are oriented towards the midwinter solstice. At Maes Howe in the Orkney Isles, as at Newgrange, the solstice sun sends its golden rays through the entrance passage to illuminate the deep, dark interior of the inner sanctum. Surely, here is a message of power and enlightenment which underpins our own, albeit now facile, festival of the midwinter season – celebrations of the birth of the light–giving hero, Jesus.

Pagan Christianity

Whatever the religion, whatever the mythology, each has had its concern with the power of place and early Christianity shared these concerns, making use, on site, of whatever preceded, and for much the same purpose. It is necessary, at this point, to generalise, for Christianity has rarely spoken with one voice.

Attitudes to megalithic and Neolithic monuments have varied considerably from use to abuse over the years. Any abusive attitudes from within the Christian community mirror the insecurities of the times rather than any genuine understanding of a bygone age. It was the poet Robert Graves who reflected this view when he wrote:

> 'Demons and bogeys are invariably the reduced gods of priests
> of a superseded religion.'[14]

Where there are signs of that from which it has emerged, myth is a good starting-point for any historical detective work. So, too, the study of linguistics and the origins of various national terms and phrases, for, as we shall see, myth and language are very intimately linked. To use one of my favourite mixed metaphors: it is a virgin field, pregnant with possibility.

Take the cairns, or *si-uns*, of the British Isles, many of which have interiors cruciform in plan. The term 'cairn' is *Carn* in Gaelic. It means simply 'rock pile'. The name of the county of Cornwall in England tells us it is a place of rock piles. In Cornish the name is even more explicit: Kernow. What interested me most about the Celtic *si-un* is that it brings us, yet again, back to the musical scale, through 'Si', the seventh note. I have mused upon the fact that in the north of England, *si-uns* were known as laws. Through 'God's laws' it brought me back to the idea of Zion and the covenant. It is as if the idea of God was implicit within place and that one had to go to these places in order to be granted a covenant. Psalm 84 is supportive of this:

> 'And they pass on from outer wall to inner, and the God of gods
> shows himself in Zion.'[15]

Moses went to a 'high place' and returned with the Ten Commandments, Abraham's covenant was signed and sealed by his remarkable composure in the attempted sacrifice of Isaac – at a 'high place'. Perhaps it is not surprising that in one of the earliest references to God in the Old Testament he is called El Elyon, 'God Most High' – 'Most High' being both metaphorical and literal, as myth seems to imply.

In Islam, the rock of Sion, over which is built one of the most famous pieces of ecclesiastical architecture, the famous Dome of the Rock, is actually called *es Sakra*, meaning literally 'the rock', this being one of a few recognised holy rocks in Islam. 'Rock' in this sense of being holy means 'sacred'. Now, also recalling chapter two, Jesus' words to Peter take on a new significance of interpretation:

> 'Upon this rock I will build my church.'[16]

As we have seen, the internal structure of a majority of cairns or *si-uns* is cruciform. At Newgrange the internal structure is not only cruciform but reflects both physically and acoustically the layout of the greatest of the European cathedrals.

For centuries, mainstream religion has looked down upon the Pagan. The term 'Pagan' means 'country dweller' and does not at first glance signify anything overtly 'heathen'. All it seems to imply perhaps is that 'civilisation' was mostly an urban affair– attitudes do not really seem to have changed much in the past 5,000 years. 'Civilisation' comes from the same root as 'city' – Latin *civitas*, thus showing that, apparently, cities and civilisation go together hand in hand, whereas in contrast the country is not civilised (i.e. citified). However, 'Pagan' means more than mere 'country-dweller'. It can also translate as 'rural district', 'the country' or, sinificantly, 'a landmark fixed in the earth'.

Nowadays these landmarks, the ancient sacred sites, are still associated with Pagans and Pagans themselves are generally taken to be those who predated Christianity and indulged in nature worship, 'Devil's work', superstition and the like. But what we are now beginning to understand is that these people had a sacred, even scientific, knowledge which was a foundation of religious activity, one which helped to 'bind back' to the divine. Their cairns, standing stones, tumuli and other megalithic-Neolithic monuments were a way of keeping in touch with the soul, the innermost nature, and its relationship to the more refined vibratory atmosphere. The early Church Fathers knew that these sites were potent and were held in veneration by locals. Even though the core of the science had likely already been lost, a tradition remained. Therefore, the Church literally built upon this tradition: churches and cathedrals were erected on sites of power. Furthermore, megaliths are quite often to be found in churches. It is as if what had been there before had then been updated, the site, in effect, 'converted' to Christianity! It is for this reason that the rise of the parish church in Britain and Europe was so overwhelming and such an obvious way for Christianity to spread.

Wherever churches were built, the local deities were absorbed only to re-emerge later as Christian saints, St. Brigid being a case in point. Originally a Celtic goddess, her *curriculum vitae* was altered to make her an Irish nun who founded a convent – all the best girls went to convents. Her name was changed to the more chaste-sounding St. Bride. Moreover, the same Brigit or Bride was, according to legend, midwife to Our Lady, Jesus' mother, the Blessed Virgin Mary. Wherever the saints were, in fact, the superseded gods of an older belief, so too were the secrets of the site consumed, to be forgotten. The irony is, I can show, that these ancient secrets were part and parcel of Jesus' original knowledge – part of the curriculum, the three Rs as one might say; radiation, resonance and ritual.

Regarding the original knowledge, we have seen how the internal plan of many sites is cruciform in nature. What is not immediately apparent is the true Christian association with the cross. As A. N. Wilson points out, the crucifix did not exist as a Christian symbol until the high Middle Ages, *but the cross did!* However, it did not represent the death of Jesus, it was a symbol of the triumph of God over death,[17] a symbolism that could be attributed to almost any of the older religions it superseded, for all religions have used the cross. Crucially, and I use this word guidedly for it comes from the Latin *crucis* , 'cross', hence the 'crux' of the situation – *the Latin term predates the advent of Christianity and yet contains the same meaning of God over death.*

In an article in a British newspaper in late 1998,[18] the Bishop of Lincoln, the Rt. Rev. Robert Hardy, spoke out against the rise of Paganism in the midst of Anglican society. The Bishop claimed that other churches had 'virtually abandoned the countryside'. In the same breath he went on.

> 'Large areas are unrecoverable for Methodism. It is a case of the Church of England or paganism.'

We look down on Paganism. It is a general term for the religions that were superseded by Christianity and we have learnt to associate it with 'Devil worship'. The Devil, in this context, is widespread throughout not just Britain, but the entire globe. Is it really possible that he could spread himself so entirely and so thinly? The answer lies in words that reflect those of Robert Graves:

> 'The God of one religion becomes the Devil of that which replaces it.'[19]

Some ancient sites have even had their component parts buried in an attempt to be rid of 'Old Nick'. At Avebury and other places, former standing stones are still being excavated, many years after they were buried in the ground by the Christian faithful. Perhaps the Avebury site was too vast for a conversion – no church or even cathedral could be built that would dominate the site. However, other sites served the Christian religion well.

In the year 601, Pope Gregory the Great wrote a letter to St. Augustine. In it, he explained:

> 'We have been giving careful thought to the affairs of the English, and have come to the conclusion that the temples of the idols among the people should on no account be destroyed. The idols are to be destroyed, but the temples themselves are to be aspersed with holy water, altars set up in them and relics deposited here. For if these temples are well built, they must be purified from the worship of demons and dedicated to the service of the true

God. In this way, we hope that the people, seeing that their temples are not destroyed, may abandon their error and, flocking more readily to their accustomed resorts, may come to know and adore the true God. And since they have a custom of sacrificing many oxen to demons, let some other solemnity be substituted in its place, such as a day of Dedication or the Festivals of the holy martyrs whose relics are enshrined there... They are no longer to sacrifice beast to the Devil, but they may kill them for food to the praise of God, and give thanks to the giver of all gifts for the plenty they enjoy.'[20]

This letter is an astute example of politics in its purest form. The Christianisation of megaliths and megalithic places became *de rigueur*; St. Gregory, as he was soon to be known, had instituted a carefully crafted policy of conversion, convincing in its authority to this day.

For example, every year, on the last Sunday in July (called Garland Sunday), up to 6,000 people make the ascent of Croagh Patrick in County Mayo, Ireland. Here, one of the Western world's great pilgrimages is made along a path first beaten by St. Patrick in AD 441. The pilgrims take with them all manner of things, and do all manner of things, in order to absorb and also to exalt the sheer holiness of the place. My grandfather was a Doherty from County Mayo and I can still remember the excitement of listening to him relate his story of the pilgrimage. Quartz crystals, called 'cure stones', would be carried to the summit, perhaps to be recharged by contact with the sacredness of the site or by the unseen presence of 'the man himself'. Others would cut strips of cloth and tie them to ash saplings for luck. Woe betide those who did not. At the first station, pilgrims recited seven Our Fathers and seven Hail Marys and then recited the Creed whilst walking round the stones seven times, in an ever-decreasing spiral. Crystals, pieces of tree, spirals and seven again! What is more, the peak of Croagh Patrick is topped by a chapel where before there was a *si-un*. The entire area is a testament to man's megalithic and mystic past. Nearby is a longstone and close to that, the old rock of Boheh, upon which is carved a plethora of concentric ring markings. Further along the way is a site known as Music Hill, where it is said that the fairies dance at night.

But perhaps the most relevant testament to the 'staying power' of older 'Pagan' beliefs, lies in the story of Sean na Sagart, or, Sean of the priests.[21] Sean was a priest killer, responsible for the deaths of dozens of priests in the eighteenth century, all of whom were tracked down and murdered for the £5 bounty[22] on their heads. Eventually, Sean himself was killed by a peddler avenging the death of his brother, who had been one of Sean's victims. It is Sean's burial that is of interest, as it reveals beliefs that are far older than the eighteenth century. Sean was interred beneath a split ash tree in the graveyard at Ballintubber. He lies facing north so that his soul will never again see the light of the rising sun. Elements of these older beliefs are present in the choice and construction of church sites:

> 'Any suggestion that the men who constructed the old churches and cathedrals could not build straight walls or construct true right angles is manifestly absurd. Why, then, did they deviate from conventional rules, and for what reasons did they decide whether a chancel should be twisted to the North or to the South, and to what degree?
>
> ...For no obvious reasons many country churchyards are raised several feet above the surrounding land. Indeed, the very position of many churches is inexplicable. Though there appear to be more convenient sites, some are half a mile or more from the villages they serve, and some are built on ground which is quite unsuitable for heavy structures.'[23]

The last point is amply illustrated by the construction of the Norman cathedral (pre-Gothic) at Old Sarum, near Salisbury in Wiltshire, England. Old Sarum is an earthwork of deep antiquity. Until the Middle Ages it was important as an administrative, religious and military centre. It now lies totally ruined and abandoned, a curious site not far from the cathedral city of Salisbury. In fact, it was to Salisbury that most of the inhabitants decamped after a débâcle unparalleled in the annals of cathedral building.

In 1070, William the Conqueror held a victory parade at Old Sarum. Having recognised the importance of the site, the Bishop's See was moved from Sherborne and a new cathedral was constructed. Five days after its completion and consecration, the cathedral was blown down in a severe storm. This warning of the inappropriateness of the site passed unheeded – the need to build upon the old earthwork must have been great indeed. Work was begun upon the construction of a new cathedral under the next bishop, Roger the Norman. The cathedral was again completed, but the weather at the particular spot was so severe that, even in its deepest recesses, one could not get away from the noise of the wind, which hurled itself against the cathedral walls without abating. Very soon, the same walls began to show signs of severe erosion. What is more, Old Sarum then found itself with a shortage of water. In the early thirteenth century the ecclesiastical authorities gave up. A new, Gothic cathedral was built on lower ground at Salisbury and Old Sarum went into terminal decline. Why the Normans should have persisted with the Old Sarum site is something that had intrigued me for a long time. Why not quite simply go to a less exposed site?

The answer is, of course, in, and on, the ground. Old Sarum is built upon a faultline, or fissure in the rock deep beneath the earth. Furthermore, it is also aligned to other sacred sites. Even the later site of Salisbury cathedral was built into this pattern. ' From Stonehenge, the spire of Salisbury cathedral, the successor to Old Sarum, can just be seen in the distance. Precisely in line between the two places is the central citadel of Old Sarum, and when one stands at the centre of Old Sarum and looks south beyond Salisbury's spire, one sees the line continue to a corner of the wooded Iron Age earthworks of Clearbury ring.' What we have here is a sacred alignment and, as John Michell makes clear in *Sacred England*, the legend that the building of Salisbury cathedral was given as an instruction to the Bishop in a dream is, in all likelihood, an allegory of a system of divination by which these sites were traditionally chosen.

In the year 1200, Lambert, the parish priest of Andres, put quill to parchment, having bore witness to the work of a master. What follows is of great interest:

> '…many oftentimes came together to see these great Earthworks; for such poor people as were not hired labourers forgot their penury in the joy of beholding this work; while the rich, both knights and burgesses and oftentimes priests or monks, came not daily only, but again and again every day, to refresh their bodies and see so marvellous a sight. For who but a man stupefied or deadened by age or cares could have failed to rejoice in the sight of *that master Simon the Dyker, so learned in geometrical work, packing with rod in hand and with all master's dignity, and setting out hither and thither, not so much with that actual rod as with the spiritual rod of his mind, the work which in imagination he had already conceived?*'[24]

Onward, Christian Dowsers

The above quotation is a clear reference to dowsing. Dowsing has for a long time been dismissed as the extreme edge of the lunatic fringe. However, in the light of greater understanding of the forces beneath our feet, it is at last being taken seriously as a responsive tool. The tenet of this research shows that water-diviners, or dowsers as they are better known, are sensitive to electromagnetism.[25] A little less than 200 years later (*c*.1400) and the Rev. Lambert's observation of dowsing in practice would be dismissed as witchcraft and the practice of heresy; in other words, Paganism had outlived its usefulness. But how useful it had been.

Guy Underwood, in a posthumously published book, *The Pattern of the Past*, was amongst the first modern commentators to observe that those who built sacred monuments, be they henges or churches, knew more about geodesy – earth measure – than has been generally assumed.

Before the construction of a monument could go ahead, water had to be located. The most natural siting of any place of power was near a spring or well. Water, of course, makes the land fertile. It was also seen as having curative powers in the treatment of illness and as, we have already noted, the water at these sites is indeed more potent, both minerally and electromagnetically. The water shortage at Old Sarum must have played a larger role than has previously been recognised. As Underwood points out, the building of a church could only go ahead once a source of water or aquifer had been located. An aquifer is a fault line in the earth's crust, a rock formation in which water has become trapped and is, to a certain extent, recoverable. The water gives off a charge, being a carrier of electromagnetism, and this charge is 'sensed' by the dowser as he walks over the site with the tools of his trade, usually a hazel rod or rods, sometimes copper rods or ordinary steel wire. Underwood sensed that beneath each altar spot he came across, there was an 'altar spiral'. Altar spirals are effects in dowsing caused by terminal blind springs, terminal in that they came to a halt. Blind springs are the esoteric centres of the old religion – and, to some extent, the new.

In the ancient period, the blind spring seems to have formed what I shall term the 'G-spot' – G in this case is for God on the earth – and thus around this spot a monument would be erected. Before churches came along, sites of this nature would be marked by the erection of a phallic stone, demarcating the spot's particularly resonant and fertile nature. These stones were known as Betyls, which is derived from the Semitic, *beth-el*, or 'house of God'. The church or kirk – both words derived from the early Greek *kuklos*, meaning 'circle' – would be marked out and distinguished as holy, consecrated ground. Gods and heroes are the stuff of such places – a quick consultation of any book on Greek myth will very quickly reveal these sites as places where the oracular hero was consulted, oracular in the sense that he would speak via an oracle. In myth, the connection to water is often strengthened when the hero himself consults, or is even married to, water nymphs. Perhaps the most famous example is the legend of the god Pan, where Pan encounters Syrinx, a water nymph. (The legend is wonderfully expressed by Debussy's music of the same name.)

Pan encounters Syrinx one day, bathing in a woodland stream. He is, at once, smitten with love. Shocked by his half-man, half-faunlike appearance, Syrinx reacts in panic (note the word derivation) and flees. Pan pursues her all the way from Mount Lycaeum to the River Ladon, whereupon she invokes the gods to aid her escape. The gods, with more than their usual irony, turn her into a water reed. Pan is distraught, for he cannot determine one reed from another and, clutching at straws, he cuts a whole sheaf of them. These are in turn transformed into the famous Pan pipes. Now it should be iterated here that, aside from his appearance, there was another aspect of Pan that made people react in panic – his voice, which was heard as a high-pitched squeal or a low resonant boom at the most unexpected of times. In the myths of Pan, he is described as sneaking up on people unawares and terrifying them. Also related to this is the fact that Pan's voice was quite transformed when it was diverted musically via the Pan pipes; what is of interest is the fact that the Pan pipes are made of *seven* component reeds. Seven yet again!

Pan was later demonised by the Christians. In some cases he became the Devil incarnate. As already mentioned the name of Tammuz, another 'Pagan' god demonised by the Christians, means 'child of the seventh'. This theme of seven is one which we shall explore later in some detail; however, it is no secret that the seven relates to frequency – of light, as in seven colours, and, more particularly, regarding ritual application; frequency of sound. Music and chanting, we know, were used to heighten the effect of sacred sites at particular times. These times, as any dowser will relate, are connected to the cycles of the moon and sun. This implies a changing charge of electromagnetism and indeed, there seems to be an alternating charge at various points on any site. At the Rollright Stones, these rings of charge spread out from the centre of the circle in a series of concentric circles of alternating charge. In fact, as Tom Graves points out, 'whole areas can also be polarised in relation to others, mainly at ground level'.[26] This is a very widely recorded phenomenon which only adds to the complexity of the sacred site. Mineral veins and the movement of water through faults and fractures cause small perturbations on a geophysical level and these in turn can affect the strength of the magnetic field. It is thought that what makes dowsers more than able to pick up signs of these perturbations is a higher than average sensitivity within the pineal gland.[27]

I have watched many dowsers at work. It is fascinating to see their rods moving inwards and outwards as if by magic as they slowly pace up and down, tracking lines of charge. When we consider the subject of dowsing, it is apparent that Western science has been very reluctant to even consider such degrees of sensitivity within man. Life, however, came into being and developed within the earth's geomagnetic field and naturally has a sensitivity to it. The incredible sensitivity of life on earth to even extremely low levels of magnetism should therefore come as no surprise (see chapter five). Fortunately, due to the early groundbreaking work of scientists like Duane Chadwick, this area of study is now being taken more seriously:

'In 1970, Duane Chadwick of Utah State University conducted a series of experiments that fully met the critics' requirements. He tested 150 people and he carried out control experiments. The results were startling; the dowsers' rod movements showed an apparent link with tiny changes in the intensity of the Earth's magnetic field.'[28]

The charges picked up by dowsers at various sites indicate an uncanny sense of knowing on behalf of the early Christian authorities, for whereas the charges at stone circles such as Rollright fluctuate on an hourly basis:

'...churches and Christian sites in general are different: the altars of those that I've tested are almost invariably positive and stay that way.'[29]

Oddly enough, in the same text, Tom Graves goes on to relate an exception to this rule: the many Lady Chapel altars are fixed at negative. Therefore, in cathedrals we have the same alternating positive–negative charge. As Guy Underwood was to note, this displays all the functions of a pattern, radiating outwards like a halo in steps of negative–positive charge. As Tom Graves notes:

'...[Church buttresses], particularly at the East ends, for some reason, are more like standing stones, as their charges wander somewhat; and other points within churches that tend to be strongly polarised are fonts and piscinas.'[30]

Buttresses ... 'more like standing stones'? Do we have here a possible further reason why, across Europe, many churches have incorporated standing stones into the fabric of their construction? At the church of Chapelle des Sept-Saints, Planaret in France, this is precisely the case, as it is at Maplescombe church in Kent, at St Mabyn's church in Cornwall, the Church of Buhel at Latsch, Germany, at Arrichinaga in Spain and a host of other sites.[31] Quite plausibly, the belief may have been, at the inception of these buildings, that the incorporated megaliths would somehow recharge the environment on an occasional basis, for this is indeed what appears to happen. Following the lunar cycle, energy moves up and down the stones in a system of ever-increasing energy release. The lowest points of the cycle occur on the sixth day after the new and full moons. Underwood noted, in *Pattern of the Past*, that this coincides very accurately with the actual structure of the Celtic calendar. According to a bronze tablet of the first century, found at Coligny in France in the nineteenth century, the months started on the sixth day after a new moon.[32]

These incorporated stones would, of course, originally have been used by the Ancients, and not superstitiously, but scientifically, for evidence is growing of their scientific interests. Some rather simple carvings on a rock at the Neolithic site of Knowth, have been shown to be a representation of the moon. Canadian scientist Dr. Phillip Stooke carefully placed a copy of the carvings over an image of the full moon and came up with an exact match. The carving is approximately 5,000 years old. Interestingly, the carving seems preoccupied with the major 'seas' of the moon rather than an overall outline of the whole body. Dr. Stooke observed that: 'The people who carved this moon map were the first scientists, they knew a great deal about the motion of the moon. They were not primitive at all.'[33]

Perhaps one of the most famous of incorporated megaliths still resides at the place to which it gives its name. The Latin verb, *vaticanate*, means 'to prophesy' or 'to utter prophetic inclination'. In the year 204 BC a stone was brought via the good offices of King Attalus of Pergammon to Rome. There it was led in a triumphal procession to its new home, high on a hill – the Vatican hill, the hill of prophecy. The stone was the holy aniconic, that is to say, 'representing without image', stone of the Great Mother herself, Cybele. Her new temple was exactly where St. Peter's Basilica stands today. The goddess whom this stone represents gave birth to a son, who, by tradition, is born yearly, every 25th December. Because of the winter solstice (on the 21st of December), the days begin to get longer around this time, light increases, darkness is in retreat – it is a time of renewal. The son, the god Attis, otherwise known as Tammuz, was, unsurprisingly, worshipped by the Romans as the redeemer.

Cybele's stone has since disappeared and where it might be to this day nobody knows ... not for sure. I wonder if it is still there, somewhere on the Vatican hill, recharging the environment?

The Journey of the Hero

Unfortunately, the many generations who have looked upon ancient stones and their markings have assumed that our ancestors were ignorant savages, particularly if the markings were simple line drawings such as spirals. Previously I have mentioned the common spiral markings at some length. I will now return to them by way of introduction to labyrinths and the journey of the hero.

One day, at my home, I received a very excited telephone call from some friends who had just visited the caverns at Wookey Hole in nearby Somerset. I had been discussing my ideas of the resonance of ancient sites with them and much, to my joy, had set them thinking. They urged me to go to the caverns at once and witness one of the wonders of nature. They had obviously caught the bug. Unbeknown to them, I had been there many years before, but their wild enthusiasm brought back the memory to great effect.

Caverns are wonderful places and were held in the highest esteem in ancient times. How Gothic these places look. They were thought of as entrances to the womb of the Mother herself. If you ever see a river flowing through a cavern you cannot but help notice the spinning vortices the water creates in its journey through darkness. This water was seen by the Ancients as the lifeblood flowing through Mother Earth's veins in much the same way as blood flows through our own. But those spirals of the dark waters also imitate the passage of energies flowing through the cosmos. It is easy to understand why troglodytes were drawn to these places and left their marks and their paintings. These caverns seem to be telling us, as are the spiral markings of the people who once frequented them, that the forces of nature, from galaxies to the flow of the blood in our veins, move in spirals, as does sound[34] – the very word from the voice of the divine.

That these things were understood by our ancestors seems clear enough. Besides the very many spiralling and labyrinthine markings on petroglyphs, the turning of the circle and the spin of the spiral are age-old fundamentals to ritual dance – and, of course, we have the spirals of pilgrimage. At Nazca, not only were the famous animal shapes walked, but also the many spirals, and for thousand of years, pilgrims to the sacred site of Mount Meru in Tibet have approached it in the path of an ever-decreasing spiral. More recently, since the advent of Islam, pilgrims to Mecca have approached the Ka'aba in the same way, as do pilgrims on the path up to Croagh Patrick – seven times around in a slowly decreasing orbit, where the ultimate intention is that, should such be the focus, that the mind, the body and the spirit become as one with God.

It was for this reason that the labyrinth was an important part of the cathedral interior. Labyrinths were often processed, barefoot, as a sort of ritual dance. This is borne out by the testimony of the tradition at Auxerre (see chapter six), however, the most famous labyrinth is at Chartres. I mentioned it earlier. Measuring 40 feet across it is to be seen set in the floor of the nave. Apparently, it used to have a bronze plaque at its centre with a depiction of Theseus and the Minotaur – Theseus being the hero of the most famous labyrinth myth of all.

> 'For a Christian justification of the use of this ancient Cretan legend we have to go to Lucca, where a similar labyrinth is incised on a pier of the west front with an inscription speaking of the labyrinth of sin which is so easy to enter...'[35]

This pious analogy is a little difficult to swallow in the light of the phenomenal use of Pagan imagery at these places, for, in chapter six, we noted other non-Christian images – Pythagoras, Aristotle, etc., – amongst the traditional Christian figures at Chartres. It seems to me that what is really being expressed is unity of belief and therefore unity of purpose; in the case of Theseus, belief in the hero and the purpose of the hero.

The Ancients appreciated that human beings are, first and foremost, individuals and that the journey of the hero is an individual act where success is based upon the calling up of great inner resources. However, in contrast, nowadays in the West we live a cossetted and increasingly uniform life. Mass production and mass marketing have changed our lifestyles and attitudes, and not necessarily for the better. Modern medicine works to generalised measures of human tolerance, mass inoculations and summary dispensation of antibiotics. Little room for heroics here, even with the common cold. In this and other spheres, the much vaunted rights and strengths of the individual appear to have been overridden by scientific uniformity.

It is almost as if, in failing to conquer himself, his own weaknesses and failings, man (and I use the masculine purposefully, for here we are discussing male dominated actions) opted instead to conquer the environment, with the disastrous consequences of pollution and global warming that are now upon us. This viewpoint that man was somehow separate from nature and could therefore conquer with impunity still dominates uniform scientific practice where, until late, scientists have been obsessed with the reproduction of key findings on site *in the laboratory*. Such attitudes have prevented science in general from recognising the extraordinary power of the sacred site and its effect upon people as individuals, for when it comes down to the power of place, it is the entire planet that is the laboratory, and man can no longer be a detached observer. Thankfully, the development of acutely sensitive instrumentation, and the work of a relatively few, dedicated mould-breakers, is waking us up to our connectivity to everything. We have been caught in a labyrinth of our own making, a labyrinth of ignorance, and at last, we are becoming alert to it. We are recognising our responsibilities, and by this very act of recognition, beginning to absolve ourselves of some of the more criminal excesses performed in the name of science and, almost always, for great profit.

'What goes around comes around' is an old saying meaning, in the biblical sense, 'ye shall reap what ye sow'. If this polluted pathway is the 'labyrinth of sin', the shedding of ignorance and the taking up of responsibilities will make it a place of hope – for the more that I have pursued the path of this research, the more I have come to see that each member of humanity is making the hero's journey to the centre of a vast maze or labyrinth.

The labyrinth at Chartres takes us from the outer to the centre, not in a direct spiral, but in a complex series of arcs which quite quickly bring us tantalisingly close to the centre but then take us away, back toward the perimeter – the path seems to reflect the 'two steps forward, one step back' of life. Moving away from the centre without instant fulfilment, one learns to let go of the 'goal'. Indeed, as we 'let go', the process(ion) becomes all important and in the 'here and now', the atmosphere of the sacred site is allowed to do its work.

Whenever I have walked the labyrinth at Chartres[36] I have always felt, towards the end, in a particularly passive, open, state of mind. From a spiritual point of view this serves as an excellent way to focus the whole sense of being upon the question of God. The placement of Theseus and the Minotaur – the famous monster that was half bull, half man – at the centre indicates that the pilgrim was undertaking the journey of the hero Theseus to the centre of the labyrinth. In the legend, the structure of the labyrinth was so complex that victims would easily get lost within it, lose their composure and be overcome by the Minotaur. Theseus' ingenuity overcame this problem by the use of a thread supplied by Ariadne. This gave him the ability to retrace his steps, he retained his composure and the Minotaur was easily overcome. Furthermore, Theseus was a hero, his name means, 'he who lays down'. I was struck by the similarity of the name Theseus to that of Jesus, and the comparison is strengthened by its meaning. Jesus is most famous for having laid down his life. My experiences have led me to wonder, is this really to do with the loss of self as one gains the perfect peace at the still centre of being and realises God?

Meanings within meanings. The enigma of Chartres is a revelation. The labyrinth at Chartres was called 'the Jerusalem'. The heavenly Jerusalem is called the City of Revelation and it seems that each of the European cathedrals has its own particular 'Jerusalem'. At Aachen cathedral in Germany, the Jerusalem is to be found in the form of an orb suspended from the centre of the octagonal dome, which itself surmounts an octagon. At noon, every 21st of June – the summer solstice, the longest day – the sun's rays enter the dome and strike the orb (which hangs on a chain above the Barbarossa chandelier). In contrast, the rays of the midwinter sun alight at noon upon a mosaic, situated above the north window; the mosaic depicts the Chi-Rho symbol of Christ situated between the letters Alpha and Omega – the beginning and the end.

However, the mysteries of Aachen cathedral go deeper. About 20 years ago, Hermann Weisweiler discovered a reflection of Britain hidden within the construction of Aachen cathedral. He noted that both Aachen and Stonehenge were very near the line of latitude 51° North, Stonehenge, slightly above and Aachen slightly below. Looking for further connections between the two, he soon discovered that the inner trilithon horseshoe pattern of the sarsen stones at Stonehenge was of the same dimensions as Aachen's Palace Chapel ground plan, in fact an extraordinarily close fit. This correlation is further underlined by further comparisons of the environment of the cathedral to that of

Stonehenge. There is an alignment that runs northeast at Aachen, running through some very significant sites, all of which are places of power; wells, springs, churches and various megalithic tumuli. To me, these things again infer something of the utmost importance – are we being told by the masons that Christianity is much older than is generally believed?

But there is more, in this case a phenomenon which manifests physically, one normally only related to Egyptian sites – that of mummification.

Pyramid Power

The idea of mummification extends over a far wider area than is generally assumed. Mummification zones are to be found at various sites worldwide, including parish churches and cathedrals in Britain and Europe. Mummification occurs in organic material that, instead of decomposing, desiccates. Desiccation is preservation by drying. In 'Earth Currents as a Causative Factor of Cancer and Other Diseases', Gustav Freiherr von Pohl quotes Edward Bush from the *British Society of Dowsers Journal* 1994–5:

> '...bodies buried above underground streams of Geopathic Zones
> do not rot in the normal fashion but become mummified...'

Geopathic zones are areas of natural electromagnetic vibration distorted by the action of subterranean running water. All of the sacred sites so far mentioned in this chapter have an association with subterranean running streams, the pyramids of Giza included. The bodies found at a number of sites in a mummified condition are exceedingly well preserved and have a very 'leathery' look about them. These 'mummification zones' can be partially explained by looking at the construction elements of the monuments. These same elements are to be found as the fundament of almost all the significant sacred sites of the world and where they are not found, there are variations that move towards the same effect.

The phenomenon occurs at Neolithic sites such as the long barrows at West Kennett, near Avebury, and Winterbourne Stoke, near Stonehenge, as well as at the sepulchre of Kerlescan, the tumulus of Mustair and the Dolmen of Mane Groch, all at Carnac, Brittany.[37] The mummification zones in the Brittany mounds are the size of the whole mound area! These zones are no accident or coincidence of construction. They are there by design in Christian churches and cathedrals too! At the ruined Glastonbury Abbey, this zone may be witnessed as the burial ground situated between the Lady Chapel and the

Abbot's house. Another such zone exists at Westminster Abbey, burial place of the English kings; it stretches over the King Henry VIII chapel and St Edward's chapel. Significantly, all the royal tombs are within this zone.

When workmen of the Caliph Abdullah al Mamun c.AD 820 broke into the Great Pyramid they were to discover nothing but empty chambers constructed in a supremely skilled yet mysterious fashion. Furthermore, these walls were described by subsequent explorers 'to have been coated with a layer of salt sometimes as much as half an inch thick'.[38] Salt, as we well know, aids the process of desiccation, but it is not only to be found in such dramatic form at the Great Pyramid; it occurs, in the same form, inside the crypts of many of Europe's churches and cathedrals.

The site upon which the three pyramids of Giza stand is perhaps the most powerful geodetic centre on earth . It is a site of great potency underscored by the existence of watercourses that radiate from the Nile. This, along with local seismic activity, makes Giza exceptionally active with electromagnetic emissions. This activity has then been enhanced by the construction of the most fabulous monuments on earth. The overall effect is one of energy enhancement, both inside and outside the buildings. Indeed, the Pyramid Texts tell us that the Nile, aside from feeding crops, was being used to enhance the spirit and the health of man.

In the 1950s, a Frenchman, Monsieur Bovis, visited Giza and whilst in the Great Pyramid could not help but notice that the more organic rubbish, left there by untidy tourists, had a tendency to dry out rather than rot. He also noticed the dead bodies of bats, rats and cats, all of which were mummified. Returning to France, Monsieur Bovis constructed a small wooden pyramid to the scale of Khufu's pyramid in Egypt. He aligned it north–south, took his final ingredient – one dead cat – and positioned it in the pyramid, approximately one third of the way up. He left the body there and went back three days later. What he discovered has continued to intrigue scientists the world over .... Monsieur Bovis' dead cat was mummified! Bovis went on to try a whole catalogue of organic comestibles from sheep's brains to other inglorious items; the effect was always the same.

Chasing quickly upon the heels of this new idea, a Czech radio engineer, Karl Drbal, took out a patent, no. 91304, and proceeded to manufacture cardboard Cheops Razor Blade Sharpeners.[39] These devices utilise the same proportions as those found in the Great Pyramid – the ratio of base-to-sides, 15.7:14.94cm – and, famously, they work. 'My record so far with Wilkinson sword blades is four months. I have a feeling that the manufacturers are not going to like this idea,' writes Lyall Watson. He points out in the same text: 'The pyramid shape itself is very much like that of a crystal of magnetite, so perhaps it builds up a magnetic field...'[40] Indeed, the electromagnetic field in and around the pyramids of Giza is strong enough to promote crystal growth, hence the salt. It is crystal growth that sharpens razor blades, with the help of Mr. Drbal's device.

> 'Structures having these geometrical proportions have been described as "generators of energy". Any electromagnetic rationale behind such *propositions must derive from similarities with the geometries of acoustic and electrical resonators..'*[41] (My italics)

Interestingly, the polarised light that comes from the moon has an undesirable effect upon razor blade sharpeners. This is because polarised light vibrates in one direction only. For crystal growth to take effect it has to vibrate in a variety of directions:

> 'Crystals are found in only seven symmetrical forms. In decreasing symmetry, these are called cubic, tetragonal, hexagonal, rhombohedral, orthohombic, monoclinic, and triclinic. There are no more than seven crystalline forms because crystals consist of units of atoms. These units, all of the same shape and size, must pack together without leaving gaps between them. Five-sided units and all other shapes of six or more sides cannot be interlocked without leaving gaps that are unsatisfactory according to the laws of crystal structure.' [42]

There is no polarised light deep inside a pyramid, but there is plenty of electromagnetism and so the crystal growth is made to come 'alive' because it is able to resonate within a given shape into a particular form: salt . (In Britain, many sacred sites are aligned upon what were, until recently, called 'saltlines'.) The various shapes – spheres, semi-spheres, pyramids and squares, etc. – act differently as resonators of the various energies around us. In human terms, the sphere and the pyramid forms are particularly good. Architects around the world are realising this:

> 'Architects in Saskatchewan, Canada, have created trapezoidal rooms and unusual corridors in a hospital for schizophrenics and found that the new environment was beneficial for them.' [43]

Further to this, in late 1999, I was delighted to hear an article on a BBC radio programme that described the activities of a Russian who is building fibreglass pyramids for use over quite a wide area. His stated aim is to 'change the energies of the earth'! A crackpot? Maybe, but with the support of the Russian army behind him I would not dismiss the story too lightly, for the army believes that he is doing precisely what he claims.

Up until quite recently, the popular conception was that pyramids were confined to Central America and Egypt. However, during the 1990s, this limited view was transformed. It is now known that pyramids or pyramid remains are to be found worldwide. There are some fantastic examples in China, not far from Xian – 125 in all! In New Zealand, pyramid remains of impressive size have been uncovered. The local Maoris, principally the Ngapuhi tribe, refuse to go near them. They have declared them to be *tapu*, that is to say sacred, and thus 'forbidden'. These pyramids are like the Central American step pyramids, though a little smaller and with a large flattened top. Remains of ancient pyramidal structures have also been found in Peru, Brazil and southern Africa as well as off the West African coast, on the island of Tenerife, where the great anthropologist Thor Heyerdahl has been responsible for the restoration of six ancient step pyramids. The remains of similar monuments have also been located in Italy and Turkey (see the Anatomy of the Hero).

Elsewhere, ancient mound builders have used a similar approach to proportion and construction. A British example is Merlin's mound, in the grounds of Marlborough School, Wiltshire; it is said to be the gateway to King Arthur's tomb. Again in Wiltshire, a much larger mound, Silbury Hill, has a huge circular terraced structure beneath its earth covering. A very interesting article in the British antiquarian magazine *3rd Stone* in the summer of 1999 pointed out some interesting similarities between it and various stupas in the Indian subcontinent. Silbury is much like some of the Buddhist stupas. R.W. Morrell points out that, although Buddhism is much too young for any influence to have been extended Silbury's way - *c*.600 BC for Buddhism as compared to *c*.2750 BC for Silbury – the cult of stupa mound building is inherited from a much older belief system. He further points out that at Silbury a 'large piece of wood was excavated and came to be known as the 'Druid Oak'. Likewise at the stupa mounds at Lauriya-Nandangarh stumps of wood were found, pillars that bore all the signs of having been placed in those positions. Interestingly Morrell goes on:

> 'Contrary to what is popularly believed, stupas are not specifically Buddhist, or, as Martin Brauen (1998) puts it, representative of "The Buddha's teaching and also the Buddha himself". But there is little doubt that Buddhism put them on the map, so to speak. In the Asokavadana the Buddhist emperor Asoka (spirit of Asa) is said to have had no fewer than eighty-four thousand dharmarajikas (stupas) built ... From the majestic temple of Borabudar in Java to the graceful stupas which dot the Indian landscape stretches a schematized reminder of the seven heavens, the seven notches, the seven levels.'

In Bhutan there are stupas with eyes painted or carved on the apex, in a symbolism that echoes the masonic 'eyed-pyramid' to be seen famously on any US $1 bill. Furthermore, in association with local belief, there is an annual display of the sacred curtain that covers the Holy of Holies, a rite that echoes the story of the youthful Virgin Mary in the nativity story. An involvement in it is apparently an excellent way of cleansing away sin.

Pyramidal shapes and their proportions are worldwide phenomena and perhaps unsurprisingly they are also to be found within the tradition of church and cathedral building in Europe. They are proportions which 'resonate' favourably with us. This goes beyond artistic taste and into electromagnetic interaction. Furthermore, as I have established, the earth below and the building materials, give off favourable vibrations. We are invited to resonate with them, for sound, in the form of chant and hymnal, is prescribed at sites the world over as an important part of ritual. I should add that what is not generally known is that the Egyptian pyramids themselves had their own choirs.[44]

The King's Chamber in the Great Pyramid is known for its incredible acoustics and needless to say, the builders have made sure that the radon count is high:

> 'Radiation counts taken of the air … were in fact higher than on the surface of the granite walls, presumably as a consequence of radon being emitted from all sides…'[45] REF?

The effect of standing inside the King's Chamber is a good example of the power of this particular material. Much of the emotional and spiritual heightening felt by many there is likely to be in response to the high radon content. I had often been intrigued by a comment of the poet William Blake: 'Every rock is deluged with a deity.' Now, as a result of my researches, I was beginning to understand what he meant.

The Power to Uplift

Returning to the architecture of the medieval masons; churches, and particularly Gothic cathedrals, have an aspect not usually shared by the more ancient buildings – that of space and, with it, light. This is why I personally believe that sacred architecture reached a height of power and of glory in the form of the Gothic cathedrals: the space, and what those master masons did with it! The power of the sun streams into the space through stained glass, and, as you read in chapter six, not just any stained glass. Again, atmosphere was optimised, this time by radiations of light.

There is one more particular aspect of churches and cathedrals to which we should attend. The masons had set up the atmosphere through choice of site and materials, and by filling the space with light. But that space was created to harness the acoustic science of the Ancients. We have seen how it worked in those far-off days, but those older structures did not usually have much space – in fact, acoustic technology can be used to great effect in small areas, as we shall see later when we return to the King's Chamber. But the medieval buildings were made for larger groups of people. Not only are these buildings wide, they are also tall. Added to that, though, are the soaring structures to which we pay so little regard in the modern world: bell towers.

The standard explanation is that bells in towers are essential in order to call the populace to prayer. But, I wondered, why build such mighty towers – and mighty expensive towers at that – at great cost to life and limb, when an external, simpler structure, perhaps even made out of wood, would have sufficed? A quick survey of an ecclesiastical interior confirmed that the calling to prayer was only a part of the answer. A bell tower helps the fabric of the building to become a giant sound box. You will remember that this is how Newgrange was designed, only on the horizontal. Looking around at the décor and seeing how many mysterious patterns and shapes carved by the medieval masons resembled sound waves and sound waveforms, I felt that the entire cathedral building programme had been a giant exercise in the practice of cymatics, the study of waveforms, and that this motive could arguably be extended outwards to the fabric of sacred architecture worldwide.

All of these sites were erected to the glory of, in one form or another, God, the Great Mother and their son, the hero. The faithful came and would need little encouragement to chant and sing, for, practised aright, the effect would be most uplifting. Congregations still have words to sing in praise of God, but there is something amiss. Some things have changed. The sounds themselves were very important and part of an underlying science which has been long forgotten. In fact, surveying the evidence now emerging regarding sacred sites, we seem to have forgotten a great deal.

Intermezzo

At the close of chapter six I posed the question, 'Who or what is God?' and went on to identify God with 'voice'. I also asked, 'Who was, or is, God's son?' Continuing the quest, we investigated the evidence on the ground, particularly in the 'power of place'. We looked at the continuity of ancient belief, its sites and the choice of building materials and techniques,and the relation to waveforms, resonance and the all-pervading subtle energies. Now, we can surely have no doubt in our minds that, whatever the era and creed, these choices were made with radiation and therefore atmosphere – quite literally, power of place – in mind. We have seen how some designs optimised the radiation by using, for example, layering techniques and we have noted the effects of the radiation, not only the subjective results upon individual consciousness, but also the material effects in the mummification zones. Here,ancient Egypt and its pyramids came into focus, but there was also the realisation that these zones are to be found beyond Egypt. They are present, not only at our Neolithic sites, but at Gothic churches and cathedrals too. This fact further highlighted similarities between cairns, fogous, pyramids, churches and cathedrals.

During this investigation, we naturally looked at Paganism afresh to find that Christianity was not only literally built upon it, but also absorbed many of its ways and, of course, symbols. That the cross is a universal symbol, much older than the crucifixion is significant, so too the labyrinthine symbolism of the hero's journey. And here we returned to God's son, for, on site, we have espied the hero in the centre of the labyrinth and identified him with Jesus. From thence, I introduced the idea that the universal hero loses the self in order to gain realisation of God.

We are gathering together the pieces of the puzzle and although we do not have the answers yet, a pattern is emerging. Praised the world over by peoples of every land and of every era, the hero is the key. It is now time to investigate him, his deeds and his legacy more thoroughly, but above all that it is time to have a closer look at his name.

8

Enigma at the Heart of Mystery

'God and I both knew what it meant once; now God alone knows.'
Friedrich Klopstock 1724– 1803

*'When words lose their meaning, people lose their
freedom'*

Confucius, 551-479 BC

HEROISM is a much-used term in Western cultural iconography. The idea of someone who can, often by virtue of necessity and in almost impossible circumstances, exceed their own humanity to become a 'superman' or 'superwoman' is a familiar one. One of my favourite films is *Superman*, starring Christopher Reeve. I particularly like the part where he rescues Lois Lane as she plunges earthward from atop a skyscraper where she has been involved in a little contretemps with a helicopter. Superman grabs the helicopter as it too plummets downward and the scene is rendered all the more heroic by the soundtrack and by the fact that onlookers are gathered to admire the hero's prowess.

However, like all heroes, Superman has his weak spot, his Achilles' heel and one gains a sense of the close proximity to tragedy that is redolent within the tale, even if it is averted at the last minute. In modern mythography this tragic element in the hero's tale is that, because of his identity and because of his prowess, he seems doomed to be a lonely outsider. This is usually reduced to a 'will he, won't he, get the girl' scenario that veils the real message within the myth: that the hero is necessarily tragic, for only a hero can overcome tragedy. Nonetheless, within these stories, we do find metaphors that appeal directly, if indistinctly, to the heroic sense in each and every one of us.

In Eastern cultures, the messages are deeper and clearer. The hero is more than metaphor, he is more than just a cultural icon, he is hope, he is justice, he is the rescuer of humanity from the ravages of time, decay and inevitable defeat. He is a poetic image that appeals directly to the spirit as a model of initiation, transition and inspiration. There may seem little difference between East and West in these aspirations, but there is one subtle difference that stands out, and it is a modern one: in the West we seem to have allowed ourselves only one universally recognised superhero – Jesus. By contrast, in the East, there are many such heroes and this has been the case for many thousands of years. This is a difference that can be overcome in the light of the hero's true identity.

Sir Isaac Newton held the view that all nations originally subscribed to one universal religion. Because of what we have seen that links the hero to sacred sites on a worldwide scale, this may not be far from the truth. Furthermore, there is a great sense in every one of the world's religions and mythologies that the hero is born 'of the earth', and yet whilst tied to it, his journey is one of the breaking of bonds in the name of freedom.

The great mythologist Joseph Campbell believed that human beings are 'the consciousness of the earth' and it is compassion for the earth that will call forth from the depths of our shared humanity a new 'mythology of this unified Earth as of one harmonious being'.

It is in this way that the heroic cycle plays its role within the human condition – by aspiring to go beyond ourselves we are linking into something profound, gaining a momentary glimpse into the nature of everything, for the hero is both mortal and divine. He is doomed to die a terrible death, but in death he will set the legions of hell atrembling and afeared, and in doing so he will inspire man beyond the deathly state and upon the road to immortality and paradise. More often than not he is the son of a goddess and a not so divine father, although in Western mythologies there is the tendency to make him a son of God, bestowed upon a virgin mother.

The tone of the myth is one of culmination; in any body of religious tradition the creation is described and then various series of events unfold beyond that. These events describe more or less the affairs of the gods or the angels and the wars of mankind. Very common to all of these traditions is the intervention of the divine. It is with the story of the hero that such intervention comes to a head and an air of both inevitability and anticipation sets in; it is precisely this sense of anticipation that defines the hero myth and marks it out as different from anything else. This is a distinction that I have noticed across the wide spectra of the world's mythological traditions, but further, too, into the heartland of Western culture itself, in its histories, its songs, its paintings, even in the way that sports journalists comment about football matches with anticipation for the game quite often centring around the deeds of one particular player. If a certain 'star' player succeeds in scoring a goal, great emphasis is placed upon words such as 'glory', 'heaven', 'hero', 'heroic', as if the player concerned is more than human. These are terms that in the common interpretation go beyond mere metaphor and take on a sheen of brighter, almost divine, splendour.

However, the glory of the modern hero is ephemeral – once the moment is gone, so too is the hero. For the mythic hero, though, that glorious moment is ever-present in that it transforms all about him and he experiences apotheosis, he becomes one with God. In the modern world that mythic moment is associated with yesterday, it has become almost a sentiment, and yet many still wish for such heroes, hoping that some great soul may fall, like a bright bolt, earthbound from the heavens. Myth encourages this, for example, at the end of the Arthurian cycle, the mortally wounded king is taken away to the Isle of Avalon by three mysterious queens, to be healed in time to come again, 'the once and future king'. And so the anticipation is kindled.

Throughout the latter half of the twentieth century, as the millennium became paramount in Western consciousness, some religious groups became more and more fervent in their anticipation of Jesus' second coming, and they remain forever hopeful. The first, and perhaps the last, resort of these believers is prophecy. But prophecy is rarely a straightforward matter. In early Greek history, prophecy was divine advice from an 'oracle'. Often the oracles were prophetesses who, when consulted, would speak as the particular divinity concerned. The fundamental problem with such prophesy was that it was not always as clear as it might have seemed, for the oracles often spoke in riddles, so it was all a simple matter of decoding the riddle in a fit and proper fashion in order to get at the kernel of wisdom that it might contain.

A good example is to be found in the legend of Croesus, the last king of Lydia, in what is now modern Turkey (*c.* 560–546 BC). Croesus' empire was prosperous and strong and he had ambitions to expand his territory further. With these ideas in mind he put in place preparations to campaign against the might of Persia. As a note of caution he consulted the Delphic oracle, who famously replied that:

> 'If Croesus attacked the Persians, he would destroy a great empire.'[1]

The oracle went on to advise, in all fairness, that the Lydian king should ally himself with the most powerful of the Greek states. This should have brought an air of foreboding into Croesus' mind but, in the best traditions of political spin-doctoring, he was relayed the advice in optimistic tones and was thus delighted with it. Needless to say, the oracle proved right. Croesus' vain expedition destroyed his own great empire. Correct interpretation is all, and without it, we are on a road of ignorance. Let us see where my dual-carriageway of mythology and etymology takes us. This expedition will not be in vain, the road is broad and it traverses the world, but there is a distinct and rewarding destination.

I will begin this journey by reiterating that elements of the hero myth are the same worldwide. To give an idea of the various proceedings, here is a general resumé. Within the broad framework of the eternal quest, a need arises. It is never stated, but is implicit within the story. In the Grail mythos this need is linked to fertility. In the Gospel of Matthew the coming of Jesus is anticipated by a lengthy genealogy, whereas in Mark, Luke and John it is through the mouthpiece of John the Baptist that we learn of the needed hero's imminent arrival. In other texts, ranging from the Greek and Egyptian myths to the Sanskrit Puranas, the land is ruled by a tyrant, a wicked king whose ruthlessness knows no bounds, the air is thick with oppression and darkness reigns. The stage is set for miracles and wonders, including, of course, the birth of a miraculous child.

Nativity

The father god, Vishnu in the Hindu myths, Zeus in the Greek (see Anatomy of the Hero) miraculously inseminates the prospective mother, a virgin, in a process famously known within Catholicism as the Immaculate Conception. In some versions of the myth, the mother is a goddess and, after delivery of the child, she renews her virginity by bathing in a sacred pool or river. In the myth of Perseus, Zeus appears to Danaë in a shower of gold. In a legend of Buddha, his mother, 'Maya' conceives him after having had a dream in which she witnesses Buddha descending from Heaven and entering her womb in the form of a white elephant.

The imminent birth of the hero is proclaimed by the heralds – a title derived from the word 'hero' – much to the displeasure of the reigning king, who can only see it as a threat to his kingship. Little does the king realise, however, how close to home the threat lies. It is usually a daughter or son who has given rise to the birth and there is a flavour of what is to come in the announcement of the forthcoming child as a 'king in waiting'. The earthly, non-divine father is soon disposed of as the forces of darkness gather, and the mother of the child is forced into exile. The exile is brought about because of a decree banning the rearing of male children. This is a motif familiar to the stories of Sargon, King of Akkad (c. 2370 BC), Alexander the Great and Augustus, Emperor of Rome.[2] In the myth of Perseus, Danaë and her babe-in-arms are cast adrift in a box, whereas in the Old Testament story of Moses it is the child alone who is cast adrift. As we can see, there are variations upon a theme.

The child is born amidst great wonders: a bright star shines forth and angels herald the miraculous child. Three kings come to visit and pay homage to the child and in some versions, three shepherds are told by an angel of the wondrous birth, as time stands still. In the mysteries of Adonis and of Osiris, a star 'of salvation' dawns in the east.[3] In many traditions this 'star' is actually the planet Venus, known in ancient Egypt as a representation of the goddess Isis. The stories, of course, are full of metaphor and symbolism.

In the early Christian period there was already a well-entrenched tradition of teaching the sacred mysteries through the use of drama. This is a very ancient practice, one that was common to the Orphic mysteries and the Eleusinian mystery rites, as well as to Christianity. Within them we get a good idea as to the use of symbolism, particularly that used in association with drama.

> 'The third scene, for instance, opens in the Bethlehem stable on
> a darkened stage.
> The Cock (crowing): Christ is born!
> The Bull (lowing): Where?
> The Ass (braying): In Bethlehem.'[4]

To an untrained, unfamiliar eye, 2,000 years later, the above scene looks straightforward enough, if a little simplistic. The three animals concerned are the same three animals to be found near the manger of the holy child. But they are sacred animals and it is what they represent that is important. The cock announces the dawn, the coming of light after the darkness. It is sacred to Hermes, conductor of souls. This is interesting, for the hours before and during dawn are the hours when the frail and the elderly are most likely to pass away.[5] The cock crowing three times is an omen of death. The bull is a symbol of the coming holy child, who is the 'Baal' of his father. In Canaanite-Phoenecian mythology the son of the father god, El, is called Baal and is symbolised by a bull, hence the word.

The ass or onager represents all that is wild and disorderly and is symbolic of the Egyptian god Set, mistakenly called the god of evil or the representation of evil by many writers. Set personified ignorance and all that was uncultured, he was man in need of a makeover. In some versions of the hero myth, the ass is ridden by the hero on the road to his coronation, a sign that he has tamed his wild self, that it is under control. All of these animals were used as a means of relaying to initiates the trials and tribulations to come. This is the reason that they appear in the story of the nativity and in nativity plays the world over.

The hero is brought forth in a grotto. In the Gospels and in early Christian nativity traditions, Jesus is either born in a manger or a cave. The time of the year is important, as the hero represents light emergent from darkness. In various traditions the dates are close, ranging from 21st December to 7th January. Significantly, the day celebrated as the birth of Osiris-Dionysus, 6th January, is also the likely date, though heavily disputed in early Christian circles, of Jesus' birth. The dispute centred on whether the birthday was 25th December or 6th January, 25th December was also the birthday of the god Mithras, who also represented light, truth and justice. An epithet of Mithras was Sol Invictus, the invincible sun. In Britain in the year 1752, people did not take kindly to the introduction of the Gregorian calendar and stubbornly clung to the old date of Christmas – 6th January. This is now the feast day of the Epiphany when Jesus manifested himself to the three wise men of the east.

The birth of the child hails the dawn of a new age. With the advent of Christianity the sun began to rise at the spring equinox in the sign of Pisces the fish, whereas some 2,000 years before, it begun to rise in the constellation of Taurus the bull. That this is beyond supposition is borne out by the reliance upon myth during these respective eras of the signs of both fish and bull.[6] The symbol of the early Christian community was that of the fish, whose geometry of two interlocking circles is also known as the *vesica piscis*: ◯ .

In Greek, the word for 'fish' is *icthus* and was used as an acronym for Jesus Christ, Son of God, Saviour (see illustration). Icthys was also the Greek name for Adonis.[7] Interestingly, as the sign of Pisces formed the background to the rising vernal sun, its opposite sign was the sign of the virgin – Virgo. According to many commentators, ancient and modern, this provides the reason why many in the Pagan world expected the coming saviour to be born of a virgin; there is, however, more to the role of the constellation of Virgo that will be discussed later.

It is at the point of the hero's birth that the old king, the tyrant that we came across earlier, has a portent whereupon he issues his decree. Both mother and child go into exile. In the story of Isis and Osiris, Osiris has at this point been killed and Isis, in order to protect her newborn son, Horus, from the ravages of the jealous Set, decamps to the Nile delta where she hides in the papyrus reeds, away from the prying eyes of Set and his spies.

Again, there are variations upon a theme. In the Gospels, the family of Jesus cannot return to Palestine until Herod is dead. In other texts, the family must wait for the child to grow older, stronger and vengeful. To necessitate the child's waxing strength and his mission of revenge, he is educated either by shepherds, whereupon he becomes a great hunter with the bow and arrow, as in the cases of Orion and Apollo; by centaurs, with much the same result, as in the case of Achilles; or by wise and learned men, as in the case of Alexander the Great, who was tutored by Aristotle. Similarly, it seems from some of the non-canonical gospels that, as is hinted in the Gospel of Luke, Jesus spends a part of his time being tutored by the doctors of the law.

The divine child grows and matures to full adulthood. There is surprisingly little within the mythologies that covers the intervening gap between childhood and adulthood. Not surprisingly, the Gospels are no exception to this rule and a considerable industry has built up surrounding Jesus and the 'missing years'. Some say he was in Egypt for the duration, others that he was in India and yet more that he journeyed to Britain.

With the passage of time the hour of the hero comes, for the old king must pass away and a new king take his place. At the due moment, almost without exception, from out of foreign quarters, the hero returns to his homeland, the land of his birth, as a stranger in a strange land. The old king dies or is killed and his place is taken by the very child he tried so desperately to be rid of. The hero undergoes the rite of anointing and this necessitates, at some stage in the proceedings, a full immersion in water or sometimes fire. In the myth of Achilles, he is held upside down as a child over a fire, wherein his mortal self is burnt away to reveal the immortal portion. In Achilles' case he is rendered invulnerable except in the heel – the place where his mother, Thetis, held him. This is an important aspect of the hero's tale, for often, if he is not crucified, he is killed by being stung in the heel.

Baptism is, of course, more familiar to us as a water-based activity. As Joseph Campbell observes:

> 'The rite of baptism was an ancient rite coming down from the old Sumerian temple city Eridu, of the water god Ea, "God of the House of Water". In the Hellenistic period, Ea was called Oannes, which is in Greek Ioannes, Latin Johannes, Hebrew Yohanan, English John.'[8]

The Buddha bathes in the waters of a stream before going on to sit under the tree of initiation. Like fire, water plays the role of purifier; it is in the waters that the goddess bathes in order to renew her virginity. In the legend of Actaean, as so brilliantly portrayed by the artist, Titian, the unfortunate hero espies the goddess Artemis bathing in a stream and stays to watch. What follows is poetic justice. In order that he should not boast of his adventure, Artemis transforms him into a stag, whereupon he is torn to shreds by his own hounds.

At the Eleusinian mysteries, initiates ritually purified themselves in the sea.[9] The narrator of *The Golden Ass*, Lucius Apuleius, also underwent a purifying bath and was anointed by sprinkling.[10] It is after the baptism, wherein the holy child is anointed saviour and becomes 'God made man', that the most miraculous period is entered into.

Miracles

As with Mithras, Adonis, Osiris, Dionysus and a host of other heroes, Jesus gathers about him 12 disciples. These are generally assumed to be symbolic of the 12 tribes of Israel which, as Sir William Drummond points out in *Oedipus Judaicus*[11], are in turn, symbolic of the 12 signs of the zodiac. As Timothy Freke and Peter Gandy observe:

> 'The zodiac was an extremely important symbol in the pagan world. Osiris-Dionysus is symbolically represented as the still spiritual centre of the turning wheel of change represented by the twelve signs. As Mithras, Dionysus, Aian and Hellos he is often depicted at the centre of the circling zodiac. During the initiation ceremony in the Mysteries of Mithras, twelve disciples surrounded the godman, just as the twelve disciples surrounded Jesus.'[12]

Quetzlcoatl, the Central and South American saviour god, had 12 disciples or companions too.

Surrounded by his disciples, the hero begins to manifest the superhuman aspect of his character. Being a saviour 'god-man', it is only reasonable that the most dramatic of the hero's powers should be his aptitude for healing. Miracles of healing were attributed to Apollo, Dionysus and Hermes as well as to other, non-European based hero-gods, from the South and Central American saviours Viracocha and Quetzlcoatl to Krishna in the East. Perhaps the most famous non-Christian healer was the first-century Apollonius of Tyana. So impressive are his feats of miracle working, that he has been described as 'a plausible Pagan Christ'.[13] Apollonius shares other, similar traits:

> 'There is, however, no reason for us to suspect an invention, save as regards the details of the biography recast by Philostratus in the third century. It is likely enough that he was a devout Pythagorean, a student of medicine and astrology, a universalist in his creed, and a believer in immortality. He may conceivably have travelled in India, though there are no details available.'[14]

Apollonius was a miraculous seer and is mentioned as such by the early Christian writer Origen. In an even closer echo of the Gospel narrative, Apollonius is said to have brought back to life the daughter of a Roman consul. Beyond this he is also credited with the casting out of evil spirits and the feeding of a multitude in much the same way that Jesus, from a few loaves

1.   Trethevy Quoit. c. 3000 B.C., an example of a Neolithic barrow, Cornwall, Britain.
(Paul Broadhurst)

2.   Rocky Valley, an ancient Labyrinth. c. 3000 B.C., Cornwall, Britain.
(Paul Broadhurst)

3. The Amphitheatre at Delphi. The soporific atmosphere of this extraordinary place is due to the fact that it is densely permeated by natural earth radiation – radon gas. Greek, 8th–9th century B.C.

    (Paul Broadhurst)

4. The Amphitheatre at Dodona, where the voice of Zeus rustled through the trees. Greek, 9th–10th century B.C.

    (Paul Broadhurst)

5. Bourges Cathedral, France. 11th century, Gothic. Note the
    similarity between the whiskers of a head of barley and the
    buttressing.

    (Paul Broadhurst)

6. The Tympanum at Chartres Cathedral, France – Christ enthroned
    at the beginning of all creation. 12th century.

    (Paul Broadhurst)

7.   Chartres Cathedral, France. 12th century, Gothic.

(Paul Broadhurst)

8.   Wells Cathedral; the stairs to the Chapter House, Somerset, Britain.
     12th century, Gothic.

9. 'The Triumph of the Name of Jesus', Baciccia's Renaissance masterpiece in the Gesu, Rome. 17th century.

10. The Step Pyramid of Djoser, the first of the pyramids. c. 2630 B.C.

11. The Gisa Plateau. *Left to right* The Pyramid of Menkaure, the Pyramid of Khafre and the Great Pyramid of Khufu. 4th Dynasty, c. 2500 B.C.

12. The Valley Temple, c. 2600 B.C. Note the use of massive granite slabs.

13. A view of the Great Pyramid behind the Pyramid of Khafre.

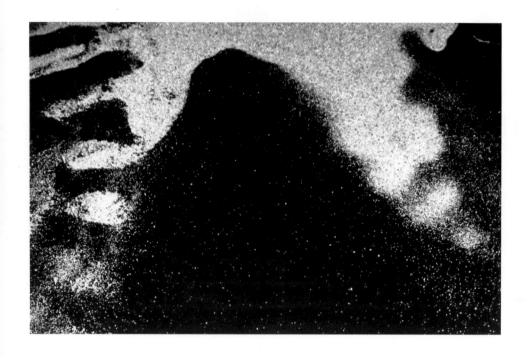

14. 'Nemes' – 271Hz. The headdress of the Pharoahs, by John Reid.

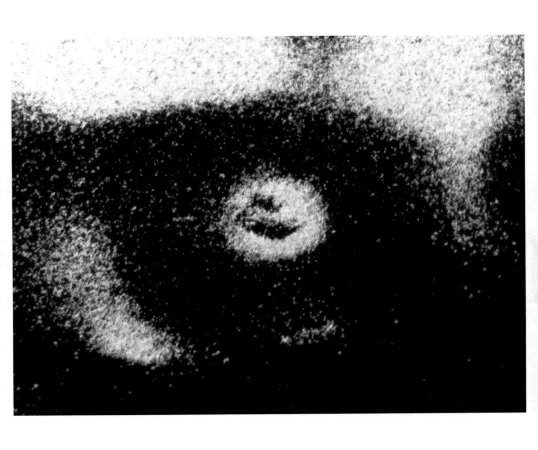

15. 'The Eye of Ra' – 198Hz. "These images kept trying to appear in the sand as the tone reverberated, this is a detail of one of them." – John Reid.

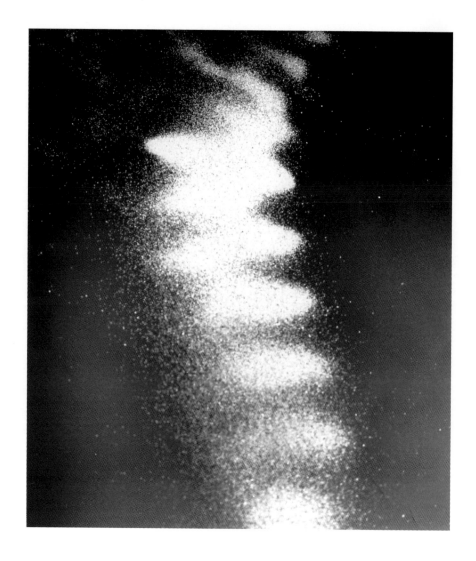

16. 'Djed' – 190Hz. The body of Jesus. The culmination of John Reid's research to date.

17. The Grand Gallery; deep within the interior of the Great Pyramid. Note it's similarity to a head of Barley.

(Peter Renton)

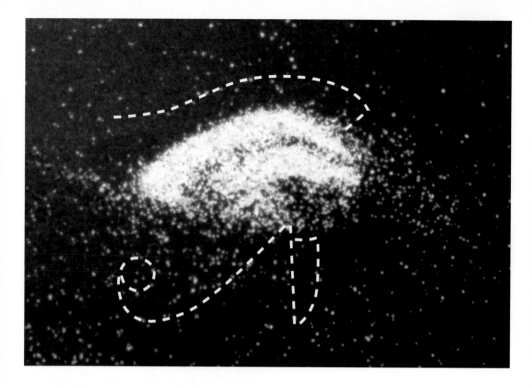

18. The Cymatic 'Eye'. The wadjet-the sacred eye of Horus.

19. The cymatic 'Key of life'-the Ancient Egyptian Ankh.

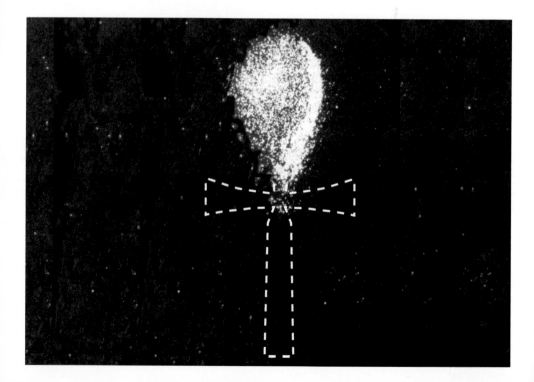

20. The oldest church in the world: the Djed Pillar and the King's Chamber complex overlaid by an English Parish Church, by Dean Baker.

21. The Eagle Nebula, 7000 light years away in the constellation of Serpens.
    Note the rising pillars of dust and gas.

(NASA. – HST)

and fishes, fed the 5,000.[15] Another shared miracle is the feat of turning water into wine. This was performed by Dionysus at his marriage to Ariadne. Dionysus was the Greek god of wine, called Bacchus in Rome, and celebrated for the famous Bacchanalias. The feat of raising people from the dead is another common aspect of the hero myth. Isis raises Osiris from the dead after he is torn to pieces by his wild brother, Set. In Greek mythology, it is Aesclepius who performs the same deed, as well as other acts of healing. Another of the famous healers was Pythagoras. In his stories of Pythagoras, Iamblichus tells us that he was born of a virgin, had a golden thigh, called upon the birds, who obeyed him and that he could calm stormy waters. In some versions of the stories, Pythagoras walked upon them.

However, the tales of Aesclepius' feats of healing go further. He is made to pay by an angry Hades, the King of the Underworld, for stealing away his denizens, for in bringing them back from the dead, Aesclepius was taking away from Hades that which he considered his own. Aesclepius was a son of Apollo. His punishment was to be killed by a thunderbolt from Zeus and, in revenge, Apollo killed the Cyclops, the one-eyed giant. When it came to writing this story down, I could not help but notice a connection between the legend and the letter of the Greek and Hebrew alphabet, *el Ayin* (see chapter six). The symbol of this letter, as we have seen, is 'o' and is derived from the hieroglyph of the eye. This is a reference to the third eye, the pineal gland, and I wondered whether the legend was relating that with the death of Aesclepius the healer, the sun, represented by Apollo, was on its way to the summer solstice – 21st June – and thus, fullness. With the death of the hero, the sun's (and the son's) rise to full glory is assured, for the hero and his father, the sun, are become one.

This is where we come to the most poignant aspect of the hero myth: his death and resurrection.

Death and Resurrection

Quite often in mythology, the hero is accompanied in some way by a dog. In certain parts of southern Europe and the Middle East, dogs are associated with death to such a degree that death is known as 'the power of the dog'.[16] In other areas of the world similar associations are to be found.

In myth, dogs are carrion eaters, they dispose of dead things. In nature, this is precisely the role of the jackal and other canine species. It is the dog, Cerberus, meaning 'Spirit of the pit', who guards the gates of Hell in the Greek mythology. In Egypt, the dog was Anubis. In Celtic myth, Dormoth, 'Death's door', and so on. In the story of the hero, the fact that he has a companion who is a dog is a metaphor for the hero's journey in the underworld; for as part of the process, all saviour hero-gods must pass through hell.

Many of the hero myths are unspecific about the reasons for the hero's death. Remember, though, that we are in a fantastic domain and not in our comfortable world of reason. However, there are motives beyond the later interpolations of classical Pagan and Christian commentators. The myth is the story of life and its journey through eternity and therefore the earliest forms of these myths were guides to the potential of the soul in life and in death. Hidden within this format was the arcane element that speaks of astronomy, mathematics and geometry as a link between man and God. It is in this light that we must look upon them, and ultimately, upon their profound significance.

Our hero has been through many trials and tribulations, but in death he comes to the greatest trial of all. The hero at the end of his mortal life becomes, in effect, a scapegoat. Upon his shoulders he bears the burden of the people, their sins, their crimes, their guilt. As a part of this process, he is expelled by the people, he becomes the messiah rejected by his nation.

> 'They will make fun of him and spit at him and whip him and kill him.'[17]

The hero willingly goes to his terrible death – crucifixion, either by being nailed to a cross or a tree or, as some motifs describe it, being hung on a tree. There is a remarkable similarity in world mythology about the mode of death. It begins with a feast, one that is familiar to every Christian as the Eucharist. The Eucharist is officially the 'Sacrament of the Lord's Supper'.

> 'He who will not eat of my body and drink of my blood, so that he will be made one with me and I with him, the same shall not know salvation.'[18]

This is how a Persian Mithraic text runs; it is almost indistinguishable from the words of Jesus in the Gospel of John (6:53–58). This aspect of the eucharistic meal, wherein the bread and wine represent the body and the blood of the saviour god, is a common motif to be found in the myth of the hero's death. It figures within the major mythologies of the Middle East and southern and northern Europe as well as in Central and South America, and in Africa, the Dogon of Mali, famous for their extraordinary rituals revolving around the star Sirius, worship the figure of a crucified man in their religion, a resurrected saviour, of whom different clans 'partake' in a symbolic, but unmistakable, Eucharist[19] (see The Anatomy of the Hero). Incidentally, the idea of the condemned man's last meal comes from this body of tradition.

This sacred meal was, in all actuality, a holy communion with the god concerned; it was, to a certain extent, the act of taking upon oneself the powers and prescence of that god. It was for this reason that priests and priestesses at the many oracle centres would eat, drink or imbibe intoxicating substances before 'communing with the god'. We know the gruesome fate of the Christian hero following the Eucharist: crucifixion. There are further gruesome trials in world mythology.

In the legend of Dionysus, the eponymous hero is torn to shreds and boiled in a cauldron, whilst pomegranate trees, symbols of the underworld, sprout from the soil where his blood has fallen.[20] There are echoes here of an agricultural purpose. The Eucharist and death of the hero-god are as inextricably linked as man is to the soil. In a less painful episode, in China, the Emperor, after having ploughed the first soil of the year, would turn to the east and to the west, in precisely the same manner as the genuflecting priest in the Catholic mass. This 'ceremony of the Guiding Light' took place at the same time as Easter in the West, and was much the same as its Catholic counterpart, even down to the niceties of the ceremonial dance that is the Holy Sacrifice of the Mass. Furthermore, the musical accompaniment is similar to Gregorian chant, and in the light of the effect upon the brain that Gregorian chant has (see chapter seven), we can see how powerful this ceremony would have been. At its culmination, three grains of rice were placed upon the Emperor's tongue and a cup of rice wine was drunk, thus completing the eucharistic ritual,[21] a ritual that paid homage to the earth. This is the ritual that has echoes all around the world. In South America the blood of sacrificial victims was given to the earth as an act of fertility and sometimes the body and the blood of the victim were consumed eucharistically. Cannibalism has largely been eradicated, with the odd exception, amongst native peoples, but this was often the thinking behind it. The word 'cannibal' is derived from *Caribe* meaning 'brave and daring', the properties of the hero – hence Caribbean, the area the etymology came from. By the same token these occasions were, and still are, celebrated within religious communities with carnivals, from Latin, *carn* and Italian *carne*, meaning 'flesh'; 'carnival' meaning literally 'the cessation of flesh eating'.

The most ancient record of the Eucharist followed by the death of the god is to be found in the Egyptian Book of the Dead. The initiate 'eats' the gods in order to take upon himself some of their powers. The main objective of this is, particularly where the deceased Pharaoh is concerned, to become one with Osiris. In the Egyptian legend, Osiris too has been torn to pieces by his wild brother, Set. In the version related by Plutarch,[22] Set tricks him into a sarcophagus which is duly sealed and cast adrift. Landing at Byblos, it sprouts leaves and becomes a tree. In some mythologies, it is a tree that the hero is hung from or nailed to. In others, heroes are crucified. Dionysus is crucified, as is the Gaelic Esus. The god Attis was known as 'He on the tree', whilst images of Adonis were often hung on trees. In Scandinavian mythology, Woden goes through a bizarre process of self-crucifixion as an act of renewal. In other legends, the image of the tree or cross is very much in evidence, but the hero does not die upon it, instead, death is usually delivered in the form of the hero falling upon a sword,[23] or being stung in the heel by a scorpion as in some versions of the story of Osiris. It is Achilles' heel that is his downfall. He is 'stung' by a poisoned arrow,[24] so too Krishna, when mistaken for a deer by a hunter. Attis, son of Cybele, is gored to death by a wild boar. In some versions of the crucifixion story, it is not the hero that suffers crucifixion, fate has something else in store for him – instead, it is his brother who is crucified. Yet another version of the legend of Osiris has his wicked brother Set crucified.[25] Set, by virtue of being wild and uncultured, would appear to be symbolic of man's lower self and so the act of crucifixion represents an act of transcendence, of rising above bodily desires. As stated in the previous chapter, a motive for the death of the hero is atonement, literally, at-one-ment – the ultimate act of communion with God. Atonement for some great sin brings him to this state. For example, in some legends the hero must pay the price, or atone, for the great sin of, albeit unknowing, committing incest with his sister.

The most famous case of incest in the history of the West passes almost without notice because we are inclined to think of the protagonists as mere 'man and woman'. Yet, in catechisms and the writings of Aquinas, we are told that, in the eyes of God, not only are they man and wife, but they are also brother and sister, and the result of their actions is not only the human race, but *the* original sin. These sources tell us that Adam and Even were cast out of Paradise for this very crime.

Jesus was called 'the second Adam' (see chapter one), in order that he would atone for his predecessor's sin. This is also what happens in the Arthurian mythos, where King Arthur has acted in the same way and must rectify the deed, laying down his own life in the process.[26] In the Finnish legend of Kullervo Kalevanpoika, the hero unwittingly sleeps with his sister and later falls on his sword.[27]

In the Gospels, Jesus utters his harrowing last words, 'My God, my God, why hast thou forsaken me?' In the original Greek of the Gospel of Mark, these words are 'Eloi, Eloi, lema sabachthani?'[28] This echoes 'Euoi, Euoi', the last cry of Dionysus, the saviour god who also was sacrificed. The Roman version of Dionysus is Bacchus. He, too, is sacrificed: 'After Bakchos (sic), who cried 'euoi' is struck, blood and fire and dust will mix'.[29] These words echo the earthly nature of the sacrifice, that it is from the earth that we came and to the earth we shall go. In a peculiar, but somewhat significant, way, the last words of Jesus are echoed in the Mayan tongue. According to a Guatemalan monk,

Antonio Batres Jaurequi, their equivalent in Mayan is: '*Hele, Hele, lamah sabac ta ni*'', meaning, 'I faint, I faint and my face is hid in darkness'.[30]

The hero harrows hell, and meanwhile, on earth, his body is placed in a sepulchre. In the legend of Orpheus, the hero walks the infernal paths to rescue his beloved Eurydice, as does Dionysus, who plunges into the dark depths of Hades to rescue his mother, Semele. On the third day after his death, the hero reappears in the greatest miracle of all, resurrection.

> '...when night had fallen, the sorrow of the worshippers was turned to joy. For suddenly a light shone in the darkness: the tomb was opened; the god had risen from the dead; and as the priest touched the lips of the weeping mourners with balm, he softly whispered in their ears the glad tidings of salvation...'[31]

In ancient Rome, as I have already noted, the carnival celebrating the rise of the god from the dead was called the Hilaria. The date was 25th March and the particular hero-god concerned was Attis/Tammuz.

In this brief overview of the myth of the hero, I think that we have now run through sufficient examples to see that it is an extraordinary and worldwide phenomenon. As had transpired with others before me, the more I sought, the more I uncovered many correspondences that were beyond mere coincidence. Unfortunately, because of these similarities and the reliance upon particular dates, such as the solstices and equinoxes, the various heroes of world myth have been reduced in status to mere vegetation deities, in the view of Sir James Frazer, or psychological archetypes, in the opinions of C. G. Jung and his followers. I do, to a certain point, agree with these estimations, but there was for me, from the outset, a growing doubt that these really were answers in any complete sense.

The Eternal Hero

The world has always needed its heroes, in whatever shape or form, but more than this, the hero is relevant to all societies and all cultures throughout history. History meanwhile insists that we have progressed, that the whole process of history is a progression of humanity and its ideas, from out of the mythic into the 'real'. And yet, wherever we look for real meaning, the hero stares back at us poignantly, and with a smile, transcends time and defies linear 'progress'.

Even amongst the least spiritual, the power of the hero story is grasped. Communism, in the form of the Soviet state, was repressive, monolithic and totalitarian; it was also officially atheistic. How strange, and how ironic, that the architect of the Soviet state should have been interred in a mausoleum that has the classical hallmarks of a pyramid. As if to confirm these suspicions of Lenin as some kind of religious focal point, a book published in 1938[32] asserts that, like a mythic hero, Comrade Lenin too had a golden portion – his shoulder – and that he was born of the moon and the sun, and so on. This of course is a perverse exploitation and yet it serves to show that everywhere I looked, there was the hero, staring out at me, beckoning me on, as if challenging my every move, forcing me to explain the inexplicable. Needless to say, despite the Communist attempt, I was convinced that the hero was not simply some primitive political ploy leftover from the archaic past.

Earlier I mentioned Sir James Frazer and the idea of heroes as vegetation deities. Whilst there is some substance to this thinking, I believe it is merely a pointer. The view of the hero and of religious belief as mere metaphors of agriculture and the turn of the seasons has been aptly summed up by many writers:

> 'The religious experience of primitive peasant societies was conditioned by their close contact with the mysteries of life and growth and by their dependence upon the rhythm of the seasons and the fertility of the soil. Whereas pastoral and hunting peoples thought of the divine powers as formidable and incalculable, to be propitiated or obeyed...'[33]

That this is the case cannot be denied, but the real solution to the enigma of the hero lies very deep within this answer. In chapter five we saw that at certain places, due to radon emissions, plants thrive and that this, having been noticed, could have led into the development of a science of sacred sites. The stuff of the hero is the very life-force, which naturally both includes and transcends the idea of of fertility within the soil. The very presence of a science of acoustics in sacred architecture is a testament to this transcendence and gives the lie to claims that agriculture is as far as the hero goes.

It seemed to me very early on that there was a source for the myth and that it was something actual, not merely symbolic or metaphorical. It was in this light and with this attitude in mind that I approached some of the supposedly wilder claims of the early Christian Fathers, though not before gaining a little context.

> 'When, as frequently happened, pastoral peoples overran agricultural communities, the old vegetation gods were considered as having been overcome by the sky gods (worshipped by the incomers), just as the peoples were subjected to their new warrior overlords. From the fusion of cultures which

resulted, new syncretistic pantheons were developed in which
the old gods tended to be relegated to the underworld, where
they ruled over the dead…'[34]

There are two points to be reminded of here. As society changes, so too does our view of our ancestors. The idea of the Ancients being anything other than primitive, ignorant savages was, until recently, widely dismissed as 'romantic'. Observations about their monuments have, to a considerable degree, changed all that. It seems that the more we discover about ourselves, the more that there is an echo of it in the past (see Appendix – Robin Heath). Point number two is the observation that the underworld, the substratum, is exactly where the hero belongs – he went there of his own volition. The later chapters of this book will show quite how important this point is; for now, it suffices to say that it can more or less be ascertained that, sky-god and earth-god, were seen as intimately and necessarily connected in order that they could be transcended. This is what the hero myth is all about and this is also the very point of Christian belief. When one takes a look, as we have, at ancient sacred technologies which relate to consciousness – the experience of altered states and the manipulation of the experience to higher levels – this shows us that the real primitivism lies within our 'progressive' view of history. We are now rediscovering much, and this indicates that civilisation and the knowledge that goes with it are cyclical. 'What comes around, goes around' is a phrase that springs to mind. This phrase is also an apt illustration of the cycle of birth, life, death and rebirth that the hero seeks to rise above. I was never more aware of this cyclical nature than after I had read the extraordinary works of St. Augustine of Hippo (AD 354–430), one of the great forces of the early Church:

> 'That very thing which is now designated the Christian religion
> was in existence among the ancients, nor was it absent even from
> the commencement of the human race up to the time when
> Christ entered into the flesh, after which true religion, which
> already existed, began to be called Christian.'

These words made me more than a little suspicious about the claims of syncretism. Syncretism is the reconciliation, or the attempt to reconcile, different systems of belief. I have no doubt, especially in the face of the giant corpus of evidence, that syncretism took place between many different and not so different cultures – it was in the interest of certain powers to do so. Syncretism is precisely what the Romans did, to a large extent, to the Greek gods. Zeus became Jupiter, Aries became Mars, Aphrodite Venus, Hera Minerva, and so on. Syncretism took place, yes, but it was not the answer to a worldwide phenomenon, only a part of a much bigger picture. For me, Augustine's words have a ring of truth about them, but needless to say, in the early centuries, there was much propaganda which exasperated Pagan reason. Celsus, a second–century Pagan philosopher, is the author of the oldest literary attack on Christianity of which details have survived. Amongst other comments which were perhaps too severe, the following is clearly justified:

> 'Good Lord! Is it not a silly sort of argument to reckon by the same works that one man is a god whilst his rivals are mere sorcerers?'[35]

Certain of the Christian rites, beliefs and gospel stories were already very familiar to the first Christians. In fact, many of the early Church commentators are insistent that their rites are exceedingly ancient, inferring that Jesus was there all the time. Justin Martyr (AD 100–165) writes:

> 'In saying that the Word was born for us without sexual union as Jesus Christ our teacher, we introduce nothing beyond what is said of those called the Sons of Zeus.'[36]

These admissions, whilst not negating that there is a uniqueness to what we call the Christian experience, indicate one that echoes outwards from deep antiquity. This was a fact very well concealed and known by few, even within the Church. What St. Paul had started out with, Constantine had completed, and the rise of the Church became inexorable; but in the light of politics and the aims of empire building, the archaic past of Jesus in myth was to remain hidden (see part one) until at last the whole question of the mystery could be approached more dispassionately, as now. It is Jesus himself who raises the question in the Gospel of Mark:

> 'Jesus and his disciples set out for the villages of Caesarea Philippi; and on the way he asked his disciples, "Who do people say I am?" They answered, "Some say John the Baptist, others Elijah." "And you," he asked, "who do you say I am?" Peter replied, "You are the Messiah". Then he gave them strict orders not to tell anyone about him.'[37]

It is indeed odd that the Jesus of the Gospels is so overt and yet so secretive. The whole mystery is nonetheless blown wide open by an explosive comment from the one–time chief editor of the Dead Sea scrolls team. Professor John Strugnall had been working on the enigma of the scrolls since 1952. In 1990, however, he was sacked in a somewhat dramatic move that cited failing health and emotional distress as the reason for his removal. There may have been another motive, an arcane but obvious one.

The Dead Sea scrolls are a very sensitive matter, given their position within the volatile cauldron of Middle Eastern politics. In 1990, a few weeks before his dismissal, Professor Strugnall gave an interview to an Israeli newspaper in which, with a grave air of insouciance, he made some remarks which, to Jews at least, would have been extremely offensive:

> 'Judaism is a horrible religion ... based on folklore ... it is a Christian heresy.'[38]

Whether Professor Strugnall was under a certain amount of distress or not, it is hardly believable that a scholar in his position should forget what most of us take as a simple fact of history – that Christianity postdates Judaism. Or does it?

Clearly, from the researches that I had conducted, a doubt had arisen about the true age of Christianity, a significant doubt. The reasons noted so far centre around the power of place and the consequent Christian adoption of Pagan sites and either the conversion or demonising of the old gods. But what of the focal Christian personality, the Son of God? It was time to take a still closer look at the myth of Jesus in relation to the hero.

The figure of Jesus seemed to me to be at least half as old again as the Christian era within which we live. Thus, if Jesus is far older than the dates given, there must be a variety of reasons. The notion of syncretism was a point in question. It has been postulated in a remarkable thesis[39] that, via this process, Egyptian deities became transformed into Greek deities and that these in turn influenced the identities and practices of the Roman mythos; furthermore, that the Egyptian influence spread out over a very wide area indeed.

I was beginning to think that the idea of religious pluralism had indeed stemmed from a single definable source and that even this source was derived from something exceedingly archaic.[40] Jesus' words, 'No one can come to the Father but by me' (John 14:6) began to take on a new hue. So, too, did the observation by A. N. Wilson in his book *Jesus*::

> 'Theology has concerned itself almost exclusively, from the beginning, with the risen Christ.'[41]

Certainly, the early Church was at pains to distance itself from the mythic Christ:

> '...when Eusebius recorded his memorable boast that he had virtually made "all square" for the Christians, it was an ominous announcement of what had been done to keep out of sight the mythical and mystical rootage of historic Christianity.'[42]

Moreover, Eusebius:

> '...and his co-conspirators did their worst in destroying documents and effacing the telltale records of the past, to prevent the future from learning what the bygone ages could have said directly for themselves.'[43]

Despite borrowing arguments from Greek mythos to bolster the concept of immaculate conception, to Justin Martyr, the similarities between the Pagan mystery religions and the Church were, 'the results of "diabolical mimicry" which blinds the foolish to the essential differences between Christianity and Paganism.'[44] There is more than a hint of motive when we view the extraordinary claim of St. Ambrose, Bishop of Milan, c.370, in an attempt to refute the Pagan claims of plagiarism, he announced that Christianity had not borrowed from Plato, rather that Plato had borrowed from Moses.[45] So, whilst Professor Strugnall thinks that Judaism is a Christian heresy, St. Ambrose says that Pagans borrowed from Moses, and by now we know the similarities of the hero stories worldwide – surely, everything is all too interchangeable!

Many scholars, from the first to the twentieth centuries, have commented upon the similarities of the world's many deities and it is well accepted that the gods represent attributes such as love, wisdom, etc., and also aspects of nature such as wind and fire. But this explanation does not solve the riddle of the heroes, Jesus and those like him.

The Name of the Hero

During the first century, by a shift of focus, Christianity transformed itself from a religion based upon the heroic cycle, the wheel of birth, life, death and rebirth, into a religion based upon the power of love. Unfortunately there was a down side, for this removal from the traditional hero cycle marked the beginning of a loss of knowledge – that God is within everyone, that everyone has the potential to be a true hero and undertake the journey back to divinity. Nevertheless, the love ideal proved most potent. What some of the early martyrs suffered upon the basis of this remarkable philosophical principle was extraordinary. That they should have endured, suffered and died, often in the most appalling agony, is a great testimony to the power of this focus of belief.

But, again, this was not the first manifestation of such a focus. The religion of love bears many striking similarities to the Orphic philosophy, which was one of high moral purity. The ethic of non-injury and of purity is there, as is the theology of redemption and the doctrine of original sin. The focus on love is manifested in the form of the Greek god Eros. The Orphics believed that at the creation Eros was the first god to emerge from the womb of darkness, in which a silver egg had been laid by Rhea. Eros, once born, set the universe in motion.[46] Significantly, Eros was, according to Plato, not only the oldest of deities, but also the one who inspired strength enough within the soul to ascend the heavenly heights after death. In Greek the word *eros* denotes a hero or demigod. Eros was the beginning and the end - the Alpha and Omega and the original hero. What the Orphic myth makes quite clear is that the hero goes hand in hand with the concept of love; you cannot have one without the other.

It is clear that the word 'Jesus' is from the same family of names as Eros and Hero. The link is made clearer with the help of another rendition of the Jesus story, this time with the name Esus. Lucan, a first-century authority, makes mention of the Druidic god, Esus as 'uncouth Esus of the barbarous altars'. He is also a crucified god, in some accounts he is even depicted as a woodcutter.[47] One can grasp the Jesus-Esus-Eros-Hero link, both through similarity of story and name. But much more is concealed.

At this juncture it is worth remembering that many of the Ancients, the Hebrews and the Egyptians for instance, did not generally write down vowels. Consonants only were written. When consonants are uttered, the vowels emerge gently and naturally, depending on the precise shape of the mouth and lips as the consonants are sounded We all know how regional accents make the same words sound different. Some accents are nasal, some gutteral, others rounded, etc.. In this way, for example, one's 'hog' is another's 'hug'. Amongst the many reasons why names change from region to region and era to era, this is one of the most important.

To return to the connectivity of names, Esus is also known as Hu-Esus, Hesus or Hu for short.[48] Hu was an exceedingly ancient god and of prime importance in the mythologies of the ancient Britons and Gauls. The link with Eros is that 'hu' is a primal vowel sound in the European languages of the period. It indicates darkness, in terms of the womb of the earth. The form of the name Hesus means literally 'healer'. Hesus is also associated with the bringing of music, in Celtic myth. The indication here is that music is light, for Hu also means 'light'. This is a complex theology, but it is also science.[49] The feast day of Hu still bears his name, Hogmanay. It is of course the Scottish New Year. In the past it was celebrated as a 'kind of Saturnalia'.[50] But where does the name Hu take us?

Hu also means, 'Lord' – 'the Lord'. It is to be found in the long Hebrew version of Jesus' name Jehos*hua*. Jehoshua means 'The Lord is salvation'. The variant: Yahu means 'Lord God' – Ya is 'God', Hu is 'Lord'. In this way the heroes are inextricably linked to the identity, the very sense of being that we call God. 'Hero' is also one of the oldest words still extant with the English language. Its source is shared by the name of one of the greatest heroes of classical myth, Hercules.

Hercules is the Latin version of the original Greek, Heracles, meaning 'Glory of Hera'. There is, however, an older derivation. I believe that the Greek Hera is a later feminisation of a god name that is derived directly from ancient Egypt. It is a god name that was used to describe the very identity and nature of the Pharaoh himself. For Heracles, perhaps we should read Heru-akhty – the living image of Horus, known more familiarly today as Horakhty,[51] whose image is famous to the world as the Sphinx. When linked to Ra, a composite name is formed, Ra-Horakhty, which is illustrated by the hieroglyph of a hawk-headed male divinity. Thus the word 'Hawk' too contains the element of 'the Lord'. Horus is the Greek spelling of the Egyptian Heru – Horus is the oldest known form of the hero.

In the Greek myth, Heracles ascends to heaven in a blaze of glory, as does Jesus in the Gospel of Mark. In the legend, Heracles is reborn into heaven to sit at the table of the gods. In Egyptian myth, Horus is the original holy child, the son of Osiris and Isis. He was the embodiment of the Egyptian pharaonic kingship; a pharaoh was the living image of the Lord, of Horus, and when a pharaoh died he ascended to the heavens as Osiris.

Taking our investigation just a little bit further, in the Old Testament Book of Genesis, Abram, by virtue of his loyalty to God, changes his name to Abraham. The insertion of the *ha* element is significant, for in Hebrew, 'ha' means 'the'; it is the definite article. Hu, Ha, Ho and He, as in Heru and all the other variants, at root, mean precisely the same thing: 'the Lord'. For 'the Lord', read 'the The'.[52] This is reminiscent of the Vedic definition of the divine: 'I am That, Thou art That, all This is That.' There is no doubt that each p*haraoh* was a hero whose goal was to move beyond the realm of 'the' and into a higher realm, the realm of the 'The'. The 'ha' is a reference to higher things. The hero lets go of the small 'the' and moves into 'The', away from the small self into the universal Self. Jesus, by being a hero, was partaking of this same mystery. His story relates more than can be read literally. In understanding the meaning of the term 'hero', we can understand more about the nature of the mythic Jesus, and some of the extraordinary correlations with archaic Egyptian myth.

I must admit that I had never expected things to turn out like this. The more

I dug, the more there was to dig. One thought did occur to me, though, and it was one that, rather than stir my suspicions, began to allay them. The observation was that some of the actual iconography of Jesus from within the Catholic Church is very striking in the way that he is portrayed as standing cloaked with his arms outstretching in a pose of welcome reconciliation, a pose that is very similar to statues that I had seen of Isis and Nephthys in the tomb of Tutankhamun. Jesus' pose is very Egyptian. Furthermore, whether the protagonist is Horus or Jesus, both are called 'Lord' and both are known as 'sons of the widow', for this is exactly what they are. This is another common motif to the hero myth worldwide.[53]

That Jesus is a hero in the vein of the Ancients is borne out by the mythic quality of his story. A summation of the telltale elements demonstrates just how obvious this really is, even down to the finer points:

Jesus is the anticipated messiah, the Son of God, God made flesh, the Saviour.
He is born in a grotto amidst wonders, of a virgin, on either 25th December or 6th January.
He is attended by three kings.
He goes into exile, pursued closely by agents of the jealous king.
He is baptised by a wild man, after being tempted by the Devil.
He has 12 followers or apostles.
He performs the miracle of turning water into wine at a marriage ceremony.
He raises a man from the dead and performs other miracles, such as walking on water.
He rides into town on a donkey and is triumphantly acclaimed king.
He is put to death upon a cross at Easter.
His lifeless body is placed inside a rock tomb.
He harrows hell and releases the spirits of the dead.
He rises from the dead three days later.
He is found by the woman who mourned him, having escaped miraculously from the rock tomb.
These events are then celebrated with the feast of the Eucharist.

We have looked at some of these aspects across myth in a general manner. Let us now focus more on the Jesus story, this time using the Gospel stories as our springboard.

Jesus, by being brought forth from a grotto, in symbolic terms represents light from darkness. The myth is also denoting that he is a son of the earth, in Greek, Gaia or Ge, in ancient Egypt, Geb, the father of Osiris. By the same token, Matthew describes the events of the crucifixion in equally earthly terms:

'...from midday a darkness fell over the land, which lasted until three in the afternoon ... and about three Jesus cried aloud, "Eli, Eli, lema sabachthani?" which means, "My God, my God, why hast thou forsaken me?" Hearing this, some of the bystanders said "He is calling Elijah". One of them ran at once and fetched a sponge, which he soaked in sour wine and held to his lips on the end of a stick. But the others said, "Let us see if Elijah will come and save him."

'Jesus again cried aloud and breathed his last. At that moment, the curtain of the temple was torn in two from top to bottom. The earth shook, rocks split and graves opened; many of God's saints were raised from sleep and coming out of their graves after his resurrection entered the Holy City...'

Matt. 27:45-52

The last sentence is interesting, given that Christian saints were only numbered from the inception of Christianity and there are few in the canon who predate Jesus.

Jesus, before ascending to heaven, must cleave at the crack of doom, at the very doors of hell itself. 'Hell' is an interesting word and does not mean what it implies, certainly in the dogmatic sense. We have touched upon this before, but now I shall reiterate from a slightly different angle. In Greek, and in certain of the old European languages, it is *helle*. Greece is, to this day, the land of the Hellenes. The Hellespont is the natural land bridge that cojoins southern and mainland Greece. Helle herself was a maiden and a sister of Phrixus. It was whilst fleeing abroad with the famous Golden Fleece that Helle fell overboard and was celebrated in the name of the Hellespont. This is significant, for it was Jason, another form of the name Jesus, who went after the Golden Fleece with the twelve Argonauts. As we have seen, a meaning of Helle is 'womb', in the sense of 'womb of regeneration' and Hel is associated with rebirth, usually through purification, often by fire, hence *helios*, Greek for the sun. Hel or Helle was a goddess. The Jewish version of Hell, called Sheol, is also feminine, as are other versions. There have been times in this project when I have gone through hell, particularly in the sense that in pursuing it, changes have been wrought in me. Going through hell is all about change.

Heracles ascended Mount Olympus in glory. Buddha ascended the mountain Pandava, in Sri Lanka, whereupon heaven opened and he was bathed in light – he shone as the brightness of sun and moon. Wherever we look, we see comparisons. The temptation in the wilderness? Look no further than the Persian account of the Devil tempting Zarathustra on the mountain (*c*. sixth Century BC). Walking on water? We have mentioned Pythagoras, but again in the Greek mythos, Poseidon does the same.

Besides the similarities in storyline, there are also the comparisons to be made between Jesus' words and the words of earlier heroes:

Jesus:

> 'You know the commandments: You shall not murder; you shall not commit adultery; you shall not steal; you shall not bear false witness; you shall not defraud; honour your father and mother.'

Mark 10:19

Buddha:

> 'Abstain from killing and from taking what is not given. Abstain from unchastity and from speaking falsely. Do not accept gold and silver.'

Khuddakapatha 2

Jesus:

> 'Do to others as you would have them do to you.'

Luke 6:31

Buddha:

> 'Consider others as yourself.'

Dhammapada 10:1

Jesus:

> 'This is my commandment, that you love one another as I have loved you. No one has greater love than this, to lay down one's life for one's friends.'   John 15. 12–13

Buddha:

> 'Just as mother would protect her only child at the risk of her own life, even so, cultivate a boundless heart towards all beings. Let your thoughts of boundless love pervade the whole world.'

Sutta Nipata 149–150

When speaking of himself, Jesus says, 'I am the Alpha and the Omega', Buddha says, 'I am the letter A'. In another example, Krishna says, 'I am the light, I am the life, I am the sacrifice', words echoed by Jesus. We are in heroic territory and a comparison of the facts of the myth demonstrates that Jesus is a hero in the ancient sense. No matter what the early Church Fathers may have said, or how they said it, their refutations appear to fall flat.

The above comparison of quotes comes from the work of Gerald Massey. Massey was an interesting man, unique in fact. He was primarily a poet and came from a poverty-stricken background. He was born in 1828 to illiterate parents who are described as having lived in a hovel, barely able to feed and clothe their children. Massey's education was a few months at a school, where he learned to read and write, but at the age of eight he was put to work in a local silk mill for 12 to 13 hours a day. In the ensuing years, Massey's main secondary occupation was reading. When he was 15 years old, he moved to London, where, though always struggling against the hardships of poverty, he thrived intellectually, producing some very important insights into the origins of historical Christianity. What particularly stirred me was the following:

> 'According to the unquestioned tradition of the Christian fathers, which has always been accepted by the Church, the primary nucleus of our canonical gospels was not a life of Jesus at all, but a collection of the Logia, oracles or sayings, the logia Kuriaka, which were written down in Hebrew or Aramaic, by one Matthew, as the scribe of the Lord.'[54]

Unremarkable stuff, you might think, until that is we come to Massey's identification of St. Matthew:

> 'The logia or sayings are *mythoi* in Greek... The sayings were the oral wisdom and, as the name implies, that wisdom was uttered by word of mouth alone. They existed before writing, and were not allowed to be written afterwards... In Egypt the sayings were assigned to various divinities, that is, mythical characters.
> 'Among the sayings of Jesus, or Logia of the Lord, is the saying that "the very hairs of your head are numbered"; In the (Egyptian) Ritual, every hair is weighed; also the night of the judgement day is designated that of "weighing a hair".
> 'Matthew alone of the evangelists represents this drama of the Egyptian ritual.'

Massey goes on to relate the copyist of the Egyptian version:

> 'These sayings, or Logia of the Lord, were written by Hermes or That (Thoth), the scribe of the Gods.
> 'This is the part assigned to Matthew, the called one, the Evangelist and Scribe, who first wrote down the sayings of the Lord. *Now, the special name or title of Hermes in the particular character of the recorder is Matthew in Egyptian – that is, Matiu.*[55]

> (My italics)

This is remarkable. In the same paragraph, Massey goes on to relate that the original sayings of the Lord are none other than the original sayings of Horus, whose very name means 'the Lord'.

Were the apostles' names merely symbolic titles of ancient Egyptian deities? That this is a distinct possibility I will demonstrate further on. Meanwhile, there is another familiar legend that I wish to relate before we go any further, the legend of Adonis, whose name also means 'the Lord'.

The saviour called Adonis comes from Syria and his name is a Greek variant upon the magical name of the Hebrew God, Adonai. Adonai means literally 'Lord God' and is a variant of the name of God, Yahweh, sometimes known as Jehovah. The myth of Adonis is exceedingly ancient and, not surprisingly, bears many familiar hallmarks. He was born at Bethlehem, the same Bethlehem as Jesus. Earlier I mentioned Hogmanay. The celebration is never complete without the oatcakes, sometimes wheatcakes, that are symbolic of Hu. Oats or other cereal crops figure quite prominently in the story of 'the Lord'. Bethlehem means 'House of bread'. Adonis was a god of the corn[56] and was symbolised by loaves of bread. The significance of this will be revealed later on.

Adonis was born of a virgin, Myrrha, sometimes Mari, and shortly after his nativity he was hailed by cries of 'The Star of Salvation has dawned in the East.'[57] The date of his nativity is 6th January or 25th December.[58] The legend is particularly beautiful in its description of an event known as the Adonia. Adonis died at Eastertime, he was gored to death by a wild boar and where his blood dropped, there sprouted anemones, the flowers of the underworld. Adonis harrowed hell and rose again from the dead. During the days that he harrowed hell, the sea was literally blood red. In the ritual of Adonia, the 'blood' element was supplied by the spring rains loosening particles of haematite – bloodstone – in the mountain soil, which would then be washed downstream and into the sea. Maidens would sail out to sea at this time and there sprinkle the 'blood' with anemones, which grow wild in the Syrian hills.

Significantly, Adonis' sepulchre is exactly the same place where Mary nursed Jesus, the same cave that was Jesus' sepulchre. Adonis was particularly revered by the Orphics, who composed hymns to him, and like Jesus, Adonis and his variants, Attis and Tammuz, are all 'sons of the widow'. Interestingly, this is also a term common to Freemasonary.

It is now, as we come again to look at the myth of Attis and his mother, Cybele, that we arrive closer to home and get a sense of scale as we approach the very heartland of the mystery. The cult of Attis had a considerable influence upon early Christianity, and for a good reason, too: its headquarters were what is now known as the Vatican. The goddess, Cybele, mother of Attis, was brought to Rome in 204 BC from Phrygia, now Turkey (see chapter six).

The earthly incarnation of Cybele was Nand. By eating an almond, Nan conceived Attis, the saviour. Attis was eucharistically eaten as bread, which was washed down with his blood, wine.[59] Attis' father was never known, hence he was called 'the Virgin's son'. After his death, he was resurrected as 'The Most High God, who holds the Universe together'.[60] His epiphany, his ascent into heaven, is greeted with the words: 'Hail Bridegroom, Hail, new Light.'[61] Significantly, Attis was crucified on a pine tree, whence his blood, shed upon the earth, redeemed man and the fertility of the soil. The date of his passion is 25th March, Lady Day in the Christian calendar – the feast of the annunciation of the Blessed Virgin Mary. The Church Father Lactantius puts the date of the crucifixion of Jesus as 23rd March and the 25th as his resurrection.

As if to hammer home the point, the day of Attis' death is a Friday, called Black Friday, the Day of Blood. The cry of Attis upon the cross is recorded in a hymn of the Naasenes of the third century AD:

"Euhai, Euhan, he is Pan, he is Bacchus".[62]

Attis' cult remained at its Vatican hill site for at least 200 years into the Christian era. The Vatican is described by a Roman churchman called Gaius, who lived in the time of Pope Zephyrinus (AD 198–217), as the place where 'you will find the trophies of those who have founded the church', rather an interesting statement considering the importance of Attis to this site. According to Pliny the Elder (AD 23–79) the Vatican had long been an unhealthy, poor and somewhat squalid area outside the hills of Rome. Pliny complained that it was full of snakes and according to Martial (AD 41–104), it was renowned for its disgusting wine. However, in the era of Caligula and Nero it soon found itself fashionable again. It was during the persecutions of Nero that it is believed that St. Peter suffered crucifixion. In the 1940s, during excavation under the high altar of St. Peter's Basilica, organic material was discovered, including fragments of a skeleton and the remains of various animals. Margherita Guarducci, an archaeologist and epigraphist who worked on the material in the 1950s, believed that she had found the remains of St. Peter himself. Given her devotion to the faith, her enthusiasm and professionalism were very highly commendable; however, I could not help but notice that amongst the animal remains were those of a mouse, a cock, an ox, a sheep and, interestingly, a pig. All of these animals were sacred to Attis, particularly the pig or boar, the very animal that had done Adonis so much injury. The explanation of these remains was that they were pilgrim offerings – pilgrims come to adore 'the Lord', perhaps? But which 'Lord'? Attis, Adonis, Tammuz? Bacchus, Dionysus, Mithras? Hercules, Heracles, Horus? Hu–Esus, Esau or Jesus? Excepting the latter, of course, none of these names could be tolerated by the early Church Fathers, even if comparisons with Christianity were admitted.

In the Name of God

So many ancient holy names, linked through common sounds and ancient tales, had drawn me into the relationship between spoken and written words. Mythology and the alphabet, I was soon to discover, are inextricably bound together in a way that is deeply profound. Many commentators have made this observation over the years and it is nicely summed up by Leonard Shlain:

> 'One explanation for the Israelites' intense hostility towards images is that, having discovered the immense utility of alphabetic writing, they considered iconic information to be a threat to their new-found skill. Learning to think without resorting to images is indispensable to alphabetic literacy. "Make no images" is a ban on right-brain pattern recognition.'[63]

The Judaic, Christian and Islamic religions all banned the worship of images and became more and more dependent upon the written word. Inevitably, the oral tradition suffered. In contrast to the written word, the oral tradition's riches lie in the personal transmission of poetry, metaphor and symbolism. Such ingredients entrain both left and right hemispheres of the brain and encourage mental imagery and emotional response. Thus the spoken word can make the intangible seem real and give rise to greater overall awareness. This is a gift of spoken mythology. But more influential still can be a single word of appropriate vibratory power, used knowledgably and purposefully. This is the true role of words in religious ritual. We are reminded of, and inspired in, our purpose through correct understanding of myth, this understanding and strength of purpose then helps empower the words of ritual. Myth tells us of our origins and the ultimate source of all – the divine. The practices of religion bind us back to that source.

There is, for instance, an element of this in a very interesting correlation of names of power that I came across when looking again at the Celtic god, Esus.

Esus, in being a Celtic god, is also a son of God. In the Celtic creation myth, God pronounces his name with 'the Word'; this is reminiscent of St. John's Gospel. The letters of the holy name are called the three columns of truth. These three columns, /|\, spell out God's secret holy name as A W E.[64] How close this is to Yahweh – all that is really missing is the 'y' sound as the mouth opens to enunciate the 'a'. Yahweh is still recognised as a name of power today in Judaism (sometimes Jehovah). Can this similarity of Esus and Awe – Jesus and Yahweh – be put down to mere coincidence? When we look further, the coincidences begin to look more than a little familiar.

The greatest of the Irish gods, the Dagda, is called 'the Good God', not 'good' in a moral sense, but 'good at everything' (RuadRo-Fhessa or 'Lord of perfect knowledge').[65] However, the Dagda has an alternative name meaning 'Father of all' – Eochaidh Ollathair. The pronunciation of Eochaidh begins by compressing the first two vowels together in order to speak them. The last two consonants are relatively silent, giving us a soft 'd' sound verging on a 'th'. The result of all this is to give us a name remarkably close to that of Joseph, who in the Gospels is also called a 'good' man.

As if in a confirmation of these correlations, in the Irish Christian tradition it is St. Brigid who is the midwife at the nativity (see chapter six). On that night she was miraculously transported to Bethlehem, where she assisted dutifully at the birth. In Irish myth it is Brigid who is the Dagda Eochaidh's consort. At the coming of Christianity, Irish writers refused to demote their powerful goddess to the rank of a mere saint, insisting that she was the Queen of Heaven herself, Mary. She was called 'Mother of my Sovereign, Queen of the South', 'Prophetess of Christ' and, significantly, 'Mother of Jesus'.[66]

Just across the water from Ireland, in Wales, the mythologies, though much censored by the ravages of evangelism, have been preserved in a body known as the Mabinogion. This comprises tales from the White Book of Rhydderch and the Red Book of Hergest. The Mabinogion[67] has been dismissed as a meaningless term related to 'juvenile romances', however it has been suggested by Gwynn Jones that, rather than being meaningless, 'Mabinogion' means 'tales of the son of a virgin mother',[68] and that the 'son' concerned is the child always born at the winter solstice.

Whilst we are on the same subject, the Welsh term, *Dodman*, means 'the man who came' and is the same in Arabic. The name Dod is given in the Old Testament as one of King David's forebears. It is the same as David, in Arabic, Daud. Thus we have in Welsh a 'man of David', a Dodman. Dodman is also a system of measure;[69] in other words, the 'spirit' of Dod is upon one when using it.

All of this is intriguing, but where does it bring us to, beyond mere similarity? Myth is trying to tell us something, something of great value and of exceptional importance. That these names, so familiar to us, are to be found over a wide area, is fascinating, but their very presence denotes an importance of meaning. Names in myth are not given in a random manner and it seems that later, when the first scribes set to work, they were most concerned to record the terms aright.

> 'Now that documents of the earliest ages of writing are available, one is truck with a wholly unexpected feature. Those first predecessors of ours, instead of indulging their whims with childlike freedom, behave like worried and doubting commentators... They move among technical terms whose

meaning is half lost to them, they deal with words which appear
on this earliest horizon already "tottering with age"... experts
have noted the uncertainty prevailing in the successors of old
texts, the attempts in them to establish correct names and their
significance...'[69]

It was at this point that I was struck by a great sense of the obvious, as if
everyday things are so shrouded in mist that we very rarely see their
significance. I had been poring over a book about churches in Rome[70] when I
noticed the church that is the headquarters of the Society of Jesus, the Jesuits.
It is called the Gesu. something about the name struck me as being plural,
though I could not quite put my finger on it, something that tacitly implied
many Jesuses, not one. In the sense of the order being a missionary one, the
many Jesuses would be spread out worldwide, all of them being in essence
the same figure, but again with regional variations. I was fascinated that the
idea of an archaic worldwide Jesus hero-figure was again being reflected here.
I was further intrigued when I discovered that inside the headquarters resides
one of the greatest masterpieces of the Renaissance. It is a mural by Bacciccia.[71]
If the word 'God' means 'voice', then the title of this masterpiece revealed
much; it is: 'The Triumph of the Name of Jesus'. In the mural, where the name
should be, there is a glorious flash of light and, barely discernible in its midst,
a cross (see plate). Again, this reflected my thoughts about the power of names
and acoustic phenomena. Inspired, I strode forward in my researches with a
renewed *raison d'être*.

The 'Gisa' Correlation

The name of Jesus is the Greek form of the Hebrew Joshua, sometimes spelt
Jeshua. This in itself is a foreshortening of the longer Yehoshua. 'Jesus' does
not mean 'saviour' as is often stated, but 'the Lord is salvation'. Sometimes, in
very old writings of the Jews, called 'Toldoth', there are variants such as Jeshu
or even Jesha, but they are the same name regardless. My eyes wandering
through the Old Testament, I noticed that there seem to be variants of this
name throughout, but the one that came to my notice most readily was the
name of Esau, the unfortunate brother of Jacob who, in one of the grubbiest
episodes in biblical mythology, has his birthright stolen through a cheap trick
played by his younger brother upon their father, Isaac.

In phonetic Arabic, the names of Jesus and of Esau (who gave his name to
the land of Edom, from whence Herod came), reduce down to Gi-sa and

Gi-su respectively.[72] Now, if all of this seems unnecessarily complex, there is a method to my madness in that this transcription raises an interesting anomaly. The name of Esau, to which the name of Jesus is clearly linked historically as well as linguistically, has no Hebrew etymology or source. In other words, both names precede Hebrew history and are therefore very, very ancient. This age indicator is significant and is supported by another venerated source.

In the Koran, one might expect that the name used for Jesus would be derived from the Hebrew, Jeshua. Quite clearly, it is not. Jeshua in Arabic would be 'Jeshu', but the Koran calls Jesus 'Issa'. This is reflected even in early Christian–Arab translations of the name: instead of 'Yasu' we have 'Isa'. The Jesus of the Koran is different from the Jesus of the gospels; he is older by far, for the Nasara, the Nasarenes of the Koran, are a sister sect of Judaism, not an offshoot of it. A god called Issa was most certainly recognised during the first century period right up until the coming of Islam[73] and, going back further, Isa (pronounced 'Eesha'), is the name of an Upanishad of the Indian Vedic tradition. The Upanishad scriptures were recorded between 800 and 200 BC.

The *Isa Upanishad* focuses on 'Self' or 'being'. Throughout scripture the favoured definition of being is 'I am'. These are words uttered at the outset of many a creation myth worldwide and this act is described in the same myths as the act of creative purpose. On an individual level, the statement 'I am' means that the speaker is 'at one' with the divine. This was a favoured term of Jesus. 'I am the light' would therefore mean 'I am at one with the light which is divine' – light, of course, is vibration at a high level. 'I am the way' would be understood as 'The attainment of heaven is only available through the divine.'

The attainment of the divine was the goal of the hero and from that place of power, great things could be accomplished. As if to confirm the ancient understanding of 'at-one-ment' and the hero, in some languages we can see a very clear link between hero names and the term 'I am'. For example, the French, *Je suis*, is close to the name Jesus.

There are some further interesting correlations which lead us onto the most controversial aspect of the thesis. The Greek mythological horse, Peg*asus*, means 'source of water'. In the legend, Pegasus flies to Mount Helicon and strikes a rock with his hoof to create a flow of ice cold, crystal clear water – the Hippocrene spring (from the Greek *hippo*,'horse').[74] This is reminiscent of the Old Testament story of Moses where he strikes the rock of Meribah and water gushes forth to ease the thirst of the Israelites (Exodus 17:1–7). This water saves the wanderers in their parched state; it is the water of life. We will see the significance of the name Meribah a little further on.

So it is that we have come to the connection of the name with the actual elements of the earth. We have already seen the importance of holy water in various religious rituals, and its presence at sacred sites. Now we can see the beginnings of a link between the site *and* its hero, and more specifically, the name of that hero.

In Greek, both Issa and Jeshu are rendered 'Iesous'. This indicates that they spring from the same source. Jeshu means literally 'God-man' – 'Yah' we know is 'God', 'ish' or 'esh' is 'man'. However, 'god-man' doesn't tell us much, but Issa or Isa does, it gives a clear indication of age and, as I will show, a clear indication of origins.

In the Greek and Hebrew myths the names of particular heroes begin with 'Y', 'I','J' or 'G'. When I investigated the origins of these letters, much was revealed about the nature of the name, much that seems familiar. The letter 'G', the seventh letter of our alphabet, is derived from the letter Zayin of the proto-Siniatic alphabet, where again it is the seventh letter.[75] In short (see appendix) the letter Zayin represents a face-to-face encounter between two people, two armies or two situations; at its highest level, a meeting between God and man. However, it also denotes' skin pierced with a shaft' and the hero in myth is almost always pierced with an arrow, a lance or with nails. This is borne out by the fact that in the alphabet now known as proto-Canaanite (*c.*1200–1050 BC),[76] the sign was transformed into a'T'. This 'T' is the cross or crucifix. Within the Phoenician royal house, this same letter was branded upon the forehead of the royal princes, some of whom were said to have been sacrificed as sons of God. In Greek, Zayin becomes Zeta, also the seventh letter of the alphabet. Seven again seems to be intimately connected to the hero. Tammuz, who, as we have already seen, is the child of the seventh (see chapter six), was also a pierced hero.

The letters 'I', 'J' and 'Y', which in Latin and Greek are sometimes interchangeable, are all derived from the tenth letter of the proto-Sinaitic alphabet, Yod,[77] This in turn comes from the Egyptian hieroglyph of a hand. This letter is pronounced 'tot' or 'Dod' – Dodman again. In the Jesus story, 'I', 'J' and 'Y' are connected to 'G', because when the hero is crucified it is the hand that is pierced by a nail. This may help answer the various disputes over whether Jesus was nailed through the palm or the wrist.

In being the tenth letter, Yod is a sign of unity or completeness, 'I am', hence its use in the name of God, Jehovah or Yahweh. There is another interesting observation to be made. The name Jesus is the late Latin translation of the Greek Iesous, which is itself a translation of the Hebrew letters: 'Yod', 'Heh', 'Shen', 'Vav', 'Heh'.–This is the holy Tetragammaton 'Yod', 'Heh', 'Vav', 'Heh', or JHVH, written around the additional letter 'Shen'. The former is of course the representation of the secret name of God, Yahweh or Jehovah. In common with other ancient scripts, written Hebrew omits the vowels and reciting Hebrew scriptures requires great dedication, since the text has to be virtually learned by heart. The vowels required for pronunciation are passed down the generations. In the case of JHVH, the proper pronunciation of the unpronounceable name of God was passed down from high priest to high priest and was believed to have been lost around 500 BC. This is not surprising, since it was only uttered once a year on the day of Atonenent when the high priest alone was allowed to enter the Holy of Holies in the Temple of Jerusalem. Here on the site of the old Temple of Solomon he prayed on behalf of his people.

The significance of 'Shen', the letter added to the middle of the tetragrammaton to make the word that eventually becomes Jesus, is 'fire' or 'light'. This therefore renders JHSVH as 'the fire or light of God', and could equally be pronounced Jesu or Joshua. Note, too, the closeness to Issa. The letter 'Vav' represents and means 'nail'. (Its symbolism is a spiral denoting cosmic forms in motion, the word of God spiralling outwards in manifestation.) What is extraordinary is that these elements come together not only in the name of Jesus, but also in the name of one particular Roman patrician family.

The name Caesar has bequeathed us the words for 'Emperor', in a few European tongues – Kaiser in German and Czar in Russian. Originally the Latin letter 'C' was pronounced as a hard 'k', but it could also be pronounced as a 'g'. It was this 'g' that later became the seventh letter. The Caesars wished to be respected as hero-gods; indeed, Julius Caesar's divine pretensions were foisted upon all. Now we will see the ancient heritage of Caesar's name, it is really Gaesar, pronounced 'Gisa'.

The gods are divine, they are of heaven, but they are sought after here on earth. Ancient Egypt has been shown to have been particularly intent on the bringing of heaven to earth. In ancient times, the divine, as we have seen, was sought to be embodied in place, as at sacred sites, and in people – the heroes. The heroes embody the heavenly here on earth, creating a link and setting an example. What linguistic device would be used to ground the divine attributes to earth? The prefix of the letter 'G', the ancient letter which denotes the divine on earth, the 'G' of Geb and Gaia. *Now 'Isa' becomes 'Gisa' and we see that Gisa is the embodiment and the place of Isa.*

In modern Egyptian Arabic, *Gisa* means 'proximity' or 'nearness'.[78] if we realise that originally languages related the highest meanings in relation to the divine, 'nearness to God' would be implicit. For myself, I felt that at last I was getting near to something approaching a source, after many years of searching.

Oddly enough, whilst researching this thesis I came across the London slang term for a man, 'geezer'. I thought that I was taking obsession to new lengths by looking it up but, much to my astonishment, I learned that this term had been brought back from the Sanish Peninsular Wars by soldiers of of the Duke of Wellington's army. It is a Basque word and it means 'man' or 'the man who came'. The god-man who came? I wondered. Basque is probably the oldest European language, its roots are unknown and it lies outside the remit of the Indo-European language table.[79]

Further applying the Gisa key, somewhat tentatively at first, I began to follow other clues and uncovered an overall correlation pattern. We have already encountered many heroes, including Jesus and Esus, but there are more to follow. Eshu is the messenger god in the myths of the Nigerian Yoruba people. He could speak every single language, and, like Jesus, he brought God's instructions to earth and took back to the gods the smoke and the scent of sacrifice. From the tales of the Creek people in the southeastern USA comes Esaugeteh Emisee, whose name, meaning 'Master of breath', is a reflection of Latin *spiritus,* meaning also 'breath'. He modelled people out of mud, as God did with Adam.[80]

We have seen how, in the ancient Middle East, these names would likely be prefaced with a 'G' in order to confirm the 'earthing' of the heavenly power. Thus we would have Geshu and Gesaugeteh. It seems that this was also the case in ancient Tibet, for there we find Gesar of Ling, the early Tibetan saviour god whose second coming is much anticipated.

Naturally, I was looking for the oldest of these correlations and for obvious reasons my focus became firmly settled upon ancient Egypt.

Through a study of names we have come to the conclusion that 'Gisa' is the root name of heroes, but Gisa is a also a place. Usually spelt 'Giza' to match the local phonetics, it is the site of the world's most fabulous monuments, the three great pyramids of Egypt. However, even before I discovered the Gisa/hero connection, there was one thing of which I was already certain: where there are monuments there is a hero. Gisa/Giza has been the name of the pyramid plateau area since long before the arrival of the Arabs *c.*AD 600 [81]. Although it is disputed in some areas of Egyptology, the area has an intimate association with the god, Osiris, the ultimate 'prince of the earth'.

Osiris is the Greek translation of the Egyptian, Asar. Asar is the son of the earth, Geb. Once again, we shall preface the name with 'G', affirming that the divine is present on the earth. It gives us, Gasar, also known as Gisa. Gisa can also be spelt Gesa or Gesu. These are variants that do occur with myth, for reasons that we shall soon see. The name means 'Prince of the earth' or 'Blood of the earth' and is the key to unlock a considerable amount of the world's mythology.

Osiris, to use his later and more familiar Greek name, is almost always portrayed as carrying a djed pillar, a mysterious-looking object reminiscent of a Greek column. *Djed* is an Old Kingdom word. The Old Kingdom is one of the oldest periods in Egyptian dynastic history. Within it there were two kings, the oddly named Djer, and Djet, both meaning 'Horus' the son of Osiris.

The syllable *Dj* represents in 'Horus' in Old Kingdom hieroglyph. When the living Horus, the regnant Pharaoh, passed on, he became Osiris. Osiris, you may recall, is the Greek name for the Egyptian Asar. This meant that Dj became Asar[82] (sometimes called and spelt Wsir or User).This process would also be recognised where the hero was considered to have attained immortality whilst still alive, that is, to have moved from the small self to the universal Self, from 'the' to 'The', in other words, to have become a man-god, a god on earth.[83] This, of course was the mark of the true hero. The composite term would be 'Djasar' or 'Djoser'. A recognisable offshoot is Zoser, (sometimes spelt 'Djasor'; 'dj'and 'z' are cognate), a king of the Third Dynasty. Zoser's step-pyramid at Saqqara, Egypt is the first known structure built with masoned stonework rather than rough stone.[84] Jesus was called the Alpha and the Omega, so too is this present in Zoser's name: 'Z' we know is the last letter of the alphabet, whereas Asar the Egyptian name of Osiris, here present as 'oser', means also 'Prince Alpha' in Greek translation. Thus the earthly Horus, at one with Osiris/Asar and therefore expressed as Djasar, would be the forerunner of Gasar, Gisa and Gesu.[85]

Von Dechend and de Santillana in *Hamlet's Mill* make the significant comment that:

> 'Once having grasped a thread going back in time, then the test of later doctrines with their own historical developments lies in their congruence with tradition preserved intact even if half understood... And universality is in itself a test when coupled with a firm design. When something found, say, in China turns up also in Babylonian astrological texts, then it must be assumed to be relevant...
>
> 'Take the origin of music. Orpheus and his harrowing death may be a poetic creation born in more than one instance in diverse places. But when characters who do not play the lyre but blow pipes get themselves flayed alive for various reasons, and their identical end is rehearsed on several continents, then we feel that we have got hold of something ... where the Pied Piper turns up both in the medieval German myth of Hamelin and in Mexico long before Columbus, and is linked to both places with certain attributes like the colour red, it can hardly be a co-incidence.[86]

We find precisely these similarities in the Gisa correlation pattern. A case in point is the ancient figure of Zoroaster (sometimes Zarathustra). The founder of an ancient Persian religion, Zoroaster's teaching is a dualistic one of the continuous, eternal battle of good against evil. Good is represented by Ahura Mazda and bad by Angra Mainyu. These are the usual elements to be found incorporated with the sacred text of this religion, known as the Avesta. The Avesta, as it is named, bears elements of the secret word that God spoke at the creation, God's own name, AWE. The good god, Ahura, is again another form of 'the Lord'; it has the element of 'hu' within it. It is Zoroaster's name that is here of particular interest. This is underlined by certain elements of his myth in which his birth is attended by marvels. He inherits the 'glory' of Yima – in other words he is a son of Yima, Judge of the Dead, and he has the tenets of the faith revealed to him by Ahura Mazda.

Zoroaster's name seems in itself dual. Zoroastrianism as a historical phenomenon has been much disputed. The Parsees, its followers, believe it to be as much as 8,000 years old. More realistically, a conservative dating puts it at *c.*1200 BC. Needless to say, at its height in the first millennium BC, Zoroastrianism's impact upon the development of Palestinian religion would be telling. It is essential to be aware of this when looking at Zoroaster's name: 'Zr' in ancient Egyptian is *Dj* – Horus. 'Aster' is related to Astarte, goddess of love, whose symbol was the bright shining star of the morning, Venus. Looking for a root we find that *Ast* in ancient Egyptian is what the Greeks have translated to us as 'Isis'. What is fascinating is the fact that this Isis name is still alive and well today within the scientific world, particularly *ast*ronomy.

Zoroaster's name then would seem to mean 'Horus, son of Isis' and to be based upon the theme of the ancient mythical cycle. It was whilst coming to terms with this aspect of the correlation that I came across other extraordinary anomalies that could only be answered, with any ease, by the formula described above. I was struck by a comment in Leonard Shlain's book, *The Alphabet versus the Goddess*:

> 'Many historians have puzzled over the rapid and enthusiastic conversion of Egyptians to Christianity in the second century. Egypt was, after all, an immensely ancient culture whose principal characteristic was *resistance* to change. Despite having been conquered by diverse foreigners throughout its three thousand year history, Egyptians retained their fealty to Osiris, Isis...'[87]

Shlain then goes on to make the interesting point that, whoever the conqueror might have been, it was *they* who were converted, not the other way round. In a similar vein, it could be that the incoming Christian religion, being the old tradition recycled, was too close to Egypt's own to be worthy of great resistance.

In the Old Testament, King David's father is called Jesse, a name quite often spelled Isai. In the Book of Isaiah 11:1,10, the first reference appears of 'the stump of Jesse', an interesting metaphor, seen as a major component of some of Europe's greatest stained-glass windows, all of them inside Gothic cathedrals. In the legend of Osiris, the hero is trapped inside a coffin which, having been sealed with lead, is cast adrift and ends up at Byblos, whereupon it sprouts leaves and becomes a tree; upon its discovery by Isis, *it is cut down.*"[88] [89] Jesse is clearly a Jesus name and the Osiris link is no coincidence, how can it be when we compare other aspects of Osiris' myth to that of Jesus? The term used by the people of Byblos to pay homage to the wood within which Osiris hung is rendered in the Greek Toxilon.[90] Exactly the same term is used repeatedly in the New Testament for the cross.[91] Trojan history (*c.*3000–1250 BC) also recalls this term, for the Trojans prayed to God and his son, an angel called Tas or Tasya, to resurrect them through the 'wooden' cross, the figure of which appears in effigy on various amulets.[92]

The Nazarenes

In an image that is strikingly reminiscent of the god Osiris in the Egyptian mysteries, St. Paul says the following of Jesus:

> 'In him everything in heaven and on earth was created, not only things visible but also the invisible orders of thrones, sovereignties, authorities and powers. The whole universe has been created through him and for him. He exists before all things and all things are held together in him. He is the head of the body, the church. He is its origin, the first to return from the dead, to become in all things supreme.'[93]

Everything in this statement applies to Osiris (see chapter ten), the god-man of the early Egyptian period, whose death hailed the coming of the nascent Horus. 'Nascent' means 'being born' and comes from the Latin root *nasci*, 'be born'.

In the Gospel of Matthew (2:15), a prophecy is made to come true in the exile of the holy family to Egypt. Quoting Hosea (11:1), Matthew describes the words of God; 'I have called my son out of Egypt.' Upon the return of the Holy family from out of exile they settle in Galilee, so that again, prophecy comes true: 'He will be called a Nazarene.' As Kamal Salibi points out, the followers of the Arabian Issa were called the community of Nasara, in other words, the Nazarenes.[94] This particular god, Issa, had been born at Mecca (in the period before the rise of Islam), which is interesting because Mecca, as well as being famous now as the central shrine of Islam, has always been famous for the Ka'aba, the cube-shaped black meteoric stone. As we have seen, the holy child is invariably the son of a mother goddess, and what can be more explicit than the fact that Cybele, whose name gives us the derivation of the word 'cube', was worshipped as a black meteoric stone?

Scholars have long pointed out the textual differences between various of the Gospels and have narrowed down the file to three possible sources, Q, M and L. It is generally assumed that Q is a lost Greek source that gave rise to the Gospels of Matthew and Luke and that additionally, Matthew drew quite separately from another source, M, whilst Luke drew from source L. It has been suggested that L and M were Aramaic. I contend that it is quite possible and entirely plausible that the 'source gospels' were derived from one original source, the story of Issa, from the oral tradition. We focused on Issa earlier as one of the 'Gisa names'. His hero mythology is rooted in Arabia and predates Christianity by as much as 1,200 years. Issa was born of Maryam, he worked miracles, he was crucified and he rose on the third day.

It is a widely-held view that the oldest of the gospel texts was the Aramaic Nazarene gospel. The origins of this gospel would have been from within the oral tradition. I have already pointed out that, in the Islamic faith, Jesus is known as Issa. Now we see that Issa's story is very close to Jesus' story as accepted by Christians and yet may be 1,200 years older than Christianity itself. This is a puzzle until, noting that the story's roots are in Arabia, we learn that St. Paul spent a mysterious three years in there, a point that is enlarged upon by Kamal Salibi, in *Who Was Jesus*. Salibi's argument is that whilst in Arabia, St. Paul had access to the original of the gospel sources, the Nazarene Gospel, and that it is from this that he gained his image of Jesus. Early writers confirm the Nazarenes as the source of gospel knowledge:

> 'The introduction to Luke and the accounts quoted by Eusebius from the early second century writer Papias ... show that all the gospels except the patently fictitious ones were based on notes taken by Greek speaking converts from the Aramaic Gospel orally current among the Nazarenes; and that each evangelist, as Papias reports, "interpreted them as best he could" – that is to say, uncritically, and, in general, with studied ignorance of their historical background.'[95]

Paul would therefore be the foremost evangelist of the Nazarene gospel, working hard to bring coherence to the beliefs and practices of the fledgeling Church. Furthermore, it is highly likely that Paul's work strongly influenced the canonical gospels. His own letters predate any of them and in these letters there are few references to anything approaching an historical Jesus; as we have already seen, St. Paul's preoccupation is with the divinity. There is also little doubt that Paul knew of at least one other Jesus, otherwise in Corinthians, why does he refer to 'another Jesus', as opposed to another saint, teacher or Christ?

'For if he that cometh preacheth another Jesus, whom we have not preached, or if ye receive another spirit, which ye have not received, or another gospel which ye have not accepted, ye might well bear with *him*.'[96]

As we know, the problem with transferring the oral to the written is that, from then onwards, its meaning becomes subject to editorial niceties and misinterpretation and the essential mystery lost. I have already pointed out some of the inconsistencies of the editorial hand, but there is a further, more modern illustration that goes to the heart of the matter. When James Joyce wrote *Ulysses*, he did so in his illegible longhand. For years, he was lauded for some of the most surreal but effective imagery in the history of literature – 'The man wrapped his beard in a piece of newspaper' summoned up a truly absurd image - until the corrected text was published and Joyce's irregular spelling was exposed. The real text read: 'The man wrapped his bread in a piece of newspaper.'

Regarding this period of transition from the oral to the written, I was intrigued by the fact that 'No illustrated Christian manuscript survives of a date earlier than the fourth century AD, but the tradition of sacred illustration, in the Book of the Dead style, had been firmly established among Greek Jews from pre-Christian times'.[97] It is highly likely that there would have been such early Christian manuscripts and I wondered that perhaps the content was not to the later Church's liking and so done away with. I say this in the light of the existence of early manuscripts of the Egyptian Coptic Church which use illustrative religious symbolism that relates both to older Jewish work and to the unfortunately named Egyptian Book of the Dead.[98] I suggest that scholars should be looking at the iconography rather than the text of these works, for I venture that they may well reveal hidden links and meaning.

You will have noted that here, although the 'root gospel' has been dated back to 1200 BC, it is still named the Nazarene gospel. Significantly, there are Nazarenes and there are Nazirites in both books of the Bible. Eusebius, in quoting from a source, now since lost, relates the probability of the two being one and the same thing. My contention, too, is that Nazirites and Nazarenes are one and the same thing and that they are extremely ancient religious orders whose influence upon the rise of cultural belief and religion has been lessened and to some degree diminished by later editorial incursion. Joseph, he of the many coloured coat, is called a Nazirite, as is the hero Samson. This is interesting in the sense that Joseph is described as such only *after* he had been in Egypt, not *before* he went there. Quoting from the memoirs of Hegessipus we see that, like Samson before him, James, brother of the Lord, was born '... holy from his mother's womb; drank no wine, strong drink, nor ate animal food; no razor came upon his head; he neither oiled himself nor used the bath; he alone was permitted to use the holy places... He was called "the righteous".' All of these are Nazirite values, as Hegessipus makes clear, yet St. James was, according to the official view, the leader of the early Nazarene Church in Jerusalem. The implication here is that whatever or whoever the Nazirites and Nazarenes were, they were older than the traditional founding date of the Church, and that they were one and the same thing.

It was at this point that I discovered another interesting anomaly. The early Church Father, Clement of Alexandria, states that:

> 'Alexander, in his book 'On the Pythagorean Symbols', relates
> that Pythagorus was a pupil of Nazaratus the Assyrian.'[99]

This strongly infers that Pythagoras was a Nazarene 600 years before St. James, the Lord's brother. It is another Church Father, Epiphanius, a very important authority on the sects within early Judaism, who describes the Aramaic 'Natsaraya' – the Nazarenes. He also willingly admits that they are pre-Christian.[100]

In the Old Testament, in the Books of Ezra and Ezekiel, the Israelite heirs of King David are accorded the title of *Nasi*, meaning 'prince' or 'chief'. In other words, sons of David, which is how Jesus is described when, in the Gospels, he is welcomed into Jerusalem. The title, however, is probably older than King David (c.1200–1000 BC), and comes from a land not too far away, Egypt. Here I offer you two quotes. The first is a stern warning regarding Jesus from the Jewish commentary Talmud Babli 'Sanhedrin' 103a:

> 'That thou shalt not have a son or disciple who burns his food
> publicly, like Jeschu ha-Notzri.'

And now, Plutarch, from *Of Isis and Osiris*:

> 'When every one of the rest of the Egyptians eats a broiled fish
> before his front door, the priests do not taste it, but burn their
> fishes to ashes before the doors [of the temple].'[101]

Placed together, not only do these two quotations identify the practices of Jesus the Nazarene with those of the Egyptian priests, but also, the latter quotation shows the sacrificial offering of the fish before the entrance to the house of God. We know that for the Christian Church, from the earliest times, the fish represented Jesus himself; this points to Jesus enacting a role originally cognised in Egypt. Let us therefore go with Plutarch's lead, into the land of Egypt, where there is much that comes to light.

In early Church iconography Jesus was always portrayed as a king. He was never portrayed as dying upon a cross, certainly not before the medieval period. In Egyptian hieroglyphs, the word for 'king' is spelt :[102] This equates to the letters 'N','S','W', in the Western alphabet.

This is the origin of related words in Arabic and Aramaic and Hebrew. *Nasi* in Hebrew means 'Prince' or 'chief', whereas in Old Semitic, *nazar* means 'keep', 'guard' or 'protect'. A quick glance at the Old Testament Book of Kings reveals that the ultimate guardian of religious secrets was none other than the king himself. The first king of Egypt, after whom all of the other kings followed, was Osiris. The followers of Jesus were the followers of the king. If we now apply what we have learnt about the actual identity of the mythical Jesus and utilise the older version of his name, we will soon realise that the term Nazarene contains the original Egyptian name of Osiris, Asar. In short, to be a Nazarene is to be a follower of Osiris.[103]

That Jesus was a Nazarene is widely accepted. That he was so called because he was of a village called Nazareth is contentious, to say the least. Recent archaeological evidence has suggested that although there may have been a settlement called Nazareth at the time of the early first century, it was hardly a thriving town or village even! The Nazareth of the Bible is not only a misinterpretation, it is a piece of wishful thinking and if a tiny settlement did exist, it would likely have been a dwelling-place of the sect of Nazarenes. The Nazarenes were a very ancient sect, often mentioned, by Epiphanius for example, in a pre-Christian light. They were influential, too, and their influence was feared, as is made clear in Acts 24:5 where St. Paul is accused of being 'a ringleader of the sect of the Nazarenes'. Both Jesus and Paul were members of a sect called the Nazarenes whose roots stemmed from ancient Egypt.

Initiatory Titles

Having arrived at this position it became very necessary to step back and cast a sceptical eye over the mountain of facts. However, the sceptical approach only served to yield more and more information, substantiating what I had already found. It was not as if the idea of Jesus and Christianity existing at the time of Egypt's Old Kingdom, 3,000 years before the established date, was shocking; it was just the fact that it took a considerable while to sink in. The thought had never occurred to me before and it was a measure of the effectiveness of my early education that I found it difficult to cope with. Nevertheless, once it did sink in, more pieces began to fall into place. It was this latter process that struck me as being almost miraculous and once my resistance was surmounted, a breath of fresh air began to blow away some of the cobwebs of my mind.

The very thing that dissolved any lingering dissatisfaction was the aspect of the sacred site and its link with consciousness and the hero. I saw that an even broader view was required, broader than I had as yet applied, one that encompassed the sites, the mythos and the linguistic angle as well as the angle of faith and its expression within ritual. This broader view bore fruit. Now I was beginning to think that the names of the 'Gisa correlation', give or take regional variations of culture, geography and climate, were all somehow universal, representing the same thing. They were universal but, of course, more than that, they were meaningful, to my mind representing something deeper and more valuable than mere deeds. But what deep values did they represent? My findings regarding acoustic phenomena at sacred sites, earth frequencies and brain frequencies, and especially the links between name and form and the relation of chanted names to higher states of consciousness, led me to the idea that the names of important hero figures of the past were very important and bestowed as titles, descriptive of a state of being. This is clear in the case of 'Buddha' which means 'the enlightened one'. It is related to the Sanskrit *buddhi,* the universal intellect. So too, even in the modern day, with the use of 'Maharishi', a title bestowed when one is accepted as a 'great seer' or 'great sage'.

Seership and enlightenment are descriptions relating to consciousness. In the same way, the idea of 'Jesus' and 'Christ' seemed to me to be a state or quality of consciousness rather than simply an individual who did great things. This is to some extent borne out by Clement of Alexandria when he admits that the Christ familiar to him did not require to be nourished, to be fed.[104] Now, God might work in mysterious ways, but the bodily Son of God, as recorded, is required to munch his way through copious amounts of bread, wheat and whatever else, let alone drinking wine and Adam's ale – water. Clement's Christ, however, sounds distinctly metaphysical, more to do with a state of consciousness or being. Now I have no doubt that the names are titles, descriptive of a state of being and given in relation to the sacred sciences that we know the Ancients had and some of which are practised today. The Gisa/ Jesus names are initiatory titles, their root is the same, whereas the localised mythology, as well as pronunciation and hence spelling, has helped the truth to be long obscured through plain ignorance, contrived deception or, in all likelihood, both.

I now felt at a plateau as far as my Jesus research was concerned – indeed, the Giza plateau. Now, my attention turned again to Mary, mother of Jesus. It was one of the small pieces that fell into place around this time that prompted me to look in that direction.

In Iran, the power of Mother Earth was called Geush Urvan, another variant upon the Gisa name 'Ge-ush', meaning literally 'man of the earth', but when Ge-ush was given form as a bull, the god Mithras killed him to transfer his energy to the sky.[105] We are back again to energy, to the vibrating powers of the sky and the earth, powers related to the Great Goddess, the Divine Mother, represented in the Christian faith as Mary, mother of Jesus.

Mary, Mary Quite Contrary

In the books of the Bible, the name of Mary, in its various forms, occurs with regularity. In the Old Testament Book of Exodus 15: 20–21, mention is made of Miriam, sister of Moses and Aaron. It tells of how she led the women of Israel in a hymn of victory to Yahweh, after the red (or reed) sea crossing:

> 'Miriam the prophetess, sister of Aaron, took the drum in her
> hand. All the women went out after her with drums and dances.
> Miriam declared to them: "Sing to the Lord, for he has triumphed;
> horse and its rider he has hurled into the sea."'[106]

This relationship between Miriam and her brothers is now seen by scholars as an embellishment upon various early traditions; in other words, it is a piece of later propaganda, either inserted or even mistranslated in order to show quite how spunky Miriam was, but also to put her quite firmly in her place – a lesser place in comparison to Moses and Aaron. This belies the degree of prominence that she quite probably had in the original legend. The role of women and of goddesses is a controversial one within all areas of ancient study and religion, and there are very relevant questions that have still to be raised over the 'masculinity' of much of our view of history. I am entirely sympathetic to the view of the Greeks that 'god without goddess is spiritual insufficiency',[107] and without a doubt one does not have to have feminist opinions to see that women do remarkably badly between the covers of the Bible.

From Eve onwards there is an antipathy towards women that at its worst is positively virulent and at best downright condescending. It is with this in mind that we must approach the biblical feminine gently and with hesitancy, for there are surprises afoot. In the disputed non-canonical book of Jasher, Miriam's story is given an entirely new slant. Here she is not just a briefly-mentioned sister of Moses and Aaron, but the actual spiritual leader of the Israelites in exile. For many scholars this, understandably, seems to be an exaggerated point of view, to say the least, but it is not unlikely, as we shall see.[108] A key to Jasher's legitimacy is that in the Books of Joshua (10:13) and Samuel (2 Sam, 1: 18), it is cited as an authority. Significantly, the actual theme of the Book of Jasher is open to discussion, for rather than being a book, it was in all likelihood originally a collection of archaic poetry, much of which has since been lost. Many commentators dismiss Jasher as having been 'primarily in oral form', but this was the case with all of the books of the Old Testament until they were written down at a relatively late stage.

Miriam or Mary as a name has led some commentators to conclude that this woman was Egyptian in origin and of the tribe of Levi. This is reflected in the New Testament, where Jesus and his mother come out of Egypt. Furthermore, there is even a St. Mary of Egypt whose biography is doubtful, a mark of the early Church carefully covering its tracks. It was the theme of this St. Mary of Egypt that led me to a vital aspect of the overall correlation pattern that we are now entering into for, as I will reveal, that Egypt had a saint called Mary is a clever subterfuge that deflects the enquirer's gaze away from a contradiction. In many versions of her biography, this Mary lived the life of a hermit in Palestine. According to Cyril of Scythopolis, in his *Life of Cyriacus,* two of Cyriacus' disciples first came across her in the desert beyond Jordan. Upon their second visit, they found her dead and therefore they buried her. Christian tradition explains that Mary was an Egyptian who left home at the age of 12 and went to live in Alexandria, where she was a prostitute for 17 years. It was on a subsequent pilgrimage to Jerusalem that she found herself being prevented from entering a church by a powerful and irresistible 'force'. Lifting her sight upon a statue of the Blessed Virgin, she was told to go across the Jordan where she would find rest. She spent the rest of her life there, subsisting upon a diet of dates and berries, and the divinely communicated Christian faith.[109] Significantly, the imagery of St. Mary is often confused with that of Mary Magdalene – this is because, in all likelihood, St. Mary of Egypt and St. Mary Magdalene are one and the same entity. The story of St. Mary of Egypt is no mere fantasy, simply concocted as a reason for a Christian presence in Egypt, it contains a kernel of truth that is surprising and reveals much.

However, before the revelations can begin, it is necessary to show how ancient Mary really is. The Catholic Church calls Mary by the sacred title of 'Theotokos', 'God-bearer' or, as is more renowned, 'Mother of God'. Wherever one goes it is always the same, wherever there is Mary, there she is as 'Mother of God'.

In the Eleusinian mysteries the virgin-born hero is introduced with the cry, 'Rejoice, rejoice, we have found our king, son of the daughter of the sea, lying in this basket among the river reeds!' The sea, in Latin, is *Mare. Mare Nostrum* can mean either 'our mother' or 'our sea'. This is a word that still thrives within modern discourse in the words 'maritime', 'marine' and 'meridian'. Debussy's wonderful music *La Mer* is French for 'the sea'. The French *mercredi,* or

Wednesday, is 'Mary's Day', a haberdasher is a *Mercier* and so on. Many readers may have tried another entrance into Mary's mysteries; the narcotic we call cannabis. In other cultures it is called marijuana. It seems that it may be considered a less mature approach toward the divine than the secret, sacred science I had uncovered; marijuana means 'Young Mary'. Enlightening stuff!

That the origin of this terminology is very ancient is borne out by the guiding lights of the ancient navigator, the stars of the sea, the Stella Maris, a reference that is even older than those great seafarers, the Phoenicians. There was even a land, an entire nation, called Mari, the land of the Amurrites, *c.*2600 BC, The very presence of this people demonstrates quite how archaic the name really is. The name may also be a reference to a star, the brightest star in the sky, Sirius.

Sirius was called Sothis by the ancient Egyptians and was the personification of the celestial Isis, whom they called Ast, or sometimes Aset. As I have already noted, from this we get the prefix 'ast' in astronomy, astrology, etc. It is also a component of the word 'pastoral', from which comes the word 'pastor,' meaning 'shepherd'. Pastors, we know, are priests who busily attend their flocks. Many within the Church are devoted to Mary, but in this, are they unknowing devotees of Isis? I felt that there was possibly a connection between the two.

I decided to dig a little deeper, for what was to become a 'marvellous' answer – the etymology of the word 'marvellous' is the old French *merveillos*, meaning literally, 'veil of Mary'. Significantly, in the mysteries, Isis wore a veil too. We are now about to part that veil, to reveal the face of great splendour and of grace. First, though, I must explain an apparent anomaly. *Mer* in Egyptian has many meanings, one of which is 'death'. This is reflected in the Latin *morte* of the same meaning. The Slavic Mara (sometimes Mora) was viewed as a destructive female spirit who actually drank the blood of men, an activity that she pursued in the depths of night, thus inducing her own form of 'night*mares*'. In the Old Testament we have Marah.[110] and as Maranatha, she is even given her own slot in the New Testament in St. Paul's Letter to the Corinthians. The 'death-dealing' Mary, though, must be seen in the context that she who takes life not only gives life, but can also bestow immortality.

In this light, it is all the more significant that, at the crucifixion, all of the requisite Marys are gathered. Furthermore, it is within this part of the Gospels that the story comes about full turn, for Jesus' body is anointed with myrrh, the very substance given to him by the three wise men at the nativity. Christians call Mary 'Myrrh of the sea'. It was Myrrha who was the mother of another crucified hero, Adonis; at precisely the same place that Jesus was born, she too was delivered of her holy child. It was thorny Myrrh twigs that thorny were used as the crown of thorns. Myrrh, as we can see, is a variant upon Mary's name. Mary, therefore, is older than the Gospel tradition.

Thus it comes as no surprise that Mary appears within the Nazarine tradition as the mother of Issa.[111] We have seen who the Nazarenes really were, the actual identity of Jesus and the hitherto unsuspected tradition dating back to the earliest days of ancient Egypt, however what I uncovered next absolutely amazed me.

Mary was beloved of God. Isis too was 'Beloved', it was one of her oldest titles, possibly even more antique than her usual Egyptian name, Aset. Isis' 'Beloved' title was also the very ancient name for the land that is Egypt, the beloved land, was called by the ancient Egyptians, Ta-Mery or Mery-ta [112] I was astonished to learn that this means 'the land of Mery'.

Another piece of the puzzle has fallen into place and with it comes other confirmation. Concurrent with ancient Egypt we find the land of Sumer, sometimes spelt Shumer.[113] Some of the kings of Sumer bore the name of Mery: A*mar*-sin of Sumer was recorded as having suffered the fate of the hero – he was stung in the heel by a scorpion in Sinai and was killed. That this is a mythic motif for death is beyond question, it is heavily symbolic, also recall the death of the Hindu Christ, Krishna, by poison in the heel (see earlier).

Within the Hindu and Buddhist traditions the divine mountain, Mount Meru, is prominent.

> 'Hocart writes that "the Sinhalese frequently placed inside their topes a square stone representing Meru. If they placed in the centre of a tope a stone representing the centre of the world it must have been that they took the tope to represent the world".'[114]

A tope is a Buddhist stupa or domed reliquary. They can be quite massive and are generally pyramidal in form. This is significant. Meru/Mery, the beloved, we are being told, is linked to the cube. Cybele, we have already seen, is the mother of Attis, Tammuz, and her name literally means 'cube'. What is interesting is that Isis' hieroglyph is a throne and in representations of Pharaoh enthroned, we see him actually seated upon a *cube within a cube*. Moreover, the land of Mery-ti also translates as 'land of the Mr'. The hieroglyph for Mr is $\triangle$, a pyramid. Pyramids then, are the personification of this hieroglyph. In chapter ten, we will see the lengths that the ancient Egyptians went to in order to make the Great Pyramid represent the earth. To all intents and purposes, it is 'Mery'.

In very archaic times the pyramidion illustrated by the hieroglyph may have been the sacred ben-ben or bennu stone. The bennu bird is the Egyptian version of the phoenix, the mythical bird that immolates itself upon a pyre of its own building and then rises from the ashes, fully resurrected. The place where the rituals of the bennu bird took place was amongst the oldest and most sacred in the long history of Egypt. Today it is sadly a mere suburb of the increasing sprawl of Cairo. Its name is Heliopolis, known to the Greeks as On-Heliopolis, the very place where, in some of the non-canonical infancy gospels, as well as some of the Gnostic gospels, the holy family came to reside on the flight into Egypt. In very ancient times On-Heliopolis was known as Annu. Christianity holds that the mother of Mary is St. Anne.

Divine Substance and Place

The names of Mary and of Anna or Anne are the names of the spirit of place. They have been used as the names not just of locations but of whole countries. The appearance of these names is no coincidence, no accident, for, as we shall see, they occur worldwide with a regularity that is, to say the least, breathtaking.

In Rome, the Blessed Virgin Mary was worshipped as the 'House consecrated to God', 'The Tabernacle of the Holy Ghost' and as a 'dwelling-place'. The very title of the king of Egypt, 'Pharaoh', means 'great house'. Isis' hieroglyph is Mr, the pyramid. Mary carried within her the divine power, the energy of the holy child. In 1997, I travelled to Ta–mery, the beloved land, and as I looked upon the greatest monument in the whole history of mankind, the Great Pyramid of Giza, I pondered upon what it all meant.

Surely, I thought – merely in a metaphorical sense (at least that's how it started), if Mary is portrayed always as the expectant mother, or as the mother who has just brought forth, she has brought forth something wonderful; grace has given rise to beautiful things. I thought back to 'marvellous things' and then suddenly the veil of Mary parted and the answer came to me, as quick as thunder. In a surprising amount of the world's mythology, the name of Anna appears. In the Middle East, Ana is the mother of Mari. The Dagda of Newgrange, whose other name, Eochaidh, when pronounced correctly, bears a remarkable resemblance to Joseph, is married to Boann as well as being intimate with the Morrigan – Mary again.[115] There is Anat of Canaan, Anath of Syria, even the Romans had Anna Perenna, eternal Anna, Mother of the Aeons, and the Celts had Anu, sometimes called Danu.

In the Babylonian myth of creation, known as the Enuma Elish, An is heaven and Anu is the underworld. This realm is called the underworld because it is the substratum which underpins and upholds our world and all worlds. Following this line of enquiry, I found that, in the Sanskrit, *anu* means 'atomic', *ana* means 'to live' and *anna* itself, taken in its most subtle and mystical sense, is the food upon which the whole of existence depends. But this food or energy is not yet embodied. The embodiment is named *murti*: 'Any solid body or material form, embodiment, manifestation, incarnation, personification'.[116] Sanskrit has the term *anna-maya-murti*, 'body of food' or 'embodiment of Anna'. How close this word *murti* is to that old name for Egypt, Mery-ta. The Anna names relate to that which gives birth to and nourishes substance. Mary names relate to the substantial, the embodiments of heaven on all levels, including of course the earth itself, especially in areas of sacred power, where the finer energies may be felt, and also at the personal level, where those energies may be embodied and, it seems, may give birth to something more. Incidentally, on the planetary level, we should realise that some 'earth-gods' are not merely associated with this planet, but with all planets by virtue of association with all embodiments on that level.

Mary names do not only relate to planets and people. We have seen how the hieroglyph for Mr is a pyramid and how sacred buildings are positioned at places of power and designed to enhance that power. If the Egyptians' beloved Mery–Isis is the pyramid, then she manifests that power. She represents that power, but what will she give birth to, what is it exactly that she carries inside her? Perhaps a clue might come from the Egyptian scriptures:

> 'In the beginning there was Isis, Oldest of the Old. She is the
> neter from whom all becoming arose.'

Isis was, like Mary in the Catholic Church, Queen of Heaven and Theotokos, Mother of God. From the Egyptian word for 'a divinity' or 'divine emanescence' (not god or goddess), *neter*, we get our word, 'nature'. We are looking at the identity of some exceedingly ancient powers, the most powerful of which, as far as man is concerned, is carried inside the womb of the mother.

Mery, the daughter of Annu, gives birth to Gisa. Who or what is the power of Gisa? This is the answer we will come to in due course; however, before we do, it is necessary to step back and view the correlations that have come to light in a table that I call 'The Anatomy of the Hero'. This will help prime us for a resurrection.

But first, another intriguing point. After his own resurrection, Jesus ascended to heaven upon a cloud of glory, in an event testified by the apostles within the Gospel texts. The Great Pyramid was known in its day, 2,500 years *before Christ*, as the 'Place of the Ascension'.[118] Here in the heart of mystery such things are not mere coincidence.

Intermezzo

In chapter eight, the hero-god stepped to the fore in fullness. In fact, in relation to the nativity, life, death and resurrection as told in the Jesus story, very many hero-gods stepped forward. They have similar births, similar lives, deaths and resurrections.

Regarding the death of the hero, as a matter of course, the ancient role of the cross was revealed as representing the tree of life in perfect balance, the hero upon it having attained that state through the 'death' of limited mortal consciousness and a rebirth into an expanded divine consciousness – a being at one with the transcendent stillness of God and yet still very much alive. Osiris is revealed as the most ancient hero, his state of at-one-ment being the goal of all of Egypt's pharoahs. Osiris was the original Jesus.

After all of this, no doubt should be left that Jesus is a hero in the vein of all of the ancient hero-gods: Apollo, Adonis, Bacchus, Tammuz, Horus, Krishna, Esau, Esus, Gesar, Isa, Djasar, Jizu *et al.* Too many of these epithets are so obviously similar to Jesus and those that seem distant have now had their mythic and linguistic links revealed. Through a closer look at the nature of the names and the relationship between spoken and written words, we traced the Jesus name and the other names to a correlation based around 'Gisa' which, of course, led us to the enigmatic Giza plateau. Then the Nazarenes stepped forward as followers of Osiris and we found St. Paul in action once again, this time in the realms of Nazarene knowledge and the ancient Arabian hero Issa. From the ranks of the Nazarenes, unsurprisingly, that great sage and mathematician so beholden to the ancient Egyptians, Pythagoras, yet again stepped forward.

Now it was made clear that the hero names were initiatory titles, for the heroes were high initiates. Here, too, Jesus' mother Mary and her mother Anna (Hannah) are seen in their fuller role as Great Goddesses, representing the substratum and substance of all manifestation. The presence of the Great Goddess at the Egyptian pyramids became obvious when it was revealed that the ancient name for Egypt was Ta-Mery and that the pyramid was the Mr or Mer, the beloved. This helps us to understand that the initiate becomes at -one with the divine in the Place of Ascension – a name given to holy places such as the Great Pyramid and the temple site at Jerusalem. The message is that the Divine Mother, the holy substance who gives birth to all of life, can also be called upon to give rebirth in consciousness to all of her children who follow the ways of the hero and that the hero-gods have, from time immemorial, been set forward as role models for all of humankind.

It is now time to summarise the main hero correlations in the form of the 'Anatomy of the Hero' and then we shall take a closer look at the mystery of Egypt, before moving into the vibrant core of that great mystery.

The broad fabric of support for this thesis having been woven, this will be the final *Intermezzo*, for as we close in on the Giza Plateau, the momentum builds toward resolution.

The Anatomy of the Hero

A Comparison to a Similarity

THIS compendium of hero-myths worldwide is a fairly general presentation that only dips its toes into the very deep waters of mythology. Furthermore, the hero-myth has a close association with the power of place and should not be separated from this essential root, for if it is, context is left behind. A more specific investigation, one that goes into greater depth, must remain the preserve of a future book, so I make no apologies for the lack of specific detail. Although detail is not lacking, having investigated each myth, I have chosen the choicest cuts.

Each of the myths shares certain specific features with Christian belief, in the sense of the original story and the ritual surrounding it. They are not all by any means the same; geography, culture and language seem to be the main reasons behind such differences, but the essential elements are there:

- The holy child is born of virgin, in a cave or grotto.
- The birth is foreshadowed by the light of a star.
- Three wise men or shepherds pay court to the wondrous birth.
- The child is the mystical 'Son of God'.
- The parents are necessarily forced into exile because of a certain tyrannical king who is usually, with very few exceptions, a relation of the holy child, an uncle or grandfather perhaps.
- The holy child performs superhuman deeds on the way to adulthood.
- Little is told of the childhood of the hero.
- The child appears in adult form, to be baptised by a holy man, as in the case of Jesus or Achilles who is schooled by a holy man called Cheiran–the cross.
- This same holy man is associated with water and is born usually at the summer solstice.
- Quite often the hero is portrayed as a long–haired bearded man with blue eyes, and arrayed in white or blue.
- The hero performs miracles ranging from walking on water to changing

water into wine.
- He heals the sick, but is not honoured in his own town or country.
- He has 12 disciples and is transfigured before them.
- The hero celebrates in triumph and soon after is accused of a misdemeanour that leads eventually to his death.
- A last supper takes place in eucharistic fashion.
- The hero is put on trial by a man known as the Pilot – the navigator who will set him on his way to the stars.
- The hero is crucified or hung on a tree and dies.
- He descends into the underworld and harrows hell.
- On the third day he rises again from the dead, having redeemed the sins of the world.
- He appears before his disciples and ascends to heaven.

These are the basics of the myth of the hero, but of course, within the worldwide telling of the myth there are variants. As I looked further afield I noted, very easily, the common similarities and also the outstanding dissimilarities. Looking closer I realised that perhaps the most important detail of all was the names themselves, their similarity not only to the type of myth, but to the type of place. The rough etymologies given are based upon the meanings of specific syllables, which appear to be universal. Because of the very widespread presence of the names, one basic assumption that I have made is that the basic syllables concerned are intimately linked to the power of place; in other words they are 'of it', they are an emanation of all of the forces that I have written of in chapters five and six and seven.

The nature of the place varies from location to location, but again the variation is tempered by the human response. The earliest of those responses are pyramidal in structure, or approximate, the same elements of pyramidal architecture within their proportion and view. In 1996 it was announced that archaeologists had discovered the world's oldest pyramids – on the Atlantic coast of southern Brazil. Dating from 3000 BC, these pyramids predate the earliest Egyptian example by several centuries. Astonishingly, whereas the Egyptian variety is built entirely of stone, the Brazilian ones have been constructed exclusively of seashells. For this reason these massive monuments lay undiscovered for centuries. Initial research suggests that they were originally more than 160ft high and up to 37 acres at the base. Furthermore, in terms of volume these monuments far outstrip their Egyptian counterparts. 'Our new research shows that Brazil's Indians, 5,000 years ago, were more sophisticated than we had thought and were capable of producing truly monumental structures,' said Professor Edna Morley, Director of National Heritage Institute.[1]

In the past 15 years pyramids have been located the world over, from Siberia to New Zealand, all of them very ancient, all of them a seemingly primal response of, indigenous people to the landscape around them – a response that echoes throughout their various mythologies (see Appendix – Geolinguistics).

It is one of the great tragedies of world history that the *conquistadores* were allowed to deliberately destroy much of indigenous Central and South American history. They also wiped out, quite deliberately, the knowledge that would allow Mayan hieroglyphs to be deciphered. Why? Could it have been for reasons of mythic similarity? An historical–cum–mythical messiah-king of the Mayans was a king by the name of Yax K'uk Mo, the Lord of the West, who was interred deep inside a pyramid within a pyramid and whose name approximates to 'The Blue Green Quetzal' (or 'Great Sun First Quetzal Macaw'). At first this meant very little to me, but returning to the theme much later, I noticed that, in pronunciation, the name Yax was very similar to the Middle Eastern word for a man, *ish* or *esh*. In fact it was very, very similar to the name of Jesus, Jeshua, Joshua, Yeshua, etc. The difference begins to fade. Looking in closer detail at the myth of Quetzalcoatl, the plumed serpent, I again noticed elements of the name. The *Qu* syllable was probably pronounced very softly, approximating the 'G' sound – the earth syllable. *Coatl* means 'twin'. Thus we are left with 'Itza', another version of Issa. Again, the myth is linked to the site by the explicit fact that the hero is the son of the earth.

Pyramids proliferate throughout Central and South America. Teotihuacan is a city full of them, the grandest of which are the Pyramids of the Sun and of the Moon. In Uxmal in Mexico there are seven pyramids ranged in a form approximating the seven stars of the Great Bear, and so on. The list is long. At Tucume in Peru, the Inca built pyramids and depicted alongside them a sacred stone, very much like the Egyptian benben stone, as well as a mythical bird in association with it, much like the Egyptian bennu bird – the phoenix. Quite probably the indigenous peoples of South and Central America took their knowledge with them in the migration to North America (*c.* 1500 BC) and there it remains as a cultural memory. Could the teepee be a cultural memory of the pyramids, a portable vestige of their latent power? Other similarities, some quite extraordinary, also occur, some of which I will raise now in a very general manner.

The Sequorno Indians of Teso dos Bichos call their female shamans *Ameru* an obvious link to the landscape and an intriguing one given that the wider continental land mass is today called America. The idea of America being named after Americo Vespucci never did make sense to me. Why was it not calle, Vespuccia? Most people denote their surnames, not their first names, in order to be remembered. Like the Egyptians and their obsessions with wheat and barley, the Anasazi, who disappeared from history long ago, were great cultivators, in this case of maize. It is clear from archaeological evidence that they saw within this process a metaphor of the dying and rising god. The Anasazi, whose name means 'the Ancient Ones', built *kivas* in what is now the southern United States, for purposes that to this day remain unclear. However, what is known of the buildings is their extraordinary resonant properties which, when harnessed, can induce altered states. But perhaps the most astonishing things about the northern Native American peoples are the names that they give to their gods. There is something about them that is very familiar.

The great god of the Navajo is a hero by the name of Yesha. He is one of the holy ones whom the Native Americans call the *Yei-eden-na*. The hero Hiawatha was called 'the feathered one' – the syllable *hia* is another form of *Hu*, the Lord. Another great divine being of these peoples is Ya-weh-node – 'She Whose Voice Rides the Wind'. Resonance again. There are further synchronicities that occur which bring elements of Egyptian and Middle Eastern cosmogony to mind, in a way that intimately links the myth to the site, and they care the little known fact that there are pyramids in North America too. In Cahokia, Illinois, there are mounds, pyramidal in form and intent, placed there because the building of them brought a closer proximity to heaven. The people wanted to be closer to God, whilst still inhabiting the earth. In this sense – and the builders were quite explicit about this – the mound represents the godly power upon earth; it is the son of the earth mother and the sky father. The symbols that have been located at these sites are all symbols that have by now become familiar to us: spirals, crosses and other hieroglyphs. Wooden posts have also been located that act as markers of time, as sundials seeking out the hour of sunrise, which the Native Americans saw as symbolic with the reawakening of life, of resurrection.

Everywhere the hero, the names of the hero, the names of gods and goddesses, and everywhere monuments that revealed much about these names. They are monuments to the divine in humankind, the sound of the human voice and, on this, myth has much to say.

THE ANATOMY OF THE HERO

Compiled by David Elkington and Robin Whitlock

Hero: **Osiris. The original Jesus.**

Region: Egypt (and abroad from the third millennium BC).

Etymology: Osiris is Greek. Egyptian: Asar. As a son of the earth god, Geb, Osiris inherits the 'earth' part of his father's name, becoming Gasar, or Gesu.

Legend: For details of the legend see chapter ten. Asar's coming was announced by the three wise men. Angelic voices hailed his coming and time stood still. A star (Orion) rose in the east, called by the Tibetans Rishi-Agastya, after a holy king in very ancient times. In Persia this same star was called Messaeil, in other words, the Messiah.

                  Osiris had a twin, Set, and who was wild and uncultured, who in some versions of the legend is crucified. Osiris was killed by his jealous brother and harrowed hell before rising from the dead and ascending to 'the Father'.

Symbols: The *djed* pillar. The ankh or ansate cross. The tamarisk tree (Ta-mar-Isis).

Monuments: The Oseirion at Abydos. The Great Pyramid of Giza.

Hero: **Krishna.**

Region: India.

Etymology: Called 'The Black', 'Dark', 'The Dark One'.

Legend: The deified hero of Indian legend, born of the goddess Devaki. His birth was announced by a star with the attendant voices of angels. Krishna was attended by three wise men and given gifts by shepherds. He was hailed as the Redeemer, Firstborn, Sin–Bearer, Saviour, Liberator and, significantly, he was called the Universal Word. Krishna's legend tells of a slaughter of the innocents and a tyrannical king who was closely related to him. Krishna was killed by being shot in the heel, his only vulnerable spot, by an arrow (as in the legend of Achilles). He was then hung between heaven and earth where his blood fructified the soil.

Symbols: The Elephant, called in the Hindu pantheon Ganesha, 'Man of the Earth'. The Tree of Life.

Monuments: Various, throughout India.

Hero: **Mithras.**

Region: Persia, first millennium BC onwards.

Etymology: Latin: Missa and Mitre; Mizd, the Mithraic sacramental meal; English; Mass; comp. 'maize' (see Etymological Glossary): Indian Mitra.

Legend: God of Light. Born on 25th December – the birthday of the 'unconquered sun'. Born miraculously of a rock (*Petra Genetrix*), a female rock, representing the Earth Mother. His birth was witnessed by shepherds, and by Magi bringing gifts. Mithra performed miracles, healed the blind and cured the lame. He cast out devils. After his triumph he ascended to heaven, an event celebrated at Eastertime.

Mithra's spouse was Anahita, the Mother of Waters, also known as Ma. The Mithraic high priest's name was the *Pater Patrum*, *Papa* or Pope.

Symbols:	The Cross of the Invincible Sun. The Chi Rho.
Monuments:	Various. A temple to Mithra may be seen under the Vatican.

Hero:	**Adonis.**
Region:	Syria, *c*.3000 BC.
Etymology:	From *Adon*, meaning 'Lord' or 'Master'.
Legend:	Born from a myrrh tree (Myrrh – Mary) at Bethlehem, Adonis was placed in an ark or coffin. His mother, called Myrrha, was a virgin and is identified with Mary. Myrrha, too, was a temple-woman.
	Adonis died at Eastertime. Associated with the grain-harvest, he rose again on the third day. He is also associated with the sun.
Symbols:	The cup or grail. Wine.
Monuments:	Various. See Tammuz/Dumuzi.

Hero:	**Sarapis. Osiris-Apis.**
Region:	Ptolemaic Egypt, *c*.300 BC. Mesopotamia, 3000 BC.
Etymology:	Sumerian Sar Apsi, Easar Apsi – Esa the bull (of the underworld), also known as Ptah-Hephaistos (the repetition of Ptah – resonance?)
Legend:	Sarapis is the fusion of Osiris with the Apis bull, lord of generative fertility, and a universal God, uniting within his person, characteristics of Zeus and Hades.
Symbol:	A kalathos – a basket-shaped head-dress.
Monuments:	Various.

Hero:	**Aleyn, also known as Baal. Storm god.**
Region:	Phoenician, western Semitic.
Etymology:	Baal – 'Lord'. Aleyn, sometimes Aleyin, *El Ayin* – the pineal gland or letter 'o'. Irish: Bel, hence Beltain. Scandinavian: Balder.
Legend:	Aleyn/Baal was the son of the Father God of the Phoenicians, El (a general term meaning 'God'). Baal had a twin brother, Mot, his mortal twin. He killed Mot (who had been forsaken by his father, El) by driving a curved knife (the moon) under his fifth rib. In another version it is the goddess Anath who kills Mot, threshes him and burns him. Mot then is the grain. Baal, having been tricked into the underworld, was under the thrall of Mot. Anath tried to persuade Mot to release him. Baal rose from the dead.

Symbols: The moon, also thunder.

Monuments: Oak groves, Ashera – stone circles – and many other sacred sites dotted throughout the region.

Hero: **Attis.**

Region: Anatolia, Rome and Phrygia (*c.*3000 BC–*c.* fifth century AD).

Etymology: Attis is very similar to Adonis in myth. It is a foreshortened form ('t' and 'd' are cognate).

Legend: Born of the virgin Nana and lover of the great goddess Cybele. Born on 25th December. A beautiful youth, he was killed by a boar while out hunting; in other versions he is crucified on a pine tree to bring salvation to mankind. A god of vegetation and healing, he was resurrected as 'The Most High God'. His passion was on 25th March, usually a Friday, called Black Friday, the Day of Blood. He descended into the underworld and the third day he rose again from the dead.

Symbol: The pine tree. Attis' feast day is called the Hilaria.

Hero: **Tammuz. Hebrew-Canaanite version of Dionysus or Adonis. Also called Dumuzi.**

Region: Mesopotamia, modern Iran-Iraq. Later, throughout the Middle East.

Etymology: Dumuzi – Sumerian, 'True Son', 'Good Son'. Greek form: Thomas. Also called 'Esos' in Greek, sometimes Ta-us, a grain god. Also called Eshmun, Ish, Issa, Ish-sar.

Legend: Tammuz was the original Anointed King, or Christos. He was also the original Good Shepherd. Sometimes called Usir (a title of Osiris). Son of Ishtar-Mari – a virgin gave birth to him. He was the lover of Inanna, who handed him over to the demons of the underworld. His twin was Azazel or Asar-el. He was killed on the Day of Atonement in the form of a lamb. At his death the 'Halleluiah' went up, with ululations of despair. Tammuz was the only begotten Son of God, who rose from the dead on the third day. A god of healing and of vegatation.

Symbols: Corn, cereal grain.

Monuments: Various. Sumerian and Babylonian ziggurats, pyramid-type structures. [Note: This mythology is very similar to the South American legend of the Calina people involving the twins Tamusi and Tamulu, respectively Light and Dark. The twins hated each other. They were the sons of Amana (Ana) the Creator, who sent them from her sea-kingdom (Mer) in the Milky Way to protect earth. In the Sumerian myth Dumuzi's mother is Ama'usumgal, whose mother is a heavenly dragon.]

Hero:	**Esus. Hu-Esus. Hes-us.**
Region:	Celtic Europe, second millennium BC.
Etymology:	Esar, Aesar; Phoenician: Izr, Iasar.
Legend:	There are many variants of this god throughout Europe. Esus was born of a virgin, was a healer god and was crucified. Although the name Esus does not occur on the British mainland, other variants do. On a carving from Roman Gaul, Esus appears in trinity, as Teutatis and Taranis. In Ireland he is Oengus or Angus, the earthly prince in the underworld, son of the Dagda. The Dagda's other name was Eochaidh the Hereman (Joseph the Herod-man). In another version of this myth, Eochaidh marries the Morrigan (Mary-anna). In Britain she was called Eseye, another probable form of Isis.
Symbols:	The cross. The bull. The crane – usually in triple form.
Monuments:	Newgrange and various.

Hero:	**Quetzalcoatl, the Plumed, or Feathered, Serpent.**
Region:	Central and South America. Aztec and Toltec.
Etymology:	An ancient Mexican god. The Aztec Saviour-God. *Coatl* means 'twin' or 'earth'. 'Etza' is the central element of the name, 'Qu' qualifies it under the rule that god names could not be progressed by a vowel. Also called Xolotl (it is to be noted that the name begins with a cross, 'X').
Legend:	Quetzalcoatl was born of a virgin. He represented corn or maize, and thus his life was symbolic of planting, growth and the harvest. His other symbol, apart from the serpent, is the dove. He was the Lord of Knowledge, the god of the wind and of the zodiac. Quetzalcoatl's twin is the typical red-haired, wild warrior twin that we have come to expect, called Tezcatlipoca (*Tezcatl*, 'mirror', *popoca*, 'smoking'). He tempted his brother, as Satan tempted Jesus in the wilderness. It was the representative of this wild twin on earth who was sacrificed by having his heart torn from his chest. Quetzalcoatl died, descended to hell and rose again from the dead. His second coming was always expected imminently. He was crucified between two thieves.[2]
Symbols:	The moon and the sun, represented by the pyramids at Teotihuacan.

The Pyramid of the Sun   *A salt crystal*

The Pyramid of the Sun has the shape and form of a salt crystal.

Hero: **Jesus. Variants Gesu, Gsu, Esu. Issa. Greek: Joshua. Hebrew: Jeshua.**

Region: Originally from Palestine and Sinai.

Etymology: Jehoshua – 'God saves', 'God is salvation'. Direct route from Asar, Greek. Osiris.

Legend: Massacre of the innocents. Born of a virgin, Mary, herself born of a virgin, Anne. Returned to Galilee, performed various miracles, then entered Jerusalem and, for an unknown reason, was crucified, harrowed hell, rose on the third day and then ascended to heaven.

Colour: White and blue – in the human bio-energy field these colours represent calm states, peace and overall good health.

Symbols: *Vesica piscis.* Cross.

Monuments: Places of Christian worship worldwide, notably cathedrals.

Hero: **Gesar of Ling.**

Region: Western China, Tibet, *c.*2500 BC–present.

Etymology: Ga or Ge (Greek: 'earth'). Tibetan: *Sar* – 'blood'. Issa, Essa, perhaps Esses or Eshe, literally, 'the man'.

Legend: The rescuer of Tibet from foreign invaders. A demi-god who lies sleeping in a cave, but who will return at the time of greatest crisis. A wonder-working Arthur-type figure who had 18 uncles. He could render himself invisible. Led a quest for the Chiata Mani – a sacred stone, jewel or cup, most often a stone in a tower in the city of Shambala. He was an architect.

Origin: Pre-Buddhist, possibly the old Bon religion of Tibet.

Colour: White and blue – red at times of war.

Symbol: Cross.

Monuments: The famous lost pyramids of Xian, approx. 125 of them in these very ancient pyramid fields. The Potala Palace.

Hero: **Gesar, Geser Khan, 'King Geser', Ge-sar.**

Region: Asia – Mongolia and Tibet.

Etymology: See Gesar of Ling.

Legend: A deity of the Mongols and Tibetans, and the hero of a lengthy epic known in different versions throughout an area which stretches from Lake Baikal to Bhutan and from Peking to Hunza in north Pakistan. Gesar's form is that of an equestrian deity, wearing a helmet and cuirass. He is rooted in pre-Buddhist religion. He was among the protective deities of Lama-ist Buddhism and entered the Mang cult *c.*1600. In the nineteenth century Gesar became identified with the Chinese god of war and protector of the Manchu dynasty. Gesar's role was as an oracular deity. In Tibetan belief, Gesar is the divine hero-king who descended in ancient times from heaven to the centre of the world in order to restore order on earth.

Hero: **Esaugeteh Emissue (Master of Voice, of Breath).**

Region: North America (USA), *c.*1500 BC–present.

Etymology: Esu, Esau – 'the red one'.

Legend: The Creator, the First Principle. Very reminiscent of the legend of the Egyptian Creator Atum, who, like Esaugeteh, hovered over the surface of the waters (cf. Hebrew creation story). Esaugeteh built a hill to reside in and in which he created people – out of mud.

Symbol: Cross

Monuments: There are many variations upon the name and legend in ancient America. The prime existing monuments are the pyramidal Cahokia mounds, Illinois.

Hero: **Al Issa, son of Arabian Mara, sometimes Mari.**

Region: Arabia, *c.*1800 BC–AD 600.

Etymology: Arab *isa* – 'God saves', 'prince of God', 'son of God'.

Legend: A good spirit raised from death, a god of fertility and of the creation.

Symbol: Cross, Phallic pillar.

Monuments: Before the advent of Islam, the Ka'aba at Mecca and various monuments throughout Arabia.

Hero: **Ise, Jizu, sometimes Joshi. Son of Maia, Maya or Mary.**

Region: Japan, Okinawa (the Ainu, re: Anna).

Etymology: 'Earth kami' or 'spirit'.

Legend: A good spirit raised from death.

Symbol;   Cross.

Monuments: The Ashitake pyramid, the Temple at Ise.

Hero: **Esus, Hesus, son of Anu.**

Region: Gaul – modern northern France – and Britain.

Etymology: The good God, earth spirit. Called Merlin – 'Follower of Mary'.

Legend: God of the harvest, of wine and grapes. Walks on water.

Monuments: Various. Silbury Hill, the British pyramid-like mound, and Merlin's Mound, a smaller one 20 miles from Silbury.

Symbol: Cross.

Hero: **Marduk, also called Esa, grandson of An.**

Region: Mesopotamia – ancient Sumer (modern Iraq).

Etymology: Man, Prince from the Sea (the rising sun).

Legend: God of the sun (bull-calf of the sun). Born of a virgin, Anu. Performed heroic deeds. Put on trial, dies and harrows hell. Is resurrected threedays later at Eastertime.

Symbol: Cross.

Monument: Ziggurat called Esa-gila, meaning 'Esa's song or glory'.

Hero: **Nimrod.**
Region: Babylon, Mesopotamia.
Etymology: Greek: Orion. Egyptian: Asar (Osiris). The hunter.
Legend: Patriarch of the Babylonians and Assyrians, called Assur, another form of Asar. A renowned king, portrayed as an oppressor in the Old Testament.
Monument: Mount Nimrod, a tumulus, resembling a pyramid, of white limestone.

Hero: **Iasius, Triptolemus, Iasion, Jesus, Jason.**
Region: Crete.
Etymology: Triptolemus means 'Three Ploughings'.
Legend: The young god with whom Demeter lay three times in the ploughed fields of Crete.[3]

Hero: **Jason, Iasion.**
Region: Greece.
Etymology: Greek: Iason, from *iasthai*, 'to heal'. A form of Joshua.
Legend: The *Argo*, or ark, refers to a building and its 'crew' are, possibly, astronomical markers in the sky. Jason has his Argonauts, 72 of them, whilst Jesus too has his disciples, at first 12 and then 72 much later in the New Testament. Jason was killed in later life by one of the timbers of the *Argo* falling on his head, therefore, like Jesus, Jason's death is associated with wood.
Symbol: The boat or ark, *Argo*.

Hero: **Eshbaal.**
Region: Ancient Israel – Palestine.
Etymology: 'Baal's man', 'man is the Lord'.
Legend: Son of Saul, the first King of Israel.
Symbol: The moon.
Monuments: Various: Asherim, oak groves, stone circles, etc.

Hero: **Aiza.**
Region: Dahomey.
Etymology: Asar, Ai sar.
Legend: One of the most important spirits in Dahomey religion, a protector of groups. Every village, region, compound and market place has its *aiza* or guardian spirit and its mound or shrine. To'aiza is a spirit of the founder of a place. Xwe'aiza is the spirit of a compound and Ax'aiza of a market place.
Monuments: Mounds or shrines.

Hero: **Woden.**
Region: Scandinavian.
Etymology: Unknown.
Legend: Wounded himself with his own spear and hung himself on the 'Windy Tree' – the great ash Yggdrasil. For nine nights the god remained hanging and bleeding, until he noticed some runes engraved on a stone below him. He managed to lift the runes and was immediately released from his ordeal and filled with new life.

Hero: **Issaki (Goddess).**
Region: Hindu (Epic and Puranic).
Etymology: Issa-ka, 'soul of Isa'.
Legend: Depicted carrying a headless child.
Origin: *c.* third millennium BC.
Monuments: Various, Indian subcontinent.

Hero: **Obassi Osaw and Obassi Nsi.**
Region: South Nigeria.
Etymology: *Ab assi* – literally, 'the heart of Issa'.
Legend: Two gods who created everything together until Obassi Osaw decided to live in the sky and Obassi Nsi to live on the earth. Osaw gives light and moisture but brings storms. Nsi is a nurturer. Nsi taught man and woman about planting. The people learned to grow and eat the fruit of the palm tree.

Hero: **Assur. Asura (India) – Kansa;[4] Suriakos (Greek);**
Surios, Sur Io, Sar ya or io – Isis, 'moon', hence 'sin'.
Region: Assyria.
Etymology: Asar, Osiris, etc. Known as the Great Mountain.
Legend: God of storms and of war. Overseer of the Law.
Symbols: The winged disc of the sun. The bow.
Monument: Was the Holy City of Harran also known as Assur (*Adrian Gilbert, Magi, p.180*). Harran was the city of Abraham, father of Isaac (the light of Issa).

Hero: **Izanami and Izanagi.**
Region: Japan.
Etymology: 'She who invites you to enter' and 'The Lord who invites you to enter'. *Iza* – 'Lord' or 'Lady'.
Legend: Male - female creators. One version says the male twin Izanagi reached down from heaven and stirred 'the deep' with his spear.
Symbols: The sun and the moon.
Monuments: Various throughout Japan. Caves and grottos.

Hero: **Amaterasu.**
Region: Japan.
Etymology: A form of Anath?
Legend: The sun goddess born from Izanagi's left eye.

Hero: **Susa No-Wo.**
Region: Japan.
Etymology: Unknown.
Legend: The dragon-slaying hero born from the nose of Izanagi.

Hero: **Ganesha.**
Region: India.
Etymology: 'Lord of Hosts(seeKrishna).
Legend: Hindu elephant god, father of Buddha. Begot Buddha on the virgin
            Maya. At Elephantine in Egypt he appeared as a form of Yahweh,
            consort of Anath or 'the Virgin Zion'.[5]

Variants of the Name of the Hero

Abassi: African deity in the myths of the Efik people of Nigeria. Associated with ploughing, sowing and harvesting. (Literally, 'the Heart of Issa'.)

Aesir: A race of gods in Norse mythology.

Amaterasu: Daughter of Izanagi.

Anasazi: A Native American tribe.

Ansar: The Babylonian totality of heaven (cf. Egyptian ansate cross).

Asa: A king of the Israelites.

Asaph: A famous musician of David's time. He is supposed to be the founder of the hereditary choir of the Bene Asaph in the Second Temple. Psalms 50 and 73 - 83 are ascribed to him.

Asia: Derives from Hittite Assuwa.

Asil: A Norse god.

Asoka: Indian Emperor (third century BC).

Assario: A tribe of South American Indians.

Asura: The old gods of the Vedas.

Azan: A son of Arcas.

Azar: The name of the patriarch Abraham's father, a vizier to King Nimrod (Orion).

Azariah: A king of Judah, whose name gives away Osirian connections.

Azerbaijan: A place name, in the former Soviet Union, now a sovereign state (Asar baijan).

Azirru: A Phoenician king with seemingly Osirian connections.

Azure: Blue, also lapis lazuli. Jesus was robed in blue.

Brizo: A goddess of Delos.

Dusaris: The chief deity of Petra in Edom, 'the Red Land'.

Edessa: 'Place of Essa', 'Place of Essa's Feast'. A site in Northern Turkey (also known as Urfa) where there was a temple to the Mesopotamian god Marilaha – 'the Lord of All'. His chief ambassador was the moon god. If Abraham was born at Edessa/Urfa then this had to be the original home of the moon cult.[6]

Elissa: 'Issa is my god.' An alternative name of Dido, Queen of Carthage c. 800 BC.

Eshu: Aka. Yoshi or Yoshu, a god of the Ninjas.

Eshu: Messenger god of the Yoruba people of Nigeria. He brought the gods' instructions to earth and could speak the languages of every living thing.

Essa: An Arcadian word for an ear of corn.

Essen: Alternatively Hashen. A word for the breastplate worn by Hebrew high priests.

Ezana: Ethiopian. King of Axum, c. fourth century AD. A convert to Christianity.

Ezekiel: The prophet. The name probably means 'Spirit of the God that is Isa'.

Gaesa or Geis: A taboo or oath in Irish Celtic society.

Gaesum: A Celtic weapon. Its exact form is unknown.

Gagsisa: A Sumero-Babylonian term for the star we call Sirius.

Gaza: The temple demolished by Samson.

Gazarii: A term used for witches in the Pyrenees.

Ge-ez: Ethiopian, a Semitic language with no known etymology. The word means 'self-awareness' as in 'I am', the creative context of God.

Geezer: 'The man who came.' Slang, but Wellington's soldiers picked it up from the Basques during the Peninsular Campaign of 1814.

Geisha: As in Geisha girls (Japan) – Ge Isha – mother of Isha?

Gerizim: A mountain in Samaria. The word means 'navel of the earth'.

Gesso: A kind of plaster *which is trodden with grapes* in the making of wine in Spain.

Geza: A king of Rumania, immediate post-Roman period.

Gisan: A province of Japan. Noted for the monastery of Shigatse.

Gizo: The Spider/man of Hausa folklore; Trickster Hero (West African).

Gusi: A cult followed by the Dusun of Borneo incorporating the veneration of green porcelain jars that are inhabited by the spirits of ancestors. (Vase from Latin *vas*, earlier form of which was *vasus*, plural form *vasa*.)

Hesi: A name of the heifer goddess.

Hissar: A range of mountains north of Turkmenistan, thus implying the presence of Isa within the mountains.

Hza: The serpent god of the Incas.

Hzamna: Enlightener of Yucatan, recognised by the Mayan Indians as founder of their civilisation and 'Master of the Dawn'. (Another variant of *Itza* or *Issa*.)

Iaso: A son of Aesculapius.

Iasus: Greek. Son of Phoroneus, brother of Io (Isis).

Iazges: A tribe of Sarmatians (fourth – sixth centuries AD).

Ibiza: The popular Mediterranean resort, meaning literally 'the Heart of Isa'.

Iosheka: One of a pair of twins (means 'the Good One') Tawiscara (Tau = Hebrew cross). Iosheka is 'the Good Twin' or 'the Godly One'. He serves the needs of nature and vanquishes his evil brother. (North America.)

Isa: A mountain in Queensland, Australia.

Ise: A Shinto shrine in Japan.

Isha: A title of Shiva.

Ishnya: A place in northern Iceland.

Issa: Collective term for the initiates of the Mysteries of Isis.

Issapoo: An island off Fernando Po. The people of Issapoo regard the cobra as their guardian deity and it is hung tail downwards from a branch of the highest tree in the public square.

Issas:	Djibouti is the territory of the Affars and the Issas.
Ixian:	Crucified on a fiery wheel, a symbol of the sun (Greek).
Iyasu:	Emperor Lij Iyasu, Emperor of Ethiopia in the early twentieth century.
Izanagi:	Japanese deity.
Izanami:	Consort of Izanagi.
Izzarra:	A Basque liqueur.
Jehosaphat:	A king of the Israelites.
Jesi:	Latin Aesis, a town on the Esino river in central Italy.
Jesse:	The father of King David.
Jester/Geste:	'Deeds' or 'exploits' (geste), hence 'jester' – 'a trickster'.
Kozi:	A name for Nimrod, another variant of Orion – Egyptian Osiris in cosmic form. The Canaanites called him Baal-Hadad.
Krishna:	A deity of India.
Lhasa:	Capital city of Tibet. The Potala (the palace which is a focus of Tibetan Buddhism) is pyramidal in structure. Elements of its design, such as the stupas, reflect aspects of Egyptian architecture and religion, particularly the Osirian djed pillar.
Masar:	A Hopi word meaning 'the Creator'.
Massi:	A Maori legend of a hero thrown into water (comparable to Moses).
Mizos:	A people of Mizaram in Burma.
Ningishzida:	Sumerian, 'Lord of the Right Tree'. An earth god. A healer god. Like Anubis he is portrayed as dog-headed, the spirit of the hero in the underworld.
Nizir:	The World Mountain of the Chaldeans.
Oisin:	An Irish hero, member of the Fianna, the warband of Fionn MacHumail (Finn MacCool).
Omphaloessa:	The omphalos of Essa (Essa being the power within the stone).
Orissa:	A state on the western coast of India.
Osain:	Yoruban (African) deity of leaves and herbs, conceived as living in the forest and giving medicines to man. He has been retained in the Afro-American cults of Brazil, Trinidad and Cuba, and as Ossange in Haiti.
Oshossi:	Yoruban deity of the forest and the chase. His devotees dance for him carrying the miniature bow that is his signature. (Compare to Jesus' dance in the Gnostic Acts of John, see chapter three.)
Ossa:	A mountain mentioned by Herodotus.
Phrixus:	Boeotian prototype of Isaac who was almost slain by his father as an offering to God. A ram with a golden fleece suddenly appeared to take his place.
Sesa:	An Indian snake demon who bears the earth or enfolds it. He is King of the Nagas and under the name of Ananta is the symbol of eternity.
Shigatse:	Buddhist monastery in Gisan province.

Sire:	Form of address for royalty etc. in medieval English – meaning literally 'prince' (Assire-Asar).
Sraosha:	Persian, 'Saresha', God manifest.
Tesup:	A form of Atabyrius, a Kassite god *c.* second millennium. Syrian.
Triptolemus:	The triple name of Jason, the Eleusinian form of Osiris (Greek).
Ulysses:	Greek hero (El-issa, probably a Phoenician etymology).
Vishnu:	A principal deity of India.
Yasu Kun:	'Country at Peace'. A Shinto shrine to and of the Emperor in Tokyo.
Yeshe:	A king in Tibet.
Zar:	Ethiopian demon, may be related to an ancient name of Osiris, worshipped during the first Dynasty at Abydos as the God-King Zer, who became Lord of the Underworld.

Part Three

JESUS BC

Ancient Egyptian Christianity

9

Salvation and the Soul

'When Israel was a child, then I loved him, and called my son out of Egypt.'

Hosea 11:1

'Neter means principle of life, and the Temple is its house.'

R. A. Schwaller de Lubicz[1]

In 1922 the world was electrified by the discovery of the greatest ever archaeological hoard, which was unearthed by the fifth Earl of Caernarvon, the Egyptologist Howard Carter and their team. Up until that time, the name of Egypt was almost singularly associated with pyramids. From now on it was the magnificent solid gold death mask of the young Pharaoh Tutankhamun, *c.*1400 BC, that would dominate the image of Egypt. For the first time, a tomb had been discovered intact. It was a discovery that led to many surprises, some of which are only at last being understood, three quarters of a century later.

In a posthumously published book, Simone Weil has commented that:

> '...Ezekiel expressly compares Egypt to the tree of life of the Earthly Paradise, and Phoenicia, at least at the beginning of his story, to the cherub standing by the tree. If this view of the matter is correct, a current of perfectly pure spirituality would have flowed across antiquity from pre-historic Egypt to Christianity.'[2]

Indeed, many of the contents of Tutankhamun's tomb had a direct link with Christianity, a belief system that only seemed to rise over 1,400 years after the

Pharaoh was interred. Some of the items found within the tomb were personal ritual objects – a pair of gloves and a gala robe. Both bear a striking similarity to ritual items found within both the Roman Catholic Church and the various Orthodox churches.[3]

I now quote in some detail from the work of my friend, the writer, Ahmed Osman:

> 'The two garments, which I have chosen to call gold robes, recall official vestments of the character of priestly apparel, such as the dalmatic worn by deacons and Bishops of the Christian church, or by Kings and Emperors at coronations... They take the form of a long, loose vestment, having richly ornamented tapestry-woven decoration with fringes on both sides. In addition to this ornamentation, one of them has needlework of palmette pattern, desert flora and animals over the broad hem at the bottom. The openings of the neck and at the chest are also adorned with woven pattern. One of the vestments, with field quite plain, has narrow sleeves like the tunicle; the other, with the whole field woven with coloured rosettes as well as figures of flowers and cartouches across the chest, has its collar woven in the design of a falcon with outspread wings, and it also has the titulary of the king woven down the front...
>
> 'Perhaps they were worn on special occasions ..... and ..... they were a symbol of joy, very much in the manner of the dalmatic placed upon a deacon when the holy order was conferred, whereby the following words were repeated: "May the Lord clothe thee in the Tunic of Joy and the Garment of Rejoicing" *Moreover, these robes may well have had the same origin as the Roman garment* whence the liturgical vestment – the dalmatic – of the Christian Church derives.' [4]
>
> 'The pair of gloves, according to Carter, were in a much better state of preservation, neatly folded, also of tapestry-woven linen. They were possibly intended to go with the robes (a Roman Catholic bishop wears gloves when pontificating – also buskings, tunic and dalmatic under his chasuble) and are similarly woven with a brilliant scale-pattern and have a border at the wrist of alternate lotus buds and flowers.'

Other objects were also found that related to later Christian beliefs and practices:

'There were also a number of ostrich feathers, recalling the flabella still used at a papal procession in Rome, such as was witnessed in the Eucharistic procession of His Holiness the Pope in July 1929. These fans, like the pontifical flabella, were carried by grooms-in-waiting in Pharaonic processions, or were held beside the throne, and appear always on either side of the king or immediately behind him.'[5]

These observations by Ahmed served to heighten my suspicions regarding further Egypto-Christian connections. They were not difficult to find.

Popes are, upon death, interred in full regalia within three coffins, as were the pharaohs. Both the papal tradition and the pharaonic tradition share the celebration of jubilee years, the wearing of similar crowns, the celebration of the same kinds of rituals, the practice of confession and so on.

The ten tablets of the law, better known as the ten commandments, are in fact the negative confession to be found inscribed upon the walls of the pyramid of Unas, otherwise known as the Pyramid Texts.[6] Also, a whole litany of miracles performed by Moses is attributable to Isis, sister and wife of Osiris, including the famous parting of the seas, in order to walk dry-footed between them.[7] Oddly enough, this miracle is performed by the Egyptian goddess Hathor, too, whilst on her way to Byblos.[8] Even the idea of the 'son of God' is particularly Egyptian in flavour. Osiris, as the son of Ra, was an exceedingly ancient concept. Osiris was the original 'Lord' and was addressed as such. Pharaoh, who was the living Horus, the son of Osiris, or, if you like, the son of the son of God, had many titles, foremost amongst which was his Horus name and his golden Horus name (see chapter ten). He was the mouthpiece of the gods and was the ultimate truth teller.

The Egyptian word for 'truth' is *heka*. One of Pharaoh's titles was 'Heka', meaning both 'Lord' and 'truth'. The name is a pun, meaning that both 'Lord' and 'truth' are the same thing. Pharaoh as the emanation of God is both 'Lord' and arbiter, the truth. The term *heka* is in hieroglyphs denoted by the shepherd's crook, another symbol of the god, Osiris, the good shepherd.

Pharaoh's title as King of both Upper and Lower Egypt was 'Lord of the City of the Sun'. (There were two such cities, Thebes in the south and Heliopolis in the north, now a modern-day suburb of Cairo). In its original hieroglyphic form, the title translates as 'Heka Iunu' and 'Heka Iunu Shmau'.

The hieroglyphic symbol of *heka*, the shepherd's crook, is always found upon sarcophagi belonging to Pharaohs.[9] It can be seen being clutched in Pharaoh's crossed hands. In his left hand is the crook, in his right the flail. This association of Heka with Osiris more than implies that the syllable *he* is a sign of the hero. When split into its component parts *he* and *ka*, we come to the essence of the term. *Ka* is spirit in ancient Egyptian. The 'Heka' means 'spirit of the hero' or even 'heroic spirit'. It can also mean 'Spirit of He', 'He' meaning 'the Lord'. This is interesting because the Hebrew letter 'He' appears in the name of God, Yahweh, quite often spelt as Yod, He, Vav, He.

Heretics of every era have been aware of Christianity's Egyptian links. The former Dominican friar and missionary for the Hermetic movement, Giordano Bruno (1548–1600), who was burned at the stake for his beliefs, viewed the Christian cross as really being just another version of the Egyptian ankh or ansate cross:

> 'A fellow-prisoner reports him as having said that the cross on which Christ was crucified was not in the form shown on Christian altars, this form being in reality the sign which was sculptured on the breast of the goddess Isis, and which was stolen by the Christians from the Egyptians. In reply to an inquisitorial question about this, Bruno acknowledged that he had said that the form of the cross on which Christ was crucified was different from the way in which it is usually "painted", adding these significant words:
> "I think I have read in Marsilio Ficino that the virtue and holiness of the character [caraterre, by which he means 'cross'] is much more ancient than the time of the Incarnation of Our Lord, and that it was known in the time in which the religion of the Egyptians flourished, about the time of Moses, and that this sign was affixed to the breast of Serapis."' [10]

In a very intriguing and important work published in 2000, *The Pharaohs Shadow*, Anthony Sattin makes some extraordinary observations. In a conversation with Professor Chancellor Dr. Zaki Shenouda, Director of Egypt's Institute of Coptic Studies, Sattin records the following information:

> '...there were prophecies that the Messiah would come. Osiris is the Christ and Isis is his mother, the Virgin. There are other things we've taken. Christians talk about the fallen angel, while in ancient Egypt there was the god Seth who killed Osiris and went on to become the god of Evil. The pharaonic temple resembles our churches. In the construction of the temple and church we find high walls and no windows, because life is supposed to be like heaven.' [11]

This is the beginning of a host of similarities from which Sattin concludes that pharaonic culture and tradition are still very much alive, though sadly encroached upon by the modern world.

Coptic churches are fascinating repositories of the deeply ancient. They have a Holy of Holies hidden behind a screen, away from the eyes of the profane. Above many of these hang oil-lamps and beautifully crafted ostrich eggs which, as any Coptic priest will gladly point out, are a symbol of resurrection, a very ancient one, going back to the Osirian era. Quite often, in Coptic iconography, the god Horus is used as the figure of Jesus. Horus is the son of Osiris, called the Logos, or the Word, by the Copts. Yet again we are back to resonance, the Word of God.

In fact, there is some very interesting iconography throughout Coptic culture. There is a statue of Horus at Koptos that portrays him grasping the phallus of the god Set. This interesting image would appear to symbolise the desire of man to overcome his wild, primal, somewhat fecund self. Osiris, the higher god, was somewhat predictably canonised out of existence by the early Church as St. Onuphris, taken from Osiris' ancient title of Unnefer, the Beneficent. This reminded me of the origins of St. Benedict, whose name was given to a monastic order – the Benedictines. Monasticism, we must not forget, was Egyptian in origin, whereas St. Benedict is of uncertain origin – it is very doubtful whether such a person ever existed. Does it come as any surprise therefore to learn that one of the titles of the Greek sun-god Apollo was Benedictus, so similar to Osiris' 'Beneficent' title! The ancient monastery at Monte Cassino, Italy, is today Benedictine; in former, pre-Christian times it was dedicated to Apollo Benedictus. The legend of St. Benedict equates him, like Apollo and Osiris, with the sun.

It is significant that until fairly recently, but especially in the ninth and tenth centuries, it was believed that the Coptic Church held the secret of the pyramids. This was no mere fantasy. One of the reasons why I believe this to be a fact comes in the form of the Humboldt Fragment, no. xvi. This fragment shows an illustration of a three-stepped pyramid, surmounted by a cross. In ancient times, the ancient Egyptian primordial cross was representative of Amsu or Min, the spirit of Horus the Elder (Heru-ur), who died and rose again from the dead. This was later converted by the Coptic Christians into the cross of Jesus by the simple expedient of making the upright slightly longer.

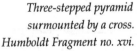

Three-stepped pyramid surmounted by a cross. Humboldt Fragment no. xvi.

Something else that intrigued me greatly was the Herodian connection with the Coptic Church. It is interesting to consider that, within a generation of the destruction of the Jerusalem Temple, the main players in the story of Jesus' crucifixion had all been canonised within the Egyptian Church.

The attitude to this today is to dismiss the habit of making saints out of almost everybody directly connected with Jesus, as early Christian over–enthusiasm. If meeting Jesus was enough to turn someone into a saint, why wasn't the Devil canonised too? Or, on a less facetious note, some of the more overtly 'dodgy' characters in the story?

The fact of the matter is that they were – even Pontius Pilate – but for reasons other than those suggested by detractors of early Egyptian Church policy. Even before the terrible destruction of Jerusalem in AD 71, there was a very strong rumour within Alexandrian Gnostic circles about Jesus' true parentage. The fact that the Herods were made saints within the Egyptian Church to my mind confirms the rumours, particularly as religions of the period had the habit of demonising rather than canonising anything or anybody who stood in the way of the hero. Could the Herods have been worshippers of an older form of Jesus, of Issa?[12]

It must again be admitted that, historically speaking, it is remarkably difficult to conceive of Christianity as having existed before its allotted historical time. Theological speculation has moulded the stuff of Jesus into its present shape, but as we have observed, theologians tend to work within, and so inflate, the accepted framework. After centuries of working according to this basis, one is likely to end up with something more akin to belief than experience, more fantasy than fact.

The Denial of Egypt

The reluctance to accept an older date for Christianity can perhaps be explained in part by the way the views of scholars have changed over the last 200 years. The emphasis has gradually shifted from the idea that the origins of civilisation lay in the Middle East to the idea that they lay in northern Europe and Asia. The older view is the 'Ancient' model, the latter is the 'Indo-European' thesis. According to this latter view, at some stage in the second millennium BC the Aryans invaded Europe and swept down into the south, bringing about Greek culture as a result. This Aryan invasion overwhelmed the local Aegean 'pre-Hellenic' culture. The Ancient model was almost precisely the opposite geographically speaking, recognising that Greek culture, the 'mother' culture of Europe, arose as a result of Egyptian and Phoenician colonisation c.1500 BC.

The Greeks themselves, of the periods of Pythagoras and of Socrates and Plato (*c*.600–300 BC), took precisely this view, as many of their writings testify. Archaeologically speaking, there is plenty of evidence for either theory; it is all a matter of interpretation.

It is this shift of view that in the past century has obscured Christianity's real origins by largely ignoring the tremendous influence of Egyptian civilisation, thus aiding the balance of opinion to remain in favour of the first-century dating of the Christian 'myth'. I do not deny that some very important historical events took place in Palestine, indeed they are crucial to my thesis. However, the idea that the myth itself – the myth of God manifest in the hero-god – dates solely to this period is absurd, as many writers contemporary to the period, Celsus *et al.*, have been at pains to make clear.

The consequences of adopting the Aryan Indo-European thesis are significant. In effect, it sidelines the Egyptian and Phoenician cultures. They are hardly accorded the status of players in the grand scheme of things after the second millennium BC. Egyptian settlements outside the geographical areas of Egypt and Palestine are denied, as are Phoenician settlements in later manifestations of the thesis. These manifestations, the product of the extreme edge of twentieth–century far-right political philosophy, eventually necessitated a change of the original name of the Aryan theory, Indo-Germanic, to its more innocuous title of the present era.

The publication in 1987 of *Black Athena* by Professor Martin Bernal caused a storm of controversy. By highlighting the anti-Semitic angle of the Indo-Germanic view, Bernal caused annoyance in academic institutions throughout the world. In showing that 'fundamental challenges to disciplines tend to come from outside', Bernal, himself an outsider, began to lay bare the Indo-European dream. He pointed out that archaeological evidence actually supported an Egypto-Afro-Asiatic model. This is not to deny that invasions from the north took place. However, these may well have been less dramatic than has been suggested, and their influence was nowhere near as great as that of the Egyptians and the Phoenicians. As Bernal points out in his book, the most surprising thing about the Aryan model is that not only does it go against all of the evidence of the ancient Greeks themselves, but at heart it is a racist theory – racist, at least, in what the extreme elements of the theory led to.

> 'If I am right in urging the overthrow of the Aryan Model and its replacement by the Revised Ancient one, it will be necessary not only to rethink the fundamental basis of "Western Civilization" but also to recognise the penetration of racism and "continental chauvinism" into all our historiography, or philosophy of writing history. The Ancient Model had no major "internal" deficiencies, or weakness in explanatory power. It was overthrown for external

reasons. For 18th and 19th century Romantics and racists it was simply intolerable for Greece, which was seen not merely as the epitome of Europe but also as its pure childhood, to have been the result of the mixture of native Europeans and colonizing Africans and Semites.'[13]

Bernal tentatively accepts the Aryan model's hypothesis of invasions by Indo-European speakers. However, according to his new model, the Revised Ancient Model, the earlier population were speakers of a related Indo-Hittite language, which left little trace in the rise of later Greek. (See language table.)

Indo-European is the favoured claimant to the throne of the 'master–language' so long sought by scholars. They hypothesise that the earliest form of Sanskrit itself arose from a much older Vedic language, from which the sacred texts, the Vedas, were derived. For Western scholars and romantics Sanskrit became a kind of *Ursprache*, in the sense of an original or ancestral tongue. The influence of Sanskrit upon other languages has indeed been immense; however, most of those languages are Eastern, not Western. The languages of Japan, China, Borneo, Tibet, Cambodia, the Philippines and Java all share significant roots, both spiritually and culturally, in Sanskrit. During the eighteenth, nineteenth and twentieth centuries the European intellectual class became collectively fascinated by all things Eastern. The rise of the Western Empires and their policies of colonisation saw to it that such fascination was deep and abiding.

It was in the inter–war period of the 1930s that this fascination was to bloom into a profoundly ugly flower, one that would leave its taint all over the world. The non-Semitic bias of the Aryan model, together with the extreme economic conditions of a severe post-war depression in Germany, came together in a poisoned chalice held up by the Nazis as the grail of racial purity.[14] Throughout the mid to late 1930s parties of Nazi fanatics trooped up and down the Tibetan highlands looking for the origins of the Aryan peoples and Germanic racial consciousness. What they discovered was specious to say the least, but it was put to extremely good use in propaganda against all Semites. The consequences were terrible and deeply tragic, but what must not be forgotten is the fact that the National Socialists could not have furthered any of their spurious researches without the guiding hand of elements within German academies many of whom kept their posts after the war. It was in the wake of the war that 'Indo-Germanic' was simply changed to 'Indo-European'.

Researchers of the past decade have had a tendency to lean towards Bernal's view that before we study our ancient origins it is necessary to study 'the history of history'. Our civilisation changes and adapts the past in its own likeness. In my view, the Aryan thesis has served to obscure an essential element in the history of myth and of Christianity. That element is the spread of myth and the mystery of Christian origins.

If I am correct that historical Christianity was based on very firm but very ancient origins, then there are two points to be made. The manner in which language spread may have been heavily influenced by both the Egyptians and the Indo-European peoples – the history of this linguistic migration is to be found in the various mythologies of these diverse regions. However, language itself may actually have stemmed from particular sites, as an interaction between man and the site, hence the extraordinary similarity of certain primary syllables and linguistic trends worldwide. The apparent spread of language across Europe, Asia and Africa may be, at least in part, an illusion. At some point in deep antiquity (c.30,000 BC), there may rather have been a coming together of linked but superficially disparate elements. This theory dispenses with the necessarily problematical and thorny issue of 'racial' influence, an issue that ever since the close of the Second World War scholars have been understandably reluctant to discuss. It would also resolve a number of linguistic quandaries.

One of the striking stumbling blocks of any theory of linguistic spread is the existence of Basque. Basque is an embarrassment to many scholars because it does not fit in anywhere and thus defies convention. It is a language to be found among the peoples of the western Pyrenees, in both Spain and France (the Basques and the Gascons). It is a region on its own, with its own culture as well as its own language, which has no Indo-European root. So where does it come from?

Basque has as one of its ancestors the old language of Aquitaine, which the Romans called Aquitania, but before that we are in very uncertain territory. However, it is interesting that Basque is a language of a particularly mountainous area, for mountainous areas being particularly powerful places, can have the most extraordinary effect upon humans. Furthermore, the name 'Pyrenees' comes from the same Greek root as 'pyramid', both forms having their own particular power. Pyramids are, like the Babylonian ziggurats and the mounds of North America, man-made mountains, using the same materials that make up mountain structure.

Incursions from other lands curtailed the spread of Basque and thus inhibited its use as a national language. However, another interesting thing about the Basque region is that throughout history it has been an area attractive to many peoples fleeing from the East. Many Solomonic Hebrews found their way there in the upheavals of the first millennium BC, for example, and more came after.

Whatever historians may say, the idea of the power of the place drawing these people to it must be taken into account. Mountainous areas have commonly given refuge, but they are also recognised to be physically, emotionally and spiritually health–giving. This is largely to do with better air quality, for not only may the air be more 'charged' due to emissions from the rock itself and high ion counts from rapidly moving waters, but the more rapid movement of the air itself elicits clarity of mind. There is a legend, prevalent over almost the entire Basque area, that certain members of the Holy Family either visited or were exiled to it. However, even before all of this, it was an area that legend says was frequented by Phoenician traders in search of tin and gold. No doubt they were also attracted by the sheer power of the place. We in the West have a very commercial point of view and the tendency is to see the Phoenicians solely as a trading nation travelling only for commercial gain. This is possibly a misleading view, because the Ancients seem to have had an holistic attitude towards their Mother Earth and neither she nor her inhabitants would have been looked upon simply in terms of exploitation. Also, the flat-Earth view of our ancestors that is held today is a stilted one; discoveries have shown that the Ancients travelled very far afield. Early in the twentieth century evidence appeared that the Phoenicians may have been regular visitors to the Americas and in the light of this there is no reason to doubt that they were familiar with Western Europe.[15]

The Phoenician tongue was closely related to Egyptian, and it is only reasonable to assume that, as the Phoenicians travelled further and further afield, so too did their language, which may have changed as it spread geographically to fit in with new experiences and ideas of the world. Thus, although the roots of Basque remain uncertain, it is known that Phoenician elements do appear both in the language and in Basque history. Although details of the Phoenician civilisation are unfortunately few and far between, enough is known of the language to see where its origins lie – in Egypt. (See language table.)

Although the Aryan theory of European civilisation has seen the influence of both Egyptians and Phoenicians minimised and, in some respects, trivialised, in the past decade things are being seen a little differently. Like Martin Bernal, Julian Baldick, a lecturer at King's College, London, sees the origins of Jewish, Christian and Muslim traditions in Afro-Asiatic roots.[16] He has observed that elements from all these religions, such as God as creator, circumcision, sacrifice, marriage rituals, a divine obsession with snakes and the Ten Commandments, are not distinct – they come from an Afro-Asiatic source, which has until now been disregarded. Baldick thus places much of this heritage back into a black African context, arguing that there is a common Afro-Asiatic language base. However, whilst I broadly agree with Bernal and Baldick's arguments, I believe that the term 'language base' should be elaborated on to become 'the outward spread of a civilisation to permeate, and be permeated by, the various elements of language that crop up in the landscape'. I believe that the origins of a language emanate from its environment, initially from the human body's subtle interaction with the planetary locale, especially its vibratory atmosphere.

The development of myth would be intrinsic within the development of language, for as language developed beyond the 'immediately practical' into the 'longer term practical', i.e. articulating a developing philosophy of life, so too would myth. To the Ancients, myth was the natural representation of the greater forces at work in and around them. Their philosophy of life lay within and behind their mythology. As peoples and ideas migrated, language would be removed from its natal environment and separated from its myth. It would spread outwards, sometimes to be assimilated successfully, sometimes to be regarded as 'uncouth' or perhaps 'inappropriate'. In other words, man's response to his landscape differs wherever he goes. Furthermore, whilst in linguistics it is accepted that syllabaries might remain the same or similar, something that has been completely overlooked is their punning nature.

The knowledge to be derived from understanding the punning nature of early language should not be underestimated. We saw the pun at work in the story of Robin Hood. Wordplay is still a major feature of modern humour, but in the past, when language more clearly reflected the law of 'as above, so below', its interpretation was deliberately multilayered. This inbuilt humour (*hu-mour*, the love of God), was meant to, literally, illicit a 'tickling' effect, a physical realisation of a greater truth in everything.[17]

In the case of Egypt, it is quite clear that, over its thousands of years as a pre-eminent civilisation, the nation became somewhat multicultural and that its influence through language and mythology would have had a tremendous potency and spread, so much so that the effects should still be easily comprehended today. Unfortunately, the currently accepted Indo-European language theory has obfuscated an honest and open search for the laws behind the origins and spread of language and therefore obscured the truth.

As we know, the Ancients were particularly interested in the power of place for practical purposes. From the earliest times, language and song were the most essential human components in the working mechanism of a site, a spiritual-linguistic technology. In essence, what we have is a man–environment interaction, where language is 'geo–linguistic'. The outward spread of this effect is thus earth-based: language is where the earth bears fruit and seeds (Greek, *pyren*, from the same root as both 'pyramid' and 'Pyrenees'). It is man who has gathered these fruits and spread the seed.

If we apply what I call the 'geolinguistic' argument to the civilisation of Egypt, we find that elements of early Greek and Hebrew support it very nicely, particularly in terms of the religion and mythology of those lands. Cultural and geographical differences still arise because of the influence of the 'power of the land', the local planetary atmosphere, as resonated within the mind.

Geolinguistics infers that the co-joining of language, myth and religion was, from the earliest times, complete. If the Indo-European thesis obscured the direct Egyptian roots of archaic Christianity, then it is the Greeks who must be given the credit for initiating the process. What made the Greeks so totally different from any other civilisation before them was the fact that they were the first to separate myth and science in terms of language, by coining the language now commonly used for scientific description. Suddenly life became less divine in origin and more a case of varying phenomena. Physics, biology and chemistry began their ascent to divinity, replacing the now overthrown gods.

For me, and this is entirely a personal view, the Ancient Egyptian mythology was, from its outset, a language of science. The very fact that the meanings of the Egyptian language have been ignored is incomprehensible; the fact that they have been wilfully mistranslated, woeful. I cannot understand why the credit for the development of monotheism should have been given to relatively recent people (by Egyptian standards). This is not to deny that the Jews were monotheistic, which they were from a later date than is thought, it is just that the Egyptians got there before them. The Pyramid Texts are quite explicit about the worship of the One. Those we label 'gods' were actually *neters* – 'principles' or 'forces' of nature. ('Nature' as mentioned earlier is derived from *neter*.) These same forces were scientific principles expressed as mythical and metaphorical concepts. To my mind the Greek separation of the two was actually a backward step! In Egypt everything was permeated by the divine, the divine was within 'all' things (Greek, *pan*). If there really is an essential difference between these two cultures, it is, I suppose, that the Egyptians saw God in a pantheistic way. The Jewish God reflects more an objective than a subjective view, in that God is totally outside human experience and the human *nous*. This was eventually how things came to be seen in Greece, though, unlike the Jewish texts, the Greeks do not deny their Egyptian origins. Unfortunately, the Indo-European language table seeks to minimise and even deny the importance of Egyptian religion and theology, which had a very telling influence upon the rise of Greek civilisation:

> 'Plotinus (*c.*205–270 AD) conceptualised Supreme Divinity as a trinity that manifests itself in three hypostases: as One, as Mind and as Soul. The prototypes of these hypostases still can be traced in the history of Egyptian thought to the first three divinities who make up the basis of the Heliopolitan Ennead: Atum-Ra, Tefnut-Mahet and Shu.'[18]

In many ways the philosophy of Plotinus was neo-Egyptian, to paraphrase Luckert, whose work, quoted above, demonstrates the fluidity with which Egyptian theology survived into Greek philosophy. Plotinus was relatively late, but Luckert also makes an important observation about Plato (428–348 BC):

'Christian theologians naturally preferred the *Timaeus* to other Platonic works. In the dialogue's underlayment of Egyptian ontology they discovered a natural affinity with their own Christology and theology. After all, Christendom was born from, and overtaken by, the same Alexandrian-Hellenistic undercurrent of Egyptian theological notions that entrapped a Porphyry and a Saint Augustine.'[19]

Elements of Egyptian Christianity survived into Greece and into the rise of historical Christianity before being ignored and the least acknowledgement overridden by the racist Aryan theory. The irony of this is that in trying to 'purify' the racial roots of the Greeks and their irresistible rise, the very foundations of such a rise are being woefully undermined to the detriment of the entire Grecian edifice by the Indo-European school.

Egyptian Masonics[20]

The denial of Egyptian influence by European scholars in the mid to late nineteenth century followed hot on the heels of the decipherment of the Egyptian script by Champollion in 1822. As a result, the mystery of Egypt began to diminish rapidly. Ironically, the hieroglyphic language had become a mystery in the first place as a consequence of Christian denial. In the fourth century AD the Christian Church banned the use of Egyptian hieroglyphics in an attempt to sever a living link with the country's 'Pagan' past. With a touch of further irony, it was to be a Jesuit priest, Athanasius Kircher, who would attempt to decipher them again, 1,300 years later.

Kircher saw the pharaonic civilisation as the fount of all wisdom and wrestled with the language of the pharaohs unsuccessfully for years. Modern hindsight has long since demonstrated that Kircher's approach was wrong and unfortunately his idea that Egypt was the source of wisdom is also dismissed, a little too eagerly, thanks to modern fashions of introspection and comparison. In reality, the sheer power of the language and its potential are only just being discovered. The 'wisdom' is in the application, and the application survives in forms of ritual that, over the years, have been inherited in many guises by many different cultures. To my mind, language and ritual developed together from the very earliest days, the sense of ritual being akin to a 'divine inflection' of the language at its optimum frequencies. When speaking our everyday language we use nuances of sound to intone and differentiate, and to give a sense of mood. Divine language was used and imparted in similar ways, but differently in that evidence points to it being sung, and at particular frequencies, with all of the brainwave changes this involved (see chapter ten). The ancient Vedic Gayatri hymn (see also chapter six) is still very much in use today and increasingly taught to Westerners. An initiate showed me a letter from his teacher, who had written:

> '..the lips must move as you pronounce the Mantra (the Gayatri hymn), which you should do in a very accurate and correct manner as I showed you, as the varying pitch of each word is also important.'

The role of language in ritual and as ritual is as ancient as the hills, as most of the world's religions still testify. However, the survival of Egyptian ritual and tradition has borne fruit in a number of surprising ways. The Coptic Church is the first and least surprising of these survivals. The other is Freemasonry.

The impressive decipherment of Egyptian hieroglyphics stemmed directly from the French Egypto-Masonic tradition, rather than from any Romantic impulse. The length of Egypt's history far outstrips anything comparable and therefore it is not surprising that the influence of Egypt was perceived by eighteenth century orientalists as conservative, a view shared by the Freemasons:

> 'Egyptian priesthoods had in fact appealed to the conservative thinkers at least since the time when Plato had modelled his Guardians on them. In the 18th century this line of thought was taken up by the Freemasons; but even in the Middle Ages, Freemasons appear to have been especially interested in Egypt because, following ancient tradition, they believed it to be the home of geometry or Masonry.'[21]

As Bernal goes on to observe:

> 'With the formation of Speculative Masonry at the turn of the 18th century they drew on Rosicrucianism and Bruno to establish a "twofold Philosophy". This entailed superstitions and limited religions for the masses but, for the illuminati, a return to the natural and pure original religion of Egypt, from the debris of which all the others had been created.'[22]

Freemasonry played an important role during the years of the French Revolution. Many of the leading Jacobins were Freemasons: Camille Desmoulins, Emmanuel Sieyes and Georges Danton. More prominent than them as a high-ranking and long-established Freemason was the Marquis de Lafayette, hated by the others for his moderation. The Revolution brought down the king but raised up an Emperor, Napoleon, whose attempt to conquer Egypt in 1798 was a military fiasco of major proportions, but on a scientific level an unqualified success. Egyptology was born, and immediately the race to decipher hieroglyphics was on.

The importance achieved by Masonic influence during and immediately after the French Revolution posed an acute threat to the stability of Christianity. But it was the work of one person in particular that presented the greatest menace; Charles François Dupuis, revolutionary, anti-cleric and scholar. His great work, *The Origins of all Cults,* is undeservedly obscure today.

Dupuis' idea was that all mythologies and religions could be traced back to one source. Furthermore, he believed that nearly all mythologies and religions were based upon one of two principles: the miracle of sexual reproduction, and the intricate movements of the stars and other heavenly bodies. He demonstrated with extraordinary, and somewhat massive, detail the Near Eastern mythological background of the Gospels. For Dupuis, Egypt was the source of Near Eastern and hence world culture.

Dupuis was active in politics during the Revolution and became the Director of Cultural Events during the Revolutionary Directory of 1795–1799. Later, during the Consulate under Napoleon, he was President of the legislative body. When Napoleon became the undisputed master of Italy and arbiter of papal affairs, it was Dupuis who was sent in to examine the Vatican records, which, in their entirety, were at his disposal. The Vatican has never been so exposed to scrutiny since. In his resulting work, *Was Christ a Person or the Sun?,* Dupuis was scathing about Christianity:

> 'If, however, it be demanded whether existed a charlatan or philosopher who called himself Christ ... nevertheless we disbelieve the reality of Christ..'[23]

Dupuis was just as harsh about his contemporaries:

> 'There are many among our readers who ... will persist in the supposition that Christ really existed, whether wise or foolish, great legislator or impudent impostor, because before reading our book they have accepted that idea, never for a series of years so much as suspecting its falsehood. Belief with such persons is a habit difficult to get rid of.'[24]

Dupuis' comments were enormously influential in the years after the publication of his work, which even 200 years later still impresses with its shrewd eye and dangerous promise – that religion is sun-centred. Dupuis and the Freemasons sent shudders of fear down the spines of those within Christianity, as well as those opposed to the Revolution – the very thing that threatened the old social order of Europe, of which Christianity was the bastion.

Christianity, it should be mentioned, had specified very precise dates for various Biblical events – 2200 BC for the time of Abraham, and exactly 4004 BC for the Creation - courtesy of Archbishop James Usher of Armagh, who calculated the dates by following a somewhat hazy trail through the Old Testament, wherein dates are exceedingly rare. A measure of the absurdity of the date of the Creation is its exactitude: 26th October 4004 BC, at precisely 9.00 in the morning! (Did God have a wristwatch?) It is an indication of Christian desperation at this time that the strict adherence to this date was seen as a means of confounding the arguments of those who, like Dupuis, opposed the fundamental tenets of Catholic Christianity.

By revealing the language of Egypt, Champollion, the decoder of the Rosetta Stone, was actually thought to be helping the Church's cause. His first discovery, in 1822, was that the date of the Temple of Dendera was not as ancient as had been thought; it was Roman. It had been a follower of Dupuis who had first posited a speculative date of many thousands of years BC. Edme-François Jomard had accompanied Napoleon to Egypt and been a leading scholar on the expedition. He had based many of his ideas on detailed surveys of Egypt and measurements of the Pyramids. In the ancient world these measurements were cited as evidence of Egypt's great antiquity. Greek sources claimed that Egyptian measures of length were based on a knowledge of the world's circumference. Jomard published his findings at a period of passionate Hellenism, Hellenism that rejected even the ancient Greeks' own view of Egypt. Champollion's discovery delighted the Vatican. In a letter to the Holy Father, the French ambassador wrote:

> ' [Champollion] has ... humbled and confounded the pride of this philosophy which claimed to have discovered in the zodiac of Dendera a chronology earlier than that of the Holy Scriptures ... M. Champollion establishes ... that no monument exists from before 2200 BC, dating back, that is, to the time of Abraham, so that, in accordance with our faith, there remain approximately eighteen centuries of darkness through which interpretation of the Holy Scriptures alone can guide us.'[25]

The Revolution in France had shaken Europe to its core. The cry of 'All men are free' had resounded heavily within the thick walls of St. Peter's, too, and as a frenzied spirit of emancipation was surging through the Continent, the Vatican reeled from blow after blow. The sheer desperation in the French Ambassador's letter is palpable. A period of enlightenment had begun, the Age of Reason had arrived, and, as far as the Vatican was concerned, the blame for it all lay squarely at the door of Freemasonry. It was Freemasonry that, under the guidance of Napoleon and with the help of Dupuis, had ransacked the Vatican and exposed its archive. Freemasonry had now risen to such eminence that it threatened the very existence of the Church and its influence upon the state.

Pope Clement XII had already singled out Freemasonry as an enemy of the Church in 1738, when he issued a Papal Bull condemning and excommunicating all Freemasons, many of whom were practising Catholics. In a letter released and published for the first time in 1962, Clement, addressing an unknown correspondent, reveals the reasons behind his condemnation of the Masons, asserting that Masonic thought rested on a heresy – the denial of Jesus' divinity. The inference was that the Masons saw all men as being divine, also a heresy. Clement also noted that the intellects behind Freemasonry were also the same minds behind the Lutheran Reformation.

Less than 70 years later it was Masonic forces that had the upper hand. Whether or not Napoleon himself was a Freemason is uncertain. That he was deeply involved in things Masonic is undeniable; many of the higher-ranking Freemasons were in his army, and under his rule they flourished. According to Bernal:

> 'His initial behaviour in Egypt also indicates this influence: he tried, for instance, to transcend Christianity and appear as a champion of Islam and Judaism, and he dutifully went into the Great Pyramid and had a mystical experience.'[26]

Freemasonry comes, ostensibly, from the guilds of masons of the great cathedral-building era of the medieval period. The acute learning of these masons is embodied within the grand corpus of their work and yet to a large degree they remain an enigma, as mysterious as the actual rise of the Gothic. Freemasons themselves claim a direct Egyptian influence and ancestry. The first Masonic Lodge is said to have been convened by Moses at the foot of Mount Horeb. At this same meeting the Tabernacle and the Ark of the Covenant and the Sacred Tables of the Law were delivered to Moses. The Second Lodge was held later by Solomon, Hiram of Tyre and Hiram Abiff, in the bosom of Mount Moriah. It was at this period that the legendary Hiram Abiff started work on the construction of Solomon's Temple. According to Masonic tradition, inscribed above the Temple balustrade (in the very place where the Slavonic Josephus states that the name of Jesus was inscribed), was the legend 'Jah-bul-on'. This translates directly as 'the Lord God of On' – On relates to the sun[27] and in ancient Egyptian times was the name of a place now known as Heliopolis, the City of the Sun. The God of On (or Annu) was Osiris, in his Ra aspect. This too is viewed as heresy by the Church.

Perhaps it is not surprising, given Freemasonry's putative origins, that elements of heresy are to be found, care of masons, inside many cathedrals. The long disused west door of King's College Chapel, Cambridge, contains much symbology linking the Christian and Judaic mysteries to ancient Egypt. The letters JHVH are carved in Hebrew within a sun symbol upon the door. Although it is known that the chapel was constructed during the reign of Henry VI (1421–71), these symbols, as well as the proportions of the chapel, have never been satisfactorily explained – it is only by reference to Freemasonry that they can be. In fact its plan was based upon the Temple of Solomon and the vaulting resembles Egyptian papyrus plants, as does much of the vaulting in Gothic cathedrals, for that matter.

Freemasonry, with its theme of the brotherhood of man, harks back to Gnosticism and its recurrent theme of knowing thyself. Shakespeare takes up the idea in *Henry VI*:

> 'Ignorance is the curse of God, knowledge the wing whereby
> we fly to Heaven.'[28]

It would appear also that such knowledge came via sound and language. A cursory glance at the term 'Masonic' suggests it is a simple combination of 'Ma' and 'sonic', meaning 'the sound of Mother' – inferring that the Masons worked with the Mother-sound, which takes us back to the idea of architecture as frozen music. Such an etymology is purely speculative; however, it is supported by the fact that the word 'mason' has an Old High German origin in *mezzo* , a musical term meaning 'neither loud nor soft, half'. From this comes *steinmezzo* , 'stonemason'.

This terminology is interesting in relation to the Masonic obsession with the Rock of Sion, the cornerstone of the Temple. This is described as a particular stone or rock that is, in the many variants of the story, at first overlooked and then retrieved and used as the keystone of the Temple. In the New Testament Jesus is compared to the cornerstone, having been rejected by his people:

> '...by the Name of Jesus Christ of Nazareth, whom ye crucified...
> This is the stone which was set at naught of you builders, which
> is become the head of the corner.'[29]

Variations of this quotation appear throughout the New Testament, in Matthew, Acts, Romans and Ephesians. What is remarkable is that as these references appear, they seem to become ever more explicit, stating that Jesus is in the Rock, as well as being it. The culmination comes in 1 Peter 2:3–8:

> '...the Lord is gracious.
> To Whom coming, as unto a living stone, disallowed indeed of men, but chosen of God, and precious.
> Ye also, as lively stones, are built up a spiritual house, an holy priesthood, to offer up spiritual sacrifices, acceptable to God by Jesus Christ.
> Wherefore also it is contained in the scripture, Behold I lay in Sion a chief cornerstone, elect, precious: and he that believeth on him shall not be confounded.
> Unto you therefore which believe he is precious: but unto them which be disobedient, the stone which the builders disallowed, the same is made head of the corner.
> And a stone of stumbling and a rock of offence, even to them which stumble of the word, being disobedient...'[30]

The scriptures tell us that Peter is 'the rock'. The above texts go further; in stating '..by the Name of Jesus Christ.....This is the stone,' the name – the sound – is related to the stone: you will note too that the faithful are addressed as 'lively stones'. I came to realise that there is a practicality here; the text that for so long I read as metaphorical, as many others had done, was being literal. The depth of it is that the Rock represents the Substance, the Great Mother, the substratum of life upon which all rests (see chapter eight). This is a clear example of 'as above, so below' at work in ancient language. A hero-god would, in consciousness, be at-one with this divinity. Jesus is in the Rock; the Rock is in Jesus. The relationship is that of resonance, a synchronous vibration with the most subtle force which permeates and upholds all of life. This is not a metaphor; to the initiated, it can become a reality.

As far as the physical rocks that are chosen and used in temples and cathedrals, those monuments to the human voice, again, the meaning is practical. The power lies in the site, the stone and in the building design. All of this is related to resonance, the vibratory key of life. The masons knew of this. The closing message is, of course: 'If you ignore "the stone" and "the word" , there will be problems.'

In the late eighteenth century different forms and variants of Freemasonry began to appear. It was at this time that the Oriental Rite of Memphis came into vogue amongst certain of these groups. According to the Oriental Rite, an Egyptian Wise Man, Ormus.[31] said to have lived in the first century AD, founded what was to become known as Freemasonry. This he did by amalgamating certain of the Pagan and Christian Mysteries; via this he founded Rosicrucianism. Not surprisingly, it is very difficult to substantiate any of these traditions and at first glance, they do seem rather fanciful. However, the sheer number of Freemasons and the success of the society throughout the world demands that we take at least a cursory glance.

'Ormus' suggests 'Hor-mose', literally 'Child of Horus' – 'Horus', of course, being another version of 'the Lord'. This suggests 'Hrm' or 'Hiram' – the legendary King of Tyre or Hiram Abiff, builder of Solomon's Temple. In the pictographs of ancient Mexico, the deity, the One God, is shown precisely as the God Ra is in Egyptian hieroglyphics, as a dot with a circle around it. This is a symbol common to world mythology, where the dot is the divine seed of infinite potential and the circle represents the infinite whole within which all exists. It is a symbol of the First Principle, the 'I Am'.[32] In Persia this High God was called Ormuz. The Assyrians called the God Assur. It seems therefore that the Freemasons, in citing Ormuz/Asar as their founder, are indeed harking back to an incredibly ancient tradition - the power of the Name of God.

Perhaps this is why 'the Craft' is riddled with Egyptian symbolism. It was Freemasons who drafted the United States Constitution, and intriguingly the symbols on the dollar bill are very Masonic and very Egyptian. The obverse side to the portrait of George Washington shows the Great Seal of the United States. This Seal, accepted as such by the signatories of the Declaration of Independence on 20th June 1782, features an eye in a pyramid with the legend *Novus Ordo Seculorum* – 'A New Secular Order'. This extraordinary symbol reminded me immediately of the letter 'o' of *El Ayin*, the Eye, the all-seeing Eye of God.[33]

A deep vein of Egyptian symbology runs all through Freemasonic tradition. The 'Cleopatra's needles' in London and Washington – obelisks actually dating from before Cleopatra's reign, of New Kingdom origin (c.1500 BC) – are topped with pyramid-shaped benben stones, as depicted on the dollar bill. In Masonic lodges a blazing star shines forth and is considered by Masonic authorities to represent the star Sirius. To the Egyptians this star was the embodiment of the cosmic Isis, consort of Osiris. Even the secret sign is of Egyptian origin, and is something also familiar to practising Catholics – the Tau cross.

It is difficult to ignore the Freemasons, particularly in the light of all this. But what all these survivals demonstrate is that Egypt's influence upon the course of history, and Western civilisation in particular, cannot be ignored. And yet the history, the beliefs and the mythology have been ignored within what must surely be their proper context.

History, it seems, is inclined to reveal more about ourselves than the proper context of our ancestors' achievements. Indeed, the broad mass of scholars and theologians have stood together, ignoring the witnesses of the past and the brave dissenters of the present.

Masonry at the Core

Let us now look at the core philosophy behind the ancient masonry that inspired, and continues to inspire, so many. We need not only rest our eyes upon Egypt for clues. So far, little mention has been made of ancient Babylon. The Babylonian era is, of course, a book in itself, some relevant aspects of which are noted in the Appendix. For the present, though, our attention is on the philosophy behind the temple structures.

The Esa-gila, the Temple of Esa or Asar, was the most important temple complex in ancient Babylon and was dedicated to Marduk, the supreme deity. The name Esa-gila would appear to mean 'Esa, Lord of the Earth'. Esa is the same as Asar. This is borne out by the fact that Marduk was later superseded by the god Assur, yet another form of Asar. Assur was the supreme god of the Assyrians, who it would appear took their name from him.

The massive buildings were ziggurats, basically 'step' or unfaced pyramids. Ziggurats were effectively graves or tombs of the suffering god and Marduk is precisely this form of god. In Sumerian, Marduk's name was Amar-utuk, 'the Calf of the Sun-god', in other words a bull calf. In Sumer he was probably a minor god, but in later times he became, as Baal, the chief god of Babylon. His other name is Bel. Marduk thus replaced the Sumerian Enlil, the 'Lord of the Wind', whose other name was 'Kur-gal' meaning 'Great Mountain'. (Assur was also called the 'Great Mountain'.) Marduk was the son of Enlil's brother Ea, meaning 'House of Water'. In Hebrew, the Jews of the exile (c.586 BC) called him Bel-Merodach.

Marduk has 50 names, a number of which are strikingly similar to that of the Egyptian Asar, who you will recall is Osiris. These names are: Asaru, Asarualim, Asarualimnunna and Asaruludu. Robert Temple comments:

> 'We have already seen how the An of Egypt was known in Sumer not only as An but as Anu, picking up a "u" ending. It is therefore not so senseless to see in Asaru a Sumerian form of Asar, with the same "u" ending added. But the Egyptians themselves also had an Asaru, or more precisely, an Asar-uu, whom Wallis -Budge describes as "a form of Osiris worshipped in lower Egypt".' [34]

Wallis-Budge also tells us that Asaruludu, means 'Osiris of the growing plants'.[35]

The Enuma Elish, the creation myth of the Babylonians, tells the story of Marduk's victory over Tiamat (Akkadian, meaning 'Sea'), the universal mother,[36] and also states that the ziggurat is the god.[37] In Egypt, the Great Pyramid was also accorded the same status; that of the god. The following utterance from the Pyramid Texts, carved on the walls of the Pyramid of King Unas (2375-2345 BC), state:

> 'O Horus, this King is Osiris, this pyramid of the King is Osiris, this construction of his is Osiris; betake yourself to it, do not be far from it in its name of Mr... O Horus, as your father Osiris in his name of "Mansion of the Monarch".'[38]

On seeing how Christian terms have been misinterpreted in the past, the assertion in the Roman Catholic Catechism that the Church is the body of Christ now becomes a reflection of the ancient viewpoint.

This, at last, reveals the real purpose of Freemasonry. It also reveals its extraordinarily ancient provenance. For in Masonry, God is the temple. Jesus, the hero-god, is the cornerstone. It is a simple case of God, temple – temple, God. It is probably for this reason that the Egyptian hieroglyph of the throne, is the symbol for the goddess Isis and a partial symbol for the god Osiris/Asar.[39] The throne is the seat of power, a king might have his throne in his great palace; the gods, however, have theirs in their great mansions or temples – quite often their pyramids.

To the Ancients, the sacred site was the meeting-place of heaven and earth, a place where humankind could more easily come into contact with those gigantic forces that play upon and within the earth. A temple or a church is today still called 'a house of God', and indeed, it is still a place wherein the consciousness of the people is meant to meet the divine consciousness of the cosmos, to meet God – although much of the means have been forgotten. To come into conscious contact with God and to remain and grow in that contact was a prime attribute of the heroic life. We have noted how Gisa is not only the hero name but also, as Giza (local phonetic) it is the name of the world's most wondrous, ancient sacred site. This may have been the origin of the traditional naming of Christian sites after saints, those men and women deemed heroic by the Church.

That as maybe, the temple was effectively a point of consciousness, a point or a location wherein God could be experienced. In this sense the sacred place was numinous and consciousness-expanding. God is everything, literally. God is both immanent and transcendent, in all things and beyond all things. By the act of communication with the divine in a prepared place, humanity could gain much. Via ritual and its attendant disciplines one could gain control of one's senses and direct them toward the divine experience. To the Ancients this was magic, to us today what is known of this is called psychology, what is unknown remains magic. However much we have dismissed both, they are really sciences and belong together, especially at the points on the planet where the subtle incoming and emanating energies are strongest.

Often, when the Ancients directed their senses toward the divine, they might begin by focusing upon various representations of the chosen god. This would help provide a bridge to the subtle, unseen realms. Provided one's intentions were pure, using these symbols or statuettes did not constitute a lapse into idolatry. In later years, with the loss of much of the wisdom that had gone before, idolatry would be a correct description, for, in ignorance, the image itself would be worshipped. By that time humanity had, to a large extent, lost touch with what God truly is – the immanent, divine spark within each one of us. We give divinity a particular name and form because it helps focus our intent. We can become conscious of this divinity and, as I will demonstrate, it is conscious of us.

In chapter one we saw how the ancient priest-king system created and sustained a gene-pool of those who were 'sensitives' – born to be sensitive to the divine and trained in order to be of service to the divine for the benefit of the people. The ruler was expected to be the nation's greatest servant and was associated with the sun. 'As above, so below': the sun was seen as the all-giving ruler of the solar system, the earthly monarch's function was the same – the all–giving ruler, embodying divinity. Thus, images of the king or queen could be used as objects of worship, not as an end in itself, but as a psychological tool *en route* to the unseen Lord. However:

> '...the solar king was no mere symbol, ornament or tax-eater, but
> a working instrument, a kind of electric generator or conductor
> of the positive current by which the spirit of the people and the
> fertility of the earth itself were maintained.'[40]

Of course, well before Herod's era, royalty had 'lost the plot', service was out, greed and arrogance were in. However, in more ancient times, the priest-king system saw to it that society remained very much a theocracy – a society based around God. Unfortunately, to merely describe it as such is not to do it justice. Theocracy is not a term that in any way helps us to understand a God-based society in ancient times, because in modern times the connotations are very different, particularly where man has lost touch with the planetary forces, let alone those of heaven. There was a difference in the approach of the Ancients that today we find very difficult to appreciate. I suggest that it lies in the lack of a differentiation between subject and object.

It is apparent that to the Ancients, divine unity was seen to uphold diversity and their day-to-day welfare was best served by understanding their relationship to the whole of life – working with nature to grow food, merging with nature in order to hunt. Confirmation of this relationship with natural forces and of a king's role comes from the hand of King Gudea of Lagash, a Sumerian who lived *c.*2400 BC:

'...with an astonishing directness, he (Gudea) depicts the gods as natural forces. All sources agree in presenting the king as instrumental in procuring for the community the boon of a harmonious integration with nature.'[41]

The Ancients' mythologies were filled with relationships between divine beings and with tales of heroic mortals become immortals. As we have seen, their ultimate goal lay in merging with the divine, a sacred acoustic science being used for this purpose. This difference in approach, compared to that of modern times, implies a greatly lessened sense of ego on the part of the individual in their society. The Ancients accepted that the creative life-giving force, God, was everywhere. Their highest goal was to experience God at all times, hence humility was a prerequisite, for how can one see something's true nature, the God within, if one considers oneself above it? The Ancients were humble before their gods. You will recall that 'Hu' is the Lord; to humble oneself is to approach the Lord, it is to be in the right state of mind. Humility enables a shaman to become his or her totem animal, taking on, for example, the attributes of an eagle and soaring above the Nazca Lines (see chapter five). Such attributes would often be reflected in the shaman's name, Great Eagle or similar. Of course, it was recognised that there was a bodily difference between a human and an eagle, but what was important to these very practical people was function. Here, we can see the relationship between name, form and function. In ancient language, although the form may be different, if the function is the same, then the name will be the same or similar, hence the Gisa correlation.

Here we return to the idea of names as titles and we can see that the function of a sacred site, as a place filled with divine atmosphere, is the same as that of the immortal hero, again, a body filled with divine atmosphere. For 'atmosphere' read 'vibration'. The vibration of the temple and of the hero are the same. The body of manifestation is different, but the function is the same, they both embody divinity and they resonate together. It should come as little surprise that, in this way, the Ancients viewed the hero and the temple as one! Again, we come to the fresh interpretation of the Roman Catholic catechism: if the hero is the temple, then *the temple is the actual body of Christ*. Further on I shall discuss just how extraordinary this concept really is, for the actual body of Jesus here on earth will be revealed and, what a revelation it truly is!

The point of regularly returning to a sacred place is to share in and retain its atmosphere. Here we should note the difference in the two embodiments, the temple and the hero, and the importance of the temple to the aspiring hero. The sacred building is sited, designed, constructed and used in a very particular way in order to embody divinity – to reveal the atmosphere of God. The aspirant must see him or her self as a temple too, but not as an edifice that can be built from 'scratch'. The aspirant already has an atmosphere that must be changed and a body which must be subtly restructured. The mind and body must be purified in order to manifest divinity. The temple and its rituals would be prime tools.

We now know that in these specifically sited and specially designed places, through acoustic-based ritual, the participants raised their consciousness to merge with what many have called 'the higher realms'. I reaffirm my earlier deposition that the names Jesus and Christ, like Buddha, are titles relating to levels of consciousness. The title holders manifest higher levels of consciousness than the norm and this benefits mankind. How one can ascribe consciousness to a building, however sacred, may require a shift in understanding. One needs to accept the understanding of the Ancients that consciousness is everywhere, embodied in different forms and hence expressed at different levels. Embodiment is expression. It is the unexpressed, universal form which sustains the expression.

God created Adam out of red clay. From the ground we come and back to it we return. This is a cycle that the temple reflects; as the human body is constructed from earth, so too the temple. Jesus is the cornerstone of the temple, he is the rough-hewn stone that the builders almost neglected. With these metaphors we are familiar, they are all about embodiment. What we are not familiar with, though, is the fact that in the Ethiopian 'Legends of Our Lady Mary',[42] Jesus' grandmother, Hannah (or Anna, Ann, Anu, etc.) is described as the 'twenty-pillared tabernacle of Testimony'. The Egyptian *Annu* also means 'pillar'. In chapter eight I pointed out that the Babylonian *Annu* means 'the underworld'. So what is the relationship between the pillar and the underworld? Simple. A pillar is a support and the underworld is the world's support. In effect the ancient builders were endeavouring to make manifest the unseen levels of life. This was not merely symbolism – because of site positioning, design, materials and ritual activities – it was practical. The uplifting divine atmosphere was there to partake of, even the atmosphere of the all-pervading, all-sustaining one. Let us now gain some further insight into the ancient ritual activities.

Wind, Gas and Vowel Movements

In the Gospels Jesus exorcises seven 'devils' from Mary Magdalene. The most ancient form of this tale (and yes there is one!) appears to be about the seven spirits of the Anunnaki or Maskim, the Sumerian-Akkadian spirits of the seven planetary spheres, born of the goddess Mari. There was a sacred drama, dating back to the third and fourth millennium BC, that told of their multiple birth. An Akkadian tablet says of them:

> 'They are seven! In the depths of the ocean, they are seven! In the brilliancy of the heavens, they are seven! They proceed from the ocean depths [Mary-Maria-Mer], from the hidden retreat.'[43]

According to Walter Scott, in his commentary on the Hermetica, and to recent research, the system of planetary spheres was believed to be the body of God the Father, in which he dwelt as the human soul dwelt in the human body.[44] According to the testimony of Al-Shahrastani (d. AD1153), the indwelling of God in the planets and in individual men

> '...is the personification... Sometimes they say that God personifies himself only by means of the celestial "habitations" [i.e. the planets or planet-spheres] in general; but that he remains one, for it is only his action (and not his essential being) that manifests itself in each of the "habitations", according to the measure of his workings on it and his personification through it. It is as if the seven "habitations" were God's seven members, and as if our seven members were God's seven "habitations", in which he manifests himself...'[45]

This is reflected in something Sir Isaac Newton (1642–1727) wrote shortly before the publication of his *Principia* in 1687. Newton had developed a theory that matter was an emanation or outpouring of the will of God, a theory that the imprint of his will upon space was what we regard as impenetrability and movement.

> '...so God may appear [to our innermost consciousness] to have created the world solely by the act of will, just as we move our bodies by an act of will alone.'[46]

These interesting quotations demonstrate the philosophical influence of myth down through the ages, and the influence of the idea of the seven planetary resonances on subsequent scientific development. But what about the effect of this mythology at the actual temple site?

Seven is an interesting number, particularly in terms of music. The seventh note of an octave is the leading note, it 'hangs on', as if demanding to be led forth. It also reconciles: it gives a sense of something that might come after, of imminence. The seventh note is the note of completion.

Furthermore, the number seven seems to be related to the body in many ways, just as the seven planetary spheres represent the body of God. Contact between man and the cosmos is said to be made via the seven chakra points that run from the base of the spine to the crown of the head. In Western medicine the existence of these areas or energy spots within the body is a moot point. In contrast, in the East they are an accepted reality. Recent photographs, using super-sensitive machinery, have shown that these points do indeed exist.[47]

The aim of Tantric yoga is to awaken Kundalini and to bring it to fruition (also see chapter four). Kundalini is known as the 'energetic serpent' that rises up through the chakras to the crown of the head. If the Kundalini energy awakens and rises to the crown, the 'thousand-petalled lotus', then the adept may attain a blissful union of the self with the Infinite. The way of awakening this energy, and creating of the body a true temple, is held by Tibetan lamas to be through words of power, the *hekau* of the Egyptians. The most famous mantra of power is the *Om*, the word of creation; another is *Om mane padme hum*, known as the Jewel in the Lotus.

The chakras are analgous to elements of a subtle circuitry which bears an energy charge which may be activated by a word of power at the correct frequency. They are centres of subtle energy, which, with the aid of subtle-energy technologies, are now being measured. Each of the chakras is associated with either a major endocrine gland or a major nerve complex. For example, the throat chakra lies over the thyroid gland, the gland that controls metabolism. The others are the crown (third eye/pineal gland), heart (solar plexus), sacral and coccygeal. Interestingly, each of these points is also 'associated with a particular type of psychic perceptual functioning'.[48] As Richard Gerber observes:

> 'The chakras translate energy of a higher dimensional (or higher frequency) nature into some type of glandular-hormonal output which subsequently affects the entire physical body.'[49]

This fascinated me. The idea that incoming frequencies from the outer spheres could be retuned to frequencies many octaves lower is very intriguing. And it is not as fantastical as some would have us believe, particularly in the light of what we have seen in chapter five about the influence of sun and moon on human physiology. In this sense the mantras of the Tibetan lamas and others, the extraordinary words of power that can have such a radical effect are themselves like points of frequency. They are transformers that help the spirit to ascend, but also help the higher frequencies to descend to what for us are edifying levels of reattunement.

Perhaps in this way the alphabet is ancient man's legacy to us – his transmission, in symbolic terms, of this innate and archetypal power. The alphabet is very much a development of earlier pictographic hieroglyphs, although the view is widely held that the letters in themselves, the individual shape-forms and characters, have no transcendent external meaning. However, this is because in translating them we have actually fixed their value and therefore their meaning. As Schwaller de Lubicz pointed out:

> 'Each hieroglyph can have an arrested, conventional meaning for common usage, but it includes (1) all the ideas that can be connected to it, and (2) the possibility of personal comprehension.'[50]

Language, in the ancient sense, is not a metaphor; it directly imparts or expresses what it wants to say. It is this that gives us a clue as to the application of language in the temple, language as frequency.

Hieroglyphics were ever and always a sacred language, the language of religious philosophy and metaphysics. Hieroglyphics did, however, enter into the realms of other written languages, and were later to provide philologists with important clues to their eventual decipherment. Hieroglyphs were of course translated, along with the stories they tell, and the similarity of these stories to tales worldwide is remarkable. They had obviously been told and retold for many millennia before being committed to parchment and wall stelae.

The myth of the hero is the most prominent among these similar tales, the similarities being so clear that the differences must be due to nothing more than local cultural and linguistic interpretations. One gains the impression that the myth was there at the outset, but was given a specific form by each culture according to those people's custom and language. Language expresses ideas and differing languages can make them appear to be different, but ultimately the only difference may be in the language itself. The story, from the Book of Genesis, of the Tower of Babel and the confusion of languages makes this point.

However, having by this time encountered a broad range of facts, I was firmly of the opinion that the myth of the hero, associated with the power of the place, induced language as a physiological response committed to history in pictographic form, as hieroglyphs, literally 'sacred language'.

Our bodies are the best bit of technology in this particular area of the galaxy. We have the inbuilt technology for transformation, but, in modern times, seem little prepared to use it. Or perhaps we have lost the knowledge of how to? To my mind, it seemed that religion was the last remaining vestige of an ancient spiritual technology. Using it and understanding it in the context of the workings of the universe helps us to gain benefit, but the benefit is gained through attending to detail.

There seem to be certain basic and fundamental syllables that contain all meanings within language. The names of Jesus, Mary and Anna are cases in point. Variations of these names appear throughout religious mythology and have certain meanings, just as the words for the spirit and the soul seem to appear on the same basis: Ba and Ka. That this syllabalary was used in a punning fashion I think is rather obvious, and the reader will no doubt have noticed my own use of puns within this text!

Certain of these syllables were used by the hierophant or priest as he or she entered the temple, walking sunwise, that is to say clockwise, having made an offering at the entrance, and gradually raising the tone and volume of his/ her voice in order to attune to the right effect. The presence of other people participating in, or merely observing, the ritual would only have added to the ambience of the site and its power.

At particular frequencies it seems that the body becomes a vessel, a receptacle for other frequencies of vibration, a meeting–place wherein opposing forces unite. Macrocosm and microcosm meet. The Temple of the cosmos meets the temple of the earth to help form the temple of man.

> 'If we listen to the audible frequency of this planet, it may be possible for us to resonate and entrain with it despite the fact that the actual vibratory resonance created may be thousands of times faster or slower than the frequencies to which we are listening. This same principle applies to the frequencies of the human body which may be far removed from those sounds which we can hear but which can be affected by audible vibrations. Through the Principle of Correspondence, we may use harmonically related sounds to influence the vibrations of atoms or the stars.'[51]

> 'Audible sound was believed to be a 'reflection', within the world of matter, of the Cosmic Tones.'[52]

Music, to ancient man, was the carrier of a divine super-physical energy, which one could draw down into oneself at certain levels of frequency.

'In the spoken or intoned rituals of many of the world's religions there is again a similar concept: that the voice of the priest within the realm of time and space becomes a vehicle for the energizing Voice of the Creator to manifest its forces through.'[53]

As David Tame goes on to observe,

'The role of music and the role of religious intonation and liturgy was to release into the earth a form of cosmic energy which could keep civilisation in harmony with the heavens.'[54]

In the light of the revelation that temples, cathedrals and pyramids were monuments to the male voice range, this is significant stuff. But music and chant do not only help to maintain the fabric and morals of society. They also heal. (See also chapter five.)

I have two good friends who are living testimony to the power of music, of sound, to heal. One of them, Bear, uses the didjeridu to this effect. Bear has been journeying and performing for the past decade. At one event, a festival in India, as part of a troupe, he played to an audience of staggering proportions – two and a half million people! As a music therapist, healer, spiritual counsellor and ceremonial leader, he has worked with the didjeridu in many contexts. He explained to me that he was particularly drawn to its use as a tool in promoting grounded, gentle relaxation and as an aid in healing sessions.

In the mid 90s he used the didjeridu in music therapy with physically and mentally challenged youngsters. It was through this work that he discovered the extraordinary healing power of this instrument. He found that the vibrational harmonic resonance produced had a deep and profound effect that uplifted and relaxed the most complex of energies, and that the low harmonic tone of the instrument married with and complemented the vibrational resonance of the human body, releasing what Bear calls 'stagnated energy', thus promoting balance and harmony.

It is the same too for my friend Jaye Stilwell. Jaye has the ability to tone and overtone at the most remarkable frequencies, in the way that Tuvan throat singers do and have done throughout history. Jaye is also a healer and is a very strong believer in the power of resonance. At particular sites his gift seems amplified, and when I first experienced it I was utterly amazed. Toning at these places makes them come alive in a way that I had never before realised.

I asked Jaye about the power of his voice. He uses different tones to effect different modes of healing, some of which are more powerful than others. When I asked him what the form of these sounds might look like, he looked me in the eye and burst out laughing. Slightly perplexed, I pressed him further, and discovered the source of his laughter. He said that one of the forms begins with the letter 'e' and concludes with an 'a' sound. The two are divided by a barely defined space, a letter 's'. As the overall sound is started by the throat, the initial 'e' is initiated by a barely audible glottal 'g'.

So, 'Gesa' is a healing sound as well as the very sound that defines man as the Temple.

The Birds and the Beings

In October 1998, I read an article in *New Scientist* magazine[55] that asked the question: 'Were the Mayan pyramids designed to capture the quetzal's cry?' In a fascinating article, acoustics engineer David Lubman, a consultant from Westminster, California, suggests that these pyramids were built to copy the cry of the quetzal, a wonderfully beautiful species of bird, sacred to the Maya. It is a trick of local tourist guides to clap a pair of rocks together and listen to the resonant echo. The echo is uncanny and comes back as a 'descending chirp of "EE-OO" '. This cry is remarkably like some of the incantations that contain variant spellings of the holy secret name of God, a name that was chanted by the heirophant or high priest. Chanting the name would drive down brainwave frequency, induce an Alpha state and open up a higher consciousness.

Research into birdsong may eventually lead to some revelations about the internal process involved when humans chant and sing. The part of a bird's brain which is responsible for song enlarges as the spring days lengthen. This process, originally thought to be controlled by testosterone, has now been shown to be controlled by melatonin. Gregory Ball and George Bentley of John Hopkins University, and Thomas Vant Hof, of the Max Planck Institute, have demonstrated this in experiments with starlings. *The Times* newspaper quoted Dr. Bentley:

> 'We would never have discovered this if we had started out trying to see what melatonin is doing in humans," he says. "Now, with this discovery, we can feed back the information to other scientists and perhaps help them to understand what is happening in other species."' [56]

I would like to offer some observations for consideration in future research: The parts of the human body that are stimulated most by changes in brainwave pattern and by fluctuations in the electromagnetic field are the pituitary and pineal glands. The major reason why they are more sensitive than other areas is due to the presence of a tiny quantity of magnetite within the ethmoid bone, within which both of these glands are situated. This seems to be the pattern within life in general – even bacteria have been shown to carry tiny crystals of magnetite. It is interesting that in the case of human beings, the magnetic source should be located close to the pineal gland. The pineal gland has long been associated by magicians, shamans and diviners with the occult and with the psychic. A tiny cone-shaped gland, situated deep within the brain, the pineal is responsible for the secretion of melatonin and seratonin over each 24 hour period. Melatonin is associated with relaxed states. Seratonin acts in the opposite way. Esoterically speaking, the pineal gland is associated with the third eye, *El Ayin*, the eye of Horus.

Returning to the cry of the quetzal, what is extraordinary is that it is very like the cry of Dionysus, or even the cry of Jesus upon the cross. The Dionysion cry is *'Euoii, Euoii'*, whereas that of Jesus is *'Eloi, Eloi'*. However, the strangest and most startling correlation is to be found within the mysteries of Mithras:

> 'I invoke the immortal names, living and honoured, which never
> pass into mortal nature and are not declared in articulate speech
> by human tongue or mortal speech or mortal sound:
> 'EEO OEEO IOO OE EEO EEO OE EO IOO OEEE OEE OOE IE
> EO OO OE IEO OE OOE IEO OE IEEO EE IO OE IOE OEO
> EOE OEO OIE OIE EO OI III EOE OYE EOOEE EO EIA AEA
> EEA EEEE EEE EEE IEO EEO OEEEOE EEO EYO OE EIO EO
> OE OE EE OOO YIOE.'[57]

There is plenty more of this within the same text, much of it in the same repeatable binary code-type system.

The god of healing, the saviour god of the Aztecs, was Quetzalcoatl, the god of spirit of life, symbolised in the breath of the wind. He was the son of the Sun and of Mother Earth. To the Mayans he was Kukulcan, to the Yucatecs he was Itzamna. As we can see, the Gisa name is again present (a 'G' prefix would have been used in the Middle East, giving 'Gitza'). Quetzalcoatl, Itzamna, both names mean 'feathered serpent'. This reminded me of the Sumerian god 'Ningiszida', the great healer who watches over the underworld. His symbolic creature is the horned snake. As if in confirmation of yet another global mythic connection, Quetzalcoatl rescued humanity from the depths of the underworld.

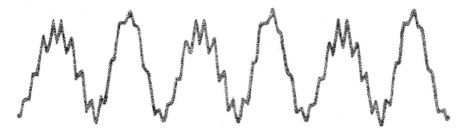

A graphic representation of the sound 'ee'. Note the terraced pyramidal forms.

The 'EE-OO' of the Mayans is a version of their secret sacred name of God. David Lubman gained his insight into the Mayan pyramid through seeing a representation of Kukulcan in Mayan art where Kukulcan was portrayed holding a large quetzal. In comparing his recording of the echo to the cries of the quetzal, he found that not just the cry was familiar but so too the range of frequencies involved. Lubman has gone on to find other examples of the cry matching the site.[58] The downside is that there is little independent evidence that Mayan civilisation based its ceremonies upon quetzal cries. However, we have seen that it is not customary for secret holy names to be well advertised. I, for one, would be very interested to see what the effects of rending such cries, *in situ*, would have upon brainwave frequencies.

The name of the god was a mantra, and as such it went abroad, outwards from its source. In this form it was secure, for it was so entirely holy that, quite often, only those who were holy in themselves could carry it. As we have seen, in Hebrew script the vowels were sacred and concealed, whereas in speech they filled in the consonant-formed words with vowels in order to give those words their real power and meaning. As Jonathan Goldman explains:

> 'The vowels were originally very special sonics indeed, being mostly used for "God names" and other sacred purposes. Consonants gave words their bodies, but vowels put soul into them. Taken together in combination, the vowels will "spell" the Name of the Living One: I.A.O.; IEOA; HU; YAH; etc. Whichever way they are connected, they signify Divinity enlivening Existence and hence were sacred in all Magical practices... Thus the vowels are to language what Life and Consciousness are to Existence.[59]

As Jonathan Goldman further points out:

'In traditional Hebrew Kabala, there are certain sacred names associated with specific spheres. These are names which, when chanted like a mantra, will cause the reciter to resonate to the frequency of the sphere. This is another aspect of sacred sonic entrainment similar to the practices of tantra, utilized by Tibetan monks, in which the practitioner, working with vocalization and visualization, recites a specific mantric form designed to invoke a particular deity. While visualising this entity the practitioner writes with it.'[60]

The act of chanting the vowel sounds can have a considerable effect upon states of consciousness. Each one of the vowels, chanted in a specific combination, can create particular forms of resonance. In the Western alphabet there are five vowels: 'a''e''i' 'o''u', whereas in ancient Egyptian and Hebrew and other ancient languages there were quite often seven, the additional vowels being a simple doubling: 'aa' and 'oo'. William Grey has done much work on this.

'In Grey's work, the vowel A (ah) is equated with the element of Earth and the direction of the North; the vowel E (ee) is equated with the element of Air and the direction of the East, the vowel I (ai) is equated with the element of fire and the direction of the South, and the vowel O (oh) is equated with the element of Water and the direction of the West and the vowel U (oo) is equated with the element of the Aether (which he called the element of Universal truth) and the direction is "around and about".'[61]

The ancient Egyptians, amongst others, believed that the human body houses seven souls. It is known that they used choirs within the pyramids and that they also used seven vowels to enliven states of consciousness within the body. Could these seven bodies and seven vowels be related to the seven musical notes? I believe that we should realise that there is a direct correlation between the various states of energy around us, music, consciousness and the divine. This would be confirmed by my sojourn in the land of the pharaohs.

10

In the Realm of the Mer

'I am the eye with which the Universe
Beholds itself and knows itself divine;
All harmony of instrument or verse,
All prophecy, all medicine is mine,
All light of art or nature; – to my song
Victory and praise in its own right belong.'

Percy Bysshe Shelley
Hymn of Apollo

A Little History of Ancient Egypt

THE origins of Egypt lie deep in the mists of prehistory. From out of these unknown depths came arguably the greatest of all civilisations, certainly in terms of longevity.

There is evidence of human activity in Egypt as long ago as *c.*700,000 BC. twentieth-century archaeology has revealed much about the landscape and its people before what is termed 'civilisation'[1] came to the region. There are, however, aspects that remain deeply enigmatic, particularly as regards Egypt's role in the development of civilisation and how that development came about. Perhaps one of the greatest mysteries is the cultivation of grain and the domestication of animals. Neolithic (New Stone Age) culture is said to have existed at more or less the same level the world over at approximately the same period, *c.*6000 BC. According to the archaeological evidence, which must necessarily be material in form, these people were at a rudimentary stage in their development, culturally they were simple, and language, it is assumed, did not exist in any written form and was thus at a basic level of sophistication. Very little has been found that might counter this view. This, as I have implied, is the firmly materialist view, but the evidence of grain and cattle suggests a greater antiquity for 'civilised' man. As John Anthony West most lucidly explains:

'The manner in which wild grains were originally cultivated and wild animals permanently domesticated is one of those questions that cannot be satisfactorily answered, but a period of long development is assumed. The fact is that throughout recorded history, no new animals have been domesticated; our domestic beasts have been around since the beginning, and no new grains have been cultivated.

'The cultivation of grain and the domestication of animals probably represent – after the invention of language – the two most significant human achievements. We can fly to the moon today, but we cannot domesticate the zebra, or any other animal.'[2]

Whatever the current archaeological view might be, the question of domestication and cultivation remains largely unanswered. I agree with John Anthony West when he suggests that attributing these great achievements to those we perceive as flint chippers and crude potters is a little premature. We do not have enough evidence, as yet, to prove the argument either way, so rich is the land of Egypt in archaeological terms and so small is the profession of Egyptology. So far, recognisable elements of a culture have been discovered that may date back as far as 7000 BC. However, what we today recognise as the ancient Egyptian culture began to emerge in what archaeologists call the Pre-Dynastic period (see appendix for Dynastic Table). The formative years of this period were the third and fourth millennia BC.[3] From out of these early times arose the Early Dynastic period, although as a preface to this era, which saw the rise of the first pharaonic dynasties, recent excavations have revealed a 'Dynasty 0' c.3300 BC. The first evidence of writing dates from this period – hieroglyphs from the era of 'King Scorpion'.[4] These glyphs portray natural features of the landscape, plants, animals and mountains, and are recognised as part of a complex written language. This implies an even greater antiquity for the rise of language and the surprise for archaeologists was that these writings demonstrate that the early Egyptians were far more developed than previously thought.

Dynasty 0 gave rise to Dynasty 1, and it is believed that somewhere between these two dynasties northern Egypt and southern Egypt were unified, hence the title of the pharaohs from this time on was 'Lord of the Two Lands'. The kings of the First Dynasty are semi-mythical characters with names like Narmer, Aha, Djer, Djet, Qaa, and so on. When I first saw the fabulous palette of King Narmer in the Cairo museum I was riveted by the fact that I was standing in front of an artefact probably used by a known historical character over 5,000 years ago. The names of these people and the beautiful artefacts that they left behind fascinated me – I was hooked.

The First and Second Dynasties (*c.*3000–2650 BC) gave rise to the Third Dynasty, and it was this Dynasty that saw Egypt begin a swift ascent to a glorious peak, before entering into a long, slow decline. King Djoser (see chapter eight) oversaw the construction of the first stepped pyramid at Saqqara (*c.*2667–2648), designed by the royal architect Imhotep, quite possibly the greatest genius in history. However, it was the next Dynasty, the Fourth, that saw the rise of the greatest monuments on earth – the three huge pyramids at Giza. There is, though, a fourth huge pyramid, the Red Pyramid at Dahshur, built by King Sneferu, the father of Khufu, who was the builder of the largest of the three mighty pyramids at Giza.

It was this period that interested me most and was to be the focus of my attention when it was drawn to Egypt. The entire era from the Third Dynasty until the close of the Seventh and Eighth is called the Old Kingdom (see table). After this, Egypt went into an intermediate phase that saw a brief cultural decline, before rising again in the Middle Kingdom period (*c.*2055–1650 BC). It is amazing to consider that it was to be another 300 years before the era of Akhenaten and Tutankhamun began, an extraordinary 1,300 years after the construction of the Giza pyramids.

After the era of Tutankhamun and the Ramesside kings, Egypt went into a third intermediate period and a swift decline, which saw the onset of invasion, first by the Persians and then by the Greeks and Romans. In 30 BC Octavian came to the throne as Roman Augustus and Egypt became yet another province in the Roman Empire. One of the major factors that made ancient Egypt so attractive to the invaders was the very same thing that made Egypt survive over so long a period – her fertility.

Egypt was called 'the Black Land' by her people, because of the silts washed down from the Ethiopian highlands, over 1,500 miles upstream. The 'inundation' took place during the month of June and fertilised a strip of land. It was a narrow strip which, less than two miles out on either side of the river, turned immediately to desert. It is in this sense that the Nile was Egypt. Egyptian life revolved around the Nile and the Nile was mother of her people. Unlike the land of the two rivers, further east in Mesopotamia, which flooded at irregular intervals causing chaos, death and destruction, the Nile was reliable, as reliable, in fact, as any modern timepiece. If the Nile rose, it must be June. This sense of constancy pervaded all things Egyptian. To her people, Egypt was 'the beloved land' as well as 'the land of the beloved', a reference to the goddess Isis, hence the oldest of the names for the land of Egypt – Ta-Mery. This is the name mentioned in the Old Testament story of Judah and the rape of Tamar – i.e. Egypt.

Literally, Ta-Mery means 'the Place of the Mr'[5] and 'Mr' has been understood as meaning 'canal' or 'waterway'. However, given the definite article, '*the* Mr', 'Mr' must translate as something more specific. In chapter eight we saw that the hieroglyph of 'Mr' is a pyramid △ , meaning a tomb,[6] it is also the name of certain specific royal pyramids, most notably those of the Giza plateau. This hieroglyph encompasses the concept of the divine power of the 'Mr', in other words, Mary carrying the divine child. 'Mr' is another hieroglyph for the goddess Isis, although rarely used outside the Old Kingdom period.[7] It simply means 'beloved', the title of Isis, whose name in Egyptian is Ast (sometimes Aust). This is represented by the hieroglyph for the throne, ⌐ .[8] Isis was therefore the Egyptian throne, and the pharaohs were seated upon her lap, protected by her outstretched winged arms. Isis carried upon her crown the symbol of 'Mu'at', meaning 'the foundation of the throne'.

We have already established the great mother goddesses as the substratum of life. In the same way, we can see that the power of the beloved, Mr, who is Isis, is actually the underlying principle behind the throne. We will come to the actuality of this power shortly. It is, however, significant that the man sitting in Isis' lap, the Pharaoh, is in fact a 'great house' – the precise meaning of the word 'pharaoh'. In other words, the power of Isis runs through that same house; and as if to underscore this, a pharaoh was the living embodiment or incarnation of Horus, the child of Isis and Osiris, the same divine child that the Mr – Mery – carried in her womb. The essence of this mystery is beautifully summed up by Timothy Freke and Peter Gandy:

> 'To the initiates of the Mysteries, a human being consisted of a material body and a spiritual soul. Our divine "father" is God, who gives us our immortal soul, our material "mother" is the Earth (matter), who gives us a mortal body. Matter cannot give birth alone, but is mysteriously impregnated by invisible Spirit to produce Life, and so is portrayed as a perpetual virgin.'[9]

Matter is the 'rock', the feminine, the substance which is impregnated by that which moves, the 'lifestream', also symbolised as blood, that which streams throughout the body to give life. As we can see, the language of the ancient Egyptians can seem very complex, but it need not be.

When I first saw hieroglyphs carved upon a stele, I was entranced by them, but the first thing that struck me was how 'unconscious' they seemed. Now this may be an odd thing to say about these enigmatic symbols, but something about them went straight into the depths of my mind, as if something primordial were trying to get through to it. In a word, the experience was 'magical'. In contrast, in the modern world – the Western world of the twenty-first century – 'magic' is a word largely disapproved of. It is almost unthinkable to use it when trying to explain the phenomenal world. This leads me on to the separation of magic, religion and science. The Church is losing its power because it is losing its magic – a word that it abhors. I remember from my boyhood the magical quality of *The Book of Common Prayer*, its beautiful language and the sheer grace of it. Many years later the misnamed ancient *Egyptian Book of the Dead* (actually, *The Book of Coming Forth by Day*) did the same for me, and the two are easily comparable, for the magic is in the language.

For the Egyptians, hieroglyphs were most certainly a living link between the cosmic mind and the human mind. By now I was entirely convinced that the key to myth lay in language and also its representation in fundamental form: hieroglyphics – the representation of actual images as a means of thought transference, the same kind of symbolic language that speaks to us in dreams and in visions, and which is the basis of all religious thought and inspiration. Language is an expression of that which is conscious, and consciousness is, for me at least, expressed in myth. The hero myth, about birth, life, death and regeneration, about the cycle of the seasons and the crops and their fertility, as conveyed in the purest linguistic terms, actually represents the divine power of the earth and the cosmos.

Hieroglyphs are an emotional expression of a universe built upon patterns of sand. I will come to an explanation of what exactly I mean in a while, but as you will have noticed in reading this work, time and again many strange things boil down to language, as if we are being told something. A practical example of this is cymatics – the study of waveforms. When a voice intones into a tonoscope which feeds the vibration onto a membrane covered with scattered sand, the sand, in response to the vibrations, accumulates within the areas of little or no vibration. The patterns formed often express various religious meanings. Chanting the 'Om' produces a mandala in the sand. In another example, I have seen a chanting male voice, intoning an 'o' sound, produce a ⊙ hieroglyph. This fascinated me; in fact it produced an emotional response within me (not an unremarkable event, given my English upbringing!) As we have seen, resonance does some remarkable things and this hieroglyph is indeed remarkable – it is the glyph for Ra, the Egyptian sun god. Furthermore, recent astronomical observations carried out by the Soho satellite have confirmed that the sun does indeed 'sing', at a very low resonance.

From the very brief accounts of things Egyptian that I have given, it is easy to see why the Egyptians were held in such high esteem by the Greeks, the Romans, by scholars, geniuses and by ordinary men and women. When Champollion finally managed to break through the enigmatic facade presented by hieroglyphs in 1822, it is said that the great mystery of ancient Egypt faded away. But the truth is that, if anything, Egypt became yet more of a riddle – for it was obvious from the outset that hieroglyphic was a very complex language. What's more, it seemed to confirm another popular misconception – that ancient Egypt was a land full to the brim of gods but with no overall

'One God'. Again, within the concept of 'the gods' we come to a superb demonstration of ancient Egyptian logic – that the concept of God is so vast that a man cannot encompass it, except perhaps in the abstract, and therefore, what could be more useful than the idea that God is expressed as the sum of every divine part? The gods of Egyptian theology were expressions of the many divine aspects of God:

> '... for learned ancient Egyptians, there has persistently been a single God who has staged the entire combined polytheistic show. No less than nine divine names were fused at Heliopolis into a single Ennead, a Ninefoldness. On what basis could a Christian scholar classify his own theological "Trinity" as monotheism and keep insisting that the Heliopolitan "Ennead" belongs to polytheism?'[10]

To say that the ancient Egyptians had 'gods' may, though, be an exaggeration, for the many aspects of one God were not referred to as 'gods', but as *neterw* (pronounced 'net-er-oo'). The singular of this is *neter*. A *neter* was a divine principle. The fact that many of these *neters* were portrayed as animal-headed is not a sign of a primitive society, but rather of a sophisticated one (*soph* meaning 'wisdom'), for animals themselves represented principles within nature, principles that were divine and that served as functions. The falcon-headed god Horus represents, for example, the principle of resurrection, as does the scarab beetle. The stork, which in fairy tales is the bringer of babies, is actually the symbol of the migrating soul, and so it goes on, for there are many examples. This in itself is a wonderful illustration of the complexities of meaning within the hieroglyphic language, which, if understood properly, can reveal some amazing things.

This brings to mind a point that I believe is cogent. Today we have words for virtually everything, from the merest flicker of emotion to the vastness of outer space, and in its way language has evolved into a tangled bundle of specificalities. It is almost as if the poetry of language is fading fast, in that we can reduce a thing by labelling it. Man has labelled himself into a corner by almost removing the unconscious from language. When we see a thing we have a word for it – a specific word, a direct word, not one which implies connectivity – and enquiry stops with this word's existence. Conversely, when we observe the collective achievement of ancient Egypt, is it really fair to label the Egyptians 'primitive' because one word could mean many things? Rather, such a word, because of its subtle application of meaning, would encourage the speaker to give it the proper expression and refined intonation, thus developing a deep understanding of its subtlety and its breadth. These people designed and constructed pyramids, whilst in the modern world, where we have machinery to do the hard work for us, we struggle to understand how the Ancients accomplished such a thing. Why then should we look down upon their language?

I am not denying our own achievements, nor am I trying to laud our ancestors and give them credit for ideals that come purely from my mind. The point is that the average ancient Egyptian would have considered a problem from such an entirely different perspective: their view was probably less specific than it was whole. Language, the gods and their temples, the very act of living, were all intimately associated with and within the divine principles, and the sense that these selfsame principles were eternal and infinite. Whatever sense of time the Egyptians had, the gods, and ultimately God, were beyond it. Everything that happened did so in an eternal sense of now – the *neterw*, or gods, were not associated with the past or future tense.[11] In the Egyptian scriptures no references have been found to the limitations of time. The present tense conveys the eternal sense of immanence, the actual feeling of the numinous. It is this very same feeling that brings man to the edge of understanding the gods and the greatest mystery of all – for throughout the long life of ancient Egypt there was only ever one real mystery: the creation itself.

Creation, Resonance and Awareness

The creation of matter *ex nihilo* – out of nothing – ranks as the greatest of mysteries, not only for the ancient mind but for the modern mind too. For physicists it has become a holy grail, as they seek a theory that unites the very large – relativity and gravity – with the very small, the quantum world of sub-atomic particles, so far unsuccessfully. But perhaps a clue to the unravelling of the mystery can be found, after all, in the ancient Egyptian *Pyramid Texts*, collectively known as the *Book of the Dead*. What they seem to reveal is an idea that has only recently begun to appeal to physics, the idea of consciousness manifesting as energy.

'Energy' expresses the principle of something active. It comes ultimately from the Greek *energeia* meaning 'activity', this being two syllables, *en* and *ergon* meaning 'in' and 'work'. Energy as a concept thus expresses a kind of movement or motion. This is interesting because physicists are beginning to theorise that even before the hypothesised 'Big Bang' that gave rise to the universe, there must have been some kind of movement within the pre-primordial energy fields whereby Creation was brought about.

However, if we now extend this concept to accommodate the ideas of the ancient Egyptian creation mythos, we will see that at the beginning of all things the god Tum became aware of himself, and in so doing created Atum, the creator god, out of Nun, the primeval waters. In this sense, Tum is transcendent cause; in becoming self-aware he not only regards himself but all the universe too. This is expressed by the primal vowel, 'a', hence, Atum. Furthermore, Tum, in becoming self-aware, becomes self-conscious. Reality is born. If this all sounds rather tricky, bear with me, because when I express it differently the penny will drop.

This basic concept of the creation bears a striking resemblance to the Gnostic idea of matter and creation. Tum is the unknowable, ineffable, unspeakable Godhead, who in becoming self-aware creates, or becomes, the Gnostic 'demiurge'. Required in all of this is the image of the feminine, of Isis the goddess, who was called, even in the earliest days, the Oldest of the Old. From a cursory look at the creation texts, Isis would appear to have been the concept of the whole, just as Gnosticism informs us. However, the whole needs to stir, to vibrate, something needs to 'move across the waters' ('the waters' being a common term for the cosmic expanse). An explanation would be that consciousness would be there before creation, for it is the 'I AM', the ever-still, knowing, observer. The creation then arises through a duality represented by male and female. The female is the substance, the male is that which brings movement. Another analogy is the receptacle and that which fills it. Both of these explanations are reflected in the sexual act. Through the motion, relativity begins, worlds are created and the 'I AM' observes itself in the myriad forms. In Christianity we have seen how 'the rock' is related to the substratum and the substance, but in Christian ritual, the substance is usually represented by bread and the movement by wine which, as I have mentioned, represents the lifeblood of the creation reflected in the ever-moving lifestream of the human body. Wine is used because it also represents the divine intoxication which can be experienced by the individual when these godly forces are at work.

Thus the concept of a great god and great goddess in motion brings us to another important expression referred to earlier – emotion.

Emotion is from the Latin *emovere*, which consists of two elements, 'e' and *movere*, meaning 'to move'. The 'e' is taken as meaning *ex* – 'out of'. So emotion is, or arises, 'out of movement'. However, the involvement of the letter 'e' does not end there, because it is also an expression of the third note of the diatonic scale of C major. This note corresponds to 'Mi' in the 'Doh-Ray-Mi' notation. Furthermore, 'Mi' (or 'Me') was, according to the *Oxford English Dictionary*, originally the first syllable of the Latin *mira*. We are back to pyramids again, to ancient Egyptian – Mr.

The exploration goes yet further, for 'Mi' is the third note of the hexachord, a row of six notes ('hex' from Egyptian *heqa* – 'lord of'). 'Doh-Ray-Mi', etc., originally gave their names to the six notes of the hexachord. This was a formulation brought about by an eleventh–century monk by the name of Guido d'Arezzo (*c*.AD 995–1050). What intrigued me about Guido was that he was no ordinary monk, but a Benedictine, a follower of St. Benedict, who as we have seen was, in all probabilty, none other than Apollo Benedictus – Apollo also known as 'the Good Speaker'. Resonance again – and here the voice of the God and of gods in general becomes exceedingly interesting. The names of the six notes of the hexachord may be found in the hymn for St. John the Baptist's Day' (24th June), which happens to coincide with the annual flooding of the Nile. Oddly enough, it was St. John's father, Zacharias, who, upon hearing of his wife's pregnancy, sang the Benedictus as a hymn of thanksgiving. The hymn to St. John features all of the musical syllables and key encoded words so far revealed within this text:

'*Ut* queant laxis *re*sonare fibris *Mi*ra gestorum *fa*muli tuorum, *So*lve polluti *la*bii reatum, Sancte Iohannes.'[12]

A translation would be, 'So that servants may sing with loose strings and can sing of your wonderful deeds, St. John, loosen the charge of defiled lips.' A request for purification before the singing of praises?

It seems, though, that the outer meaning is secondary to the sounds and the effects they may have. Within these lines we not only have the six notes of the hexachord, (see the italicised syllables) but also various expressions of the names of the gods. We have here *resonare* , resonance; *Mira* , Egyptian Mr, the beloved of God, Mary; and directly after that *gestorum*, which, as it relates to the holy guest or ghost – the divine in the body – is also used as another expression of the name of Jesus. So what is it that I am getting at?

In the beginning God is said to have uttered the Word. The movement of energy needed to utter that Word, no matter how infinitesimally small, would have created motion, energy motion: e-motion. And out of (Latin *e* or *ex*) this would have come the expression of the Word and Creation. To the ancient mind this was and is an ever-continuing process. Plato expressed it thus:

'Pure being was confronted with non-being, and the result was becoming.'[13]

This is the fundamental ancient Egyptian concept.

Something from Nothing

A few years ago I found myself in the Valley of the Kings. I was visiting the tomb of Pharaoh Ramesses VI (reigned *c*.1141–1133 BC). As I entered the tomb and began the slow descent into the darkness, I could make out murals. These murals give a picture of Ramesses' soul in the afterlife and his perilous ascent into the Duat, guarded and guided by various incantations from the *Book of the Dead*.

The hieroglyphs signalling the beginning of this journey are sited very close to the entrance, and amongst the first of them I noticed the symbols of the *neterw*, looking rather like the flags on a golf course. There were seven of them in a row – ⌐⌐⌐⌐⌐⌐⌐ .These were preceded and followed by the royal crowns of Upper and Lower Egypt. The crowns, I was sure, marked the beginning and ending of a cycle, so that their combined value would have been a whole, a unity. I realised that what this opening hieroglyphic sequence was expressing, taken as a whole, was the cosmic octave – the hieroglyphs in this tomb were meant to be sung or chanted. It was only after my return from Egypt that I learnt that hieroglyphs were known as 'Words of the God'.[14] What this said to me was quite revelatory: that all sound and all language is but a further emanation of the very first primordial Word uttered by God.

This was reflected by one of those nice synchronicities that happen from time to time. I was listening to a piece of music by the American composer Edgar Varese (1885–1965), when I picked up the CD case and read the accompanying information. Apparently, Varese had a strong belief that sound had an intelligence of its own. The more I looked at the myths of creation, the more I realised that this is precisely what these myths are trying to tell us. The organising powers of nature, the gods, are sound, subtle vibration. The more I looked, the more everything fell into place.

The hieroglyphic symbol for unity, for the figure 1, is ⬯ . It represents the open mouth and the creation of all from nothing by God. Its meaning is 'primordial scission', being the division and separation from out of the ineffable, and is philosophically unfathomable and incomprehensible. For '1' is the absolute whole – from out of the One, multiplicity came forth, all matter, all words, all number.

The ancient Egyptians held that before all things there was a primeval abyss of waters, everywhere and infinite, endless, with no boundary and no direction, a limitless void, the infinite, as yet unmoving, substance.

This sounds amazingly like recent scientific speculation about the nature of the universe. It is estimated that a vast quantity of the universe, known as dark matter, which has been sought over the decades using a whole gamut of experimental equipment and data, might actually be made up of hydrogen, the chief component of water. On 8th May 2000, it was announced that the Hubble Space Telescope had at last located some of this missing water.[15] The hydrogen was to be found in the spaces between clusters of galaxies and it accounts for nearly half the known matter in the universe.

Now, interestingly, water is one of the greatest carriers of energy, if not the greatest, and the universe is a sea of energy. Within this there is a phenomenon known as 'zero-point energy', which is contained within a 'zero–point field'. This is an all-pervading electromagnetic field that exists within a quantum vacuum. Zero-point energy is basically the vibrational energy associated with matter as the matter itself is defined all the way down to zero. In effect a zero point is a point of stillness in a universe that is totally in motion. Now, if all of this seems complex, let me get to another point: that zero is defined as 'neuter', meaning 'neither masculine nor feminine'. 'Neuter' is from the Latin and beyond that its etymology is uncertain. But given its definition it seems obvious to me, particularly considering its spelling, that its origin is Egyptian: *neter*. The reason why others have hesitated to come to the same conclusion is that it has been taken for granted that none of the historical peoples of the Middle East had a concept of zero. This is based upon a dearth of proper evidence, but no evidence does not mean that they did not have it. My speculation is that as a theological and mathematical concept it was considered so secret, so dangerous even, that the understanding of it was limited to a select few, the initiates of the mysteries. To understand a point of zero is to come close to a greater understanding of creation, for Nothing defines Everything.

As we have already discovered, water, called *hydras* by the ancient Greeks, was associated with strange qualities and was a prime ingredient in the construction of the sacred site. It was with this in mind that I visited one of the most mysterious and possibly one of the most ancient temples in Egypt – the Osireion. Quite literally it is deluged in water, so much so that little of it can be seen. To my mind this was a part of its actual purpose; the Egyptians were very good at pointing to the completely obvious. The Primeval Hill in the centre of the great hall is totally covered with water. This reflects the myth of the creation, for, in the beginning, God created a primordial mound or bennu which rose up out of the waters. It was from this first dry spot that God went on to polish off the task.

As we can see, the hieroglyph of unity – ⬯ – resembles, in fact *is*, a *vesica piscis*, exactly the same as the cathedral tympanum, in the centre of which sits Jesus enthroned. Jesus is again being implied as sound. Furthermore, the glyph looks like a vibrating string. It has recently been speculated that the universe is nothing but a gigantic standing-wave pattern, vibrating to the tune of billions upon billions of frequencies. It is this vibrational energy that is set in train from the finest to the gross level; and everywhere this energy continues to be moved by the initial breath of God – the Word. Another thing that caught my attention was the similarity of this glyph to an eye. In fact what really struck me was its resemblance to the perceived shape of a flying saucer. We are back again at the Hebrew-Greek-Egyptian *ayin*, the eye, in this case the eye of God. If we place within it, the hieroglyph for the sun god Ra, the determinative that means light and time, we end up with what is clearly an eye – . Thus we now have, from the initial Word of Creation, light and its measure, time.[16]

So, if we now look at the texts in the order of the story that they are telling, the first thing that must be corrected, from the standpoint of their subsequent influence, is the opening line to the Book of Genesis, which has been translated as:

'In the beginning God created the heaven and the earth.'

The more direct translation is:

'The Lord of the beginning created...'

This is more sophisticated: Tum, the transcendent, becomes aware as Atum, this is the beginning. From the self-aware Lord, come all of the pantheon. The divine breath is facilitated or given form by the god Ptah. And this divine breath is the sound of the Om, sometimes spelt Aum – this seems to be a variation of Atum's name, with a silent 't'. Atum is the Word. Ptah is the creative power immanent in Atum – the demiurge. Atum appears in the Bible as Adam, whose son is Cain, the Hebrew equivalent of Ptah. Atum is the god who fell to earth, whose name means 'the complete one'. Ptah's facilitation of the Word is reflected in the sheer power of the opening to St. John's Gospel:

'In the beginning was the Word, and the Word was with God,
and the Word was God.
The same was in the beginning with God.'

John 1:1–2

According to Egyptian belief, the heart and the tongue represented thought and speech, attributes of the Creator that were deified as Horus and Thoth. By bringing forth thought and speech Ptah brings forth order from chaos, and the gods come into existence.[17] This is well expressed in the idea that the Word, vibration, facilitates self-luminosity as exemplified by the sun. This is where Ra, the self-luminous one, comes into his own. The disc hieroglyph representing Ra, who at the creation is Atum-Ra, is also the 'eye' of 'Khepera', the Egyptian verb 'to be'. Ra sails around the heavens in his boat of millions of years, with all the other gods in tow. He is the pilot, the navigator of the celestial waters. The boat of Ra was sometimes called Ur or Uru, or even Makaa, which means 'great protector' – literally calling self-luminosity the great 'AA', the double vowel of Creation. So in this sense, creation is a process of quantum sound expanding ever outwards. It is interesting that the later word 'sound' is related to that for 'sun'. In Anglo-Norman the word is *sun*, whereas 'sun' in the English of the Middle Ages is *son* or *sonne*. Here we see the relationship between all three: 'sound' is the child of God, so is the sun and so is a son (or, of course, a daughter, the tradition of sexism now being over).

In the *Corpus Hermeticum*, Asclepius warns King Ammon not to translate the Egyptian mysteries into Greek. The quotation is a good analysis of the nature of words:

> 'For the Greeks, O King, who make logical demonstrations, use words emptied of power, and this very activity is what constitutes their philosophy, a mere noise of words. But we [Egyptians] do not use 'words' *[logoi]* but 'sounds' *[phonai]* which are full of effects.'[18]

This reflects my own earlier expressed sympathies.

The power of the Word is expressed in another version of the creation myth wherein a heron-like bennu bird flies over the waters of the primeval abyss and alights upon a stone or rock. It then emits a piercing cry to break the silence of the abyss. The bennu bird is the bird recognised by the Greeks as the mythical phoenix, also identified as Osiris, who is said to have uttered his name at the creation. The *Edfu Texts* are explicit in stating that it took seven words or sounds to create the world. In the Old Testament, God takes six days to create all things and on the seventh rests. Oddly enough the 'seven words' of the *Edfu Texts* become trapped in a chest, rather like Osiris, who is also trapped in a chest. Is this a reference to God's secret powerful name being made up of the seven primal notes? Is this the original name of Osiris?

This brought me back to Guido d'Arezzo's hexachord, which, as the *Oxford Companion to Music* points out, is in reality a heptachord – seven notes, not six – Doh-Ray-Me-Fah-Soh-Lah-Te. There seems to be a long religious tradition of preserving the sacred words of God, a tradition that tells that all is music.

This struck a chord, which in turn brought something else to mind. In Greek the word 'chord' also reveals a certain amount about the mechanics behind creation. Spelt χορδε, transliterated as 'chorde' and meaning 'of the emotions', the Greek word contains the letters Chi, Omicron, Rho, Delta and Epsilon.

The Chi Rho was of course the symbol that Constantine saw, the great cross in the sky, but here in this instance we have the two separated by Omicron, O. This is symbolic of the pineal gland, the *Ayin* of Hebrew and Egyptian. The cross is symbolic of matter. Rho is the creative female principle; it is the power of fertility, of reproduction. This aspect of 'chord' suggests 'awareness', in the form of the 'O', of the two creative principles, Chi and Rho. The ChiRho represents the cross of the hero and the 'O' our awareness of it – God within us. The philosopher Iamblichus (second century AD) stated that the names of the gods were impressed on souls before birth and that theurgic chants awakened them. Theurgy was the magical system practised by the Egyptians for the invocation of beneficent spirits.

At the beginning of time it all came down to words and music. When I looked at the words I could see why: God, whose name means 'voice' (see glossary and chapter six), 'expressed' the Word – 'ex' meaning 'out of' and 'press' as in 'pressure'. This gave rise to the 'universe', literally 'one' – 'uni', 'word' – 'verse', one word. Thus the Word 'reverberated', from 'verb' – 'word' and 're' – 'back'. In other words, the Word bounced back and forth like an echo. The Word, the thought of God musing upon the state of self-awareness, became music, from 'muse', 'to reflect in silence'. This music shattered the silence. The music was a reflection of the 'experience' of awareness, in Latin *expriri*, 'out of trying, effort'. This is related to 'expire', in Latin *expirare* – 'to breathe out'. That which was breathed out was the spirit, literally the breath, of God. It is this in its form of music that 'resounded' around the newly formed universe – resonance. These elements were the 'humour' of God, 'the love of the Lord'. Now at last I could understand my 'enthusiasm' for the task, literally *en theos* – 'in God'. The next time I meet any enthusiastic atheists I'll correct them!

Suddenly, I was 'exhilarated', literally *ex hilare* – 'out of laughter'. No wonder the old Roman festival celebrating God's son was called the Hilaria, where the Romans made 'merry' (from the word 'Mary', 'the beloved of God'). Something had emerged out of nothing – ex ni*h*ilo . And the gods laughed. So did I!

The Power of the Word

The Word is all around us, within the universe. Within one word – universe – there are billions of vibratory permutations that give the universe its momentum. As these words spin around the cosmos, they form little vortices, giving rise to matter, to mass, volume, weight, gravity and quanta (the very small). And all of these cross-correlations of frequency make the universe what it is – home.

Science and religion are, it appears, speaking the same language. The universe, both will admit, is a mass of eternal creation. The recent research of

Professor Andre Linde of Stanford University, California, has suggested that the 'Big Bang' is a bit of an exaggeration. Rather it was a seething foam of Creation that, he suggests, will refresh and renew itself for eternity. Professor Linde believes that there was more than one bubble and that even though our section of the universe is created, other parts are still going through the process of Creation.[19] This view accords well with ancient conceptions of the Creation – that it is an ever-expanding, ongoing event. Another thing that accords is the structure of the hydrogen atom, which has a single proton and a single electron in orbit about a nucleus. The hieroglyph for the god Ra is startlingly reminiscent of this: ⊙ . Without hydrogen, there would be no water and thus no life.

Electrons, protons and nuclei have even smaller particles, sub-atomic particles, at their core. These bundles of quanta are in fact bundles of energy, vibrating at different but incredibly high frequencies. Frequency describes the rate of energy flow or the amount of energy in a particle or a bundle. It has also been suggested that gravity is an effect due to standing waves (see chapter five), moving in towards the ultimate structures of matter – in other words the interaction of different bands of frequency.[20] What seems to have happened throughout history is that these ideas[21] have been redefined, as language and understanding have changed their perspective over the course of millennia.

'Being is change, motion and rhythm, the irresistible circle of time, the incidence of the "right moment",' say de Santillana and von Dechend,[22] and I for one agree with them. Furthermore, it seems to me that resonance, the resonance of the Word, defines each moment by a deft act of consciousness.

The breath, *spiritus*, is released, and the primal substance moves, giving rise to cause and effect; the eternal is in motion, and time is born as a consequence. This description has barely changed through the centuries:[23] the Ancients' discovery is our rediscovery.

Even particle theory existed all those years ago. According to Sextus Empiricus (second century AD), it was not Democritus who first formulated atomic theory, but Moschus, a Phoenician, who, unlike Democritus, rightly believed that the atom was divisible. This is exceptional stuff given that Democritus is always given the credit for the discovery. The idea that even atoms are divisible is too often thought to be a modern discovery. Similar scientific observations were not rare. The philosophers Thales and Anaximenes both saw the Milky Way as being made up of an infinite number of stars and planets – just as astronomers, now discovering planets beyond our solar system, are beginning to realise.

There are many other instances where it is being revealed that the Ancients had more depth than we previously thought. The Kabalah, for example, is not just pure mysticism, but may have been describing complex mathematical concepts in a philosophic vein, the origin of today's scientific paradigm. The ten Sephiroth of the Kabalah, the ten branches of the Tree of Life, mean 'numerical emanations'. They are, as is now being discovered, 'nothing less than a mathematical blueprint of the cosmos'.[24] These branches are linked by 22 paths, which represent the psychological states of experience that are encountered as the Logos – the Word – descends into matter, or as the monad (soul) ascends to higher worlds.

> 'As can be done with most complex symbolism, the same glyph of ten sephiroth can be used to represent Dionysus' nine celestial hierarchies (plus a tenth for mankind), with seraphim or lords of love in Kother (the Crown), cherubim, the lords of harmony, in Chokmah (Wisdom), and thrones, or spirits of will in Binah (Intelligence). The rest follow in descending order into ever greater density ... which, according to Phillips, denotes equally the outer organic form of the Cosmic logos, the entire universe, this solar system, a human body, or a single evanescent subatomic particle.'[25]

Perhaps deeper even than this is the principle of the spin of the electron. Without it life and matter would be quite different – non-existent even.

The rotation of the sun gives off energy in the form of the solar wind – positive and negative particles that take about 48 hours to reach the earth. As the earth travels around the sun she receives this fertilising seed, which in many ways correlates closely to the 'breath of life'. The sun has two very distinct magnetic fields – the equatorial and the polar. The equatorial field consists of alternating negative and positive polarities and rotates at a different rate from the polar field. It has been calculated that every seven days the sun's radiation alternates in polarity. This correlates nicely with the description of God making the world in six days and then taking the seventh day off. This led me to the idea that perhaps, here again, the Ancients expressed the same concepts as us, but in a different, more poetic, language. It follows then that the ancient language of religion may well be an old language of science, a science based upon pure observation with an inherent subjective element. I decided to take a closer look.

In the Temple of Pharaoh Seti I (r.1291–1278 BC), the Pharaoh is shown receiving the 'water of life' from the gods. What is interesting about this is that the water is not portrayed as one might be inclined to think, as a torrent, but as a series of tiny ankhs. The ankh is the Egyptian cross, symbolic of life, and of matter. As can be seen, the ankh has a strange looping shape, reminiscent of a teardrop. Strange

The Ankh

looping figures like this also appear upon the
pyramid capstone of Amenemhet III, a Middle
Kingdom pharaoh (r.1842–1797 BC). They appear
right next to the figure of the celestial Osiris,
holding a star in his hand. The meaning of this
glyph varies, but in this context it means 'in the
neighbourhood of' (m-s ht): it is a variant spelling
of 'Sahu', the celestial Osiris. The glyph is telling
us that he is near.

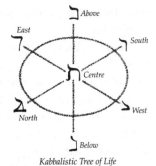

Kabbalistic Tree of Life

This reminded me of the later Hebrew tradition
regarding the origin of the double vowels. These seven double vowels, the
original elements of the primordial Word, were specifically related to the seven
directions of space, which they are also believed to have formed.

If we exclude the centre, these six directions correspond to the six types of
quark, the fundamental particle of matter. Scientists call these six types,
arbitrarily, 'strange', 'top', 'up', 'bottom', 'down' and 'charm'. Quarks combine
in twos or threes to form other particles, including electrons; in other words
they decay into larger particles, as all particles do.[26] However, it was when I
stood back to look at the Hebrew idea of the double vowels that I noticed
something really striking. Here we seem to have all the elements of the spin
ratio of a particle as it manifests in space. The particle concerned is the electron,
and electrons, as far as matter and life are concerned, are fundamental for the
negative charge. Electrons will give off radiation, unless they are in a stable
orbit. When giving off radiation, they are moving from one orbit to another.
Electrons, however, also absorb radiation; that means they move farther out
from the nucleus. It is this that defines the make up of the elements. This
behaviour of electrons gives rise to an easily observed set of spectral lines,
which can be used to identify the atoms of different chemical elements. When
electrons absorb energy, their frequency changes, thus changing the chemical
that they form, to a greater or lesser degree. Of all the particles so far defined,
it would seem that the electron is the one most responsive to other frequencies
and prone to change its own.

However, it is the spin ratio of the electron that is most of interest here, for
all particles spin in various orbitals. It is the nature of these electron orbitals

that gives a substance most of its physical and chemical
properties. Electrons, unlike most other particles, do not
follow a definite path around a nucleus. Instead they can
be found within orbitals, and these are arranged around
the nucleus of an atom like shells. There are 'S' orbitals,
'P' orbitals and 'D' orbitals. It is the 'D' orbital that is of
interest to us (*see illustration, left*), because it and the
Egyptian ankh are similar in shape, especially if you

imagine that the orbital is edge-on. Significantly, they both refer to the same thing – life.

The 'D' orbital consists of a 'bubble' that is actually a torus, a doughnut-shaped ring that has a rapid rotation. From within this rises a teardrop shape, through which flow spinning particles, sub-elements of the electron itself. Energy does not enter in, but rises up from the inside of this orbital. Without the 'D' orbital spin of an electron the spark of life would not exist, for this orbital defines the wavelength of the electron, as well as its frequency.

The other intriguing phenomenon that the shape of the ankh resembles is the teardrop shape of the earth's magnetic field, which extends outwards towards the sun as the magnetosphere. The lines of magnetic force flow downwards at the North Pole and upwards at the South Pole. Also part of the magnetosphere are the doughnut-shaped Van Allen radiation belts, which consist of highly energetic charged particles trapped within the earth's magnetic field. This most closely resembles one of the many variations on the theme of the ankh, in form and in motion, the variation from which, it is thought, the *fleur de lys* originated.

The fleur de lys

There were other cultures that used symbolism as a precise way of describing life. The Druidic and Celtic cultures spring to mind (see Anatomy of the Hero). Although seemingly less sophisticated than the Egyptians, they used a symbol, a 'cross of matter', very similar to the ansate cross or cross of Osiris. As a representation of creative power, as if from the cross, they used a trinity of rays, this was the AWE, /|\.

I find it quite extraordinary that modern theory should have been so accurately foreshadowed by the philosophical and also the alphabetical symbolism of the Ancients. Both Krishna and Christ declared that they were the first letter of the alphabet, the letter 'A'. Jesus stated, 'I am the Alpha and the Omega' (Revelations 1:8.). Omega is the sound of a long 'o', as in 'eau'. 'O' symbolises unity, the boundary of the universe, the world-egg of the Orphic Mysteries. *Eau* is the French for 'water', the water abyss of the primordial universe, until it was broken by the newly self-aware God, uttering the double vowel 'aa', the beginning. This 'aa' coming out of the toroidal 'o' again assimilates electron spin. What Jesus and Krishna are both stating is that they are at-one with the Lord of the beginning – God.

Prince Alpha and Omega

The name of Osiris in its later native Egyptian form – Middle Egyptian – is Asar. *Sar* means 'blood' or 'prince' (princes generally being 'of the blood'). Thus Osiris' name translates as Prince Alpha. Osiris' name in hieroglyphs is a throne above an eye, signs representing the syllables *as-ar*. Sometimes this is transcribed as Usir, or more commonly Wsir. There are many variations of the name; one has a *neter* symbol, ⌐, another has the symbol of Ra, (•), and yet another shows the crown of Upper Egypt, but all contain the throne and eye symbols.

Wallis-Budge concedes that the meaning of the name in its original sense is not known, and doubts that it is ever likely to be.[28] However, as I have already revealed, the myth and its location at a place of power offer us more than enough clues. The site itself would have inspired the initial human response in terms of a language with a mythic value that sprang from both the site and its direct experience. Hence the early hieroglyphic form of language. The key to the language was cross-correlation, at the site and beyond. This would have resulted in a lordly and inspired reaction – humour. Puns would have been the order of the day, without the barriers created by one word having only one particular meaning.

The key glyph in Osiris' name is the eye – *Ar – el Ayin*. The throne – *As* – is symbolic of the centre of all things, the axis. In hieroglyphs it is a determinative sign that embraces the concepts of equilibrium, support and exaltation. In Asiatic symbolism the throne stands midway between the mountain and palace on the one hand and the head-dress on the other.[29] If anything symbolised the pharaonic history of Egypt it was the crown – the head-dress, known as the *Nemes*.

The pun of Osiris' name Asar, is that it translates as Prince Alpha, yet, in its form Wsir, it also translates, much to the bemusement and annoyance of Egyptologists, as Prince Omega. In Greek the 'w' is a double 'u' and is cognate with 'w', and Hebrew 'Vav', represented by the glyph for the nail, ⌐, with which Jesus and the other heroes are crucified. In being the Alpha and Omega, Osiris is all things: it is his name in its seven-vowelled form that gave rise to all creation, and still does, for it is an ongoing process. In other words, it is a name of most considerable power.

There is a reflection of this in other mythologies of the world. In Mayan mythology, the god of death (Osiris too was a god of death), Yum Cimih, was also symbolised by the hieroglyph meaning 'completion'. He too was both a lord of the beginning and a lord of completion. There seem to be many striking parallels between Egyptian and South American culture, even though the two are separated not only by an ocean, but also by several millennia, with

South American culture dating to a much later era. The Mayans believed, like the Egyptians, that when they died their souls travelled to the underworld, facing trials along the way. Furthermore, rather like the Gaelic-Arabian linguistic similarities, Mayan and Egyptian language share extraordinary resemblances, even though both have many dialects. For example, the word *bak* in both languages means 'chickpea'. There are other correlations too that are mythological, architectural (pyramids) and linguistic.[30]

Alphabetically speaking, the shape of a pyramid is similar to that of an 'A'. The great German Rosicrucian, Jacob Boehme, proposed the idea that God could be represented by the letter 'A'. 'A' in German is Auge, meaning 'eye'. This is the all-seeing 'eye of God' that reflects the divine expression throughout the cosmos, and is the key to consciousness. The 'A' of *auge* would reflect its own 'A' which, as Boehme is quick to point out, gives a diamond-shaped glyph:

For Boehme, this was the image of the interpenetration of cosmos and man, of macrocosm and microcosm – the very large and the very small. This is an image to be found in many Kabalistic texts, as well as in Rosicrucianism and also in Freemasonry.

You may recall that Jesus, known to us as a carpenter, was actually a *tektos* – a builder. In Masonic imagery, God may be seen as the Great Architect, the builder of the 'great house' (in Egyptian, 'pharaoh'). In his hand are the callipers with which he sets out the measure of all. In Freemasonic symbolism there is a reflection of the imagery used by Boehme. The compass and the T-square of Freemasonry are shaped as *fig. 1* and *fig. 2* respectively. When placed together they form an ideogram *fig. 3* . This is one of the heretical symbols of the early medieval Albigensians, also known as the Cathars. This symbol appears in many watermarks of the period. It means, 'Thy kingdom come' and was expressed as an 'aspiration', literally the 'desire to rise up on the breath of God'. This drew my attention to its resemblance to a pyramid. The connection seemed obvious in view of the significance of architecture within Freemasonry and also in view of the pyramid name of Mr – Mary, the beloved of Osiris.

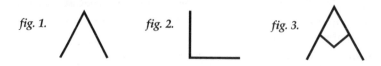

fig. 1.   *fig. 2.*   *fig. 3.*

Isis and Osiris, Jesus and Mary too

The legend of Isis and Osiris is amongst the most curious and the most beautiful in world history, as well as being amongst the most archaic. The earliest references to the legend appear in the fifth Dynasty *Pyramid Texts* (2498–2345 BC), which are so named because they are inscribed upon the interior walls of the Pyramid of Pharaoh Unas (r. 2375–2345). Until recently it was doubted whether the religion of Osiris had developed in archaic times. George Hart stated that the earliest known mention of Osiris is dated to the fifth Dynasty.[31] However, in contradiction to this, Professor Walter Emery[32] said in 1961 that Osiris' religion was already well advanced by the inception of what today we recognise as ancient Egypt. The discovery at Helwan of a girdle with the name of Isis was supplemented by the discovery of a hieroglyphic symbol of the god Osiris, a *djed* pillar, both of which dated to the first Dynasty. These symbols in themselves confirm the already well developed character of the religion.

It is in the Pyramid Texts that the story of Isis and Osiris is given its most complete airing. Isis and Osiris were the offspring of the earth god Geb and the sky goddess Nut. Geb and Nut were themselves the children of Shu, meaning 'air' or 'space', and Tefnut, the goddess of moisture. These two sprang from out of the Creator, Atum. Thus Osiris was a great-grandchild of the Creator, and was destined to become the lord of the underworld. So human is the story of Isis and Osiris that some commentators have suggested that it may in fact be based upon real historical figures. However, this element of humanity had a higher purpose – to draw man nearer to the gods and, ultimately, God. Osiris was the human aspect of God. After all, humankind was made in God's own image and Osiris was seen as the full realisation of that image. As the eldest son of Geb and Nut, Osiris inherited the right to the throne of Egypt. Osiris was a prototypical messiah, establishing the tradition of all heroes and all messiahs that came after.

The ancient texts tell us that, as the first Pharaoh of Egypt, after whom all other pharaohs were heirs or 'sons of Osiris' (Horus-Kings), Osiris set about civilising the barbarian[33] world by becoming its king. He taught the world how to grow and cultivate corn, how to worship and how to live in general; more importantly, he also educated the world, giving it wisdom and the alphabet (the hieroglyphic language). For these deeds he was called *wennefer* – 'eternally good'. Because of these things, Osiris' brother Set (Greek Typhon) became insanely jealous and plotted Osiris' downfall. Set gathered a gang of conspirators and they hatched a plan.

A magnificent wooden chest was constructed to Osiris' specific dimensions, and he was duly asked to come and view it. Set and his companions tried to fit themselves into the chest, but each, in turn, was unsuccessful. At last it was

Byblian palm tree

Osiris' turn, and, fitting into the box perfectly, he fell victim to the ploy. Set and his conspirators nailed down the lid of the chest and, with Osiris inside, threw it into the Nile. Osiris drowned, but the box made its way past the delta and across the sea to Byblos (modern-day Lebanon), where, mysteriously, it sprouted leaves and turned into a palm tree.[34] This palm tree was subsequently cut down and taken to the royal palace where it was used as a pillar.

In the meantime, Osiris' beloved wife Isis, distraught at the disappearance of her husband, went in search of him and, after much travail, ended up at Byblos, where she saw the pillar for what it truly was. Isis disguised herself, became a handmaiden to the local queen and in token of the queen's generosity immortalised her children. However, just as she was finishing off the process on the last child, she was caught in the act – holding it by its heel over a sacred flame. To the total astonishment of the royal court, Isis was forced to reveal herself. Then, taking the pillar with her, she returned to Egypt.

However, the angry and murderous Set once again managed to get his hands on the body of his dead brother and tore it into pieces, 14 in all, and scattered them all over Egypt. In great sorrow Isis and her sister Nephthys, the wife of Set, gathered up all the pieces and put them together again, as the first mummy.[35] Isis then hovered over the body as a kite, and, with the help of Thoth and Anubis (the guide of souls to the underworld), she breathed life, *spiritus*, into the body. Unfortunately, though, the body was incomplete, for Osiris' phallus had been swallowed by a fish. This did not stop Isis, who manufactured another, and Osiris, resurrected as the ithyphallic god Min (sometimes Men or Menu), the equivalent of the Greek Pan, was able to impregnate Isis, who conceived the divine child Horus. Horus would later avenge his father, who, resurrected in spirit, became lord of the underworld, the Duat, and the judge of the dead. This then, in brief, is the legend of Isis and Osiris, and at first glance it seems most unlike other myths, until we begin to take a closer look.

The first comparison that came into my mind was one that must ultimately remain speculative. At the beginning of the myth, Geb, the earth god, and his wife Nut, the sky goddess, had a curse placed on them by Ra, who feared usurpation by any of the children in Nut's pregnant womb. Ra forbade her to give birth on any day of the 360-day year. Thoth subsequently played chequers with the moon and won sufficient light for five extra days, during which Nut gave birth to Osiris, Isis, Set, Nephthys and Horus (called Apollo by the Greeks). This is very similar to the story of the birth of Jesus. Herod, as the king, represents the sun; Jesus is his heir. Herod, as we saw, in his final days tried to find the prophesied child and have it killed. He recognised it as a probable grandson, and suspicion fell on Antipater, his eldest child. Then Herod is thought to have died and Antipater is killed. Herod, though, manages to live on for a further *five* days. It is likely that during these five days Jesus was born. This too would be the birth of the hero-god during the intercalary period. As I have already stated, this is speculative, but probable, given what we have already seen of the broader evidence.

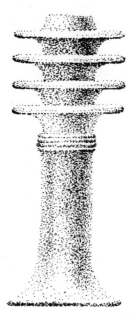

The djed pillar

The other thing that struck me was that Osiris became a pillar at Byblos. I could not help but notice that, as we have seen earlier, Josephus mentioned that Jesus' name was carved above the balustrade, which was itself supported by pillars, the most famous of which had names – Jachin and Boaz – sacred within Freemasonry. In an early form, Osiris was known as Andjeti, or was at least identified with the god of that name, taking from Andjeti the symbols of the shepherd's crook and the flail. Actually, I believe that from the outset, the two were the same, for the Egyptian texts claim that, originally, Osiris came from Djedu, the capital of the ninth nome (administrative district) of Lower Egypt. The Greeks called this town Busiris, from its Egyptian name, Per-Asar, literally 'House of Osiris'. (Later on, during the first and second Dynasties, Osiris' cult moved to Abydos.) The only difference between Osiris and Andjeti is that the latter was always represented as a living king, whereas Osiris was always dead. However, Osiris was not really dead, but resurrected, and as such represented a living force both within the body of his own son, the Horus-King, as well as within the land and the cosmos. This is reflected in the name Andjeti, literally 'pillar of the underworld, of Annu'. The very word is talking of these forces immanent within the earth.

The Egyptian word for pillar is *djed*, and this is a component of Thoth's name in its hieroglyphic form. 'D' and 't' are cognate, hence the Greek form Dod or Tot – Thoth. In Egyptian the name is Djehuti.[36] The component 'hu' – the Lord – is within the name, within the pillar, the *djed*. Djehuti is a pun upon Osiris' title reflecting Isis' search – 'My Lord is in the pillar'.

This reflects the legend of Adonis, whose name means 'the Lord', and who was said to have been born from a myrrh tree – 'myrrh' being another form of Mary.[37] Thus Adonis' mother was Myrrh.[38] What we have here is an age-old myth, one that can be found the length and breadth of the Middle East and beyond; such as the myth of Aleyin and Mot, the rival twins of Canaanite mythology. Aleyin we have encountered before as El Ayin; another of his names is Baal – the Lord. Mot simply means 'death'. Aleyin, like Adonis and Osiris, is Life, whilst Set and Mot are Death. Going back to the tree/pillar, at the base of it, or curled around it, is a serpent, the Egyptian hieroglyph for 'goddess', the goddess concerned being Isis. Could it be that this became the story of the temptation of Adam and Eve? Adam is Atum, the Creator, and Eve is Hebe, darkness, mother goddess and mistress of the Tree of Life. Any icon displaying these elements could easily have been misinterpreted in later years.

Another thing that struck me was the story of Osiris' missing bit – his phallus. Apparently it had been swallowed by a fish – a letos fish. The letos fish is a curious thing, and certain parts of it, particularly its liver, were used in ritual purifications. The fish is of course a symbol of Christianity, but the name of this fish suggests that it had something to do with Apollo as well, for Leto was Apollo's mother. As we have seen, Horus was equated with Apollo. We are back to 'the Lord' again – the meaning of Horus' name.

The very archaic Egyptian mythos would appear to be the forerunner of them all; recognisable features of it appear in quite a few mythologies from other countries. Isis' search for Osiris and her later anguish over her dead son Horus (who in some versions of the myth is, as an infant, stung by Set, disguised as a scorpion), resemble the Eleusinian Mystery of Demeter and her search for the lost Persephone,[39] in that Isis' anguish halts Ra in his tracks, thus causing the world to become dark and infertile. The similarities are almost limitless. However, it would be unfair to label Egypt as unquestionably the oldest source. It is just that so many thousands of years later Egypt has the most intact remains, and what came after appears to be but a remnant of an older, more complex theology, out of which emerged what today we term 'religion'. Egypt as she stands now, allows us to penetrate deep into the mysteries of belief, into her way of life, which was so totally permeated by the gods,

I now felt that I had entered the Holy of Holies and was about to have numerous mysteries revealed to me. There was so much. My sense of intrigue was heightened – I was getting ever nearer to an answer. Having drawn apart the veil of Christianity, a greater mystery loomed before me, one closely related to Church dogma and doctrine, which in its youth had risen like a phoenix from out of the ashes of ancient Egypt.

We have seen how Osiris' name in Egyptian is Asar, represented in hieroglyphs as a throne and an eye. The former means 'to have power', and given the nature of Osiris' myth, the implication appears to be 'power within'. Osiris/Asar, as we have also seen, was the mythical Jesus, the names being the same – Gesa or Gesu.[40] Also, like the Indo-Aryans, the Assyrians and others, the Egyptians had a solar dynasty of kings represented by hawks or falcons. Also common to these mythologies is the myth of the phoenix, which Jesus is often compared to, as is Osiris, and a plethora of other gods worldwide.

The myth of the phoenix, the bird that sets itself alight and then arises, reborn, from its own ashes, is a potent one. It is a motif that recurs to this day, a rare survival of ancient thinking, possibly more than 5,000 years old. The word 'phoenix' comes from the Greek *phoinikos* (generative). There is some dispute as to whether this word is related to *phoinos*, also a Greek word, meaning 'red'. Even if it is only a pun, I think that it is related, for in Phoenician phoinix means 'purple', from the dye of the mollusc murex. This same dye also produced the red hues that may be seen in the robes of modern, medieval and ancient cardinals of the Roman Catholic Church. The dye was a very expensive commodity in the ancient world and was much sought after. (See chapter one and its footnotes.)

What is interesting is that 'phoenix' is a masculine form of *phoenissa*, 'the red one' or 'the bloody one'.[41] This would appear to be a reference to the hero, whose fate is indeed bloody. However, 'phoenix' also refers to the date palm, which brings us back to Osiris again and his sojourn at Byblos. The Persian form of the mythical bird is called the *huma*, and it is quite probable that this comes from the same root as 'human' (Latin *homo*).[42] The incarnation of God into human form is symbolised in the Egyptian glyph for the phoenix – a stork or heron, the bennu bird. The bennu bird was the carrier of the soul of Osiris.[43] It represents the divine Logos – the Word of God. The bennu bird also initiates a new world age, where order is saved from cosmic entropy. As if to underscore the wide mythic connections that have so permeated my quest, it was believed by the ancient Egyptians that the phoenix/bennu bird wrapped up its father's ashes in an egg of myrrh – the tree from which Adonis/Osiris was born. Furthermore, the phoenix utters a cry from its mythic pyre, the cry of the soul, just as Jesus, Dionysus and Quetzalcoatl too utter a death cry. The heroes die to rise again, like the sun and phoenix.

Osiris was the original 'Good God', whose 'thrones are the stars which never rest.'[44] He was the 'King of Kings' and 'Lord of Lords' and 'God of Gods'.[45] More than this, he was the Resurrection and the Life, the Good Shepherd, Lord of Eternity and the Everlasting, who made men and women to be born again. According to the ancient Egyptian scriptures, 'As truly as Osiris lives, so truly shall his follower live; as truly as Osiris is not dead, he shall die no more...' The great scholar Sir Edwin Wallis-Budge wrote, 'From first to last, Osiris was to the Egyptians the god-man who suffered, and died, and rose again...'.[46] For the devout Christian, unaware of things Egyptian, this is profoundly surprising stuff, for it is also deeply familiar – as the life of Jesus from the Gospels.

For the ancient peoples, of at least the second and third millennia BC, there was no distinction to be made between myth and history. Together, with immanence and numinousness, they provided the ongoing sense, the perception of creation, the everlasting now, the universe unfolding to the story of the gods. In a Jungian sense these gods represented archetypes, and the greatest and the most human of them all was Osiris, whom today we call Jesus.

The story of Osiris/Jesus was about the burden of life, the burden of getting to know oneself. To the Egyptians, the journey of the soul in death was a reflection of self-knowledge in life. The journey to heaven of a pharaoh's soul was actually a reflection of his philosophical journey through life's experience. These similarities are not limited to Christianity, but, of all the world's religions and mythologies, it is Christianity's doctrine and theology that most approximate to the ancient Egyptian mode of the sacred. In fact, so very similar are the two that the more ancient way should be labelled 'ancient Egyptian Christianity', for that is precisely what it was.

Osiris was the Redeemer at the centre of the ancient Egyptian belief system. As in the modern Church, hymns cry out to his glory, exulting him beyond all compare. Here is an example:

> 'He is born! He is born! O come and adore Him!
> Life-giving mothers, the mothers who bore Him,
> Stars of the heavens the daybreak adorning,
> Ancestors, ye of the Star of the Morning,
> Women and Men, O come and adore Him,
> Child who is born in the night.'[47]

There are other verses, and the whole thing reads like a Christmas carol.

Osiris' nativity was announced by three wise men, who were represented by the three belt stars of the constellation of Orion. In the Greek mysteries of Adonis, a cry of celebration went out that the Star of Salvation had dawned in the East. In myth, the nativity of the saviour is often marked by the dawning of a 'new' star. This motif also occurs in the legends of Krishna, Pythagoras, Yu and even Caesar, of all people. Zoroastrianism, too, shares the same legend. In a historical context we have the first century rebel and messianic pretender, Simon bar Kochba – 'the Son of the Star'. This motif appears in South American tradition, too, in the legend of the hero saviour-god Quetzalcoatl, who appears as the morning star.

The three wise men, having found the child, pay homage to it and its mother. In the Egyptian mythos this divine child is the reborn Osiris, the hawk of his father, called Horus. Another comparison that I noticed was that the newborn child's father was dead before the child was born. It was also at this point that I realised that I was not alone in recognising Isis as Mary. In 1933 Sir Edwin Wallis-Budge, Head of Egyptian Antiquities at the British Museum, published a book, *Legends of Our Lady Mary, the Perpetual Virgin, and her Mother Hanna.*[48] In the third section of the introduction he makes a comparison between the cults of Isis and Mary, and comes to much the same conclusion as I; though, on account of the era in which he was writing, he was less explicit.

These Christian similarities are underscored by Pilate's accusation to Christ, *Chrestos ei!* which, translated from the Latin, reads, 'What a simpleton you are!' *Chrestos* means 'simple', as in innocent and gentle, whereas *Christos* means 'anointed'. It is thought that the two words became confused in the early Greek texts. 'Chrestos' is one of the traditional epithets of Osiris, and on the island of Delos, sacred to Apollo, there is an inscription to Chreste Isis. Pilate may well have known these things.[49]

But what of the name Pilate? How odd it is! It means 'pilot' and this immediately drew my attention to another Egyptian connection. The sun–god Ra sails through the heavens in his boat of 'millions of years' and in this boat are the assembled gods. It is Ra who navigates it, Ra who is the pilot, Ra whose son Osiris was the 'Word made flesh' and Ra who decreed that the flesh should go through the wheel of suffering, just as Pilate condemned Jesus. There are various maritime references in the New Testament. The Gospel of John contains the following:

> 'And he said unto them, "Cast the net on the right side of the ship, and ye shall find." They cast therefore, and now they were not able to draw it for the multitude of fishes.'
>
> John 21:6

Needless to say, the fishing motif is one that occurs regularly within Egyptian sacred iconography, scenes that are trivialised as 'everyday' by some Egyptologists, who fail to see the symbolism. Much is missed.

The modern idea of Jesus represents two different aspects of Egyptian thinking: the dead and resurrected Osiris, and the living Horus, the son of Osiris. Pharaoh was the incarnation of Horus, and when he shuffled off this mortal coil he would become Osiris and his heir the new Horus. Thus it was that the mythic cycle lived on in the pharaohs and the pharaonic bloodline. Horus,

> '... represented the soul of life, which came by water to a dried up world, upon the verge of perishing with hunger and with thirst. Here the fish, as the first fruit of the earth, was a sign of his incorporation in matter; hence the typical shoot, the green

ear of corn, or the branch that were imagined in Child Horus –
the Saviour who came by water.

'The Saviour who came in fruit as a product of the tree was the
Natzar. *[Nzr.] [Hence 'Nazarene'.]* The Saviour who came by spirit
was the soul of the sun. This was the earliest rendering of the
incorporation of Horus, as the primary of life and light of the
world...'[50]

The Egyptian element which might seem out of place is Osiris' opposing
brother, Set. Whilst it is of note that there are some stories of Jesus having a
twin,[51] it is interesting to discover that the pharaoh was the incarnation of
them both. He was at once the living Osiris – Horus – and he was Set. During
the nineteenth Dynasty there were two kings named after this wild god. This
raises an interesting point, one often overlooked by researchers, and one that
thus leads to innumerable misunderstandings.

Set is generally held to be the god of, or an incarnation of, evil. Quite simply,
this is only half-true. The only evil about Set was his wild nature and thus his
ignorance. Kings of Egypt would hardly have named themselves after evil! In
calling themselves, or associating themselves with, Set, they were
acknowledging their all-too-human characteristics. Set was the man of the
wilderness, wild, red and hairy, unkempt and vicious – Osiris as man in his
lowest form. When a pharaoh died he longed to rise to the heavens, homeward
bound as the higher Osiris – knowledgeable, cultured, meek and mild, saintly
and godlike.

If there was ever a god of evil, it is more likely to have been the serpent who
opposed the passage of the boat of Ra in the underworld, the Duat. For Ra,
the sun god, to rise and fill humankind with his divine breath, he had to
overcome this serpent, called Apophis. However, to the Ancients, the serpent's
obstruction was functional, for they understood that wisdom is gained through
dealing with adversity. Hence the serpent's traditional association with
wisdom.

Apophis was chaos, disorder from order, the swallower of light. As if to
prove my point, in the myth, as the boat of Ra ploughs on through the cosmos,
there at the prow is a marksman with a spear, the spear destined to kill the
serpent. And who is the marksman? None other than Set. The very act of
spearing the serpent illustrates how Set is destined to overcome his own chaos,
his 'dark side' and to ascend as one with his brother Osiris. That is why Set is
in the divine boat of Ra, who as Atum fills the universe with the sound of his
holy voice.

There is a red hairy wild-man in the Old Testament too. He is also one of
two brothers. His name is Esau, brother of Jacob. It is Esau who is tricked out
of his rightful inheritance through the gift of a bowl of red lentil potage. Red

lentils were always ritually offered to Horus (see chapter one, f.25), and, as if to confirm the Egyptian origin of Jacob and Esau, Set too is tricked of his rightful inheritance of the land of Upper Egypt, even after Geb, the earth god, adjudicates and decides that he should have it. Horus gains it at Set's expense.[52]

Set, who probably gives his name, his red-hairy name, to sunset, the red, dying sun, was the god of primal regenerative power. From 'Set' is derived 'Satan', known to Hebrews and Jews as 'God's adversary', and also 'satyr', an early Greek variation on the theme of Set, portrayed as part–man, part–goat.

However, as always seems to be the case, something else came to mind at this point: Set's name. It is the only one of the Egyptian divine names that, although male, is actually spelt in the feminine form – with a 't' at its end. The female inside Set is Aset – Isis. This would be the primal expression of the letter 'a', as in Aset, giving us the alchemical base matter, the matter that needs to be transmuted. Is this the reason why in Christian iconography the devil is sometimes portrayed as a woman, a woman with the hoof of an ass, the animal that sometimes represents Set? Is this why on the Christian Palm Sunday (palms were sacred to Osiris), Jesus is set on an ass? To represent that he has overcome his bestial nature?

The myths and scriptures were there to encourage everyone to overcome their lower nature, but how might the process be best represented in myth? It is back to the cross, but not in the way that the Church sees it today. I found a good example in the Greek hero, Chiron, the boatman of the infernal River Styx. Chiron received a wound and although he was able to heal others he was unable to heal himself. He therefore bequeathed his own immortality to someone else and then died. However, by virtue of his actions, his wound was healed and he became immortal. His action was one of complete selflessness, offered without thought of personal gain, one without guile. Chiron is, of course, our old friend the Chi Rho, the cross. In the ancient myths the hero-gods are nailed or pinned to the centre of the cross. The centre represents the still point from which all movement proceeds. This aspect of the cross therefore represents innocence in action.

Further to this, on my first visit to the Valley of the Kings, I saw, in the tomb of Pharaoh Tuthmosis III, a hieroglyph of a strange ram-headed god, which looked nothing like the only other ram-headed God of my acquaintance, Amon. It was in fact Lwf[53] – Ra in the form of a lamb, the gentle creature which, in its newborn innocent activity, represents the Word made flesh. This seemed to confirm my thinking. Lwf was the soul of Ra, the Word of consciousness. Innocence in action.

The ancient symbols and gods not only represent all of the powers and attributes of nature, but in the form of the hero-gods, they also supply us with instructions for the betterment of our estate.

11

Epiphany

'Science must begin with myths, and with the criticism of myths.'

Karl Popper (1902-1994) [1]

'Any sufficiently advanced technology is indistinguishable from magic.'

Arthur C. Clarke

The Science of the Soul

In previous chapters, I have indicated the components of an ancient and sacred spiritual technology, one that seems, like the gods, to be somehow inherent within language – a language that the sensitive Ancients translated as an expression of the power of place and their understanding of the evolutionary process. Human beings, as we have seen, seem to be able to tune in, like radio receivers, to certain frequencies and thus gain inspiration (literally, 'in spirit'). And yet in the modern world we have little realisation of this. I do not wish to seem too harsh, but it seems to me that modern man has been scrabbling around in the dust in an attempt – a doomed one at that – to tie down the ancient gods and the mythic heroes to history. It has invariably led down a false trail. This is not the only false trail. In many ways the so-called 'breakthrough' idea (as modern historians have described it) of monotheism has turned out to be a retrograde step. This is beautifully summed up by Professor Bob Brier:

> 'No war was ever fought between polytheistic countries over
> whose gods were the true ones. Compare this with the number
> of wars fought on behalf of the Jewish, Christian and Islamic
> religions.' [2]

If these monotheist religions become more scientific, I believe that they will have to acknowledge the science of the Ancients, where the gods, as the aspects and attributes of God, represented the activities of nature in all its forms and in all things. This new polytheism would take us beyond blind belief and into universal surety. At its core, the activity of Osiris-Gesu is as the life-force, the hero-god who 'dies' in order to give life to others and, in dying, realises immortality. The hero's association with nature was not just with the daily round of the setting and rising sun, but also the seasonal solar aspects. Ancient Egyptians would beat their breasts and sing a lament to the god as they threshed the corn. The god was dying, this was the season of the harvest, and the life-force was withdrawing back into the earth, leaving only seed-heads behind, seeds that carried the hope of the future. Earthen corn dollies would be made and buried at this time; when excavated later they would be found to have sprouted – an omen of the resurgence of the spirit of life, immanent within the earth. Hieroglyphics are quite explicit about Osiris/Gesu as life itself, and as such he was defined by death, a concept familiar within Christianity.

The 'science' of the ancient Egyptians has become the faith of today:

> 'He that eateth my flesh, and drinketh my blood dwelleth in me, and I in him.'
>
> John 6:56

In Mithraism the same passage reads:

> 'He who will not eat of my body and drink of my blood, so that he will be made one with me and I with him, the same shall not know salvation.'[3]

Both the ancient Egyptians and the followers of Mithrais used communion wafers. The Mithraic wafers even bore the sign of the cross. I believe, though, that the followers of Mithraism had a deeper understanding of the workings of nature as represented in the communion, the celebration of the Eucharist, where the knowledge that the active principle and the sustantive principle were at work within was well understood.

A question that one may ask at this stage is, 'In what sense were the ancient peoples aware of this as science?' The answer is that science was looked upon differently by the Ancients. It was not removed from life in the objective sense. It was inseparable from daily living and personal, subjective experience. This does not mean that these 'scientists' were unaware of the finest realms of nature; the evidence to the contrary is plain to see. 'Science' as a term means 'knowledge', from the Latin *scientia* (from the present participle of the verb *scire*, 'to know'). For the Ancients, knowledge came from within – gnosis. And ultimately, knowledge in this form was godly: information was transmitted by those cosmic powers, the gods who permeated all things.[4] The very names and symbols of the gods expressed the scientific principles I was looking for.

The hieroglyph denoting the name of the Egyptian god of wisdom, Thoth (pronounced 'T-o-te'), is referred to by Egyptologists as an ink-jar. This is a reasonable assumption, for Thoth (in Egyptian, Djehuti, pronounced 'Joe-tee'), was the scribe of the gods.[5] However, the ink-jar is also the hieroglyph for the heart, symbolic of the conscious mind, the very thing that Thoth represents.[6] Egyptian water–jars were quite frequently moulded in the form of the heart hieroglyph, for reasons that, until recently, remained unknown. Until, that is, Bruce Mace, an American enthusiast of things Egyptian, got his hands on some ancient Egyptian pottery and subjected it to an analysis. Having analysed it, he blended certain clays into the right admixture and consistency and made a water–jar, heart-shaped, of course. What he discovered was remarkable. Tainted water, when poured into the jar, was rendered clean by an extraordinary process of reverse osmosis. Inside the jar the water spun at a frequency counter to its various polluting agents. These were absorbed by the clay and expelled as waste through its outer shell. The water inside was of such purity that it became almost sweet to the taste – at least that's how it seemed when I tried it. This reflects a discovery about blood-flow, announced in May 1998. Surgeons have realised that as the heart pumps blood around the body, the blood forms swirls as it rushes through the arteries. Furthermore, nature has designed arteries with a helical 'twist' to encourage the swirl. There is a further observation to be made. The earth's core spins at a much faster rate than the rest of the planet, whilst generating the planet's magnetic field. The same observation can be made of the sun, whose inner core spins at a rate phenomenally faster than its surface. In chapter seven, we looked at the importance of the spiral to the Ancients. Here, through the symbolism of the heart, the ink pot, and the rediscovery of an ancient technology, we see that the Egyptian god Djehuti (Thoth), whilst relating to the conscious mind at the heart of matter, relates to the spiralling force which directs the blood in microcosm and the galaxies in macrocosm: e-motional intelligence.

For me, this was remarkable stuff, the kind of knowledge that reaffirmed the nature of my journey. I was getting somewhere; the scientific and the magical had merged to reveal a greater truth, and this brought to my mind some remarkable words of Pierre Teilhard de Chardin:

> 'A truth once seen, even by a single mind, always ends up by imposing itself on the totality of human consciousness.'

Surely, it is now time for this ancient knowledge to be accepted as a spiritual science and to be respectfully researched as such!

In the mid 1970s, at the annual conference of the World Education Fellowship, Professor Sir Alister Harding (1896–1985) made:

'... a powerful appeal for the building of what he called a scientific theology for the era that lies ahead of us, and on three separate occasions in the course of his address he reminded his audience of the dangers of dogmas of materialism which were supposedly built on secure scientific foundations. He remarked upon the fact that our civilisation had been built upon a spiritual interpretation of the world... His concluding words stressed the need for "an experimental faith which can regenerate the spiritual that has been the driving force of all the great civilisations of the past".'[7]

This recognition of past civilisations by an eminent scientist, pre-eminent even, gives a novel perspective upon the issue of our origins and a rare accreditation of the spiritual intelligence of the Ancients, an intelligence not based purely upon the rational elements of the mind, but upon the emotions too.

The seat of emotional intelligence may have been the heart as presided over by Thoth, but the seat of spiritual intelligence was marked upon the forehead by the uraeus of the Pharaoh's crown. One of the finest examples of the uraeus may be seen upon the golden likeness of King Tutankhamun in the Cairo museum. It protrudes from the forehead part of his *nemes* head-dress. The uraeus, from the Greek *ouraios*, 'cobra', was exactly that – the cobra goddess Wadjet. The uraeus was the archetypal serpent-image of kingship and was often seen in tandem with the vulture goddess Nekhbet. Together, Wadjet and Nekhbet offered the Pharaoh protection against all-comers. Significantly, Wadjet was sometimes portrayed in leonine form and as such was known as the Eye of Horus.

I was back at the 'Eye' again, *El Ayin*. Oddly enough, looking at the crown of Lower Egypt, the red crown, I saw a strange-looking proboscis protruding from it (see illustration). There were four main crowns of Egypt: the blue *khepresh* crown,[8] the ostrich-feather-like *atef* crown, the crown of Upper Egypt, called the white crown or *hedjet*, and the crown of Lower Egypt, the red crown or *deshret*. From the First Dynasty onwards the crowns of Upper and Lower Egypt were united, but still had the strange proboscis.

The crown of the Emperor of Japan is almost exactly the same as the pharaonic crown of Lower Egypt, and as the Emperor himself ritually and mythically represents the mysterious force of fertility, the creative force of life itself. I found myself at once intrigued and fascinated. It was only when I found myself looking at Tutankhamun's fabulous golden mask in profile that I realised that I had come across an answer. Side on, the uraeus cobra has a similar line of flow to the old Egyptian letter (hieratic) rendered as 'r', 'l' or 'n' in Semitic scripts. Its shape infers the movement of energy:

*The united crowns
of Upper and Lower Egypt.*

*The red crown of
Lower Egypt.*

The exact sound of the letter in old Egyptian is not known. However, it does have a marked resemblance to the Hebrew *ayin*, the letter 'o' (Greek Omicron).[9] Its sound probably varies with the different meanings of the glyph, though the Semitic rendering 'r' gives a broad hint that its divine meaning was the double vowel 'aa', representing the breath of God. (Just say the letter 'r' and you'll see what I mean!) The confusion over which letter it represents may be solved by the application of a little Egyptian theology – the fact that the holy, inexpressible name of God was made up solely of vowels. Ancient languages can only be written as consonants, but the very sound of these is what gives the clue.

The letter 'a' when doubled means 'primal energy' and 'possibility' in terms of 'potential'. These are the very things that are said to have spurred on the creation and to have been behind it.[10]

The uraeus appears to be protecting the *ba* or soul of the Pharaoh. The first thing that I noticed about it was its position over the spot approximating to the third eye or pineal gland, the fount of consciousness. Oddly enough, Heliopolis was called Ayin esh Shems – 'the fountain of the sun' – by the Arabs. Heliopolis was, from the very outset of Egyptian history, the greatest cult centre of them all and the most ancient. Ayin is also the fountain of the soul. In ancient Indian tradition the gland associated with the pineal, the pituitary, was called the 'cave of Brahma'. In ancient Egypt it was the 'cave' or 'grotto of Ra'.

In researching the connection between the cobra/uraeus and the pineal gland, I came across the following by Manley P. Hall, written at the beginning of the twentieth century:

'Did the Egyptians know that reptiles present the highest development of this gland and for this reason coiled the serpent upon their foreheads where the third eye of the Orientals is placed by symbolic license? Was not the Uraeus the symbol of wisdom and is not the pineal gland the organ of a method of acquiring knowledge...'[11]

This is followed by a further intriguing comment:

'As an emblem of divinity, the pineal gland would naturally be associated with royalty, for the kings were the shadows of the gods upon earth. The crown of Lower Egypt and also the Pschent, or crown of the Double Empire [consolidated Egypt], were surmounted by a curious antenna, feeler, or very thin curved horn, which is most reminiscent of the descriptions of the structure of the third eye that have descended from the first ages.'[12]

From what we have seen so far regarding the pineal gland and its symbology, it is fairly obvious that the Ancients had a detailed knowledge of its workings and abilities, and knew it to be the seat of the soul. To quote Manley P. Hall once again concerning the occult knowledge of ancient man,

'The pineal gland is regarded as a link between the objective and subjective states of consciousness: or, in exoteric terminology, the visible and invisible worlds of nature.'[13]

My guess was that this knowledge, gained first hand via the ancient technology of the sacred site, was put to supremely good use and preserved via the mythology that has come down to us many thousands of years later. I have described various aspects of those mythologies in order to demonstrate their extraordinary similarities across the world and we have only skimmed the surface of those generally uncharted waters. That Christianity emerged out of Egypt many thousands of years ago seemed to me to be the only obvious conclusion that one could draw. However, it was also obvious that many and various aspects of it were drawn directly from the power of place, no matter where that place might be. It was now time to name names and point the finger in a more definite direction. Reflecting upon the pharaohs of Egypt and the symbolic nature of their power, I came across something that quite took my breath away, something as controversial as it is extraordinary. Suddenly, after many years of research, much hardship and many questions, the answers came thick and fast – answers that I never dreamed would appear in the way they did. And yet, as always, it was only a matter of looking.

The first of these answers was the beginning of a short trail that would take me to the summit of the mountain. It dealt with the tragic figure of Mary Magdalene. The truth of who she was and what she represented could not be farther from how she is perceived today, and yet the clues were all so near. And it was ever so.

Nuts about Mary

Mary Magdalene is one of the most prominent characters within the New Testament. A follower of Jesus, she is famous for being a reformed prostitute, though the text that describes her is not at all explicit. The passage, in the Gospel of Luke, merely states:

> 'And certain women, which had been healed of evil spirits and infirmities, Mary called Magdalene, out of whom went seven devils.'
>
> Luke 8:2

The name of the Magdalene does not appear in any text earlier than the Gospels and no historical documents of the period mention her either, not even Josephus. However, this does not mean that she was not historical. As usual, we need to examine in what sense she was historical. The Magdalene was said to be a prostitute, a whore. My first real clue came from ancient temple practices, but by way of a remotely related term.

A prostitute is a tart, in common English parlance. *The Oxford Dictionary of Slang* states that 'tart' is probably short for 'raspberry tart', the rhyming slang for 'sweetheart'. However, it reminded me of Astarte, who appears in the Old Testament as Ishtar, the Babylonian goddess of love and sexuality. Among the Greeks she was identified with Aphrodite, another heavenly goddess of love, called Venus by the Romans.

Astarte is one of the oldest forms of the great goddess in the Middle East. Intriguingly, she was also known as the Lady of Byblos, the place where Osiris was transformed into a palm tree and where Isis went in search of him. In Hebrew, Astarte was translated into Esther, meaning 'star' or 'soul'.[14] Esther is the word from which we derive 'Easter', the pivotal time for our dying and rising god.[15] But why was Mary Magdalene described as a whore?

It seems that some priestesses gave themselves over to sexual activities of a Tantric nature in the service of the goddess, before going on, perhaps, to other things. Initially they were temple virgins and it is at this point that we come to a very delicate comparison, because Mary the Mother of God was a temple virgin, at least according to some accounts. But this is where things begin to get a little interesting.

The word 'whore' comes from a variety of European sources: Low German *Hore*, Middle Dutch *hoere*, Old Norse *hora*, and so on. These probably come from the Greek term *choron*. The nearest in meaning to the Gospel term (which is from the Greek) is the Gothic *hors*, meaning 'adulterer', which is what the Magdalene is implied as having been. However, the argument is sealed by the Latin term *carus* (from an Indo-European base, *qar*). Car, Q're, Kar and Qar are all early forms of the Greek Kore. (There was even a nation named after her, the Carians, who were formidable seafarers.) The male version of this name makes the answer entirely obvious – Horus. A whore was an Egyptian temple woman and would be a temple dancer at that. Remember the Dance of the Seven Veils by Herod Antipas' niece Salome? 'Whore' has the same etymology as 'hour', and it was the Hourae who performed the dances of the hours and also acted as midwives to the gods. If I am right in my thinking about the close correlation between the story of Jesus and the family of Herod, then it is significant that Salome was lusted after by Herod Antipas and was, in thought at least, an adulteress. Was Salome the historical Magdalene? Is this the reason why Salome is portrayed in the Gospel of Mark (15:40) at the foot of the cross? To delve into the question of an historical Magdalene is beyond the scope of this book, but who or what was the mythical Magdalene?

In the early Christian treatise *The Shepherd of Hermas* (second century AD), Christ is compared to a 'cube-shaped mountain, upon which a tower is erected'.[16] The cube-shaped mountain's name is Mount Meru. The origin of the word 'cube' is Kubaba, another name of the goddess Cybele. Cybele is traditionally associated with the pine tree and the pineal. Cybele means 'Beauty of the Waves' or 'Lady of the Waves' and she is also known as the 'hairy woman' (see chapter six). This is interesting, for this is precisely what Mary Magdalene is said to have become, on vacating the Holy Land post-crucifixion. Of course the legends are apocryphal, but relevant nonetheless. So where does all of this take us?

In the tomb of Tutankhamun a wonderful representation of his birth – his ritual birth – was discovered by Howard Carter and his team. It portrayed the newborn Tutankhamun emerging, headfirst, out of a lotus. This was representative of the god Osiris/Gesu/Horus arising out of the primordial state. As a piece of statuary it is quite breathtaking, but it also has great implications. It was believed that the lotus seed and the almond seed were containers of the spirit of the unborn divine child. I thought back to the Festival of Cybele, which fell on 4th April, the Megalensia (which was in all likelihood a mistranslation of Megdalensia), the celebration of her conception of the divine child. Suddenly I knew that I was getting somewhere.

In the brain the seat of the emotions is the amygdala,[17] and it has been suggested that the amygdala may use the earth's ELF channel in association with the environment of the power of the place (see chapter five). Electrical stimulation of the amygdala and hippocampus can induce a whole range of paranormal sensations, which include out-of-the-body experiences. These experiences often involve the consciousness moving through a tunnel or tower of light towards a brighter light. This is especially so in 'near-death' experiences.[18] In the Old Testament Book of Micah the following can be read:

> 'And thou, O tower of the flock,
> the stronghold of the daughter of Zion,
> unto thee shall it come, even the first dominion;
> the kingdom shall come to the daughter of Jerusalem.'
>
> Micah 4:8

In a motif common within mythology, when the hero wishes to leave earth and 'join his fathers' he does so by entering a tower. This could be a reference to a monument where the dead king is entombed, but the near-death evidence and the Ancients' focus on the otherworldly should encourage us to look a little deeper.

In Hebrew, 'tower of the flock' is *magdal-eder*. The epithet *magdala* means literally 'tower'. It also means 'elevated, great, magnificent, high'. *Amygdale* is the Greek word for 'almond', from which we derive 'amygdala'. In French the word for 'almond' is *amande* – the origin of the Christian name Amanda. This means, appropriately, bearing in mind the Magdalene connection, 'fit to be loved'. The very similar Sanskrit word *ananda* means 'bliss'.

The almond is curiously shaped, like a *vesica* or standing-wave pattern, with nodes and antinodes. Recall the story of Jesus driving seven devils out of the Magdalene? Seven is the number of music, the notes of the scale, and music heightens the emotions, identified within the brain with the amygdala.

The Book of Micah, chapter four, relates to the healing of afflictions and the return of all, particularly the feminine, the substance of life, to God. In other words, the translation of emotion from pain to bliss, a process that can be stimulated by ritual and all that ritual entails.

In pharaonic ritual, when a pharaoh was crowned, the spirit of the hero-god entered into him. The Pharaoh became Horus – the living Osiris/Gesu. His wife became the symbolic Isis/Mary. In the coronation ceromony, he was anointed with almond oil and his marriage became a covenant with the beloved goddess, for that was who the queen was.

Interestingly, the eating of almonds can increase the production of semen (called the 'water of life' by ancient peoples). Almonds were not only understood to be an aphrodisiac, but also associated with consciousness and the powers of the mind. They were the fruit of immortality and, as such, their use in ritual was paramount. In some of the non-canonical gospel texts, the young Mary was given an almond seed or sometimes a lotus seed to swallow – the seed was the newly conceived foetus. The myth was fairly widespread. In some texts it is Mary's mother Hannah who swallows the seed in order to give rise to Mary. The virgin Mary, being pure, gives birth to the hero who must attain the heavenly state despite the adversity of this material world. The fallen aspect of Mary as attributed to the Magdalene may well be due to a fall into materialism and the subsequent loss of the use of *El Ayin*, the 'third eye', for, as we see, Mary Magdalene is also Mary 'Amygdala' who falls and then reclaims her divinity through devotion to the way of the hero-god. Through this, the pathway to higher consciousness, the tower to the heavens, is reinstated. Based upon near-death experience research, this tower may not be an analogy, but a real attribute, perhaps available through the correct functioning of the amygdala and the pineal. Mary relates to the substance of life. The story of Mary Magdalene could well be urging the end of gross materialism and the recognition, rejuvenation and integration of the spiritual attributes into human life. The tower which rises to the divine would be operative. But what is a tower? Could it not also be talked of as a column or a pillar?

Churches Hor–us

By 1997, my research had developed out of all recognition from my initial innocent enquiries. The proportion, too, was staggering. I had amassed over 10,000 books, papers and other documents and more information was flowing in to confirm my thesis. I had uncovered an ancient spiritual technology and traced Christianity to the Giza Plateau. I already had more than enough material for publication but, to me, that was not the point. I was not fulfilled, for I sensed that there was a missing ingredient. I didn't know what it was, but all the evidence told me that I would find it at Giza. At that time, as an impoverished researcher, getting there was not a simple matter. However, the fates were to lend a hand. It was early summer when I received a call from a tour promoter asking whether I would be available to co-host a special tour of ancient Egyptian sites, scheduled for November. Giza, of course, would constitute a significant part of the itinerary. Needless to say, I accepted and felt that someone, something, was assisting me in my quest. And so it was, that a few months later, that a grateful David Elkington could be found standing at the edge of the village of Nazlet-el-Sammam, gazing toward the Sphinx and the pyramids beyond. The late afternoon sun was warm and I was musing gently upon the overall nature of the site and the ceremonies that may have been associated with it.

Although no overall description of a pharaoh's coronation ceremony has survived into the modern era, enough research has been done to show that a procession around 'the walls' and then inward toward the temple would take place. The walls referred to may relate to the boundary of the long disappeared city of Memphis, but it is more likely to be the boundary of the sacred Giza complex. As we saw in chapter six, the idea of sacred sites being 'processed' in an ever-decreasing spiral is worldwide and still operative.[19]

According to the Gnostic group known as the Sabians, the three Giza pyramids were the three kings come to pay homage to the holy child. In the Osirian legend, Osiris' coming was announced by the three wise men, the three stars of Orion's belt, Mintaka, Al-nitak and Al-nilam. The terrestrial positions of the pyramids at Giza reflect the stars' positions,[20] but not fully. As Herald and Lawton point out, the magnitude of the stars does not match the size of the pyramids.[21] This does not mean ,though, that the synchronicity of their siting would have been lost on the builders.

There is, however, a distinctive mathematical correlation to the siting which has a clear association with the tradition of spiral procession. Rostau,[22] the very ancient name of the area, means both 'the place of the cross' and 'symmetry'. The symmetry is this: the apexes of the three pyramids of the Giza Plateau lie along the curve of a Fibonacci spiral[23] (see illustration). The Fibonacci spiral is based upon the 5:8 ratio, a ratio that is found widely in

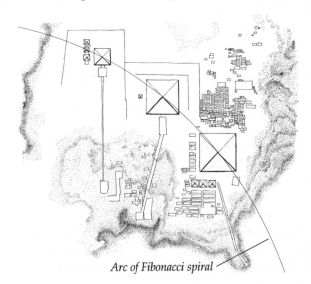

Arc of Fibonacci spiral

nature, especially in relation to growth. The siting of the pyramids in this way seems to confirm that in being houses of life, they follow the patterns of life, exude it even. Almond and lotus seeds too, the seeds of immaculate conception, reflect the pattern of the Fibonacci spiral as it flows ever outwards. I cannot help but feel that there are overt statements being made here. It is as if the ancient Egyptians are saying, 'We know what we are doing, for we are attuned to the powers of nature.' Oddly enough, the Fibonacci proportion of 5:8 also betrays the proportions of cereal grain. It also relates to the workings of the harmonic overtones of a vibrating string as well as the golden proportions of a piano keyboard, all of this illustrating wonderfully well the outward flow and proportions of life itself.[24]

Prior to my Giza visit, I had been looking into the names of holy places and their relation to the Giza site. The word 'church' comes from the Greek *kyriakon*, 'belonging to the Lord', and if anything belonged to the Lord, the Giza Plateau did. In fact, the entire plateau is nothing but a massive church, a church of 'the horizon'. Horus, of whom the Sphinx is a representation, is, apart from being 'the Lord', also known in a different aspect as Ra Horakhty,[25] 'Horus of the Horizon'. In Greek, *horos* means 'limit', and this is the root of 'horizon'. However, 'horizon' also implies a circle, one's circle of vision into the distant landscape, as far as the eye can see. 'Horizon', therefore, suggests 'the Wheel of Horus' – the God was often called 'Horus of the Double Horizon'.[26] The symbolic horizon represents the ultimate limit of creation, the limit of all that is godly, the limit of Atum-Ra. The beginning and the end of the circle are the Alpha and Omega, and within this boundary Atum-Ra is manifest as Osiris, and as Osiris' son, Horus, the Lord. In Greek mythology it was the Father God Zeus who was the guardian of boundaries and limits, just as the Greek word for 'horizon' is from *horos*, 'limit', and *kuklos*, 'circle'.

Choros (the 'c' is silent, hence the spelling *horos*) is, according to Liddell and Scott's Greek lexicon, a word meaning 'circular' or 'cyclic chorus', in the sense of 'any which were danced around a ring, round an altar'.[27] This is interesting, because the English word 'orison' (from Old French *orison*, French *oraison*) means 'a prayer'. The root of this is the Latin *orare*, 'to pray'. Hence oratories and musical oratorios. Everything to do with this word implies the sacred. In Egyptian hieroglyphs this is underscored by the sign for 'horizon': the sun rising over a mountain,[28] properly, 'the place in the sky where the sun rises'. In Greek, *ori* means 'mountain'. The fact that *choros* means 'cyclic chorus' brings together two concepts here, one is entirely to do with the idea of measure and the other with music within that measure. We are back at resonance again.

The church is a house of God and we resonate within it, both on a physiological level and by chant and the singing of hymns. 'Church' in Gaelic is *kirk*, in German it is *Kirche*, in Dutch *kert*, and so on. In Old English the terms are *circe* and *cyrice*. Circe was a Greek goddess. She was the daughter of the sun. Recalling the religions of the dying and rising gods – all associated with the sun – and the fact that Jesus too was a dying and rising god, the term 'church' is well chosen. *Cyrice* comes direct from the Greek *kuriakon*, which pertains to 'the Lord' and his house. However, all of the former terms – *circe*, *kirk,* etc. – imply a circle, and indeed many of the oldest churches were circular, as were medieval Templar churches. 'Circle' in Greek is *kirkos.* But there is another Greek word for 'circle', and it is *kuklos,* more in the sense of a cycle – hence we now have the aspect of continuation, of time. There is much about all of these words that fascinates and thrills, for indeed all of them have mythical implications.

'Horizon' is the circle of Horus, the Lord; it is the horizon of the circle of the church. In Hebrew, *hug* means 'circle'. 'Hug', of course, contains the lordly syllable *hu.*

St. Peter was the legendary holder of the keys to the church whose original site I had now located at the Giza Plateau. But this may have been a variation on the theme of 'Petosiris', meaning 'Osiris within the rock'. This Petosiris is likely to have been the root of the Latin *petra* revealed in chapter three. Recall the Roman god of the underworld, Dis-pater. ('Dis' is cognate with *deus* and *divus* – 'divinity'.) Dis-pater means 'divine father', or 'divine Peter'.

Dis was represented by a dot within a circle: $\odot$. This is precisely the same as the Egyptian hieroglyph for the father god Ra. I was brought immediately full circle, to Circe and the Church.

Now, if all this sounds convoluted, let me sum up, and thus come to the point: we have a circular boundary, *horos,* meaning a 'dance around an altar' – which altar? We have 'orison' from the Latin *orare,* from which we derive 'oratory' – what was this oratory, where prayers were sung? We have the Egyptian glyph of the sun rising over a mountain – but where on the Giza Plateau will we find a mountain? We have a church within a circle – where? And finally, we have Dis-pater, the power within – within what?

Of course, they were all in front of me: the altar, the oratory, the mountain, the church and the circle. The power? Certainly, one of attraction: I stepped into the circle and began to walk through the site.

When Plutarch writes in *On Isis and Osiris* of the visible and calls it Isis, he is pointing to a particular spot within the circle, the Mr, $\triangle$, Mary – the pyramid, whose holy child is within. By the same token I had begun to believe that, somewhere within the building that I was now approaching, there was a body, the body of the 'Son of God'. All of the indications were that the whole of the Giza Plateau was a temple to this man. It was earlier in the year, whilst I was perusing a dictionary of Basque, probably Europe's oldest surviving language – older even than Latin, Greek and Hebrew – that I discovered another synchronicity. For most Europeans, the word 'church' is some variation of *kirk;* but not for the Basques. Their word 'church' is *eliza,* literally, 'the God Isa'.

The Womb of the Mer

The Great Pyramid of Khufu is probably the most extraordinary place on the planet. Photographs cannot do it justice; they only serve to minimise both the size and the impact of this incredible monument. Standing before it, cupping one's hands over one's brow and looking up at layer upon layer of stone until its peak meets the sky, is quite simply a breathtaking experience. Although the white tura limestone casing has long since been stripped off, the pyramid stands firm, the ultimate enigma of the Ancients, whose construction all those thousands of years ago we can only guess at.

It is astonishing to consider that London's St. Paul's cathedral, St. Peter's in Rome and a whole host of Gothic cathedrals could easily be incorporated into the Great Pyramid, such is its volume. Sir William Matthew Flinders-Petrie, the father of modern archaeology, estimated that this immense building consisted of 2,300,000 stones, weighing an average of 2.5 tons each. Others have noted that some of the stones may weigh up to 50 tons. The stepped exterior is made of limestone, whilst the interior chambers are made up of both limestone and granite.

How this gigantic monument was completed in approximately 20 years is a problem that has vexed historians and architects alike. The figure of 20 years comes from the *Histories* of Herodotus, who was informed of the figure by the Egyptians themselves, when he visited the region c.450 BC. The logistics of completing this task in a mere 20 years, without anything approaching modern technology, are staggering. It has been calculated that, even taking a period of 30 to 32 years, one block would have had to have been put into place every two or three minutes in a ten-hour working day!

The term 'pyramid' is Greek. Individually, each of the ancient Egyptian pyramids had a different name and, in short, seemed to be 'horizons' of their respective pharaohs. In the previous chapter we have seen that the pyramid is the god to whom it was dedicated. Therefore, by being dedicated to a priest-king, a pharaoh, the pyramid represented the meeting–place on earth of humanity and the divine. The Great Pyramid was called Akhet Khnum-Khuf, or Akhet Khufu for short. This translates as 'the Horizon of Khufu'. However, the other pyramids of the Giza Plateau, those of Khafre and Menkaure, are simply referred to, in their original glyphs, as $\triangle$, Mr. Khafre's monument, in its day, was called the Great Pyramid, whereas Menkaure's was the Divine Pyramid. Khufu's, now known as the Great Pyramid, was actually 'the Pyramid which is the Place of the Sunrise and Sunset', in effect, the place of the dying and rising god. All of the pyramids of Egypt still have names, most of them very beautiful: the Pyramid which is Flourishing of Places, the Pyramid of the Ba Spirit, the Purified Pyramid, and so on.[29]

In the *Hermetica*, reference is made to the pyramids. Ibn Zulaq (d. AD 997) states:

> 'Among the wonders of Egypt are the two great pyramids ... of which one is the grave of Hermes, i.e. Idris, and the other is that of Agathodaimon, the pupil of Hermes; and the Sabians used to go on pilgrimage to these pyramids.'[30]

A little earlier (about AD 987), An-Nadim writes:

> 'According to some, Hermes is said to have been one of the seven temple-priests who were appointed to have charge of the seven temples [of the planet-gods]; and it is said that the charge of the temple of [the planet] Mercury was given to him, and that he was thence named Hermes... They say that he was a wise man, and that after his death he was buried in the building which is known in Cairo under the name of Abu-Hermes, and which the people call "the two Hermae [pyramids]"...'[31]

To the Egyptians, theirs was a sacred landscape, highlighted by equally sacred landmarks, their additions to a land given them by the gods. It so happens that Osiris was entombed upon or within this landscape, in the House of Sokar, a realm that lay within the fifth division of the earthly Duat, or underworld. According to the Shabaka Texts, the House of Sokar was in the realm of Sokar, a land that Sir E. A. Wallis Budge recognised as 'a large extent of territory ... in the deserts around Memphis'.[32] According to R. T. Rundle-Clarke, this area was the modern Giza, which is the burial place of Memphis and 'the home of a form of Osiris known as Sokar'. This area is also known as Rostau. This point is confirmed by various texts and stelae, but perhaps the most telling of all is the stele that stands between the paws of the Sphinx. This identifies Giza as 'the Splendid Place of the First Time' and demonstrates that the Sphinx stood beside the 'house of Sokar'. Sokar was a falcon god of the dead, indigenous to Memphis. Apparently, according to some Egyptologists, he was taken over by Osiris at some time in the past. The Egyptologists' conclusions remain hypothetical, but, needless to say, the 'house' beside the Sphinx is the Great Pyramid of Khufu.

In chapter nine we saw that the temple was the god. So, too, with the pyramids.[33] But were the pyramids tombs? I shall answer this in a way that might seem prevarication, but stems from the fact that I think the 'pyramids as tombs' theory is all down to a misconception. Yes they were, but no they were not!

Whilst the Giza site was certainly a necropolis, all of its pyramids have been discovered to be devoid of human bodies. The same is true for other pyramids too – perhaps the odd bone or two has been found, but no bodies in any state of completeness. Even when untouched, fully intact sarcophagi have been uncovered, they have proved to be empty when opened. The pyramids were empty tombs.[34]

The step-pyramid ziggurats of Mesopotamia were not used as tombs either. So, how to explain this riddle? Well, it's easy. 'Tomb' in Middle English is *tumbe*, sometimes *taumbe*, in Old French it is *tambe* and then there is the Latin *tumba*, hence 'tumulus' and 'tumuli'. These are recognisably related to the Greek word *tumbos*, meaning 'mound' as well as 'tomb'. And here we come to the crunch: a Greek *temenos* was a place dedicated to a god, a mound, from the same root, *tumbos*. This shrine was a place apart, hence the Greek *temnein*, 'cut off'. We have come across 'Tum' before, and Atum – in the Egyptian pantheon. This is, I believe, the origin of the Greek word. The pyramids are places of Atum, so in a way they are tombs, but the meaning has, at some stage, been misinterpreted. By being taken too narrowly, the god-given meaning has been lost.

At present the common consensus is that the Great Pyramid was erected during the reign of Khufu. This dates it to approximately 2589–2566 BC. However, an assessment of the site reveals that it was busy hundreds of years before Khufu. There is even the possibility that Khufu's pyramid itself may have been constructed over an older site.

The Giza Plateau was an important site from at least the First Dynasty, *c.*3050 BC, and possibly before. Several archaeological finds have confirmed this.[35] Several of the mastaba tombs found at Giza, dating to this period, are known to have influenced certain aspect of design in the later Fourth Dynasty pyramid building era. There are undoubtedly other archaic elements, such as the boat pits, and the remains of several recently discovered pyramids, in the style of the Third Dynasty, but believed to have been constructed in the Fourth. However, what is of interest is the fact that the entire necropolis is exactly that – a city of the dead, littered with tombs, graves and mastabas, right back to the earliest period. But none of them encroach, or have ever encroached, on the most sacred area of the plateau, the pyramid area itself. Aerial photographs and satellite pictures have confirmed that the pyramid area has remained separate throughout, untouched by the mundane. It is as if this area was so incredibly sacred that it was a kind of *Sancta Sanctorum*: it exuded a power all of its own.

Geological analysis has revealed that at a short distance beneath the sands there are a few rocky outcrops, which, if they had been built upon, would have provided a massively unstable foundation. It is in the space between these outcrops that the three great pyramids have been built.[36]

It is beyond the scope of this present work to go into details as to how a pyramid was constructed, but needless to say it is a debate that has raged on.

Many Egyptologists, most of them without any experience of the building profession,[37] have opted for the theory of a gigantic ramp, which once the monument was completed may have served as the main causeway. I do not think that the ramp theory is a wholly tenable one, particularly when the logistics of its mass are taken into consideration – it would far exceed the volume of the pyramid itself. Other, more cost–effective methods must have been put into operation, especially in the light of the speed with which the monument was constructed.[38]

I was also interested in the causeway and its similarities to other sites worldwide. In ancient Egyptian there is a word *pdwt*, which means 'something that stretches, like a rope or line'. The Westcar Papyrus contains a story about King Khufu and a magician called Djedi. (I will come to this name soon.) The story revolves around Khufu's search for the secret chambers of Thoth. The Egyptologist Sir Alan Gardiner made a translation of the papyrus in the 1920s, in which he suggests that Khufu was looking for the number of the chambers of Thoth. This, however, has been countered by the Egyptologist F. W. Green, who observes that Gardiner may have confused two words: *pdwt* and *ipwt* – 'account', 'archive' or 'plan'. The two words have a similar sound and *ipwt* can mean a stretched string for marking a wall.

This is interesting because from time immemorial, hemp ropes were used to join sacred sites to their associated settlements, if these were any distance away. It was believed that the hemp aided the conduction of the site's energy into the settlement.[39] This brings to mind the pyramid causeways which link each pyramid to its associated mortuary temple. The causeways are composed of very conductive quartz – surely a medium used precisely for this purpose.

Standing now before Khufu's Great Pyramid, I looked up toward its peak, recalling that in the nineteenth century, its amazing conductivity was demonstrated by Sir William Siemens (1823–1883). Siemens was a British electrical engineer who visited Egypt and climbed the pyramid. While he was standing on the summit,

> '... an Arab guide called his attention to the fact that whenever he raised his hand with his fingers outspread an acute ringing noise was heard. Raising his index, Siemens felt a distinct prickling in it. When he tried to drink from a wine bottle he had brought along he noted a slight electric shock.'[40]

Siemens moistened a newspaper and converted the bottle into a Leyden jar by wrapping the newspaper around it.

> 'It became increasingly charged with electricity simply by being held above his head.

'When sparks began to issue from the wine bottle, Siemens' Arab guides became distrustful and accused him of practising witchcraft. One of the guides tried to seize Siemens' companion, but Siemens lowered the bottle towards him and gave the Arab such a jolt that he was knocked senseless to the ground.'[41]

Whilst a similar effect can be observed at a host of domed structures and even cathedrals worldwide, given what I had already uncovered about the technology of the Ancients, I could only suspect that this column of energy atop the pyramid was a goal of the designers. Both the Egyptians and the Greeks believed that power – real power – resided in the pillar or column. To the Greeks the actual place of power was the space above the column called the 'attic'. It is interesting that in classical mythology, the hero-god Attis was also strongly linked to the earth, in the form of the goddess Cybele. Columns of the Attic Order were square and it was believed that the column co-joined the earth's power to anything constructed above it, perhaps because static electricity would accumulate on top of the columns, either from the earth or to be absorbed by it. I wondered if this was a symbolic co-joining of earth and sky, or perhaps something related to the 'tower to heaven' often featured in near-death experiences.

As the evening approached, the Giza air was cooling and so I took a walk around 'the Pyramid which is the place of the Sunrise and Sunset' and then returned to my hotel to prepare for a spot of tour hosting the following day. Needless to say, though, my mind was on the Great Pyramid and an item called a *djed* pillar, mentioned briefly in chapter eight. I will now relate to you the gist of the research I have undertaken regarding this pillar, my thinking and where it was to lead.

12

Communion

THERE is a story of King Khufu and his search for the secret chambers of Thoth, and the deeds of the magician called Djedi. Intriguingly, in *The Antiquities of the Jews*,[2] Flavius Josephus tells of how Herod the Great had sought out the Tomb of David in order to take money from it so that he might pay for the rebuilding of the Jerusalem Temple. Money he found none, but apparently he desired to go further into the Tomb, when suddenly two of his guards were slain by a mysterious burst of flame, and Herod, frightened, turned tail and ran.

This story of Josephus is spurious and William Whiston (1667–1752), in his translation, makes it abundantly clear that he thinks so too. So, where did Josephus get it from? Well, if we look at the stories of Khufu and Herod they bear remarkable comparison. Khufu consulted a magician called Djedi wanting to know about the secret chambers of Thoth. Djedi responded by stating that he did not have the information himself, but that he knew where it could be found – inside a box in a room called 'Revision' in Heliopolis. As Sir Alan Gardiner writes:

> '...what ambition could have fired Cheops (Khufu) more than to possess in his own pyramid a replica of the mysterious chambers in the hoary sanctuary of the god of Wisdom?'[3]

At the time of his supposed raid on the Tomb of David, Herod was rebuilding the Temple of Jerusalem, the home of Yahweh. Thoth is often transcribed as

Dwd and is the root of the name David. However, Thoth is the Greek transcription, in Egyptian it is Djehuti. Another form of this root name of David is Djedi – a foreshortened form of Djehuti. For the tombs of Thoth and David, read the same thing; it is really the same story. Furthermore, no remains of any Davidic tomb have ever been located at the Temple site in Jerusalem, nor is it by any means certain that the historical David of the Old Testament ever existed.

Khufu's pyramid took 20 years to build, so too the inner Temple at Jerusalem by Herod's builders. Both kings raid a tomb involving a chap called David. Khufu asks the help of a magician. Herod has magic occur unaided. Khufu wanted to seek information about Thoth's sanctuary, so too Herod, who wanted to complete the magnificence of his own refurbishment of David's Tomb, his monument being constructed around it, mythical though its existence seems to have been. The same too of Khufu, whose pyramid, it is suspected, was erected over the mythical sanctuaries of Thoth. Khufu was a Horus king. Herod's name is not too far from the same spelling.

All of this made me wonder if there was, during the first century, an ancient tradition of sorts permeating the religious culture of Jerusalem. Was Josephus perhaps responding to an older Israelite tradition, one with its origins in Egypt? This made me think about the story of Jesus' name over the temple balustrade – a reference to Osiris of the Great Pyramid, perhaps? Was it the continuation of an age-old tradition, hence the name of Jesus in Israelite tradition? With all of this in mind, the title of Josephus' *The Antiquities of the Jews* seems all the more pointed, because in Josephus' day the Jews were not really all that old as a people; the name only dated back to 600 BC. The fact that Josephus was relating a story which originated prior to this period highlights the point. In all likelihood Josephus was himself of the more ancient tradition. He too had hidden within his story a mythic cipher.

The simple hint that it gave me was, 'The Djedi will lead you to the secrets of Thoth.'

The Return of the Djed and I

Heliopolis, the City of the Sun, was known in deep antiquity as Iunu or Annu. Literally, it was the City of the Pillar. In full, it was Annu Mehret, the City of the Northern Pillar. Tradition had it that atop this pillar was the benben, one of the most sacred and powerful objects in all of the realms of Egyptian belief. This benben, with its pillar, is very intimately associated with Osiris, whose pillar is called the *djed*. The bennu atop the pillar symbolises, in this case, the power of the phoenix within the pillar.

The story of Khufu and the magician Djedi brought me back to this point, for I felt that the secret of the tale was in the magician's name. The *djed* itself is heavily associated with magic. Quite often in Egyptian religious iconography the *djed* is portrayed linked to the key of life, the ankh, thus underlining life's magical qualities, but also underscoring its mystery. On a cosmic level the *djed* represented the backbone of the universe, the axis around which everything spun. So in a way the *djed* also symbolises stillness, the only point of 'no motion' in the entire cosmos. This equates with the point of perfect balance at the centre of the cross. The word *djed* means 'to endure' in Egyptian; the enduring one, everlasting, immortal. Recall that in the myth of Byblos it was Osiris who was sought by Isis, the beloved, and that he, the immortal one, was in the pillar. Extending my point further, this in turn brings us back to the role of the column in Greek, Roman and Egyptian architecture. It did not merely hold up the higher sections of the building, but extended the power of the earth, the numinous, throughout it.

The following line appears in the King James Bible – it is part of the Lord's Prayer, part of the very same text that is to be found inscribed on the interior walls of the pyramid of Unas:

'Thy will be done in Earth as it is in Heaven.'

In the Aramaic tongue the text reads:

'Nehwey, tzevyanach aykanna d'bwashmaya aph b'arha.'

The point of introducing this now is to demonstrate again the fact that, in many ancient languages, words had multiple interpretations, which followed a meaning from subtle to gross, from macrocosm to microcosm. Unfortunately, not only is the reader offered just one interpretation in the King James version, but it has come to be looked upon in a very literal sense. The 'earth' spoken of is taken solely as the title of our planet. The text is very dry and does not reflect the poetry and 'multi-levelled' approach of the ancient wordsmiths.

Alternative Aramaic meanings include: 'Your one desire then acts with ours; as in all light, so in all forms' and 'Let all wills move together in your vortex, as stars and planets swirl through the sky.'[4]

The Aramaic word for earth is *arha*, and its Hebrew roots carry the meaning of *all* nature, *all* gatherings of mass and form produced by universal force. The ancient traditions associate this force with the feminine. 'Mother' and 'earth', as we have seen, have the same connotations and share the same essence. Thus we follow the feminine path from microcosm to macrocosm: earth is the firmament on which we live, in turn the earth lives within the cosmos, which lives through the universal force, which, as the ultimate Mother, gives births to all, and, as the ultimate firmament, nurtures all. This firmament is the substratum, the primal substance that upholds all.

As if to underline this, Sanskrit has the word *artha*, meaning 'substance'. We find the same root, 'ar', here, as we do in the midst of the word 'Mary'. How does the Mother give birth to all? Through the Father, the movement, the lifestream, equated with that oft-used term 'spirit'. It is this that is the essence of the myth of Isis and her search for Osiris, the lifestream that arises within the *djed,* within all living things. Isis and Osiris, the two together as substance and spirit, bring about life.

When we see the word *djed* and its pictorial symbolism, we have to understand that its meaning is very significant and very male, but that it has been interpreted quite differently in a number of contexts, particularly as the symbol has passed into history.

The Osirian *djed* pillar was essential to kingship. There are many representations of it depicting it as the backbone of Osiris/Gesu, with human arms at each side holding the royal regalia. The kingly ritual of the 'raising of the *djed*' was symbolic of the royal power or *puissance*, as well as the resurrection of Osiris.

The prophet Jacob raised a pillar at Mizpah and the first King of Israel, Saul, was acclaimed at this very same place. So we can see a continuation of the tradition beyond Egypt.

The architectural element and its close connection with the life-giving power of the *djed* pillar intrigued me. The force in cosmic terms went beyond life and death and implied consciousness and rebirth, in the form of Sokar, the cosmic Osiris. This was also associated with the god Ptah, who was sometimes referred to as 'the noble *djed*'. The fascinating thing about this association is that Ptah was a god associated with creation, whose instruments were his heart and tongue – through the power of the Word he created the world, but the world could only come about through the *djed,* hence Ptah's connection with it.[5]

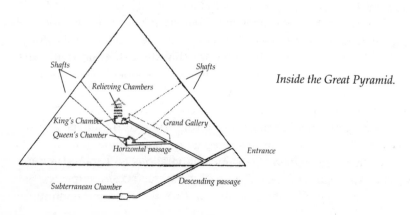

Inside the Great Pyramid.

The Backbone of God

For those who do not know the Great Pyramid, there are three accessible chambers on three distinct levels (see illustration). The lowest is a crypt or grotto which is directly accessible from the pyramid entrance via a descending passageway. It lies beneath the base level of the building and is therefore named the Subterranean Chamber. In myth, the grotto, is often where the divine child is born. This subterranean grotto is in a rough and unfinished state. I wondered if it had been used as an abaton.

In the era of the pyramids the 'earth mother' was held to be the source of dreams. A process of dream incubation was used at many temple sites, as a means of escaping from the conscious mind and receiving guidance from the spirit of the place. The abaton was the pit or dream-chamber where the dream was incubated. The initiate would be sleeping a womb-like sleep within the realm of the earth mother. This was a means of seeking remedy for physical, emotional and mental distress. Release from these burdens would be a purification, a kind of 'birth' or initiation. But one might go through a personal 'hell' first.

In Hebrew and medieval demonology, the lowest pit of hell is called Abaddon. Literally, this means 'the heart of the Lord' (ab-Adon). As 'd' and 't' are cognate, Abaddon and abaton are the same word. The Subterranean Chamber is the deepest 'pit' in the Great Pyramid and we should remember that the pyramid is the Lord – Osiris. We should also not forget that 'hell' is associated with transformation.

The Queen's Chamber comes next in ascending order. To get to it one moves up the ascending passageway to the foot of the Grand Gallery and from there along a horizontal passageway which leads directly to the chamber. The name 'Queen's Chamber' does not seem to have been based upon any particular evidence. It is said that the incumbent Arabs named it so because their women were buried in places with sloping roofs, whilst their men were laid to rest under flat roofs. The Queen's Chamber has a sloping roof and the King's has a flat roof and this simple reason is given as the origins of their names. If this is the case, these designations may be accidentally correct. The masons used limestone in the Queen's Chamber and granite in the King's. It is likely that they saw limestone as feminine compared to granite as masculine. Limestone is relatively permeable, being the prehistoric residue of great sea beds and therefore associated with water, recognised as a feminine element by ancient peoples worldwide. On the other hand, granite is harder and is created as a consequence of the earth's heat, the fiery element being associated with masculinity. Furthermore, whereas granite seems to have been used for its overtly radioactive properties and was therefore a stone of the spirit, limestone has no such qualities, it was everyday building stone and as such probably represented *ma*terial things (see chapter five).

A fascinating pyramid puzzle is that the Queen's Chamber's narrow (eight inch square) 'ventilation shafts' defy their description, having been sealed at both extremes. Moreover, one shaft features a mysterious 'door' some 200 feet up its ascent from the chamber wall. Anomalies abound in this pyramid. Were they deliberately planned as anomalies, or do they just seem anomalous because our minds, our goals and perceptions are so very different from those of the pyramid builders?

Of course, I was looking for concrete evidence that this great building was designed with acoustics in mind. Anecdotal evidence from friends and associates Peter Renton and Paul Ellson, who have an interest in the aformentioned mysterious door, had raised my hopes. Whilst on a research trip, Peter was taking measurements in the horizontal passageway when Paul began to chant in the King's Chamber. Peter relates that he was:

> '...hit by a powerful wave of sound, which flowed past me, entered the Queen's Chamber, and came back out again, mixing with the reverberations which were following in its wake. The effect was very eerie.'

To me, this effect inferred a strong acoustic relationship between the two chambers and adjoining passageways. Soon I would be proved correct.

Before entering the King's Chamber, with its silent ever-haunting sense of 'presence', the Grand Gallery has to be ascended. This great corbelled hall is a breathtaking sight. Such is its scale, design and position, that the pressures bearing down upon the masonry must be immense, to say the least.

At the top of the Grand Gallery is a high step and then one must duck and dive before entering the King's Chamber, a granite-clad chamber of striking simplicity and no adornment whatsoever. However, it is above the King's Chamber that the mystery deepens. Constructed, it was thought, to relieve the enormous pressures bearing down from on top, the so-called 'relieving chambers' are five in number, and from the bottom up are named Davison's, Wellington's, Nelson's, Lady Arbuthnot's and Campbell's Chambers. But to call them 'relieving' chambers is a misnomer. Relieve pressure they inevitably do, but the relief only comes from the presence of the upper chamber – Campbell's Chamber. Here there occurs the inconsistency of the ceiling being formed of sloping limestone slabs – everything else in these remarkable chambers, including the King's Chamber itself, is composed of granite. Furthermore, as has been pointed out,[6] that the architect of this pyramid need not have incorporated five relieving chambers. To relieve the pressure bearing down upon the flat ceiling of the King's Chamber it would only have been necessary to insert pairs of angled limestone beams above it, forming a pitched roof which would withstand the pressure. However, in the King's Chamber there seems to be a purpose at work that suggests at once the symbolic and the acoustic. Other chambers in other pyramids have been constructed using local limestone, whereas the granite used for the King's Chamber was brought from Aswan which is 500 miles up the Nile. Granite, as we have established, tends to be saturated with fairly high doses of the earth's natural radioactivity in the form of the gas radon, which has been implied to 'spirit' stone; this is perhaps reflected in the glyph for granite, ▭, whereas ordinary rock is ▭. The glyph implies a sense of greater solidity and something within making it so.

The pitched limestone ceiling of the Queen's Chamber is enough to sustain the pressure bearing down from above. These pitched beams remain uncracked, whereas the granite beams in the King's Chamber are all cracked. So far, to Egyptologists, the reasons for constructing the King's Chamber in granite remain unclear, as does the reasoning behind the 'relieving' chambers. The bafflement of the casual observer and of Egyptologists continues when we address the King's Chamber sarcophagus, also made of granite. Limestone and alabaster, used in other pyramids, are far easier to fashion. Granite, in contrast, must have been very difficult, and yet the task has been completed with seeming and accomplished ease. The choice of granite is significant – in all areas of the King's Chamber. Having been at Newgrange, at Chartres and a host of other sites, I knew why: the quartz content and the radon emissions. The only thing that really left me baffled was the interior plan – why were the relieving chambers present, if in reality they were not relieving that much?

This puzzle had baffled me for quite a while. In early 1997, I had mulled over it for days, looking and looking again. The answer was there in front of my eyes, but my mind unable to let go enough to see it. Then, one day, having let the issue slip to the back of my mind, as I drank tea at the house of a friend, the gods deposited a thunderbolt into my neocortex. 'The pyramid is Osiris,' flashed in the back of my mind. 'Eureka!' I thought. 'Of course, and it is all so simple!' The pyramid is the god Osiris. Pyramid Text no. 600 confirms this. If we could zoom in on the magnificent edifice with X-ray eyes, we would see the King's Chamber and the chambers above forming a significant pattern. In a mystical sense the Great Pyramid was constructed as the body of the god and whatever the god represented. This pyramid was the house of life, a symbol of living sovereignty. And what representative symbol may be seen in the hands of both gods and pharaohs? A *djed* column – the backbone of the god Osiris. The King's Chamber and its associated relieving columns are in fact a massive *djed* column.

It also struck me at this point, although it must remain purely in the realms of conjecture, that Khufu's quest to find the number of the secret chambers of

A cross-section of the King's Chamber and Relieving Chambers.

Thoth may have borne fruit in the form of these very same chambers.

The *djed* concerned is one with five crossbars. Normally the number of crossbars is four (see the illustration in chapter eleven), though sometimes there are three. Though five-elemented *djeds* exist, they are a rare sight indeed. The only one that I know of resides in the British Museum, and is of a late date. Thinking further about this correlation, and pondering upon the function of the relieving chamber/*djed* complex, there was, I realised, another answer: the *djed-ankh* co-joining upon 'the key of life and of heaven' (see plate 20). Thus the uppermost chamber, Campbell's Chamber, with its gilded roof, would represent the ankh – life itself. If granite is 'spirit' stone, then limestone (being representative of that which is material and being the component of the Campbell's Chamber ceiling) would seem to be symbolic of the divine manifesting in the material world.

Radiation readings taken inside the King's Chamber are really quite high and are similar to those taken at Europe's granite-built sacred sites. In terms of the living sovereignty of the Great Pyramid, the internal cladding of granite, heavily crystalline in nature, is a living, breathing thing – 'breath' in Latin being 'spirit'. Many scientists in recent years have drawn parallels between crystals and living organisms – we must not forget that it is being suggested that at the outset of evolution, life itself was crystalline (see chapter five). Granite, being full of semi-conducting crystals, is a container of the breath of the god, and, as we have seen, people were, and still are, capable of interaction within and with this environment, hence the reason and the realisation that the architectural *djed* is not unique to the Great Pyramid.

In various of the Chinese languages there is a glyph similar to the *djed* hieroglyph, and this led me to realise that Buddhist stupas are very *djed*-like in structure, as are Chinese pagodas, some being five-layered and others seven-layered. I also arrived back at the pineal gland, whose root is the same as 'pine', for in seeing the *djed* I could also see that it was a stylised version of the pine-tree. The same symbol occurs in the realms of Native American creation myths as the 'Tree of Great Peace' (see Anatomy of the Hero), also a fir tree.[7] Again with the Native Americans, the Navajo creation myth tells of four-columned clouds,[8] reminiscent of the *djed* symbol.

It was whilst looking at the Native American traditions, which have much in common with ancient Egyptian thinking and culture, that I came across petroglyphs depicting the shaman and his rattle – a depiction that is at once pine-like and *djed*-like, associated as it is with wisdom. In Egypt the word for 'wisdom' was *djehuti* – literally, 'the Lord within the pillar'. In east and central Arizona these glyphs are particularly vivid. Can it be a coincidence that the shaman's rattle was used for healing or that many of the hero-gods in Native American tradition bear the names Yeshe, Esa or Esu? What is more striking is that the name of many a father god is Yawe, like the Jewish Yahweh.

Shaman and rattle petroglyph

The resonance of the shaman's rattle made me think more about the acoustic connection between sound and healing. The healing hero-god who used words of power to bring about transformation had fascinated me throughout my journey. The fact that he had occurred almost everywhere had astonished me. And it was often in the most unlikely places. The Australasian Aborigines provide one of the most important of these correlations. Taking a wider view of things, though, that should not be in the least bit surprising, given their closeness to the earth and their incredibly well-tuned gifts of mind, body and spirit.

The Aborigines have always interested me. As a boy in Australia I thought that they were angels, with their marvellous painted instruments and panoply of boomerangs and throwing sticks, and, of course, their painted selves. However, it was back in England, many years later, that the obvious would hit – with striking results.

I had a visit from my good friend Bear the didjeridu player (see chapter nine). He brought out of its wrappings a five-foot-long hollowed tube of wood and boomed out a few low-resonance sonorations. Such was the power that, being directly at the other end of it, I felt distinctly overwhelmed. However, when Bear said that this instrument was made from sycamore, which he had found to be one of the best woods for 'didg' making, I nearly fell off my seat. Sycamore was commonly used in Egyptian culture, but its mythic association with Osiris and Isis is what it is most famous for. The holy sycamore at Mataria in Egypt was the Shrine of the Tree, sacred to Isis-Hathor of Dendera. It was also the place where the Holy Family are said to have stayed when they first entered Egypt. This tree was said to be a receptacle for the spirits of the dead, especially Osiris, for this reason mummy cases – coffins – were made out of it.[9] One of the didjeridu's ceremonial uses is in fact as a means of connecting with the ancestral beings of the Australian Aboriginal 'dreamtime'.

The didjeridu is, in effect, a column of air, a pillar. It is a type of *djed*. A *djed*eridu! The name of the dreamtime deity is sounded by the didgeridu master down the hollow tube, to low-resonant effect. What this can do for brainwave patterns we have already seen. Musical pillars like these are used the world over in varying shapes and sizes, in Tibet, Switzerland, South America and so on. Like the Osirian column at Byblos, the god is within the pillar – present as resonance.

That night, in my Cairo hotel, I considered the wheres, the whyfores and the coincidences of my *djed* journey, and, as I settled down to sleep, my mind wandered back to the plan of the King's Chamber complex. I figured that whatever was manifesting itself here was doing so with a deep mystical purpose. I remembered the American dollar bill with its pyramid and the eye – *el Ayin*, the symbol that appears just beneath the pyramidal apex. I tingled. Little did I know that what I was waiting for would soon manifest, in the most unexpected fashion.

The Body and the Blood of Christ

On the following day, I was introduced to an independent researcher, John Reid. John had come to Egypt with a mission. Like myself, he believes that the pyramids of Egypt were designed to be resonant at specific frequencies. I immediately warmed to John's friendly, relaxed and easy-going manner, and tried, in the brief time available, to tell him a little of my own way of thinking. I described to him my suspicion that the Great Pyramid was the finest example of a building constructed to aid the alteration of individual states of consciousness. I explained how I even felt that the building itself was in some way 'conscious', mainly through the building materials used, and how the idea of 'the gods' was a description of the powers within.[10] I told him that I believed that the Great Pyramid was spiritual technology at its peak.[11]

However, I didn't tell John of the Osiris connection. I felt that perhaps I might seem a trifle crazy if I did. I need not have worried – that day he would undertake the first of two, pre-arranged, acoustic experiments in the pyramid. What he was soon to discover would actually have seemed incredible to me, had I not known the Great Pyramid so well.

John is a sound engineer who has spent a lifetime analysing, as a part of his profession, the acoustics of cathedrals, churches and other structures of like use. When he returned to our hotel after this session, he confirmed to me that the prime resonant frequencies of the Queen's Chamber, the King's Chamber *and* its sarcophagus were *all* close to 125Hz, well within the male voice range. He is the first to admit that, given the disparate dimensions of the two chambers and the much smaller proportions of the sarcophagus, this cannot be a coincidence.

John also carried out a test for 'prime resonance' in the Grand Gallery and discovered this to be 250Hz, exactly double the frequency of the King's and Queen's Chambers. The acoustic link between the chambers could hardly be firmer – this would be the reason for Peter Renton's eerie experience, mentioned earlier. The Grand Gallery is a layered structure of seven corbels of four feet each. It has all the appearance and acoustics of having been built to reflect the diatonic ratio. I have never had the opportunity to experiment, but I have often wondered what would happen to the brain if pentatonic chant was sung therein. I pondered over this Fibonacci dimension to the resonance within – 5:8. Is this what happens inside the King's and relieving chambers? My hunch is an educated one, for until recently, with the introduction of air-conditioning, salt would accumulate on the ceiling of the King's Chamber – crystalline salt, which grows following the 5:8 ratio.

In any complex tone, harmonics can be heard as part of the overall frequency. They are an integral multiple of the fundamental tone so, for example, with a tone of 100 Hz, you may hear a harmonic frequency of 200Hz and 300Hz, etc. There is a strong relation to resonance here. If you pick up an acoustic guitar and intone a note into the sound-hole, you will find that, subject to the frequency intoned, sympathetic tones come from the strings, some higher than the note given. These are harmonics.

Of more interest regarding the King's Chamber are sub-harmonics. A sub-harmonic is officially described as 'an integral submultiple of the fundamental'. So, in the case of 100Hz, that number can be divided by whole numbers – 2, 3, etc. – in order to find the sub-harmonic. Actually, sub-harmonics are not recognised in science as being implicit to a complex tone.

John Reid published his figures in the winter of 1999/2000,[12] and subsequent to discussions between us, he provided me with figures which include important predictions regarding sub-harmonics. We thought that until we returned to Giza, these would remain predictions. However, recently published details of experiments in the King's Chamber by Tom Danley and his team[13] have helped to confirm figures given in the charts overleaf. Tom Danley described the moment dramatically:

> 'What really made everyone get up and run to the exit was the resonance near 30Hz. At that moment, I aborted the test. This was a good resonance, it got nice and strong and scared the wits out of several crew members.'[14]

Now, if we extrapolate some of the sub-harmonics from the frequencies that John discovered, we obtain the following results:

Area	Prime Resonance**	1st Sub Harmonic 2:1	2nd Sub Harmonic 4:1	3rd Sub Harmonic 8:1	4th Sub Harmonic 16:1	5th Sub Harmonic 32:1
Grand Gallery	250Hz	125 Hz	62.5 Hz	31.25Hz	15.62Hz	[†] 7.81Hz
King's Chamber	125Hz	62.5Hz	31.25Hz	15.62Hz	[†] 7.81Hz	3.9 Hz
Queen's Chamber	125Hz	62.5Hz	31.25Hz	15.62Hz	[†] 7.81Hz	3.9 Hz
Sarcophagus	125Hz	62.5Hz	31.25Hz	15.62Hz	[†] 7.81Hz	3.9 Hz

The 3:1 and 6:1 harmonics are also significant:

Area	Prime Resonance**	3:1	6:1
Grand Gallery	250Hz	83.33Hz	*41.66Hz
King's Chamber	125Hz	*41.66Hz	20.83Hz
Queen's Chamber	125Hz	*41.66Hz	20.83Hz
Sarcophagus	125Hz	*41.66Hz	20.83Hz

**Prime Resonance is to the nearest centre frequency of analysis.

If we look at the frequencies marked [†] under 16:1 and 32:1, we find 7.81Hz. This is the frequency known as Schumann resonance. In her book, *Sounding the Inner Landscape*, Kay Gardner cites the work of Michael Hutchinson,

> 'When a meditator reaches the rare point of oneness with All That Is, the EEG reading is around 7.83Hz. This is also the frequency rate of the electrical field resonating between Earth and the ionosphere (the Schumann resonance). Hutchinson writes that this frequency has the unique power of "seemingly integrating and harmonizing one's body and brain with the Earth's electromagnetic energy." This helps the meditator attune with Earth energy through the synchronization of vibrations.' [15]

And here, firmly built into every room of Khufu's Great Pyramid is that very resonance. Coincidence?

Paul Ellson has pointed out another potentially important inbuilt frequency. In the 3:1 and 6:1 columns of the chart, 41.66Hz is asterisked. There is evidence to suggest that frequencies in the region of 40Hz are consciousness related.

A device called a magneto-encephalograph (MEG), which can measure the brain's holistic magnetic activity, has enabled scientists to identify brain-wide oscillations in the region of 40Hz and clearly associate them with the presence of consciousness. Research by Rodolfo Llinas and his team at the New York University School of Medicine has also confirmed that these oscillations cover the whole cortex and move in waves from front to back. In *SQ, Spiritual Intelligence, the Ultimate Intelligence*[16] Danah Zohar and Ian Marshall further report that:

> '...these oscillations "bind" individual perceptual and cognitive events in the brain into a larger, more meaningful whole and there may be a quantum dimension to the ion channel activity that generates the oscillations...'[17]

This reference to ions is particularly interesting given that the granite in the King's Chamber exudes ions as part of the 'radon package'. The inbuilt harmonic of around 40Hz could well have been used by chanters to stimulate and increase brain coherence, and the presence of ion-exuding stone may well have helped to facilitate this.

As we can see from the chart, the frequencies are precise, moving in octaves of earth and brainwave frequency. The effect upon the mind and the body when these frequencies are intoned, would be potent. The pyramid – the Mr – is a meeting place of Earth Resonance and humanity for purposes of interaction. The earth resounds to the cosmos. The pyramid is a gateway to God; when individuals enter it, God may enter them – which is perhaps why so many people have reported life-changing experiences within its chambers.

Further to these acoustical enquiries, John Reid was also the first person to carry out cymatic experiments in the Great Pyramid. Many inquisitive visitors have noticed that the sarcophagus rings like a low-pitched bell when struck. He suspected that the ancient Egyptians had deliberately tuned it for ritualistic purposes and he decided to set up an experiment to 'see' the sound waves circulating within its interior, in the hope of gaining some insight into this theory. However, its south-east corner has been badly damaged by generations of souvenir hunters so he had first to carry out temporary repairs using a pre-formed aluminium corner. He then placed a small loudspeaker into the sarcophagus and stretched a plastic membrane over its open top, which was then weighted down with 63 small bags of sand to create a taut, drum-like, surface. Onto this John sprinkled a layer of fine quartz sand (using a cappuccino chocolate shaker!) The speaker was connected to a sine-wave oscillator in order to create a range of pure tones.[18] He turned on the equipment and slowly adjusted the control on the oscillator whilst closely observing the sand grains for movement.

Even though John had taken something of a leap of imagination to create such an experiment, he had no idea that the sand would reveal something quite so extraordinary. As the images began to form he couldn't believe what he was seeing. One by one, in an atmosphere of intense anticipation, archaic motifs appeared – **a whole series of ancient Egyptian symbols**: the *Nemes*, ritual headdress of the pharaohs (see plate14); the *Ankh* or key of life (see plate 19); the hieroglyph for Ra, the sun god (see plate 15); the *Wedjat* or sacred eye of Horus (see plate 18); they were all there and many more.

John rushed back to our hotel in great excitement, eager to share his revelations with me. Sitting in the hotel lobby, he was breathless as he told me of his news – I shall never forget the look upon his face. I listened intently and I caught his excitement as he recounted his experiences. Of the eye of Horus, I remember quite vividly what he said:

> 'The chamber was filled with the low-pitched tone of the oscillator and I was watching the sand intently; it sat lifeless and motionless on the membrane. I slowly adjusted the pitch and suddenly all the sand grains jumped into life and began to move. I began to see what looked like two eye images trying to break through within a few centimetres of each other, giving me the eerie feeling that I was being watched. One of them formed more fully and momentarily pulsated, almost as if blinking. I told myself to remain objective but I was so mesmerised it is a wonder that I had the presence of mind to take a photograph. Only a second or so after I did, the eyes melted into oblivion.'

He went on to tell me that almost every tiny adjustment of the oscillator brought new images to the sand in a seemingly never ending stream but he lacked both the time and the film stock to record them all. It was, he said, one of those rare events, which may come only once in a lifetime, when you know with every cell of your being that what you are witnessing is far greater than yourself and belongs to humankind. He likened the sarcophagus to Arthur C. Clarke's monolith in *2001 A Space Odyssey*, frozen from the dawn of time, waiting with infinite patience for someone to trigger the message that it had been programmed to deliver. The cymatic images had convinced John that the sarcophagus contains ancient data, locked into a matrix of quartz crystals, embedded within the living stone. But whilst the scientist in John struggled with the inference that the ancient magician-priests had somehow 'encoded' data within the stone, I knew without doubt that his work was an amazing confirmation of my own research.

It was his description of the image which formed at 190 Hz which excited me most (see plate16). This tone is yet another significant harmonic, being exactly ten times 19 Hz, the frequency which triggered the visionary experience investigated by Lawrence and Tandy referred to in chapter six. John told me that the image strongly resembled a 'human backbone', complete with curvature; he said that it slowly pulsated in a state of flux, as if it was a living organism. Stunned, I asked him to repeat his description; I thought that perhaps my ears had deceived me. But there was no change in his description and a shiver ran up my own backbone with the realisation that my quest was finally over. After almost 20-years, after thousands of hours of study and research, destiny had brought me to Egypt to meet the man who could unlock the secrets at the heart of the pyramid and provide answers to so many questions. His 190 Hz image was a *djed* column! but it represented much more than that. It was a spine, a pillar, the trunk of the world tree. It was the image of Osiris and of Gesu, and it had imposed itself upon the sand for all to see. Even if it had been the physical remains of Jesus himself that had been found, the moment would not have been sweeter for me. This image, the image of the *djed*, had been derived through the action of sound, thus confirming my understanding that 'the Word' was far more than a philosophical concept.

Standing back to take stock of this news, I realised that I had come to a milestone on my journey. I had sought and, as I write this, it seems to me a wonder that I found. Yet there was the evidence. Not only the presence of conciousness-expanding frequencies, but also an acoustically obtained language – the icons of religion – all gained in a 4500 year-old building that bore the name of the divine mother, Mary. I could imagine the priests stretching the animal skin over the sarcophagus and sprinkling the sand over it. The pyramid choir would chant and the images would appear. These sacred images would, in time, influence the design of many of their symbols and hieroglyphs, some of them ultimately becoming stylised versions of the cymatic forms. A technology so simple yet so profound.

But the revelations do not end here. I remembered an image, from an Egyptian papyrus, of the fifth division of the Duat, the House of Sokar.

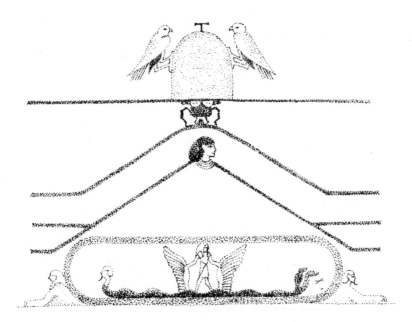

The cosmic Osiris, Sokar-Osiris (see illustration overleaf) is shown in his boat beneath a pyramid form that has as its apex a head. Above this there is what I can only describe as a waveform, and indeed, the pyramid seems to reflect this too. And where is this resonance being emitted from? An omphalos-shaped bell, held high by two doves. From out of the bell emerges the scarab, Khepera – the Egyptian verb 'to be'. The resonance is 'becoming', and upon it rides Sokar, who is within it.

The King's Chamber *djed* is a tower to the Lord, known to the Phoenicians as Baal: a Baal tower or bell-tower, 'bell' and 'Baal' having the same root. Bells are the voice of the Lord and if a plan of a church bell-tower is overlaid on a plan of the King's Chamber complex, we get a match (see plate 20) – both serve the same purpose. Sitting with John and discussing the images, it occurred to me that the famous Egyptian Book of the Dead was meant to be sung, in honour of the gods, and ultimately in honour of the One God. The word 'oscillate' comes from the Latin *oscillum* – the mask of Bacchus. He was the Roman version of Osiris-Dionysus, the god who 'trod the wine-press alone'. Surely, the ceremony in Khufu's Great Pyramid was an acoustic Eucharist!

> 'I have eaten from the tambourine: I have drunk from the cymbal.'[19]

These words, from the Mystery Schools, suddenly made sense. The substance and the motion, the bread and the wine, the body and the blood of Jesus, Adonis, Aleyin, Apollo, Bacchus, Dionysus, Esus, Gesar, Issa, Osiris and more! The power had manifested, in the name of the gods!

Afterword

Acoustic Consciousness

– The End of the Journey

'The act of faith is an act of acceptance, not an explanation.'

Morris West, *The Shoes of the Fisherman.*

'Only a fool rejects what he cannot understand.'

E. D. Elkington

The End of the Journey

LOOKING back over the Giza plateau later on that day I saw the bright globe of the sun turn from white hot to warm yellow and then to red as it perched upon the horizon. My emotions were running at a premium as the events of the day sank in deeply enough to become accepted as reality. I had never envisaged my hypotheses bearing fruit in this way. The research had drawn me to Giza, where a chance meeting with a fellow Englishman had resolved the matter at a stroke, but with a huge bonus – not only was the Great Pyramid built for acoustic purposes, but also, there was a visual element too!

Everything made much more sense. The female and the male, the substance and the motion – Life arising from the Word, and the symbols of life made visible through acoustic ritual. For the first time in my life I felt that I could understand the nature of it all, including the yearnings that I had had to pierce the veil and gain a vision of a wider reality.

As if in answer to my prayers the powers that be, the *neters*, had bestowed upon me the gift that, through this book, I share with you. The gift though, was not there simply for the taking, it was hard fought and hard earned. I felt as if my mind, body and spirit had, over a course of two decades, been battered into submission and that having come through it all, the highs and the lows, the joys and the sorrows, the black and the bright, I was ready for the gift. Yet to find that the answer was oh so simple was the greatest wonder of all. My reaction was to laugh, for the love of the Lord (hu-mour), brings the joy of laughter.

It was only later, back in England, that a sadness crept in. A sadness that modern science seems to be so far from the divine. And yet, once the Church's suppression of open enquiry had begun (see Part One), it was inevitable that the development of science would be separate from religion, leading in turn to the crucial dislocation of science from spirituality, and to the era of rationalism and objectivity. However, rationalism seems more about ration that ratio, as it has foreshortened the spirit of enquiry to within the empirical mean. Yet hope prevails, for even as I write, new technologies are being nurtured which will measure the subtlest of energies. The coming generation of researchers will be like hungry children suckling upon the food of the gods as they are taken into the hitherto unexpected realms of the spirit.

Space technology, too, will extend our boundaries. As the astronauts orbited around the dark side of the moon, and thus beyond the influence of the earth, some reported transcendental experiences and others reported UFO phenomena, pointing perhaps to a change of perceptual awareness on their part. Furthermore, many of those taking part in the Apollo missions of the sixties and seventies commented upon 'the womb of space' – an almost mythological turn of phrase. By virtue of their situation, these people were naturally tuning in to a greater awareness.

At a far greater distance, deep in space, there is an ongoing ever-present mystery that we have been able to view only recently. Courtesy of the Hubble Space Telescope, we can now see the most profound images of gargantuan pillars of dust and gas, many light years across. Great fists arise, as if clutching fate itself; the gods rise up, aeons old, to illuminate an Olympus that humanity hardly suspected existed.

Deep inside the Eagle nebula, a super-massive pillar, 13 light years long, there is a cosmic miracle happening: the birth of stars. The image taken by the Hubble Space Telescope displays the illumed knuckles of a giant's fist – a Titan perhaps? – and at the edge of these knuckles, bundles of light, pockets of compressed dust and gas that have fused and ignited, are to be seen drifting off into the ether, giving light to the dark reaches of the universe. These things have been named extraneous gaseous globules or 'EGGs' by astronomers, and indeed, that is what they are – eggs in the birthing fields of the cosmos.

To my mind, this is the real mythology. This is the expanse of the Greek gods, of the Egyptian gods too, and the Assyrian, the Aztec and so on. It is a living mythology, universal and pertinent. Here, from the birthing fields of the macrocosm to the birthing fields of the microcosm, Osiris' holy pillar is at work. In the earth's own birthing fields it is seen in the pillar shape of cereal heads, the barley and the wheat so venerated by the Egyptians.

I am aware by now that the ancient Egyptians equated the djed, the pillar shape, with the most potent conduit of divine energy on every level.

From the Ancients' point of view, all of existence fitted into an inter-connected poetic context. This spoke of all things emanating from a source and reflecting one another. In this sense, the Word, potent with frequencies, octave upon octave echoes from star to star across the entire extent of the universe. It is possible that these are frequencies that we could become attuned to. Given that 'God' is 'voice', the hypothesis of acoustic consciousness is not so much an exaggeration, but perhaps a 'super-reality' worthy of serious research.

Could this be reflected in the context of ancient mythology? One wonders about the birthing fields and the pillars of the Eagle nebula and the ancient belief that the dead, if pure, are reborn as stars. Could humanity have picked up knowledge from a source many octaves higher and then transmitted it as only humankind can? As language? As poetry?

To me, the poetic quality of myth in its telling is a real display of an awareness of immortality, the resonant power of the soul and the subtle rhythms that underlie nature. In the words of the late poet R. S. Thomas, 'God is a poet who sang creation.' Yet within creation each individual soul has its equally individual sound – its own song, its own link with the Voice, God. We all have that poet within us and from time to time, we sense a something that dwells within, intelligent and arcane, divine, imperishable, universal and yet so deeply personal.

This seems at odds with modern science, but science today is at odds with itself. Objectivity can only go so far. One can reduce a thing until it is virtually, on a sub-atomic level, no longer a 'thing', but a tangle of rhythmic vibrations. Who ,then, is best to describe the dance of life but the poet, whose rhythmic flow of musical language can so naturally define the ever-moving world and resonate to the heartbeat of the universe itself: the rhythm of love.

Objectivity is an illusion. What we perceive is subjective. Consciousness itself is what we perceive, clothed with a little help from the outward, liquid flow of the Word. That the Ancients knew this is all too obvious. Perhaps it is about time that we listened to them and moreover, perhaps it is time that we awakened to their wisdom.

*　　　　*　　　　*

Appendices

Contents

Footnotes and references follow each appendix, where required. This section is not featured in the main index.

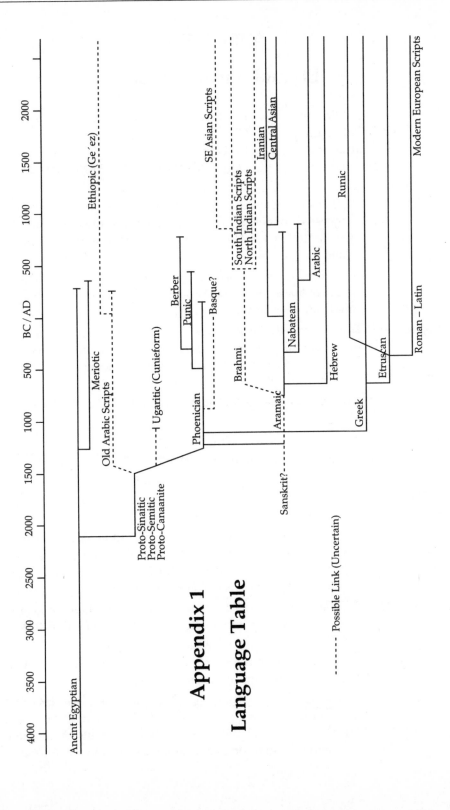

Appendix 1
Language Table

Appendix 2

Etymological Glossary

OE – Old English	Fr. – French	cf. – compare
OS – Old Saxon	Gk. – Greek	f. – from
IE – Indo-European	L – Latin	OF – Old French
Heb. – Hebrew	ON – Old Norse	AN – Anglo-Norman

Alien L *alienus* – belonging to another person or place; f. *alius*. Suggested etymology *El Ayin* – the Heb., Gk. and Egyptian letter 'O'; the 16th letter. The Eye of Horus, the third eye, the pineal gland.

Anatomy L *anatomia*, Gk. *anatomia* (in early use often *anath* or *anoth*), aphetic forms of 'natomy', 'atomy' and 'otomy'. Anat or Anath was, in myth, another form of the goddess Isis.

Balustrade Baluster, Fr. *balustre*, Italian *balaustro*, L *balaustim*, one of a series of short moulded shafts supporting a coping or rail. Ultimately f. Gk. *balaustion* – the blossom of the wild pomegranate.

Barley 1184-85 *barli*, OE *baerlic* (966), *baere*, *bere* (beer).

Bell OE *belle*, *bellhus* – bell-chamber, Icelandic *bjalla*; cf. Phoenician Baal.

Cereal L *cerealis*, f. Ceres, goddess of agriculture.

Chorus L *chorus*, Gk. *khoros*, dance or band of dancers; cf. Horus and hour, Arabian *houris*, Persian *huri*. Music and the Gods.

Church OE *cirice*, OS *kirika*, *kerika*, OE *kirk*, Gk. Circe, English circle, Gk. *kurikon*, f. *kurios* – master, Lord.

Earth Gk. *Ge*, *Gaia*, Egyptian *Geb*, OS *ertha*, cf. Hertha. *Gaya* – in Hindu myth an *asura*, everyone touching him was purified. *Pahlavi, Gayomart* – in Iranian cosmology the first man; literally 'Earth of the Earth'. Re: Heb. *Adam, Edom* – red earth.

Exhilaration L *exhilarare*, L *ex* and *hilaris* – hilarious, out of laughter. Gk. hilaros, related to *hilaos* – gracious, kindly. Cf. Hu – the Lord. *Exhilare* – out of grace, poss. the Lord's grace.

Experience L *experiri* – out of trying, effort (implying the expelling of air through effort). L *ex* – out of, *periri* – to go through.

God German *Gott*, ON *God*, OE *God* (pl. Godu), Goth. *Guda* (pl.), Old High German *Got* (or *Goth*), Gothic *Guth*, f. Germanic *guth* – voice. 'The Goth. and ON words always follow the neuter declension. The neuter sb., in its original heathen use, would answer rather to the L *numen* than to L *deus.'* (OED) Cf. Egyptian *neter.* IE *ghu*, repr. by Sanskrit *hu* – invoke the Lord, the gods.

Harlequin   16th century, *harlicken, harlaken*, Fr. *harlequin*, later var. of *herlequin*. Medieval L *hellequini*, cf. herald. Gk. *helle* – metamorphosis or change (see Herald).

Herald   Middle English *herauld, heraud*, OF *herau*, OS *heridd*, ON *haraldr*. Officer who delivers proclamations (the task of the herald is to announce change). Cf. Hermes, herald of the gods, heroetc..Ultimately, *Hu, Hero, Horus* – the Lord.

Humour   OF *humor, umor*, L *umor. Hu* – the Lord, *-mour* cf. Fr. *amour* (var. of hieroglyphic *Mr*) – love. Originally meant any of the four chief fluids of the body (blood, phlegm, choler and melancholy), as in Fr. *mer* – sea.

Mass   OF *masse*, L *massa*, Gk. *maza* – barley cake (cf. maize) (cf. Ahura Mazda).

Music   Fr. and OF *musique*, L *musica*, Gk. *mousike* (fem. of *mousikos*) – pertaining to the Muse or Muses; f. Gk. *Mousa* – Muse. The Muses were daughters of Zeus and Mnemosyne (which combines *mnemonikas* – mindful, remember, and syn – with).

Nature   Italian *natura*, L *natura* (f. poss. stem of *nasci* – natal; birth or nativity). Poss. Egyptian *neter* – the gods (or principles) within nature. Essential qualities of innate character. Vital powers.

Ogham   *Ogam, Ohm, Om* – various. The Druidic alphabet, the original expression of the Word.

Pine   L *pinus*, Italian *pino*, Rumanian *pin*, f. base pit, Gk. *pitus* – pine (as in pituitary). L *pituita* – gum. A tree of coniferous variety much described in myth, hence pineal.

Real   AN *real*, OF *reel*, Vedic Ram. To exist, or L blood.

Science   L *scientia*, Spanish *ciencia*, Portuguese *sciencia*, f. L *scire* – to know. Orig. from the root *sapientia* (early Roman).

Scion   OF *sion, cion*. A descendant or offshoot, esp. by grafting; a young member of a family.

Star   OS *sterro*, L *stella*, Gk. *aster*; re: astronomy, astrology. Egyptian Ast – Isis.

Tragedy   L *tragaedia*, Gk. *tragoidia*, f. *tragos* – goat, and *oide* – ode, cf. the Hebrew scapegoat, re: Greek myths of Zeus in the Dictyean cave (Bernal, *Black Athena*, vol.i, p.65).

Wheat   OE *hweate*, OS *hweti*, hw-hu (830).

Zion   Celtic *Si un*, L *Sion*, Gk. *Seon*, Heb. *Tsiyon*. One of the hills of Jerusalem, a fortress of stone.

Appendix 3

Dynastic Table of the Pharoahs

Archaic Period (c. 3150 - 2686 BC)

Pre-Dynastic (c. 3150 - 3050 BC)

Dynasty O
King Scorpian
Narmer

Early Dynastic Period

1st Dynasty (c. 3050 - 2890 BC)	2nd Dynasty (c. 2890 - 2649 BC)	3rd Dynasty (c. 2649 - 2575 BC)	
Menes	Hotepsekhemwy	Zanacht	2649-2630
Ajd	Raneb	Djaser	2630-2611
Djer	Ninetjer	Sekhemhet	2611-2603
Diet	Peribsen	Khaba	2603-2599
Den	Khasekhemwy	Huni	2599-2575

Old Kingdom (2575 - 2150 BC)

4th Dynasty (2575 - 2465 BC)		5th Dynasty (2465 - 2323 BC)	
Sneferu	2575-2551	Userkaf	2465-2458
Khufu (Cheops)	2551-2528	Sahure	2458-2446
Djedefre	2528-2520	Neferirkare-Kakai	2446-2426
Khafre (Chephren)	2520-2494	Shepseskare-Ini	2425-2419
Menkaure (Mycerinus)	2494-2472	Neferefre	2419-2416
Shepseskaf	2472-2465	Neuserre	2416-2392
		Menkaukar	2396-2388
		Djedkare-Izezi	2388-2356
		Una	2356-2323

6th Dynasty (2323-2150 BC)

Teti	2323-2291
Pepi I	2291-2255
Merenre	2255-2246
Pepi II	2246-2150

First Intermediate Period (c. 2150 - 2040 BC)

8th - 10th Dynasties

Middle Kingdom (2040 - 1783 BC)

11th Dynasty (2040 - 1991 BC)		12th Dynasty (1991 - 1783 BC)	
Mentuhotep I	2040-2061	Amenernhet I	1991-1962
Mentuhotep II	2061-2010	Sesostris I	1971-1926
Mentuhotep III	2010-1998	Amenemhet II	1929-1892
Mentuhotep IV	1998-1991	Sesostris	1897-1878
		Sesostris III	1878-1844
		Amenemhet III	1844-1797
		Amenemhet IV	1799-1787
		Sobek Neferurd	1787-1783

Second Intermediate Period (1783 - 1550 BC)

13th - 17th Dynasties

New Kingdom (1150-1070 BC)

18th Dynasty (1150 - 1307 BC)		19th Dynasty (1307-1196 BC)	
Ahmost	1550-1525	Ramesse I	1307-1306
Amenhotep I	1525-1504	Seti I	1306-1290
Tuthmosis I	1504-1492	Ramesses II	1290-1224
Tuthmosis II	1492-1479	Merneptah	1224-1204
Tuthmosis III	1479-1425	Seti II	1214-1204
Hatshepsut	1473-1458	Amenmesse	1202-1199
Amenhotep II	1425-1401	Siptah	1204-1198
Tuthmosis IV	1401-1391	Twosret	1197-1196
Amenhotep III	1391-1353		
AmenhotepIV/			
Akhenaton	1353-1335	20th Dynasty (1196 - 1070 BC)	
Smenkhare	1335-1333		
Tutankhamun	1333-1323		
Ay	1323-1319		
Horemheb	1319-1307		

Third Intermediate Period (1070 - 712 BC)

21st Dynasty - Tanis (1070-712 BC)
22nd Dynasty - Libyan (945-712 BC)
23rd Dynasty - Nubia and Thebes (878-712 BC)
24th Dynasty - Soris (724-712 BC)

Late Kingdom (712 - 332 BC)

25th - 30th Dynasties

Graeco - Roman Period (332 BC - AD 395)

Appendix 4

A Chronology

10,000 BC	Mesolithic or Middle Stone Age begins.
	The earliest stages of the city of Jericho built.
8000 BC	Neolithic age begins.
	The domestication of animals and the cultivation of cereal crops is established.
7500 BC	The ice covering much of the earth has now mostly melted away – the separation of the British Isles from the European mainland occurs at about roughly this period.
5000 BC	The rise of the city-state secures the importance of religion within society; belief in the importance of the harvest and the planting of the corn reflecting the human life cycle becomes paramount.
4200 BC	Sumerian civilisation takes root. Language in its written form takes a little longer. Settlements appear along the banks of the Nile. The putative Tasian and Badarian periods begin.
4000 BC	The Amer-Indians begin to develop their way of life.
3500 BC	Newgrange in Ireland constructed. Egyptian towns in the Nile delta are also developing. In Upper Egypt towns and settlements develop along the Nile. The development of hieroglyphs.
3100 BC	Stonehenge built. Silbury Hill in southern Britain constructed. In Egypt the two kingdoms are unified by the mysterious King Scorpion and later by Narmer, the first king of the Old Kingdom first dynasty.
3000 BC	Egypt and Sumer develop systems of numbering. Bronze is produced in Egypt.
2900 BC	Sumerian influence extends everywhere, including the Indus Valley civilisations (known as the Harappan).
	Work starts on the first of the ziggurats, work that is continued by the later Chaldeans.
2700 BC	Sumer is at its height. The city of Ur comes to prominence.
2686 BC	The rise of the Third Dynasty in Egypt. Djoser builds the first pyramid – the step pyramid at Saqqara.
2675 BC	Egypt is importing cedar from Lebanon. The Epic of Gilgamesh.
2600 BC	The beginning of the Bronze Age in Crete - the early Minoan period.
2550 BC	The fall of the Sumerians. The Akkadians begin their ascent to power in the old city of Ur.
2575 BC	Pharoah, Khufu constructs the Great Pyramid at Gisa.
2550 BC	Pharoah Khafre constructs the second of the great pyramids at Gisa.
2331 BC	Sargon of Akkad conquers Sumeria, Elamite Susa, and possibly Cyprus.

2190 BC	The empire of Sargon is swept away by barbarians from the north, whom the Sumerians call the Guti – 'the vipers from the hills',
2060 BC	Stability is brought to Egypt during the Middle Kingdom period by Pharaoh Mentuhotep II, of the 11th dynasty.
2050 BC	The destruction of Troy II.
2000 BC	The Palace of Knossos is built on Crete.
1950 BC	The autobiography of the scribe Sinuhe reveals that pharaohs are considered to be living gods.
1842 BC	Amenemhet III, the greatest pharaoh of the Middle Kingdom, comes to the throne.
1800 -1400 BC	The Patriarch Abraham leaves the city of Ur.
1792 BC	Hammurabi creates the first Babylonian Empire. A golden age of peace, prosperity and law making ensues.
1700 BC	The Hyksos – The Shepherd Kings – invade Egypt and rule for two hundred years.
1600 BC	The Minoans change from a hieroglyphic style of writing to the style now known as 'linear A'.
1590 BC	The beginning of the liberation of Egypt from Hyksos rule takes place under Pharoah Seqenenre Tao. The task is completed under Ahmose, founder of the 18th dynasty.
1350 BC	The Amarna period in Egypt under Pharoah Akhenaton.
c.1200 BC	The Exodus from Egypt of the children of Israel under Moses. The commandments of Moses, like Hammurbi's, are said to be God-given.
1190 BC	The entry into Palestine of Joshua.
1183 BC	The final destruction of Troy by the Greeks.
1025 BC	Saul is made the first King of Israel.
1003 BC	David becomes King of Israel. He makes Jerusalem his capital.
970 BC	Solomon is King of Israel.
959 BC	Solomon completes the Temple of Jerusalem.
925 BC	Rehoboam succeeds his father. Israel splits into a double kingdom – Judah and Israel.
733 BC	The Assyrians invade Israel – the end of the northern kingdom - the prophets Micah and Isaiah having already given their warnings.
722 BC	The fall of Samaria after a three year siege; 27,290 Israelites are deported wholesale into Mesopotamia.
715 BC	The traditional date of the founding of Rome by Romulus and Remus.
705 BC	Hesiod writes the Theogony, both he and Homer are believed to have given the Greeks their unique view of the gods.
640 BC	King Josiah reigns in Judah; many reforms take place.
586 BC	The fall of Jerusalem to the invading army of the Babylonian king, Nebuchadnezzar. Many are exiled to Babylon. The end of Judah as a nation.

538 BC	Cyrus releases the Jews from their captivity, the end of the exile.
323 BC	The death of Alexander the Great. The Ptolemies rule in Egypt.
202 BC	The end of the second Punic war between the Romans and the Carthaginians.
200 BC	Palestine is under Seleucid control.
175 BC	Antiochus IV imposes Hellenistic principles upon the Temple of Jerusalem.
167 BC	The beginning of the great revolt under the Maccabees.
166 BC	The revolt succeeds under Judas Maccabeus.
164 BC	Judas Maccabeus defeats the Seleucids, and cleanses and rededicates the Temple.
161 BC	The Maccabees ally themselves with Rome.
59 BC	Caesar is consul of Rome.
40 BC	Herod the Great becomes king, all Maccabaean opposition having been removed.
27 BC	Octavian becomes the first Emperor of Rome, taking the name Augustus.
c.4 BC	The birth of Jesus, son of Antipater and Miriam. Herod dies, and so too does his son, Antipater.
AD 1	Beginning of the Christian era.
c.AD 30	The death of Christ upon the cross.
AD 33	The conversion of Saul; he becomes Paul. St. Stephen is stoned to death by a mob: the first Christian martyr.
AD 36	Pontius Pilate is recalled to Rome.
AD 45	The first of Paul's missionary journeys.
AD 55	The death of Paul.
AD 66	Revolt breaks out in Judea.
AD 70	Jerusalem is taken by the Romans and destroyed.
AD 71	The first of the Gospels are written.
AD 73	The seige of Massada.
AD 132	Simeon Bar-Cochba (The son of the Star), declares himself the Messiah and the final revolt of the Jews begins. Two years later the revolt is utterly defeated and the diaspora begins with the Jews being forbidden entrance into Jerusalem.

Appendix 5

Herodian Lineage

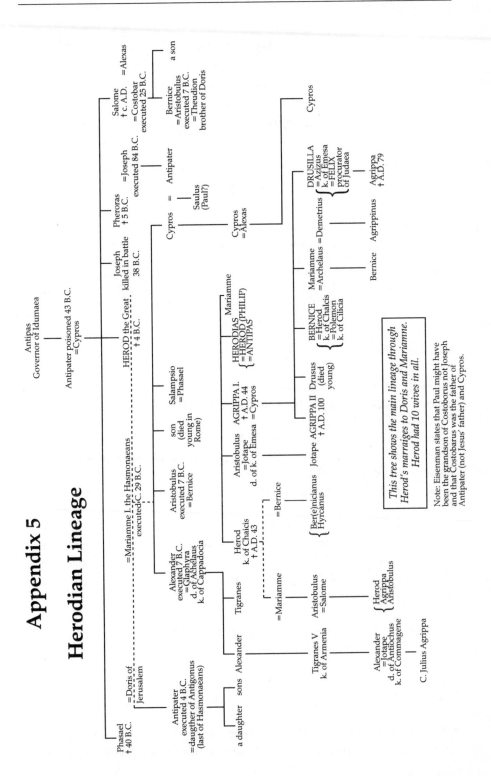

Antipas
Governor of Idumaea

Antipater poisoned 43 B.C.
=Cypros

Phasael
† 40 B.C.

Antipater
executed 4 B.C.
=daughter of Antigonus
(last of Hasmonaeans)

=Doris of
Jerusalem

HEROD the Great
† 4 B.C.

=Mariamme I. the Hasmonaeans
executedC. 29 B.C.

Joseph
killed in battle
38 B.C.

Pheroras
† 5 B.C.
=Joseph
executed 84 B.C.

Salome
† c. A.D.
=Costobar
executed 25 B.C.
=Alexas

Cypros
=Cypros

Saulus
(Paul?)

Antipater

Bernice
=Aristobulus
executed 7 B.C.
=Theudion
brother of Doris

a son

a daughter   sons   Alexander

Alexander
executed 7 B.C.
=Glaphyra
d. of Archelaus
k. of Cappadocia

Salampsio
=Phasael

son
(died
young in
Rome)

Aristobulus
executed 7 B.C.
=Bernice

Cypros
=Alexas

Herod
k. of Chalcis
† A.D. 43

Tigranes

=Mariamme

AGRIPPA I.
† A.D. 44
=Cypros

Aristobulus
=Jotape
d. of k. of Emesa

HERODIAS
=HEROD (PHILIP)
=ANTIPAS

Mariamme

Mariamme
=Archelaus

Bernice   Agrippinus

Tigranes V
k. of Armenia

=Mariamme

=Bernice

Drusus
(died
young)

AGRIPPA II
† A.D. 100
=Cypros

Jotape

BERNICE
=Herod
  k. of Chalcis
=Polemon
  k. of Cilicia

DRUSILLA
=Azizus
  k. of Emesa
=FELIX
  procurator
  of Judaea

Demetrius

Cypros

Aristobulus
=Salome

{ Herod
  Agrippa
  Aristobulus

{ Ber(e)nicianus
  Hyrcanus

Agrippa
† A.D. 79

Alexander
=Jotape
d. of Antiochus
k. of Commagene

C. Julius Agrippa

*This tree shows the main lineage through
Herod's marraiges to Doris and Mariamme.
Herod had 10 wives in all.*

Note: Eisenman states that Paul might have
been the grandson of Costoborus not Joseph
and that Costobarus was the father of
Antipater (not Jesus' father) and Cypros.

Appendix 6

John Reid

EGYPTIAN SONICS

An extract from the forthcoming publication *Egyptian Sonics*
(publication due in summer 2001)

The foundations of many sciences were laid by the ancient Egyptians and some
of their discoveries influenced Greek and Roman science. It is well documented that
acoustic enhancement of public buildings was common practice in both Greek
and Roman cultures[1], but were their architects inspired by acoustical knowledge obtained
from ancient Egypt? This preliminary study takes a first step towards answering this
question; early results have yielded some suggestion of sonic knowledge.

Introduction

Many of Egypt's pyramids have chambers which are highly resonant, possibly
the best examples being Snefru's 'Red' Pyramid at Dahshur and Khufu's 'Great'
Pyramid at Giza; it is believed that both monuments were constructed in a 47-
year period, *c.* 2575-2528 BC in the 4th Dynasty[2]. Snefru, Khufu's father, chose
a 50-feet high, cathedral-like, corbelled limestone main chamber whilst Khufu
chose a simple rectangular, granite-lined space; granite has also been used to
fashion Khufu's sarcophagus. Whilst there is no evidence that these two
pyramids were designed by the same architect, the disparate choices of
construction material and style were both successful in creating a long
'Reverberation Time', (the time taken for a sound to decay to one millionth of
its original intensity). The results below show that the King's Chamber, in
Khufu's Pyramid, benefits from an even longer Reverberation Time (R.T.) than
Snefru's main Chamber.

Snefru's Red Pyramid (limestone, main chamber):
R.T. = 2.72 seconds. Volume = (approx) 350 cu metres

Khufu's Pyramid (granite- lined King's Chamber):
R.T. = 4.47 seconds Volume = 329 cu metres

The main body of data obtained from Snefru's Red Pyramid will be the
subject of a future paper. However, from the results set out above, it can be

concluded that it is the granite linings of Khufu's King's Chamber which are responsible for the increased R.T. Such long reverberation times compare well with those found in large cathedrals and churches, where this feature was, and is, an important element in the design in order to enhance the organ and choir performance.

All Saints Church, Newcastle (Sandstone):
R.T. = 3.5 seconds Volume 6000 cu metres

Newcastle Cathedral (Sandstone):
R.T. = 3.9 seconds Volume = 14,000cu metres

If high levels of reverberation were purposely designed into Snefru's and Khufu's main chambers (to enhance the ritual chanting of priests and, possibly, for other reasons to be discussed later), it will be seen that the architect(s) achieved this objective with chamber volumes which are a small fraction of present day churches and cathedrals.

It may be relevant that, whilst limestone was available locally at both work sites, the granite for Khufu's King's Chamber had to be brought from Aswan, 500 miles south of Giza. Given the great cost and difficulty in its acquisition, it seems likely that the architect considered the material to have some major advantage.

It is unlikely that granite was chosen for reasons of structural strength since the Queen's Chamber, which was constructed in limestone, is located lower in the pyramid's superstructure than the King's Chamber and is, therefore, subjected to even greater imposed loads.

In unventilated areas, as was the case for the King's Chamber, granite can produce levels of Radon, a toxic gas which, in sufficient concentrations, can induce altered states of consciousness. This factor could have influenced their decision to employ granite, assuming that they desired the effect and had knowledge of it; however, the lack of consistency in the use of granite for subsequent pyramids presents us with an unclear rationale.

It could be argued that granite was chosen because it provided the best available security against intrusion, much like that of a modern day bank vault. Whilst pyramid portcullises and plugging blocks were obviously fashioned from granite for this reason, the fact that many other contemporary pyramid chambers were lined in limestone suggests that its large scale use for the walls, floor and ceiling of the King's Chamber was not connected with security concerns.

Only three possibilities would appear to remain: the choice was either a personal preference, an egocentric demonstration of wealth, or an experiment in acoustic enhancement.

The case for personal preference is, of course, impossible to prove directly and it is only by weight of evidence toward other possibilities that it may be seen as unlikely. Although the very existence of the pyramid suggests an egocentric owner, the case is confused by a lack of the internal inscriptions which would have been expected to proclaim the ownership of such a massive and costly monument. It is these arguments which open the possibility for granite to have been chosen for its acoustical properties, possibly as an experiment in acoustic enhancement, this being the basis of the present study.

Textual indicators

The following quotation from Demetrius, c. 200 BC,[3] suggests that purity of sound was, apparently, important in his era and that the rendition of sound for its own sake, or for ritual purposes, was of concern to the ancient Egyptians.

> 'In Egypt, when priests sing hymns to the gods, they sing the seven vowels in due succession and the sound of these vowels has such euphony, that men listen to it instead of the flute and the lyre.'

Such 'euphony' would, no doubt, have been enhanced by singing in reverberative chambers, just as artificial reverberation is an important function of sound equipment in churches and places of entertainment today. Although the date of this quotation is much later than the Pyramid Age, it should be remembered that vowels were considered sacred throughout ancient Egyptian history and that Late Kingdom customs invariably had their roots in early or even pre-dynastic times. It seems reasonable to suggest, therefore, that the ancient Egyptians of the 4th dynasty may have used vowel sound chant as part of their ritual. However, even if their chant was not specifically vowel sound oriented, studies of prosodie and metre, in which ancient Egyptian religious texts have been examined by scholars in the context of rhythm and poetry, have concluded that in many cases, they were intended to be sung or chanted [4].

Dr. Lise Manniche[5] provides confirmation of this, in some measure, with the following quotation from Nikaure in the 5th dynasty:

> 'Instructor of the singers of the Pyramid of King Userkaf'

This title, given to Nikaure, seems to indicate that a group of singers were retained specifically to maintain song or chant-based rituals at the pyramid of Userkaf, although whether the singers performed inside or outside the pyramid cannot be determined without further evidence, nor do we yet know their gender. Also, it cannot be confirmed that all pyramids were similarly served although this is certainly a possibility and it may be that the reverberant chambers were the focus for such activities.

Although no Critical Distance Test was carried out (the distance from a given sound source at which the level of direct energy, reaching one's ears, equals the level of reflected energy), speech intelligibility, even when two people are as close as one metre, is extremely poor in the King's Chamber. However, this effect works very much in favour of chanting or singing, where continuity, *not* intelligibility, is the prime concern.

Now consider the following extract from the ancient *Egyptian Book of the Dead*, translated by R.O. Faulkner[6].

> 'The Mighty One appears, the horizon shines. Atum appears on the smell of his censing, the Sunshine-god has risen in the sky, the Mansion of the pyramidion is in joy and all its inmates are assembled, a voice calls out within the shrine, **shouting reverberates around the Netherworld.'**
>
> Spell 133
>
> [Emboldened words are my emphasis]

One could interpret this spell as being suggestive of a ritual performed within a pyramid, in which vocally generated sound played an important part, though clearly, further research in which a corpus of ancient Egyptian texts is examined for clues, is needed.

R. A. Schwaller de Lubicz[7] also believed that the ancient Egyptians used sounds, as distinct from words, in their rituals. In the last sentence of the following passage he quotes from *Corpus Hermeticum*:

> 'Sacred or magical language is not to be understood as a succession of terms with definite meanings...the excitation of certain nervous centres [cause] physiological effects [which] are evoked by the utterance of certain letters or words which make no sense in themselves.'
>
> 'The Pharaonic texts are rich in examples of litanies playing a magical role through the repetition of sounds... and through word play. The hieroglyphic writings allow us to confirm this although their transcription into our language is impossible since the pronunciation of this language is unknown... **In a letter from Asklepios to King Amman** [he says]: **'As for us, we do not use simple words but sounds all filled with power.'**
>
> [emboldened words mark the *Corpus Hermeticum* reference.]

Discussion

In addition to the core of the hypothesis, several other linked possibilities exist.

Sounds created in the highly reverberant King's Chamber may have been intended to have an energising effect on the sarcophagus during sacred rituals which were connected with foetal symbolism. Such a possibility is based on Professor I. E. S. Edwards' hypothesis that the sarcophagus symbolised the womb of the goddess Nut[8]:

> 'According to one of the most popular myths... the sun god Re entered the mouth of the sky goddess Nut every evening, passed through her body and was reborn at dawn. When he died, the King was assimilated to Re and was thought to undergo the same nightly process of gestation and rebirth as the sun-god. Spell 430 addresses the god in the womb thus: 'You are restless, moving about in your mother's womb in her name of Nut'. It is particularly indicative that Djedefre, [Khufu's] immediate successor, should have chosen to have an oval, not rectangular, sarcophagus; **it is really a representation of the human womb**... As these texts show, the actual sarcophagus was regarded as identical with Nut and it possessed her maternal attributes.
>
> [Emboldened words are my emphasis.]

When sound is generated in the King's Chamber at its Prime Resonant Frequency (refer to my end notes), the sarcophagus resonates in sympathy. This phenomenon would occur even if the prime resonant frequency of the sarcophagus was substantially different to that of the King's Chamber but in such a case, the excitation level of the sarcophagus would be of relatively low amplitude. The actual prime resonance of the chamber (identified by the technique in which Pink Noise is generated in the space and the resulting reflected energy is analysed) was found to be 125 Hz ± 4Hz. This was later refined, by calculation, to be in the order of 121 Hz; that of the sarcophagus was identified, using the same technique, as 117 Hz. However, the south-east corner of the sarcophagus is severely damaged and it is, therefore, possible that it was once tuned exactly to the chamber. Even today, the two prime resonances are so closely matched that any powerful intonation produced in the chamber, especially if executed at or near musical note 'B2' (123 Hz), causes a massive excitation of the sarcophagus, via acoustic coupling. The similarity between the two resonant frequencies could be viewed as either coincidental or as a possible indicator of acoustics design. The process of tuning may not have been as difficult as one may imagine since granite is highly resonant and most large pieces of the stone emit a clearly audible sound when struck. The architect would have had access to expert stone masons who would be adept at hollowing out large blocks of stone; the process of grinding off material to alter its ringing tone is one which was well within the limits of their known technology.

The concept that the sarcophagus was deliberately 'tuned' suggests a further possibility: that of a womb-foetus correlation. I discovered by experiment that the pitch of the sound of a new-born baby's heart is also centred around 125 Hz. The ancient Egyptians could easily have identified this, simply by placing an ear against the baby's chest, as one can do today, and then attempted to mimic it in the resonance of the sarcophagus. Two further items lend some support for this:

1. Some ritualistic instruments were found in the northern 'star shaft' of the Queen's Chamber in 1872. These items were found by Wayman Dixon, a British engineer; prior to his visit, both shafts in this chamber were concealed from view, i.e they had not been cut through into the chamber but ended approximately 100mm behind the wall face. One of the instruments he discovered was a small bronze tool, described then as a 'grapnel hook' but now thought to be a ceremonial, non-functional, 'Pesh-en-kef'. The word *peshen* means to divide, to split, to cut, to separate, and such instruments were used during the 'Opening of the Mouth Ceremony' in which the deceased was symbolically reanimated. They were also used as birthing knives, i.e. for cutting the umbilical cords of new born babies. In their archaic form, they were probably fashioned from flint, consisting of two curved blades which meet at a point, thus cutting through both sides of the umbilical cord as it was circumflexed around it. In effect, the tool was an early form of scissors.

2. The second item concerns the pyramid's 'star shafts'. It is well known that 'false doors' which the ancient Egyptians used as a symbolic device through which the 'ka ' or spirit body could pass were invariably constructed to normal door proportions, as if to accommodate a 'ka ' which matched the proportions of the living Pharaoh. However, the shafts, which are now believed by many authorities to be conduits to the stars for the Pharaoh's 'ka', are only around 200mm square, well suited to the symbolic transit of a foetus or the 'ka' of a foetus, but not to that of an adult. Also, if the sarcophagus can be considered as the womb of the sky goddess, it is possible that the shafts were constructed as symbolic fallopian tubes; the ancient Egyptians were almost certainly aware of the existence and main functions of the female reproductive organs. It may be relevant that, in the human female, the necks of the fallopian tubes remain closed and dormant until the time of ovulation, just as in the Queen's Chamber, the shafts were originally closed off at the chamber end.

Both these shafts terminate within the body of the pyramid, perhaps symbolising the connection between the fallopian tubes and the ovaries. The southern shaft, connecting with this chamber, was explored by Rudolf Gantenbrink in 1996 by robot, resulting in the discovery of what has come to be known as 'Gantenbrink's Door', 200 feet from the chamber.

Many authorities believe that the King's Chamber shafts were also originally closed off at the chamber end. However, there is no historical evidence to substantiate this. By carrying out a microscopic examination of the area around the mouth of the northern shaft, within the King's Chamber, it may be possible to find chisel marks which would indicate a rude opening, as opposed to the careful sawing which would be predicted if the work had been carefully planned.

Both shafts from this chamber originally terminated in gold-sheathed meteoric iron plates, near to the outer casing stones, perhaps indicating that the symbolic ovaries associated with the King's Chamber lay within the celestial goddess, Nut. I base this possibility on the assumption that the ancient Egyptians were aware of the source of meteoric iron, i.e. a rock that had fallen from the sky.

There are other examples of concealed symbolism within and adjacent to Khufu's Pyramid, most notably the sea-going Solar Boats which, it is generally believed, facilitated the Pharaoh's sailing on the celestial sea. Such examples demonstrate that the ancient Egyptians were fond of symbolic devices and would go to extreme lengths to produce them; construction of the shafts would certainly have been a very difficult engineering problem and must have held a powerful symbolism.

If we find behind Gantenbrink's door a statue of Khufu looking out to the stars, as was suggested by Professor I.E.S. Edwards, might this be of foetal proportions? It would indeed be ironic if the only statuette of Khufu in existence, which is truly miniature in its proportions and displayed in the Cairo Museum, turned out to be one of two, the other being behind the portcullis. The ancient Egyptians' artistic representation of a foetus would, almost certainly, be represented by an adult in miniature.

Let us return for a moment to the possibility that the sarcophagus was tuned to match, as nearly as possible, the prime resonance of the King's Chamber. It was considered important to examine if there was an acoustic reason why the sarcophagus is currently off-center on both the north-south and the east-west axis of the chamber. Athough Piazzi Smyth's 1865 plan of the chamber and Maragioglioa and Rinnaldi's 1965 plan both show the sarcophagus as being skewed from the north-south axis, its present-day position is in perfect alignment with the east side of the floor slab, which I have designated as 'A1'. There is probably no scientific technique which could identify the precise original position of the sarcophagus. However, given its general arrangement toward the east end of the chamber, it would seem reasonable to conclude that the intended placement of Khufu's sarcophagus was close to its present site. Assuming that the chamber and its sarcophagus were intended to 'acoustically couple', when acoustic energy produced in the chamber is transferred with good efficiency into the sarcophagus, then a full modal analysis of the chamber should be able to highlight any acoustics design intent.

Due to time constraints, it was not possible to carry out a full modal plot in the chamber, but some unusual features can be seen in the data obtained. For example, the series of axial modal points, regions of high and low pressure, showed fairly even spacing in the central area of the chamber. However, the modal points near to the sarcophagus appeared to be relatively cramped and two of the antinodes were suspiciously close to the east and west walls of the sarcophagus. Why such cramping occurs will probably not become clear until a full modal analysis of the chamber has been carried out. The entire top edge of the sarcophagus measured as high pressure, i.e. an average of 86dBA, yet the air at the centre point of the top opening, point 27, was a definite node of 75dBA. The entire inside bottom of the sarcophagus measured as high pressure, peaking at 88dBA. From this data, we can see that in its present position, the sarcophagus and chamber are very well coupled when using the 125 Hz frequency, which was identified as being dominant in the chamber. If we were to use any other frequency, the modal points would be rearranged to different locations, probably resulting in poorer coupling; such an experiment will be carried out on a future visit, if access is granted. If acoustic coupling is subsequently confirmed to be at an optimum when using a frequency at, or close to, 125 Hz, the correlation between the corresponding modal pattern and position of the sarcophagus would be a further indicator of acoustic design. That is, the sarcophagus may have been deliberately positioned to straddle specific antinodes. To identify the most favourable spatial orientation of the sarcophagus, several techniques were available to the ancient Egyptians. For example, by introducing a small volume of water into it, ripples could have been observed on the surface of the liquid whilst priests intoned the prime resonant frequency of the chamber-sarcophagus. The sarcophagus could have been made mobile by use of rollers, thereby permitting a variety of locations to be tried for maximum excitation of the water.

One further feature of the chamber points to a possible acoustics design intent. The architect's choice of a simple 2:1 ratio (20 and 10 royal cubits respectively for the chamber's length and width) is significant, particularly at bass frequencies where distinct room modes (dominant resonances) would be expected to arise. The actual width and height, at approximately 5.25 and 5.85 metres respectively, are also important as the following reference source on acoustics[9] indicates.

'In smaller rooms, where some of the dimensions are less than 10m, it is found that the resonant frequencies become widely spaced out at the low frequency end of the range. This is particularly so if two or more of the room dimensions are the same, or are related by simple ratios such as 2:1 or 3:1... When widely spaced frequencies occur, sounds [made in the room] can occasionally be strongly influenced by [such dimensions].'

My final experiment concerned the possibility that the ancient Egyptians had used the acoustically resonant sarcophagus as a means of divining future events. It is well documented that they believed in and practised 'dream sleep' from which readings of future events would be given by a priest versed in this skill. In 'classical' and present day shamanism, the taut skin of a drum, sprinkled with sand, produces sonorous patterns which are then interpreted for the recipient. The drum itself is thought of as a living spirit helper and serves as an object as well as an agent of life cycle rituals[10]. In ancient Egypt, the drum was one of the earliest musical instruments and although we have no textual indicators as to its use as an instrument of divination, it is possible that the ancient Egyptians experimented in this way.

Merely by stretching an animal skin across the open top of the King's Chamber sacophagus and tensioning it with small, sand-filled, leather bags, it would have been possible to create a cymatic membrane. A sprinkling of sand would then have been applied to the skin and the priests would have sounded a number of sacred vowel tones at frequencies which would excite the sarcophagus-skin system. In this way, sonorous patterns could have easily been produced.

For my own experiment, having made temporary repairs to the sarcophagus' south-east corner, I stretched a P.V.C. membrane across its open top. A loudspeaker was placed in the base of the sarcophagus and connected to a sine wave oscillator which was slowly swept through the full audio band. A wide variety of sonorous patterns emerged, three of which are reproduced in this book. Their future analysis may help us to understand how granite behaves in acoustic fields. It seems likely that the millions of tiny quartz crystals, embedded in the stone, contain coded information, stored in the form of piezo electric charge, which can be released by acoustically exciting the sarcophagus. It may be that the sand grains, which are themselves small particles of quartz, are given positional 'instructions' by a combination of sonic eddies and electrostatic charge patterns. I believe that the electrostatic mechanism is evidenced by what appear to be sweeping parallel curves on some images. They are actually areas of greater electrostatic charge, created by my hand movements in clearing away the sand for the next test frequency. This may be a type of data storage and retrieval system, hitherto unsuspected, and worthy of further investigation.

Conclusion

The choice of granite as the lining material for the King's Chamber is clearly responsible for the long Reverberation Time, and, from the range of possible reasons identified for its selection, acoustics enhancement seems the most likely when viewed in the context of other results. For example, the close correlation between the prime resonant frequency of the chamber and its sarcophagus is remarkable and suggests that it could have been deliberately engineered. Also, the architect's choice of chamber length and width are ideal for establishing powerful low frequency resonances and, again within context, could be viewed as acoustic design intent.

If the ancient Egyptians thought of the sarcophagus as the womb of Nut, the foetal correlations with the *pesh-en-kef* instrument and the small area of the shafts could be seen as indicators of the extent to which they developed the symbolism. The correlation with the heart-sound of a new born baby is less likely, but nevertheless interesting.

The deliberate concealment of the shafts in the Queen's Chamber (and probably also in the King's Chamber) has hitherto not been explained, but it does seem possible that this was an attempt on the part of the architect and/ or priests at symbolising the closed necks of fallopian tubes.

The current modal data seems to point to the sarcophagus having been deliberately positioned, presumably in order to maximise its acoustic coupling with the chamber. A more detailed modal analysis could ultimately confirm this although, at this stage, we should adopt caution in interpreting the current data, which was incomplete due to time restrictions.

The Demetrius quotation is important and may help in establishing a link between the sonic science of the ancient Greeks and Romans and that of the ancient Egyptian, assuming that the case for the existence of such a science in ancient Egypt is ultimately proven beyond reasonable doubt. It is also important in demonstrating that the ancient Egyptian priests, at least in the Late Kingdom, were concerned with the creation of sound for its own sake; given such a mind-set, it seems likely that they would have desired reverberant spaces in which to chant.

Future research, in addition to continuing with the acoustics study of pyramids, should therefore seek to examine the acoustics of temples, particularly those of the Late Kingdom, some of which feature highly reverberant spaces and were constructed whilst the country was under Greek or Roman occupation. I would welcome the assistance of other researchers in this endeavour.

Finally, the Cymatics experiment showed how richly resonant the sarcophagus is. Whether the ancient Egyptians used it in a manner similar to that practised by classical and present day shamans, we may never know but the images revealed need careful study and interpretation from the scientific viewpoint; the acoustic 'lock and key' mechanism needs to be fully understood. The spiritual nature of the pyramid will, no doubt, give rise to many interpretations of these images; my friend and colleague, David Elkington, has, at the date of writing this document, already drawn his own remarkable conclusions.

Notes concerning my definition of Prime Resonant Frequency

In any enclosed space, but particularly one of regular proportions and with parallel facing walls, many dominant resonances (modes) will occur. They can be predicted mathematically but, when found experimentally, there is always one wherein the amplitude of the resonance is seen as being the most powerful; it occurs when the maximum acoustic energy in the room is reflected back to source. Conversely it can be thought of as occurring when there is least absorption of acoustic energy by the room. These are two definitions of 'Prime Resonant Frequency' and typically the prime will be of low frequency. However, the roll-off frequency of my test loudspeaker was 63 Hz, thus I was unable to analyse frequencies below this figure. The highest amplitude of energy reflected from the chamber, using pink noise as the sound medium, was 125 Hz and calculations refined this to 121 Hz. This frequency is very near to a musical ' B2' (123 Hz), is easily sung or chanted by a male priest (see below for specific reference to the male gender) and its dominance would have been discernible to anyone with a 'musical ear' simply by walking slowly around the chamber whilst a vocalist performed a slow bass glissando. The sound of greatest loudness would have been around 125 Hz. The lowest frequency that can be sung by an adult male is about 80 Hz and for the purposes of discussing male chant, I have, therefore, redefined the Prime Resonant Frequency as *the lowest frequency mode which can be sung by an adult male.* The true Prime Resonant Frequency of the King's Chamber may prove to be a sub harmonic of 125Hz, say at 66 Hz or 33 Hz, but if so, a 33 Hz mode could not have been discerned by the ancient Egyptians and neither of these frequencies could have been vocalised by their priests.

Note concerning the gender of priests

From what is known of the priesthood in ancient Egypt, those of high rank were almost always of the male gender. If it was the architect's intention to engineer spaces in which male priests were required to perform chant-based ceremonies, then we can predict that low frequency modes would have been desired since the general inclination of the male voice is toward the bass register. The dominant resonance in the King's Chamber, circa 125 Hz, is below the vocal range of most female singers and it is, therefore, likely that it was designed primarily, although not necessarily exclusively, for male priests.

Notes concerning plotting of the Mode Map

1. There was some difficulty in identifying the exact locations of some nodes and antinodes due to a slow throbbing beat frequency which affected the stability of the meter's pointer, as did the movement of the two assistants as their bodies interacted with the acoustic field. I estimate the node-antinode tolerance to be in the order of ± 2cm at best, though possibly much greater in some instances. Only a repeat mapping will remedy this uncertainty and ideally it should be carried out by one person to minimise disturbance to the acoustic field.

2. Whilst modal points were briefly noted around all the walls, there was not time to record them, and only three east-west lines of points were recorded.

3. The speaker was set up in the centre of the chamber, propagating due east, at a height of 1-metre above the floor. It was driven with a 125 Hz sine wave, generating a 100dBA sound pressure level at 1-metre on axis, a level which I considered appropriate in order to produce well defined modal points.

References and Bibliography

1   Marcus V. Pollio Vitruvius, *Vitruvius on Architecture*,
     Loeb Classical Library, ISBN 0-674-99277-6, p. 293.

2   John Baines & Jaromir Malek, *Atlas of Ancient Egypt*,
     Time Life Books, p. 36.

3   Aristotle, *Poetics*, Loeb Classic Library,
     ISBN 0-674-99563-5, p. 395.

4   Gunter Burkard, *Ancient Egyptian Literature*,
     (ed. by Loprieno), 1996, p. 447-463.

     Waultraud Guglielmi, *Ancient Egyptian Literature*,
     (Ed. By Loprieno), 1996, p. 465-497.

     Fecht and Osing, *Lexicon der Agyptologie*,
     vol. IV, cols 120-121. Also cols 1127-1154.

5   Lise Manniche, *Music & Musicians in Ancient Egypt*,
     British Museum Press, ISBN 0-1741-0946-0, p60, p. 162.

6   R. O. Faulkner, *The Ancient Egyptian Book of the Dead*,
     British Museum Press, ISBN 0-1741-0946-0, p. 121.

7   R. A. Schwaller de Lubicz, *Sacred Science*,
     Inner Traditions International, ISBN 0-89281-222-2, p.167, p. 168.

8   I. E. S. Edwards, *The Pyramids of Egypt*,
     Penguin, ISBN 0-14-013634-7, p. 62.

9   P. H. Parkin, H. R. Humfries & J. R. Cowell,
     Acoustics, Noise & Buildings,
     Faber & Faber, London, ISBN 0-571-04953-2..

10   Mircea Eliade (ed.), *Encyclopaedia of Religion*, vol. iv
     Macmillan Free Press, p. 498.

Appendix 7

Robin Heath

A 'Language' of Number and Geometry

History consists, as Arthur Koestler neatly puts it in The Sleepwalkers, of 'the engine-drivers', conquerors like Alexander the Great and Genghis Khan, while 'the conquerors of thought are perhaps the pointsmen who, less conspicuous to the traveller's eye, determine the direction of the journey'. Our present culture, like all before it, attempts to hold a tight rein on thought, informing us as to how we must all think, and keeping us on rails that support a world belief that we represent the supreme pinnacle of civilisation. Central to the upholding of this patently untrue stance, is the need to belittle the achievements of the past. To do otherwise would expose the lie, that, in some essential respects our culture has devolved.

Because of this, David Elkington and I both choose to work outside the normal boundaries of academia, as independent researchers. Academics tend to uphold the status quo. We both work with historical artefacts, and we are both passionately interested in alternative models of history and the origins of human consciousness. David works essentially with the 'software' of language, whereas my artefacts are primarily the 'hardware' associated with the neolithic stone circle builders. Because the megalithic culture was preliterate, there is an inbuilt essential difference in our perspective and approach to ancient culture. As a consequence, both of us have undertaken quite different processes of exploration, well beyond the present boundaries of historical research.

David Elkington's work relies for its impact on a significant cultural artefact which does not, or appears not to, undergo radical change at times of war, revolution, pestilence or other catastrophe. The thread of language weaves back through history and may be unpicked to reveal a remarkable landscape of cultural commonality. Within the weft of this ancient garment of language lies the hidden material which is the subject of this book. If we all spoke Japanese, or if texts had either not been written or had not survived, David's route would have been, to a large extent, blocked.

Reckoning with the circle builders is rather like finding oneself in foreign parts unable to speak the language. The megalithic culture of northwestern Europe is initially quite impenetrable and quite different from our own, having apparently arrived quite suddenly, ousting the earlier long barrow culture. From about 3000 BC, this culture built stone circles – many thousands of them

– reflecting outstanding astronomical and geometrical sophistication. Then, after about 1500 years, it suddenly disappeared, almost without trace, into the dark gloom of pre-Celtic Britain. Yet one can hardly state that the stone circles are hidden or occult, for on a foggy day, one can still quite literally walk into them on moor and fell, throughout western Britain. But neither can a waning culture be said to have hurriedly constructed them in order to preserve their secrets. They were built for over one and a half millennia. Their importance must have been immense, yet stone circles belong to a culture no longer extant. It is reasonable to ask, what was once their purpose and their message?

To understand the circles, one must understand both astronomy and geometry to quite a high level. Those things are, in effect, the 'language' of many circles, encoded within their shapes and their locations. Imagine if no-one alive today knew anything about astronomy or the simple rules of geometry – then there would indeed be no message emanating from the circles. To the circle builders, such ignorance would be considered barbaric, yet that, unfortunately, is just about the present position upheld by academia. Regretfully, the archaeological establishment is largely unaccommodating to any messages coming from other disciplines or from alternative research into this culture, and thereby the layman has been encouraged to think that the circles are merely a challenging feat of stone moving, a curiosity of the past, with no real underpinning meaning. A visit to Stonehenge will amply confirm this state of affairs, yet as we shall shortly see, the astronomy and geometry of the circles is truly a 'language' which reveals some of the secrets of the culture which undertook their construction and, remarkably, this 'language' is found to totally support David Elkington's linguistic research.

In a society increasingly repulsed by its shameful history of religious intolerance, the story of Jesus is quite wrongly seen as irrelevant by most moderns. Similarly, myths and legends of kings, sacrificial hero-victims and resurrected saviours are seen at best as quaint or charming and at worst the superstitious ramblings of a well forgotten past, for reasons I have suggested earlier. So, David's seminal work, in showing the common and vastly more ancient cultural story of the Christ figure as an archetypal pattern of human development, lands in the lap of a society largely unaware and unappreciative of the implications such a discovery may have on our future understanding of the purposes and meaning of human life. Our essentially solar culture has turned its back on the ancient myth of the solar hero, supplanting it with modern ersatz versions – Superman or Jimi Hendrix. The social consequences of such a dilution of the myth and the archetypes are self-evident to anyone who seeks to discover such things.

Our culture demands or appreciates objectivity through numerical proofs, and the research I have undertaken possesses, by its very nature, a far more direct numerical and objective nature than does semantics and linguistics. Many of David's conclusions are astonishingly well supported within the hard geometrical and astronomical evidence bequeathed to us from the megalith builders. The combined picture which emerges when one places our respective findings side by side reveals a remarkably coherent historical landscape. When mathematics joins hands with language, myth embraces geometry, and music and astronomy dance together with semantics. We can then recognise in the ancient world a wisdom which has subsequently been lost and certainly been denied to our own world-view. Like Christ's seamless garment, a holistic picture is revealed of a *gnosis* or cosmology which may not be torn apart nor partitioned. It is this *gnosis*, however imperfectly we discern it at present, which David reveals within this book.

It cannot be over-stressed that the very nature of this original research makes it appear somewhat weird and out of place, for there is as yet no space for it within our current cultural paradigm as it emerges into consciousness - just as there was 'no room at the inn' – no room in the material world for anything Christ-like to be born. But then along came the precessional *Age of Pisces*, and exactly on cue, it made room for a re-enactment of the archetypal theme of 'saviour/victim'. Three wise astrologers recognised the signs of the times, saw the star, and arrived at the nativity.

However unlikely this story may appear to the modern mind, the *Age of Pisces* was an astronomical reality coincident with the beginning of the Christian era. The historical Jesus appears to both have recognised and then acted out the archetype of the 'Fisher king', and the rest would have been history, as they say, but for the repackaging of most of the Jesus story some centuries after his crucifixion. In some versions of the Christian faith, Jesus even becomes God himself within an entirely masculine and entirely bizarre Trinity that typifies all the imbalances of a Patriarchal culture. At least, the misogyny is out on the surface for all to see!

Even a casual or skeptical reader will find sufficient hard evidence in the material which follows to support and augment the major claims made by David's thesis. However, it is also true that the treatment afforded within the space here precludes any great depth, and three of my published works* offer fuller treatments with supporting evidence for many of the points which follow.

Astronomy and a 'Language' of Number & Geometry

The ancient world cultures of Egypt and Greece were obsessed with number and geometry. To them, God was recogniseable through being primarily a geometer and mathematician. In the ancient past, the wise believed in the adage, 'as above, so below', from which amongst other things, the subject of astrology evolved. But this essentially Pythagorean viewpoint harks back much further than the 5th century BC. If we study megalithic stone circles, we may find solid evidence for both their astronomy and metrology, dating back beyond 3000 BC, for many stone circles are not circular at all, and require the pegging out of Pythagorean triangles to replicate their complex geometry. As a further example, the two inner circles at Avebury suggest the two lunar monthly cycles, with 27 and 29 stones, whilst the huge outer circle appears to define the presently forgotten solar-lunar calendar synchronicity of 8 solar years, being synchronous with 99 lunar months. And it is true that an engineer asked to design an analogue of the Sun and Moon in the sky would inevitably come up with the numbers and shape of the Aubrey circle at Stonehenge, whose 56 markers enable eclipses, moon phases, seasons, tides and dates to be instantly 'read off' like the time from an analogue watch.

These isolated examples demonstrate ancient human recognition of the cycles that wash around our world, and whilst not proofs in the modern scientific sense, they suggest the 'words' of a numerical and geometrical language. And like all languages, the grammar can only take certain forms, forms limited in this case by the numerical realities. Thus a realistic working calendar may only be fabricated from very few numbers, notably 360, 364 or 365 days. History furnishes examples of all three, each with its limitations and each demonstrating the problems of marrying the apparent motion of the Sun to that of the Moon.

Because the lunar year does not fit nicely within the solar year, a calendar must choose either 12 or 13 months for its year. Either a calendar designer opts for 12 months of 30 days, which is what the Egyptians and Babylonians and early Greeks did, or opts for 13 months of 28 days, as very ancient cultures appeared to have done, particularly in Europe. The simple playing card set is an analogue of this old 364 day, 13 month calendar. Our present, and quite dreadful, 365 day calendar, holds to the inner structure of the 364 day calendar, with seven day weeks, four week months and 52 weeks to the year, all shoved within a 365 day overlay; originally (45 BC) to minimise bad Roman timekeeping across the Empire. Whilst nearer to the actual solar year, this wretched artefact generates irrational numbers throughout its use and rotates the days of the week on any particular date.

Because there are between 12 and 13 lunations (new moons) in a solar year, our folk-stories are filled with heros or spiritual teachers who associate themselves with twelve disciples or knights. Jesus, Arthur and the Mayan wind god Kulkulcan are the best known 'thirteens', but there are others. Twelve around The One: like nested spheres, the twelve accrete around the central thirteenth, and interestingly, the myths parallel the geometry. The One, or thirteenth member, is usually the missing saviour, or the wise woman in some older folk tales. Because, in all cultures, the sun and moon, are associated with male and female deities (though not always carrying the same gender), the concept of the 'sacred marriage', permeates much of human society. In our time, the Templars, Alchemists, Rosicrucians and Freemasons have preserved material which alludes to the marrying of male and female, sun and moon, spirit and matter, father and mother within one unified being. Not surprisingly, some of the lost and forgotten gospels and codices of the Bible carry the same theme.

Calendars are the end products of hard won observations to determine the length of the year or the month. The observatories of megalithic culture, used to that end, have been explored by Professor Alexander Thom, who discovered that ancient astronomers had wrestled from the skies the length of the year, the length of both the sidereal and synodic months and the period of rotation of the lunar nodes (18.6 years). There were even complex stone devices to estimate the moon's tiny wobble – which causes eclipses – and its maximum monthly declination, when this failed to coincide with the nearest moonsets. These, and the extensive use of 'Pythagorean' or whole number geometry to define the complex shapes of many types of stone ring, led Thom to state, about the megalith builders, on the BBC's *Chronicle* programme... 'I think they were, as far as brain power is concerned, my superiors.' Perhaps the reader can see just how dangerous a remark this was. Thom's work was quickly marginalised, despite the retired Oxbridge professor being better qualified in surveying, astronomy and experience of megalithic sites than anyone else around at the time.

I have shown elsewhere[1] that those same solar observatories, from which the length of the solar year could be found to within a few minutes, would also have showed that, after 33 years, the Sun rises *exactly* where it did 33 years previously. This closest repeat rising behind a foresight stone matches with the many myths of the solar-hero, a divinely inspired male figure who is often numerically linked to the number thirty-three. In Irish mythology particularly, this number takes precedence within the tales of Cuchulainn's battles with the Labriads, the Tuatha de Danaan and other heroic accounts of battles and kingships. The inscribed pictograms of Irish megalithic chambers (2500 BC) confirm 33 as a significant number. In Scotland, at Brainport Bay, two archaeologists, Col. Peter Galway and Dr. Euan MacKie, discovered a tightly packed cache of 33 quartz pebbles at an equinoctial sunset alignment: They knew nothing of my work and the astronomical connection between the number 33 and the realities of equinoctial sun-watching revealed here.

In our culture, our solar-hero, Jesus, is seen to be crucified and resurrected in his 33rd year. The son (sun) rises from the stone blocking the tomb (underworld) at the easter rising, that same equinoctial rising most suited to observing the repeat solar cycle. Whatever spiritual message is conveyed by the Nazarene's death and subsequent resurrection, the numbers above clearly show a link between astronomical realities and the story of the Resurrection. The astronomy which fuels this story was evidently being applied in megalithic Britain, perhaps prior to 3000 BC. Apparently, our ancestors could count and were adept in astronomy. On both counts, this is denied by our archaeologists.

Units of Length and Flattened Circles

We might take another symbol of Christianity – that of the fish. There is already much evidence to show that the linking of Jesus to the dawning *Age of Pisces* is confirmed by gematria and other symbols. One of these symbols is the *vesica piscis*, a geometric construction which both divides a line into three equal parts, and which generates within itself the three irrational numbers, √2, √3, and √5. The *vesica* is also an essential part of the construction of a genre of stone ring termed by Thom a 'flattened circle'. The diagram here shows this elegant shape (*Fig. 1*). The lengths of the ropes used to produce the flattened arcs create the ratios 1 : 1.72 : 2.72. These ratios are identical to those of the foot, royal cubit, and megalithic yard, which is remarkable. Yet even more astonishing is the fact that the 'flattened circle' may also be used to extract important astronomical constants to better than 99.9% accuracy. The length of the eclipse year may be found directly against the solar year and the disparity between the lunar year and solar year may be found and then used to predict eclipses in advance. As a single symbol of the sun, moon and earth system, Thom's 'type B' flattened circle would be impossible to match, whilst the neolithic culture that built them is still thought primitive, incapable of such miraculous feats. Yet there they are, over thirty of them, in Britain, still in good enough shape to recover the original geometry!

These units of length are still recognisable today. The royal cubit was used to build the Great Pyramid – two examples of the length may be seen in the Louvre. The foot is still hanging on, despite its recent illegality, and may still be purchased as a ruler in Woolworth's stores. The megalithic yard, used to measure out the stone circles of northwestern Europe, is believed to be unique to that region in prehistory. Yet here I have uncovered a connection between all three units of length. We might reasonably ask what, if any, is the connection between the Great Pyramid and a 'type B' flattened stone ring? The former is Egyptian, the latter found throughout the British Isles, Ireland and Brittany. And the foot originates from Sumeria. Is there therefore a cultural connection? What might that mean? Like a sentence made up entirely of nouns, these units of length appear to be strung together without sense, without a verb or sentence to show an underpinning meaning.

Once more we may turn to astronomy to elucidate matters. The foot and the royal cubit add to make the megalithic yard. If one now takes the megalithic yard to represent a lunation period, more specifically the time between the lunar year (12 lunar months) and 13 lunar months, then the foot and the royal cubit, meet precisely at the point which defines the end of the solar year, as the illustration shows (*Fig. 2*). Here is our verb, a 'doing word' or phrase which informs us of some intent. Let us try to make a sentence here: *The metrology of the ancient world is defined and connected through the astronomy of the Sun and Moon's annual cycles.*

We may dive deeper into what is going on here and attempt to construct a bigger sentence, perhaps a paragraph, from all this material, one which will link us to the stories of the New Testament. It may be shown that the royal cubit and the megalithic yard are further connected by the geometry of the vesica and its double square, where each side has the length of the Egyptian 'remen' (1.2167 feet, another ancient unit of length). The $\sqrt{2}$ and $\sqrt{5}$ diagonals take the length of the royal cubit and megalithic yard respectively. What this indicates (to this writer) is the following: *There was a whole metrology of the ancient world based on simple astronomical laws unbeknown to us moderns, where the measurement of land areas could be undertaken by the simple factors 2 and 5.* The irrational square roots disappear in such calculations. Thus we may write, $2\,MY^2 = 5\,RC^2$.

The 153 Fishes in the Net

It then becomes true that if the diagonal of any rectangular plot of land is measured in megalithic yards, the square reveals immediately its area in square Royal cubits. This allows us to define our second meaningful sentence, for the astronomy of the solar year is that it contains 12.368 lunations or full moons. The square of this number is 153, the number of fishes 'caught in the net' in the final chapter of *St. John's Gospel*. This is exactly correct from a metrological perspective, because a length of 12.368 megalithic yards, whose square is 153 MY^2, produces 'a net' which does indeed contain 153 RC^2 (*Fig. 3*). We are now forced to rethink what to make of an earlier Bible story,the feeding of the five thousand, where five loaves and two fishes now suggest something other than a miraculous tale of God meeting human needs. We might suggest both to the linguist and to Bible scholars that 'fishes' relate to royal cubits, whose existence springs from the *vesica piscis*, whilst 'loaves' relate to megalithic yards.

Thus we arrive at another conclusion: *The story in St John includes, by its numerical content, the solution to the secret of the calendar, which is actually about marrying solar and lunar cycles.* When Jesus is said to 'break bread', might not he have been undertaking a ritual more consecrated to accurate calendrical measurements than to eucharistic communion? These meanings connect the stories in the Bible to practises which pre–date that book by more millennia than it predates ourselves.

These previous few paragraphs, convey a most interesting meaning, and open up new areas for research, but they could never have come about from the specialised knowledge of an etymologist or linguist, nor from the axioms of present day archaeology. They needed the researches of a retired professor of engineering, who was an excellent amateur astronomer and a maverick mathematician and amateur astronomer who knows the Bible fairly well. The result is clear: *the Bible carries a hidden cargo of metrological and astronomical techniques which date back to beyond 3000 BC. Stories in both the Old and New Testament contain accounts of megalithic astronomical practices in Britain. The latitude of the prophet Enoch's observations of the sun may be calculated from his data and suggest an observatory in northern Europe, perhaps even Stonehenge. The connections between the units of length of the prehistoric world suggest a common cultural origin in prehistory.*

These sentences suggest a sophisticated and integrated science operating from prehistory, a science, remnants of which later became absorbed into the Jesus myth. Other myths, legends, language and folklore enable us to both validate and appreciate the ancientness of this story. The examples I have presented above dovetail perfectly with David's material and, quite separately, our two spheres of activity have led to more or less the same conclusions. Whilst David has deliberately been asking uncomfortable questions which have enabled him to restore the core features of the 'Jesus story' and determine its origins, my own discoveries have led to the same place, largely by accident, as a by-product of research into neolithic astronomy and geometry. We have, of course, both been asking unreasonable questions and 'all progress depends on the unreasonable man'.

As the new millennium dawns, let us recognise the value of non-compartmentalised and inter-disciplinary research. Such a step will surely help to pull back the veil concerning our past, and will assure further progress in the future.

1. *Culture and Cosmos*, Vol one, No. 1. 'An Astronomical basis for the myth of the Solar Hero'.

* Books by Robin Heath referred to in this appendix are, *Sun, Moon & Stonehenge* (Bluestone Press, 1998); *Sun, Moon & Earth* (Wooden Books, 1999) and *A Beginner's Guide to Stone Circles* (Hodder & Stoughton, 1999).

Robin Heath is an independent researcher into cosmic cycles. Previously a senior lecturer in mathematics and engineering he is now director of Megalithic Tours, operating specialist and custom designed tours to megalithic and other sacred sites throughout Britain and Ireland. He has made many radio and TV appearances and has lectured widely on matters megalithic.

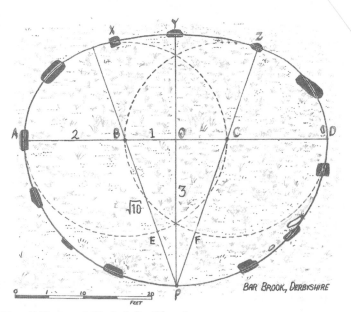

Fig. 1. Type B Flattened Circle (after Thom)

1) $\dfrac{OP}{BP} = \dfrac{\text{Eclipse year}}{\text{Solar year}}$ 2) $\dfrac{BE}{BP} = 0.368 = $ Solar year - Lunar year (in lunations)

3) $\dfrac{BP}{BP-AB} = 2.72$ $\dfrac{BP}{BP-AB+OP} = 1.72$ - Foot: Royal Cubit: Megalthic yard = 1:1.72:2.72

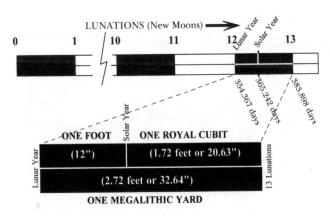

Fig. 2. The Ancient Metrology of the Calendar

If each rectangle is of one lunation (one megalithic yard), then the Imperial foot becomes the length between 12 lunations and the end of one tropical (seasonal) year - the solar year of 365.242199 days.

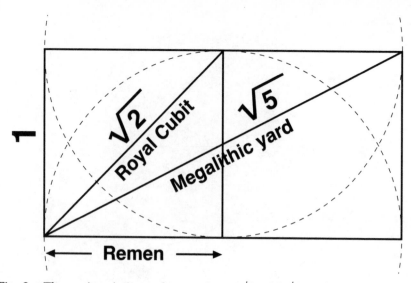

Fig. 3a. The *vesica piscis* used to generate √2 and √5 and its application in ancient metrology.

1 : √2 : √5 = remen : royal cubit : megalithic yard
(The remen: An Egyptian unit of 1.215 ft.)

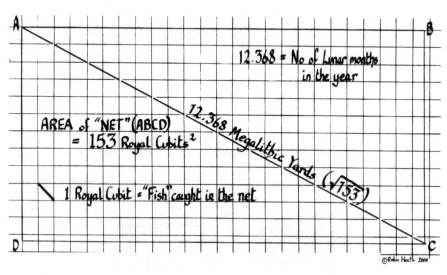

Fig. 3b.
The 153 Fishes caught in the Net

Appendix 8

The Didjeridu

My name is Christopher Cann. My friends call me Bear. I have been journeying with the didjeridu for the past nine years, travelling widely and playing to audiences sized from a solitary person to two and a half million people. I have played as a solo artist, street performer and teacher . . . in ceremonies and in healing sessions. From all my many areas of work with this beautiful instrument, I am particularly drawn to its use as a tool to promote grounded gentle relaxation. The harmonic vibrational overtones created by the didjeridu are a tremendous aid during healing sessions. In the mid-nineties I used the didjeridu in music therapy with severely physically and mentally challenged youngsters and discovered that the sound of the didjeridu has its own magical spirit that can uplift, yet relax, the most complex of energies.

The didjeridu, also known as the *yidaki,* is a sacred Australian Aboriginal instrument traditionally made from a termite-hollowed branch of a eucalyptus tree. It is used in a ceremony called Corroboree, for celebrating the Dreamtime. The Dreamtime is the expression of the Australian Aboriginal peoples' connection and oneness with the universe. The method of playing the didjeridu is simple yet complex. The hollowed branch is cut to the required length and the soft termite nest is scraped out, leaving a simple wooden tube. The smaller end is then circled with a ring of beeswax to form a mouth piece. Playing the instrument by vibrating the lips into the mouth piece sounds simple, but one then has to learn a method of breath control called 'circular breathing'.

In essence, when the player feels he is about to run out of breath, he keeps the vibration of his lips going by squeezing air forward using the muscles of his cheeks. At the same time he snatches in a quick lung full of air through his nose. He then immediately returns to lung pressure again to sustain his lip vibration. This cycle of changeover from lung pressure to cheek pressure, and then back again to lung pressure, produces a pulse that is used to create many varied rhythmic patterns. This is a simplistic over-view, but in practice, mastering circular breathing can take many years of dedication.

The instrument itself is thousands of years old, and truly creates one of the most ancient musical sounds known to man. The Australian Aboriginal people themselves have existed for at least 120,000 years, and their culture is one of the oldest living on the planet today.

During my research into sacred sound, I have discovered that many other ancient cultures throughout the world have used a didjeridu-like instrument for ceremonial use. For example, the Tibetan monks use the dungchen, the ancient Celts had the dawed, and the Swiss still have and use the alpenhorn. All of these instruments produce a deeply haunting harmonic resonance, and are used for spiritual connection.

In my work as a music therapist and healer, I have witnessed, while playing the didjeridu, some of the most moving and beautiful transformations in people. It appears to me that the harmonic vibrational resonance created by the didjeridu can literally, energetically transform the human body. I have witnessed people with muscle seizure unlock static limbs and stand up and walk while the didjeridu is played around their bodies. I have worked with private clients who have moved through deep mental and physical traumas assisted by the sound of the didjeridu. The sacred resonance produced by this magical instrument, seems to facilitate enormous energetic change, and promote harmony and balance within the human mind and body.

I took all of this knowledge and experience and produced *Monolith*, an album of harmonic sound. Its aim: to assist people's natural ability to heal themselves and others. To further empower the project I decided to record it live at a sacred location. My research into sound and the healing potential of vibrational harmonics has led me to many sacred places and structures. I have found that the acoustics in such locations naturally amplify the sound of didjeridu, gong, Tibetan horn and voice, and are perfect for such a recording. In October 1999, after two years of searching for the venue best suited for the project, I finally found the 'Abbot's Kitchen'. When I first stood in this remarkable place, I was deeply touched by the presence of spirit, which seemed to me to seep through the very walls. The 'Kitchen' itself is an ancient solid rectangular stone structure, approximately 50 feet square and 60 feet high. It was constructed in AD 1340, and is the only roofed building left standing intact within the ruins of Glastonbury Abbey, probably the oldest Christian sanctuary in the United Kingdom.

The album *Monolith* is a great success, and has brilliantly captured the essence of harmonic sound along with the awesome acoustic power of this sacred structure.

I conduct workshops in the UK using harmonic sound as a means of carrying people through their own transformational healing journeys. Since *Monolith* has been incorporated into these sessions, the results have been stunning. I have received many letters recounting people's positive experiences within the workshops and many of these letters say that the writer has been opened up to new ways of being, and to a greater understanding of self.

If you would like a copy of the album *Monolith*, or would like more information on my work, please contact me by e-mail: <shiningbear@altavista.net> ,or see my website: www.didgeridoodreaming.com

Appendix 9

Overtone Singing by Jayson Stillwell

The term overtone singing broadly refers to any singing style which incorporates the feature of producing two or more notes simultaneously. Geographically, it is most commonly found in Central Asia – Mongolia, Tibet, Tuva and Siberia. However, varying examples of these techniques can be found in many different cultures, from Africa to the Middle East. Within this singing style there are two basic techniques. One is the ability to produce bell-like tones which can be manipulated to produce a tune which is separate and distinct from the sound of the 'normal' fundamental note of the voice. The other is a deep and physically resonating sound comparable in tone to a didjeridu. Both of these techniques are known under a variety of names. The former is often referred to as 'throat whistling', 'harmonic singing' or 'sygyt' (in the Tuvan language). The latter is known as 'khoomei', 'kargyraa' or in the case of the Tibetan monks, 'the one voice chord'.

In all cultures where these techniques are encountered, there is a strong link to shamanic and religious practice. There are a number of documented applications for these sounds, ranging from meditation and healing to the movement and manifestation of objects. My own work has been largely concerned with these effects of sound and the voice.

In my opinion, the human voice can be used as a way of converting thoughts and feelings into something physical. If you consider that sound from our voice is the one thing we truly create without the use of any external tool, then each of our voices is like a sonic fingerprint, a bridge between our internal and external world, containing the power to bring about change by converting our intent into a physical waveform which travels outwards from us. As this is quite a conceptual approach to sound, I would like to share some personal experience to illustrate my point.

My first attempt at healing with sound involved working with a man who had undergone keyhole surgery on his knee two days before I met him. He was very friendly but totally sceptical. I started by internally saying that it was my intention to bring through the highest energy of healing available to this man using sound. At this point, much to his amusement, I began to sing to his knee. I did this for approximately twenty minutes. When I had finished both of us sat quietly for a few moments. Then, he said that his knee had totally stopped hurting. That night he slept for the first time since his operation and the next day he went back to work six weeks ahead of schedule. He told me that there had been no pain in his knee since I had sung to it. Another anecdote I would like to share, is about my time in America. I was attending a week long 'sound intensive' held by Jonathan Goldman (President of the World Sound Healers Association). My friend Nancy Byers and I had started the week by jointly saying that it was our intention to effortlessly experience magic in our lives. This was something we reaffirmed on a daily basis. A few days into the event I went outside and sat on a bench by a pond. I began to make high overtones and immediately, about eight or nine fish converged from different areas of the pond and just floated in the water all facing me. They stayed in this position as I continued to sing for approximately five minutes. The moment I stopped the fish swam away.

To me, such events illustrate the idea of combining the energy of sound and intention to manifest in our daily lives. It is also important to add that I believe this type of experience is available to all who are willing to experiment and have fun with it. I feel that the significance of these sounds is that they make available to us divine states of being, such as the alpha wave pattern of brain activity. This is the state of mind one enters during meditation; the sound frequency that the brain emits at this time is the same as that of the earth.

Overtone singing creates forms of vowel sound which allow other sounds to magically appear from within them. For example, when moving gradually from one vowel sound to another, the harmonic naturally appears in the place where the two sounds join, a sort of zero point that is neither one sound and yet is both sounds plus one other. In fact, overtone singing could be viewed as a kind of holy trinity of sound, a place where heaven and earth meet to create something new.

*   *   *

Jayson Stilwell has been overtone singing for several years. He has toured the UK and USA performing and running workshops on the healing power of sound through voice and rhythm. He has recorded music for film and software soundtracks and has appeared on HTV's *No Naked Flames* demonstrating the relationship between vocal harmonics and the stones of Avebury. Jayson's album *Brand New World* is on general release through Rotator records from March 2001.

To find out more about forthcoming releases and workshops in your area contact the following email address: <Jaysonstilwell@yahoo.co.uk>

Appendix 10

Notes on Sumer

The origins of the Sumerians are shrouded in mystery, and so too is the enigmatic departure of this civilisation in the 3rd millennium BC. Even to attempt an answer presents difficulties that have yet to be investigated in any due detail, either archaeologically or ethnographically speaking.

It might be that the Sumerians, as a people and as a culture, had their origins in the Tibetan Highlands. At the time of writing, this seems to be one of the most viable theories and one with a certain basis of fact. However, the evidence is too sparse to offer conclusive support to the idea of the Sumerian culture being a mass-Aryan invasion. The evidence provided by the religious ideas of both does, however, offer a crumb of comfort.

In Tibet, long before the era of Buddhism, which arose c.600-500 BC, the religion of the day was the ancient belief called Bon. Bon involved a combination of revelation and esoteric knowledge, the holders of which were shamans, the elite of the religion. Some have speculated that it was elements of this 'proto-religion' that emanated southwards c.4000–3500 BC, and formed the core of Sumerian civilisation in the Mesopotamian lowlands. It might be that the early wanderings of these peoples contributed to the rise of Egypt herself at approximately the same period. The Sumerians called themselves the Black-Headed Ones, whilst the Greeks called the Egyptians the Melampodes, the Black-Footed People. This might be a reference to the fertile qualities of the Nile silts, for the Egyptians called their land Kemet, the Black Land, whilst those from the outside were labelled Dushratim, foreigners, red-haired ones, implying that they were wild and uncultured, like the Egyptian god Set, brother of Osiris.

There are similarities between all three religions, of Tibet, Sumer and Egypt. In the Bon religion one of the supreme gods bears the name Esses (sometimes Eshe). Esses was a wonder worker, of the kind we are very familiar with. An ancient Bon book describes him thus:

> 'The wonder-worker Esses then came to the land of Shanshun-Mar [North Tibet].'[1]

This same Esses was mentioned in later Buddhism as Gesar-ling.[2]

How interesting it is that the syllable 'mar' should occur again in the context of the land! In Egypt the legend of Osiris tells the same story, with geographical variations; for as the story travels south its land-centred motif must also change, though the monuments built to these hero-saviour-gods remain very similar.

The land of Tibet, and the lands round about, are exceedingly rich in varying forms of sacred architecture. If we follow the migratory route of ancient times we also see that it is a route littered with site after sacred site. Almost immediately after arriving in their new homeland the Sumerians began to construct huge monuments, culminating in the great ziggurats and temples which were later subsumed into the Akkadian Empire and its culture.

Sumer was a conglomeration of city-states that arose gradually from a period starting in approximately 4500 BC. Where the Sumerians came from initially is unknown, but by 3100 BC the city-states of Kish, Erech, Ur and Uruk were thriving along the banks of the Rivers Tigris and Euphrates, in what is now modern-day Iraq. It was in these Sumerian city-states that hieroglyphic and, later on, cuneiform writing were developed. The excavations of Sir Leonard Woolley in the 1920s revealed a high level of technological achievement within Sumerian society, and evidence suggests that the civilisation in Egypt may have had contact with Sumer. If this was indeed the case, then the Bible's recorded migration of Abraham up towards Horan and then south towards Egypt may have been along a well-worn trail.

In around 2300 BC Sumer was invaded by King Sargon of Agade, and the unique language and culture of Sumer was absorbed into the wider Akkadian Empire. Over the course of the next two centuries Akkadian replaced Sumerian in all things. For although the two cultures used the same writing system, cuneiform, their languages were completely different. Sumerian has, as far as linguistic theory goes, no known cousins, and, for the present, stands on its own. Akkadian, by contrast, is a member of the Semitic language table, and is clearly related to other contemporary languages of the area.

Sumerian is an agglutinating language. In other words, one syllable can mean many things, depending upon what one chooses to put at the end of it to determine its overall character. Akkadian, by contrast, although it borrowed heavily from Sumerian, did not take up Sumerian verb forms. Like other Semitic languages, it modifies verbs by making internal changes, not by adding to them.

Another interesting thing that I have noticed about these languages is their pronunciation. As a Semitic language, Akkadian is harsh on the tongue. It is gutteral, at least more so than Sumerian, which seems to me to be an 'open mouth language', a language of the fertile plain. With Akkadian, one can imagine its use in hotter, drier places as it has plenty of 'ish' and 'esh' sounds, as if one is trying to spit out the desert sands.

Sumerian as a language is out on its own. To this day no known relative of it has been uncovered. This lack of a derivation makes the Sumerians a very enigmatic people, the more so because of what they brought with them into the West: language, culture and an amazing propensity to construct huge but eminently durable buildings. The Sumerians provided ancient culture with a huge leap forward before vacating the scene as enigmatically as they arrived.

A little earlier I mentioned the 'open mouth' style of their language, as opposed to the guttural quality of Semitic languages. Because the mouth has to expand in order to speak it, it is only reasonable to speculate that they might have been a people of high places, where the air is cool and fresh and the native can breathe with impunity, as opposed to the air in lowland, dry areas, which is full of dust and particles of sand. The evidence of the contents of certain Egyptian pharaoh's stomachs demonstrates that such conditions might have been a factor in the rise of certain forms of language. Not only do a majority of the mummies display all the evidence of grit being an unwanted part of their everyday diet, but quite often their stomachs are full of sand. As a consequence, language of hotter, drier realms was, I believe, shaped by anatomical necessity: it was short, concise and designed to keep one's mouth closed as much as possible.

This now brings me briefly to the Sumerian hero–god, Enki. 'Enki' is a pun. Its two syllables, 'en' and 'ki', mean 'soul of the underworld', and thus it intimates some kind of immanent power. Enki was actually the Lord of the earth, or the nether regions. In Sumerian legend he was the ruler of the life-giving springs, and was also a healer. In addition, he was the god of wisdom, of vegetation and of man. The Sumerians are being explicit here; all of these aspects are related, and the god is the power that defines them. The pronunciation of Enki's name, along with those of all the other gods and goddesses, is very close-mouthed in nature; again this perhaps highlights more the geographical nature of the Mesopotamian landscape, and, crucially, the role of the God's name within it. The other (probably, in its time, secret) name of Enki was Asar – the Egyptian form of Osiris. The Akkadians and Babylonians, when they took over from the Sumerians, called Enki 'Ea', known to the Hittites as 'Aias'– yet another form of Asar. The name Ea is very likely a foreshortened form of Esa or Asar.

In both Sumerian and Babylonian mythology it is related that Ea and Marduk are one and the same god, and there is a prophecy that runs:

> 'His name shall be Ea. All my combined rites he [Marduk] shall administer; all my instructions he shall carry out.'[3]

When the Sumerains arrived in what is now modern day Iraq they began to construct the great ziggurats and temples; and during the great days of the Babylonians, who were the eventual heirs to the Sumerains, there arose some of the greatest of these buildings, foremost amongst which was the curiously named Esa-gila, home of the great Babylonian hero, Marduk and also the probable site of the Bible's Tower of Babel (from *Bab-ilu*, 'Gate of God').[4]

Before we go on to investigate the Esa-gila, there is a detail to the story of Marduk that is, in the light of the Gisa-correlation (see chapter eight), more than a little interesting.

Marduk is referred to as a 'Lord of Salvation' in the sacred 'Kyrie Eleison', a hymn that was sung before dawn during the rites of Atonement at Babylon.[5] In the myth, he harrows the underworld, as do all suffering hero-gods, and then he is liberated from the 'mountain' of the netherworld by his son, Nabu. Marduk thus obtains a 'destiny beyond compare', in other more familiar words, resurrection. Marduk, in an episode reminiscent of Moses, then goes on to inherit the sacred tablets of the law.

Marduk is equated with the Sumerian Asariluchi, the son of Enki, (in Babylonian, Ea) the lord of the earth. We have already seen that 'Gisa' is 'prince of' or 'blood of' the earth, and that the oldest form of this name is Asar. That Marduk is yet another form of this name is confirmed by the fact that like Asariluchi he is the the saviour and the god of exorcism. He is also a healer and in his legend he walks on water. Interestingly, a part of his name comes from one of his attributes, the symbol of the pick axe, a sickle, the *marru*. We have seen that 'mr' is, in Egyptian, the pyramid, in Babylonian myth, the pyramid-like ziggurat constructed as Marduk's tomb is associated as being the god himself. The Kings of Babylon and of the Assyrians even bore the name of Asar. Esarhaddaris is one such name. He was a king of Assyria, *c*.680-669 BC. His name is translated by scholars as 'Ashur-Aha'Iddina' which means 'Ashur has given me a brother', which is not a translation that I agree with. First and foremost it makes very little sense. My way of looking at it is 'Ashura-Ha-Ittina' which would translate as something like, 'the power of the Asura, (the gods or forces of the earth) surges forth (from Anu-the underworld). The many kings who bore elements of the name included Nabopolassar, Belshazzar, Ashur-Ubalit, Tiglath-pileser and so on. All of these kings claimed the earth as their dominion. If they themselves were not gods, as in Egypt, then they were god's arbiters; or at least this was the official view of the time.

The hero's father in Sumer's case is the 'lord of the earth'', Enki, whose name is a pun meaning 'spirit from heaven', for the spirit from heaven, in our terms 'energy from the cosmos' (mostly coming from the sun), is indeed the lord of the earth, for our planet is utterly dependent on the sun and the wider cosmos. The hero-son is called 'Esa', 'Esar' or 'Asar', a Gisa name of course. The name of the major temple, the Esa-gila would appear to mean 'Esa, prince of the earth'. The early god, *Marduk* (note the Mary connection) was superceded by the god, Assur – yet another form of Asar. Assur was the supreme god of the Assyrians, who, it would appear, took their name from him. He was also called the 'great mountain', as if his power in some way resided in the mountain.

This now brings us to the identity of the 'God Most High', (whose son was

Jesus/Esa) and where that God might be found. The Babylonian creation story begins: 'Enuma Elish....when on high...' The God of Abraham was El Elyon; also a 'God Most High'. Can both 'Elish' and 'Elyon' mean entirely the same thing? It is not unreasonable that it should do so, for as we have seen, there are elements of a shared mythology.

Now I do not want to stretch the point, but there is a flavour of what the god-man truly is in the term 'Ely*on*' a point that I believe the ancients were making via an elaborate pun, or double meaning. For 'on' read also 'an'. In Annu (Sumerian - 'An' or 'Anu') we have not simply 'sun' but 'heaven'; more familiar in this guise as the underworld. The God Most High of Annu is the very same hero (or Horus in Egyptian) who harrows the underworld, Hel – the dark black womb of the goddess – on the road to heaven. We are talking here of strange forces from heaven that are immanent within the earth, for the hero is borne of the earth; his coming is, in all religions, endlessly foretold. He is foretold in prophecy (one look at the Old Testament book of Isaiah, so beloved of the Gospel authors, will confirm this point), there is always the sense of anticipation of expectation.

The Ancients were not so uncouth as to give their words one simple meaning; they endowed them with great subtlety and cunning. An understanding of their punning mechanism could only reveal that the speaker was an initiate, that he or she had made the grade. To normal people not endowed with a knowledge of the workings of myth, they remained as simple words that told simple tales. The hero is born of the earth, which, as we have seen, has a great breadth of meaning. The earth is also 'substance' and the 'substratum of all'. However temples were engineered to make the substratum more easily accessible, more 'present'. This is why, in masonry, God is the temple. The hero is the cornerstone. It is probably for this reason that the Egyptian hieroglyph of the throne is the symbol for the goddess Isis and a partial symbol for the god Osiris/Asar. The throne is the seat of power. A king might have his throne in his great palace, the gods, however, have theirs in their great temples, quite often their pyramids.

The song or hymn, called the 'Kyrie Eleison',[6] that was sung before dawn of the second day of the Babylonian holy season, was also known as the 'Secret of Esagila':

> 'Lord, without peer in my wrath;
> Lord, gracious king, lord of the lands;
> Who made salvation for the great gods;
> Lord, who throwest down the strong by his glance;
> Lord of Kings, light of men, who dost apportion destinies!
> O Lord, Babylon is thy seat, Barsippa thy crown;
> O Lord, with thine eyes thou piercest the Universe...

...With thy glance thou grantest them grace,
Makest them see light so that they proclaim thy power.
Lord of the lands, light of the Igigi, who pronouncest blessings:
Who would not proclaim thy, yea, thy power?
Would not speak of thy majesty, praise thy dominion?
Lord of the lands, who livest in Eudul, who takest
The fallen by the hand;
Have pity upon thy city, Babylon;
Turn thy face towards Esagila, thy temple;
Give freedom to them that dwell in Babylon, thy words'.[7]

This prayer, sung at dawn, during the rites of atonement, the festival known today as Easter, has a charm all of its own. It is an attempt at humility by the mass of the people, a plea to allow Babylon to thrive for another year; it is a song of power. When chanted by the priests in its original form of Babylonian, and within the temple precinct, the idea would be to drive down brainwave frequency and bringing about an altered state of consciousness. There is a reference made in the hymn to all sorts of things with which we are familiar: the eye of the Lord, the idea of enlightenment, and the wrath of God. Perhaps though we are not so familiar with the Igigi.

The Igigi are the celestial version of the Anunnaki, the original gods of Sumer and Akkad. The precise meaning of Igigi is unknown, and has remained beyond the true grasp of any Sumerologist. It is, according to Temple, 'terribly imprecise and confusing'[8]. Before I go on and attempt an understanding of this term we ought to have a look at what is known about the Anunnaki.

There were seven Anunnaki and they are specifically mentioned in association with the underworld, they are gods of destiny. Yet again we have arrived at the figure seven in association with divinity. The Sumerian tale of King Etana mentions the divine seven, and from all appearances this tale would appear to be a myth based upon a core of fact. Etana has to ascend to heaven in order to be cured of a rather delicate ailment which is subsequently put right, from which point the king becomes morally upright and most certainly erect!

The Igigi would appear to be cosmic giants. 'Giant' is derived from Greek, 'Gigas', and this is almost matched by the like terms in other languages. The biblical 'Gog' is very familiar to Western eyes as one of the most famous of giants. In Akkadian the term is 'gg' and in Amharic, a Coptic dialect, the game is given away; 'g...gg' – meaning 'tooth that pushes under another', again we are back to the idea of a substratum. This 'tooth' has a dual meaning. In this instance, it implies a force within the earth, the very force harnessed by the Ancients at temple sites. But, as if to underline this usage, the Canaanite, Ugaritic and Akkadian versions mean also 'roof, gallery or top', the encapsulating architecture, holding in the force like a faraday cage. One might wonder why the Ancients would equate teeth with these forces and structures until we remember that in chapter five we saw how our own teeth are crystalline structures, they have subtle energy transference properties, on occasion even acting as radio receivers!

We know that the favoured material for use at sacred sites was granite, 'A very hard, granular, crystalline, igneous rock consisting mainly of quartz, mica and feldspar and often used as a building stone' (The Oxford Dictionary).

The 'ig' of igneous takes us to the Igigi, and the Igigi take us straight into the domain of the permeating electrical forces. 'Gi' as we know is part of the Gisa name and means 'of the Earth'. 'Ig' can be followed through igneous to the Latin 'ignis' meaning fire and then on to its root in the Sanskrit, 'Agni', the god of fire. But this is not simply fire as we know it, as 'the all-pervader', Agni is 'the mediator between men and gods'.[9]

> 'The shining quality in anything is the quality of Agni, hence, worshiping him, man gains the brilliance of intelligence, of strength health and beauty... As a cosmic principle, Agni is the chief deity amongst the spheres-of-the-elements, but when he is envisaged merely as the earthly fire, the leading role may be attributed to two of his aspects, Indra, the thunderbolt, the form of fire dwelling in the intermediary sphere of space, and the solar Vishnu, the All-Pervader, who is the ruler of the heavenly sphere, as well as the inner fire hidden within all things, within all beings, as their power of devouring and digesting... The science of fire is the key to all knowledge. Agni is the power of all inner as well as all outer illumination, the power of knowledge as well as perception. He is the lord of knowledge. The 'Ancient Lore of Agni' (Agni Purana) is the encyclopedia of all the traditional sciences.' [10]

Clearly this is not simply tongues of flame, not fire as we know it. What fire can pervade all things? In its earthly aspect we have 'Indra, the thunderbolt, the form of fire dwelling in the intermediate sphere of space'. This sphere is situated between the earth and the sky and Indra is not only the thunderbolt, he is also the god of atmospheres. Indra is called 'Chief-of-the-Maruts' or immortals and all of these earthly immortals relate to light, including of course, lightning.[11] Without doubt, we are again dealing with the pervading electrical fields and forces!

I had recognised electric deities elsewhere. It was when reflecting upon a Greek myth where Hercules so easily overcomes the gigantic Antaeus by simply lifting him from the ground, that I recognised a scientific analogy:

when electricity has no earth connection, it lacks potency – the giant is disabled.

Now the Igigi themselves may be celestial, but like the solar Vishnu, they have an influence over the Earth, a vibratory influence that may be detected by the priest-shaman, in particular at the sacred site. The hero-god Marduk was clearly related to the vibratory powers. He was not only a bringer of light, as are all heroes, he was also a god who could annihilate and create out of sound by the power of his voice alone.[12]

Notes and References

1. A. Faber-Kaiser, *Jesus Died in Kashmir*, 1894.
2. Evans-Wentz, *The Tibetan Book of the Dead*.
3. de Santillana and von Dechtend, *Hamlet's Mill*, p.267.
4. Pritchard, *Ancient Near East Texts*. vol.i.
5. Frankfort, *Kingship and the Gods*, University of Chicago Press 1948. p. 318.
6. '"Kyrie Elesau" is the Greek "Lord have mercy", it is the song of the Lord, special to the ceremony of the eucharist - the blood and body of the Lord.' (See Cross and Livingstone: *The Oxford Dictionary of the Christian Church*.)
7. Henri Frankfort, *Kingship and the Gods*.
8 Robert Temple, *The Sirius Mystery* p. 190.
9. Alain Danielou - *The Gods of India*, p88. Inner Traditions International, New York, 1985.
10. Ibid.
11. Ibid. p. 104
12. Funk and Wagnall, *Dictionary of Folklore and Myth*, p. 677. Pritchard, *Ancient Near East Texts*.

Appendix 11

The Ancient Peter

By removing the vowels from Peter we get 'Ptr'. This looks very much like the Russian Cyrillic version of Peter – Piotr. By reducing it in this way we get a direct connection with Ancient Egypt, for Ptr is one of the great gods of the Egyptian pantheon – Ptah, sometimes rendered as Ptar.

Ptah was the chief god and creator in the Memphite pantheon (from Memphis, halfway down the Nile). Ptah created the universe by speaking, `by saying the words that named what he willed to create.'[1] This is extraordinary stuff, reflecting as it does the opening of St. John's Gospel, `In the beginning was the word and the word was with God.' Ptah also carries the Ankh in his hand as Peter carries the key of heaven. There is a further correlation in that, like Peter, Ptah was said to be enrobed in white, assisting in the birth of the `white ones', that is to say, the purified or enlightened; Ptah would seem to be an aspect of consciousness.

In Hebrew and Aramaic the name is transcribed `Patar'; there is in fact no precise translation, but in the New Testament it becomes Petra, `rock'. The Aramaic *kephas* also means `rock', but also implies `head' as in *cephalos*. This is, I believe, a pun implying consciousness within the rock, or consciousness being altered by something within the rock. *Cephalos* does seem to imply `living earth'. For long ages past ancient Man worshipped rocks as symbols of the deity. Peter, the rock, seems to imply an omphalos or navel stone of some sort. A navel stone is an aniconic link between man, the earth and the cosmos; it is a stone of some considerable power, an umbilicus for humanity, certainly in the ancient world. Generally they were phallic in shape, connected as they were to Mother Earth, who in mythology is sometimes portrayed as Kore the virgin, who in the Coptic Christian church was celebrated as the virgin-mother of God. In the Old Testament book of *Exodus*, Moses' mysterious sister Miriam (an ancient form of Mary) is compared to a rock, for the striking of which Moses eventually forfeits his life.

St. Patrick, the patron saint of Ireland, is another form of the name Peter. According to the Welsh *Iolo* manuscript, the native name of Patrick was Maenwyn, meaning `sacred stone'. Furthermore, he was the son of one Maewon, meaning, similarly, `a stone'. From the same root *men*, we get *menhir*. *Petra*, the Greek for `rock', becomes in Latin *patera*, which also means `disc' or `circle'. According to Bayley, `both owe their existence to "pater A", the rock, or Jupiter, whose way is perfect.'[2]

The connection with Egypt is an interesting one; however, there was another contemporary belief that is likely to have derived from ancient Egypt, and from which Christianity borrowed much. The Father god in Mithraism is called Pater Patrum (father of fathers), and, as we can see, it is a name not a million miles from Peter. Perhaps then it is not surprising that Pater Patrum is both a rock and a father. The bishop of Rome became assimilated into the very same Mithraic title of Pater Patrum, particularly in its shortened version of Papa or Pope. As J. M. Robertson observed, `The tradition came to transfer from Jesus to Peter, the reputed founder of the Roman See, the attributes of the Persian god (Mithra), and of those with whom he was identified in Rome...' The very chair upon which the pope was enthroned was called the chair of the Pater Patrum, the Supreme Pontiff of Mithras at Rome.

With the fall of the Empire the pope became, as supreme Pontiff – a title of the former emperors – the virtual king of Rome and all things Roman. Within his person there was much that had been brought together from sources other than Christianity. The bishop's mitre, for instance, by virtue of its very name, gives the game away: it comes from the Latin *Mitra*, another version of Mithras. Even Mithras' birthday, 25th December, is an example of this sharing.,In fact, deep beneath the modern-day Vatican there still exists an ancient temple to Mithras.

In AD 315 Constantine formally recognised Christianity with the Edict of Milan. He ordered the construction of a basilica to be named after St. Peter - not so much the founder of the roman church as its god and the god of the religion that Christianity both absorbed and superceded, Mithraism.

Mithraism was very ancient indeed, as Franz Cumont explains in the opening to his seminal study, *The Mysteries of Mithras*. `In that unknown epoch when the ancestors of the Persians were still united with those of the Hindus, they were already worshippers of Mithra.'

The Order of Carmelites are also known as the White Friars. Founded in the twelfth century, the official name of the Order is `The Order of the Brothers of Our Lady of Mount Carmel'. They are contemplatives who see Elijah as their model, and are dedicated to the pursuit of mystical theology. There is also an order of nuns. It was upon Mount Carmel that Elijah defeated the prophets of Baal; however, Mount Carmel is very much an Old Testament site, not New Testament, so how is it that Our Lady had come to be associated with it? According to tradition the Carmelites originated in the days of Elijah (*c.* 9th century BC), almost a thousand years before the official date of Christ!

I was also struck by the Pagan names of the first popes of Rome. History states that these are legendary figures with hardly a basis in fact, but why have their names not been altered along with everything else? Evaristus, Eleutherius (meaning `Freedman'), Telesophorous, Soter, Zephyrinus, Cornelius, are all Pagan; and some are positively Mithraic, like Soter, which means (in Greek) `saviour', and was a title of Mithras.

There is more Peter-related material in footnote eight of chapter three.

Before closing this piece, I should also mention that the famous papal triple crown looks very suspiciously like an omphalos stone; such things are often called pierre-stones or Peter stones.

References
1   Funk and Wagnall, *Dictionary of Folklore and Myth,*p. 908
2   Bayley, H., *The Lost Language of Symbolism.*

Appendix 12

The Geolinguistics Aspect of Myth

As I have related in chapter eight the earliest forms of hieroglyphic writing seem to have penetrated myth and legend from the earliest times. Elements of this are borne out by the history of the letter 'G' given in the same chapter. It is derived from the seventh letter of the Proto-Siniatic alphabet, Zayin - symbolic of a face to face encounter between two people, armies etc., and at the highest level, between the individual and God. Moreover, and in true mythic fashion this same letter is symbolic of the 'skin pierced with a shaft'. The 'G' signifies the earth and the hero's necessary connection to it. It is the letter that begins to describe many of the earth gods of antiquity. The word 'Jesus', which in its proper form is 'Gesu' or 'Gisa', also contains in its Hebrew spelling the letter 'Vav', which represents and means 'nail'. In denoting that the original form of the god, Osiris, name is 'Gisa', there is another link to be made. Osiris's real name was, I believe, secret. It was a secret held by those who were trained to a priestly level and who could commune with the gods, the gods who were in, and were, everything. Osiris's common name, 'Asar', also translates as 'Prince Alpha' and like all heroes he was the alpha and the omega. Omega was and is the last letter of the Greek alphabet, which shares many of its meanings and possibly, its derivations with Hebrew. The last letter of the Hebrew alphabet is 'Tav', the letter 'T', the cross, upon which the hero was hung.

It seems only too obvious to me that language (like its cousin, myth) is a thing of place – the power of place. Myth arose as a living expression of such power; it was both a conscious and unconscious expression by the Ancients of the site and it was derived from it. Recent researches have revealed that the early nature of language was not entirely linguistic, literal and monotone, but was in fact musical.[1] Furthermore, in the form of chant, the male voice has a broad range of effects, when performed within the environs of a sacred place. The mind enhancing capacity of music under this circumstances has been well demonstrated down the ages. It was with this is mind that I recalled the tales told me of how these sites were generally associated with fairies, spirits who are also invariably linked in some way to sound, song and resonance. The tales involve the visit by certain characters to these sites and tell how they are enchanted by the fairy people and lulled into a deep sleep, waking the next morning with only a memory to remind them of their experience. Now, the one thing that I and dozens of people noticed is the soporific effect of these places. I have visited hundreds of these sites and often the effect is the same. The folklore elaborates further in some instances that if the place doesn't get you, the drinking water will. Well water is particularly associated with curative properties (see chapter six). Looked at as a whole these sites have a tendency to be situated in places of high radon emission levels, readings from the water can tell us so. The fact that our ancient ancestors chose to construct sacred monuments at sites such as this can only lead one to the conclusion that he too was sensitive to them and used them with a purpose in mind. Russian research (see chapter five) has demonstrated the increased psychic awareness in individuals at these sites, an effect that cannot have been lost on megalithic man. Myths arose at these sites, which were quite often the palaces and habitations of the gods. Language arose as the expression of myth and reflects it almost uncannily. Could language and myth be responses to the radiation found at these sites?

Myth is based around landscape; a close look at myth reveals all sorts of fine landscape details essential to the telling of the story and the information contained therein. As a schoolboy I was particularly partial to the Arthurian legends, for they are indeed enigmatic in this respect. The stories of Arthur and the Knights of the Round Table are the heirs to the particularly strange landscapes of Celtic myth and the tales of the Mabinogian. Whether told by French minstrels or English romancers, the stories invoke the land. The king and the land are one. It is as if the myth is expressing the language of the land in all its glorious physicality. The land shapes us and leaves many shapes for to remind us and inspire us. From it we get the forms of language. 'Inspiration' is an interesting world, being derived from Latin spiritus, 'breath'. It is as if, in order to be inspired, one has to imbibe the charged atmosphere of the site, like the people who constructed it. In fact it is interesting to think just how much landscape has breathed a resonant power into our language; we may still reflect back some of that power and experience its effect. Is it as a result of such experience that our myths and legends relate to living principles called 'gods'? Is this why the Ancients referred to our planet as the 'Earth Mother' – upon an experiential basis?

In his book, *The Cosmic Serpent, DNA and the Origins of Knowledge*, the biochemist Jeremy Narby related how, on a journey through a rainforest, searching for new pharmaceuticals, he sampled some of the substances his shaman guides carried with them all to unusual and revelatory effect. His mind expanded and he went on a fantastic journey that ultimately revealed to him the structure of plant DNA, which he was able to verify upon return to his Paris laboratory. His shaman friends were, by virtue of their substance induced experiences, devoted to and on good terms with the great earth spirit who apparently related all sorts of information to them, including the whereabouts of the drugs that Dr Narby was seeking. This is but one example of many of the nature of the earth spirit.

The shaman, in his otherworldly existence, is the hero; in spirit he descends to the underworld and communes with the womb of Mother Earth and there learns great things; of paramount importance in these great things are language and its communication through song. It is often said that language is the gift of the gods. What fascinates me is that in myth it is the hero-god, immanent and numinous within the womb of the great mother, who brings the alphabet to humanity. Thus by Geolinguistics I mean specifically the emergence of language as a direct result of humankind's physical interaction with the environment, particularly the sacred enviroment.

'Hieroglyph' means 'sacred language', the gift of the Egyptian gods. As I have observed in chapter twelve, it is extraordinary that certain sounds,uttered in a situation such that their physical wave pattern may be observed, either in smoke or sand, reflect the shape that certain hieroglyphs and cursive script have been given. That the Mayan pyramids were quite possibly constructed to the 'EE-OO' cry of the quetzal is no more extraordinary than the fact that the sound 'EE' on an oscilloscope makes a wave pattern – approximately a silhouette of precisely those pyramids. The Ancients built in response to their landscape, because such a response redounded within their brain wave frequencies. The goddess or god was speaking to them through the subtle emanations of the environment, namely, dare I say, via that godly power, radiation.

Work on this intriguing new aspect of linguistic theory will be continuing over the next five years and will be conducted by the C.L.E.A.R. group at the host of ancient sites worldwide. C.L.E.A.R. is an acronym for Consciousness Linguistics Energy Acoustics and Resonance. The team comprises, Dr Keith Hearn, David Elkington, John Reid and Paul Ellson.

Reference:
1. David Attenborough, Song of the Earth, BBC TV, 23rd December 2000 and various.

Postscript

by Dr. Keith Hearne

Human Wrongs and Human Rights in Scientific Inquiry

In evaluating ideas based on concepts and information coming from great antiquity, it is salutary to consider that current public opinion, and even 'scientific' opinion, has very often resulted from considerable and deliberate political and/or religious distortions imposed in the past. Further, several natural psychological factors operate within us so that over time we tend to look uncritically (more than we would comfortably accept) upon the imposed view – so limiting our acceptance of a more truthful perception of the world. It is convenient to conform to mass thinking.

Within this framework we can begin to see how there may be an initial reluctance to countenance new ways of thinking – for instance, that the Ancients had a profound knowledge of acoustics. We assume too much and are cruelly disrespectful if we think them too 'underdeveloped' to have known such things.

Ancient knowledge was staggering. For example, the ancient Greeks knew the circumference of the earth and the distance of the moon. It was appreciated that the earth was a globe, with the sun at the centre of the planetary system – a concept that in the west took was only rediscovered by Copernicus in the 16th century. Unfortunately, many great truths that the ancients knew have been ignored and no doubt many of them lost.

We should not automatically think that our social and technical advances over the past two thousand years or so are the first that have occurred to humans or human-like creatures on earth. There is good evidence that humans exactly like you and I have been around for hundreds of thousands of years. There may have been several such progressions, followed by vast set-backs - such as mass destruction by super-volcanoes (the last such event happened some 75,000 years ago in the Pacific region and reduced the human population, it is estimated, to a few thousand or so – hence the limited variance in mitochondrial DNA), or impacts from outer space, or even self-destruction. We all know of the rumoured existence of Atlantis, a highly advanced society destroyed seemingly by natural forces.

It should not surprise us if we were to find on here on the earth, or even on the moon and the planets, evidence of ancient technologically advanced inhabitation – not by distant alien beings, but by earlier earth civilisations of human beings like ourselves.

The hypothesis also exists that alien beings have visited this planet in the past and disclosed their insights to our ancestors.

Apart from the possibility that there have been repeated cycles of progression and regression in human development, we have in our own recorded history suffered other types of disaster.

We are familiar with catastrophic military conquests in history. However, there have been equally calamitous intellectual events with the resultant persisting 'thought biases' acting on people like some long-lasting nuclear contamination having a 'half-life' of centuries or millennia.

Until fairly recent times, a way of thinking could be readily and specifically imposed by powerful institutions, or a few powerful individuals, on whole areas of the world. In subtler ways, we are still manipulated.

Unfortunately, once an attitude has been inculcated for centuries, the original, motivated, suppressive reason is lost and people actually accept the idea as based on common sense. The attitude adopts the same status as folklore and wisdom. We find ourselves unwittingly giving lip-service to someone else's self-motivated attitude from long ago.

This may be illustrated in two areas: the notion of reincarnation; and the area dealing with persistently reported anomalies – parapsychology. Both were recognised areas of understandings in the ancient world, but became virtually forbidden topics in the west.

The early Christians could accept repeated lifetimes. It was a natural notion, eminently sensible at a spiritual level, perhaps coming from ancient Egypt. It was favoured in ancient China and was found strongly in ancient Greece. Pythagoras was a particular exponent of the idea. Metempsychosis (rebirth) was part of the teaching of the Greek mystery schools, and Plato's Academy in Athens promulgated the idea. It was also present in the Gnostic teachings and Cathar thinking in the Middle Ages. Such groups were wiped out by the official church.

The concept of a cycle of life, death and rebirth has, however, thrived elsewhere in world. It was, and is, a perfectly acceptable and reasonable belief to Hindus and Buddhists.

One man, the Emperor Justinian, was responsible for the willful destruction of the idea of reincarnation in the west. In May AD 553 , he convened the Second Council of Constantinople, also known as the Fifth Ecumenical Council. For his own reasons he wanted the Council to ban certain popular ideas. The Pope, Vigilius, refused to co-operate and was jailed. The Western bishops did not attend.

In one of the great 'fixes' of history, the council 'voted' to put an official curse, or anathema, on the topic. Anyone supporting the idea would be automatically excommunicated and damned to eternal hellfire.

There have been arguments about what really happened, and there is evidence that some documents were later altered, but effectively, the council banned the idea of repeated existences.

At this same council, official anathemas were placed on the equally ancient concepts that the sun, moon and the planets possessed a spirit. In one act, the accumulated wisdom and feeling about the nature of things that had sustained whole cultures was eradicated from western thinking. The many-lives notion remained taboo to the western world for some 1400 years, until it was reintroduced along with various eastern teachings . However, in the west many people consider it to be an unacceptable idea, their attitude directly repeating the dictates of the Emperor Justinian.

The area is a seminal one, but conventional western science, labouring under its own backward-looking restrictions, has no framework in which to encompass any kind of research in this field. Only a few brave scientists, like Ian Stevenson in the U.S., have tried to gain an understanding of this topic. He has, for instance, found strong links between birth defects or birth-marks in children reporting a previous life, and injuries sustained during the previous reported incarnation.

In science, anomalous observations are extremely important and are usually seized upon because they indicate that the current theory is flawed in some way. There are actually many anomalous phenomena that science has studiously ignored because of a strict bias. The area includes paranormal effects such as telepathy, precognition, psycho-kinesis, and dreams.

That amazing block – like some gigantic neurosis – on the investigation of these fields was also engineered by the Church. As a result of several Papal Bulls, notably that of Pope Innocent VIII, against witchcraft, such topics were considered to be forms of sorcery and therefore heresy. That suppression had consequences that still warps and stunts science today.

We like to think that we have complete freedom of thought, and assume that science must be completely open-minded, but biases from centuries ago affect the thinking and attitude of all of us concerning many issues.

Censorious and authoritarian impositions on thinking from the past are, it could said, kept alive by modern motivated and organised 'skeptics'. Paradoxically operating with religious zeal, they unwittingly echo the restrictions on thinking imposed ages ago. Unfortunately, such skepticism never advances science; quite the opposite, it actively obstructs its natural progress.

Looking sensibly at counter-hypotheses to a new finding is a natural part of the scientific method. However, it is reasonable to assert that organised, motivated skepticism is an infringement on the freedom of those who seek an understanding of the curious situation of sentient existence in which we all find ourselves.

At a time when far-reaching human rights legislation is becoming part of ordinary law in more and more countries (recently in Britain, for example) the same analogous concept of the human right to scientifically investigate any area, without undue and campaigned bias against that research, is bound to follow – just as racism and sexism have had their day. Organised skepticism is perhaps the last resort of the chauvinist.

This is not a book for the scientific chauvinist. I hope it marks the start of an awesome re-evaluation of the wisdom of ancient peoples. The notion itself opens the doorway to vast mysteries and new vistas of possibilities concerning what happened on earth long, long ago.

Dr Keith Hearne BSc MSc PhD
Surrey, England. January 2001.

Dr Keith Hearne (BSc MSc PhD) is an internationally known innovator in science. He conducted the world's first research into 'lucid' dreams for his PhD and invented the 'dream machine'.

Notes and References

Fuller details of the sources given below may be found in the Bibliography.

Introduction

1   George F. Jowett, p.60.

Chapter One

1   Quoted in Robert Graves, *King Jesus*, p.1.

2   A. N. Wilson, *Jesus*, p.239.

3   The reconstructed Slavonic Josephus in R. Eisler, *The Messiah Jesus and John the Baptist*, quoted in Rupert Furneaux, *The Other Side of the Story*, 1953. Also there is a description by Publicus Lentulus in the annals of Rome, although it is a later Christian forgery.

4   Furneaux, ibid.

5   Ibid.

6   The West is obsessed with the image of Jesus, to the extent perhaps that the image *is* the religion; not that Jesus is our idol, but that his image exudes an infinite sense of 'goodness', of the eternal, of belief and, ultimately, the divine. On the other hand, in Native American myths Eshu or Esqu is ugly – he has yet to create beauty.

7   John of Damascus, St. Augustine, etc.

8   Rt. Rev. Richard Harries, *The Independent*, 24th December 1999.

9   You will note how the current Dalai Lama was taken from his peasant family background into training at Tibet's capital, Lhasa, his family being given status and all their needs met.

10   During prolonged periods of upheaval and uncertainty, however, the holy ones often found places of remote seclusion to be safer and more condusive to their goals.

11   As it did in the years postdating Solomon's reign; indeed, to such a wide area that the later centralisation of Temple practice imbued the legends with an even greater mystique.

12   J. Allen Godbey, *Lost Tribes: A Myth*.

13   Margaret Barker, *The Great Angel*.

14   Burton L. Mack, *The Lost Gospel: The Book of Q and Christian Origins*, and *In Search of Alexander the Great*, BBC TV, 18th May 1996.

15   There is an interesting observation to be made here, that Jeroboam, in becoming king, had become the focus of northern opposition to the dynastic ambitions of the Davidic royal house, which was already tending towards centralising the faith on Jerusalem.

16   Assyrian records indicate a figure in the region of 27,000.Tiglath-Pileser III was the king of the Assyrians who incorporated substantial parts of Palestine into his empire.

17   Expanding the city to four times its size into the bargain.

18   The Talmud and A. N. Wilson, *Jesus*, p.55 and p.247.

19   Quoted in Morton Smith, *Jesus the Magician* and *The Secret Gospel*.

20   Ibid.

21   See introductory quotes at head of chapter.

22   Babli, sanhedrin 43a.

23   Hugh Schonfield, *According to the Hebrews*.

24   Ibid.

25   The Jerusalem Bible. In the King James version, the colour is not mentioned. Instead, the word 'richly' is used, meaning the royal colour, which is purple/red. Regarding Horus, Set and the lentil, there is a very interesting reference to this given in Flavia Anderson, *The Ancient Secret*. Lentils occur throughout world mythology, and in the same context.

26   Dr. N. Kokkinos, *The Herodian Dynasty*, p.28 and p.125.

27   Phoenicia, a name given by the Greeks, *phoinikos*, means 'purple', 'red' or 'crimson'. It is likely that Bozrah was closely associated with the selling of the famous Phoenecian red and purple dyes, items that were exclusive to the Phoenician tradesmen. The actual location of Bozrah and the Phoenician dyeing industry is much disputed by scholars and archaeologists. It has been suggested, for instance, that the town of Basra in Iraq might have been the location. I have no intention of joining the fray as I believe that Isaiah's words are explicit enough. Whatever the probabilities, Edom was connected intimately to Phoenicia.

    'Born to the purple' is a term often used to describe a person or prince of royal blood. The Phoenician trade in the colour harvested from the marine mollusc, murex was indeed ancient. In ancient Egypt, even back to the earliest times only kings were allowed to wear red, for it was an extremely holy colour. Of all the colours of the murex, red was the oldest; purple was only to become fashionable at a much later date. The sea snails of the family Muricidae from which murex comes were also the source of the famous Tyrian purple worn by Emperors and Kings, for the Tyrrenians were themselves of Phoenician origin. In fact there is a remnant of Phoenicia on the Italian coast to this day. A Middle Eastern 'Ph' becomes a relaxed European 'V' to give us Venice and the Venetians.

    English sources, William of Malmesbury for example, mention that Joseph of Arimathea was allied to the Phoenicians, in relation to Joseph establishing the first Christian church in Glastonbury, England, and the possibility that, as a child, Jesus visited England with Joseph. The Phoenicians are known to have traded in the west of England on a regular basis.

28   This name is derived from the Greek and Latin words given to descendants of the Philistines.

29   'El' was used as a proper noun or as a common noun, as Baal too was used.

30   See, for example, Gen. 16:7–14, Gen. 17:2, Gen. 21:33, Gen. 31:13, Isa. 14:12–15, Judges 9:46.

31   Margaret Barker, *The Great Angel.* p.3, 37 and 101

32   Keith Whitelam, *The Invention of Ancient Israel*, p.3. See also L. Ginzberg, *Legends of the Jews*, vol.5, p.223, note 82.

33   *The Talmud*, quoted in Robert Graves, *The White Goddess*, p.150–1.

34   *Whiston's Josephus*, W. P. Nimmo et al, 15:10:5.

35   Ibid. 15:10:4.

36   Robert Graves, *King Jesus, The White Goddess*, p.138–9.

37   Rupert Furneaux, *The Other Side of the Story*, p.116.

38   J. Allen Godbey, *Lost Tribes: A Myth*, p.512.

39   Nicolaus of Damascus and Josephus, *Works*; Julius Africanus; *The Talmud*; Nikos Kokkinas, *The Herodian Dynasty*.
It is worth noting that in all their other provinces, the Romans' policy of 'divide and rule' was the basis of their success. What they divided were the royal families. Never did they put a foreigner, an outsider, on the throne, with one supposed exception: Herod the Great. 'Supposed' because Herod's geneaology was known to the Romans and upon that basis his claim to the kingship was verified.

40   Josephus, op. cit.

41   That many Indians immigrating into 20th century Britain changed their surnames in order to climb up in the caste system is a recent example of a similar situation.

42   Although called derisively a 'half-Jew' or a 'foreigner' by his many opponents, it is interesting to note that when it furthered their interests they would refer to him as by birth a Jew. Philo, *Ambassadors*, XXXVI, Yongl, IV, p.160; Josephus, *The Antiquities of the Jews*, XX, viii.

43   A temple slave, though not a slave in the ordinary sense of the word. *Hieros* in Greek is 'sacred'.

44   Whilst Josephus claims that one Antipas was Herod's grandfather who became governor of Edom (Idumaea), Epiphanius, and Africanus etc. claim that it was Herod's father, Antipater, who was governor of Idumaea. Either way, all are agreed that Herod's father held high rank.

45   Tetrarch of Lysanias, later King of Judeae and Samaria.

46   Philo, *Ambassadors*, XXXVI.

47   Josephus, *Kokkinos*, ibid.,p.95-100

48   Robert Graves, *King Jesus*, pp.52f. I am fully in agreement with Graves' argument about Herod's lineage – all of the myths and symbols, and the linguistic aspects point to its inexorable logic.

49   Ibid., p.54 and p.59.

50   Ruth 4:20–22. This book is explicit about King David's Edomite-Moabite ancestry and provides quite a few surprises mythologically. Whatever its dating, it reveals much about the ancestry and the kingship in Israel.

51   The Semitic 'Milku' meaning 'king'. 'El', we have already discussed.

52   Robert Graves, *King Jesus* and *The White Goddess*, p.328, and Josephus.

53   Ibid.

54　Thus the Phoenicians and the Philistines were historically the same people.

55　Margaret Barker, *The Risen Lord*, T + T Clark, 1996, p.xi.

56　Ibid.

57　Ibid.

58　Prof. Sam Berry, *Daily Mail*, 20th December 1996.

59　Isaiah 7:14, King James version.

60　Quoted in Giorgio de Santillana and Hertha von Dechend, *Hamlet's Mill*, p.244–5.

61　Graves and Podro, *The Nazarene Gospel Restored*, p.62, note x.

62　Robert Graves, *King Jesus*, p.48; Josephus, *Africanus*.

63　Anthony Spawforth, BBC TV, 1999.

64　Josephus, *The Antiquities*, xvii, 6:5.

65　Graves and Podro, op. cit., p.56.

66　J. G. Frazer, *The Golden Bough*, p.293.

67　Kokkinos, op. cit., p.114ff; Josephus, *The Jewish Wars*, 1.186; *Antiquities*, 14.126, in *Whiston*, op. cit.

68　Josephus, ibid.

Chapter Two

1　Here, as for other Bible quotations, the King James version is used unless otherwise stated.

2　A. N. Wilson, *Paul: The Mind of the Apostle*, p.28.

3　Acts 21:39 and 22:3 in Salibi, op. cit., p.16.

4　Josephus, The Jewish Wars, 2.4–18, pp.556–8.

5　Kokkinos, op. cit., p.166, note 75.

6　'Foster', as in children of the same family and approximately the same age but from different parents, being brought up together.

7　If this is the family connection, there is always the possibility that young Saul may have been in the room during that meeting. This is intriguing.

8　See the Herodian Family Tree in the Appendix.

9　Wilson, ibid., p.26.

10　Ibid., p.26.

11　Furneaux, ibid., p.142.

12　*Slavonic Josephus* in R. Eisler, ibid.

13　"by the Jews" is a later Christian insertion into the text. Crucifixion was not a Jewish mode of execution, it was a Roman method.

14　As with other events described in the Bible, there are a number of different versions of this story included in the text. In cases such as this, the intellect cannot be satisfied with regard to what happened. However, the very existence of the various versions should tell us that factuality was not always the point behind the oral tradition, or scriptural storytelling and that something other was at work. I am reminded here of the anthropologist who was told the explanation behind a local landmark by a Native American Elder. Later, a young member of the tribe told the anthropologist that a quite different explanation had been given him by the same Elder. Angry, the anthropologist confronted the Elder, who explained that the story, as told to the young man, contained just what he needed at the time. The ancient storytelling tradition, be it oral or scriptural, is a teaching tool on many levels.

15   Wilson, ibid., p.78.

16   The local Dimshq is transliterated as Damascus. The 'Da' and 'ma' are self-evident; 'scus' relates to Mother Earth, but, quite frankly, has cruder connotations nowadays, relating to parts of the female anatomy. In more respectful terms, 'the place of the Father-Mother [i.e. God] on the earth' would be a reasonable material interpretation of the place name.

17   'Father, Son and Holy Ghost' in Christianity, 'Brahma, Vishnu and Shiva' in Hinduism etc. An interesting thesis regarding the number three and the elements from a mathematical point of view is to be found in Dr. Peter Plichta, *God's Secret Formula*.

18   Sir Monier Monier-Williams, *A Sanskrit-English Dictionary*, originally Oxford University Press, 1899; now Motilal Barnarsidass, Delhi.

19   Kasimukti-viveka of Suresvara [412], quoted in Alain Danielou, *The Gods of India*, p.220.

20   See, for example, Evelyn Underhill, *Mysticism*.

21   Danielou, ibid., p.215.

22   Eusebius, Diodorus and A. B. Cook, quoted in Robert Bauval and Adrian Gilbert, *The Orion Mystery*, Heinemann, 1994, p.119–120.

23   A good description of this concept is given by the Cistercian monk Thomas Keating in his book *Intimacy with God*.

24   Published by the Order of the Cross, London.

25   Sometimes Saul is depicted as being thrown from his horse. It is significant that across many cultures, the horse is a metaphor for state of mind, especially relating to desires and intent. In the mythology of Greece, Belleropheron rides Pegasus, the flying white horse which embodies purity of desire. This example would have been known to Saul.

26   A. N. Wilson, *The Sunday Times*, February 1997.

27   *Encyclopaedia Britannica*, p.812.

28   In addition, Professor A. T. Hanson points out in his book *The Acts in the Revised Version* that we cannot be absolutely certain that Acts was recognised and used widely by Christians before AD 170. Acts is first mentioned by Irenaeus, Bishop of Lyon and an early Church father (AD 130–202). This gap has led scholars to conclude that the book was subjected to a great deal of editing in the second century. There are two extant copies of this book, the earlier of which dates to the fifth century and comes from Alexandria, and the later of which is a Greek text. Textual differences between the two revealed the extent of later editing.

29   Josephus, *Jewish Antiquities*, 20.

30   Mark 15:43–46.

31   Rupert Furneaux, *The Other Side of the Story*, p.91.

32   The year is c.AD62. Christianity is still in its putative stage and yet it is not only the people who believe, but the rulers of the people too! This is remarkable. Political leaders in the ancient Middle-East were shrewd and wily operators who knew a good thing when they saw it, but Christianity? Given the particularly tense political situation it seems unlikely, unless the belief in question was related to the old established order. The inscription in the Temple at the 'door of Jesus' makes that connection, describing Jesus as a king who did not reign but a king all the same and, what is more, a dying and rising god, a Messiah of the House of David.

33   Furneaux, op. cit., p.164.

34   A. N. Wilson, *Paul*, p.14.

35   Bishop of Caesarea (c.AD260–c.340) and the 'Father of Church History'.

36   Eusebius, *History of the Church*, 3, 20, pp.1–6.

37   Ibid.

38   See chapter one, reference 3.

39   Wilson, op. cit., p.185.

Chapter Three

1   Giorgio de Santillana and Hertha von Dechend, Hamlet's Mill, p.174.

2   Marcus, in Cicero, *De Legibus*, 2.14.36.

3   Suetonius, *The Twelve Caesars*.

4   Otto Betz and Rainer Reisner, *Jesus, Qumran and the Vatican*, p.87.

5   Matthew 16:18–19.

6   Also said to be St. Paul's place of burial.

7   Peter de Rosa, *Vicars of Christ*, p.31–32.

8   I also pursued the etymology of the word 'saltpetre'. It is *sal petrae* – 'salt of rock'. Christ called Peter the rock upon which his Church would be founded, so *petra* and 'Peter' are the same word. 'Saltpetre' is a younger word than the Vatican Peter, from about the sixteenth century (according to the *Oxford Dictionary of Etymology*), but given the actual properties of saltpetre, also known as potassium nitrate, as a component of gunpowder, it is not difficult to suppose that both the property and the name were known to the alchemists, most of whose activities the Church deemed heretical. I shall write of the alchemists a little further on, but for the moment I wish to illustrate how certain of their practices reveal their very ancient foundation and its link to the Church, via symbolism and mythology.

9   Brewer.

10   Daily Telegraph, 2nd July 1997.

11   M. Bernal, *Black Athena*, vol.I, p.51.

12 *Oxford English Dictionary.*

13 See Evelyn Waugh, St. Helena and others, R. W. Morgan, Isabel Hill Elder and Geoffrey Ashe, various et al.

14 H. Chadwick, *The Early Church*, Harmondsworth, 1978, p.125.

15 Bayley, *The Lost Language of Symbolism*, p.329.

16 T. P. Wiseman, *Remus*, C.U.P.

17 Actually, there were three major frontrunners bidding to become the official religion of the Roman Empire: Christianity, the cult of Sol Invictus and the cult of Isis. It is when we come to the imagery associated with the worship of Isis that we realise just how great the Christian borrowings really were. Perhaps the most recognisable is the image of the Virgin and Child, which originally was a portrayal of Isis and her son Horus. Christian versions of this statue proclaim, 'Immaculate is our Lady.' This is a direct borrowing, for the original statuettes of Isis bore the inscription, 'Immaculate is our Lady, Isis.'

    Isis was also known as 'Stella Maris', the star of the sea. It is interesting that the early Christian St. Jerome should also have referred to the Blessed Virgin Mary by exactly the same epithet. The similarities do not stop there. Priests of Isis were tonsured and shaven-headed. They celebrated Matins and Evensong (Vespers), with the use of bells and holy water, as jewelled images of Isis as Mother Goddess were carried around in solemn processions.

    All of these images are aspects of what today is familiar to us as Catholicism. By the time of its meteoric rise in the fourth century, Catholic Christianity's vision of Mary had merged with much of the cult of Isis.

18 After a brief period of Pagan revival during the reign of Julian 'the Apostate', AD332–363.

19 Porphyry was a leading neo-Platonist philosopher c.232–303. Neo-Platonism flourished in the Roman Empire from the third to the sixth centuries and was a strong influence on metaphysical thought.

20 Rupert Furneaux, *The Other Side of the Story*, p.86.

21 Peter de Rosa, *Vicars of Christ*, p.60.

22 Graves and Podro, *The Nazarene Gospel Restored*, Introduction.

23 In AD435, one Theodoretus also wrote of Paul preaching the Gospel to the Britons.

24 If we replace 'Jews' with 'Israelites' the whole thing makes a lot more sense. The advent of a separate 'Jewishness' coming long after the Israelite exodus from Egypt (see chapter one).

25 The most ancient name of the Palatium Britannicum – the Palace of the British – was the Church of Pastor Hermas, in other words Hermes, the messenger of the gods, who would take the souls of the dead (and sometimes the living) to heaven.

26 R. W. Morgan, *St. Paul in Britain.* p.55 ff

27 The Vatican Hill in Rome was the home, until the Middle Ages, perhaps even the nineteenth century, of a large dolmen, called a perron or, interestingly, pierre. Pierre is, of course, the French version of Peter. The stone had a phallic shape and

strange powers were attributed to it. Quite often a pine-cone was placed at its tip – symbol of the dying and rising God Attis, whose home was also the Vatican Hill. In later years the Church replaced the pine-cone with a cross.

28 This is one of the Oxyrhynchus sayings, found in the form of papyri at Oxyrhynchus, west of the Nile near modern Behnessa, around 1897. Scholars believe that these sayings are extracts from a Hebrew gospel. See S. Caiger, *Archaeology and the New Testament*, in Birks and Gilbert, p.140.

29 Timothy Freke and Peter Gandy, *The Jesus Mysteries*, p.17.

30 Plato, *Phaedrus*, cited in Freke and Gandy, ibid., p.17.

31 Devereux, Steele and Kubrin, *Earthmind*, p.30.

32 Ibid., p.30, Ovid and Plutarch.

33 William Kingsland, *The Gnosis*, p.97.

34 See Robert Graves, *The White Goddess*, p.147, and M. Bernal, *Black Athena*, vol. I, p.69.

35 E. C. Krupp and J. D. Westwood, *Atlas of Mysterious Places*, p.48f.

36 W. Hone, *Lost Books of the Bible*, quoted in Adrian Gilbert, *Magi*, p.18.

37 The Zoroastrian first man is Gayomart, literally 'divinity from the earth' (see chapter eight).

38 Simone Weil, *Intimations of Christianity among the Ancient Greeks*, p.151.

39 Plato, *Philebus*.

40 Gordon Strachan, *Jesus the Master Builder*, p.98.

41 Cited ibid.

42 Clifford Longley, *Daily Telegraph*, 7th July 2000.

43 Justin Martyr, *First Apology*, chapter 60.

44 Elaine Pagels, *The Gnostic Paul*, p.2.

45 Timothy Freke and Peter Gandy, *The Jesus Mysteries*, p.159.

46 Tobias Churton, *The Gnostics*, p.54.

47 Ibid.

48 Robinson, *Nag Hamadi Library*, p.153.

49 Hugh McGregor Ross, *Jesus Untouched by the Church*, William Sessions, p.34.

50 If this evil god be devilish, he was originally a servant of the Most High God. This is borne out by the Devil's name – Lucifer, meaning 'light-bearer'. Another form of this name is Luke, as in the Gospel of Luke. From the same root comes 'lucid' – 'clear, intellectually bright, shining'.

51 Although few have actually seen it since. It is an enigma.

52 Quoted in W. Barnstone, *The Other Bible*, p.341.

53 Edward Lane, *The Manners and Customs of the Modern Egyptians.*, A.Sattin, The Pharoah's Shadow p.173-174.

54 John Baines and Jaromir Malek, *Atlas of Ancient Egypt*, p.111.

55 G. R. S. Mead, *The Hymn of Jesus*, and M. R. James, *The Apocryphal New Testament*, p.303ff.

56 Ibid.

Chapter Four

1   Francis Hitching, *The World Atlas of Mysteries.* p232.
2   The university at Cordoba was effectively the great mosque, to which students flocked.
3   This Cyril was canonised in 1882, as a Doctor of the Church.
4   Also called 'Maria Prophetessa'; Lyndy Abraham, *A Dictionary of Alchemical Imagery.*
5   Distillation gives us, where wine – the blood of Christ – is involved, another Arabic word – alcohol. The Arabic 'alkoh'l' was a fine metallic powder used to stain the eyelids; this powder was produced after a distillation of spirit of wine. So again, the blood of God takes us to ever higher heights. My personal experiments with alcohol – performed under the strictest of experimental rules, with observers talking me through the whole agonising process of consuming a bottle of red wine – have revealed that it has a wonderful, though all too temporary, effect upon the mind. Spirits, too – an interesting term, both religiously and alchemically – have a short-term enhancement effect, for me, transmuting the purely physical into a wider sense of awareness. When I consume alcohol I have always noticed how it enhances and heightens my overall awareness of colour and the sense of colour vibration.
6   B. Walter Warren, *Encyclopedia of Myths and Legends,* p.19.
7   Joseph Campbell, *The Mythic Image,* p.254.
8   Joseph Heller, *Catch-22.*
9   Evelyn Underhill, *Mysticism,* p.206.
10 Ibid., p.210, quoting Schmolders, 'Essai sur les Ecoles Philosophiques chez les Arabes', p.54.
11 From Charpentier, *Mysteries of Chartres Cathedral,* p.69.
12 During the course of researching this book, I have discovered so much about this mission from so many angles that it would be best explored in the next book of this series.
13 Wolfram von Eschenbach, *Parzival.*
14 Ibid.
15 Within the same period as these events, as the foundation of a Kingdom of Jerusalem, Hildegard of Bingen (1098–1179) described in a poem, 'Cosmos: the Manifestation of God', the Earth as the 'mother of all, for contained in her are the seeds of all'. The earth is 'the fleshly material of people, nourishing them with its sap, as a mother nurses her sons or daughters'.
16 Professor J. Yahuda, *Hebrew is Greek.*
17 The Assassins were in fact Hashishim, an Arabic word meaning 'hashish takers'. The Ishmailis were said to have intoxicated themselves with hashish when preparing to despatch their victims, hence the modern meaning of the word 'assassin'.
18 In *The Song of Roland,* an 11th century retelling of a 778 battle that took place in

Northern Spain, 'Sarrisins' are mentioned. This has been taken to mean the Basques, but the *Song*, composed much later, has transformed a relatively minor military manoeuvre into an anti-Islamic rallying cry. It is obvious that it refers to the 'infidel hordes' that by that time had conquered most of Spain. It is also interesting, whilst upon this theme, that the mythical horn of the hero Roland had, within its blast, the power to shatter rock. In folklore the horn has the magical power to make the desert bloom. (Bayley, *Lost Language of Symbolism*.)

19   *The Letters of St Bernard of Clairvaux*, trans. Bruno Scot James, and *Focus* magazine, June 1998.

20   Paul Broadhurst and Hamish Miller, *The Dance of the Dragon*, p.219.

21   Ibid.

22   *The Cambridge Illustrated History of the Middle Ages*, ed. R. Fossier, Vol.II, pp.440-1.

23   M. Starbird, in ibid., p.xxi.

24   Notably, I believe, by Buckminster Fuller. Malcolm Stewart, personal communication.

25   The name Richard also translates as 'Hud' or 'Hood', 'the hooded one' (*The Oxford Dictionary of Names*).

26   See J. W. Walker in Graves, *The White Goddess*, p.349, and Dobson and Taylor.

27   *Oxford English Dictionary* and *Oxford Arab Lexicon*.

28   Auslan Cromb, *The Sunday Times*, 6th December 1997.

29   There was, however, an influential group of Templars who continued to operate in Scotland after the demise of the Order on mainland Europe.

30   Otto Betz and Rainer Reisner, *Jesus, Qumran and the Vatican*, p.40, and O. M. Burke, *Among the Dervishes*, p.12.

31   *Fortean Times*, October 1999.

32   *The Times*, 10th March 1999.

33   Again, as with 'Rabbie', the Scottish pronunciation, which is more forceful than the English, gives a good representation of the sound made.

34   Details of these practices vary from teacher to teacher, but breathwork and sound usually play a large role.

35   *Scientific American*, September 1999.

36   1066.

37   *The Oxford Dictionary of Names*.

38   The figure of Robin Hood, or just plain Robin, is often addressed as 'the King of the Witches'. In southern Europe, on the Spanish-Franco border, in the Pyrenees, witches were called Gazarii. These witches were also Gypsies of Romany origin. Gypsies are in fact Hindu in origin, although they were supposed to have come from Egypt, hence their name – Egyptians, Gypsies for short. In Southern France Gypsies are called Czigane (sometimes Tzigane). This is very like the Russian 'czar'. We will see the connections later. Gazarii is obviously a form of Catharii, after the Cathars of the Languedoc region of France, from *cathari*, the Greek for 'pure'.

Skeats' Etymological Dictionary gives 'witch' a derivation from medieval English *wicche*, a form of the more familiar Anglo-Saxon *wicca*, the term by which the craft is known today. However, all of this comes from Anglo-Saxon *witan*, the root word of 'wit', in other words, 'to know', and this brings us full circle to the Gnostics, from the Greek *gnosis* – 'to know'.

39 Cymbals and flutes can produce the same effect.

Chapter Five

1 The title of a poem published in 1885.

2 Pierre Teilhard de Chardin, *The Phenomenon of Man*.

3 For example, the Institute of Noetic Sciences.

4 Maxwell Cade and Nona Coxhead, *The Awakened Mind*, describes details of research in this area.

5 Becker and Selden, *The Body Electric*. p.249.

6 Elizabeth Rauscher, *The Power of Place*, p.300.

7 Gabriel Cousens, *Spiritual Nutrition*, pp.81–91.

8 Paul Devereux *et al.*

9 Serena Roney-Dougal, *Where Science and Magic Meet*, p.140.

10 Cousens, op. cit., p.84.

11 Jacques Benveniste et al., *Nature*, 1998.

12 Quoted in Guy Lyon Playfair and Scott Hill, *The Cycles of Heaven*, p.218.

13 Dr. Mike Ibison, personal communication.

14 Robert G. Jahn, Paul Devereux and Michael Ibison, 'Acoustical Resonances of Assorted Ancient Structures', Princeton Engineering Anomalies Research, School of Engineering and Applied Science, Princeton University, USA, March 1995.

15 Ibid.

16 Ibid.

17 Ibid.

18 Valerie Hunt, *The Infinite Mind*. p.65-66.

19 *Frontier Perspectives*, vol.VIII, no.1, p.44.

20 Lyall Watson, *Supernature*, p.99.

21 Lawrence Blair, *Rhythms of Vision*, pp.126–7.

22 Ibid.

23 *Science Now*, BBC Radio 4, March 1999.

24 Katharine Le Meé, *Chant*, pp.123–5.

25 I have heard from a number of sources that in an experiment performed in the 1980s a human 'guinea pig' was monitored for changes in brainwave patterns as a response to Gregorian chant. As an added bonus the experiment took place within the environs of a monastic building. It is said that the results were dramatic, displaying a lowering of brain rhythms to precisely the rhythm of the interior wherein the experiment took place. I have to admit that, to date, I have not been able to trace related published material and therefore am planning EEG research

on a similar basis with my associates in the CLEAR Research Group.

26   David Ash and Peter Hewitt, *The Science of the Gods*, p.123 (now retitled as *The Vortex*).

27   Ibid.

28   Gabriel Cousens, *Spiritual Nutrition*, p.85.

29   Ibid. and Serena Roney-Dougal, *Where Science and Magic Meet*, p.129.

30   Some fascinating interplays have been noted, especially with crystals. For example, it has been demonstrated that ruby and emerald vibrate in sympathy with the liquid crystal structures of the heart muscle system.

31   Persinger *et al.*

32   Ibid. and Ronay-Dougal, op. cit., p.140ff.

33   Aisling Irwin and Roger Highfield, *Daily Telegraph*, December 1998.

34   Ibid. and Lyall Watson, *Supernature*, pp.94-5.

35   Dr. Tony Scott-Morley, personal communication.

36   Laurence Blair, *Rhythms of Vision*. p.132-3.

37   Cited in A. T. Mann, *Sacred Architecture*. p.92.

38   Ibid. and Dr. Tony Scott-Morley, personal communication.

39   Devereux, p.105ff.

40   A. T. Mann, op. cit.

41   Ibid.

42   Paul Devereux, *Secrets of Ancient and Sacred Places*, p.27.

43   Devereux, *Earthmind*, p.107.

44   Geoffrey Ashe, *The Ancient Wisdom*. p.82.

45   Dr. Keith Hearne, *Visions of the Future*, p.132, and personal communication.

46   Antonio Damasio, *New Scientist*, 11th March 2000.

47   Paul Devereux, *Earth Memory*, p.298.
     Pierre Teilhard de Chardin, cited in Lyall Watson, *Supernature*.

48   From the Aitareya Brahmana, Aranyaka II.

49   Robin Heath, *Sun, Moon and Stonehenge*. (Also see Appendix.)

50   Sir J. N. Lockyer, *The Dawn of Astronomy*.

51   Lyall Watson, op. cit., and Hans Jenny, 'Visualising Sound', *Science*, June 1968.

52   Lyall Watson, ibid. and *The Cambridge Encyclopedia of Language*, ed. David Crystal, p.128ff.

Chapter Six

1   Robert Graves, *The White Goddess*; Joseph Campbell, 'Hercules', *The Hero with a Thousand Faces*.

2   'Occult' means, literally, hidden.

3   *Daily Telegraph*, 3rd March 1999; *Daily Mail*, 3rd March 1999; and *Fortean Times* no. 123, June 1999. Some doubts have subsequently been expressed about the quality of the security film or, more precisely, about the nature of what was caught on film. A logical explanation of the imagery might appear to be nothing other than oak leaves! However, the jury is still out, although in my opinion the explanation does indeed look credible.

4   *Sunday Telegraph*, 28th June 1998; Daily Mail, 29th June 1998.

5   David Fontana, *Visions of the Queen of Heaven*, quoted in the *Daily Mail*.

6   In pre-Islamic Arabia she was a moon goddess.

7   David Elkington, *Amateur Astronomy and Earth Science* magazine, May 1996.

8   Sri Aurobindo, *On Yoga*, Tome Two.

9   Satprem, *Sri Aurobindo or the Adventure of Consciousness*. Our thanks to the Institut de Recherches Evolutives, BP9, 14380 Hermouiville, France.

10   Dante Gabriel Rossetti, 'The Blessed Damosel', 1870.

11   Results cited in John Cornwell, *Powers of Darkness, Powers of Light*, p.49–51.

12   *Daily Telegraph*, 1st July 1999.

13   R. Gerber, *Vibrational Medicine*. A.J. Scott-Morley. *et al.*

14   Peter Tompkins, *Secrets of the Soil*, p.104.

15   Ibid.

16   Devereux, *Places of Power*; John Michell, *The Earth Spirit*; Dr. A. J. Scott-Morley.

17   Devereux, *Earthmind*.

18   The Royal College of Veterinary Surgeons, for example, undertook a veterinary project in which a herd of cows was divided and one half was subjected to a dilution, the other to a placebo.

19   Devereux, *Earthmind*, p.177.

20   *Daily Telegraph* and *Daily Mail*, December 1998.

21   Becker and Selden, *The Body Electric*. p.259.

22   Dr. A. J. Scott-Morley, personal communication.

23   *Daily Telegraph* and *Daily Mail*, op. cit.

24   Becker and Selden, op. cit.

25   Joseph Campbell, *The Masks of God*; Prof. Steven Hawking, *A Brief History of Time*; Prof. Percy Seymour, *Astrology: The Evidence of Science and the Paranormal*; Ken Wilbur, *Quantum Questions*.

26   *Russell Targ and Harold Puthoff, Mind Reach*; S. Roney-Dougal, *Where Science and Magic Meet*. p.43. ff

27   John Cornwell, *Powers of Light, Powers of Darkness*; p.17.and p.161.

28   Rt. Rev. Richard Harries in *The Sunday Times*, 22nd March 1998.

29   In addition, it may also refer to God's omnipresence.

30   Wilson, op. cit.

31   Prof. Antonio R. Damasio in *Scientific American*, December 1999.

32   Jack Spooncer, personal communication.

33   John Haddington quoted in Wilson, *op. cit*, p.29.

34   Wilson, ibid; John Michell, *The Cereologist*; Dr Valerie Hunt, *The Infinite Mind*.

35   Paul Devereux, *Earth Memory*, pp.236ff.

36   The Enuma Elish.

37   For example, the settlement of Qumran by the shore of the Dead Sea.

38   Robert Graves, *Greek Myths*, *The Nazarene Gospel Restored*; T. McKenna, *Food of the Gods*; P. Reddish, *Spirits of the Jaguar*.

39   Robin Heath, *Sun, Moon and Stonehenge* and Alexander Thom, *Megalithic Sites in Britain*.

40   Nigel Pennick, *The Secret Love of Alphabets*; Sir E. A. Wallis-Budge, *Gods of the Egyptians*; Spawforth, *The Oxford Classical Dictionary*.

41   After the goddess Anat. Egyptian Neit, Greek Athena.

42   Robert Graves, *Greek Myths*, Barbara Walker, ibid., pp.201ff.

43   Note the similarity to *belle* and *bella*.

44   *The Oxford Dictionary of Saints* and *The Oxford Dictionary of the Christian Church*, and Robert Graves, *The White Goddess*, p.175, note 1.

45   J. G. Frazer, *The Golden Bough*.

46   *The Oxford Companion to Music*. p.949.

47   L. George, *Heresies and Heretics*, p.218.

48   Jean Seznec, *The Survival of Pagan Gods*, p.149.

49   L. Charpentier, *Mysteries of Chartres Cathedral*; William Anderson, *The Rise of the Gothic*; Sir Bannister Fletcher, *Architecture*.

50   W. Anderson, ibid., p.10.

51   Ibid., p.12.

52   *Abbot Suger on the Abbey Church of St. Denis*, ed. Erwin Panofsky.

53   John D. Barrow, *The Artful Universe*.

54   Blanche Mertz, *Points of Cosmic Energy*, p.105.

55   Charpentier, ibid. p.86.

56   Anderson, ibit p.156..

57   In Sanskrit, the Vedic language believed by many to be the root of the Indo-European family of languages, 'Gaya' is 'song, and 'Gia' is Earth! Sir Monier Monier-Williams, Sanskrit–English Dictionary.

58   H. Whone, *Church, Monastery, Cathedral*; John Anthony West, *The Traveller's Key to Ancient Egypt*; and R. A. Schwaller de Lubicz, *Sacred Science*.

59   Cited in L. Blair, *Rhythms of Vision*, p.136.

60   Ibid; see also Marcel Vogel, Princeton University.

61   Wulfstan of Winchester, *De Organis*, trans. Jamie Leader.

62   Ibid.

63   Owen Barfield quoted in Humphrey Carpenter, *The Inklings*.

64   Prof. Antonio R. Damasio, *Scientific American*, December 1999.

65   St. John's Gospel.

Chapter Seven

1   Valerie Hunt, *The Infinite Mind*, pp.26, 32.

2   Dr. Valerie Hunt and Dr. A. J. Scott-Morley, *Frontier Perspectives*.

3   Hunt, ibid., p.33.

4   L. C. S. Gundersen and R. B. Wanty, 'Field Studies of Radon in Rocks, Soils and Water', *U.S. Geological Survey Bulletin*, 1971, pp.39–50; Serena Roney-Dougal, *Where Science And Magic Meet*; John Michel, *The Earth Spirit*, and various; Paul Devereux, various.

5   Jaime Bigu, *The Journal of Environmental Radioactivity*, vol. 47, p.245.

6   Lyall Watson, *Supernature*. Roney-Dougal, Devereux *et al.*

7   Granite has other properties. One of these is to be found within its magnetic record. Analysis of this record has uncovered evidence of past changes in the polarity of the earth's magnetic field, via a process of 'fossil' magnetism. As molten magma hardens upon exposure to the air, liquefied iron minerals solidify. In hardening they become magnetised at a certain critical temperature – the Curie point. It is this 'fossil' magnetism that gives us a record of past ages. Regarding enhanced sensitivity to magnetic fields at sacred sites, it should be borne in mind that many types of rock contain iron-bearing minerals such as magnetite, also known as lodestone, and thus magnetic impulses can be measured from them. Amongst these rock types, again, is granite.

     See, for example, Charpentier, *Mysteries of Chartres Cathedral*; Paul Devereux, *Earth Memory*; Nigel Pennick, *Mysteries of Kings College Chapel*; Watson, ibid.

8   Roney-Dougal, p.163.

9   Frances Lynch, *Prehistoric Religion and Ritual*, p.64.

10   Meo, *The Orgone Accumulator Handbook*.

11   An electrical charge arises within it. This is piezoelectricity.

12   'Man Made Diamonds – A Cut above Nature', *Daily Telegraph*, 21st August 1999.

13   Sometimes, seeming anomalies arise which, on inspection, turn out to be local practical applications of the resonant rule. For example, at the chambered mound of Maes Howe in the Orkney Isles and at Camster Round passage grave in Caithness, Scotland (see Appendix).

14   Robert Graves, *The White Goddess*.

15   Psalm 84:4–7.

16   Matthew 16:18.

17   A.N. Wilson, *Daily Telegraph*, 27th December 1998.

18   Rt. Rev. Robert Hardy, *Daily Telegraph*, 20th November 1998.

19   Leslie Grinsell, 'Folklore of Prehistoric Sites in Britain', *3rd Stone*, no. 32, 1998, p.23ff.

20   Bede, p.86ff.

21   Christopher Somerville, *Daily Telegraph*, 26th July 1997.

22   Paid out by the incumbent Protestant authorities.

23   Guy Underwood, *The Pattern of the Past*. p.161

24   Frayling, *Strange Landscape*, p.57.

25   Hitching, Earth Magic; Richard Gerber, *Vibrational Medicine*.

26   Tom Graves, *Needles of Stone – Revisited*, pp.34-5.

27   Roney-Dougal. Smith and Best. David Cowan.

28   Roney-Dougal, p.147.

29   Tom Graves, op. cit.

30   Ibid.

31   *3rd Stone*, no. 32, 1998, p.23; F Hitching, *Earth Magic*.

32   Tom Graves, op. cit., p.37.

33   Dr. Phillip Stooke, *Daily Mail*, 23rd April 1999.

34   Sir James Jeans calls this movement 'little whirlwinds'. See *Science and Music*, p.126.

35   William Anderson, *The Rise of the Gothic*, p.156.

36   Unfortunately, this is not so easy of late, as seating now usually covers the labyrinth.

37   Dr. G. Schneck, *British Society of Dowsers Journal*, 1994-5??

38   Herald and Lawton, p.20.

39   Cheops is the Greek for Khufu. Both are alternative titles for the Great Pyramid.

40   Lyall Watson, *Supernature*, p.101–2.

41   Smith and Best, *Electromagnetic Man*, p.121–2.

42   Ken Johnson, *The Ancient Magic of the Pyramids*, p.45.

43   Oestrander and Schroeder, p.362.

44   The Pyramid Texts.

45   Devereux, Steele and Kubrin, p.115.

Chapter Eight

1   Herodotus, *Histories*, p.21.
2   Timothy Freke and Peter Gandy, *The Jesus Mysteries*; A. Wallace-Hadrill, *Augustan Rome*.
3   J. G. Frazer, *The Golden Bough*, p.347.
4   Robert Graves, *King Jesus*, p.11–12.
5   According to Richard Knight in 'A Discourse on the Worship of Priapus' there is, hidden away in the Vatican, a bronze image of a cock with the head of a penis. Appended to this Graeco-Roman statue are the original words: 'The Saviour of the World'.
6   During the Age of Aries, preceding that of Taurus, c.3000–2000BC, it was the ram that was the favoured symbol.
7   Robert Eisler, *Orpheus the Fisher*, 1920.
8   Joseph Campbell, *Occidental Mythology*, p.350.
9   Freke and Gandy, op. cit., p.35.
10 Ibid., and Graves *et al*, *The Golden Ass*.
11 Sir William Drummond, *Oedipus Judaicus*.
12 Freke and Gandy, op. cit., p.42.
13 J. M. Robertson, *Pagan Christs*, p.97.
14 Ibid.
15 Timothy Freke and Peter Gandy, *The Jesus Mysteries*, p.41, and others.
16 Robert Graves, *Greek Myths* and *King Jesus*; Barbara Walker, *Women's Encyclopaedia of Myths and Legends*; Kerenyi, *Dionysus et al.*
17 Mark 15:17–20.
18 Quoted in J. Godwin, *Mystery Religions*, p.28.
19 Giorgio de Santillana and Hertha von Dechend, *Hamlet's Mill*, p.33.
20 Graves, *Greek Myths*, p.103; Euripides, *The Bacchae*.
21 Bayley, ii, pp.25–7.
22 Plutarch, *De Isis et Osiris*.
23 See Jesus in the Gospels; de Santillana and von Dechend, op. cit., p.33; Kullervo falls upon his sword.
24 Homer, *The Iliad*.
25 Sir E. A. Wallis-Budge, *Gods of the Egyptians* and various.
26 De Santillana and von Dechend, op. cit., p.33.
27 Ibid.
28 Mark 15:34.
29 Kerenyi, *Dionysus*, p.251.
30 Quoted in Peter Lemesurier, *The Great Pyramid Decoded*, p.272.
31 J. G. Frazer, *The Golden Bough*.
32 *Lenin Folklore*. Moscow, 1930.
33 Walter Birks and R. A. Gilbert, *The Treasure of Mont*é*gur*, p.113.
34 Ibid.

35 Quoted in Timothy Freke and Peter Gandy, *The Jesus Mysteries*, p.41.

36 Quoted in ibid., p.29.

37 Mark 8:27-30

38 Prof. John Strugnall, *Ha-Bretz*, November 1990; Michael Baigent and Richard Leigh, *The Dead Sea Scrolls Deception*, p.95–6.

39 Martin Bernal, Black Athena, vols I and II; see also Julian Baldick, *Black God*.

40 Mircea Eliade, *Encyclopaedia of Religion and Religions*, vol. XII, pp.331–3.

41 A. N. Wilson, *Jesus*, p.239.

42 Gerald Massey, *The Logia of the Lord*, p.1.

43 Ibid.

44 Quoted in Freke and Gandy, op. cit., p.63.

45 Ibid.

46 Robert Graves, *Greek Myths*, 2:b, p.30.

47 E. Merry, *The Flaming Door*, p.152.

48 Sometimes called 'Hu-Esus'.

49 Merry, op. cit.

50 *Brewer's Dictionary*, p.523.

51 The god Horus, the lord whose name is Hu, meaning 'the', became a higher form – he became a stellar deity, a cosmic god, a higher form of 'the' as it is used on earth, an all-encompassing 'The', in the divine sense of ultimate realisation, 'I am.' He was the former Horus now become Osiris, a 'Gesu', the man who had become God, giving hope to the rest of humanity, 'Gesu' being a composite of Horus the earthly, and Osiris/Asar, the father who art in the heavens.

52 See Martin Bernal, *Black Athena*, vol. II, p.106 and Appendix.

53 Giorgio de Santillana and Hertha von Dechend, *Hamlet's Mill*, p.114ff.

54 Gerald Massey, The Logia of the Lords, p.5.

55 Ibid., p.11, and *The Historical Jesus and the Mythical Christ*, p.156ff.

56 J. G. Frazer, The Golden Bough; Barbara Walker, *Women's Encyclopaedia of Myths and Legends*, p.10–11; Timothy Freke and Peter Gandy, *The Jesus Mysteries*, p.33, et al.

57 Freke and Gandy, ibid., p.33; Frazer, ibid., p.347.

58 Due to changes in the Caesarian calendar, ten days were taken off the year during the reign of Pope Gregory in 1582, giving a confusion of dates. Whereas old Christmas – 6th January – and new Christmas – 25th December – are the same.

59 Robert Graves, *The White Goddess*. p.175 and 327n.

60 Ibid.

61 S. Angus, *Mystery Religions*, p.136.

62 Walker, op. cit., p.78.

63 Leonard Slain, *The Alphabet versus the Goddess*, p.83. Shlain (p.259) submits that Christianity could never have gained a foothold in Egypt if the Gospels had been written down in hieroglyphics. This is, I feel, contentious, but possibly, if only partially, true, as (see chapter ten) Christianity could not have existed in the first

place without hieroglyphs; many of these glyphs entered Christian myth in a much misunderstood form.

64   E. Merry, *The Flaming Door*, p.143; Graves, op. cit.; Marion O'Morgan, *The Mabin of the Mabinogion*, p.70.

65   Nora Chadwick, *The Celts*, p.170.

66   Graves, op. cit; Walker, op. cit., p.602ff.

67   As put together by Lady Charlotte Guest.

68   Cited in Graves, op. cit., p.95.

69   Robin Heath, personal communication.

70   Pierre Grimal, *The Churches of Rome*.

71   Bacciccia was born Giovanni Battista-Gaulli and executed his masterpiece between the years 1672 and 1685 in the Baroque decorative style.

72   Dr. Phillip Blair, personal communication.

73   Kamal Salibi, *Who was Jesus?*

74   Adrian Bailey, *The Caves of the Sun*, p.35.

75   Marc-Alain Ouaknin, *Mysteries of the Alphabet*, p.178.

76   Ouaknin, Jacques Benveniste *et al.*

77   Ouaknin, ibid., p.200.

78   Christine and Abdul el Mahdi, personal communication.

79   Bernal, *Black Athena, et al.*

80   Also in North America, the Apache Indians have a hero figure called Herus. This figure is taken to be Jesus, and is said to have come from their first contacts with the Spanish. Their version, however, is too near to the original hero of the Egyptians, Horus, for the Spanish story to be easily acceptable. It is only when we dig deeper that we learn that in ancient times the tribe were given a book, a holy book, by a man named Herus, but that on his death, it was burned as it was the custom to burn the possessions of a dead man. What can we make of this? I am inclined to the more ancient view because many Native American Indian tribes had or still have heroes that bear striking similarities to the holy child. The Chiricahua called theirs 'Child of the water' – baptism again?

81   The Arabs adapted an existing place name.

82   *Dj* is often translated as 'Zer', this being another form of Osiris' name in archaic Egyptian – Asar.

83   In Scandinavian mythology the father god, Woden (sometimes Odin), crucifies himself upon the world tree as an act of renewal. I was hardly surprised to learn that the collective name for the Scandinavian Norse pantheon of the gods was the Aesir or Aesar – Asar, and so Gisa, again.

84   Mark Lehner, *The Complete Pyramids*, p.84.

85   As a further confirmation of the Gisa-Jesus link, in The Secrets of the Great Pyramid, p.1ff., Peter Tompkins tells us that Giza (Gisa) is transliterated by various authors as Djiseh or Jeeseh, the 'G' being pronounced hard by Egyptians and soft by other Arabs.

86 De Santillana and von Dechend, *Hamlet's Mill*, p.6–7.

87 Leonard Shlain, *The Alphabet versus the Goddess*, p.258.

88 The rendering of the Hebrew text is very interesting here. In *Jesus, Qumran and the Vatican*, p.180, note II, the translation is given as *mig-geza* – 'from the stump'.

89 Other trees that have been cut down in the same fashion feature in the myths of the Cuna Indians of Central America, wherein the sun god, Quetzlcoatl, disguises himself as a tapir and cuts down the Palluwalla tree. This tree is the world tree that stands at the centre of the universe.

90 G. R. S. Mead, *Thrice Greatest Hermes*, vol. I, p.286, note 8; Plutarch, *Isis and Osiris*.

91 Mead, ibid.

92 H. Sayce, the Hibbert lectures on the Religion of Ancient Babylonians, 1898.

93 Colossians 1:16–17.

94 Kamal Salibi, Who Was Jesus?, pp.51–52ff.

95 Graves and Podro, *The Nazarene Gospel Restored*, Foreward X1

96 II Corinthians 11:4.

97 Graves and Podro, op. cit., Introduction.

98 Better named as 'The Book of Coming Forth by Day' or 'The Book of Coming Forth by Light'.

99 Clement of Alexandria, *Stromata* I, XV, 70, 1.

100 Panarion; also see *The Oxford Dictionary of the Christian Church*, p.553 for a breakdown of Epiphanius' life. Significantly, showing the roots of the Nazarene knowledge, Plutarch states (as noted in *Egyptian Wisdom* by Naomi Ozaniec), 'There is no difference as a matter of fact, between the texts called hieroglyphs and most of the precepts of Pythagoras.' It is well known that Pythagoras spent much time in Egypt.

101 Quoted in G. R. S. Mead, *Thrice Greatest Hermes*, vol. I, p.270, and note 3.

102 Sir E. A. Wallis-Budge; Manley and Collier.

103 See Marc-Alain Ouaknin, Mysteries of the Alphabet, p.252, the letter 'N'.

104 Clement of Alexandria, *Stromatis*, Book 1–3, trans. John Ferguson

105 McLeish, *Myth*.

106 Exodus 15:1–21.

107 Graves, *King Jesus*, chapter one.

108 *The Book of Jasher*, with a foreword by the exotically named Prof. Hilton Hotema.

109 *The Oxford Dictionary of Saints*, ed. David Farmer, p.337.

110 Books of Joshua and Ruth.

111 Kamal Salibi, Who Was Jesus?, p.57ff.

112 Sir E. A. Wallis-Budge, *The Mummy*, p.2.

113 Shu is the Egyptian Heracles (see Graves in *Larousse Mythology*), thus Sumer is the land of Heracles and of Isis.

114 Giorgio de Santillana and Hertha von Dechend, *Hamlet's Mill*, p.221.

115 Robert Graves, *The White Goddess*, p.95.

116 *A Sanskrit–English Dictionary*, ed. Monier Monier-Williams.

117 Barbara Walker, *Women's Encyclopaedia of Myth and Legend*, p.453 and Sir E. A. Wallis-Budge, *Gods of the Egyptians*.

118 I. E. S. Edwards, *The Pyramids of Egypt*. p.279.ff

The Anatomy of the Hero.

1 *The Independent,* 19th November 1996, David Keys

2 *Codex Borgianus.*

3 Walker, *Encylopaedia of Myths*, p.1,020.

4 deSantillana and von Dechend, *Hamlet's Mill*, p.78.

5 Walker, *Encyclopaedia of Mythology*, p.336.

6 Adrian Gilbert, *The Magi*, p.184).

Chapter Nine

1 R. A. Schwaller de Lubicz, *The Temple in Man: Sacred Architecture and the Perfect Man*, p.132.

2 Simone Weil, *Intimations of Christianity Among the Ancient Greeks*, p.27.

3 Ahmed Osman, *In the House of the Messiah*, p.171–2.

4 Ibid., also Howard Carter and Mace, *The Tomb of Tutankamun*.

5 Osman, op. cit.

6 *The Pyramid Texts*, trans. R. O. Faulkner.

7 In the Book of Exodus, Joshua performs the incredible feat of stopping the sun in its tracks, a feat that was also originally performed by the goddess Isis.

8 Sir E. A. Wallis-Budge, *Gods of the Egyptians*, vol. II, p.191.

9 A pharaoh was also a magus, a bearer of great authority and great wisdom. In magical tradition, *Heka* signifies the spirit of God. A magical spell in witchcraft is a 'hex' and comes from the same root as *Heka* (Greek *Hex* or *Heksa*). The hexagram is the Seal of Solomon and the symbol of King David, better known as the Star of David.
     Heka still has a widespread influence today. *Hake* in the Arabian tongue means that which is right, that which is true. Any follower of rugby football will be very familiar with the magical connotation of the term *heka*. It is found in the Maori tradition as the splendid 'Haka' performed not only by Maoris but by members of the New Zealand rugby football team at the outset of each of their matches. It is an intimidating act with a magic all of its own. The hex was, of course, sacred to the goddess Hecate of the Greek Pantheon, who is derived from the Egypt Heket (sometimes Heqit). *Hekau*, the plural of *heka*, means 'magical words of power' and almost invariably the names of the gods were names of magical power, hence the Hebrew embargo upon speaking the holy name of God, Yahweh. Thus we can associate the Pharaoh with 'magical words of power'.

10 Dame Frances Yates, *Giordano Bruno and the Hermetic Tradition*, p.115ff.

11 Anthony Sattin, *The Pharaoh's Shadow*, p.171.

12 Oddly enough, the Coptic spelling of Jesus is Essa, and it dates right back to the

first century AD.

13 Martin Bernal, *Black Athena*, vol. I, p.3.

14 Michael Wood, *Hitler's Search for the Holy Grail*, C4 TV, 1998, and Nigel Pennick, *Hitler's Secret Sciences*.

15 More recently it has become known that even the Romans found their way across the Atlantic.

16 Julian Baldick, *Black God*.

17 This 'ah ha' moment is sometimes related to a feeling of something physically falling into place in the body, but more often to a tingling or tickling sensation in the spine or head. Such activity is also associated with kundalini. Some individuals, in whom kundalini is active, suffer long bouts of uncontrollable laughter. Whatever symptoms manifest during kundalini, after a period of purification – length subject to that required – feelings of discomfort give way to feelings of joy. There is much ongoing research into this subtle energy.

18 K. Luckert, p.241. See chapter ten for a quote from Luckert on the nature of the Egyptian Ennead and its relation to the One God.

19 Ibid.

20 With apologies to John Reid.

21 Bernal, op. cit., p.26.

22 Ibid.

23 C. F. Dupuis, *Was Christ a Person or the Sun?*, p.8.

24 Ibid.

25 Letter of Montmorency-Laval, 22nd June 1825, quoted in Martin Bernal, *Black Athena*, p.252.

26 Ibid., p.184.

27 John Todd Ferrier, *Herald* XXVII, p.89.

28 William Shakespeare, *Henry VI*, iv, 7.

29 Acts 4:10–11.

30 1 Peter 2:3–8.

31 *Acta Latomorum ou Chronologie de L'Histoire de la Franche-Maconnerie Française et Etrangère*, 1815, Bibliotèque Nationale.

32 In astronomy the symbol represents the sun, whilst in astrology it is used to represent the self.

33 The fact that this eye is in the pyramid is all the more telling – the Freemasons were perpetuating a tradition that the Church deemed heretical and wanted to be rid of. God was in the machine.

34 Robert Temple, *The Sirius Mystery*.

35 Sir E. A. Wallis-Budge, *Gods of the Egyptians*.

36 Lurker, *Gods and Goddesses*, p.345.

37 Henri Frankfort, ibid., p.318.

38 *The Pyramid Texts*, op. cit., no. 600, *A prayer for the King and his pyramid*, Faulkner, op. cit., p247

39   The Sumerian Anunnaki are also depicted seated upon their thrones.
40   John Michell, *The Earth Spirit.*
41   Frankfort, op cit., p.318.
42   Sir E. A. Wallis-Budge, *Legends of Our Lady.*
43   H. Wedeck, quoted in Barbara Walker, *Women's Encyclopedia of Myths and Secrets*, p.614.
44   Walter Scott, *Hermetica*, vol. IV, p.262.
45   Ibid., p.261.
46   Newton, quoted in Paul Devereux, Steele and Kubrin, p.55.
47   Dr. A. J. Scott-Morley, personal communication.
48   Richard Gerber, *Vibrational Medicine*, p.130.
49   Ibid., p.131.
50   R. A. Schwaller de Lubicz, *The Temple in Man.* p.17.
51   J. Goldman, *Healing Sounds*, p.17.
52   David Tame, *The Secret Power of Music*, p.23.
53   Ibid., p.24.
54   Ibid.
55   David Lubman, *New Scientist*, 10th October 1998, p.7.
56   Quoted in 'Birds trigger songs that enlighten', *The Times*, 21st April 1999.
57   Marvin W. Meyer, *The Ancient Mysteries*, p.216.
58   Lubman, op. cit.
59   Jonathan Goldman, *Healing Sounds*, p.42–43ff.
60   Ibid.
61   William Grey, quoted ibid.

Chapter 10
1   The word 'civilisation' comes from the Latin *civitas* meaning 'city' or 'city dwellers' (in the sense of 'the body politic').
2   J.A. West, *Serpent in the Sky*, Quest Books, 1993, p.216.
3   This is when various cultures called Amratian, Gerzean, Badarian, Semainean, Naqada I and Naqada II were spawned. These cultures are named after the places where elements of this period may still be found. Amratian is essentially the same as Naqada I (early) and Gerzean is the same as Naqada II (late); thus in recent years these names have tended to be discarded, being elements of the other named periods.
4   Vivian Davies and Renee Friedman, *Egypt*, British Museum Press, 1998, and Daily Mail, 16/12/98.
5   Wallis-Budge, *The Mummy*, p.2
6   Gardiner, *Egyptian Grammar*, p.495.
7   Old Kingdom language usage became to a degree obsolete by the time of the Middle Kingdom.
8   Wallis-Budge, *Gods of the Egyptians*, vol.ii, p.202.

9   *The Jesus Mysteries*, p.262, note 35.

10   Professor Karl Luckert, *Egyptian Light and Hebrew Fire*, State University of New York Press, 1991, p.42-3.

11   Von Dechend and Santillana, p.62-3.

12   Note that 'te' and doh', adopted later, are present here in 'Sancte Iohannes'.

13   Von Dechend and Santillana, p.149.

14   Hilary Wilson, *Understanding Hieroglyphs*, p.1.

15   *Daily Telegraph* 8.05.00 and Nature.

16   If one compares the two versions of the Creation from the Old Testament and the New, the version in St John's Gospel is much more related to the very ancient tradition of Creation Mythology, particularly the Egyptian.

17   S.H. Hooke, *Middle Eastern Mythology*, Penguin, 1963, p.73.

18   *Corpus Hermeticum*, ch.xvi, 2.

19   *Daily Telegraph*, 26/1/99.

20   *Frontier Perspectives*, vol.7, no.2, p.5.

21   Ideas which I believe are forms of inherent memory, visions of consciousness reaching out from the human standpoint to a point of infinite memory, Godhead.

22   *Hamlet's Mill*, p.57.

23   Other descriptions which have already been explained within the text include analogies wherein the breath 'spiritus' is replaced by 'the blood', 'the wine' or 'the lifestream' and 'primal substance' by 'the substratum', 'the rock' or 'bread of life'.

24   Peter Tompkins, *The Secret Life of Nature*, Thorsons, 1997, p.153.

25   Tompkins, ibid., p.155, quoting Stephen M. Phillips.

26   *Scientific American*, September 1997, p.41.

28   Wallis-Budge *Gods of the Egyptians*, vol.2, p.114.

29   J.E. Cirlot, *A Dictionary of Symbols*, Routledge, 1996, p.341.

30   For example, in Central America the Mexican King Can had a son Prince Aac, meaning 'A – the great'. This figure slew Prince Coh, meaning 'the great O'. The biblical brothers Cain and Abel mean respectively 'the great A' and 'the Lord O' (Abel in Hebrew is spelt with an 'O'). In the bible story, Cain slew Able. To my mind, this twist does not negate the connections, especially in the light of Geolinguistic theory.

31   *A Dictionary of Egyptian Gods and Goddesses*, R.K.P., 1986, p.151.

32   W.B. Emery, *Archaic Egypt*, Pelican, 1961, Penguin pbk., 1991, p.122, and Saad, 1947, p.27, plate xivb.

33   'Barbarian' means literally 'hairy man', a fitting description of various of the heros; in the Old Testament, Esau is described as a 'red and hairy man'.

34   Sometimes it is a sycamore tree. See S.H. Hooke, *Middle-Eastern Mythology*, p.69.

35   'Mummy', from the Persian *mum* meaning 'wax', in this case preserving wax.

36   Recognisable in the Indian Vedic literature as Jyoti. This word and its progeny relate to illumination and all that shines.

37   The myrrh tree was known as 'the tear of Horus'.

38   Freke and Gandy, op.cit., p.33.

39   Bernal, op.cit., vol.i, p.70f.

40   This is confirmed by the name of the Vedic god of the dead, Yama, who was also called Asu or Esu-niti, and who performed the same function as Osiris/Gesu as a guide of spirit. See Frawley, *Gods, Sages and Kings*, Motilal Banarsidass, 1999, p.271.

41   R. Graves, *The Greek Myths*, Penguin, 1992, p.196.

42   This brings us back to Thoth, who was also the herald of childbirth, a role taken in Christian tradition by the Archangel Gabriel.

43   Osiris is sometimes referred to as Herm-Anubis (Heru-em-Anpu). Cocks of a saffron colour were sacrificed to him – reminiscent of the Buddhist colours.

44   *Pyramid Texts*.

45   *Book of the Dead*, Sir E.A. Wallis-Budge.

46   Sir E.A. Wallis-Budge, *Gods of the Egyptians*, vol.2, p.126+141.

47   Freke and Gandy, op.cit., p.32; M.A. Murray, *Egyptian Religious Poetry*, John Murray, 1949, p.68.

48   Sir E.A. Wallis-Budge, *Oxford University Press*, 1st Edition, 1933.

49   Desmond Stewart, *The Foreigner*, Hamish Hamilton, 1981, p.77.

50   Albert Churchward, *Signs and Symbols of Primordial Man*, 1903.

51   Thomas Didymus or Judas. This is another theme which runs throughout the hero mythology.

52   In the myth of Osiris and Set it is Set who is crucified (R. Graves, *Greek Myths*, vol.i, pp.283-4, and J. Campbell, The Mythic Image, p.29), for Set was a king, and a ritually crucified one at that. This crucifixion is rather like that of Woden, who crucified himself so that he might gain higher knowledge of the Mysteries. Thus once again we have a motif of Set metamorphosing through his own suffering and becoming his higher self. Ass-eared Set ruled Edom, the country of Jesus' ancestry.

53   Sir D. Gardiner, *Egyptian Grammar*, p.587.

Chapter 11

1   Karl Popper in 'The Philosophy of Science'. C. A. Mace (ed.) *British Philosophy in the Mid-Century* (1957

2   Bob Brier, *The Murder of Tutankhamun*, Weidenfeld and Nicolson, 1998, p.99.

3   J. Godwin, *Mystery Religions in the Ancient World*, Thames and Hudson, 1981, p.28.

4   In Ancient Mesopotamia, the powers or properties of the gods were called *me* (pronounced 'may') and they enabled a whole host of activities central to human life, especially religion – the binding back to the source. The names given to the powers were the names of the gods, and thus the gods denoted the nature of these powers: in ancient Egyptian, *neter* – literally, the power of God in whatever

variant aspect. The Ancient Mesopotamian term that denoted how these powers really ought to be was, interestingly, *Gishur*. This term means 'play', or 'design', in the sense of how God brings things about in the grand scheme of things. Therefore it is most fitting that *Gishur* is so similar to Gisa. This sense of the word 'design' is the a theme that runs through not just the ancient Egyptian Book of the Dead, but through scriptures and Mystery Teachings worldwide. The Ancient Mesopotamian 'me' are the 'powers which make possible the powers of the Gishur and which ensure the continuation of civilised life'. See Jeremy Black and Anthony Green, *Gods, Demons and Symbols of Ancient Mesopotamia*, British Museum Press, p.130.

5   Thoth or Tot is interesting. 'd' or 't' are cognate, thus we may derive 'Dod' from the name. This is the ancient form of David. Jesus/Asar was of the line of David. 'Thoth' is Greek; in Egyptian it is Djehuti, meaning literally, 'Dje, the Lord, has come' – Dje is Osiris. Thoth was brought to Britain 4,000 years ago – hence the many 'Toots' in English place-names (Toothill, Tooting etc.).]

6   R. A. Schwaller de Lubicz, *The Temple in Man* and John Anthony West, *The Serpent in the Sky*.

7   A. Brooke, *Towards Human Unity*, 1976.

8   'Resh' in *khepresh* is the letter 'r' in Egyptian and Hebrew. It is the pronunciation of the double 'aa' – the Word of God.

9   Ouaknin, Marc-Alain, *Mysteries of the Alphabet*, p.266f.

10   Ibid.

11   Manley P. Hall, Man: *The Grand Symbol of the Mysteries*, p.209.

12   Ibid.

13   Ibid.

14   'Astarte' seems to be a reference to Ursa Major, the Great Bear, 'Ast-arte' meaning 'Star of the bear'. This is a constellation of some significance, as it may have played an important part in the funerary ceremony surrounding the dead pharaoh.

15   Esther had a consort, Mordecai, who sacrificed the god Hammon. What this story is really about is the goddess Ishtar and her consort Marduk. Hammon would seem to be Amon. This was a myth current in the civilisation of Elam, *c*.2000 BC, and seems to be yet another mythic retelling of the story of Isis, consort of Osiris.

16   Shepherd [or Pastor] of Hermas, 9th Simile.

17 '...neuroscientists using positron emission tomography (PET) have demonstrated that long-term memory for emotionally arousing events in healthy humans is highly associated with increased brain activity in the amygdaloid complex. The finding provides dramatic graphic evidence that the amygdalae – a pair of walnut-shaped structures near the hippocampus – play a critical role in the formation and modulation of emotionally influenced memory in both animals and humans.' University of California, Irvine, 22nd July 1996. Susan Menning, Press Release.

18   This is now common knowledge since the publication of *On Death and Dying* by Dr Elisabeth Kubler-Ross in 1969 and subsequent research.

19   The word 'gilgal' means 'spiral', and is part of the name of the Sumerian mythical hero Gilgamesh, said to have been an actual historical king, the fifth king of the Second Dynasty of Erech. 'Gilgamesh' means 'man of spirals'. A gilgal was also a circle of stones. (In Aboriginal, *gilgai* means 'saucer-shaped depression' – one that has formed a natural reservoir.) Gilgal is the name of a place where Joshua, Moses' heir, spent the night – it was within sight of Jericho, where ' the walls came tumblin' down'. The proper reading of the story would seem to intimate that it was the name of Joshua/Gesu that was used or invoked to such devastating effect – a great blast of air, perhaps? Or is the entire story merely the coded description of a temple ritual? The fact that Joshua, who is cognate with all the heroes so far described in this book, stayed the night is interesting. In relation to this ritual timing, I have discovered an interesting letter by the Roman governor of Bithynia in Asia Minor, Pliny the Younger. Writing of the Christians *c*.AD 111. He states: 'They meet on a certain fixed day before sunrise and sing an antiphonal hymn to Christ as a god, and bind themselves with an oath...'
The practice of antiphonal singing, a kind of alternate chanting sung by two parties, is indeed very ancient, and in ritual at certain sites, as we have seen, is very powerful. At the culmination of the *hieros gamos* within the *Sancta Sanctorum*, the name of God was ritually chanted in a rite known as the epiclesis. The epiclesis was the invocation of the spirit of God into the Eucharist, as in Greek the 'indwelling' of God was called the *eutheos*. In the heavens the term is *eutheoi*. God was called upon to send the Holy Spirit upon the bread and wine, thus making them the Body and the Blood of the Christos, his Holy Son.

20   See Robert Bauval and Adrian Gilbert, *The Orion Mystery*.

21   Chris Herald and Ian Lawton, *Giza, the Truth*.

22   In the *Shabaka Texts* (line 18), carved into a single slab of solid black granite which now resides in the British Museum, the following description of Rostau occurs:'This is the land .. [of] ... the burial place of Osiris in the House of Sokar.'

23   Named after Leonardo Fibonacci, also known as Leonardo of Pisa (*c*.1175–*c*.1250). His work, *Liber Abaci* helped introduce Arabic notation into Europe. In their simplest form, Fibonacci numbers form a sequence where, beginning with 1, each number is the sum of its two predecessors – 1, 1, 2, 3, 5, 8, 13, etc. There are clear applications in botany, psychology and astronomy.

24   There is too much evidence to suggest that the Egyptians were not aware of these things; in fact some of the imagery has come down to us, after many thousands of years, in the form of the pointy-hatted wizards wearing cloaks with stars and spirals and carrying long staves. I.E.S. Edwards observes that this was precisely the apparel worn by the Heliopolitan high priests, the greatest of whom was known as Chief of the Astronomers. His staff even had a five-pointed star on it (See I. E. S. Edwards, *The Pyramids of Egypt*, p.286.). Even the image of a magician's hat bears similarity to a pyramidal-shaped structure.

25   Churchward, A., *Signs and Symbols of Primordial Man*, p.381. Horus is Hu – in 'the

80th Chapter of the Ritual: "I have seized upon Hu..."' The Ritual is the Pyramid Text.

26   Bayley, *The Lost Language of Symbolism*, part ii, p.201.

27   Liddell and Scott, *Greek Lexicon*, p.1,006-1,251.

28   See Gardiner, *Egyptian Grammar*, p.489, sign N27.

29   Baines, J. and Malek, J., *Atlas of Ancient Egypt*, pp.140-1.

30   Quoted in W. Scott, *Hermetica*, vol.4, p.256.

31   Ibid., pp.255-6.

32   Sir E. A. Wallis-Budge, *The Egyptian Heaven and Hell*, p.131.

33   This is reflected in Mexico, where the pyramids indigenous to the area are known as *teocallis*, from *teo calli*, meaning 'house of God'. The Mexican word *Teo* is very like the Greek *Theo*, also meaning 'God'.

34   Jesus, like the Pharaohs, was entombed, and after the Resurrection his tomb was found to be empty; but even then it was Jewish custom to entomb bodies for a statutory period before re-entering and collecting the bones of the decayed corpse and depositing them in ossuaries.

35   For a detailed discussion of this there are several excellent populist books on the subject: Herald and Lawton, *Giza, the Truth*; M. Lehner, *The Complete Pyramids*, and Alan Alford, *The Phoenix Solution*. See Bibliography.

36   However, the Great Pyramid is sited directly over a huge mound of bedrock. Jean Kerisel argues that topography is not a sufficient answer to the siting of the Pyramid. Furthermore, the bedrock of the Giza plateau could not take the weight of a pyramidal structure. Nor were the three Giza pyramids built in succession – after Khufu, Djedefre built his at Dahshur.

37   In fact, to my knowledge, there is only one investigator of note looking into the enigmas of the Giza site who has the required construction background. This is the researcher Peter Renton, whose work has not only developed a noteworthy pyramid construction theory, but also generated much excitement regarding access to known but previously inaccessible chambers of the Great Pyramid. Peter is a friend who works with Paul Ellson, my collaborator and editor of this volume, hence I am privy to revelations yet to be publicised. As far as the Giza Plateau is concerned, expect the unexpected.

38   See Peter Hodges, *How the Pyramids were Built*, Element Books, Shaftesbury, 1989.

39   There are many examples worldwide of straight roads and paths of this kind, complete with threads or ropes. In fact, to impede the progress of particular types of spirit, shamans would often tie knots in the rope. (*3rd Stone* magazine, No.31, p.41, Alby Stone.)

40   Peter Tompkins, *Secrets of the Great Pyramid*, pp.278-9.

41   Ibid.

Chapter 12

1   From *On First Looking into Chapman's Homer* by John Keats (1795–1817)

2   Flavius Josephus, *Antiquities of the Jews*, Book 16, Chapter 7.

3   Sir Alan Gardiner, 'The Secret Chambers of The Sanctuary of Thoth' in *The Journal ofEgyptian Archeology*, vol. II, 1925.

4   *Prayers of the Cosmos, Meditations on the Aramaic words of Jesus.* With translation and commentary by Neil Douglas-Klotz. HarperCollins 1994

5   The whole Osirian mythos and its symbology is complex but fascinating. Through his death comes life anew – the fundamental mystery. Osiris, as the god of death, is portrayed mummiform, wrapped in a white shroud – the symbol of a dead king. And here we have another connection with the historical Jesus – the famous shroud.

6   John Reid, *Egyptian Sonics* (see Appendix).

7   In the Christian world, of course, we use fir trees as part of our Christmas celebrations.

8   My thanks to Rod Bearcloud for this and other helpful information.

9   'Sycamore' is *sycos* in Greek, meaning 'fig' – the original forbidden tree in the Garden of Eden, because it was the Tree of Death, the very thing that Adam and Eve reaped when they ate the apple.

10   Beyond the presence of a high radon content, some studies had revealed differing levels of magnetism. The upper chambers had very much lower readings of magnetism than the lower chambers, whilst at the same time the upper chambers were significantly higher in terms of frequency See Greg Braden, *Awakening to Zero Point*.

11   (Strange things had happened there, peculiar 'doublings' of energy, which generally is supposed to diminish with output – not so in the King's Chamber. But there was something else peculiar too: people with broken bones would visit the place and walk away significantly further along the road to recovery – healing that took place by coming into contact with the dying and rising god, Osiris/ Gesu.)

12   *Inscription* journal, November 1999 and January 2000. Please note that although I do not agree with some of Tom Danley's conclusions, his work has provided corroboration of the 31.25 Hz sub harmonic.

13   Tom Danley, *Live Sound* magazine, June/July 2000.

14   Ibid.

15   Kay Gardner, *Sounding the Inner Landscape*, p91.

16   *SQ, Spiritual Intelligence, the ultimate intelligence*, Danah Zohar and Ian Marshall, p73ff.

17   Ibid. p87.

18   A sinusoidal wave form enables energy to be transferred smoothly to the membrane.

19   J. Godwin, *Mystery Religions*, p.28.

Bibliography

Abegg, M., Wise, M. and Cook, E., *The Dead Sea Scrolls*, HarperCollins, 1996.

Adams Leeming, David and Adams Leeming, Margaret, *Encyclopedia of Creation Myths*, ABC-Clio, 1994.

Adams, B., *Predynastic Egypt*, Shire, 1988 (pbk).

Aesop, *The Complete Fables*, trans. Robert and Olivia Temple, Penguin, 1998 (pbk.).

Aghion, I., Barbillon, C. and Lissarrague, F., *Gods and Heroes of Classical Antiquity*, Flammarion, 1996.

Aldred, Cyril, *Akhenaten: King of Egypt*, Thames and Hudson, 1988.

Alexandersson, Olaf, *Living Water, Gateway*, 1990 (pbk.) (1st ed. 1982).

Allegro, J.M., *The Sacred Mushroom and the Cross*, Hodder and Stoughton, 1970.

Ames, Kenneth and Maschner, Herbert D., *Peoples of the Northwest Coast*, Thames and Hudson, 1999.

Andreu, G., *Egypt in the Age of the Pyramids*, John Murray, 1997.

Ann, Martha and Myers Imel, Dorothy, *Goddesses in World Mythology*, ABC Clio, 1993.

Apion, *History of Egypt*.

Apollonius of Rhodes, *The Voyage of the Argo*, trans. E.V. Rieu, Penguin, 1971 (pbk.) (1st ed. 1959).

Apuleius, Lucius, *The Golden Ass*, trans. Robert Graves, Penguin, 1990 (pbk.) (1st ed. 1950).

Ash, D. and Hewitt, P., *The Vortex* (formerly *The Science of the Gods*), Gateway Books, 1990.

Ashe, G., *The Ancient Wisdom*, Macmillan, 1977.

Ashe, G., *Mythology of the British Isles*, Methuen, 1990.

Ashe, G., *The Virgin*, Routledge and Kegan Paul, 1976.

Assman, J., *Moses the Egyptian*, Harvard University Press, 1997.

Augustine of Hippo, *Dei Civitas*, Penguin, 1972 (pbk.).

Aurobindo, *On Yoga II, Tome Two*. The Sri Aurobindo Ashram Trust. Pondicherry.

Aveni, A., *Stairways to the Stars*, Wiley, 1997.

Ayta, J., *The Oxford Dictionary of Slang*, Oxford University Press, 1998.

Bailey, Adrian, *The Caves of the Sun*, Jonathan Cape, 1997.

Baines, J. and Malek, J., *Atlas of Ancient Egypt*, Phaidon, 1989.

Baldick, Julian, *Black God: The AfroAsiatic Roots of the Jewish, Christian and Muslim Religions*, I.B. Tauris, 1998 (pbk.) (1st ed. 1997).

Bamford, Christopher (ed.), *Rediscovering Sacred Science*, Floris, 1994 (pbk.).

Barber, Richard, *The Knight and Chivalry*, Longman, 1970.

Baring, A. and Cashford, J., *The Myth of the Goddess*, Arkana, 1993 (pbk.).

Barker, M., *On Earth As It Is In Heaven*, T. & T. Clark, 1995.

Barker, M., *The Great Angel*, SPCK, 1992.

Barnes, Michael, Brightwell, Robin, von Hagen, Adriana, Lehner, Mark and Page, Cynthia, *Secrets of Lost Empires: Reconstructing the Glories of Ages Past*, BBC Books, 1996.

Barnhart, R.K., *Chambers Dictionary of Etymology*, Chamber, 1988.

Barnstone, Willis, *The Other Bible*, HarperCollins, San Francisco, 1984 (pbk.).

Barr, James, *The Variant Spellings of the Hebrew Bible*, British Academy/Oxford University Press, 1989.

Barrett, D.V., *Sects, 'Cults' and Alternative Religions*, Blandford, 1996.

Bauval, R. and Gilbert, A., *The Orion Mystery*, Heinemann, 1994.

Bayley, H., *The Lost Language of Symbolism*, Williams and Norgate, 1912.

Becker, Robert O. and Selden, Gary, *The Body Electric*, Morrow, 1985.

Becker, U., *The Continuum Encyclopedia of Symbols*, Continuum, 1994 (pbk.).

Begg, E., *The Cult of the Black Virgin*, Arkana, 1996, (pbk.).

Bernal, M., *Black Athena*, vol.i, Free Association Press, 1987, vol.ii, Rutgers University Press, 1993.

Bernheim, Pierre-Antoine, *James, Brother of Jesus*, SCM, 1997.

Betro, M.C., *Hieroglyphs: The Writings of Ancient Egypt*, Abbeville, 1995.

Betz, O. and Riesner, R., *Jesus, Qumran and the Vatican*, SCM, 1994.

Bhagavad Gita, The, Element, 1997.

Bible – Revised English.

Biddle, M., *The Tomb of Christ*, Sutton, 1999.

Bienkowski, P. and Millard, Alan, *Dictionary of the Ancient Near East*, British Museum Press, 2000.

Birks, W. and Gilbert, R.A., *The Treasure of Montsegur*, Crucible, 1987.

Black, J. and Green, A., *Gods, Demons and Symbols of Ancient Mesopotamia*, British Museum Press, 1992.

Blair, H.A., *The Kaleidoscope of Truth*, Churchman, 1986.

Blair, L., *Rhythms of Vision*, Paladin, 1976.

Blois, L. de and Spek, R.J. Van der, *An Introduction to the Ancient World*, Routledge, 1997.

Bloom, H., *Omens of Millennium*, Fourth Estate, 1996.

Bloom, H. and Rosenberg, D., *The Book of J*, Faber and Faber, 1991.

Bond, H.K., *Pontius Pilate in History and Interpretation*, Cambridge University Press, 1998.

Bowen, Merion, *Michael Tippett*, Robson Books, 1997.

Bowker, J. (ed.), *The Oxford Dictionary of World Religions*, Oxford University Press, 1997.

Bowker, John, *World Religions*, Dorling Kindersley, 1997.

Bowles, J., *The Gods, Gemini and the Great Pyramid*, Genius, 1998 (pbk.).

Brewer, Douglas J. and Teeter, Emily, *Egypt and the Egyptians*, Cambridge University Press, 1999 (pbk.).

Bridges, Marilyn, *Egyptian Antiquities from Above*, Little Brown, 1996.

Brier, Bob, *The Murder of Tutankhamun*, Weidenfeld and Nicolson, 1998.

Broadhurst, Paul, *Secret Shrines*, Pendragon Press, 1991.

Broadhurst, Paul, *Tintagel and the Arthurian Mythos*, Pendragon Press, 1992.

Broadhurst, Paul and Miller, Hamish, *The Dance of the Dragon*, Pendragon Press, 2000.

Brook, Elaine, *In Search of Shambhala*, Jonathan Cape, 1996.

Brown, Guy, *The Energy of Life*, HarperCollins, 1999.

Brown, Mary Ellen and Rosenberg, Bruce A. (eds.), *Encyclopedia of Folklore and Literature*, ABC-Clio, 1998.

Brunton, Dr Paul, *A Search in Secret Egypt*, Rider, 1969 (pbk.) (1st ed. 1935).

Bryce, D., *Symbolism of the Celtic Cross*, Weiser, Maine USA, 1995 (pbk.).

Burl, Aubrey, *Circles of Stone*, Harvill Press, 1999.

Burl, Aubrey, *Great Stone Circles*, Yale University Press, 1999.

Burl, Aubrey, *The Stone Circles of Britain, Ireland and Brittany*, Yale University Press, 2000.

Cade, Maxwell and Coxhead, Nancy, *The Awakened Mind*, Element, 1987.

Calasso, Roberto, *The Marriage of Cadmus and Harmony*, Vintage, 1994 (pbk).

Campbell, Joseph, *Creative Mythology*, Arkana, 1991 (pbk.) (1st ed. 1968).

Campbell, Joseph, *Occidental Mythology*, Arkana, 1991 (pbk.) (1st ed. 1964).

Campbell, Joseph, *Oriental Mythology*, Arkana, 1991 (pbk.) (1st ed. 1962).

Campbell, Joseph, *Primitive Mythology*, Arkana, 1991 (pbk.) (1st ed. 1959).

Campbell, Joseph, *The Hero With A Thousand Faces*, Fontana, 1993 (pbk.) (1st ed. 1949).

Camrie, B., Matthews, S. and Polinsky, M., *The Atlas of Languages*, Bloomsbury, 1996.

Capra, Fritjof, *The Tao of Physics*, Flamingo, 1982 (pbk.).

Carmichael, David L., Hubert, Jane, Reeves, Brian and Schanche, Auldhild, *Sacred Sites, Sacred Places*, Roultledge, 1997 (pbk.) (1st ed. 1994).

Carpenter, Edward, *The Origins of Pagan and Christian Beliefs*, Senate Books, 1996 (1st ed. 1920).

Carter, Howard, *The Tomb of Tutankhamun: The Annexe and Treasury*, Duckworth, 2000 (pbk.).

Caygill, Marjorie, *The British Museum A-Z Companion*, British Museum Press, 1999.

Ceram, C.W., *Gods, Graves and Scholars*, Victor Gollancz, 1952.

Charles, R.H., *The Book of Enoch*, SPCK, 1989.

Charpentier, Louis, *The Mysteries of Chartres Cathedral*, RILKO, 1972 (pbk.).

Chatwin, Bruce, *The Songlines*, Picador, 1987 (pbk.).

Chevalier, J. and Gheerbrant, A., *The Penguin Dictionary of Symbols*, Penguin, 1996 (pbk.)

Churchward, A., *Signs and Symbols of Primordial Man*, The Society of Metaphysicians, 1913.

Churton, T. *The Gnostics*, Weidenfeld and Nicolson, 1990 (pbk.).

Cirlot, J.E., *A Dictionary of Symbols*, Routledge, 1988 (pbk.).

Clark, Stuart, *Universe in Focus: The Story of the Hubble Telescope*, Cassell, 1997.

Collier, M. and Manley, B., *How to Read Egyptian Heiroglyphs*, British Museum Press, 1998.

Compact Oxford English Dictionary, The, Oxford University Press, 1994.

Cook, S.A., *The Religion of Ancient Palestine in the Second Millennium BC in the Light of Archaeology*, British Academy, Oxford University Press, 1908.

Cooke, S.A., *Origins of Early Semitic Ritual*, Schweich Lectures, British Academy, Oxford University Press, 1925.

Corbally-Stourton, Patrick, *Songlines and Dreamings*, Lund Humphries, 1996.

Cornelius, Geoffrey and Devereux, Paul, *The Secret Language of the Stars and Planets, Pavilion*, 1996.

Cotterell, Arthur (ed.), *Penguin Encyclopaedia of Ancient Civilisations*, Penguin, 1980 (pbk.).

Cousens, Gabriel, *Spiritual Nutrition and the Rainbow Diet*, Cassandra Press, USA, 1986.

Cowan, David and Silk, Anne, *Ancient Energies of the Earth*, Thorsons, 1999.

Cross, F.L. and Livingstone, E.A., *The Oxford Dictionary of the Christian Church*, Oxford University Press, 1997 (2nd ed.).

Crossan, J.D., *Who Killed Jesus?*, HarperCollins, 1995.

Crum, W.E., *A Coptic Dictionary*, Oxford University Press, 1993.

Crystal, D., *The Cambridge Encyclopaedia of Language*, Cambridge University Press, 1997 (pbk.).

Cumont, Franz, *The Mysteries of Mithra*, Dover (pbk.) (1st ed. 1956).

Cunliffe, Barry, *The Ancient Celts*, Oxford University Press, 1997.

Currer-Briggs, Noel, *The Shroud and the Grail*, Weidenfeld and Nicolson, 1987.

Dalby, A., *Dictionary of Languages*, Bloomsbury, 1998, Sterling, 1999.

Danielou, Alain, *The Gods of India, Hindu Polytheism*. Pbk. 1985, Inner Traditions International, New York.

David, Rosalie and Archbold, Rick, *Conversations with Mummies*, HarperCollins, 2000.

Davidson, H.R.E., *Symbols of Power*, D.S. Brewer, 1977.

Davies, Vivian and Friedman, Renee, *Egypt*, British Museum Press, 1998.

Description de l'Egypte, Taschen, 1994.

Desroches-Noblecourt, C., *Tutankhamun*, Penguin, 1971 (pbk.) (1st ed. 1963).

Devereux, Paul, *Earth Memory*, Quantum, 1991.

Devereux, Paul, *The Long Trip: A Prehistory of Psychedelia*, Arkana, 1997 (pbk.).

Devereux, Paul, *Secrets of Ancient and Sacred Places*, Cassell, 1995 (pbk.) (1st ed. 1992).

Devereux, P., Steele, J. and Dubrin, D., *Earthmind*, Destiny Books, 1989 (pbk.).

Dhammapada, The, ed. Anne Bancroft, Element, 1997.

Dimbleby, G., *The Palynology of Archaeological Sites*, London, 1985.

Douglas-Klotz,Neil, Prayers of the Cosmos: Meditations on the Aramaic Words of Jesus.HarperCollins Pbk 1994.

Dobson, R.B. and Taylor, J. *Rymes of Robin Hood: An Introduction to the English Outlaw*, Sutton, 1989.

Downer, John, *Supernatural: The Unseen Powers of Animals*, BBC Books, 1999.

Driver, G.R., *Canaanite Myths and Legends*, London, 1956.

Driver, G.R., *Hebrew and Semitic Studies*, London, 1963.

Driver, G.R., *The Origin of the Name 'Yahweh': Evidence and Conclusions*, Zeitschrift Fuerdie Alttestamentliche Wissenschaft (ZAW) XLVI, pp.7-25, 1928.

Drucker, J., *The Alphabetic Labyrinth*, Thames and Hudson, 1995 (pbk.).

Drummond, Sir William, *Oedipus Judaicus*, RILKO, 1986.

Drury, N., *Shamanism*, Element, 1996 (pbk.).

Duffy, E., *Saints and Sinners*, Yale University Press, 1997.

Dunford, Barry, *The Holy Land of Scotland*, Brigadoon, 1996 (pbk.).

Dupuis, Charles Francois, *Memoire Explicatif du Zodiac*, Paris, 1806.

Dupuis, Charles Francois, *Origine de Tous les Cults* (3 volumes), Paris, 1795.

Dupuis, Charles Francois, *Was Christ a Person or the Sun?*, Holyoake and Co., 1857.

Durando, Furio, *Splendours of Ancient Greece*, Thames and Hudson, 1997.

Durrani and Radomirllic, *Radon Measurements by Etched Track Detectors*, World Scientific, 1997.

Dziemidko, Dr Helen E., *Energy Medicine*, Gaia, 1999 (pbk.).

Egypt Exploration Society, The, *Journal of Egyptian Archaeology*.

Eisenman, Robert, *The Dead Sea Scrolls and the First Christians*, Element, 1996.

Eisenman, Robert, *James the Brother of Jesus*, Faber and Faber, 1997.

El Mahdy, Christine, *Mummies, Myth and Magic*, Thames and Hudson, 1989 (pbk.).

Eliade, Mircea, *Shamanism: Archaic Techniques of Ecstasy*, Arkana, 1989 (pbk.) (1st ed. 1964).

Elkington, D., Ellson, P. and Whitlock, R., *The Grail, the Green Man and the Alchemist*, Green Man Press, 2002.

Emery, W.B., *Archaic Egypt*, Penguin, 1961 (pbk.).

Empereur, Jean-Yves, *Alexandria Rediscovered*, British Museum Press, 1998.

Epiphanius, *Panarion*.

Erdoes, Richard and Ortiz, Alfonso, *American Indian Myths and Legends*, Pimlico, 1997 (pbk.) (1ˢᵗ ed. 1984).

Erman, Adolf, *Life in Ancient Egypt*, Dover, 1971.

Eusebius, *The History of the Church*, Penguin, 1989 (pbk.).

Evans-Wentz, W.Y., *The Tibetan Book of the Dead*, Oxford University Press, 2000 (pbk.) (1ˢᵗ ed. 1927).

Farmer, D., *The Oxford Dictionary of Saints*, Oxford University Press, 1997.

Faulkner, R.O., *The Ancient Egyptian Pyramid Texts*, Aris and Phillips, Oxford, 1969 (pbk.).

Faulkner, R.O., *A Concise Dictionary of Middle Egyptian*, Griffith Institute, Oxford, 1988.

Fideler, D., *Jesus Christ, Sun of God*, Quest, Wheaton Illinois, 1993 (pbk.).

Firmage, R.A., *The Abecedarium*, Bloomsbury, 2000.

Flinders Petrie, Sir W.M., *Researches in Sinai*, London, 1906.

Florescano, E., *The Myth of Quetzacoatl*, John Hopkins, 1999.

Forman, Werner and Quirke, Stephen, *Hieroglyphs and the Afterlife in Ancient Egypt*, British Museum Press, 1996.

Fossier, Robert, *The Cambridge Illustrated History of the Middle Ages*, Cambridge University Press, 1986.

Fox, M., *Original Blessing*, Bear and Co., 1983 (pbk.).

Francke, Sylvia and Cawthorne, Thomas, *The Tree of Life and the Holy Grail*, Temple Lodge, 1996 (pbk.).

Frankfort, Henri, *Kingship and the Gods*, University of Chicago Press, 1948.

Frawley, D., *Gods, Sages and Kings*, Motilal Banarsidass, 1999.

Frayling, Christopher, *The Face of Tutankhamun*, Faber and Faber, 1992 (pbk.).

Frayling, Christopher, *Strange Landscape: A Journey Through The Middle Ages*, Penguin, 1996 (pbk.) (1ˢᵗ ed. 1995).

Freeman, C., *Egypt, Greece and Rome*, Oxford University Press, 1996.

Freidel, David, Schele, Linda and Parker, Joy, *Maya Cosmos*, Quill, 1993.

Freke, Timothy and Gandy, Peter, *The Complete Guide to World Mysticism*, Piatkus, 1997.

Freud, S., *The Origins of Religion: Moses and Monotheism*, Penguin, 1985 (pbk.).

Gardam, Jane and Fedden, Mary, *The Green Man*, Windrush, 1998.

Gardiner, Sir A., *Egyptian Grammar*, Griffith Institute, Oxford, 1957.

Gaunt, B., *Stonehenge and the Great Pyramid*, Adventures Unlimited, 1997 (pbk.).

Geoffrey of Monmouth, *The History of the Kings of Britain*, Penguin, 1978 (pbk.).

George, L., *Encyclopaedia of Heresies and Heretics*, Robson Books, 1995.

Gerald of Wales, *The Journey Through Wales/The Description of Wales*, trans. Lewis Thorpe, Penguin, 1978 (pbk.).

Gerber, R., *Vibrational Medicine*, Bear and Co., 1988.

Gibb, J.H.P., *Fan Vaults and Medieval Sculpture of Sherborne Abbey*, Sherborne, 1999.

Gibson, Alex and Simpson, Derek (eds.), *Prehistoric Ritual and Religion*, Sutton, 1998.

Gilbert, A., *Magi*, Bloomsbury, 1996.

Ginzberg, L.J., *The Legends of the Jews* (2 volumes), Jewish Publications Society, 1909-46.

Godwin, Joscelyn, *Mystery Religions in the Ancient World*, Thames and Hudson, 1981 (pbk.).

Godwin, Joscelyn, *The Mystery of the Seven Vowels in Theory and Practice*, Phanes Press, 1991 (pbk.).

Goetz, D. and Morley, S.G., *Popol Vuh*, University of Oklahoma Press, 1991.

Golb, N., *Who Wrote the Dead Sea Scrolls?*, Michael O'Mara, 1995.

Goodbody, G.B.H., *An Attestation to the Resonance within the Pyramid of Khufu*, Spectre, 1921.

Goodman, Martin, *The Roman World 44 BC–AD 180*, Routledge, 1997.

Grabsky, Phil, *The Lost Temple of Java*, Orion,1999.

Grant, Michael, *Myths of the Greeks and Romans*, Phoenix (Orion), 1994 (pbk.) (1st ed. 1962).

Graves, Robert, *Collected Writings on Poetry*, Carcanet, 1995.

Graves, Robert, *The Greek Myths* (one-volume edition), Penguin, 1992 (pbk.).

Graves, Robert, *King Jesus*, Cassell, 1946.

Graves, Robert, *Mammon and the Black Goddess*, Cassell, 1965.

Graves, Robert, *The White Goddess*, Faber and Faber, 1948, corrected text, Carcanet Press, 1997.

Graves, Robert, with Patai, Raphael, *Hebrew Myths*, Cassell, 1964.

Graves, Robert, with Podro, Joshua, *Jesus in Rome*, Cassell, 1957.

Graves, Robert, with Podro, Joshua, *The Nazarene Gospel Restored*, Cassell, 1953.

Green, Celia, *The Decline and Fall of Science*, Hamish Hamilton, 1976.

Green, Miranda, *Celtic Art*, Weidenfeld and Nicolson, 1996.

Green, Miranda, *The Gods of the Celts*, Sutton, 1997 (pbk.) (1st ed. 1986).

Green, Miranda, (ed.), *The Celtic World*, Routledge, 1996 (pbk.) (1st ed. 1995).

Green, Thomas A. (ed.), *Folklore* (2 volumes), ABC-Clio, 1997.

Gregory of Tours, *The History of the Franks*, trans. Lewis Thorpe, Penguin, 1977 (pbk.).

Griffen, Toby D., *Names from the Dawn of British Legend*, Llanerch, 1994 (pbk.).

Grimal, Pierre (ed.), *Larousse World Mythology*, Hamlyn, 1965.

Grof, S., *Books of the Dead*, Thames and Hudson, 1994 (pbk.).

Gruber, E. and Kersten, H., *The Original Jesus*, Element, 1995.

Guiley, R.E., *Encyclopedia of Mystical and Paranormal Experience*, Grange, 1993 (pbk.).

Hagger, N., *The Fire and the Stones*, Element, 1991.

Hale, C., *A Dictionary of British Folk Customs*, Helican, 1995 (pbk.) (1st ed. 1976).

Hanks, P. and Hodges, F., *The Oxford Dictionary of First Names*, Oxford University Press, 1990.

Hardy and Killick, *Pyramid Energy: The Philosophy of God, The Science of Man*, Delta-K, 1987 (pbk.).

Hart, George, *A Dictionary of Egyptian Gods and Goddesses*, Routledge and Kegan Paul, 1988 (pbk.).

Hart, George, *Egyptian Myths*, British Museum Press, 1990.

Hart, George, *Eyewitness Ancient Egypt*, Dorling Kindersley, 1990.

Hart, George, *Pharaohs and Pyramids*, Herbert, 1991.

Haskins, S., *Mary Magdalen*, HarperCollins, 1993.

Hassinain, Prof. F., *A Search for the Historical Jesus*, Gateway, 1994.

Hastings, A., Mason, A., and Pyper, H. (eds.), *The Oxford Companion to Christian Thought*, Oxford University Press, 2000.

Hearne, K., *Visions of the Future*, Aquarian, 1989 (pbk.).

Hearne, K., with Melbourne, David, *Dream Interpretation*, Blandford, 1997 (pbk.).

Heath, Robin, *A Key to Stonehenge*, Bluestone Press, 1995 (Revised Edition).

Heath, Robin, *Sun, Moon and Stonehenge: Proof of High Culture in Ancient Britain*, Bluestone, 1998.

Hepper, F. Nigel, *Pharaoh's Flowers*, HMSO, 1990.

Herodotus, *Histories*, trans. Aubrey de Selincourt, Penguin, 1996 (pbk.).

Herodotus, *Histories*, trans. Robin Waterfield, Oxford University Press, 1998.

Heselton, Phillip, *The Elements of Earth Mysteries*, Element, 1998 (pbk.).

Hesiod, *Theogony/Works and Days and Theognis, Elegies*, trans. Dorothea Wender, Penguin Classics, 1973 (pbk.).

Heyerdahl, Thor, *The Maldive Mystery*, George Allen, 1986.

Higgins, Godfrey, *Anacalypsis* (2 volumes), University Books Inc., NY, 1965.

Hitching, Francis, *Earth Magic*, Cassell, 1977.

Hitching, Francis, *The World Atlas of Mysteries*, Pan, 1978 (pbk.).

Hodges, Peter, *How the Pyramids Were Built*, Element, 1989.

Holt, J.C., *Robin Hood*, Thames and Hudson, 1996.

Homer, *The Iliad*, trans. Robert Fagles, Penguin, 1990 (pbk.).

Hooke, S.H., *Middle Eastern Mythology*, Penguin, 1963 (pbk.).

Hooke, S.H., *Myth, Ritual and Kingship*, London, 1964.

Hooke, S.H., *The Origins of Early Semitic Ritual*, Schweich Lectures, British

Academy, Oxford University Press, 1935.

Hooke, S.H., *Religion in Palestine in the Light of Archaeology*, Schweich Lectures, British Academy, Oxford University Press, 1935.

Hope, Jane, *The Secret Language of the Soul*, Duncan Baird, 1997.

Hope, Murry, *The Ancient Wisdom of Ancient Egypt*, Thorsons, 1995 (1st ed. 1985).

Hornblower, S. and Spawforth, A., *The Oxford Classical Dictionary*, Oxford University Press, 1996 (3rd ed.).

Hornblower, Simon and Spawforth, Antony, *The Oxford Companion to Classical Civilisation*, Oxford University Press, 1998.

Hornung, Erik, *Conceptions of God in Ancient Egypt: The One and the Many*, Routledge and Kegan Paul, 1983.

Houston, Jean, *The Passion of Isis and Osiris*, Ballantine/Wellspring, 1995 (pbk.).

Hyginus, *Fables*.

Illion, T., *In Secret Tibet*, Adventures Unlimited, 1997 (pbk.).

Isserlin, B.S.J., *The Israelites*, Thames and Hudson, 1998.

James, E.O., *The Ancient Gods*, Orion, 1999 (pbk.) (1st ed. 1960, Weidenfeld and Nicolson).

James, Peter, *Centuries of Darkness*, Pimlico, 1992.

James, Peter and Thorpe, Nick, *Ancient Mysteries*, Ballantine, 1999.

James, T.G.H., *An Introduction to Ancient Egypt*, British Museum Press, 1979 (pbk.).

Jaynes, J., *The Origins of Consciousness in the Breakdown of the Bicameral Mind*, Allen Lane, 1979.

Jenkins, Simon, *England's Thousand Best Churches*, Penguin, 1999 (pbk.).

Jenny, H., *Cymatics* (2 volumes), Basilius Press, 1974.

Jerusalem Bible, The.

Johnson, A.R., *Sacral Kingship in Ancient Israel*, University of Wales, 1967.

Johnson, A.R., *The Cultic Prophet in Ancient Israel*, University of Wales, 1962.

Johnson, K. Paul, *Edgar Cayce in Context*, University of New York, 1998 (pbk.).

Johnson, Paul, *The Papacy*, Weidenfeld and Nicolson, 1997.

Jones, Anthea, *A Thousand Years of the English Parish*, Windrush, 2000.

Jones, Prudence and Pennick, Nigel, *A History of Pagan Europe*, Routledge, 1995 (pbk.).

Jordan, Michael, *The Encyclopedia of the Gods*, Kyle Cathie, 1994 (pbk.).

Jordan, Michael, *Myths of the World: A Thematic Encyclopedia*, Kyle Cathie, 1995 (pbk.) (1st ed. 1993).

Jordan, Michael, *Plants of Mystery and Magic*, Blandford, 1997.

Josephus, *Against Apion*, Loeb Classics, 1926.

Josephus, *Fragments of Berossus's Babylonian History*.

Josephus, *Jewish Antiquities*, Loeb Classics, 1930.

Josephus, *The Jewish War*, Loeb Classics, 1927.

Jung, C.J., *Modern Man In Search of a Soul*, Ark, 1990 (pbk.) (1st ed. 1933).

Katan, N.J. and Mintz, B., *Hieroglyphs: The Writing of Ancient Egypt*, British Museum Press, 1991 (pbk.) (1st ed. 1981).

Kerenyi, Carl, *Dionysus: Archetypal Image of Indestructible Life*, Princeton, 1996 (pbk.) (1st ed. 1976).

Kerenyi, Carl, *The Gods of the Greeks*, Thames and Hudson, 1995.

Kerenyi, Carl, *The Heroes of the Greeks*, Thames and Hudson, 1997.

Kharitidi, Olga, *Entering the Circle: Ancient Secrets of Siberian Wisdom*, Thorsons, 1997 (pbk.) (1st ed. 1996).

King James Bible.

King, L.W., *The Legends of Babylon and Egypt*, Schweich Lectures, British Academy, Oxford University Press, 1916.

King, Ursula, *Christian Mystics: The Spiritual Heart of the Christian Tradition*, Batsford, 1998.

Knappert, J., *The Encyclopedia of Middle Eastern Mythology and Religion*, Element, 1993.

Knight, Vernon James and Steponaitis, Vincas P., *Archaeology of the Moundville Chiefdom*, Smithsonian, 1998.

Kokkinos, N., *The Herodian Dynasty*, Sheffield Academic Press, 1998.

Kuhrt, A., *The Ancient Near East* (2 volumes), Routledge, 1995.

Lamy, Lucie, *Egyptian Mysteries*, Thames and Hudson, 1981.

Lane Fox, R., *Pagans and Christians*, Penguin, 1988 (pbk.).

Lane Fox, R., *The Unauthorised Version*, Viking, 1991.

Lang, A., *Myth, Ritual and Religion* (2 volumes), Longmans, Green and Co., 1906.

Laszlo, E., Grof, S. and Russell, P., *The Consciousness Revolution*, Element, 1999.

Lawlar, R., *Sacred Geometry*, Thames and Hudson, 1982 (pbk.).

Lawton, I. and Ogilvie-Herald, C., *Giza – The Truth*, Virgin, 1999.

Leach, M. (ed.), *Funk and Wagnall's Standard Dictionary of Folklore, Mythology and Legend*, HarperCollins, San Francisco, 1984 (1st ed. Harper and Row).

Leadbeater, C.W., *Freemasonry and its Ancient Mystic Rites*, Gramercy, 1986.

Lehner, Mark, *The Complete Pyramids*, Thames and Hudson, 1997.

Leick, G., *A Dictionary of Ancient Near Eastern Mythology*, Routledge, 1998 (pbk.).

Lemesurier, Peter, *The Great Pyramid: Your Personal Guide*, Element, 1987 (pbk.).

Levinson, David, *Religion: A Cross-Cultural Encyclopedia*, ABC-Clio, 1996.

Liberati, Anna Marie and Bourbon, Fabio, *Splendours of the Roman World*, Thames and Hudson, 1996.

Liddell, H.G. and Scott, R., *Greek-English Lexicon*, Oxford University Press, 1996 (with Supplement).

Livy, *The Early History of Rome*, trans. Aubrey de Selincourt, Penguin, 1986.

Lockhart, Douglas, *The Dark Side of God*, Element, 1999.

Lockhart, Douglas, *Jesus the Heretic*, Element, 1997.

Lockyer, Sir J.N., *The Dawn of Astronomy*, London, 1894.

Lorimer, David (ed.), *The Spirit of Science*, Floris, 1998 (pbk.).

Lovelock, James, *Gaia*, Oxford University Press, 1979.

Luckert, Karl W., *Egyptian Light and Hebrew Fire*, State University of New York Press, 1991.

Lurker, M. *Dictionary of Gods and Goddesses, Devils and Demons*, Routledge, 1996 (pbk.).

Lysimachus, *Commentaries on the Works of Manetho*.

MacCana, Proinsias, *Celtic Mythology*, Chancellor Press, 1996.

Mackenzie-Brown, C., *The Devi Gita*, State University of New York Press, 1998.

MacKillop, James, *Dictionary of Celtic Mythology*, Oxford University Press, 1998.

Maclagan, D., *Creation Myths*, Thames and Hudson, 1977 (pbk.).

Mahoney, William K., *The Artful Universe: An Introduction to the Vedic Religious Imagination*, State University of New York, 1998 (pbk.).

Maisels, Charles Keith, *Early Civilisations of the Old World*, Routledge, 1999.

Mallory, J.P. and Mair, Victor H., *The Tarim Mummies*, Thames and Hudson, 2000.

Mallory, Sir Thomas, *Le Morte d'Arthur*, Oxford University Press, 1954 (original 1485, William Caxton).

Man, John, *Alpha Beta*, Headline, 2000.

Manley, Bill, *The Penguin Historical Atlas of Ancient Egypt*, Penguin, 1996 (pbk.).

Mann, A.T., *Sacred Architecture*, Element, 1993 (pbk.).

Manniche, Lisa, *An Ancient Egyptian Herbal*, British Museum Press, 1989 (pbk.).

March, Jenny, *Dictionary of Classical Mythology*, Cassell, 1998.

Martin, S. and Grube, N., *Chronicle of the Maya Kings and Queens*, Thames and Hudson, 2000.

Massey, G., *The Historical Jesus and the Mythical Christ*, London, 1886.

Mathews, Caitlin, *Sophia: Goddess of Wisdom*, Mandala, 1991.

Maxwell-Stuart, P.G., *Chronicle of the Popes*, Thames and Hudson, 1997.

McKenna, Terence, *Food of the Gods*, Bantam, 1992 (pbk.).

McLeish, K., *Myth*, Bloomsbury, 1996.

McLuhan, T.C., *Cathedrals of the Spirit*, Thorsons, 1996.

Mead, G.R.S., *Fragments of a Faith Forgotten*, Theosophical Publishing Co., 1906.

Mead, G.R.S., *The Hymn to the Robe of Glory*, Theosophical Publishing Co., 1908.

Mead, G.R.S., *Thrice Greatest Hermes* (3 volumes), Theosophical Publishing Co., 1906.

Meeks, Dimitri and Favard-Meeks, Christine, *Daily Life of the Egyptian Gods*, John Murray, 1997.

Mertz, Blanche, *Points of Cosmic Energy*, Daniel and Co., 1987.

Merz, A. and Theissen, G., *The Historical Jesus*, SCM, 1998.

Michell, John, *City of Revelation*, Garnstone Press, 1972.

Michell, John, *The Earth Spirit*, Thames and Hudson, 1975.

Michell, John, *The Flying Saucer Vision*, Abacus, 1974 (pbk.).

Milanich, J.T., *Laboring in the Fields of the Lord*, Smithsonian, 1999.

Miller, Hamish and Broadhurst, Paul, *The Sun and the Serpent*, Pendragon Press, 1989.

Miller, Lee (ed.), *From the Heart: Voices of the American Indian*, Pimlico, 1997 (pbk.) (1st ed. 1995).

Miller, Malcolm, *Chartres Cathedral*, Pitkin, 1996 (pbk.) (1st ed. 1985).

Milner, George R., *The Cahokia Chiefdom*, Smithsonian, 1998.

Monier Monier-Williams, Sir, *Sanskrit-English Dictionary*, OUP 1899, and Motilal Banarsidass, India 1986.

Morgan, R.W., *St. Paul in Britain*, Covenant, 1978.

Morkot, Richard G., *The Black Pharaohs: Egypt's Nubian Rulers*, Rubicon, 2000.

Morris, Craig and Hagen, Adriana Von, *The Inka Empire*, Abbeville, 1993.

Morrison, T., *Pathways to the Gods*, Michael Russell, 1979.

Murnane, William J., *The Road to Kadesh*, University of Chicago Press, 1990.

Murray, M.A., *The Splendour that was Egypt*, Sidgwick and Jackson, 1963.

Murray, P. and L., *The Oxford Companion to Christian Art and Architecture*, Oxford University Press, 1996.

Narby, Jeremy, *The Cosmic Serpent, DNA and the Origins of Knowledge*, Gollancz, 1998.

Naydler, J., *Temple of the Cosmos*, Inner Traditions, Vermont USA, 1996 (pbk.).

Niemojewski, A., *God Jesus*, trans.V. MacDermot, Janus, 1996 (pbk.).

Noah, M.M., *The Book of Jasher*, New York, 1840.

North, John, *Stonehenge: Neolithic Man and the Cosmos*, HarperCollins, 1996.

Notes on the Cathedrals (5 volumes), London: Photocrom Co. Ltd., 1904.

Oldenbourg, Zoe, *The Crusades*, Weidenfeld and Nicolson, 1998.

Oliphant, Margaret, *The Atlas of the Ancient World*, Ebury Press, 1992.

Onions, C.T., *The Oxford Dictionary of English Etymology*, Oxford University Press, 1996.

Osman, Ahmed, *In the House of the Messiah*, HarperCollins, 1992.

Osman, Ahmed, *Out of Egypt*, Century, 1998.

Ostrander, S. and Schroeder, L., *PSI: Psychic Discoveries Behind the Iron Curtain*, Abacus, 1973.

Ouaknin, Marc-Alain, *Mysteries of the Alphabet*, Abbeville, 1999 (pbk.).

Ovid, *Metamorphoses*, trans. Mary Innes, Penguin, 1955 (pbk.).
Ozaniec, N., *The Elements of Egyptian Wisdom*, Element, 1994.

Pagels, E., *The Gnostic Gospels*, Penguin, 1982 (pbk.).
Pagels, E., *The Origins of Satan*, Allen Lane, 1995.
Palestine Exploration Quarterly.
Panati, C., *Sacred Origins of Profound Things*, Penguin, 1997 (pbk.).
Partner, Peter, *Two Thousand Years, The Second Millennium* (2 volumes), Granada, 1999.
Patai, R., *The Hebrew Goddess*, Wayne State University Press, 1990.
Peat, F. David, *Blackfoot Physics*, Fourth Estate, 1996 (pbk.).
Pennick, Nigel, *The Ancient Science of Geomancy*, Thames and Hudson, 1979 (pbk.).
Pennick, Nigel, *The Secret Lore of Runes and Other Ancient Alphabets*, Rider, 1991 (pbk.).
Phillips, Roger, *Wild Food*, Pan, 1983 (pbk.).
Piatgorsky, A., *Who's Afraid of Freemasons?*, Harvill, 1997.
Playfair, G. Lyon and Hill, Scott, *The Cycles of Heaven*, Souvenir Press, 1978.
Plato, *Timaeus and Critias*, Penguin Classics, 1977 (pbk.).
Porter, J.R., *Jesus Christ*, Duncan Baird, 1999.
Powell, Anton (ed.), *The Greek World*, Routledge, 1997.
Poynder, Michael, *The Lost Magic of Christianity*, Green Magic, 2000 (pbk.).
Poynder, Michael, *Pi In The Sky*, Rider, 1992.
Prache, Anne, *Cathedrals of Europe*, Cornell University Press, 1999.
Pritchard, James B. (ed.), *The Ancient Near East* (Volume One), Princeton, 1958.
Pritchard, James B. (ed.), *The Times Atlas of the Bible*, Times, 1987.
Procopius, *The Secret History*, trans. G.A Williamson, Penguin, 1981 (pbk.) (1st ed. 1966).
Pryse, J.M., *The Apocalypse Unsealed*, John M. Pryse, New York, 1910.
Pukarick, Andrija, *Beyond Telepathy*, Souvenir, 1962.
Purce, Jill, *The Mystic Spiral*, Thames and Hudson, 1974 (pbk.).

Quirke, Stephen, *Who Were the Pharaohs?*, British Museum Press, 1990 (pbk.).

Raney-Dougal, Serena, *Where Science and Magic Meet*, Element, 1991 (pbk.).
Rawson, Jessica (ed.), *Mysteries of Ancient China*, British Museum Press, 1996.
Read, Piers Paul, *The Templars*, Weidenfeld and Nicolson, 1999.
Redford, Donald B., *Akhenaten: The Heretic King*, Princeton, 1984.
Reeves, N., *The Complete Tutankhamun*, Thames and Hudson, 1990.
Reeves, N. and Wilkinson, R.H., *The Complete Valley of the Kings*, Thames and Hudson, 1996.
Reich, Wilhelm, *The Function of the Orgasm*, Souvenir, 1993 (pbk.) (1st ed. 1942).

Reid, Howard, *In Search of the Immortals*, Headline, 1999.

Rice, Michael, *Egypt's Legacy*, Routledge, 1997.

Rice, Michael, *The Power of the Bull*, Routledge, 1998.

Richards, Chris (ed.), *The Illustrated Encyclopedia of World Religions*, Element, 1997.

Robertson, J.M., *Pagan Christs*, Barnes and Noble, NY, 1993 (one-volume abridgement).

Robin Hood Country: The County Guide to Nottinghamshire.

Robins, Gay, *The Art of Ancient Egypt*, British Museum Press, 1997.

Robinson, A., *The Story of Writing*, Thames and Hudson, 2000 (pbk.) (1st ed. 1995).

Robinson, James (ed.), *The Nag Hamadi Library in English*, Brill, 1996.

Rogerson, J., *Chronicle of the Old Testament Kings*, Thames and Hudson, 1999.

Rogerson, J. and Saldarini, A.J., *The Cambridge Companion to the Bible*, Cambridge University Press, 1997.

Romer, John, *People of the Nile*, Penguin, 1982 (pbk.).

Romer, John, *Valley of the Kings*, Michael O'Mara, 1981.

Room, A., *The Cassell Dictionary of Word Histories*, Cassell, 1999 (pbk.).

Root-Bernstein, R. and B., *Honey, Mud, Maggots*, Sidgwick, 1997.

Rosa, P. de, *Vicars of Christ*, Bantam, 1988.

Ross, Anne, *Pagan Celtic Britain*, Routledge and Kegan Paul, 1967.

Ross, Hugh McGregor , *Jesus Untouched by the Church*. Wm Sessions. 1985.

Rowley, H.H., *From Joseph to Joshua*, Schweich Lectures, British Academy, Oxford Univesity Press, 1950.

Rowley, H.H., *The Meaning of Sacrifice in the Old Testment*, British Academy, Oxford University Press, 1950.

Rudgley, Richard, *Secrets of the Stone Age*, Random House, 2000.

Russell, Bertrand, *History of Western Philosophy*, Routledge, 1996 (pbk.) (1st ed. 1946).

Ryan, William and Pitman, Walter, *Noah's Flood*, Simon and Schuster, 1998.

Salibi, K., *The Bible Came from Arabia*, Jonathan Cape, 1985.

Salibi, K., *Who Was Jesus?*, I.B. Tauris, 1998.

Samson, Julia, *Nefertiti and Cleopatra*, Rubicon, 1987.

Sanders, E.P., *The Historical Figure of Jesus*, Penguin, 1993 (pbk.).

Santillana, G. De and Dechend, H. von, *Hamlet's Mill*, Godine, 1977 (pbk.).

Sassoon, John, *From Sumer to Jerusalem: The Hidden Hypothesis*, Intellect, 1993.

Satprem, *Sri Aurobindo or the Adventure of Consciousness*, Thomson Press, Faridabad, India, June 2000. (Our thanks to the Institut De Recherches Evolutives, BP9, 14380 Hermouiville, France.)

Sattin, Anthony, *The Pharaoh's Shadow*, Victor Gollancz, 2000.

Saurat, D., *Literature and Occult Tradition*, G. Bell and Sons, 1930.

Scarre, Chris, *Chronicle of the Roman Emperors*, Thames and Hudson, 1995.

Scarre, Chris, *Exploring Prehistoric Europe*, Oxford University Press, 1998.

Scarre, Chris (ed.), *The Seventy Wonders of the Ancient World*, Thames and Hudson, 1999.

Scarre, Chris (ed.), *Timelines of the Ancient World*, Dorling Kindersley, 1993.

Scholes, P.A., *The Oxford Companion to Music*, Oxford University Press, 1992.

Schonfield, Hugh, *The Essene Odyssey*, Element, 1996.

Schonfield, Hugh, *The Pentecost Revolution*, Element, 1985.

Schonfield, Hugh, *Those Incredible Christians*, Element, 1985.

Schulz and Seidel, *Egypt: The World of the Pharaohs*, Konemann, 1998.

Schwaller de Lubicz, Isha, *The Opening of the Way*, Inner Traditions, 1981 (pbk.).

Schwaller de Lubicz, R.A., *The Temple in Man*, Inner Traditions, 1981 (pbk.) (1st ed. 1949).

Schwaller de Lubicz, R.A., *The Temples of Karnak*, Thames and Hudson, 1999.

Schwenk, Theodor, *Sensitive Chaos*, Rudolf Steiner Press, 1999 (pbk.).

Scott-Littleton, C. (ed.), *The Sacred East*, Duncan Baird Publishing, 1996.

Sellers, J.B., *The Death of Gods in Ancient Egypt*, Penguin, 1992 (pbk.).

Settegast, M., *Plato Prehistorian*, Lindisfarne, 1990 (pbk.).

Seymour, P., *The Birth of Christ*, Virgin, 1998.

Seymour, P., *The Paranormal: Beyond Sensory Science*, Arkana, 1992 (pbk.).

Shafer, Byron E., *Temples of Ancient Egypt*, I.B. Tauris, 1998.

Shaw, Gregory, *Theurgy and the Soul*, Pennsylvania State University Press, 1995.

Shaw, I. and Nicholson, P., *British Museum Dictionary of Ancient Egypt*, British Museum Press, 1997 (pbk.).

Sheldrake, R., *A New Science of Life*, Paladin, 1983 (pbk.).

Sheldrake, R. *The Presence of the Past*, Fontana, 1989 (pbk.).

Sheldrake, R., *The Rebirth of Nature*, Century, 1990.

Shlain, L., *The Alphabet versus the Goddess*, Allen Lane, 1998.

Shorter Oxford Dictionary, The (2 volumes), Oxford University Press, 1993.

Shorto, Russell, *Gospel Truth*, Hodder and Stoughton, 1997.

Smith, Anthony, *The Human Body*, BBC Books, 1998.

Smith, Cyril W. and Best, Simon, *Electromagnetic Man*, Dent, 1990 (pbk.).

Smith, Morton, *Jesus the Magician*, Aquarian, 1985.

Smith, Morton, *The Secret Gospel*, Harper and Row, New York, 1973.

Snow, Ian (ed.), *The Oxford History of Ancient Egypt*, Oxford University Press, 2000.

Stanton, G., *Gospel Truth?*, HarperCollins, 1995.

Starbird, M., *The Woman with the Alabaster Jar*, Bear and Co., Santa Fe, 1993 (pbk.).

Stevenson, V., *The World of Words*, Sterling, NY, 1999.

Stierlin, Henri and Anne, *Splendours of an Islamic World*, Touris Parke, 1997.

Strachan, G., *Christ and the Cosmos*, Labarum, 1985 (pbk.).

Strachan, G., *Jesus the Master Builder*, Floris, 1998.

Strert, Jakob, *Sun and Cross*, Floris, 1977.

Strudwick, Nigel and Helen, *Thebes in Egypt*, British Museum Press, 1999 (pbk.).

Sullivan, William, *The Secret of the Incas*, Three Rivers, 1997 (pbk.).

Swan, J.A., *The Power of the Place*, Gateway Books, 1993 (pbk.).

Sweeney, Emmet J., *The Pyramid Age*, Domra, 1999 (pbk.).

Symes, Dr R.F., *Rock and Mineral*, Dorling Kindersley, 1988.

Symes, Dr R.F. and Harding, Dr R.R., *Crystal and Gem*, Dorling Kindersley, 1991.

Taldoth Yeshu, The.

Talmud, The.

Tapsell, R.F., *Monarchs, Rulers, Dynasties and Kingdoms of the World*, Thames and Hudson, 1987.

Temple, Robert K. G.,,, *The Sirius Mystery* Sidgwick and Jackson London, 1981.

The Book of Common Prayer.

The Interpreters' One-Volume Commentary on the Bible, Abingdon Press, 1991.

Thiede, Carsten Peter and D'Ancona, Mathew, *The Quest for the True Cross*, Weidenfeld and Nicolson, 2000.

Thieder, C.P. and D'Ancora, M., *The Jesus Papyrus*, Weidenfeld and Nicolson, 1996.

Thomas, A.P., *Akhenaten's Egypt*, Shire, 1988 (pbk).

Thomas, Keith, *Religion ad the Decline of Magic*, Weidenfeld and Nicolson, 1997.

Thompson, T.C., *The Bible in History*, Jonathan Cape, 1999.

Thubron, C., *In Siberia*, Chatto and Windus, 1999 (pbk).

Thurman, R.A.F., *The Tibetan Book of the Dead*, Thorsons, 1995 (pbk.).

Tompkins, P., *Secrets of the Great Pyramid*, Harper and Row, 1978 (pbk.).

Tompkins, Peter, and Bird, Christopher, *The Secret Life of Plants*, Allen Lane, 1974.

Tompkins, Peter and Bird, Christopher, *Secrets of the Soil*, Arkana, 1992 (pbk.).

Townsend, Richard F. (ed.), *Ancient West Mexico: Art and Archaeology of the Unknown Past*, Thames and Hudson, 1998.

Tresidder, J., *The Hutchinson Dictionary of Symbols*, Helican, 1997 (pbk.).

Tresider, J., *Symbols and Their Meaning*, Duncan Baird Publishing, 2000.

Troev, Theodor, *The Argonautica Expedition*, Ian Faulkner, 1991 (pbk.) (1st ed. 1990).

Tubb, Jonathan N., *Canaanites*, British Museum Press, 1998.

Tubb, Jonathan N. and Chapman, Rupert, *Archaeology and the Bible*, British Museum Press, 1990.

Tucker, Linda, *Children of the Sun God: From the White Lions of Timbavati to the Great Sphinx of Giza*, Gryphon Press, Cape Town, 2000.

Tully, Mark, *Lives of Jesus*, BBC Books, 1996.

Underwood, Guy, *The Pattern of the Past*, Abacus, 1972.
Upton-Ward, J.M., *The Rule of the Templars*, Boydell Press, 1992.

Vaux, R. de, *The Early History of Israel* (2 volumes), Darton, Longman and Todd, 1978.
Vermes, Geza, *The Changing Faces of Jesus*, Allen Lane, 2000.
Vermes, Geza, *The Complete Dead Sea Scrolls in English*, Allen Lane, 1997.
Vernus, Pascal and Lessing, Erich, *The Gods of Ancient Egypt*, Tauris Parke, 1998.
Vinci, Leo, *Pan, Great God of Nature*, Neptune Press, 1993 (pbk.).

Wace and Layamon, *Arthurian Chronicles*, trans. Eugene Mason, Dent, 1962.
Walker, B.G., *The Woman's Dictionary of Symbols and Sacred Objects*, HarperCollins, 1988 (pbk.).
Walker, B.G., *The Woman's Encyclopedia of Myths and Secrets*, HarperCollins, 1983 (pbk.).
Wallace-Hadrill, D., *Augustan Rome*, Bristol Classical Press, 1993.
Wallis Budge, Sir E.A., *The Book of the Dead*, Arkana, 1989 (pbk.) (1st ed. British Museum Press, 1899).
Wallis Budge, Sir E.A., *Egyptian Religion*, Arkana, 1987 (pbk.).
Wallis Budge, Sir E.A., *The Gods of the Egyptians* (2 volumes), Dover, 1969 (pbk.) (1st ed. 1904).
Wallis Budge, Sir E.A., *Legends of Our Lady Mary*, Oxford University Press, 1933.
Wallis Budge, Sir E.A., *Kebra Nagast*, London, 1932.
Warner, Marina, *Alone of All Her Sex*, Picador, 1985.
Warner, Marina, *From the Beast to the Blonde*, Chatto and Windus, 1994.
Watson, Lyall, *Lifetide*, Hodder and Stoughton, 1979.
Watson, Lyall, *Supernature*, Hodder and Stoughton, 1973.
Watterson, B., *Gods of Ancient Egypt*, Sutton, 1996 (1st ed. 1984).
Wayland Barber, Elizabeth, *The Mummies of Urumchi*, Macmillan, 1999.
West, J.A., *Serpent in the Sky*, Quest, 1993 (pbk.).
West, J.A., *The Traveller's Key to Ancient Egypt*, Quest, 1995 (pbk.) (1st ed. 1985).
Weston, Jessie, *From Ritual to Romance*, Princeton, 1993 (pbk.).
Westwood, Jennifer, *Sacred Journeys*, Gaia Books, 1997 (pbk.).
Whiston, W., *The Works of Josephus* (New Updated Edition), Hendrickson, 1987.
Whitelam, K.W., *The Invention of Ancient Israel*, Routledge, 1996.
Whittaker, Clio, *An Introduction to Oriental Mythology*, Grange, 1997.
Whone, H., *Church, Monastery, Cathedral*, Element, 1990 (pbk.).
Wilkinson, R.H., *The Complete Temples of Ancient Egypt*, Thames and Hudson, 2000.
Wilkinson, Toby, *Early Dynastic Egypt*, Routledge, 1999.
Willis, R. (ed.), *World Mythology*, Piatkus, 1997 (pbk.).

Wilson, A.N., *Jesus*, HarperCollins, 1992.

Wilson, A.N., *Paul*, Sinclair-Stevenson, 1997.

Wilson, Colin, *Alien Dawn*, Virgin, 1998.

Wilson, Colin, *The Atlas of Holy Places and Sacred Sites*, Dorling Kindersley, 1996.

Wilson, Hilary, *Egyptian Food and Drink*, Shire, 1988 (pbk).

Wilson, Hilary, *People of the Pharaohs*, Michael O'Mara, 1997.

Wilson, Hilary, *Understanding Hieroglyphs*, Michael O'Mara, 1995 (pbk.).

Wilson, Ian, *The Bible is History*, Weidenfeld and Nicolson, 1999.

Wilson, Ian, *Jesus: The Evidence*, Weidenfeld and Nicolson, 1996.

Wilson, Steve, *Robin Hood: Spirit of the Forest*, Neptune, 1993 (pbk.).

Wise, Terence and McBride, Angus, *Ancient Armies of the Middle East*, Osprey, 1981.

Withycombe, E.G., *The Oxford Dictionary of English Christian Names*, Oxford University Press, 1946.

Wood, Michael, *In the Footsteps of Alexander the Great*, BBC Books, 1997.

Worwood, Valerie, *The Fragrant Heavens*, Doubleday, 1999.

Wroe, A., *Pilate*, Jonathan Cape, 1999.

Yahuda, J., *Hebrew is Greek*, Becket, 1982.

Zink, D., *The Ancient Stones Speak*, Paddington Press, 1979.

Zohar, Danah, and Marshall, Ian, *SQ, Spiritual Intelligence,the Ultimate Intelligence*, Bloomsbury 2000.

Zohary, M. *Plants of the Bible*, London, 1982.

List of Plates

1   Trevethy Quoit *c*.3500 BC, Cornwall, Britain.
2   Rocky Valley, an ancient labyrinth *c*.3000 BC, Cornwall, Britain.
3   The Ampitheatre at Delphi.
4   The Ampitheatre at Dodona.
5   Bourges Cathedral, France.
6   Christ enthroned upon the Tympanum at Chartres.
7   Chartres Cathedral, France.
8   Wells Cathedral, England. The stairs leading to the Chapter House.
9   'The Triumph of the Name of Jesus', by Baciccia.
10   The Step Pyramid of Djoser.
11   The Giza Plateau.
12   The Valley Temple, Giza.
13   View of the Great Pyramid behind the pyramid of Khafre.
14   The cymatic image of the *Nemes* at 271 Hz.
15   The cymatic image of the Ra hieroglyph.
16   *Djed*.
17   The Grand Gallery.
18   The cymatis 'eye' of *Wadjet* – The sacred eye of Horus.
19   The cymatic 'Key of Life' – the *Ankh*.
20   The oldest church in the world.
21   The Eagle Nebula.

Acknowledgements and thanks for permission to reproduce the photographs and the illustration are as follows:

1–7, Paul Broadhurst; 9, Theo Benedictus; 14,15,16,18,and 19, John Reid; 17, Peter Renton; 20, illustration by Dean Baker; 21, NASA–HST.

List of Illustrations

All of the above illustrations are by Amanda Patten.

Index

David Elkington will return with Paul Howard Ellson and Robin Whitlock in
'The Grail, the Green Man and the Alchemist'.